ECONOMICS
FOR
BUSINESS

Prof. H.R. Appannaiah

M.Com.

*Dean of Studies, Surana P.G. Centre, Kengare
Bangalore-60.*

*Former Principal, P.A. College, Tiptur,
Founder President, Federation of Teachers'
Councils of Commerce and Management in
Karnataka.*

Dr. P.N. Reddy

Ph.D.

*Director, K.K.E.C.S. Institute of
Management Bangalore.*

*Former Dean & Chairman,
Department of P.G. Studies in
Commerce and Management,
Bangalore University.*

Ms. S. Shanthi

A., M.Phil.

*Faculty, Department of Economics,
Mount Carmel College,
Bangalore.*

Himalaya Publishing House
ISO 9001:2015 CERTIFIED

First Edition : 2004
Second Revised &
Enlarged Edition : 2005
Third Edition : 2008
Reprint : 2009, 2011, 2013, 2014, 2017
Reprint : 2019

Published by	:	Mrs. Meena Pandey for **Himalaya Publishing House Pvt. Ltd.,** "Ramdoot", Dr. Bhalerao Marg, Girgaon, Mumbai - 400 004. **Phone:** 022-23860170, 23863863; **Fax:** 022-23877178 **E-mail:** himpub@vsnl.com; **Website:** www.himpub.com
Branch Offices	:	
New Delhi	:	"Pooja Apartments", 4-B, Murari Lal Street, Ansari Road, Darya Ganj, New Delhi - 110 002. Phone: 011-23270392, 23278631; Fax: 011-23256286
Nagpur	:	Kundanlal Chandak Industrial Estate, Ghat Road, Nagpur - 440 018. Phone: 0712-2738731, 3296733; Telefax: 0712-2721216
Bengaluru	:	Plot No. 91-33, 2nd Main Road, Seshadripuram, Behind Nataraja Theatre, Bengaluru - 560 020. Phone: 080-41138821; Mobile: 09379847017, 09379847005
Hyderabad	:	No. 3-4-184, Lingampally, Besides Raghavendra Swamy Matham, Kachiguda Hyderabad - 500 027. Phone: 040-27560041, 27550139
Chennai	:	New No. 48/2, Old No. 28/2, Ground Floor, Sarangapani Street, T. Nagar, Chennai - 600 012. Mobile: 09380460419
Pune	:	First Floor, "Laksha" Apartment, No. 527, Mehunpura, Shaniwarpeth (Near Prabhat Theatre), Pune - 411 030. Phone: 020-24496323, 24496333; Mobile: 09370579333
Lucknow	:	House No. 731, Shekhupura Colony, Near B.D. Convent School, Aliganj, Lucknow - 226 022. Phone: 0522-4012353; Mobile: 09307501549
Ahmedabad	:	114, "SHAIL", 1st Floor, Opp. Madhu Sudan House, C.G. Road, Navrang Pura Ahmedabad - 380 009. Phone: 079-26560126; Mobile: 09377088847
Ernakulam	:	39/176 (New No. 60/251) 1st Floor, Karikkamuri Road, Ernakulam, Kochi - 682 011. Phone: 0484-2378012, 2378016; Mobile: 09387122121
Bhubaneswar	:	Plot No. 214/1342/1589, Budheswari Colony, Behind Durga Mandap, Laxmisagar Bhubaneswar - 751 006. Phone: 0674-2575129; Mobile: 09338746007
Kolkata	:	108/4, Beliaghata Main Road, Near ID Hospital, Opp. SBI Bank, Kolkata - 700 010. Phone: 033-32449649; Mobile: 07439040301
Printed by	:	M/s. Sri Sai Art Printer, Hyderabad. On behalf of HPH.

Preface for Third Edition

We are very happy to note the response we got for the first edition of "ECONOMICS FOR BUSINESS". The subject Economics demands a peculiar style of thinking than what we experience in other subjects. Application of economic laws for solving business problems drives us to use of assumptions to break down complex problems into simple, analytically manageable parts. Analytical style is more demanding in Business Economics than in any other discipline. Students should note that study of Business Economics is different and requires practice.

The title provides case studies to practice and analyze the business situation and apply economic laws wherever possible. Every chapter has been updated as per the needs. The shortcomings of the first edition have been looked into. We hope that the student community will well receive this title.

We thank Sri. D.P. Pandeyji, Sri. K.N.Pandy, and Sri. Niraj Pandey and the staff of HPH for their cooperation in bringing out this revised edition. We thank Sri. S. Madhu of Sri Siddhi Softtek for composing this work.

— Authors

Preface for First Edition

The theme of economic theory, from the day it was conceived in eighteenth century by Adam Smith and others to today has changed along with the growth of the economy throughout the world. We find a shift in theme from "Wealth" (Classical School -Adam Smith and Others) to "Welfare" (Neo-classical School-A Marshall and Others) to "Scarcity" (Modern School-L.Robbins and Others) to "Growth" (Samuelson and Others). This shift has taken place due to the thinking of economists and the development of the economies from time to time. In all these phrases of economic growth, many economic laws and concepts were evolved. These laws were applied to business problems to obtain solutions. Some of the laws became powerful tools in the hands of business people to forecast the demand for their products, to assess the market conditions, to study the consumer behaviour and so on. This gave way for the emergence of a new learning area of economics called "Business Economics" or "Managerial Economics."

Today, in every curriculum of business education of any University or any autonomous school of business, business economics is studied as a core subject. This title "ECONOMICS FOR BUSINESS" covers both micro and macro economic aspects and deals with the application of economic laws to business problems and cater to the needs of all business economics students. Every economic law has been analysed with graphs. Quantitative techniques are also used wherever necessary to understand the application of an economic law. Some case studies are also given to give an insight into business problem and how an economic law can solve it. Chapter summaries are included to know the Central theme of each chapter. Study questions are incorporated at the end of each chapter for self evaluation. Many works on the subject were consulted while preparing this book. We have consulted many books, periodicals and journals. We thank the authors of these works. We invite the readers and students in particular to give their suggestions to fill in the gaps of this book.

We thank Sri. D.P. Pandeyji the architect of HPH for his willingness to publish and promote this book. We also thank Sri. Niraj Pandey and staff of HPH for their cooperation in bringing out this book. We thank Sri. S. Madhu of Sri Siddhi Softtek for composing this work.

P.N.Reddy
H.R.Appannaiah
Shanthi

Contents

1 Chapter

Economics for Business

The subject "*Business Economics*" deals mainly with the application of economic laws to business problems to take sound business decisions. Business is an activity which results in economic gain or loss. To run a gainful business, businessmen take the assistance of several tools and techniques along with the human effort. Economic laws are some such tools which facilitate business decisions on problems like demand forecasting (This helps in production planning and profit projections), optimum production etc. Economics provides ground for making rational decisions. BUSINESS ECONOMICS deals with the economic utilisation of source resources of a business firm to make effective decisions.

The terms "Business Economics" and "Managerial Economics" are used as synonyms. Business economics is concerned with the application of economic theory and methodology to the decision making processes of the enterprise. In other words, business economics is concerned with the using of those aspects of economic theory which would help in maximizing profit through an increase in the production and marketing of the product. The process of application of economic analysis to the management of the firm is that of using various concepts and techniques which enable the decision maker to achieve his goal in business.

Business economics is a powerful mechanism of theoretical knowledge to the business executives in managing their organisations systematically and effectively.

1. MEANING AND NATURE OF BUSINESS ECONOMICS

Economics is a science of management of limited resources with unlimited wants of human beings. The development and happiness of human beings depend upon the production, distribution and consumption of various goods and services. Man wants food, shelter and clothing primarily. These are for his existence. He needs more in order to make his life comfortable and joyful. These lead to exploration of various resources and materials and technique of production, movement and consumption of various types of goods. Man is confronted with various problems like what to produce, how to produce, for whom to produce, are the resources economically used, the products so produced are within the reach of men, etc. Knowledge of economics helps to solve all these problems. Here lies the importance of business economics.

As population and per capita income go on increasing, the demand for goods and services also increases. These development in human civilization inspires the leaders in production, trade and commerce to take up new economic activities (With the expansion and diversification of human wants, various economic activities will result in). Here comes the role of business economics in order to direct the utilization of natural and man-made resources in a desired manner for the production of various goods and services. Business economics is now derived as a body of organised and systematized knowledge comprising of theories. Economics is often defined as the science of management of economic institutions which engage in the conversion and transformation of raw-resources into consumable products. The modern society with its complex character, exercises tremendous influence through tastes and attitudes on the production and marketing of innumerable types of goods and services. Ever increasing and changing of human wants and the existence of limited volume of resources give rise to many problems such as what to produce, how to produce and how much to produce and where to produce. In this game, business economics assumes the central role. The men behind in organizing production and marketing of the products are called the business people or business executives. The business executives now turn to economics to get knowledge which would help in formulating business policies. Thus a new branch of economics called Business Economics emerged in fifties of twentieth century. Business Economics is thus a ready made tool for the business people in shaping their business decisions. Business Economics is an indispensable tool for the business people to make proper decisions.

> *Thus, Business Economics is the application of economic theory and methodology to decision making process within the enterprise. In other words, it refers to those aspects of economic analysis which are relevant to the practice of management processes in the business organisation.*

2. BUSINESS PROCESS

a. Decision making

Modern business organisation are very much concerned with decision making and forward planning. Decision making means the process of selecting the suitable action from among several alternative courses of action. The modern business is confronted with various intricate problems such as – what goods to be produced. Here the problem is selecting from among various models. Secondly, there is again another problem regarding the quality of the products to be produced. Then again, selecting the proper technology of production, such as labour saving technology or labour using technology, which energy resource is to be used – gas, diesel or coal-based or electricity, etc. Then comes another problem – how to obtain resources or what alternative resources are there for these resources and the cost aspects. Finally the determination of prices which would give the business people a reasonable amount of profit. Thus, decision making is the central objective of business economics.

b. Forward Planning

Forward planning means preparing the perspective plan of development of the organisation. This involves capital budgeting, obtaining land for future expansion, the availability of technology, cost reduction programmes, etc. As the production of the quantity of the output increases, the unit cost is required to fall gradually. Future expansion will have to be done from the surplus derived from annual profit. Forward planning also involves plan for mobilizing raw-materials, labour, pricing, etc. Thus, forward planning and decision making go hand in hand.

Present day business functions with the cloud of uncertainty. This makes decision making and forward planning difficult and complicated. If the knowledge of the future is certain, then the formulation of business plans is not difficult. But today, since the business functions with too much of uncertainty, the knowledge of business economics helps it to incorporate suitable changes whenever necessary.

3. DEFINITIONS

Management economists have defined the terminology 'Business Economics' in various ways. Some of the definitions are really illustrative.

Spencer and Siegelman have defined Business Economics as 'the integration of economic theory with business practice for the purpose of facilitating decision making and forward planning by the management'. According to them, the decision making and forward planning are the important fields of a study of business economics.

McNairMerian says that business economics consists of the use of economic modes of thought to analyse business situation. According to them, business economics becomes applied economics since economic theory is invoked in solving business problems. In other words, it also means integration of economics theory with business practice. The linkage between economics and management will help the business people to run the organizations effectively and smoothly. Economics advocates rational utilization of resources since they are scarce and have alternative uses. The business people are aware of these problems and hence they decide to set up priorities and on the basis decide the utilization of resources.

The general laws propounded by economists are put into particular situations by the Manager. Economists develop tools and techniques to study and solve various general problems. The business managers use the same tool and techniques to solve specific problems of their enterprises. Economists are concerned with elucidating general theories while the business economists use them for organizations.

Business economics does not cover all aspects of either management or economics. It covers only those aspects which are useful in business matters. The business economists have to make proper planning for the growth of the organisation. They have to make realistic forecasts regarding the future demand, competition, availability of resources and also the mode of profit and has to secure cooperation and coordination from departments of his organisation in order to make his planning effective. Thus, Business Economics covers only those aspects of economics which are relevant to the decision making process of the firm. Business Economics is purely micro-economics. It will not bother about macro-economic aspects.

The main goal of business economics is to solve practical problems. The study of business economics is for getting knowledge to solve practical problems of business. It is pragmatic. It avoids abstract ideas. It considers only the concrete issues pertaining to business. Business is not restricted to private sector. The scope of Business Economics extends to public enterprises as well.

4. CHARACTERISTIC FEATURES OF BUSINESS ECONOMICS

The features of business economics distinguish it from both management and economics. The following are the features of business economics.

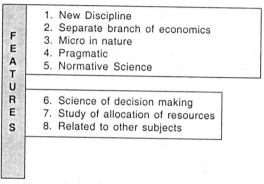

FEATURES	1. New Discipline
	2. Separate branch of economics
	3. Micro in nature
	4. Pragmatic
	5. Normative Science
	6. Science of decision making
	7. Study of allocation of resources
	8. Related to other subjects

Features of Business Economics

1. New Discipline: Business economics is a new discipline and of recent origin.

2. Separate branch of economics: Business economics is a highly specialised subject and a separate branch of economics like public finance, agricultural economics etc.

3. Micro in nature: Business economics is micro in character. It deals with the study of a unit *i.e.,* a firm. This is because a business manager is concerned with the problems of his business unit rather than the economy as a whole.

4. Pragmatic: Business economics is pragmatic in its approach. It provides solution to the problem faced by the firm.

5. Normative Science: Business economics is a normative science than a positive one. It is prescriptive rather than descriptive in nature.

6. Science of Decision Making: Business economics bridges the gap between economics and business management thereby helps the business manager to take a better decision.

7. Study of Allocation of Resources: Business economics is a study of allocation of resources made by a business firm in its production process.

8. Related to other subjects: Business economics is related to other subjects like statistics, accounting, mathematics, economics etc.

5. RELATIONSHIP BETWEEN ECONOMICS AND BUSINESS ECONOMICS

Business economics is an applied economics. Business economics depends entirely on economic analysis for getting theoretical knowledge, tools, and instruments for decision making and forward planning. It bridges the gulf between pure economics and management practice. The important subjects of study of Business Economics are demand, cost of production, pricing of products in different market structures, profit maximization, etc. In order to fully understand the above concepts, it is necessary to have a thorough knowledge of economic analysis. In order to estimate demand for products, the business economics relies on elasticity of demand. At the same time, the incomes of individuals, the production and distribution of wealth in the economy, the tastes of the people, etc. are taken into consideration. On the basis of the above, demand forecasting is made. The income and employment theory of modern economics helps the business economist to make demand forecast as accurate as possible. The prospects of the individual firms depends on the general prosperity of the economy as a whole. As such, the knowledge of pure economics is indispensable to analyse the economic prospects of individual firms. The major fields of economics which are useful to management economists are the following:

(a) Demand theory,

(b) Theory of the firm – price – output and investment decisions,

(c) Business financing,

(d) Public finance and fiscal policy

(e) Money and Banking

(f) National income and social accounting, theory of international trade and economic development.

Thus, Business Economics derives insight and guidance from economics.

6. MICRO AND MACRO-ECONOMICS

The study of economics is divided by modern economists into two parts, micro-economics and macro-economics. The terms micro-economics and macro-economics were first used by Swedish Economist Ragnar Frisch in the 1920s. An economic system may be looked at as a whole or in terms of various decision making units such as individual consumers or households, producing units such as firms, business concerns, individual factor of production such as land, labour, capital and entrepreneurs and individual industries such as iron and steel, cotton textiles, automobiles, etc. When we are analyzing the problems of economy as a whole, it is macro-economics. While an analysis of the behaviour of any particular decision making unit such as firm, an industry, a consumer constitutes micro-economics.

Micro-economics is also called Price Theory while Macro-economics is called Income Theory. "Price theory" explains the composition and allocation of total production, why more of some things is produced than others etc. 'Income Theory' explains the level of total production and why the level of production rises or falls.

Micro-Economics

Prof.Boulding defines Micro-economics as the study of a particular firm, particular household, individual price, wage, income, industry and particular commodity. It is defined as a study of economic activities of such units as consumers, resource owners and business firms.

The word 'micro' means a millionth part. It forms only a small part or component of the whole economy. The study of the behaviour of individual consumer of a product or the study of an individual firm or the individual industry is micro-economics. Micro-economic theory studies the behaviour of individual decision-making units, such as individual consumers, firms, resource-owners, etc. Micro-economics studies how the resources flow from resource owners to individual business units and the flow of goods and services from individual firms to households. It studies the composition of such flows and how prices of goods and services in the flow are determined.

Macro-Economics

Prof.Boulding defines it as "Macro-economics deals not with individual quantities as such, but with aggregates of these quantities, not with individual income but with national income, not with individual prices but with price levels, not with individual outputs but with national output."

"Macro-economics is concerned with such variables as the aggregate volume of output of the economy, with the extent to which its resources are employed, with the size of the national income and with the general price levels" says Gardner Ackley. The study of totals of important variables in the economic system such as income, consumption, saving, investment, employment, forms the subject matter of macro-economics.

Macro-economics is also called aggregative economics. Macro-economics is concerned with aggregates and averages of the entire economy. It deals with economic affairs 'in the large'. It concerns the overall dimensions of economic life. It deals with how economy grows. It establishes an important relationship between movements of income, employment and price level.

Inter-dependence of the Micro-Macro Approaches

It may appear to common minds that Micro-economics and Macro-economics are unrelated and independent. But, in fact, it is not so. Neither approach is complete without the other.

Every micro-economic problem involves macro-economic thought. How much a firm should pay for a labour is no doubt comes within the purview of micro-economy. But the wages of one firm are related to the wages of other firms in the locality. Thus, every price, every wage and every income is dependent directly or indirectly upon the prices, wages, incomes of all other products, of all other workers and of all individuals in the community. It is thus clear that every micro-economic problem involves macro-economic analysis.

Macro-economic analysis requires micro-economic analysis. A society consists of individuals. Individuals collectively make up society. In the same way, many firms constitute industry and many industries collectively makeup the economy. Therefore, to get a clear idea of working of our economy, we are required to know the working of individual units. The total production of individual firms make up the output of the entire economy. The sum total of individual income is the national income. Therefore, to understand the working of the economy, we have to study the theory of individual firm. Thus a study of macro-economics necessarily involves the study of micro-economics.

Integration of these two Approaches

What is needed is a proper integration of the micro and macro approaches to such problems. In fact, there are a few macro problems which have no micro elements involved and a few micro problems that are without macro aspects. It is therefore proper to integrate both in analyzing the economic problems and prescribing policy measures for solving them. Ignoring one and concentrating on the other gives rise to incomplete results.

Is Business Economics Micro-Economics or Macro-Economics?

Business economics essentially is micro-economics. It is concerned with business firms. It studies the problems of a business firm such as forecasting the demand for its product, calculating the cost of production, fixation of price, profit planning and capital management.

Though basically being micro-economics, Business Economics seeks the help of macro-economics. It is because that individual units function in the environment in which all firms work. If it has to survive, it has to modify its objectives, plans and programmes so as to make it in conformity with the whole economy. The firm has to function in a macro-economic environment and therefore it has to adjust its pricing policy, profit policy to national economic policies. Therefore Business Economics cannot be exclusively micro-economics in character. It has to face macro-economic issues like, tax policies, business cycles, wage policies, industrial relations, pricing and distribution policies and anti-monopoly policies of the government. Business economics in this respect becomes macro-economics. The importance that macro-economics has come to acquire is not without reasons. Macro-economics helps in understanding the economic environment in which the individual unit works. Therefore, if the individual units are studied under the broader macro perspective, suitable decisions can be taken to correct if there are any imbalances. Further, macro-economics is useful in formulating policies applicable to whole nation. It is not at all possible to frame policies to individual units. Under the guidelines shown by macro-economics, individual units can function effectively. A clear understanding of both the individual units and the whole environment is necessary to produce the best results.

Economics is both Positive and Normative

Economics associates with ethics. For example, mal-distribution of wealth is dangerous. It creates tug of war between the rich and the poor. Therefore, the purpose of economics is to promote welfare and as such it is normative science. Mahatma Gandhi said, "Economics which disregards moral and sentimental considerations is like wax works that being life like, still lacks the life of a living fresh". In order to pass value judgement, it is necessary that the problems are to be explored and explained. Since people approach economics for a fruit, economics should provide solutions which are beneficial to mankind. It is in this regard economics is called both a positive and normative science.

Economics is regarded as a normative science due to the fact that economics is an engine of social betterment. Economics, since time immemorial, have been giving suggestions regarding the welfare of human beings. For example, Adam Smith advocated the Taxation Policy. Malthus advocated population control and suggested to how to control it. J.S.Mill suggested imposition of taxes on unearned income. Keynes suggested measures to remove unemployment. In this way, economists have been advocating various measures to promote human welfare.

Hence, economics consists not merely allocating scarce resources among competing ends but is maximizing total satisfaction according to ones own judgement. The choice resulting from subjecting competing desires to judgement makes economics obviously a normative science.

Business economics is a normative science because it deals with problems of modern business organizations and offers solutions. It tells us what should be under a particular circumstance. A business economist tells the management what should be done to achieve the business objectives. It tells the businessmen what should be done in order to get results.

Business economics is considered as applied economics. It suggests how the economic principles are applied to the formulation of policies and programmes. It tells the business executives how to achieve the business objectives.

In order to pass judgements, business economics has to explore and explain the issues. It has to describe the state and operation of the firm or the economy at a point of time or during a period of time. It also develops hypothesis and explains why it has happened. Along with it also suggests how to overcome problems. In the case of normative micro-economics, one is concerned with problems like what the objectives and policies of business ought to be and how to go about them. In the macro-economic level too business economics behaves in a normative way.

In conclusion, it can be said that business economics is essentially micro-economics. It studies an individual unit namely a business firm. It is concerned with normative micro-economics. In normative micro-economics, the economist says what ought to happen rather than what happens. In attempting to study the various connected problems, he has to take up positive economics.

The main goal of business economics is to solve practical problems. The study of business economics is for getting knowledge to solve practical problems in business. It is pragmatic. It avoids abstract ideas. It considers only the concrete issues pertaining to business. Business is not restricted to private sector alone. The scope of businss economics extends to public sector enterprises as well.

Business economics is a scientific art too. Art is a system in which the rules and regulations so formulated are put into successful application. Business economics helps the management in better utilization of scarce resources for the production of commodities which are going to satisfy the needs of man.

7. DIFFERENCE BETWEEN BUSINESS ECONOMICS AND ECONOMICS

Though Economics and Business Economics are closely related to each other, yet they differ in certain aspects. The differences are listed below:

	Business Economics	*Economics*
1.	Deals with application of economic principles to the problem faced by the firm.	It is concerned with the body of principles itself.
2.	Micro in Nature. *i.e.*, it deals with the problems concerning a particular firm.	It includes both micro and macro economics.
3.	It is mainly concerned with profit theories.	It deals with different theories such as wages, interest and profit theories.
4.	Its scope is limited.	It has wider scope.
5.	Provides solution to the firm with the help of other subjects like statistics, mathematics, mathematics, accounting etc.	Economic theories are based on assumption and hence they cannot give practical solution to business problems.

8. BUSINESS ECONOMICS AND OTHER SUBJECTS

Business economics is closely related with other subjects like pure economics, statistics, mathematics and accounting.

Its relationship with Economics

In fact, Business economics is an applied economics. Business economics depends entirely on economic analysis for getting theoretical knowledge, tools, and instruments for decision making and forward planning. It bridges the gulf between pure economics and management practice. The important subjects of study of Business Economics are demand, cost of production, pricing of products in different market structures, profit maximization, etc. In order to fully understand the above concepts, it is necessary to have a thorough knowledge of economic analysis. In order to estimate demand for products, the business economics relies on elasticity of demand. At the same time, the incomes of individuals, the production and distribution of wealth in the economy, the tastes of the people, etc. are taken into consideration. On the basis of the above, demand forecasting is made. The income and employment theory of modern economics helps the business economist to make demand forecast as accurate as possible. The prospects of the individual firms depends on the general prosperity of the economy as a whole. As such, the knowledge of pure economics is indispensable to analyse the economic prospects of individual firms. The major fields of economics which are useful to management economists are the following:

(a) Demand theory,

(b) Theory of the firm – price – output and investment decisions,

(c) Business financing,

(d) Public finance and fiscal policy

(e) Money and Banking

(f) National income and social accounting, theory of international trade and economic development.

Thus, Business Economics derives insight and guidance from economics.

Business Economics and Statistics

Business Economics is not a mere theoretical exposition. In fact, it is concerned with practical problems which are started in quantitative data (in fact, after the II World War, the business people are using the knowledge and the analytical techniques of behavioural science). The data so collected and apply presented helps the management to take appropriate decisions whenever possible.

Business economics uses statistical methods to test the economic generalizations and conclusions. When the data are checked in the respective fields, the business managers will be able to take correct decisions.

Statistical data are collected frequently in order to reduce the danger of uncertainty in the minds of business people.

Business Economics and Mathematics

Mathematics is another important tool used by Business Economics. It is stated that Business Economics is both conceptual and metrical for, without measurement, the theory will be misleading in taking decisions. Mathematics helps in estimating various economic relationships, predicting relevant economic quantities and using them in decision taking and forward planning. Business economics uses considerable amount of geometry, algebra, calculus extensively in deriving solutions. Further, operational research is used in estimating demand and determining the prices of the products.

Then there is operational research which is closely related to business Economics. Operational research is the application of mathematical techniques to solving business problems. It provides all the data required for business decisions and forward planning. Techniques such as linear programming, game theory, etc. are due to the works of operational research. Linear Programming is extensively used in decision taking. Business economics is concerned with efficient use of scarce resources. Operational research is concerned with efficient use of scarce resources. There is close affinity between business economics and operational research. Business economics gives special emphasis to problems involving maximization of profit and minimization of costs, while operational research focuses attention on the concept of optimization. Business economics has made much use of optimization concept but initially started with marginal analysis taken from economics. Business economics uses the logic of Economics, Mathematics and Statistics for undertaking effective decisions, while operational research techniques based on these ways of thinking are being used to solve decision making problems in business. Again, both operational research and business economics are concerned with taking effective decisions.

Operational research is a tool in the hands of business economics to solve day to day business problems. Business economics is an academic subject which aims to understand and analyse problems and decision making by a firm. Thus operational research is a functional activity pursued by specialists within the firm. Though it is expensive, it helps to make accurate solutions by means of providing necessary data.

Business Economics and Accounting

Management accounting provides necessary financial data for suitable decisions in business. The business decisions are generally based on accounting data. For example, the profit and loss statement of the firm for a specific period will reveal how the firm has preformed. The business economist will now form future course of action, namely, whether to continue in the existing manner or to make proper improvement etc. Accounting information supplies necessary information needed for business decision making. Manager of a business concern needs market information, production information and accounting information for taking effective business decisions. Thus, there exists a close link between business economics and management accounting. The main task of management accounting is to provide the sort of data which managers need to solve some business problems accurately. The accounting data are also to be provided in such a manner so as to help the business economist to take correct decisions in business.

Thus, bsiness economics is concerned with determining the means of achieving given objectives in the most e ficient manner while considering both explicit and implicit constraints on the application of the means. The major areas of Business Economics are:

(a) Decision making,

(b) Demand analysis and forecasting,

(c) Production and cost,

(d) Pricing and market structure,

(e) Capital budgeting and profits.

Business economics is firmly rooted on the foundation provided by economics and is enriched by the growing influence of Mathematics, Statistics or Management Accounting.

9. SCOPE OF BUSINESS ECONOMICS

The scope of business economics extends to those fields of activity which are carried out by business organizations. Business economics is concerned with solving all problems pertaining to business affairs. It refers to policies of planning and development of business. The subject matter of business economics is classified under the following broad heads:

(a) Consumption analysis with special emphasis on demand analysis and forecasting.

(b) Production and cost analysis.

(c) Pricing decisions, policies and practices.

(d) Profit management

(e) Capital management and

(f) Decision-making

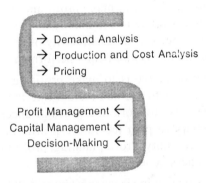

→ Demand Analysis
→ Production and Cost Analysis
→ Pricing

Profit Management ←
Capital Management ←
Decision-Making ←

Scope of Business Economics

(a) Demand Analysis: Spencer and Siegalman defined a business firm as an economic organism which transforms productive resources into consumable goods which are meant for sale in the market. As such, a firm before producing any consumable commodity, must assess the nature of demand for the product. It has to search out and measure the forces that determine sales. In order to estimate the future demand, the manager has to take into consideration the income elasticity, price elasticity, and substitution elasticity of demand. Demand analysis covers demand determinants, demand distinctions and demand forecasting. Demand analysis is an important bench mark for appraising salesman's performance and for setting up sales quotas.

(b) Production and cost analysis: The production and cost analysis is another field of study of business economics. It helps the manager to attain efficient allocation of productive resources which are scarce. The production and cost analysis is essential for effective project planning. The cost of production of a firm are estimated from the accounting records. From these records, the business manager will be in a position to compare costs of production of different periods and thereby evolves suitable policies in controlling costs and deriving suitable profits.

The production analysis is concerned with proper product mix. What factors are to be combined in what manner to produce a given product. It is done in physical terms while cost analysis is done in financial terms. The important topics discussed in this field are cost concepts, classifications, cost input relationships, economies and diseconomies of scale, production function and cost control.

(c) **Pricing decisions, policies and practices:** Pricing of the product or products produced by the firm is a very important field of business economics. The chief function of the firm is pricing. This depends upon the cost of production and at the same time the prices of substitutes and the nature of competition. Price affects profits which in turn determine the existence and growth of the firm. The Manager is required to have a thorough knowledge of the theories of production and the pricing in order to make sure that the firm gets profit continuously. The manager has to determine suitable price policies applicable to short and long term production.

(d) **Capital management:** A business firm is organized with a view to make profit. In order to organize a business firm, the most important requirement is capital. Capital management is efficient use of scarce capital. Capital management is done by means of preparing a capital budget. It includes both investment capital and working capital. It also involves short term and long term requirement. Further it deals with three things – cost of capital, rate of return and selection of project.

(e) **Profit management:** Profit management is central matter in business economics. A business firm is an organisation designed to make profit and profits are the primary measure of success. Social criteria of business relate to the quality of the product, rate of progress and the behaviour of prices. But these are tests of the desirability of the whole profit system. Within this system profits are acid test of the individual firm's performance.

The business firm's sacred objective is to make profit but it has to make profit under the situation of uncertainty. This is due to various factors like the prices of resources, the cost of production, etc. Since the firms have to work in a world of uncertainty, profit planning becomes very difficult. Yet, it is necessary to plan the future profits in a realistic manner, taking into consideration the element of uncertainty. Profit planning, profit management, profit measurement are the important areas of business economics.

(f) **Decision making:** Decision making is the most important function of the Business Manager. Faced with scarce resources, competing ends, the choice of a final end is to pass value judgement. To try and to achieve optimum satisfaction, is to realize the objective which may be considered good and reasonable. The economic agent has to act on the principle that scarce resources are put into best advantage and should not be wasted. This is obviously 'a universal human value' affecting all economic behaviour. It is in this context decision making occupies a central place in Management.

10. METHODS OF BUSINESS ECONOMICS

Since Economics is recognized as a science, it follows certain methodologies. A systematic way of approach to any problem is called methodology. In fact, method means the mode of rule of accomplishing an end. It is a procedure of examining any economic problem. Some tools are employed to arrive at a solution. These tools are used in a systematic way in business economics. A business manager is confronted with many problems. In order to solve these problems, he is required to use some tools of investigation. In other words, he uses certain methods which would help him to understand the problems. These methods are (1) Internal data, (2) The data given by associations, (3) Published data, (4) Field investigations and assistance of specialized agencies. Let us know the details of these methods.

Internal Data: Internal data refers to facts and figures available with the company or business organisation. When a manager wants to solve the problem, he should have complete knowledge of things going on in his company. He gets the latest figures and facts regarding production, inventory, sales, etc. In a modern business organisation, all major departments are expected to maintain complete records. Nowadays they are all computerized. He can get any information within minutes. Let us now see how he can use these figures in order to take a decision. Supposing the sales of a company producing soaps fell down in the previous month. In order to find out the reason and to arrive at a solution, he takes the data of several months of the year. The data from three departments such as production, inventory and sales is as follows in the next page.

Data on Production, Inventory and Sales (Year 2002)

Month	Production	Inventory	Sales (in tonnes)
January	3000	2000	4000
February	3100	1000	3100
March	2900	1000	3000
April	2800	900	3000
May	3200	700	3000
June	3000	900	3000
July	3000	900	3000
August	2000	900	2800
September	2000	100	2100
October	2000	Nil	2000
November	2100	100	3000
December	3000	200	2900

With this data, the manager is required to analyse the cause for downward trend in sales, particularly during September and October. From the table, it can be seen that sales actually fell down during September and October. Rest of the months, the sales were normal except in January. A look at the production level will reveal that in months of August, September and October production was only 2000 tonnes. The question is that why the stocks could not be met from the inventory. A look at the inventory position also reveals that the stocks of finished goods fell down from 2000 tonnes to Nil in October. This means that the inventory department met the demand of sales department to the maximum extent. In the month of September, the stock fell down to 100 tonnes and in October to nil and hence could not meet the requirement of sales department. Therefore, the problem is with the production department. The solution lies in tackling the causes for decreased production. The manager now takes up measures of increasing production. Thus internal data is of great help in solving business problems. He will now closely follow the trend in production and inventory management. Huge stocks of inventory means blocking of working capital. A meagre stock or huge stock of finished goods would have a telling effect on sales.

Associations: Manufacturers form association in order to promote their interests. Association will help the producers in obtaining raw materials, movement of finished goods, etc. The members of the association are required to furnish various data, which will compile it and publish in their annual reports. Members of the association can study these figures supplied by the association. This reveals whether a company is selling more or less. The data is useful in working where the company stands in the market. He can now take up suitable measures in improving the sales of this product.

Published Data: The data furnished by the Associations does not give a correct picture of the industry as a whole. It is only partial. In order to get the information at the national level, he has to depend upon the published data brought out either by the government or by research bodies. Data published by Planning Commission, Centre for Monitoring Economy, National Council of Applied Economic Research. The D.G.T.D publishers two books, one Annual Report and the Hand Book of Statistics. Annual Report contains the data of production of both agricultural and industrial products. The Hand Book of Statistics furnishes advance information. From these documents, the business managers can know as to how many units are manufacturing various industrial products, their installed capacity and percentage of utilization, etc. The Centre of Monitoring Indian Economy brings several publications periodically. These publications will help in arriving at two important points namely the production trend over the years and percentage of capacity utilization. From this, present supply of products can be estimated. On the demand side, the journals like Fortnightly Journal of Indian Economy publishes current as well as future demand. From this, the Managers can draw the production schedule of their products.

Besides this, factors like seasonal, economic, climatic are also to be known. The Association of Indian Engineering Industry publishes bulletins to reveal the demand and supply pattern of Engineering goods. A business economist can arrive at an agreeable conclusion as regards production, inventory and sales.

Field investigation: In addition to the above mentioned methods, it is necessary to undertake field investigation. The Company can take up this work itself by sending sales executives or personnel to the respective areas. Supposing the sales of the product of particular company in a particular area is sluggish, then the company may take up special investigation. This enquiry may be conducted to find out the various facts, such as number of rival products sold in the region, their prices, their demand, the nature of sales campaign by the rivals, etc. To get answers to these questions, one has to go to the specific area for detailed investigation. The company takes up market survey by itself. On the basis of the survey report, the company can take suitable measures to face the competition.

Specialised Agencies: If the Company finds that its officers are not equipped to undertake this type of enquiry, it can entrust this work to specialized consultancies. Market Survey is a technical job, only experts can do it efficiently. The Consultancy may also furnish many related matters such as potential buyers, their income and their consumption pattern, etc. It is also better to entrust such specially technical enquiries to those agencies.

11. ECONOMIC PRINCIPLES APPLIED TO BUSINESS ECONOMICS

Several concepts and tools are used in economic theory to analyse various problems concerned with production and consumption. These concepts and tools are very much used in Business Economics too. In fact, economics does not provide ready made answers to all problems but it offers variety of broad principles which can be applied with modifications wherever necessary to solve economic problems. In applying economic principles for solving various business problems, the business economist has to use additional skills and tools to bridge the gap between economic theory and business practices. It is because, that in actual practice there exists great disparity between economic principles and actually observed practices in business. The basic principle tools which are used business economics are as follows:

(a) The Opportunity Cost Principle

(b) The Incremental Principle

(c) The Principle of Time Perspective

(d) The Discounting Principle

(e) The Equimarginal Principle

(a) The Opportunity Cost Principle: By the opportunity cost, we mean the cost involved in any decision that consists of sacrifices of alternatives required by that decision. If there are no sacrifices there are no costs. The opportunity costs are measured by sacrifices made in the decision. This can be very well understood by the following examples. The opportunity costs of funds employed in one's own business is the interest that could be earned on those funds had they been employed in other ventures.

The opportunity cost of using a machine to produce one product is the income foregone which would have been possible from other products. If the machine has only one use, it has no opportunity cost. If the machine has a number of uses, opportunity cost of a product is measured in terms of cost of producing an alternative product. Similarly, the opportunity cost of time an entrepreneur devotes to his own business is the salary that he could earn if he would take up a job with some one else. For decision making, application of opportunity cost principle is very much useful. It is because that it is the only relevant cost.

(b) The Incremental Principle: Economists use the incremental principle in the theories of consumption, production, pricing and distribution. Incremental concept is closely related to marginal cost and marginal revenue in the theory of pricing. Incremental cost involves estimating the impact of decision alternatives on cost and revenue, emphasising the changes in the total cost and total revenue resulting from changes in prices, products, procedures, investments, etc. The two basic components of incremental principle are incremental cost and incremental revenue. Incremental cost is the change in the total cost as a result of new decision. The incremental principle is useful when the firm wants to expand the production of a commodity. If the incremental revenue is higher than incremental cost, then it is profitable for the manager to expand the business. The moment the incremental revenue is equal to incremental cost, the manager is required to stop further expansion. Incremental principle is very much used in decision taking.

(c) The Principle of Time Perspective: The time perspective such as short run and long run or market period, short period, long period and secular period is useful in determining prices of products. Economists have established through analysis, short term costs and price are higher than long run prices and costs. In this connection, they have maintained an argument that in the short term average prices may not cover average costs, but in the long run, they must be equal. The most important aspect in decision taking is that the firm must maintain right balances between short term and long term considerations. Modern economists have introduced a new time perspective called 'Intermediate run' between short term and long term in order to explain price and output behaviour of the firm under oligopoly. The principle of time preference can be stated as 'A decision should take into account both the short run and the long run effects on revenues and costs and maintain a right balance between short run and long run perspectives'.

This principle can be explained with the following illustration. If a company has idle capacity, to make use of this idle capacity, it may offer the product at a price lower than the cost. This may be alright in the short period. Supposing the demand for the product rises, then the firm comes into the problem of building sufficient capacity to increase production. This will result in increased incremental cost. In the long run the prices will have to be equal to cost. It is therefore necessary to give due consideration to the time perspective. Haynes, Mote and Paul mentioned an example of a company which followed the stable price policy, even though there was idle capacity. The reason was that the management realised that long run repercussions of pricing below the full cost would be more than offset any short term gain.

(d) Discounting Principle: Discounting principle occupies a very important place in business economics. It is because the future is uncertain. The costs and revenues may change in future. Whenever the present value of a business is to be known, the future values will have to be discounted. For example, suppose a person is offered to make a choice to make an investment on shares of a company, he will prefer the present value more than the future value. It is because of the uncertainty of the future. If the share is worth Rs.100, he will prefer Rs.100 today to Rs.100 next year. Even if he is sure to receive Rs.100 next year, one would do well to receive Rs.100 now and invest it for one year and earn a rate of interest on Rs.100 for one year. To find out its present worth, we have to find out what rate of interest he is going to earn in one year. Suppose the rate of interest is 8 per cent. Then we have to discount Rs.100 at 8 per cent in order to find out its present value. The relevant formula for finding this out is:

$$PW = \frac{Rs.100}{1+i}$$ where 'i' is the rate of interest.

Present worth of Rs.100 is 100   1 + 8% = 100   1.08 = 92.59

The same logic applies to longer periods. A sum of Rs.100 after two years will have a present worth:

The discounting principle is thus stated as follows:

If a decision affects costs and revenues of future dates, it is necessary to discount those costs and revenues to obtain the present values of both before a value comparison of alternatives can be made.

(e) The Equimarginal Principle: The Equimarginal Principle is one of the widely used concepts in economics. The law of equimarginal principle states that an input should be allocated in such a way that the value added by last unit of the input is the same in all its uses. This law can be explained with the following illustration.

Suppose a firm has to employ 50 workers in three departments such as spinning, weaving and printing. The firm has to allocate the workers in such a way that the marginal productivity of the last worker employed is the same. Supposing the marginal productivity of a labour in spinning is Rs.20 and in weaving Rs.30, it is profitable to shift labour from spinning to weaving, thereby there is expansion in B and reduction in A. The optimum is reached when the value of marginal product is equal in all the twin activities. The formula is as follows:

$$VMP_A = VMP_B = VMP_C \text{ etc.}$$

In applying the equimarginal principle or make it more practicable, certain aspects will have to be looked into. Firstly, we have to find out the net value of the marginal products before resorting to comparison. It is because, when a worker is to be added to an activity, it necessitates adding other inputs like machinery. And to find out the net marginal value of the workers, we must deduct from his VMP the value of additional materials used in the process of production. Supposing the value of the additional material used is Rs.10, then the VMP of the worker is 30 - 10 = 20.

Secondly, the future prices of the products produced by additional labour input is also to be considered. If, as a result of increased prodution, the price falls, the additional revenue earned by the firm will be less. Then we have to subtract the reduction in revenue from the VMP of the worker in order to get net marginal revenue product of the labour.

Thirdly, it is necessary to discount the revenues made available to the firm from the sale of additional production in the future. Labour is to be paid today, while the output will be sold in future. If a year is required to sell the output, we have to discount the net product for one year.

It should be noted that equimarginal principle works only under ideal conditions. For example, due to non-economic pulls and pressures, an economic activity will have to be carried on, even though additional revenue is negative. This happens especially when the government wants to keep up employment generation programme. There is also certain instances where a firm wants to expand, managers may resort to spending more than necessary. Managements may not agree to retrench workers even after the introduction of automation, simply because of maintaining good labour relations. In such cases, the equimanagerial principle has to be rendered unworkable.

Summing up, it can be stated that principles and theories of economics are of considerable interest to modern business enterrises. Economic theories as such cannot be directly applied to draw conclusions. Economic theory is meant for generalised study and application to practical situations, some modifications have to be made. There is a great need for modification of the assumptions in business economics. For example, there is an assumption in the theory of firm where the entrepreneur strives to maximise his profit. But in actual practice, the businessmen strive to attain a level of profit holding a certain share of the market for his product. Prof.Baumol is of the opinion that firms do not devote all their energies to maximising profit but they seek to maximise the sales revenue. Thus, suitable modifications have to be made to assumptions of pure economic theory.

12. ROLE OF A BUSINESS ECONOMIST

The concept Role refers to the behaviour and action of a person in accordance with specified functions.

A business economist is one who has specialised in basic economic theory and with this knowledge, he applies it to business prosperity. He is very well called adviser to a firm since the firm takes several economic decisions which are vital to the growth of a firm based on his advice. He has to study cost - price - output relationship and advise the business in fixing the prices of the products. He is required to solve various problems concerning decision making and forward planning. Nowadays all big business organisations are utilising the services of business economists. The business economist, by virtue of his expert knowledge can help the businessmen to take correct decisions.

Business economist can help the Board of Management in several ways.

1. He can assist the management in decision making process of what commodities to be produced, how are prices dtermined and to determine marketing strategy. These are external factors to the firm and are said to constitute business environment.

2. He can also assist the management in business operations. That is, regarding the amount of capital to be invested and at what price the capital has to be mobilised and to procure factors of production and at what prices and finally at what price the commodities can be sold, etc.

3. He has to analyse and forecast external factors which affect the business prosperity.

4. The business economist is required to provide necessary information and guidance to tackle problems both during inflation and deflation.

5. The business economist has also to analyse the balance of payments position of the country, exchange rate, import and export policies of the Government, etc., so that the industry which is exporting the products can very well make necessary adjustments.

6. The business economist acts as a friend, philosopher and guide to the businessmen. He should offer constructive suggestions and give proper direction and guidance to the firm.

7. Business Economist should react and respond quickly to the dynamic changes that are taking place in the modern business horizon and should come out with appropriate changes in the policies and programmes of a business unit.

8. Business Economist has to conduct national, international, inter-industry studies and product line research to assist the management to take suitable decisions.

9. Business economist should coordinate the activities of various departments of the firm and he should work in harmony with other policy makers of the firm.

The business economist is required to tackle various questions which are referred to him. Some of the basic questions which are referred to business economist are:

1. The present and future outlook of the national economy. The present phase of growth taking place in the economy whether the economy is facing inflation or recession.

2. The growth rate of population and the occupational distribution of population and the income pattern of various categories of population.

3. The demand pattern of industrial products in internal and external markets – the changes and fashions of the people in different regions of the country and the impact of these on the production and sale of durable goods.

4. The consumption pattern of people abroad and the scope of foreign trade of products produced by the firms.

5. Financial aspect namely the availability and cost of capital both in the country and outside.

6. The foreign exchange regulations and sources of foreign capital for the expansion and modernization of the firms.

   In this context the business economist has to acquire knowledge with regard to foreign collaboration.

7. The problems of institutional finance for the firms and ways of obtaining institutional finance for the development of the firm.

8. Price variations of both raw materials, finished products and the extent of competition that the firm has to face.

9. The sectional outlay of Five-Year plans and its effect on the production and sale of company's product. Supposing the outlay on agricultural mechanization is increased by 10 or 15 per cent over the previous plans outlay, then producers of machineries are required to formulate plans of development, such as quantity of steel and other materials required and fixation of prices for different categories of agricultural machineries.

10. The economic policies of the Government and how far they are helpful or affecting the growth of the activities of the firm.

11. The policies concerning the company taxation, general excise duties, import and export duties, etc.

12. The decisions of the Central Bank of the country with regard to interest rates on short term and long term borrowing and their rules and regulations, etc.

Thus, the field of enquiry of the business economist is so vast that he is required to have up-to-date knowledge of economic trends at the macro level in order to offer required advice to the industry. These are relating to external operations of the firm for which the business economist has a greater role to play in the firm. Professors K.J.W.Alexander and Alexander G Kemp have outlined specific functions of the business economist in an industrial organisation, which are as follows:

(1) Sales forecasting

(2) Industrial market research

(3) Economic analysis of competitors

(4) Pricing of industrial products

(5) Capital budgeting

(6) Production programmes

(7) Future investment programmes

(8) Advice on trade and public relations

(9) Advice on the purchase of raw materials

(10) Advice on inventory building

(11) Advice on the use and conservation of foreign exchange earnings

(12) Market survey to determine the nature and extent of competition

(13) Environmental aspects

The fields of enquiry of the business economist are so exhaustive, that he becomes a key person in an industrial organisation.

The business economist has to keep an eye on the fast changing technological developments. An economic decision is taken within the framework of technological developments. Therefore, the business economist has to make a continuous assessment of the impact of technological changes. If the firm does not make suitable changes in the production and marketing strategies it fails to face competition of the rival firms. In this context, the business economist has to find out ways and means of economizing, thereby minimize the cost of production.

Above all, the business economist has to help the management in business planning by offering guidance for the correct running of the industrial organisation. Organizationally, the business economist has to work in harmony with the policy makers of the industry, for he has to identify problems and constraints and suggest alternatives for the successful functioning of the firms.

The business economists perform varied functions. Apart from sales forecasting and market research, they have to maintain statistical records of sales performance not only of their industrial organizations, but also the rival firms. Every firm wants to sell more and capture a greater portion of industry's sales and for this purpose the business economist is required to guide them.

The fundamental function of the business economist in an industrial organisation is to supply economic information to the management. The information includes the prices of the rivals of the products, the consumers' attitude towards the price and quality of the products, tax rates, tariffs rates, etc. He is required to collect all these information, analyse them and present them to the management.

Role of Business Economists In India

Business economists in India are required to perform the following functions. The main fields of activity of the business economists in this context are as follows:

(a) Macro forecasting of demand and supply. The Planning Commission Projects future demand and supply of various commodities. The business economists are required to modify them in the light of past performance.

(b) Micro and Macro level production planning. Macro level production planning is made by the Planning Commission and also National Council of Applied Economic Research. The business economists are required to project the production trends of their units taking into consideration their production capacities and normal constraints such as transport bottlenecks, fuel and power shortage, working capital constraints and market absorption.

(c) Planning of capacity production and determination of product mix.

(d) Preparing economic feasibility of new production processes, diversification of production, etc.

(e) Participating in the planning process of Company's development.

(f) Preparing periodical economic reports on company's product sales, sales of the rival products, consumers' preferences, future growth opportunities, general price trends and national and international factors affecting the prospects of industry as well as the units concerned.

(g) Participating in seminars, conferences, workshops organized by Chambers of Commerce or Industry's Association.

(h) Preparing rules and principles which facilitate in attaining the goals and objectives of the company. These goals relate to costs, revenues and profits are important within both the business and non – business institutions.

(i) Suggesting how economic theories and methodologies can be applied in the decision making process of the firm.

13. RESPONSIBILITIES OF THE BUSINESS ECONOMIST

Business economics is a composite discipline. It contains quantitative statements as well as statements touching ethical aspect. Business economics is more practical than theoretical and as such the business economist has to study practical economic implications of any decision taking. The main responsibilities of the business economist are as follows:

1. Better Management of Resources: Though business economics is normative, it cannot ignore the positive aspect. Positive economics is a scientific discipline while normative economics is a branch of ethics. If the firm is to attain success in business, it has to produce products of exceptionally high quality and sell it at reasonable prices. This requires better management of men and resources. The utilisation of optimum production capacity, the exploitation of hidden talents in the man power, better financial management are sine quo non for success in business. It is said that the opinion of the business economist on a normative question is of no more value than guessing the result of a football match. This field rests with management itself. But the role of the business economist in the organisation is that of a pure scientist leaving the normative aspect to the management.

2. Economic forecast: The firms function in certain social, economic and political system. For example, we assume the existence of mixed economy in which individuals enjoy right to property. We also assume that law and order prevails in the country and every one is subordinate to rule of law and there exists stable political system. The existence of free markets is assumed. The markets keep buyers and sellers of a commodity in touch with one another. That is how prices are determined and a uniform price prevails for a product in the market. The business economist functions in such social and political environment and thus manage the affairs in perfect co-ordination and understanding. He cannot function in ivory tower. He functions in realities. Therefore, economists have to function in an environment where resources are scarce and technical factors put a limitation on industrial output etc. Though the business economist works in an uncertain environment, he is required to forecast, the demand for the product, the sales turnover, the net profits, etc. as realistic as possible. His analysis should indicate the probable risks that the company may experience in varied situations. The economic forecast is like weather forecast, as such, in the midst of uncertainties, the forecast should suggest how the management can adjust the production and marketing of the product and withstand the economic fluctuations.

Apart from the above mentioned responsibilities, the business economist must maintain and establish contacts with data sources for his forecasts and analysis. He should also collect information by joining in professional associations and subscribe to the journals giving him latest information. The most important responsibility of a business economist is to obtain information quickly by establishing contacts with various sources of information.

The business economist can be a successful and earn an important place in the managerial or business team only when he understands and undertakes his responsibilities in a best possible manner.

14. BASIC CONCEPTS IN BUSINESS ECONOMICS

1. Scarcity: Scarcity is one of the important concepts of economics, relevant for management. The reason for any economic problem, micro or macro, is the scarcity of resources. The managers who decide on behalf of the firm always face the economic problem and scarcity of one kind or the other. A few examples to illustrate this - A production manager may be facing scarcity of good quality of materials or skilled technicians. A marketing manager may be encountering shortage of sales force at his command. A finance manager may be facing the scarcity of funds necessary for his programme. Thus, scarcity is a universal problem.

The term scarcity in terms of economics may be defined as 'excess demand'. At any time, for any thing if demand (requirement) exceeds supply (availability) that thing or good is said to be scarce, *i.e* the demand in relation to supply determines the elements of scarcity. So scarcity is a relative concept. For example, unemployment is due to scarcity of jobs. Inflation is due to scarcity of goods. Unsold stock of inventory is due to shortage of consumers etc.

2. Marginalism: When the resources are scarce managers have to be careful about the utilisation of every additional resources. A decision about additional investment has to be taken in the light of the additional return from that investment. In economics the term "marginal" is used for all such additional magnitudes of out put or return. For example, the terms like marginal output of labour, marginal output of machines marginal return on investment, marginal costs of production etc are used in economics.

The term 'marginalism' is not similar to the concept of average. For example average product of labour is the ratio of total product to total labour whereas marginal product of labour is the ratio of change in product to one unit change in labour.

The following table will illustrate the relationship between average and marginal concepts

No. of Labourers	Total Output	Average Output	Marginal Output
L	(Q)	(Q/L)	($\Delta Q / \Delta L$)
1	100	100	-
2	180	90	80
3	240	80	60
4	320	80	80
5	450	90	130
6	600	100	150

is a symbol which denotes change.

When the average output decreases, the marginal output decreases steeper than the average output such that marginal is lower than the average. When the average output remains constant, the marginal output is equal to average output. When the average output increases the marginal output increases steeper than the average output such that the marginal exceeds the average.

The marginal principles of economists are:

(1) Each factor (labour) will be paid wages according to its marginal product

(2) Each commodity(x) will be priced according to its marginal utility

$\Rightarrow P_X = MU_X$

The basic idea is that satisfaction should balance sacrifice.

In the real business situation, it is difficult to apply the concept of marginalism. The problem is that the margin? Variable may be supplied to many (group) changes 'rather than' unit changes.

In such cases the concept of 'marginalism' may be replaced by the concept of 'incrementalism'. For example the additional cost of installing computer facilities may be called as 'incremental costs'. Incrementalism is more wide whereas marginalism is more specific. All marginal concepts are incremental concepts but all incremental concepts need not be confined to marginal concepts alone.

3. Risk and Uncertainty: Many of the business decisions involve future revenues and costs. But it is not possible to predict future with great accuracy. Future involves changes and there is no guarantee that the present will be repeated in future. The business environment changes in course of time.

All changes are not the same. The changes may be known or unknown. The result of known changes may be either definite or indefinite. The definite result or outcome related with known changes is known as "certainity". The indefinite nature of outcome or result related with known charges involves 'risk'. Such risks can be estimated and can be insured. On the other hand, if changes are unknown, their outcome is indefinite the risk element is incalculable and immeasurable. This is called as 'Uncertainty' and cannot be insured. This is the difference between 'risk' and 'uncertainty', though these two terms are used as synonyms in common parlance. (eg) The interest rate is a risk premium where as profit is a reward for uncertainty.

With the help of statistical concept of probability, the concept of risk and uncertainty is introduced in the analysis of business decision making.

4. Profits: Profits means revenue minus costs, Revenue (TR) depends on total quantity of sales (Q) and the price at which the output is sold (P). The total cost (TC) depends on the number of factors employed (F) and the average factor price (c).

Thus profits (π) can be stated as $\pi = TR - TC$

$$P.Q - C.F.$$

Since profit is a controversial subject, a distinction is made between business (accounting) profit and economic profit.

The businessman calculates his return on investment (ROI) by calculating profit as a perentage on investment. The various profit concepts such as gross profit, net profit, profit after tax etc., are used depending on accounting convention and accounting convenience.

The concept of accounting profit is wider than that economic profit, because the opportunity costs have to be deducted from accounting profit to get economic profit. Opportunity cost refers to the costs of employing self owned factors in the business. For example, suppose a businessman uses his own capital, building, labour in his business. If he rents out the same to some body's business he would have earned interests, rents and wages have to be regarded as opportunity costs.

Since it is very difficult to measure opportunity cost, most of the economists assume zero opportunity costs so that accounting profits and economic profits do not differ.

There are some more pure micro-economic concepts of profits.

Super normal profit (TR > TC)

Normal profit (TR = TC) and

Subnormal profit (TR < TC)

Normal profit refers to no profit - no loss situation where as subnormal profit refers to loss.

5. Industry: Group of firms which produces similar commodity is called an industry. The concept of an industry has been developed to include firms, which are in some form of close relationship with one another. These firms belonging to a group are behaviourly interdependent.

The concept of industry serves a lot of purposes. It helps us to group the firms, makes it possible to predict the behaviour of firms in the group that constitute industry, it provides the framework for equilibrium price and output, helps the businessmen in designing the tactics in view of the industry and the government policy is designed with reference to industry; most policies are industry-specific.

There are two criteria of industry classification:

(i) *Product criterion:* The firms are grouped in an industry if their products are close substitutes.

(ii) *Process Criterion:* The firms are grouped in an industry on the basis of similarity of processes - technology, use of raw materials, methods of production, channels of distribution etc.

6. Firm: A firm is defined as an organisation carrying on economic activities like production, distribution and marketing of goods and services with a view to earn profit. In traditional economic theory, a firm is defined as an organisation of an individual or a group of individuals formed to achieve economic objectives. A firm in modern period is defined as a joint stock company in which decisions are taken by the shareholders and they are executed by the Company Officers.

Whether the firm is owned by an individual or by group of persons, the goal is to make profit. Once this goal is ensured, the next goal, namely, expansion of the firm comes into existence. The traditional economists keeping profit maximization as the goal of the firm, formulated a theory which is called equilibrium of a firm. They said, that a firm is in equilibrium position when it is earning maximum money profits.

As regards the objectives of a firm, Prof.Galbraith in his book "The Goals of Industrial System" says, 'Any organisation, as for any organism, the goal has a natural assumption of pre-eminence is the survival of the organisation'. Survival here refers to obtain normal earnings. Once a firm accomplishes this objective, it plans to expand the activities of the firm, which means assuming more responsibilities in the organisation. The goal of expansion is followed by growth and then by technological development. This means taking up of innovation. In course of time, a business firm with a simple objective grows to a global institution with multiple objectives.

7. The Market: Market in economics means, meeting place of buyers and sellers directly or indirectly. Cournot, a French Economist defines market as "Economists understand by the term market not any particular market place in which things are bought and sold, but the whole of any region in which buyers and sellers are in such a free intercourse with each other that the prices of the same goods tend to equality easily and quickly."

In the words of Jevons, "The word market has been generalised so as to mean any body of persons who are in intimate business relations and carry on extensive transactions in any commodity."

Stonier and Hague explain the term market as, "any organisation whereby buyers and sellers of a good are kept in close watch with each other..... There is no need for a market to be in a single building.......The only essential for a market is that all buyers and sellers should be in constant touch with each other either because they are in the same building or because they are able to talk to each other by telephone at a moment's notice."

Benham explains the term market as "and area which buyers and sellers of a commodity are in close touch with each other either directly or indirectly that the price obtainable in one part of the market affects the prices paid in other part." Ely observes, "market means the general field within which the forces determining the price of particular product operate."

If we study the above definitions, we find that a market comprises of the following components.

(a) *Consumers:* The buyers of the product are called consumers. The buyers of a product are identified by means of income, need, etc. If there are high income groups and they are concerned with trade and commerce or higher government administration, they need luxuries like motor cars, VCRs etc.

(b) *Sellers:* There should be manufacturers of a product in the market. There must be industries manufacturing motor cars in a country. They form sellers in the market.

(c) *A Commodity:* A market means the buying and selling of a commodity. If there is no commodity, the market will not exist. Each commodity has a separate market, in the sense that every commodity has a separate set of buyers and sellers.

(d) *A Price:* If the commodity is to be bought and sold, there must be a price for the product. The exchange of the product between buyers and sellers take place at a place.

Thus all the four components form a market.

Market Structure

The knowledge of market structure with which a firm is to operate is useful in understanding the nature and extent of manouverability which the firm has in deciding about the price and the quantity of product.

Market structures are different. Market forms based on the degree of competition prevailing in the market. Broadly the market forms are classified into two types. (a) Perfectly competitive market (b) Imperfectly competitive market. Before we begin to study the characteristic of market structure, let us understand what we mean by market.

Classification of the Market

1. Market is classified on the basis of an area, such as local markets, regional markets, national markets and international markets.

2. On the basis of nature of transactions, market is classified into spot market and future market. Where goods are physically exchanged on the spot, the markets are called spot markets. In the case of transactions involving agreements of future exchange of goods, such markets are known as future market.

3. Market is classified into wholesale market and retail market on the basis of volume of business.

4. Market is classified on the basis of time as very short period market, long period market and very long period market or secular market.

5. On the basis of status of sellers, the market is classified into primary, secondary and terminal markets. The primary market consists of manufacturers who produce and sell the product to the wholesalers. The wholesalers who sell the product to retailers are called secondary market. The retailers who sell it to the ultimate consumers are called terminal market.

6. Market is further classified into regulated market and unregulated market. If the government stipulates certain conditions and regulations for the sale and purchase of product – then that market is called regulated markets. These are absent in unregulated markets.

7. Markets is further classified on the basis of competition as perfectly competitive market, monopoly market, monopolistic competitive market, oligopoly market, etc. If there is no competition for the product, then such a market is called monopoly market. In a competitive market, several producers are manufacturing the product. The product is homogeneous. There are large number of buyers and sellers in the market. Such a market is called perfectly competitive market.

In the table on the next page, market forms are classified on the basis of number of firms producing the product and the nature of product produced by them.

Perfect Competition

Perfect competition comes into existence when there are large number of firms producing homogeneous product. The maximum output that a firm produces is so small when compared to the industry output, that a firm cannot affect the price by varying output. With larger number of firms and homogeneous product, no individual firm is in a position to influence the price. The demand curve of firms under perfect competition is a horizontal straight line. That is the price elasticity of demand for a single firm is infinite. Joan Robinson says, "Perfect competition prevails when the demand for the output for each producer is perfectly elastic. This entails first that the number of firms is large, so that the output of any one seller is negligibly small proportion of the total output of the commodity and second that the buyers are all alike in respect of their choice between rival sellers, so that the market is perfect".

Imperfect Competition

Since perfect competition is very rare, what actually prevails is imperfect competition. In imperfect competition, the number of firms exercising control is large since the product is differentiated. Imperfect competition has several sub-categories. They are *(i)* Monopoly, *(ii)* Duopoly, *(iii)* Oligopoly and *(iv)* Monopolistic Competition

1. Monopoly: Monopoly is a market form in which a single producer producing a single product which has no close substitute. And as such, this is extreme case of imperfect competition. Since a monopoly firm wields a solid control over the supply of the product, which can have only remote substitutes, the expansion and contraction of output will affect the price. Contraction of output will raise its price while expansion of output will lower it. Therefore, the demand curve facing the monopoly is downward sloping but has steep slope. For monopoly, sometimes, the words absolute monopoly or pure monopoly, complete monopoly are used. But such a pure monopoly or absolute monopoly does not exist in the real world.

2. Duopoly: This is market segment where in only two sellers operate and more buyers exist. Price in this market moves in the same direction as it moves in monopoly. Sellers enjoy additional profit over and above the normal profit

Classification of Market Forms

	Form of market structure	Number of firms	Nature of product	Price elasticity of demand for an individual firm	Degree of control over price
1.	**Perfect competition**	Large No.of firms	Homogeneous product	Infinite	None
2.	**Imperfect compention**				
a)	**Monopoly**	One	Unique product without close substitute	Very small	Considerable
b)	**Duopoly**	Two	Substitutes	Small	Some
c)	**Pure oligopoly** (i) **Oligopoly without product differentiation**	Few firms	Homogeneous	Small	Some
	(ii) **Differentiated oligopoly**	Few firms	Differential product (Close substitutes)	Small	Some
d)	**Monopolistic competition**	Large no. of firms but less than perfect competition	Differential products but close substitutes	Large	Some

3. Oligopoly: The second category of imperfect competition is oligopoly. There are two types of oligopoly. One without product differentiation and this is called pure oligopoly, the other is with product differentiation, which is called differentiated oligopoly. Under this category, there exists competition among the few firms producing homogeneous product. Since the number of firms is few, each of them exercises some control over the price. The demand curve facing the firms under oligopoly is downward sloping.

4. Monopolistic Competition: Prof.E.H.Chamberlin defines monopolistic competition as a market from characterized by a large number of firms with product differentiation. Demand curve facing the firms in monopolistic competition is highly elastic indicating that the firm enjoys control over the price. Product differentiation is the hall mark of this market.

SUMMARY

1. Business Economics can be defined as the integration of economic theory with business practice for the purpose of facilitating decision making and forward planning by the management.

2. Micro-economics is the study of a particular firm, particular household, individual price, wage, income, industry and particular commodity.

3. Macro-economics is the study of aggregates. It is concerned with aggregates and averages of the entire economy.

4. Business economics is micro in nature and it is in normative science.

5. Business economics is closely related with other subjects like pure economics, statistics, mathematics and accounting.

6. The scope or subject matter of business economics is classified into six broad heads:

    (a) Consumption analysis with special emphasis on demand analysis

    (b) Production and cost analysis

    (c) Pricing decisions, policies and practices

    (d) Profit management

    (e) Capital management and

    (f) Decision making

7. The basic principle tools which are used in business economics are:

    (a) The opportunity cost principle

    (b) The incremental cost principle

    (c) The principle of time perspective

    (d) The discounting principle

    (e) The equi-marginal principle

8. Business Economist has an important role to play by helping the management in decision making and forward planning.

9. Business Economics is considered as applied economics and it suggests how the economic principles are applied to the formulation of policies and programmes. It tells the business executives how to achieve how to achieve the business objectives.

QUESTIONS

1. 'Business Economics has a close connection with micro-economic theory and macro-economic theory of decision making and forward planning'. Elucidate.

2. Define Business Economics and discuss its scope.

3. Discuss the functions and responsibilities of Business Economist.

4. Explain the fundamental concepts of Business Economics.

5. 'Business Economics is economics applied to decision-making'. Explain.

6. Explain how business economics is related to Economics, Mathematics, Statistics and Accounting.

7. A manager without the knowledge of Economics is like a doctor without his Medical Kit. Elucidate.

8. Explain the nature and scope of Managerial Economics.

9. Is Business Economics a positive science or normative science?

10. Is Business Economics prescriptive or descriptive?

11. Explain the uses of operational research in Business Economics.

12. What are the limitations of Business Economics?

13. What is the significance of forward planning to a firm?

14. Mention the functions of Business Economist.

15. Define Managerial Economics.

16. What is Managerial Economics? How does it differ fromn traditional economics?

17. What is the scope of Managerial Economics?

2 Chapter

Economic and Econometric Models

1. MEANING OF MODEL

The guidelines for decision making based on analysis can be provided through an alternate method called as model. The use of models is a very popular technique of economic analysis. In ordinary sense, a model is a physical specification - a protopype of an object like the model of a school building, the model of an aeroplane etc. In technical sense, a model is a system or relations which help us in understanding the reality. Each relationship can be presented in one or more alternative forms - diagrams, table, graph, flowchart, statistical distribution, mathematical functions, etc., A model symbolises the behaviour pattern of a given variable in relation to other, irrespective of the form of representation. Thus a model though a theoretical abstraction or just a conceptual construction, can explain the behaviour that is actually observed and can predict the behaviour that is likely to be observed. So, we can say that a model has both analytical and predictive value.

2. CLASSIFICATION OF MODELS

Models can be classified into three broad categories. They are:

(i) Iconic Models: These are visual or pictorial representation like design, drawings, prototype, etc., which provide information to management.

(ii) Analogue Models: These models present a set of properties of the data in the form which is easily amenable to analysis. *E.g* a flow chart, funds flow statement, statistical distributions such as bionomial distribution, poisson distributions, normal distribution, etc.

(iii) Mathematical models: In mathematical models, mathematical symbols and equations are used to express the relationship between the variables. Such models are extensively used in economic analysis. These models can be further classified into: (a) Economic Models, (b) Econometric Models

3. ECONOMIC MODELS

Economic models is a set of equations or relationships used to summarise the working of the national economy or of a business firm or some other economic unit. Models may be either simple or complex and they are used to illustrate a theoretical principle or to forecast economic behaviour. Economic models are usually theoretical constructions.

Definitions

According to Garden Ackley, 'An economic model consists simply of a group or set of economic relationships, each one of which involves, at least one variable also appears in at least one other relationships which is a part of the model – Economic models, then are succinct statements of economic theories.'

According to Mardougall, 'An economic model is a simplification of reality.'.

From the above definitions, it is clear that economic models are used to describe the complicated behaviour of the economy by means of a few simple relationships and also show how major aggregate variables are related to each other.

Economic models may consist of mathematical equations or a set of diagrams or they may take the form of a scheme such as the flow chart of the computer programmer or the electronic engineer. In recent years models are used to a greater extent in economic theories to make it more precise and realistic. Since the economists are unable to conduct controlled experiments, they have resorted to model building. If a model reproduces important features and real life, then it provides a guide to understanding and a basis for predictions.

Few Examples

The "Marshallian Demand Curve" is a simple model which deals with a single relations between two variables i.e, price and quantity demanded.

"The Marshallian Cross" consisting of two relationships, a demand curve and a supply curve, is another valuable model.

J.M.Keynes has used economic models in his work to explain his ideas. For example, static or comparative static model in the general theory, consumption function model, etc.

The mathematical economic models became more popular with the works of J.B Clark, Walras, Chamberlin, Fisher, Mrs.Robinson, Edgeworth, Harrod and Domar growth models and others. These economic models provide and opportunity for prediction and for carving out paths of economic development.

Economic models can be further classified into Micro Economic Models and Macro Economic Models.

Micro Economic Models

Models, when they incorporate individual economic units such as households and firms, often grouped into individual markets and industries and the relationship between them are called as microeconomic models. These models are used to explain the price output determination of particular commodities and payments for individual factors of production.

Macro Economic Models

These models have been extensively developed for the construction of total or national income accounts by the late Sir Arthur Bowley, by colin Clark and late Lord Stamp and from the theoretical work of Keynes and the Swedish economists. Macro-economic models are used to explain and predict the working or performance of the economy as a whole, e.g changes in the level of national income, the level of employment and inflation.

Macro-economic models are used in a larger scale when compared to micro-economic models. The British Treasury uses a macro economic model in constructing the budget. Planning bodies use these models when working out the implications of alternative rates of growth.

Macro-economic models provide a tool by which the aggregate behaviour of the economy is analysed in terms of employment, interest rates, income, prices, balance of payments etc. A macro model describes the aggregate behaviour of consumers, investors and holders of money. The simplest model consists of a simple equation where as complex model consists of multiequations. The input-output model given by W.Leontief includes both micro economics and macro economics features (models) and it explains the sources and the inputs of different industries and the distribution of their output.

Both the micro economic and the macro economic models can be further divided into (a) 'equilibrium models' and (b) process models.

(a) **'Equilibrium Models'** may specify the conditions under which the variables would be incorporated would have to tendency to change, but they are used to analyse changes in the economy. A distinction has to be made between general equilibrium models and partial equilibrium models. General equilibrium models include all the variables of the whole economy and their main aim is to provide a summary chart of the inter-related variables (eg the price of a single commodity and the quality demanded of the same) and workout the mutual interdependence of these variables and assume fixed values for all other variables.

(b) **'Process Models'** trace out the paths of adjustment indicating the conditions under which steady movement, oscillation and rebounds from 'ceilings' and 'floors' are to be expected.

Economists often frame the basic structural relationship of an aggregate economy in the form of a 'macro aggregative model'. They also focus on the structural relationship between various sectors like agriculture, industry etc., and they are called as 'Sectoral Models'. Some times economists show transactions within an economy between industries dependent on each other. Such models are called as 'inter-industry models' and are usually put in the form of an input-output table. For demand forecasting input-output models are used where as for the purpose of planning and projection for the national economy, both aggregative and sectoral models are useful.

4. ECONOMETRIC MODELS

Econometrics is of recent origin. Though marginalist and neo-classical economists stressed more and more on the use of mathematics in the field of economics to make it more scientific, only in recent years econometrics has gained its supremacy.

According to Oscar Lange, 'Econometrics is the science which deals with the determination methods of statistical methods of concrete quantitative laws in economic life. It shows that econometrics tries to picture economic phenomena statistically with the aid of quantitative economic relations. Though, it is true that econometrics is a scientific method of study which uses statistical methods and mathematical tools are also indispensible.'

5. THE ROLE OF ECONOMETRICS

The essential role of econometrics is the estimation and testing of economic models. The first step in the process is the specification of the model in mathematical form. Secondly, appropriate and relevant data from the economy or sector that the model purports to describe must be assembled. Thirdly use the data to estimate the parameters of the model and finally carry out tests on the estimated model in an attempt to judge whether it constitutes a sufficiently realistic picture of the economy being studied or whether a somewhat different specification has to be estimated. The assumptions of exact relations in equations has to be removed in econometric work. No economic data ever give an exact fit to simple relations of this kind, since linear or other simple forms are only an approximation to possibly complex but unknown forms and also since only a small subset of all possible explanatory variables can usually be included in any specification. These factors requrie the specification of a stochastic error (determined by a random distribution of probabilities) or disturbance term in each relation other than identities and indeed a very useful product of the econometric process is an estimate of the error variance in each relation. These estimates shed crucial light on the quality of the econometric relations and they are also vital for the assessment and the estimated coefficients and for the use of the estimated model for forecasting purposes.

The area covered by econometrics is given in the box in the following page.

Economists are able to present their theories more scientifically and realistically with the help of mathematical and statistical tools. There, we can say that Econometrics is a discipline combining economic theory, statistical method and mathematical precision. Econometrics uses statistical techniques to test econometric models that are developed to explain economic relationship.

The econometric models may be of two types:

(a) Single equation model as given in the regression analysis

(b) Simultaneous equations models.

Regression analysis is useful in those cases where the factors influencing the dependent variables are mutually unrelated. (e.g) demand function, production function, cost function and profit function. Simultaneous equation models are used where variables are mutually related. Eg: macro aggregative model, input-output model, sectoral models etc.

The relations among the variables in the models are stated in the form of equations. Equations are of two types:

- *Definitional equations* – These are identities and definitionally true. All equilibrium conditions are stated in this form Eg: Demand = Supply, or Savings = Investment or Marginal Cost = Marginal Revenue.

- *Behavioural Equations* – These equations explains the behaviour of one variable in terms of another. Eg. Demand depends on price.

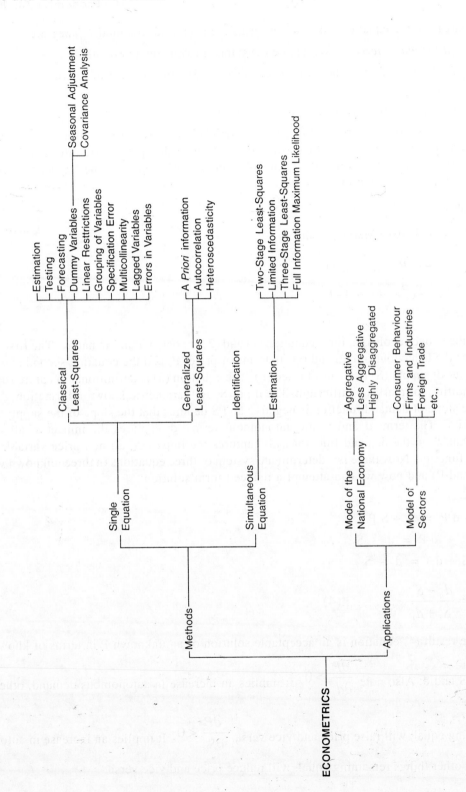

Apart from the equation, some other terms are also used in a model. They are:

- *Autonomous terms* – Which are constants influencing a variable.
- *Exogenous terms* – these are determined outside the systems of relations postulated and few other.
- Parametric information like the slope term.

Econometric models are used to derive a 'reduced-form solution' - solution of an unknown (endogenous) variable in terms of known constants and other parametric information as well as exogenous terms. i.e the econometric models can be used to predict the impact of a change in known terms on the unknown variables.

Examples:

(1) A competitive Market Model.

$$D = d_o - d_1 P ....(1)$$
$$S = S_o + S_1 P ....(2)$$
$$D = S$$

In the above set of equations, equation (1) and (2) are behavioural in nature. The first equation explains the behaviour of demand (D) in terms of price (P) and the equation second explains the behaviour of supply (S) in terms of price (P). The equation (3) is definitional in nature suggesting the condition for market equilibrium. The d_1, or S_1 are parametric known information, d_1 denotes that the slope of demand function is negative and S_1 denotes that the slope of the supply function is positive. The terms d_o and S_o are autonomous terms; d_o captures the impact of all variables other than P on the demand functions; S_o captures the impact of all non-price variables on the supply function. Now there is a determinate system of three equations in three unknown variables (D, S and P) and now we can attempt a reduced form solution.

D = S

$d_o - d_1 P = S_o + S_1 P$

$S_1 P + d_1 P = d_o - S_o$

$P(S_1 + d_1) = d_o - S_o$

$$P = \frac{d_o - S_o}{S_1 + d_1} ....(4)$$

The result (4) equation is an acceptable solution of an unknown P in terms of known terms d_o, S_o, S and d; Also note $\frac{\partial P}{\partial d_o} > 0$. It implies an increase in autonomous demand, other things remaining equal, will raise price and vice versa. $\frac{\partial P}{\partial S_o} < 0$. It implies an increase in autonomous supply, other things remaining equal, will reduce price and vice versa.

(2) A Macro Model of an Economy

$$Y^S = Y^d \qquad (1)$$

$$Y^d = C + I + \overline{G} \qquad (2)$$

$$C = C_0 + C_1 Y^S \qquad (3)$$

$$I = i_0 + i_1 Y^S \qquad (4)$$

In this model we have four equations or four unknown terms. where

Y^d = aggregate demand

Y^S = aggregate supply

C = consumption

I = Investment

$\overline{G}$ = Government expenditure

The terms C_o and i_o are autonomous; c_1 and i, are slope terms and $\overline{G}$ is exogenous. Now we can attempt a reduced form solution

$$y^s = y^d$$

$$\coloneqq C + I + \overline{G}$$

$$= C_0 + C_1 y^s + i_0 + i_1 y^s + \overline{G}$$

$$\Rightarrow Y^5 - c_1 y^5 - i_1 y^5 = c_0 + i_0 + \overline{G}$$

or, $\quad y^s(1 - c_1 - i_1) = c_o + i_o + \overline{G}$

$$\therefore y^s = \frac{1}{1 - C_1 - i_1}[C_o + i_o + \overline{G}] \qquad (5)$$

In the equation (5) (that is result), we have a solution for unknown y^s in terms of all known terms, $C_o, i_o, \overline{G}, C_1$ and i_1. And now we may operate

$$\frac{\partial y^s}{\partial C_o} = \frac{\partial y^s}{\partial i_o} = \frac{\partial y^s}{\partial \overline{G}} = \frac{1}{1 - C_1 - i_1}$$

The behavioural equations in this model can be estimated through the regression technique. Given the time-series data, we can use least square techniques to estimate the intercept term like C_o, i_o, and the slope terms (regression coefficients like C_1 and i_1.).

Conclusion

In most of empirical estimates in Managerial or Business Economics, single equation models are used to a greater extent. Other few problems of managerial economics can be approached through other types of models like Statistical Distribution models, Allocation and Transportation models, Scheduling Models, Quening models, Simulation models, Inventory models etc.

SUMMARY

1. A model symbolizes the behaviour pattern of a given variable in relation to other irrespective of the form of representation.

2. Economic model is a set of equations or relationships used to summarise the working of the national economy or of a business firm or some other economic unit.

3. Economic models can be further classified into micro-economic models and macro economic models.

4. Econometrics tries to picture economic phenomena statistically with the aid of quantitative economic relations. i.e Econometrics is a discipline combining economic theory, statistical method and mathematical precision.

5. Econometric Models can be further classified into single equation model and simultaneous equations models.

QUESTIONS

1. What is a Model? Or what does a Model refers to?
2. Classify Models.
3. What is Economic Model?
4. Give a definition for Economic Model.
5. State few advantages of Economic Models.
6. Distinguish Micro and Macro Economic Models.
7. What is meant by an Equilibrium Model?
8. Give the meaning of Process Model.
9. Give the meaning of Econometrics.
10. What is an Econometric Model?
11. Explain the area of study covered by econometrics.
12. What are the different types of Econometric Models and explain them.
13. Discuss economic and econometric models.

3 Chapter

The Theory of Consumer Behaviour

The end of all economic activity is consumption. All economic activities are undertaken with a view to produce goods and services which can satisfy human wants. Consumption refers to utilisation of the product for satisfying wants. It does not mean destruction of commodity but its utility is destroyed while consuming. Utility means the power of the commodity to satisfy human wants.

1. MEANING OF CONSUMER BEHAVIOUR

Consumer behaviour refers to the study of consumer while engaged in the process of consumption. It tells us how a consumer with his limited resources purchase different varieties of goods and services in the market and compare price and utilities of different alternatives etc.

> *Consumer behaviour refers to the study of consumer while he is engaged in the process of consumption.*

The highest possible satisfaction for him is possible when he reaches the equilibrium position.

The process of reaching equilibrium position can be explained with the help of two approaches: (i) The Utility Analysis and (ii) The Indifference Curve Analysis.

The Utility Analysis is otherwise called as cardinal utility theory of consumer behaviour and it is also known as traditional approach to the measurement of consumer behaviour. Though this approach was introduced by Jevons, Walras and Menger in early 1870s, it was popularised by Alfred Marshall and it appeared in his book "Principles of Economics" in 1890. Under this cardinal approach, the numerals like 1, 2, 3, 4, 5,.... etc. are used to measure utility. This approach is based on the assumption that the volume of utility of a commodity can be measured exactly in terms of numbers.

On the other hand, Indifference curve analysis is otherwise called as ordinal utility theory of consumer behaviour and is called as modern approach to the measurement of consumer behaviour.

This approach was originated by Edgeworth in 1881 and refined by Pareto in 1906. Later, this technique was perfected by R.G.D.Allen and J.R.Hicks in 1934. Under this ordinal approach the Roman numerals like I, II, III, IV etc. are used and they are ordered or ranked. Indifference curve analysis takes the level of satisfaction instead of measuring utility.

2. UTILITY APPROACH

People buy goods because they satisfy the wants of the people. Utility means the want satisfying power of a commodity. Utility is defined as a property of the commodity which satisfies the wants of the consumers. Utility is purely subjective in character. It depends upon the mental attitude of the consumers. Being subjective, it varies from individual to individual. It means, different persons derive different utilities for the same product. People know utility of goods by means of introspection. The desire for a commodity by a person depends upon the utility he expects from a commodity. If the desire for the commodity is greater, then its utility to the person is also higher. It should be noted that the question of morality does not influence the utility. The commodity may not be useful in the ordinary sense of the term, even then it may provide utility to some people. For example, cigarettes have no utility for non-smokers. But for the smokers, cigarettes bring utility. Thus, the concept of utility is ethically neutral.

> *Utility refers to want satisfying capacity of a commodity.*

Total Utility

Utility of a commodity or commodities is additive. It means utility of various goods or different quantities of the same goods can be added to obtain total utility. Total utility refers to the sum total of satisfaction which a consumer receives by consuming various units of the same commodity. The more units of a commodity that a consumer consumes, his total utility of that commodity is high. As a consumer goes on consuming more and more units of a commodity, he eventually reaches the maximum point and if the consumption increases beyond this point, total utility also diminishes.

Marginal Utility

There is another concept in theory of consumption namely the marginal utility. Marginal utility refers to the utility of every additional unit of a commodity consumed. Marginal utility can be defined as a change in total utility resulting from a one unit change in the consumption of a commodity at a particular point of time. Normally, when a person is buying a commodity, he consciously weighs the utility he is going to offer. He will continue buying different units of a commodity till the marginal utility of the units is equal to the price. This concept is very well explained by Stonier and Hague as "A consumer will exchange money for units of a commodity A up to the point where last (marginal) unit of A which he buys has for him a marginal significance in terms of money just equal to its money price".

3. THE LAW OF DIMINISHING MARGINAL UTILITY

Marshall, who was the famous exponent of the theory of marginal utility, defines the law of diminishing marginal utility as follows: "The additional benefit which a person derives from a given increase of his stock of a thing diminishes with every increase in the stock that he already has'. Prof.Lipsey defines it as "For any individual consumer, the value that he attaches to successive units of a particular commodity will diminish steadily as his total consumption of that commodity increases".

This means that as the consumer consumes more of a commodity, the utility of every additional unit consumed diminishes.

The Law of DMU states that if a consumer consumes more of a commodity the utility of additional unit consumed diminishes.

Assumptions of the Law of Diminishing Marginal Utility

1. Various units of a commodity are homogeneous.
2. There is no time gap between the consumption of different units.
3. Every consumer wants to maximize utility.
4. The tastes and preferences of the consumer remains the same during the period of consumption.
5. Marginal utility of money remains the same

The law can be explained with the help of the following example.

Units of a Commodity (Apple)	Total Utility	Marginal Utility
1	20	20
2	37	17
3	51	14
4	62	11
5	68	6
6	68	0
7	64	-4
8	50	-14

In the above example, total utility goes on increasing until the consumption of 5th unit. It is very important to note that the increase is in the diminishing rate. The total utility is the maximum at 6th unit (68), then afterwards it falls.

In the case of marginal utility, it is 20 for the first unit and goes on decreasing with every additional unit consumed. It becomes zero for the 6th unit and becomes negative for the subsequent unit. If the table is converted into a graph, the diagram appears as shown in next page:

The total utility curve rises gradually and reaches the maximum at the 6th unit of the commodity and afterwards diminishes. Marginal utility curve slopes downwards from left to right from the first unit onwards. Marginal utility curve cuts OX axis at the 6th unit and falls below the axis

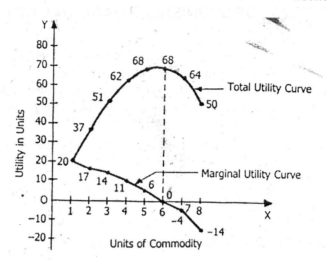

afterwards. It shows that, as the quantity of the commodity with the consumer increases, its marginal utility decreases. This is called the Theory of *Diminishing Marginal Utility*. The question now to be solved is why does marginal utility fall when the quantity of the commodity with the consumer increases. The reasons for this phenomena are – even though human wants in the aggregate are unlimited, yet a particular want can be satisfied fully. Therefore, when a person consumes more and more units of a commodity, his want is satisfied and that he does not want any more. Thus, his marginal utility decreases as consumption of that commodity increases. A stage is reached that further consumption brings marginal utility to zero.

Another reason is that goods are imperfect substitutes to one another. Different commodities satisfy different wants. When a person goes on consuming more and more units of a commodity, the marginal utility falls as his want is satisfied. But, if the commodity could be substituted for other commodities, it would have satisfied other wants. Hence, its marginal utility would not have decreased even though its quantity increases.

Limitations of the law of Diminishing Marginal Utility

The law of diminishing marginal utility suffers from certain limitations. These are discussed below:

(i) Homogeneity: It is assumed that the units of the commodity consumed must be homogeneous. The size of the unit and the quality of the unit must be the same. Unless the units are of suitable size and quality, the law will not hold good.

(ii) Suitable Time: The time of consumption should not vary. The commodity is consumed within a certain time. If you take the first cup of coffee at 8 a.m and the next cup at 3 p.m, there is no reason why the utility of the second cup of coffee is less. If the second cup of coffee is taken at 8.10 a.m, the third cup at 8.20 a.m and the fourth cup at 8.30 a.m, then the law of diminishing marginal utility will definitely operate.

(iii) No Change in the Taste of the Consumer: This is an important assumption in which the character of the consumer should not change. After taking a cup of coffee at 8 a.m., he takes a cup of tea at 9 a.m., the utility increases.

.(iv) **Normal Persons:** The law of diminishing marginal utility applies to normal persons and not to eccentric or abnormal persons. The law assumes that the consumer behaves rationally. If he behaves in an irrational manner, the law does not operate.

(v) **Constant income:** The law assumes that the income of the consumer remains the same during the period of consumption. Any change in income will falsify the law. If the income of a consumer rises in the course of a give consumption time, the presently consumed commodity becomes inferior and he goes in for a superior commodity. Even here if the person buys more and more units of a superior good, then the additional units of commodity brings less utility.

Thus, the law of diminishing marginal utility is a statement of tendency. It depends upon so many conditions – if these conditions are not fulfilled, law does not operate.

Uses of the Law of Diminishing Utility

The law of diminishing utility is very much useful in both economic theory and policy.

1. In determining the price of a commodity, the concept of marginal utility plays a crucial role.

2. The law has helped in explaining paradox of value – namely water – diamond paradox. Though water is essential for life it has no price. On the other hand, diamond is not essential, but has a high price. Water on account of its plentiful supply, is relative marginal utility is less. Therefore, it has less price. On the other hand, diamonds are scarce and its marginal utility is very high and hence it commands a high price.

3. The law of diminishing marginal utility explains the reason for the downward sloping of a demand curve. Further, the concept of consumer's surplus is based upon the law of diminishing marginal utility.

4. Another important use of this concept is in the field of direct taxation. For the rich people with higher income, marginal utility of money is low. On the other hand, the poor people with less income find marginal utility of money very high. Hence, higher direct taxes are levied on the rich while the poor are exempted.

Exceptions of the Law of Diminishing Utility

*   **Alcoholics:** The consumption of liquor is not subject to this law. The more he drinks the greater is the intoxication and hence he drinks more.

*   **Misers:** Miser gets more happiness and his greed increases with every increase of his stock of money.

*   **Money:** In the case of money, it is said that the more one has of it the greater is the desire to acquire still more.

*   **Reading:** More reading will give more knowledge and it can be increased only by reading different books and not the same one again and again.

*   **Hobbies and Rare Collections:** Hobbies like stamp collection, old paintings and antiques, coins etc. are an exception to the law of diminishing marginal utility. The more the collection, the greater is the desire to have more.

*   **Arts:** Arts like music, poetry or drama is better appreciated even after the first hearing or viewing.

4. THE LAW OF EQUI-MARGINAL UTILITY

The consumer with a given outlay of money, has to spend on various goods and services. Now, the question is, how he should allocate the given money among various goods.

Supposing he has to buy only one commodity, he will attain equilibrium at a point of units of the commodity where the marginal utility equals price. In the case of more than one commodity, the same principle is extended. It means the marginal utilities of goods and their prices should be equal. This is called the Law of Equi-marginal Utility. The Law of Equimarginal Utility states that the consumer would distribute his money income between the goods in such a way that the utility derived from the last rupee spent on each good is equal. In other words, a consumer attains equilibrium when marginal utility of money expenditure on each goods is the same. In other words,

$$\frac{\text{Marginal Utility of 'X' commodity}}{\text{Price of 'X' commodity}} = \frac{\text{Marginal Utility of 'Y' commodity}}{\text{Price of 'Y' commodity}}$$

> *The law of Equi-Marginal Utility states that the consumer would distribute his money income between the goods in such a way that the utility derived from the last rupee spent on each good is equal.*

Assumptions of the Law

Illustration

Let us take up the following example in order to understand this principle clearly.

Units	Marginal Utility of X Commodity	Marginal Utility of Y Commodity
1	20	24
2	18	21
3	16	18
4	14	15
5	12	9
6	10	3

Let us assume that price of X commodity is Rs.2 per unit and that of Y is Rs.3 per unit. Reconstructing the above table by dividing them with price, the reconstructed table will be as follows:

Units	M of X Commodity /Price of X	Mu of Y Commodity /Price of Y
1	10	8
2	9	7
3	8	6
4	7	5
5	6	3
6	5	1

Now, with a given money income, i.e he allots Rs.19 to buy these goods, he will purchase 5 units of X commodity and 3 units of Y commodity and attains equilibrium. At 5th unit of X commodity, $\dfrac{mu\ of\ X}{price\ of\ X}$ is equal to $\dfrac{mu\ of\ Y}{price\ of\ Y}$ of 3rd unit of Y commodity.

The law of equi-marginal utility is based on the following assumptions:

(i) There is perfect competition in the market and the consumer has to accept the prevailing price.

(ii) Utility is measurable in terms of money.

(iii) The income of the consumer remains constant and it is limited.

(iv) The consumer behaves rationally.

(v) The marginal utility of money remains constant.

(vi) The utility schedule of one commodity is independent of the utility schedule of the other commodities.

(vii) The law of diminishing marginal utility operates.

The diagramatic expression of the theory of consumer's equilibrium is as follows:

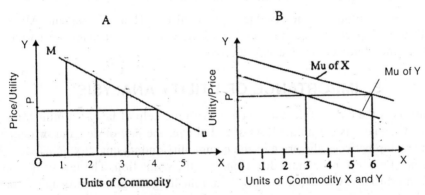

In the case of one commodity, the consumers buy (A) 4 units of X commodity because the price is equal to utility of the 4th unit. In the 'B' diagram, consumer buys two commodities X and Y. He buys 6 units of X and 3 units of Y commodity and attains equilibrium.

The Significance of the Law of Equi-marginal Utility

As Marshall says "The applications of this principle extend over almost every field of economic enquiry." Some of the applications are given as follows:

• Helps in the determination of optimum budget for the consumer.

• Helps in the distribution of earnings between savings and consumption.

• The entrepreneur can apply this law to maximise his profits.

• The ideal distribution of resources is possible in such a way that the marginal social utility in each use is the same.

• An individual can distribute his assets among alternative forms using this principle.

• It is also applicable in public finance particularly in taxation.

- It is more useful to a person who has limited time to be spent among alternative uses. He can distribute time in such a way that the marginal utility gained from those uses are equal.

Limitations of the Law of Equi-marginal Utility

This law is based on unrealistic assumption and hence this law is subjected to the following criticisms.

1. Consumers cannot act as a rational person always. Quite often he purchases a commodity under the influence of desire and rational thinking is absent.

2. Marginal utility of money does not remain constant always and for everyone. It varies between rich and poor.

3. This law cannot be applied if certain commodities are not available in the market for consumption and hence consumer cannot maximise his satisfaction from expenditure on various goods.

4. Utility is a subjective concept and it cannot be measured.

5. The equi-marginal principle can work only if goods are divisible but certain goods are not divisible. This restricts the free working of the equi-marginal principle.

Because of these limitations, the law lacks practical use. Hence Hicks and Allen have put aside Marshall's utility approach to consumers equilibrium and advanced an alternative approach which is called as the "Indifference Curve" approach.

5. IMPORTANCE OF UTILITY ANALYSIS

Utility analysis is the basis of demand theory. With the help of law of diminishing marginal utility, the law of demand is formulated. As stated above, the law of demand or demand curve shows the relationship between the price of the commodity and its quantity demanded. Marshall derived the demand curve for a commodity from its utility function. The law of demand can be derived in two ways: firstly, with the aid of law of diminishing marginal utility and secondly, with the help of equimarginal utility.

The law of marginal utility states that as the quantity of a good increases, marginal utility of the goods falls. In other words, marginal utility curve is downward sloping. Now the consumer goes on purchasing goods but the marginal utility of goods equal the price. He will be at equilibrium. His satisfaction will be maximum when marginal utility equals price. When the price of a good falls, its utility also falls. It therefore follows that diminishing marginal utility curve implies downward sloping demand curve.

According to the law of equimarginal utility, the consumer is at equilibrium in regard to his purchases of various goods when marginal utilities of goods are proportional to their prices. Thus, the consumer is in equilibrium when he is buying the quantities of two goods in such a way that it satisfies the following rule of proportion.

$$\frac{\text{mu of X}}{\text{Price of X}} = \frac{\text{mu of Y}}{\text{Price of Y}}$$ etc., where Mu stands for marginal utility of price of that commodity.

The consumer will be in equilibrium when he equalises marginal utility of money expectations with the ratio of marginal utility and the price of each commodity. Supposing the price of X commodity falls and price of Y commodity and consumer's money income remain the same, then the equilibrium position also is disturbed. With the lower price, $\dfrac{mu\,X}{PX}$ .will be greater than $\dfrac{mu\,X}{PX}$. In order to restore equilibrium, marginal utility of X must be reduced by buying more of X goods. It is thus clear when the price of a good falls, the quantity demanded of that commodity rises.

6. MEANING OF THE INDIFFERENCE CURVE APPROACH

The utility analysis suffers from certain shortcomings. It assumes that utility is measurable cardinally, *i.e.,* it can be assigned definite numbers. Since utility is a mental concept, it cannot be measured cardinally. Instead we can have ordinal measure which means that satisfaction can be compared and say that it is more or less.

Further, marginal utility analysis boasts too much and explains too little. Hence, an alternative analysis was propounded by Prof.Hicks and Allen and called as "Indifference Curve Analysis."

In indifference curve analysis, the consumer compares the satisfaction obtained from different combinations of goods. If the various combinations are marked A,B,C,D and E, the consumer can tell whether he prefers A to B, B to C and so on. Similarly, he can indicate his preference or indifference between any other combinations. The concept of ordinal utility implies that the consumer cannot go beyond stating his preference or indifference.

Indifference curve analysis does not use cardinal numbers like 1,2,3,,, but instead it uses ordinal numbers like 1st,2nd,3rd... etc. Thus, this approach was evolved as an alternative approach to cardinal utility analysis. Moreover, according to this approach, it is very clearly stated that: the consumer can only compare his levels of satisfaction in terms of degrees "good, better, best" or "bad, worse and worst" and cannot measure it in terms of numbers as assumed by Marshallian analysis. For this Indifferent Curve analysis makes use of the concept called scale of preferences.

Scale of Preferences

A rational consumer always tries to seek maximum level of satisfaction from the goods he buys. He will arrange them in different combinations in the order of their level of satisfaction or their significance. He would rank them accordingly in order to decide priorities. This kind of conceptual ordering of different goods and their combinations in a set order of preferences is called as the "scale of preferences."

> *Scale of preferences refers to the ordering of different goods and their combinations in a set order of preferences.*

For example, the consumer has the following scale of preferences formulated on the basis of level of satisfaction.

Scale of Preferences

Combinations of 2 goods	Level of Satisfaction	Order of Preference
Apples and Mangoes		
I. 5 apples and 15 mangoes	Highest	I
II. 4 apples and 12 mangoes	Less than I	II
III. 3 apples and 9 mangoes	Less than I & II	III

From the above table, we can understand that combination I gives highest level of satisfaction and hence the consumer gives first preference to that combination. For the other combinations II and III the preferences go on decreasing. The indifference curve technique is based on this principle. The scale of preference differs from person to person and it is drawn on the basis of mental attitude of consumers towards the commodities.

Indifference Schedule

An indifference curve is drawn based on an indifference schedule. An indifference schedule can be defined as an imaginary schedule of various combinations of two goods that will equally satisfy the consumer.

> *An indifference schedule is a list of different combinations of two goods which will give equal level of satisfaction to the consumer.*

The principle can be explained with the help of the following table.

Combination	Apples	Mangoes	MRS
A	20	1	-
B	16	2	4:1
C	13	3	3:1
D	11	4	2:1
E	10	5	1:1

The various combinations of two goods (apples and mangoes) shown in the above table gives the consumer the same level of satisfaction. Further, we can see that the number of apples is decreasing and that of mangoes is increasing because the consumer has to remain at the same level of satisfaction.

Indifference Curves

An indifference curve represents satisfaction of a consumer from two or more combinations of commodities. An indifference curve is drawn from the indifference schedule of the consumer. It is a geometrical device representing all different combinations of two goods which give equal level of satisfaction.

> *An indifference curve can be defined as a graphic representation of the various quantities of two goods that will yield equal satisfaction.*

The indifference curve is shown in the following diagram.

The number of mangoes is represented on the X axis and apples on the Y axis. Any combination on the indifference curve (a,b,c,d or e) will equally satisfy the consumer. Therefore, we can say that an indifference curve is a locus of the various combinations of two goods which yield the same satisfaction to the consumer. The curve is otherwise called as the "iso-utility curve" or "curve of equal utility."

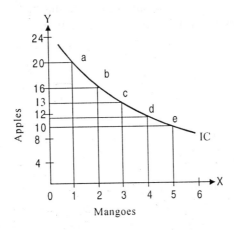

An Indifference Map

An indifference map is a collection or group of indifference curves. It represents various levels of satisfaction. In this, the higher indifference curve represents higher level of satisfaction and vice versa. Since consumer always prefers higher level of satisfaction, he always move to higher indifference curve than a lower one. The higher indifference curve will be given higher order of preference and so on. Since all the points on the same indifference curve yields the same level of satisfaction, he is indifferent.

An indifference map can be defined as a collection or group of indifference curves.

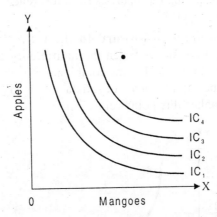

Higher indifference curve IC_4 represents higher level of satisfaction when compared with the other three indifference curves. An indifference map of a consumer portrays the consumer's scale of preference.

Assumptions of Indifference Curve Analysis

The assumption made in this technique are as follows:

(i) It assumes that consumer is in interested in buying two goods.

(ii) It is assumed that consumer will always prefer large amount of goods to a smaller amount of goods provided that the amount of other goods at his disposal remain unchanged and his income is fixed over a period of time.

(iii) The tastes of the consumer remain unchanged during the period of consumption. The consumer is rational and his choices are transitive.

(iv) The principle of diminishing rate of substitution is assumed. In other words, if a consumer prefers more and more units of one commodity, he will forego fewer units of the other commodity. The concept of marginal rate of substitution is a tool of indifference curve technique and is parallel to the concept of marginal utility in the Marshallian analysis of demand.

(v) It is based on ordinal analysis.

Properties of Indifference Curves

The basic characteristics or properties of indifference curve may be listed as follows:

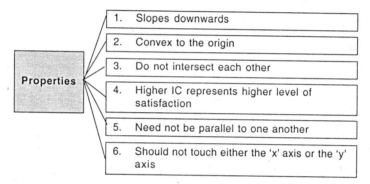

	Properties
1.	Slopes downwards
2.	Convex to the origin
3.	Do not intersect each other
4.	Higher IC represents higher level of satisfaction
5.	Need not be parallel to one another
6.	Should not touch either the 'x' axis or the 'y' axis

The first three properties are main properties of indifference curves and the remaining three are considered as additional properties.

A. Indifference curves slope downward to the right. This property implies that an indifference curve has a negative slope. When the indifference curve being downward sloping means that when the amount of one good in the combination is increased, the amount of the other goods is reduced. This must be so, if the level of satisfaction is to remain on the same indifference curve. The below diagram makes this point very clear.

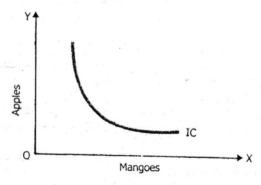

2. Indifference curves are convex to the origin. The implication of this rule is that as the consumer has more and more of X goods he takes less and less of Y goods. The marginal rate of substitution goes on falling. In the table mentioned in the previous page, it can be seen that for the second combination, the consumer foregoes 4 apples for one mango. In the third combination, he sacrifices 3 apples to one more mango. Like this, the rate of substitution between apples and mangoes goes on falling with the movement from one combination to another combination. Thus, the normal shape of the indifference curve is convex to the origin as shown in the above diagram. The curvature of the indifference curves reflects the degree of substitutability between the two commodities. If the indifference curve is flat or straight, it indicates that the two commodities are perfect substitutes. In the case of perfect substitutes, the indifference curves are downward sloping straight line (as shown in the diagram A). If the consumer is not willing to substitute one commodity for another, the indifference curve will either be vertical or horizontal as shown in the diagrams B and C.

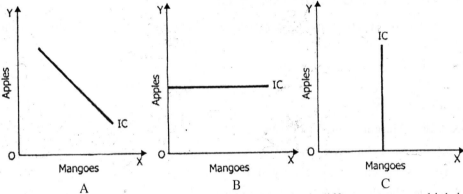

Goods which can be substituted are represented by the indifference curve which is convex to the origin.

3. Indifference curves cannot intersect each other. In other words, only one indifference curve will pass through a point in the indifference map. This property follows from the assumption 1 and 2. Supposing two indifferences intersect each other, then the whole theory becomes absurd. Let us study the following diagram keeping in mind the qualification of indifference curve.

Indifference curves represent different levels of satisfaction. IC_1 is higher than IC_2 in the below diagram. The two indifference curves cut each other at the point A. At the point B, the consumer is on the higher indifference curve and at the point C, he is on the lower indifference curve. The point A is on both the indifference curves, which in turn means that A is at once equal to B and C which as seen, represent two indifference curves. Then the question arises whether higher indifference curve (IC_1) is equal to lower indifference curve (IC_2). As such, a thing cannot

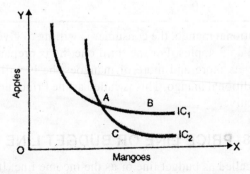

be and as such two indifference curves cannot intersect each other. Further, indifference curves can neither touch nor be tangent to each other.

Additional Properties

1. Indifference curve which lies on the right hand side of another indifference curve always represent a higher level of satisfaction.

2. Indifference curves need not necessarily be parallel to each other always. They can be drawn in any manner.

3. Indifference curves should not touch either of the axis *i.e.,* either X axis or Y axis because of the assumption that the consumer prefers different combinations of two goods.

7. MARGINAL RATE OF SUBSTITUTION

Marginal Rate of Substitution shows the rate at which the consumer is willing to substitute one commodity for another.

Symbolically

$$MRS_{xy} = \frac{\Delta x}{\Delta y}$$

where, MRS=Marginal rate of substitution

Δx = a small change in quantity of X

Δy = a small change in quantity of Y

MRS decides the slope of the indifference curve.

> *MRS can be defined as the rate at which an individual will exchange successive units of one commodity for another.*

Theoretically MRS may diminish, increase or remain constant. But practically it always diminishes. It is shown in the following table.

Combination	Apples	Mangoes	MRS
1	20	1	-
2	16	2	4:1
3	13	3	3:1
4	11	4	2:1
5	10	5	1:1

In order to get one additional mango, the consumer is willing to give up 4 apples. For the next one, he is prepared to give up 3 apples. For the third one, he is prepared to give up 2 apples. It clearly shows that, as he gets more and more of mangoes, he is willing to give up fewer and fewer of apples for each additional mango. This is called as the Principle of Diminishing Marginal Utility and it is always negative.

8. PRICE LINE OR BUDGET LINE

Price line can also be called as budget line or as the income line. It represents the maximum quantities of the goods (apples and mangoes) that can be purchased by the consumer at a given level of income and prices.

It is called as a income line because it represents the real income of the consumer.

> *The price line shows all the possible combinations of two goods that the consumer can buy at a given level of income and prices of two goods.*

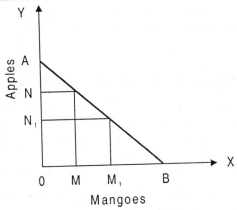

In order to determine the price line, we have to know the prices of the two commodities and the money outlay to buy these goods. Supposing the consumer has set apart Rs.30 from his total income to buy these two commodities. If we assume that the price of apple is Rs.2 and that of the mango is Rs.3 and if he spends Rs.30 on apple, he gets 15 apples or OA and on mangoes he gets 10 mangoes or OB. These points are shown in the above diagram.

AB points in the diagram are connected by a line and this is called *price line*. This line shows all the possible combinations of two goods that the consumer can buy if he spends the whole of his outlay, prices being unchanged. Supposing he buys ON of apples, he has to buy OM of mangoes. If he prefers to buy OM₁ of mangoes, he has to buy ON₁ of apples. Any combination lying beyond AB price line is not possible.

Shifting of the Price Line

If the prices of the two goods remained unchanged and this income or outlay increases, then the new price line will lie parallel to the old price line. Supposing the price of apples remain unchanged and that of mangoes fall, then the price line changes. These aspects are shown in the following diagrams.

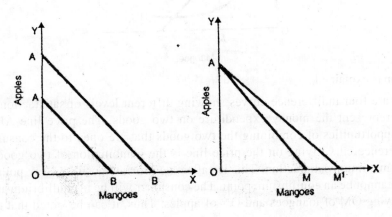

The diagram 'X' indicates change in money outlay (income) while the prices of the two goods remain unchanged. In the 'Y' diagram, the money outlay remains unchanged. The price of apples is the same and the price of mangoes falls. In the case of change in money income, a new price line parallel to the original price line comes into being. In the case of price line where the price of one commodity is constant and the price of the other commodity changes, the slope of the price line changes. The concept of price line is an important tool in the determination of consumer's equilibrium.

9. CONSUMER'S EQUILIBRIUM

As we have seen in the utility analysis, the consumer will attain equilibrium when the utility from a particular unit of the commodity is equal to its price. (marginal utility = price). In the indifference curve analysis, the procedure of equilibrium is somewhat different. In order to find out the equilibrium position of the consumer, we have to draw the price line. The price line is also called the *budget* line or outlay line.

We are now in a position to explain with the help of price line, how a consumer reaches equilibrium position. A consumer is said to be in equilibrium when he is buying such a combination of goods, as leaves him with no tendency to rearrange his purchases of goods. He is then in a balance position in regard to the allocation of money on various goods. In the Indifference curve analysis, the consumer's equilibrium is determined in respect of the purchases of two goods only.

The consumer has before him the indifference map showing three or four indifference curves. He has also a price line before him. In the diagram in the next page, the process of consumer's

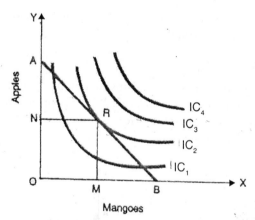

equilibrium is explained.

There are four indifference curves showing different levels of satisfaction. Price line AB is shown to represent the money expenditure on two goods. The price line AB contains all the possible opportunities of combining the two goods that are open to the consumer. Any point of the indifference curve lying on the price line is the combination of two goods which give the consumer maximum satisfaction. This is called *equilibrium* position. Any point not lying on the price line cannot be an equilibrium point. The consumer will be in equilibrium at a point R, *i.e.*, he will be buying OM of mangoes and ON of apples. Thus, it can be stated that the consumer will maximise his satisfaction and be in equilibrium at a point where the price line is tangent to an indifference curve. In the above diagram, the price line AB is tangent to indifference curve two (IC$_2$) at a point R. Any combination of two goods other than the above cannot give the consumer maximum satisfaction and equilibrium.

Conditions of Equilibrium

We can state the condition for equilibrium by saying that the given price line must be tangent to the indifference curve. The same may be stated as equality between marginal rate of substitution and the ratio between the prices of these two goods. This is no doubt a necessary condition for equilibrium. For attaining equilibrium, there is another condition which must be equally fulfilled. That is at the point of equilibrium, the marginal rate of substitution must be falling. It means that indifference curve is convex to origin. If the indifference curve is convex to the origin at the point of equilibrium, it means that at that point, the marginal rate of substitution of mangoes for apples is falling.

Thus, the point of consumer's equilibrium may be defined by the condition that the marginal rate of substitution between any pair of two commodities will be equal to the ratio of the prices of the two commodities. In other words, the marginal rate of substitution of money for any commodity must be equal to the price of that commodity. The slope of the price line and that of indifference curve must coincide.

10. INCOME EFFECT OR INCOME CONSUMPTION CURVE

In the above analysis, we have made two assumptions, namely the money income of the consumer is given and the prices of the two goods in combinations are also constant. Normally, either the money income of the consumer changes or prices of these goods change. The consequences of such changes are studied here under. Let us now take up the effect of consumer's change in money income on consumer's equilibrium. Whenever his money income rises, prices of goods and tastes of the consumer remaining the same, he will buy more quantities of these goods. This is known as income effect. Income effect shows this reaction of the consumer. The income effect means the change in consumer's purchases of the goods as a result of increase in his money income. This is shown in the following diagram.

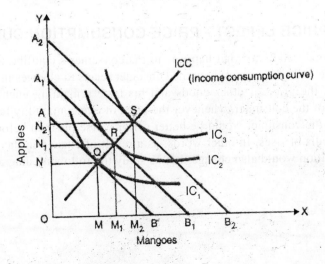

With given money income and prices of the two commodities as indicated in the price line AB, the consumer will be in equilibrium at a point of Q on the indifference curve (IC_1), buying ON of apples and OM of mangoes. Now his money income increases. The prices of the two goods are remaining the same. Then a new price line A_1B_1 comes into being. As a result of this change in money income and buying more units of the two goods, he goes to a higher indifference curve namely IC_2. The price line A_1B_1 is tangent to new indifference curve IC_2 at R. as a result of his increase in income, he buys ON_1 of apples and OM_1 of mangoes. If his income increases still further, then the price line moves further up to A_2B_2. He goes to a higher indifference curve IC_3. The consumer will be in equilibrium at point of S where the price line A_2B_2 is tangent to IC_3 at a point S. If the points Q, R and S are connected, we get a line called the *income consumption line*. The income consumption curve is the locus of equilibrium points at various levels of consumer's income. Income consumption curve traces out the income effect on the quantity consumed by the people.

Types of Income Effect

Most of the income consumption curves slope upwards to the right. This means as income increases, consumer buys more of each of any two goods he is consuming. This is the usual shape of the income consumption curve. The effect of income consumption curve may be positive or negative. If the consumption of goods increases with the increase in income, the income effect for the goods is positive. For example, if the income of wage earned i.e factory workers increases their consumption of superior goods rises. This is the positive effect of the income consumption curve. However, for some goods, the income effect is negative. Income effect for goods is said to be negative where, with the increase in income, the consumer reduces his consumption of goods. Such goods for which income effect is negative, we call them *inferior* goods. This is because the goods whose consumption falls as income increases are considered to be inferior goods by the consumer and he substitutes superior goods for them. Therefore, with increase in income, consumption of superior goods rises while the consumption of inferior goods falls. When the people are poor, they consume coarse grains such as maize, jowar bajra, etc. When they become richer, they buy superior grains such as wheat, rice, etc. In the case of inferior goods, the income consumption curve slopes backwards to the left. If the income effect is positive, it slopes upwards to the right.

11. PRICE EFFECT - PRICE CONSUMPTION CURVE

We have now analysed as to what happens to the consumer's equilibrium when his money income changes. We will now explain how the consumer reacts to changes in the price of goods, his money income, the price of other goods and his taste remaining unchanged. Price effect shows the reaction of the consumer, whenever the price of one commodity falls. When the price of a good changes, the consumer would be better off or worse off than before, depending upon whether the price falls or rises. In other words, as a result of change in the price of the goods, his equilibrium position would also change. Let us study the following diagram.

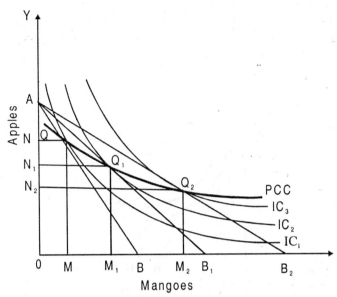

AB is the original price line and is tangent to IC_1, at Q. The consumer is in equilibrium buying ON of apples and OM of mangoes. The price of mangoes falls while the price of apples remain the same. As a result of this, the new price line AB_1 is formed. Since the consumer gets more units of mangoes for the same money expenditure, he goes to a higher indifference curve. The new price line AB_1 is tangent to IC_2 at Q_1, and the consumer is in equilibrium buying ON_1 of apples and OM_1 of mangoes. He has thus become better off, i.e., his level of satisfaction has increased as a consequence of fall in the price of mangoes. Suppose the price of mangoes falls still further, so that AB_2 is now the relevant price line. With the price line AB_2, the consumer is in equilibrium at Q_2 on the indifference curve IC_2, where he has OM_2 of mangoes and ON_2 of apples. When all the equilibrium points Q, Q_1 and Q_2 are joined together, we get what is called price consumption curve. *Price consumption* curve traces the effect of changes in the price of a commodity. It shows how the changes in the price of mangoes will affect the consumer's purchases of mangoes, price of apples, his tastes and money income remaining constant.

The price consumption curve is downward sloping. It indicates as price of a commodity falls, more units of that commodity are bought.

12. SUBSTITUTION EFFECT

When the price of a good falls, the consumer feels better off. There is an increase in the potential purchasing power of the consumer's income following a relative fall in the price of one commodity. This is called *income* effect. It is as if his income has increased and the prices of both the goods have remained the same. The income effect is the first component of the price effect. The consumer is moving along the income consumption curve.

The income effect will lead to the purchase of a better commodity. This is called *substitution* effect. Since the price of X has fallen, it becomes cheaper. Since the price of Y has remained unchanged, it becomes dearer. So, a tendency arises in the mind of the consumer to buy more units of a commodity for which the price has not fallen. In other words, he will substitute cheaper goods for the dearer one. Thus, the second component of price effect is the substitution effect. The following diagram illustrates the two components of price effect.

Initially, the consumer is in equilibrium, price line AB is tangent to the indifference curve 1. (IC$_1$)With a fall in price of X goods, a new price line AB$_1$ comes into existence.

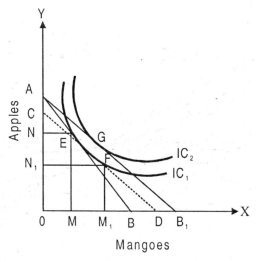

The consumer is in equilibrium at the point F at initial price line AB. When the price of mangoes falls, his price line is shifted to AB$_1$, and thus he shifts to higher indifference curve IC$_2$ and then he would attain an equilibrium point at G. If we have to measure pure substitution effect, then we should resort to compensating variation in income and hence hypothetical income line 'CD' is drawn. It is parallel to new price line AB$_1$, and tangential to the original IC$_1$. Thereby the consumer is shifted to original level of satisfaction. Now, his equilibrium position is changed to 'F'.

Thus, diagrammatically the substitution effect is measured by movement from one point to another point on the same indifference curve. Substitution effect may be small or large but it will always be positive.

Substitution effect always induces the consumer to buy more of the good when the price of the goods falls.

13. SPLITING OF PRICE EFFECT INTO SUBSTITUTION EFFECT AND INCOME EFFECT

Using indifference curve analysis we can split price effet into substitution and income effect. The price effect can be defined as the sum of substitution effect and income effect.

Price Effect = Substitution Effect + Income Effect

Diagramatically, the substitution effect is measured by a movement from one point to another point on the same indifference curve, while the income effect is measured along the income consumption curve which indicates a movement from one indifference curve to the other. The following diagram explains the separation of price effect into income effect and substitution effect.

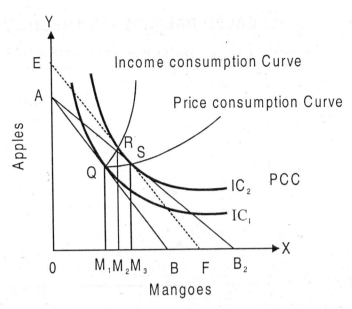

The consumer is in initial equilibraium point 'Q' on AB price line and he derives the level of satisfaction intimated by the indifference curve IC_1. He buys OM_1, of mangoes when the price of Mangoes falls, the price of apples being constant the price line is now shifted to AB_1. Accordingly the consumer reaches the new equilibrium point 'S' on a higher indifference curve. Now the consumer buys OM_3 of Mangoes. The price effect can be measured as M_1M_3. However the movement from Q to S is not direct. Firstly the consumer experiences income effect. When the price of Mangoes fall, his real income rises. This rise in income is shown by drawing a hypothetical line (EF) parallel to the initial price line AB. It is also tangent to new indifference curve IC_2 at point R. By joining this point we can derive income consumption curve.

Due to this income effect, the consumer moves from Q to R on the income consumption curve there by buying M_1M_2 more of mangoes. This is described as income effect. But it is not a stable equilibrium point. The substitution effect persuade the consumer to move from R to S. So he moves downward on the same indifference curve. Since the price of mangoes has become relatively cheaper he is induced to substitute mangoes for apple. Now, he buys more of mangoes i.e., M_2M_3.

Thus we can say that, when the price of mangoes falls, the consumer moves from Q to R along the income consumption curve and this is due to income effect. The substitution effect makes him to move further from R to S. The total effect is measured as Q to S on the price consumption curve.

Price effect = Income effect + Substititution effect

$$M_1M_3 = M_1M_2 + M_2M_3$$

The increase in demand from M_1 to M_2 for mangoes is due to income effect and increase in demand from M_2 to M_3 is due to substitution effect, so that the total price effect implies demand for mangoes to expand by M_1M_3.

14. REVEALED PREFERENCE THEORY

Prof.Samuelson's Revealed Preference Theory is superior to ordinal utility theory of Hicks and Allen. This theory analyses consumer's preference for a combination of goods on the basis of observed consumer behaviour in the market.

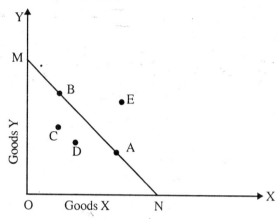

This theory is based on the logic that choice reveals preference. A consumer may buy a combination of two goods either because he likes that combination in relation to others or that is cheaper than others. Suppose a consumer buys combination B rather than combination A, C or D. This reveals his preference for combination B. He can do this for two reasons. Firstly, combination B may be cheaper than others and secondly though it is dearer than others, yet he may like it more than other combination. In this situation it is clear that 'B' is revealed preferred to A, C and D or A, C and D are revealed inferior to B.

This can be explained with the help of a diagram.

Two goods x and y and with their given income and prices, MN is the price-income line of the consumer. The triangle MON is the area of choice for the consumer. This shows the various combinations of x and y on the given price income line MN. The consumer can choose any combination between A and B on the line MN or between A and B on the line MN or between C and D below this line. If he choses 'B' it is revealed preferred to 'A'. The other two combinations i.e 'C' and 'D' are revealed inferior to 'B' because they lie below the line MN. The combination 'E' is beyond the reach of the consumer because it lies above his price-income line MN. Therefore 'B' is revealed preferred to other combinations.

Assumptions

This theory is based on the following assumptions:

(i) The consumer's taste remains constant

(ii) The consumer chooses only one combination at a given price-income situation.

(iii) The consumer choses only one combination at a given price income situation.

(iv) The consumer prefers a combination of more goods to less at any time.

(v) This theory assumes consistency of consumer behaviour. If 'B' is preferred to 'A' in one situation 'A' cannot be preferred to 'B' in other situation.

(vi) This theory is based on the assumption of transtivity. Transtivity refers to a situation where A is preferred to B, B to C and then the consumer should prefer A over C.

(vii) Income elasticity of demand is always positive which depicts that more will be demanded when income increases, and less when the income decreases.

Superiority of Revealed Preference Theroy:

This theory is superior to Hicksian ordinal utility approach.

(i) This theory presents a behaviouristic analysis based on observed consumer behaviour rather than involving of any psychological introspective information about the behaviour of the consumer. So this theory is more realistic, objective and scientific than other theories.

(ii) This theory does not include the assumption of 'continuity' which is assumed in indifference curve analysis. Samuelson believes in discontinuity because the consumer can have only one combination.

(iii) Samuelson's theory does not assume the rational behaviour of the consumer i.e behaviour of the consumer i.e behaving rationally to maximize his satisfaction from a given level of income. This is not possible in reality also.

(iv) This theory provides the foundation for welfare economics in terms of observable behaviour of consumer based on consistent choice

15. CONSUMER'S SURPLUS

In the theory of consumer behaviour the concept of consumer surplus is very important. It was first devised by French economist Dupuit in 1844 and later on developed and perfected by Alfred Marshall in 1879 in his book "Pure Theories of Domestic Values" under the title 'Consumers Rent'. This concept assumes cardinal measurement of utility.

Meaning

This concept is introduced to indicate the consumer's gain from the goods he purchases in a market economy. While purchasing he may derive satisfaction in excess of dissatisfaction he has experienced in parting with the money for paying its price. This excess satisfaction is called consumer's surplus.

In this situation he pays upto its marginal utility compared with the marginal utility of money which he has to pay. It can also be measured as the difference between the maximum price the consumer is willing to pay for a commodity and the actual market price charged for it.

Alfred Marshall has defined consumer's surplus as, 'The excess of price which a consumer would be willing to pay rather than go without the thing, over that which he actually does pay, is the economic measure of this surplus of satisfaction. It may be called 'consumer's surplus.'

> Consumer's surplus is the difference between the total amount of money the consumer would be willing to pay for a quantity of a commodity and the amount he actually had to pay for it. This concept is based on the law of diminishing marginal utility.

16. MEASUREMENT OF CONSUMER'S SURPLUS

Consumer's surplus = Total utility − (Price   Quantity)

In other words,

Consumer's surplus (CS) = TU − (P   Q)

Where,   TU = Total utility

           Q = Quantity of the commodity

           P = Price.

Otherwise,

Consumer's surplus = Price prepared to pay − Actual price paid.

The following table illustrates the measurement of consumer surplus.

Unit of Commodity A	Marginal Utility MU	Market Price Rupees	Consumer's surplus = Price prepared to pay (MU) − Actual market price
1	70	20	70−20 = 50
2	60	20	60−20 = 40
3	44	20	44−20 = 24
4	20	20	20−20 = 0
Total 4 units	TU = 194	80	= 114

Thus,

CS = TU − (P   Q)

    = 194 − (20   4)

    = 194 − 80 = 114

It clearly shows that a fall in the price will increase the consumer's surplus and vice versa.

The concept consumer's surplus is a relative concept because the term utility is relative. *(i.e)* it differs from person to person and from time to time. The consumer's surplus differs from commodity to commodity also. In the case of necessaries whose prices are low consumer's surplus will be high than high-price luxuries. For example, commodities like milk, vegatables, salt, newspapers etc., usually have high consumer surplus.

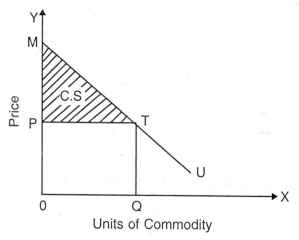

Units of Commodity

See explanation in the next page

If OP is the price, and OQ is the number of units purchased, MU of OQ = Price OP. Total money paid = OP × OQ = OPTQ

TU = OMTQ (i.e price prepared to pay).

Now the C.S = OMTQ − OPTQ = MTP

Assumptions of Consumer's Surplus

(i) Marshall assumes cardinal or numerical measurement of utility to measure the gain from the purchase.

(ii) The concept of consumers' surplus is based on the law of diminishing marginal utility and thus it includes ceteris paribus assumptions.

(iii) It also assumes that marginal utility of money remains constant.

(iv) To measure the concept of consumer's surplus, Marshall assumed that commodity in question has no substitutes.

(v) Each commodity is assumed as an independent commodity.

If all the above mentioned assumptions hold good, only then, the concept consumer's surplus is valid.

17. CRITICISMS OF CONSUMER'S SURPLUS

Various economists have criticised the Marshallian doctrine consumers' surplus. They are:

(i) Unrealistic Assumptions:

(a) This concept is based on the unrealistic assumption of cardinal or numerical measurement of utility i.e consumer's surplus cannot be expresed numerically.

(b) Marginal utility of money does not remain constant.

(c) This concept is not applicable in the case of substitutes.

(ii) Consumer's surplus cannot be measured. Critics argue that being a subjective concept, it cannot be exactly measured in terms of money and further entire concept is hypothetical.

(iii) Meaningless of this concept in the case of necessaries: In case of necessaries like water, a consumer derives infinite utility and would be willing to pay anything rather than go without it. So, in the case of water consumer's surplus may be infinite. Hence it is not correct to say that whenever a consumer drinks a glass of water, he enjoys great consumers' surplus.

(iv) The concept is imaginary: Consumer's surplus is imaginary and illusory and does not exist in reality.

(v) No evidence in support of this concept: Marshall has not provided any data in support of this concept and it is not capable of emperical testing also.

(vi) No practical utility: Prof.M.I.D.Little says that "The doctrine of consumers' surplus is a useless theoretical toy, having no practical significance".

18. USES OF THE CONCEPT OF CONSUMER'S SURPLUS

Consumer's surplus is a practical experience of all the consumers in the economy. It is not just a theoretical concept. It can be used as a guide in many fields.

(i) It helps in understanding the paradox of value: It is useful in understanding the distinction between value-in-use and value-in-exchange. The commodities like necessaries have more value in use and less value in exchange and hence the consumers' surplus is more. In the case of luxuries like diamond, the value-in-use is less as compared to their value-in-exchange and hence their consumers' surplus is less.

(ii) It is helpful to a monopoly firm: it is useful in determining the price policy of a monopoly firm. He can fix a high price if the consumers' surplus is high and vice versa.

(iii) Useful in Taxation Policy: Government can levy high indirect taxes on those commodities when consumers' surplus is high.

(iv) Helpful in measuring the gains from International Trade: We can measure it in terms of consumer's surplus obtained from the imported goods.

So, we can conclude that the concept of consumers' surplus is of great theoretical and practical value.

SUMMARY

1. Utility is defined as a property of the commodity which satisfies the wants of consumers.

2. The law of diminishing marginal utility states that if a consumer consumes more of a commodity, the utility of additional unit consumed diminishes.

3. The law of Equi-marginal utility states that the consumer would distribute his money income between the goods in such a way that the utility derived from the last rupee spent on each good is equal.

4. An IC represents satisfaction of a consumer from two or more combination of commodities.

5. The revealed preference theory analyses consumers prevenence for a combination of goods on the basis of observed consumer behaviour in the market.

6. Consumer's surplus is the difference between the potential price and actual price of a commodity.

QUESTIONS

1. Give the meaning of marginal utility.

2. State and explain the law of diminishing marginal utility.

3. How does a consumer use the law of equi-marginal utility in maximising his utility from a given expenditure?

4. Show how a consumer achieves maximum satisfaction with the help of IC techniques.

5. What is an IC? What are the properties of IC?

6. State and explain the revealed preference theory.

7. Define consumer surplus. Explain its assumptions, limitations and uses.

8. What is consumer's surplus?

9. What is a rational decision?

10. What is consumer surplus?

11. Briefly discuss the revealed preference theory and its utility in analysing consumer behaviour.

12. Explain the theory of cardinal utility.

4 Chapter

Demand Analysis

CHAPTER OBJECTIVES

After reading this chapter you will be able to answer the following:

1. Meaning of Demand
2. Demand Determinants
3. The Law of Demand
4. Changes in Demand
5. Factors Affecting the Demand Schedule
6. Elasticity of Demand
7. Types of Elasticity of Demand

People are talking about consumption and production of goods and services for centuries. Producers make goods in order to satisfy the consumption of wants of the people. If no one consumes, there will be no production at all. Consumption is thus, the end of productive activity. What goods are to be produced and in what quantities depend on what is demanded by the people. Thus, the knowledge of demand is indispensable for managers to determine what to be produced and how much to be produced. Here also lies the important thing, namely the price of the product. Demand analysis is concerned with the size of the demand for the product. There are three managerial aspects of demand – one is the Analysis and Forecasting of Demand, second is the Effect of Demand on the activities of the firm. Then the third is the Positive Approach of meeting the demand.

Demand analysis has two main managerial purposes: **(1) Forecasting sales (2) Manipulating demand.** The first is passive managerial aspects of demand because it represents factors which influence the firm the second is active which represents what the firm can influence. Forecasting implies knowledge of the factors likely to affect demand in a given situation. Sales forecasting is only passive because it estimates external economic factors and predicts the amount of sales that the firm can do. But in a free economy, since consumers enjoy absolute freedom to consume, the producers have to take up production of those commodities which people expect to buy. The demand analysis unearths the main issue of what people want and how much do they want.

1. MEANING OF DEMAND

The demand for the product is essentially the attitude of consumers towards the product. The consumer's attitude gives rise to action in buying so many units of a product at different prices. Precisely stated, the demand for a commodity is the amount of it that a consumer will purchase or will be ready to take off from the market at various prices at a given time. Demand in economics implies both the desire to buy and ability to pay for a product. It is to be noted that mere desire does not constitute demand, if it is not supported by the ability to pay for a product. Thus, demand in economics means desire backed up by adequate purchasing power to pay for the product when demanded and willingness to spend the money for the satisfaction of that desire.

> *Demand = Desire + Ability to Pay + Willingness to Pay*

2. DEMAND DETERMINANTS

Demand for the product is determined by several factors like price of the product, taste and desire of the consumers for commodity, income of the consumer, the prices of related goods such as substitutes and complements, advertising and sales promotion. These factors have the greatest influence on sales of the products. Let us discuss fully these variables which influence demand.

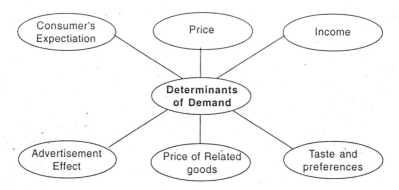

(i) Price of a Commodity: This is the basic factor in determining demand. There is a definite relationship between the quantity demanded and the price of the product. If a person wants to pay a certain price to the commodity, he must get satisfaction which is equivalent to the payment of price. No rational human being will pay for a product more than what it is worth to him in terms of utility. If the price is high, the individual has to sacrifice much, therefore he buys less. If the price falls, his sacrifice is less, he buys more. This inverse relationship between the price and the quantity demanded is called the *Law of Demand*.

(ii) Consumer's Income: The income of the consumer is another important variable which influences demand. The ability to buy a commodity depends upon the income of a consumer. The higher the income, larger is the quantity of a product that the consumer will buy. For example, a rich man can afford to buy more because his purchasing power is high. When the income of consumer increases, they buy more at a given price or at a higher price. When the income falls, the consumers are forced to buy less.

(iii) **Tastes and Preferences of Consumers:** The demand for a commodity depends upon tastes and preferences of consumers. These depend upon the cultural and social standard of consumers. If the consumers develop a taste for a commodity, they buy whatever may be the price. The particular life style influences the consumers to buy luxury goods and quality products. For example, a few years back, the demand for soft drinks was very low. But now the demand for soft drinks has increased very significantly, which is due to change in taste. Advertisement and sales campaign and improved knowledge are some of the factors which cause changes in consumers' tastes and preferences.

(iv) **Prices of Related Goods:** The demand for a product is also affected by the prices of substitutes and complements. Generally, commodities have alternatives and also they are used as complements. For example, coffee and tea are substitutes. Ink and pen are complements. When coffee becomes cheaper, the consumers substitute coffee for tea and as a result the demand for coffee increases and that of tea decreases. If the price of ink rises, the demand for pen falls. Likewise, when the price of cars falls, the demand for them would increase which in turn will increase the demand for petrol.

(v) **Advertisement and Sales Campaign:** In these days of modern civilization, the advertisement and sales campaign in newspapers and television influence the demand for products very significantly. They can change the demand pattern of the upper class people.

(vi) **Consumer's Expectations:** A consumer's expectations about the future changes in the price of a given commodity also affect its demand.

Thus, all these factors contribute for the demand for a commodity. We can analyse the concept of demand in the form of a formula as $q = f(py_1, pr, w)$, where q stands for quantity demanded, p stands for the price of the commodity, y stands for income of the consumers, pr stands for price of the related goods and w stands for tastes and preferences. If income, price of related goods, tastes and preferences are assumed to be constant, the quantity demand for a commodity depends upon the price. Then, the formula for demand is $q = f(p)$.

3. THE LAW OF DEMAND

The law of demand is based on the law of diminishing marginal utility. The law states the relationship between the quantity demanded and price. Experience tells us that ordinarily if the price of a commodity falls, the quantity demanded goes up and vice-versa there is an inverse relationship between the price of the commodity and the quantity demanded. In economics, this relationship is called as the Law of Demand.

Statement of the Law

Prof. Marshall writes, "The amount demanded increases with a fall in price and diminishes with a rise in price."

According to Bilas, "The law of demand states that often things being equal, the quantity demanded per unit of time will be greater, the lower the price and smaller, higher the price."

Prof. Samuelson writes, "Law of demand states that people will buy more at lower prices and buy less at higher prices, other things remaining the same."

The law of demand states that other things being equal, demand varies inversely with price.

Assumptions of the Law

According to Stigler and Boulding, the law of demand is based on the following assumptions.

1. There should be perfect competition in the market.
2. There should be no change in the income of the consumers.
3. There should be no change in the tastes and preferences of the consumers.
4. Price of the related commodities should remain unchanged.
5. The commodity should be a normal one.
6. The size of population should not change.
7. There should be no expectation of rise in price of related goods.

Explanation of the Law

This law can be explained with the help of a demand schedule and demand curve.

Demand schedule: Demand schedule is a state showing the relationship between the price and the quantity demanded. The following illustration shows price-quantity relation.

TABLE 1

Price	Individual Demand Schedule Quantity Demanded
Rs. 10	1 Unit
Rs. 8	2 Units
Rs. 6	4 Units
Rs. 4	8 Units
Rs. 2	14 Units

TABLE 2

Price	Market demand schedule assuming there are many buyers with different income and tastes
Rs. 10	10,000 Units
Rs. 8	20,000 Units
Rs. 6	40,000 Units
Rs. 4	80,000 Units
Rs. 2	14,00,000 Units

The demand schedule shown above reveals the relationship between the price and the quantity of the commodity bought. If the price is Rs.2, 14 units of the commodity are purchased. If the price rises to Rs.6, only 4 units of the commodity are demanded. If the price rises to Rs.10, then only 1 unit is demanded. It shows that lower the price higher the amount of the commodity are demanded, higher the price, lower the amount of the commodity demanded. Assuming there are many consumers with different incomes and tastes, by adding up all the individual demand schedules, a market demand schedule is obtained. The demand schedule if plotted on a graph map, a demand curve is obtained which is shown in the next page:

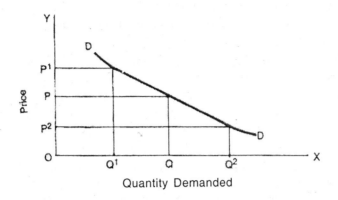

Quantity Demanded

The demand curve (DD) simply shows the relationship between the price, and the quantity of the commodity demanded. The demand curve slopes left to right downwards, indicating that when price rises, lower amount of the commodity is purchased and when price falls, more is demanded. The slope of the demand curve is negative because as price declines, more units of the commodity are bought. It is conventional to show, the quantity demanded on the X axis and the price on the Y axis. The demand curve is also known as Average Revenue Curve (AR) because the price paid by the consumer is revenue per unit for the seller.

Chief Characteristics of Law of Demand

(1) The law states that demand varies inversely with price, not necessarily proportionately. If the price falls by 10 per cent, it does not follow that demand will rise exactly by 10 per cent. It may be more than 10 per cent or less than 10 per cent.

(2) Price is an independent variable while the quantity demanded is a dependent variable. It means that demand is entirely dependent on the price.

(3) The law of demand depends upon certain conditions such as constancy of tastes and preferences, incomes of the individuals, prices of substitutes, etc. If these change, demand also changes.

Income and Substitution Effects of Law of Demand

The law of demand states that if the price of a commodity falls, the demand for the commodity rises and vice-versa. It means that demand responds to the price in the reverse direction. This aspect can be explained with reference to the behaviour of buyers. The buyers are classified into marginal buyers and intra-marginal buyers. Intra-marginal buyers are those who increase or decrease their consumption of a good but do not start or stop their consumption when faced with price variations. The behaviour of marginal buyers can be explained in terms of income and substitution effects.

(i) Income Effect: The fall in the price of a commodity is equivalent to an increase in income of the consumer, because he spends less while buying the same quantity of the commodity as before. A part of the money so gained can be used to buy more of the same commodity. When the price rises, the consumer's income is reduced since he has to spend more money to buy the same units of the commodity, by curtailing the consumption of other commodities. If the consumer does not want to buy more units of the same commodity when price falls, he may use the surplus

money to buy some units of a superior commodity. The reverse takes place when price rises. Thus, income effect of a change in price is negative for superior goods and positive for inferior goods.

(ii) Substitution Effect: When the price of a commodity falls, the consumers can buy more units of the same commodity or they can substitute that commodity for some other commodity or commodities which have now become relatively dear. If the price of tea falls, the consumers will now buy less of tea and more of coffee. It is also possible that if the price of coffee falls, others may now use coffee in place of tea. When the price of tea rises, more of tea will be used while consumption of other commodities is reduced. This is 'substitution effect'.

A change in price gives rise to both substitution effect and income effect. Income effect is positive and substitution effect is negative. The sum of income and substitution effects measure the price effect. For superior goods, both the income and substitution effects work in the same direction, while for inferior goods they work in opposite direction.

Exceptions to the Law of Demand

The demand curve generally slopes left to right downwards. But sometimes, it may rise from left to right upwards. This is called exceptions to the law of demand. It means, when prices rise, more units of a commodity may be demanded. If price falls, less units of the commodity may be demanded. This is shown in the form of a rising demand curve. Such cases are very rare. However, there are some cases in our every day life. They are often referred to *Giffen* goods. Giffen goods are those inferior goods on which consumers spend a large part of their incomes. Giffen paradox states that the demand is strengthened with a rise or weakened with a fall in price.

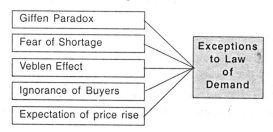

(i) **Giffen Paradox:** People spend a major portion of their income on staple foods like wheat, jowar, etc. If the price of wheat or jowar falls, the people are forced to give up buying of these goods and buy more of rice and other superior goods. When the price of wheat or jowar rises, the consumers buy more of wheat or jowar and forego the buying of other goods. Sir Robert Giffen found that in the nineteenth century in Ireland, the people were so poor that they spent a major portion of income on bread and a small amount on meat. Bread was so cheap while meat was very costly then. When the price of bread rose, they spent their entire income on bread and abandoned meat. Thus, a rise in the price of bread resulted in increased sales of bread. This phenomenon happens in all communities when they spend a major portion of their income on staple commodities.

(ii) **Fear of Shortage:** When a shortage is feared, people become panicky and buy more even though the price is rising.

(iii) **Veblen Effect:** There are some commodities which are purchased by the upper sections of the society for their 'snob appeal' or ostentation. If price of goods of ostentation rise, some people buy more units of these goods. Veblen calls this conspicuous consumption. For example, diamond. When the price of diamond rises, rich people buy more in order to exhibit their superiority in society. When the price of diamond falls, its demand will also fall for it loses its prestige.

(iv) **Ignorance of buyers:** Sometimes people buy at a higher price in sheer ignorance.

(v) **Expectation of price rise:** In the speculative market, a rise in price of shares and stocks is followed by large purchases, while a fall in their prices is followed by less purchase. When the prices of shares rise, people expect that their prices would rise further and rush to buy. When the price falls, they anticipate further fall in the price and stop buying.

Basis of the Law of Demand - Diminishing Marginal Utility (Reason for downward sloping demand curve)

The fundamental question in the demand analysis is, why do consumers buy more when the price falls and vice versa. The answer is that the consumer acting rationally, calculates deliberately the satisfaction he gets from the consumption of various units of a commodity at a given time. The goal of a consumer is to derive maximum satisfaction or utility from the purchase of various units of a commodity. In order to maximise satisfaction or utility, the consumer allocates his expenditure on a commodity in such a way that he receives the same marginal utility for the last unit of money spent on that commodity. The same is explained in the law of diminishing marginal utility.

Thus, the basis of law of demand is operation of the law of diminishing marginal utility. The consumer will buy more only if the price falls, because the more he buys, the lower is the marginal utility. Because of this reason, the demand curve slopes downwards.

4. CHANGES IN DEMAND

The demand curve shows the inverse relationship between the price and quantity demanded, i.e., how various quantities of a commodity can be sold at different prices assuming other things such as tastes and preferences, prices of the related goods and consumer's money income are remaining constant. Classical economists were quite aware that price is not the sole factor determining sales and changes in other things may change the demand schedule. The effect of changes in demand consequent on changes in other things is called *shift* in demand schedule. If the shift is upward it is called "*increase in demand*" and the downward shift in called "*decrease in demand*."

On the other hand, if changes in demand arises due to changes in price, it is called as "*expansion or strengthening*" of demand and "*weakening or contraction*" of demand. When the demand rises due to fall in the price, it is called expansion of demand. On the other hand, if the demand falls due to rise in price, it is called contraction of demand. There is vast difference between the terms of expansion of demand and increase; and contraction of demand and decrease in demand.

Expansion and Contraction of Demand

Here, the movement of expansion and contraction of demand takes place on the same demand curve because the demand schedule is fixed. The price simply goes up and down the same curve. This is illustrated in the following diagram.

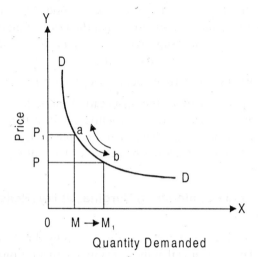

Quantity Demanded

The consumers demand curve is DD. At OP price, OM_1, is the quantity demanded. If the price rises to OP_1, his demand will be reduced to OM. If the price falls he will slide back. The consumer in this case is purely guided by price. Such a change in demand is called *expansion and contraction of demand.*

Increase and Decrease of Demand

Shifts in the position of the demand curve may take place due to the change in the conditions of demand. These shifts may be of two types - the upward shift or increase in demand and the downward shift or decrease in demand.

The demand is said to increase when the consumers are ready to buy more at the same price or willing to pay more for buying the same quantity as before.

The demand is said to decrease when the consumers buy less at the same price or pay less for buying the same quantity as before.

The increase and decrease in demand are shown in the shifting of demand schedules. In the following diagram, the changes in demand schedules are shown.

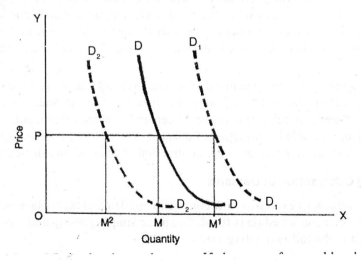

Quantity

In the beginning, DD is the demand curve. If there are favourable changes in factors determining demand, the demand curve (DD) shifts upward to D_1D_1. At price OP, the consumers will buy more, i.e. from OM to OM_1. When the other factors become unfavourable the demand curve shifts downward to D_2D_2. Then the demand falls to OM_2.

The increase in demand occurs due to the following factors -

(a) The fashion for goods increases or people's tastes and preference become more favourable for goods.

(b) Consumer's income increases.

(c) Price of substitutes of a commodity in question rises.

(d) Price of complementary goods have fallen.

(e) Propensity to consumption by people.

(f) Increase in the number of consumers owing to increase in population.

(g) Transfer of income in favour of middle and low income groups of people.

In all the above cases, the demand curve shifts upwards. Decrease in demand occurs when the following situations arise:

(a) A good goes out of fashion or people may develop distaste for the goods.

(b) Incomes of the people fall.

(c) Prices of substitutes fall.

(d) The prices of complements rise.

(e) There arises decline in the propensity to consume by the people and

(f) Income is transferred in favour of rich people.

In all the above cases, the demand curve shifts downward or backward.

5. FACTORS AFFECTING THE DEMAND SCHEDULE

1. Tastes and preferences of the customers

2. Incomes of the people

3. Change in the price of related goods

4. The number of consumers in the market

5. Changes in the propensity to consume

6. Consumer's expectation with regard to future prices

7. Income distribution.

Some explanations to the above factors:

(i) *Tastes and preferences of the consumers:* Whenever there arises changes in fashion, due to the pressure of advertisements in mass media, it will affect the demand. In the sixties of the twentieth century, when Coca-Cola was introduced to the market, the demand was very conservative. Even though the price of Coca-Cola was low, the demand was not high. But now, people's taste for Coca-Coal has undergone tremendous changes. Even though its price is high, demand is high. In economics, we would say that the demand curve for Coca-Cola has shifted upwards. On the contrary, when any goods go out of fashion, the demand for them decreases. Then the demand curve shifted downward.

(ii) Incomes of the people: The demand for a commodity also depends upon the money incomes of the people. When their money earnings are high, their demand for goods and services also will be high. for example, after planning was introduced in India, money earnings of the people have started increasing and consequently, the demand is rising even where prices are ising. Then the demand curve shifted upward.

(iii) Changes in the Prices of the related goods: The related goods are complements and substitutes. When the price of a substitute good falls, the demand for it also falls and vice-versa. For example, if the price of tea falls, demand for it also falls but demand for the substitute, the price of which has not changed, rises. Then the demand for coffee increases. The same things happen in the case of complementary goods. For example, when the price of cars falls, the demand for them would increase, which in turn will increase the demand for petrol.

(iv) The number of customers in the market: In a country like India and China, the number of consumers is vastly increasing owing to an alarming increase in population. Consequently, the demand for essential goods is also high. It is also easy for the sellers to find market for their goods in such thickly populated countries. Thus, the greater the number of buyers for a product, the greater is the market demand for it.

(v) Changes in the propensity to consume: Propensity to consume is another important factor in determining the demand for a commodity. During the period of inflation, propensity to consume is high. Consequently, the demand for goods is also high. During the depression, the propensity is low owing to fall in income and gloom about the future. The propensity is low. Then the demand curve shifts downward. Changes in propensity to consume will bring about changes in the demand schedule.

(vi) Consumer's expectation of future prices of goods: This is another important factor which affects demand. If due to some reason, the future prices would rise, the demand for many goods also will rise. During inflation, people expect the future prices will be high and start buying larger quantities at the prevailing prices. Then the demand curve shifts upward and vice-versa.

(vii) Income distribution: Income distribution refers to the equitable distribution of income among people by a Government's tax and public expenditure policies. When distribution of income is equal among the people, then the propensity to consume by the society as a whole increases and consequently the demand will be high. For example, if progressive taxes are levied on high income groups of people and the same revenue is spent on the betterment of poor people, their incomes rise and which in turn increases the demand for goods and services. If the growth of wealth and income is concentrated in the hands of the rich people, their number being small in a society, the purchasing power of a large percentage of the people will remain low and the demand for goods also will be low. Then the demand curve shifts downward.

Apart from the above mentioned factors, there are certain other factors like changes in climate or weather conditions, savings of the people, real income, quantity of money in circulation, inflation, conditions of trade prevailing in the market that also cause changes in the demand for a commodity.

Demand Distinctions

Demand analysis is studied for specific purposes. The main purpose is for the business objectives. The business people are required to make a thorough study of demand analysis with a view to solve business problems and to make business decisions. The business people have to produce goods which have great demand in the market. In order to study the demand potential for goods, they are classified into several types. They are as follows:

1. Producers' goods and consumer goods,
2. Durable and non-durable goods,
3. Derived demand and autonomous demand,
4. Industry demand and company demand
5. Short run demand and long term demand,
6. Short term demand fluctuations and long term demand trends
7. Market demand and market segments.

Producers Goods and Consumers Goods

Producers' goods are those goods which are used in the production of goods which may be consumer goods or producers' goods. Examples: machines, tools and implements, ships, locomotives etc. Consumers' goods are those goods which are in use in the final consumption. Examples of consumer goods can be given an number-food items, ready made clothes utensils and so on and so forth. There are intermediate goods such as yarn to produce cloth, steel to produce machinery which are producers' goods. There are single use goods and durable use goods. Manufactured food items are single use consumption goods. Sewing machines are a single use, durable use goods. A car, a refrigerator are consumer durable goods.

The reasons for the demand for producers' goods are the following

Buyers of produce goods are professionals. They are experts and they can make discrimination pricewise, qualitywise and are sensitive to substitutes.

Their motives are purely profit. Products are bought not for the product sake but for making profit. Their purchases are not at all influenced by advertisement, but more sensitive to price differences.

Demand for producers' goods fluctuate more dramatically than consumer goods.

The distinction between consumer goods and producers' goods though serves a useful purpose, a purely arbitrary. Whether goods are producers' goods or consumers' goods, it is based on (i) who buys (ii) why he buys. For example, if coal is used for cooking, it is a consumers' good-if the same coal is used in a railway engine, it is a producers' good. If the car is used by a retired executive, it is a consumer good and if the same car is used by a marketing executive, it is a producers' good.

Durable Goods and Perishable Goods

Durable goods are those which satisfy their owners for a long time to come if they are maintained properly. Perishable goods or non-durable goods are goods which can be consumed only once. In other words, perishable goods are themselves consumed, while in durable goods, the services are consumed.

Durable products present more complicated problems of demand analysis than the non-durable goods or perishable goods, sale of perishable goods are made to meet the current demand which depends upon current conditions. While the sale of durable goods add to the stock of existing goods which are still serviceable. Therefore, it is necessary to segregate current demand for durable goods with that of existing goods.

One characteristic of demand for durable goods is the volatile relation to business conditions, since the current production of durable goods is only a fraction of the products which are in current use. For example, normal production of autonomobiles is used – (i) to replace 10 per cent of the existing cars and (ii) to expand car production by 5 per cent, then a 3 per cent increase in demand for cars will raise the new car demand by 20 per cent. To put it more clearly, let us assume that there are 20,000 cars in use. The replacement demand at the rate of 10% means 2000 cars. (Supposing there is expansion in demand for cars by 5%, it means 1500. Then the existing total production would be 3000. If there is an extra 3% rise, then it means 600 additional cars, i.e 20% of the existing production of 3000 cars).

Demand analysis for durable goods is not simple. Both replacement and expansion have manifold set of demand determinants. Replacement demand depends on the value of existing cars as transportation relative to their scrap value. When the existing demand rises up suddenly, the prices of used cars go up higher than the scrap value, as a result, the scrapping rate falls (replacement demand falls). If the expansion demand falls, the scrappage rate will be higher than the level of new car production. The most important determinant for replacement is obsolescence due to technological developments. Obsolescence is pervasive and strategic in American economy in determining the level of business activity. Physical deterioration is rarely a deciding factor in replacement of durable goods. For durable goods, both consumers' and producers' goods, styles, convenience and income play a dominant role in demand.

Occassionally, technological upheaval can produce a blast of obsolescence that wipes out any distinction between expansion and replacement. For such innovation, demand depends upon cultural tags, financial agencies and rivalry of alternate investments.

While buying durable goods, the buyers, apart from their incomes and current prices of products, look into other things such as maintenance and operating costs in relation to their future income and other demands. They may look into the future sale prices of these products. They consider carefully whether to buy now or postpone the purchase. Thus, for durable goods, not only present prices and incomes, but their current trends and states of optimism are proper variables to include in demand functions. Expectation of proper improved designs are also important.

Derived Demand and Autonomous Demand

When the demand for a product is tied with another product, it is called *derived* demand. For example, demand for steel is related to the production of machinery. Demand for all producer's goods, raw-materials and components are derived demand. Demand for building materials like doors and windows, cement, sand etc. is derived from demand for houses. It is difficult to find recently products whose demand is all demand. In fact, independent demand is derived. There is no autonomous demand. Derived demand is supposed to have less price elasticity than autonomous demand, assuming that substitutes are equally available. For a 10% cut in the price of steel would cause only one per cent cut in the cost of a car, assuming prices of all other components are the same.

Some products are tied to others in their uses and they have no independent demand. For example, television antennas. If a commodity has a number of uses, it is difficult to tie demand down to parent products.

Derived demand facilitates forecasting when proportions of the two products are fixed. In some cases, demand may not provide a very reliable basis. For example, demand for looms in Cotton Textile Industry would normally be determined by the demand for cotton textiles. Yet, it may not give the current indicator as the looms may be used in double or triple shifts and the number of looms required may be reduced by half or one third. The recession in motor car industry forced tyre manufacturers to cut production and reduce stocks.

When the proportion between the parent and dependent goods is not fixed it is very difficult to determine demand for dependent goods on the basis of the demand for parent goods. If the number of uses to which a particular product can be put fluctuates, it is difficult to estimate the derived demand on the basis of the demand for the parent product. Electric motors and sulphuric acid are good examples for they can be used in any number of industries.

Industry Demand and Company Demand

Industry demand refers to the demand for the products used by all firms in a particular industry. For example, total demand for cotton, jute, steel etc. in an economy. Industry is composed of a group of closely associated firms. All firms manufacturing cloth are put together in order to form a cotton textile industry. The firms in the cotton textile industry are buying the same product namely yarn and selling the product (cloth) which are close substitutes. When there is considerable product differentiation within the industry and substitutes compete with other industries, then the concept of industry demand becomes irrelevant. For example, jaggery and sugar are distant substitutes excluded in the sugar industry.

An industry demand schedule represents the relation of the price of the product to the quantity that will be bought by all firms. It has a clear meaning when the firms are producing cloth substitutes. It has no meaning when the products produced by the firms differ markedly. Adding Ambassador and Premier cars and averaging their prices does not produce a meaningful demand schedule.

Industry's demand schedule can be classified into customers groupwise. For example, steel required for building construction and manufacture of machinery, etc. from the managerial point of view, mere industry' demand does not serve any purpose. What is to be recognized is to know the company's share in the industry's demand.

Company demand refers to the demand for the products of a particular company. Demand for Ambassador cars refers to the demand for the product of that company, while demand for cars refers to the total demand for cars of all firms put together. In order to understand the relation between company demand and industry demand, it is necessary to know the characteristic of different market structures. There are different market structures such as monopoly, perfect competition, monopolistic competition and oligopoly. In the case of monopoly, there is a single firm and hence there is no difference between company demand and industry demand.

In the case of oligopoly, there are two types – one is homogeneous oligopoly and the other is differentiated oligopoly. In the case of homogenous oligopoly, sellers are few and their products are standardized, the business is highly transferable among themselves. Example: aluminium, steel and cement. There is competition among rivals. The company's own demand curve is uncertain, for it depends on the rivals.

There is differentiated oligopoly – few sellers with differentiated products. (for example, motor cars, refrigerators, television sets, etc.). The company may have an independent demand function, depending upon the superiority of the product and advertisement effect.

In the case of monopolistic competition, the individual companies have their own demand curves and the industry demand curve has no meaning.

Demand Analysis in Terms of Market Share

The market share concept of company demand is now being used in demand analysis. The market demand for a product may be 10 million tones of steel. But a company's output may be 2 million tones. Then the company's share in the market demand is 20 per cent. It is started that some companies control 60 to 70 per cent of the product market, which are called *dominant* companies. The concept of market share becomes important because of the entire demand being the result of vast impersonal economic forces and is usually beyond the capacity of an individual company to control it. For example, an X company which produced say 60 per cent of the market share, cannot control the entire market but the market share enjoyed by it can be manipulated. Market share information may help in persuading people to buy the product of that company. This concept of demand indirectly is useful for the company either to increase its market share or try to retain it at least for which the company has to improve the product or change the market strategy.

The factors that determine the market share are - (1) The price differentials, (2) Promotional expenditure and, (3) Product improvement.

The price differential or price spread for product in the market determines the market share of the company. If a company's price is lower than the price charged by other companies, then that company would be able to capture a greater market share. If there is still competition in the market, a company may resort to increased promotional campaign, or it may take up product improvement by using latest technology. Thus, market share concept influences the individual companies to improve their respective positions in the market. In this cultural setting, market share objectives are often defensive.

Short Run Demand and Long Run Demand

Short run demand refers to existing or current demand. Further, there is immediate reaction to price changes, income fluctuation, etc. whereas long-term demand refers to demand which ultimately exists due to changes in prices or promotion of product improvement. For example, a cut in price of electricity will induce the existing users of electrical appliances to make greater use of them. This is short term change in demand. In the long run more people will be induced to buy them, ultimately leading to a greater demand for electricity. Thus, a temporary price cut cannot be viewed in the same light as one that is expected to stick. Competition among the producers will result in cut in the prices in the short run. This will lead to the entry of new competitors and exploration of substitutes in the long run.

Factors that cause this distinction are - (1) Cultural lags in information and experience, (2) capital investment required on the part of consumers to change their consumption patterns.

A price change today will result in a chain of adjustments in customer's attitudes and competitor's prices. There may be delayed action on the part of the buyers in response to price changes, because in practice, the consumers' use patterns are sticky. In the case of new products, price changes may not induce the buyers to buy them more. In the long run, price cuts may accelerate growth considerably, because by that time, there will have been adjustments in the use patterns.

Another factor is with regard to the new investments that will have to be made in order to take advantage of price cuts. In order to buy electrical appliances like refrigerators, T.V sets, washing machines, etc., a huge investment will have to be made, which may not be possible for many people. Thus, long run growth is not entirely dependent on price-cuts. Yet, price cuts influence the increase in demand considerably.

Demand Fluctuations and Long Trends

Fluctuations in demand cause more problems to producers since demand shifts in passage of time. There are several kinds of time patterns such as of day, month, seasonal and cyclical trends. Forecasting brief of time patterns does not pose serious problems to businessmen. But the forecasting as to how sales fluctuate from year to year and projecting long terms trends in demand post difficulties. In year to year fluctuations, much of the setting namely competitive structure, market position, quality and even prices remain constant. For long term, the trend is different, for everything is uncertain. There might be changes in tastes, technology and way of life.

Forecasts of year to year changes provide for programming firm's production plans, such as man-power requirement, raw materials requirement, inventory, cash etc. Projection of long range demand trends are useful for planning investments, choosing location, etc. Joel Dean observes that in the atomic age, long run forecast is necessarily a speculation.

Total Market and Market Segment

Total market for a product refers to its total demand. When the total market for toilet soaps is referred, it includes all the brands or substitutes of toilet soaps. Market segment refers to the part of the total market such as foreign market, local market, regional market and national market. Market segment may also be carved out by sub-products, the use of products, sensitivity to price, etc. When demand is divided into different segments, this gives rise to the market segment. Total market includes all segments.

When demand forecasting is to be made, total market has to be taken into consideration. When pricing, distribution and promotion is to be taken up, their market segment is preferred. Each of these market segments may differ in prices, packaging, promotion etc. For manipulating price, promotion, production and distribution, a segment concept of demand is appropriate.

6. ELASTICITY OF DEMAND

1. Meaning

Elasticity of demand is a common device for describing the shape of the demand function. It is a measurable concept which measures the response to change in demand. The law of demand indicates the direction of change in the quantity demanded in response to a change in price while elasticity of demand refers to the degree of responsiveness of quantity demanded to a change in its price, income of the consumer and prices of related goods. Alfred Marshall who developed this concept defined it as 'The elasticity (or responsiveness) of demand in a market is great or small according to the amount demanded increases, much or little for a given fall in price and diminishes much or little for a given rise in price'. Thus, elasticity of demand refers very much to price changes only. It is also defined as *'The contraction and extension attribute of demand by virtue of which it stretches or contracts under the pressure of a change in price is called elasticity of demand'*.

> *Thus, the term elasticity of demand refers to the degree of correlation between price and demand. Elasticity of demand is the measure of the responsiveness to a change in the price.*

Prof.Joan Robinson defines it as *'The elasticity of demand at any price or at any output, which is the proportional change of amount purchased in response to a small change in price divided by the proportional change of price'*. In simple language, price elasticity is the ratio of relative change in quantity to a relative change in price. The terms demand elasticity and price elasticity are used in the same sense.

7. TYPES OF ELASTICITY OF DEMAND

The quantity demanded of a commodity may change as a result of changes in the determinants such as price, incomes of the consumer and prices of the related goods. The concept of elasticity of demand therefore refers to the degree of responsiveness of quantity demanded of goods to a change in its price, income and prices of related goods. Accordingly, there are three kinds of elasticity namely price elasticity, income elasticity and cross elasticity or elasticity of substitution. Joel Dean introduced another kind of elasticity namely promotional elasticity.

(i) Price Elasticity of Demand

The concept of price elasticity of demand has an important practical application in decision making. Many a time, the producers are involved in a controversy whether to lower the price, to increase the sales or not. If he would come to know that a 5 per cent reduction in price will lead to a 20 per cent rise in the quantity demanded, he takes a decision of lowering of the price. Here the concept of elasticity becomes crucial.

The price elasticity of demand refers to the response of quantity demanded of a commodity to a change in its price, given the consumer's income, his tastes and price of all other goods. Thus, price elasticity means the degree of responsiveness or sensitiveness of quantity demanded of a commodity to a change in price.

> *Price elasticity can be precisely defined as proportionate change in quantity demanded in response to proportionate change in price.*

Thus, Price Elasticity $= \dfrac{\text{Proportionate change in quantity demanded,}}{\text{Proportionate change in price}}$

Price Elasticity $= \dfrac{\dfrac{\text{Change in quantity demanded}}{\text{Quantity demanded}}}{\dfrac{\text{Change in Price}}{\text{Price}}}$

In symbolic terms:

$$e_p = \frac{\dfrac{\Delta q}{q}}{\dfrac{\Delta p}{p}} = \frac{\Delta q}{q} \div \frac{\Delta p}{p}$$

$$e_p = \frac{\Delta q}{q} \times \frac{p}{\Delta p} = \frac{\Delta q}{\Delta p} \times \frac{p}{q}$$

Where e_p stands for price elasticity

q stands for quantity

p stands for price

Δ stands for a small change

If the law of demand holds good, price elasticity is negative, since change in quantity demanded is in opposite direction to a change in price. When price falls, quantity demanded rises and vice versa. For the sake of clarity, the negative sign is ignored and a numerical value is preferred. For example, if 5 per cent change in price leads to 10 per cent change in the quantity demanded of a commodity, then the price elasticity is 2. Suppose the price of a commodity is Rs.20, the quantity sold is 400 and when the price falls to Rs.15, the quantity sold increases to 600. What would be the price elasticity of demand?

Solution: Here P = Rs.20. Δp = 5 (Rs.20 − 15)

$$q = 400 \quad \Delta q = 200 \ (600 - 400)$$

$$e_p = \frac{\Delta q}{\Delta p} \times \frac{p}{q} = \frac{200}{5} \times \frac{20}{400} = 2$$

$$\therefore e_p > 1$$

If a 5 per cent change in price leads to 10 per cent change in the quantity demanded, then the price elasticity is 2. This is positive. It gives an incentive for business to increase the sales of the product by lowering the price.

Price elasticity can also be calculated with the help of a following formula:

$$\text{Price Elasticity} = \frac{\text{Percentage change in quantity demanded}}{\text{Percentage change in price}}$$

Degrees of Price Elasticity/Types of Price Elasticity

It is usual to distinguish between five cases of price elasticity - (a) Perfectly elastic (Infinite elasticity), (b) Perfectly inelastic or zero elasticity, (c) Relatively elastic, (d) Relatively inelastic, (e) Unit elasticity.

(a) Perfectly Elastic

When a small percentage change in price leads to large percentage change, in the quantity demanded, it is called perfectly elastic demand. The shape of the demand curve is a horizontal straight line. The diagram below illustrates the perfectly elastic demand curve.

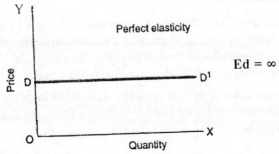

(b) Perfectly Inelastic Demand

Perfectly inelastic demand shows that how much ever the price may fall or rise, the amount demanded remains the same. It means that demand for the commodity does not show any response to a change in the price. For example, if the price rises from Rs.5 to Rs.50, the quantity demanded remains the same. This is called Perfectly Inelastic Demand. Perfectly inelastic demand has zero elasticity. The demand curve for this demand is that of vertical straight line as shown in the above diagram.

(c) Relatively Elastic Demand

It may be noted that both perfectly elastic demand and perfrectly inelastic demand are two extreme limits which are seldom met in real life and therefore can be recognised theoretically. On the other hand, in actual life, we come across elasticity of demand which is some-where between these two extreme limits. It is more zero or less than infinity. The fairly elastic demand curve is a downward sloping demand curve. The downward sloping is gradual.

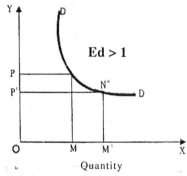

In the above diagram, the price falls from P to P^1 and the quantity demanded rises more than the change in the price to MM^1.

(d) Relatively Inelastic Demand

In the fairly inelastic demand, the quantity demanded changes by a smaller percentage than the change in price. In other words, if the price of a commodity falls, the demand increases only by a small percentage as compared with the fall in price. The numerical value of relatively inelastic demand lies between zero and one. It is also called less than one.

As the price falls from PN to P^{1}N^1, the quantity demanded increases from OM to OM^1 which is a small increase when compared with the fall in price. Thus, the demand is inelastic and it is shown in the above diagram.

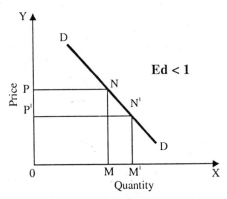

(e) Unitary Elastic Demand

Unitary elastic demand is the dividing line between elastic and inelastic demand. In this case, the elasticity of demand is equal to one. It means the response to the change in the quantity demanded is the same as change in the price of a commodity. If the price of a commodity falls by 10 per cent, the quantity demanded also increases by 10 per cent. The unitary elasticity demand curve is that of a rectangular hyperbola. The following diagram shows the unitary elastic demand curve.

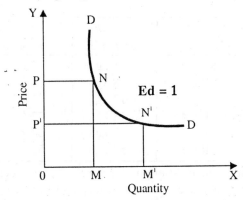

In this diagram, PP^1 equals MM^1. The area OPNM is equal to $OP^1N^1M^1$. The total amount spent on the purchase of the commodity at different prices is the same. Thus, the elasticity of demand in this case is unity.

The terms elastic and inelastic are used in relative sense. It means that elasticity is only a matter of degree. Demand for some goods is more elastic, while the demand for some other goods is less elastic. In the case of salt, it is inelastic and in the case of luxuries, the demand is elastic. Some goods of daily requirements such as milk, foodgrains etc. are unresponsive to change in their prices. Those goods which are indispensable, any rise or fall in price will not induce the customers to buy more or less. Thus, elasticities are different for different commodities.

Measurement of Price Elasticity of Demand

For practical purposes, it is not sufficient to know whether the demand is elastic or inelastic. It is very useful if we find out what exactly it is. For that purpose, it is necessary to measure elasticity. There are four methods of measuring elasticity, which are: (a) Total outlay method, (b) Proportional method and (c) Geometrical method or point elasticity (d) Arc method.

(a) Total Outlay Method

According to this method, we compare the total outlay of the purchaser (or total revenue i.e., total value of sales from the point of view of the seller) before and after the variation in price. In this method, it is possible to find out whether elasticity is unity, less than one and more than one.

Marshall has suggested this easy way of estimating elasticity of demand and to find out whether demand is elastic or not.

Total outlay (Total Revenue) = Price × Quantity

Marshall has distinguished three types of elasticities.

Unity: It is unity, when the total amount spent on a commodity remains the same even though the price has changed. The rise in price is balanced by reduction in purchases and a fall in price results in rise in his purchases.

Greater than One: It means that money spent on the purchase of the commodity increases when the price of the commodity falls and vice-versa.

Less than One: It means that total amount of money spent increases with every rise in price and decreases with every fall in price.

Example:

	Price of the Commodity	Quantity Demanded	Total Outlay (Revenue)	
1	Rs. 10	5 kg	50	} e > 1
2	Rs. 8	8 kg	64	
3	Rs. 6	12 kg	72	} e = 1
4	Rs. 4	18 kg	72	
5	Rs. 2	32 kg	64	} e < 1
6	Re. 1	50 kg	50	

As between 1 and 2 and 3, the elasticity is greater than unity because with every fall in price total amount of money spent increases and with every rise in price, the total amount of money spent decreases. As between 3 and 4, the elasticity is unity since the total amount of money spent remains the same, whatever is the price. Between 4 and 5, the elasticity is less than unity, since with every fall in price, the expenditure also decreases.

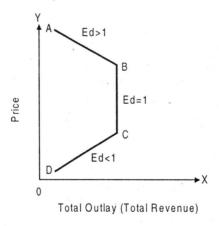

Total Outlay (Total Revenue)

In the given diagram in the previous page, the curve AB represents elasticity of demand greater than one (Ed>1). It indicates that, with the fall in the price, the quantity demanded and total outlay both increase.

But the curve BC represents no change in the total outlay though there is a change in the price and hence elasticity is equal to one (Ed=1).

The curve CD represents elasticity of demand less than one (Ed<1). It indicates that with the fall in the price, though the quantity demanded increases, the total outlay falls with the fall in the price.

Thus, elasticity is a warning signal to the businessmen. It tells them that in the case of inelastic demand, reduction price will reduce his revenue and increase in price will increase the revenue. The effect will be opposite if the demand is elastic.

(b) Proportion Method

In this method, the percentage change in the quantity demanded is compared with the change in price. The formula is:

$$\text{Price Elasticity} = \frac{\text{Percentage change in quantity demanded}}{\text{Percentage change in price}}$$

For example:

The original price of radio is Rs.500.

New price is Rs.400.

[Fall in price is 20%]

Quantity demanded of radio at Rs.500 is 400

Quantity demanded at new price Rs.400 is 600

[rise in quantity demanded is 50%]

$$\text{Price Elasticity of demand} = \frac{50\%}{20\%} = 2.5$$

(c) Point Method

This method measures elasticity at a given point on a demand curve. It takes into consideration a straight line demand curve and measures elasticity at different points on the curve. Elasticity of demand is different at different points of demand curve. It is because that it is a realative measure of change. The formula for measuring elasticity at different points is as follows:

$$\text{Elasticity of demand} = \frac{\text{Lower Segment}}{\text{Upper Segment}}$$

Elasticity of demand measured in a straight line demand curve is as follows:

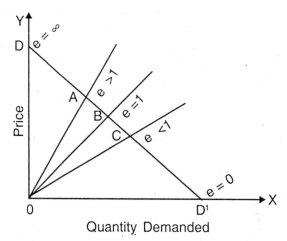

Quantity Demanded

At point A, the elasticity of demand is greater than one and hence demand is elastic. *i.e.*, D¹A/AD. D¹A is greater than AD.

At point B, the elasticity is equal to unity, because at B, D¹B = BD.

At point C, the elasticity of demand is less than one and hence the demand is relatively inelastic. i.e, D¹C/CD (DC is lesser than CD).

At the top left i.e., at point D on the Y axis, the elasticity is infinity.

At the bottom right, i.e at point D¹ on the X axis the elasticity is zero.

If the demand is a curved line, a tangent has to be drawn at the point and then elasticity is measured.

(d) Arc Method

Point method can be used when the changes in price and quantity demanded are small.. Arc method can be used when the changes are large. According to Prof.Baumol, "Arc Elasticity is a measure of the average responsiveness to price change exhibited by a demand curve over some finite stretch of the curve". According to Watson, "Arc elasticity is the elasticity at the mid-point of an arc of a demand curve". According to Leftwitch, "when elasticity is computed between two separate points on a demand curve the concept is called Arc Elasticity".

The formula for Arc Elasticity is as follows:

$$\text{Arc Elasticity of Demand}(E_A) = \dfrac{\dfrac{\text{Change in Demand}}{\text{Original Demand} + \text{New Demand}}}{\dfrac{\text{Change in Price}}{\text{Original Price} + \text{New Price}}}$$

Arc elasticity of demand in notational form can be expressed as:

$$E = \frac{Q_1 - Q_2}{Q_1 + Q_2} \div \frac{P_1 - P_2}{P_1 + P_2}$$

where Q_1 = original quantity demanded
            Q_2 = new quantity demanded
            P_1 = Original price
            P_2 = New Price

Arc elasticity can be shown with the help of a diagram given below.

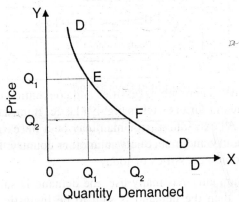

In the figure, quantity demanded is measured along X axis and price is measured along Y axis. DD is the demand curve. We take the average price of OP_1 and OP_2 and the average quantity of OQ_1 and OQ_2 are considered for measuring arc elasticity. In the diagram the arc elasticity is measured in terms of the dotted line EF, which is taken as approximation of arc elasticity measure. E and F is an arc on the demand curve. Its elasticity is called arc price elasticity. To measure arc elasticity, we have to take the average of two prices OP_1 and OP_2 as well as quantities namely OQ_1 and OQ_2.

$$\therefore E_A = \frac{Q_1 - Q_2}{Q_1 + Q_2} \div \frac{P_1 - P_2}{P_1 + P_2}$$

Factors Determining Price Elasticity of Demand

It is not possible to classify goods according to the nature of their demand and lay down rules to determine whether demand in any particular case is elastic or inelastic. However, some general rules can be formulated in this direction.

Elasticity is always relative. For one person or at any one place, the demand may be elastic, and for another person and at another place, it may be inelastic. The factors governing elasticity of demand are as follows.

Factors determining price elasticity of demand.

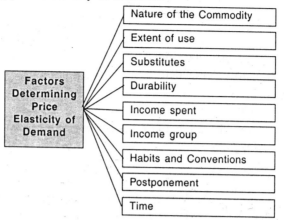

Factors Determining Price Elasticity of Demand
Nature of the Commodity
Extent of use
Substitutes
Durability
Income spent
Income group
Habits and Conventions
Postponement
Time

(i) **Nature of the commodity:** There are necessities and convention of necessities for which the demand is inelastic. The demand for luxuries is highly elastic. It must be remembered that the term luxury is a relative term. A luxury to a poor man may be a necessity to a right person. A thing may be luxury in one country and a necessity in another country. It may also be true that luxuries of yesterday have become necessities of today.

(ii) **Extent of use:** If a commodity has many use, the demand is said to be elastic and if a commodity has a specific use, then the demand is said to be inelastic. For example, there is electricity. It has a number of uses like lighting, cooking, ironing, etc. A fall in price increases demand, a rise in price decreases demand and hence demand for these goods is elastic.

(iii) **Substitutes:** The main cause for the difference in the responsiveness of demand for goods to change in their prices lies in the fact that there are more competing substitutes for the same goods than others. When the price of coffee rises, we may curtail the consumption of coffee and take to tea and vice-versa. In a case like, this a change in price will lead to contraction in demand or expansion in demand.

(iv) **Durability:** Durable goods have higher elasticity than non-durable goods, because the durable goods satisfy the consumers over a period of time. When the consumption of a commodity can be postponed, the demand is said to be elastic.

(v) **Proportion Spent on a Commodity:** If a person spends only a small percentage of his income on a commodity, the demand is said to be inelastic. It is due to the fact that his consumption of that commodity is a small amount, he does not bother about spending some more amount if its price rises.

(vi) **Income Group:** Elasticity also varies with income. People with high incomes are not affected by price changes than people with low incomes.

(vii) **Habits and Conventions:** If the consumption of a commodity has become a matter of habit, it is not much affected by the price changes. Hence the demand is inelastic.

(viii) **Goods that can be postponed:** The demand for goods whose use can be postponed is elastic. Most people postpone their purchases during war periods.

(ix) **Time:** The elasticity of demand will be less in the short period than in the long period because, with the fall in the price the demand will not increase in the short period.

Business Applications of Price Elasticity

The concept of price elasticity of demand is of great practical importance in the field of business, government, finance as well as commerce.

- It is an important piece of knowledge for managerial decision making.
- If the businessman know the elasticity of demand for their commodities, they can determine the prices accordingly.
- It is helpful for the finance minister for imposing taxes on commodities and to have an idea about government revenue.
- To determine terms of trade between the countries, the concept of elasticity of demand is of great help.
- The concept is also useful in the determination of rewards to the factors of production.
- The concept of price elasticity is useful to labour unions in wage bargaining.
- Elasticity of demand enables the government to declare and decide as to what industries should be made as public utilities.
- Fixation of the rate of exchange between two currencies of countries depends on the elasticity of demand for imports and exports.
- The concept explains the "paradox of poverty" in the midst of plenty. The farmers remain poor despite a bumper crop because foodgrains have inelastic demand.

Thus, the concept of elasticity of demand is of great use to businessmen, farmers, government, trade unions and policymakers.

(ii) Income Elasticity of Demand

As a result of economic development, the per capita income of the people is increasing every year. In the developed countries, the rate of growth is between 5 and 8 per cent per annum. In the underdeveloped countries, it is around 4 per cent per annum. Consequently, the demand for goods and services is also rising. If the income of the rich people rises, the demand for luxury goods increases. In the case of common people, the demand for comforts rises. This will result in investment of capital on new industries. This will further result in increase in employment, income and so on. Thus, the demand for goods and services is positively influenced by the level of income, employment and production. What will be the extent of influence of economic development on the sale of particular goods can be known with the help of co-efficient of income elasticity of demand. If the co-efficient is greater than one (unity), sales of the product will increase more than the rate of growth of economic development. The co-efficient of income-elasticity to inferior goods is negative, sales of such products decrease with every increase in economic development.

The knowledge of income elasticity of demand is very much useful in forecasting the influence of possible future changes in economic activity on demand. If the changes in income is long standing, then the demand for superior goods also increases. If the changes in income is all of a sudden, either owing to emergence of war or some inflationary situation in the economy, the demand for goods is very cautious.

What is Income-Elasticity of Demand?

As explained before, income elasticity of demand shows the degree of the responsiveness of quantity demanded of a good to a change in the income of the consumers.

> *The income elasticity of demand is defined as the ratio of proportionate change in the purchase of goods to the proportionate change in income*

$$\text{Income Elasticity} = \frac{\text{Proportionate change in the purchase of a commodity}}{\text{Proportionate change in income}}$$

Example 1

If the income of a consumer rises from Rs.1000 to Rs.1200, his purchase of goods X increases from 10Kg to 12 Kg. The income elasticity of demand in this case is:

$$\frac{\frac{2}{10}}{\frac{200}{1000}} = 1. \text{ Income elasticity of demand is } 1$$

Example 2

Increase in the demand for electricity is from 100 units of electricity to 200 units per month with an increase in income from Rs.3000 to Rs.4000. Then his income elasticity is:

200 − 100 = 100 units; Rs.4000 − 3000 = 1000 income.

Increase in the demand for goods is 100. Increase in income is Rs.1000. The income elasticity;

$$\frac{\frac{100}{100}}{\frac{1000}{3000}} = \frac{100}{100} \times \frac{3000}{1000} = \frac{3}{1} = 3\%$$

The income elasticity of demand is 3,

There is a useful relationship between income elasticity for goods and the proportion of income spent on it. The relationship between the two is described as:

(i) If the proportion of income spent on the goods remains the same as income increases, then the income elasticity of demand for the goods is equal to one. It is Unitary Income Elasticity.

(ii) If the proportion of income spent on goods increases as income increases, then the income elasticity of demand is more than one. It is also called High Income Elasticity.

(iii) If the proportion of income spent on goods decreases as income increases, then the income elasticity for the goods is less than one. It is Low Income Elasticity.

(iv) If a change in income will have no effect on the quantity demanded, then it is negative income elasticity. It is also called zero income elasticity. Goods having negative income elasticity are known as inferior goods. Commodities widely differ in terms of their income elasticities.

Income Sensitivity of Demand

Modern economists have propounded a concept called "income sensitivity" of demand. This is almost similar to income elasticity of demand. The difference between these two concepts is only slight. The income elasticity of demand is concerned with changes in physical units purchased as a result of changes in income, while income sensitivity deals with changes in rupee expenditure due to change in income.

Types of Income Elasticity

The various types of income elasticities are shown in the diagram below:

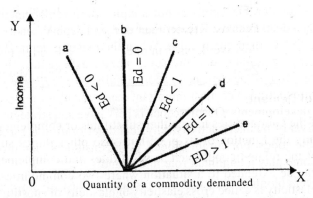

a = Negative income elasticity   b = Zero income elasticity
c = Income elasticity is less than one,   d = Income elasticity is equal to one,
e = Income elasticity is greater than one.

(a) Negative income elasticity: If the demand for a commodity decreases with an increase income, the demand is said to be negative income elastic. The demand curve will be sloping downwards like 'a' in the diagram. The income elasticity co-efficient in this case is Ed<0.

(b) Zero income elasticity: When the change in income do not bring about any changes in quantity demanded, i.e., quantity demanded remain the same, it is said to be zero income elasticity of demand. In this case, the shape of the demand curve is vertical straight line like 'b' in the diagram. So, income elasticity co-efficient is Ed=0.

(c) Income elasticity less than one: When the propositionally or percentage change in quantity demanded is less than the proportionate or percentage change in income, the income elasticity is said to be less than one. The demand curve in this case will be steeper like 'c'. Thus, Ed<1.

(d) Income elasticity equal to one: If the proportionate or percentage change in quantity demanded is equal to percentage or proportionate change in income, it is said to be unitary income elastic and the shape of the demand curve will be 45° angled like 'd' in the diagram. In this case, the co-efficient is Ed=1.

(e) Income elasticity greater than one: When the proportionate or percentage change in quantity demanded is greater than the proportionate or percentage change in income, then income elasticity it is said to be greater than one. The demand curve will be flatter like 'e' in the diagram. The co-efficient will be Ed>1.

Usually income elasticity is positive because there is a positive relation between income and quantity demanded. Other things remaining the same, there will be an increase in demand when there is an income and vice versa. However, negative income elasticity is also observed sometimes. In the case of inferior goods *i.e.,* Giffen goods the income elasticity is negative. In the case of luxury goods, income elasticity is always positive and greater than one. For normal goods, income elasticity is always positive. When income elasticity is zero the commodity is said to be neutral. For essential goods, income elasticity is positive but less than one. The following table will give a clear idea regarding types of income elasticity.

Nature of goods	Types of income elasticity	Examples
1. Normal goods	Positive	Fruits, Vegetables etc.
2. Inferior	Negative	Jowar, Bajra etc.
3. Luxury	Positive, greater than one	TV sets, Cars etc.
4. Essential	Positive, Less than one	Foodgrains etc.
5. Neutral	Zero	Salt, Matches etc.

(iii) Cross Elasticity of Demand

Generally, most of the commodities have either substitutes or complements. The demand for a commodity is not only the function of its price but also other things such as income of an individual and price of the related goods such as substitutes and complements. The concept of elasticity of demand can be extended to a situation where two commodities are related to each other. This concept of elasticity is called cross elasticity or elasticity of substitution. Cross elasticity of demand is useful in handling inter-commodity demand relations.

> *Cross elasticity of demand is defined as the ratio of the percentage change in demand for one good to the percentage change in the price of other goods.*

Cross elasticity of demand tells us how the demand for a good, say coffee depends upon the price of a substitute tea. It may be a complement also. The quantity of bread depends upon the price of butter or jam, because these goods are complements. The formula for cross elasticity of demand is:

$$\text{Cross elasticity of demand of X and Y} = \frac{\text{Percentage change in demand for commodity X}}{\text{Percentage change in the price of commodity Y}}$$

Example 1

The price of coffee increases from Rs.60 to Rs.80 per kg and as a result of this, demand for tea rises from 5 kg. to 10 kg. What is the cross elasticity of tea for coffee?

Solution:

Change in the price of coffee: Rs.80 − 60 = 20

Change in the quantity demand of tea: 10 − 5 = 5

Cross elasticity : $\dfrac{5}{10} \div \dfrac{20}{60} = \dfrac{5}{10} \times \dfrac{60}{20} = 1.5$

$$\therefore \ Ed > 1$$

In the above example, coffee and tea are substitutes. Increase in the price of coffee results in increase in the quantity demanded of tea. If the two goods are substitutes, the value of cross elasticity is positive. If the two goods are perfect substitutes, the cross elasticity is infinity. If the two goods are unrelated (like sugar and salt), then the cross elasticity is zero.

Example 2

Torino and Thums-Up are good substitutes. If the price of Thums-Up rises, many of its customers go in for Torino. The cross-elasticity in such a case is positive, because change in the demand for Torino and change in the price of Thumps-up move in the same direction. If the two substitutes are very much closer, the greater is the size of cross elasticity. If the two commodities are poor substitutes (Coffee and Torino) then the cross-elasticity is low.

In the case of complementary goods, a fall in the price of butter increases the demand for bread. If the price of one commodity rises, the demand for other commodity falls. In the case of two complementary goods such as sugar and tea, the cross elasticity will be negative. If the price of sugar goes up, its demand also falls and consequently the demand for tea also falls.

In conclusion, it may be stated that cross elasticity of demand for perfect substitutes is highly positive, and for perfectly complementary goods, it is highly negative.

Relationship Between Price Elasticity, Income Elasticity and Cross Elasticity

As already discussed, price effect, that is the effect on the quantity demanded of a commodity due to a change in price depends upon income effect on the one hand and substitution effect on the other. In the same way, the price elasticity of demand depends upon income elasticity on the one hand and cross elasticity on the other. Thus, price elasticity is a compromise between income and substitution elasticity of demand. The relationship between these elasticities can be expressed in the form of a formula. The price elasticity of demand for X goods is given by the formula:

$$ep = KX. \, ei + (I - KX) \, ec$$

where, ep = stands for price elasticity

ei = stands for income elasticity

ec = stands for cross elasticity

KX = stands for proportion of income spent on goods X.

The first part of the formula $KXei$ represents the influence of income effect on the price elasticity of demand. This shows that the change in quantity demanded of x due to fall in price depends in part upon the magnitude of income effect of the change in price. This income effect of the change in price depends on the one hand upon proportion of income spent on good X (i.e KX) and income elasticity of demand for good X that is (ei) on the other. The proportion of income spent on good X determines what amount of income spent on goods X will be released as a result of fall in the price of goods X. The income thus released is spent on buying more of good X as well as other goods. Given the income elasticity of demand, the greater the proportion of income spent on good X, and greater the amount of income released for purchasing good X and other goods as a result of fall in the price of good X and consequently greater the increase in the amount demanded of good X. The amount of good X demanded is due to income effect of the price fall depends on the income elasticity of demand for good X. This is because the income elasticity of demand for good X determines how much of income obtained by the fall in the price of X, will be spent on good X, whose price has fallen and how much will be spent on other goods. Proportion of income spent on good X being given, greater the income elasticity of demand for good X, greater the part of income released will be spent on good X. Consequently, there will be a greater increase in the quantity demanded of good X. So, the first part of the formula shows the impact of income effect on the price elasticity of demand.

The quantity demanded of X good does not increase, only because of income effect of the fall in price but also because of substitution effect. When the price of a commodity falls, it becomes a cheaper good and consequently he buys other goods of which the price has not fallen. The second part of the formula (1 KX) ec shows the influence of substitution effect on the price elasticity of demand for goods X. The magnitude of the substitution effect in turn depends in part on the cross elasticity, i.e., to which extent the goods X can be substituted to other goods which were being purchased before the fall in the price of X good.

Some Recent Developments in the Theory of Demand

Distributed Lag Models: At present demand function is used in dynamic form. It expresses that the present purchasing decisions are influenced by past behaviour. The present purchasing behaviour depends on the income and demand in the past. In the case of durable goods the current and the future purchases will be definitely affeted by the stock of past purchases of this commodity. In the case of non-durable goods, the current and the future patterns of demand is influenced by the past habit of the consumer. The recent past influences (e.g. past income levels) will affect the present consumption pattern to a greater extent. The demand functions which incorporates lagged values of variables like income, prices, demand etc. are called distributed lagged models. For example:

$$q_t = f(p_t; \ p_{t-1}; \ y_t; \ y_{t-1} \ .... q_{t-1}, \ q_{t-2})$$

where

q_t = quantity purchased at present i.e. in period t

q_{t-1} and q_{t-2} = quantity purchased in past period t-1 and t-2.

p_t = present price i.e. in period t

p_{t-1} = price in the past period

y_t = present income

y_{t-1} = past income i.e. income in t-1 period

Nerlove's model is based on stock adjustment principles which is mostly used in demand function and in investment function. The model is related to the study of demand function of consumer durables. The past purchase of consumer durables (stock) determine the purchase of other products. For example, the consumer durable like tape-recorder determines the likely purchase of other products like cassetes.

The extension of stock adjustment principle to non-durable consumer goods is made by Houthakkar and Taylor and named it "Habit reaction principle." According to them the previous purchases reflects the habit of the consumer and in turn that influences his present purchases of non-durable goods like food tins, vegetables, milk, cigarettes etc.

Linear Expenditure System (LES): LES Models do not deal with single commodity but with group of commodities. Total consumer expenditure can be obtained by adding such groups. This was first suggsted by Prof. R. Stone.

The LES are formulated on the basis of utility function from which the demand functions are usually derived. In this context, LES is similar to indifference curve approach. But it differs slightly because it deals with groups of commodities between which no substitution is possible. The total utility is derived by adding the utilities derived from the various groups of commodities.

For example, all commodities bought by the consumer are grouped into five categories. They are:

1. Food and Beverages (Non-durables)
2. Clothing
3. Consumer durables
4. Other Household expenditure
5. Services

The total utility $U = \sum_{i-1}^{n} u_i$

$\therefore U = U_1 + U_2 + U_3 + U_4 + U_5$

This shows that utility of various groups are independent and no substitution is possible between the goods but substitution is possible within the group. Irrespective of the prices, the consumer may buy minimum quantity of each group. They are called as 'subsistence quantitative (minimum requirement to keep the consumer alive). The left over income is spent among the various groups on the basis of prices.

Hence, the income of the consumer is divided into 2 parts one, subsistence income which is spent on the bauying of minimum quantity and various commodities and the two supernumerary income which is left over income to be spent on other commodities.

In LES approach, the income effect is given a new dimension and importance.

SUMMARY

1. The demand for anything at a given price is the amount of it which will be bought per unit of time at that price.
2. The Law of Demand states that other things being equal, demand varies inversely with price.
3. Elasticity of demand is the percentage or proportionate change in quantity demanded of a commodity in response to a given percentage or proportionate change in price.
4. The demand functions which incorporates lagged values of variables like income, prices demand etc. are called distributed lagged models.
5. The Linear Expenditure systems are formulated on the basis of utility function from which the demand functions are usually derived.

QUESTIONS

1. What is meant by demand? Explain the factors which influence demand.
2. Examine the role of price, income and price of the related goods in affecting demand.
3. What is the significance of demand analysis to the managerial economist?
4. Explain the law of demand. What do you mean by shifts in demand curve?
5. Explain the concept of elasticity of demand. What factors are influencing in making the demand for a product elastic or inelastic?

6. "If the demand is elastic, it will pay a businessman to charge a low price. If the demand is inelastic, he would be better off with a high price". Discuss.

7. Explain the concept of cross elasticity of demand. How would you measure such elasticity?

8. Distinguish between the following:

    (a) Producers goods and consumers goods.

    (b) Durable goods and perishable goods.

    (c) Superior goods and inferior goods.

    (d) Complementary goods and substitutes.

    (e) Company demand and industry demand.

9. Give an explanatory note on distributed log model.

10. Distinguish between incremental revenue and marginal revenue.

11. Distinguish between demand schedule and demand function.

12. Distinguish between price elasticity and income elasticity

13. Distinguish between substitution effect and income effect of a change in price.

14. Give a note on linear expenditure system.

15. Give a note on each one of these concepts.

    (i) Demand Function (ii) Demand Schedule (iii) Demand Curve (iv) Individual Demand (v) Market Demand (vi) Change in Demand (vii) Shift in Demand (viii) Elastic Demand (ix) Inelastic Demand (x) Autonomous Demand (xi) Derived Demand (xii) Increase in Demand (xiii) Decrease in Demand (xiv) Extension of Demand (xv) Contraction of Demand.

16. Give your opinion (based on economic laws) on the following statements with reasons.

    (a) Law of demand has no exceptions.

    (b) When the price of steel rises, demand for cement decreases.

    (c) The concept of "Demand" is an absolute term.

    (d) Price is the sole determinent of demand.

    (e) Desire is not a demand.

17. What is the usefulness of demand in managerial decision making?

18. The recent Census of India exhibits a vital statistics. The male-female ratio is 1:0.95. This indicates that female population has increased over the previous census. This has resulted in:

    (i) Increase in female workers in business houses.

    (ii) Social habits in society are changing, giving more prominence to dress, comforts of all kinds.

    In this backdrop analyse the demand position in the market for goods and services consumed by female population (your analysis should be purely on economic aspects).

19. Give a mathematical attribute (Demand equation) for X brand television.

20. Define elasticity of demand. Explain its variants.

21. Differentiate between direct demand and derived demand.

22. What are the determinants of price elasticity of demand? Explain.

23. Explain what happens to demand curve of a certain product when the following changes occur.

    (i) The price of the commodity falls.

    (ii) Income increases and the commodity is normal.

    (iii) Income increases and the commodity is inferior.

    (iv) The price of a substitute increases.

    (v)   The price of a compliment decreases.

    (vi)   The income of the consumer decreases.

    (vii)   The price of the good is expected to fall in near future.

24. Distinguish between extension of demand and increase in demand.

25. What is unitary elasticity of demand?

26. What is income elasticity of demand?

27. Explain the factors affecting demand.

28. What are the determinants of demand?

29. "The demand for the product of a firm within a given industry is influenced by the nature of market structure and sources of demand". Discuss.

Illustration on Demand Analysis

Illustration 1:

The demand function for a brand of radio in a city is Qd=3000-5p. where Qd is the quantity demanded of radio sets per year. "P" is the price per set of radio. From this equation

(a) Develop a demand schedule (and plot it on a graph) at prices Rs.150, Rs.250, Rs.325, Rs.400 and Rs.500.

(b) At what price Qd=0.

(c) If the seller wants to sell 2500 sets what price should be fixed?

Solution:

(a) P=150, Qty=3000-5x150=2250
P=250, Qty=3000-5x250=1750
P=325, Qty=3000-5x325=1375
P=400, Qty=3000-5x400=1000
P=500, Qty=3000-5x500=500

(b) If Qd=0, applying the equation, 3000-5P=0 will be the new equation.

By substantiation;

5P=3000

P=3000/5=Rs.600

This means, at price Rs.600, demand will be zero (3000-(5x600)3000=0).

(c) To sell 2500 sets, the price to be fixed is Qd=3000-5P.

Quantity to be sold or demanded is 2500 sets.

∴Qd=2500=3000-5P

  5P=3000-2500

  P=500/5=Rs.100

At price Rs.100, the producer can sell 2500 sets of radio.

Mathematical attribute or usual demand function is as follows:

$$D=f(P): \text{ where } \frac{\Delta D}{\Delta D} < 0$$

This equation implies inverse relationship between price and quantity demanded.

DEMAND ANALYSIS IS THE BASIS FOR MANAGERIAL DECISION MAKING RELATING TO PRICE POLICY.

Illustration 2:

Construct a demand schedule for a washing soap "Quick Clean" (Qc) at alternative prices of Rs.6, Rs.7, Rs.8 Rs.9 and Rs.10 per cake. Given demand function $100-4P_{QC}$.

Solution:

$Dx=100-4P_{QC}$

At price Rs.6; $Qd=100-4(6)=76$

Rs.7; $Qd=100-4(7)=72$

Rs.8; $Qd=100-4(8)=68$

Rs.9; $Qd=100-4(9)=64$

Rs.10; $Qd=100-4(10)=60$

(Plot this data on graph)

Illustration 3:

Demand equation for a TV is determined as follows based on market price.

$P=48000-4Q$

From this find the following:

(1) Marginal revenue when Q is 20 and 30.

(2) Price and quantity when total revenue is maximum.

6. (a) Construct a demand schedule for a newly released computer at alternative prices Rs.30,000, Rs.32,000 Rs.33,000, Rs.35,000 and Rs.40,000 for a given Demand function is $90000-2P_{NC}$

(b) Plot this schedule on a graph.

(c) Give the price at which demand becomes zero.

Demand Forecasting

5

Chapter

CHAPTER OBJECTIVES

After reading this chapter you will be able to answer the following:

1. Meaning and Nature of Demand Forecasting
2. Types of Forecasting
3. Determinants for Demand Forecasting
4. Objectives of Demand Forecasting
5. Approaches to Demand Forecasting
6. Methods of Demand Forecasting
7. Forecasting Demand for New Products
8. Some of the Difficulties in Forecasting of Consumer Durable
9. Importance of Demand Forecasting

Forecasting is a prediction about a future event which is most likely to happen under given conditions. Demand forecasting means estimate of expected future demand conditions. Kotler remarked that 'forecasting is like trying to drive a car blindfolded and following directions given by a person who is looking out of the back window'. Looking into the future which is uncertain, is really a difficult task. But it has been so in the experience of mankind. Assuming that future would be bright, every man takes some risks in life and tries to advance further. In the business field, there was lack of forecasting in the past. It was only after the depression in 1930s, that systematic forecasting was realized as a tool of management.

1. MEANING AND NATURE OF DEMAND FORECASTING

Forecasting is defined as a study with scientific prediction in regard to an event which may have future demand for goods, services either at the micro level or at the macro level. Forecasting deals with the likely shape of future events. It is scientific guesswork.

Forecasting is useful for managerial decision making, effective and efficient planning. It helps to assess the probable demand for goods and services in different periods of time. Demand forecasting translates the demand functions into quantitative guesses. A theoretical demand function seeks to include all the forces that influence sales. If these are to be translated into actuality, some of the demand determinants have to be selected and a formula for forecasting sales has to be evolved. This is the function of demand forecasting. Since the management operates under conditions of uncertainty, a probable estimate of future demand for the products is absolutely essential. This helps in reducing the risk of uncertainty to the absolute minimum. Forecasting is required in all areas of enterprise. Since future is uncertain, no forecast is hundred percent certain. However, it is necessary for every firm to make forecast as correct as possible. Henry Fayol was the first to lay emphasis on forecasting as an important function of business management. A good forecast reduces the scope of uncertainty to the barest minimum.

> *Demand forecasting refers to the prediction or estimation of a future situation under given constraints.*

2. TYPES OF FORECASTING

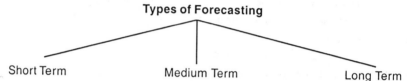

Types of Forecasting

Short Term   Medium Term   Long Term

Short Term Forecasting: Short term forecasting covers a periods up to one year. It relates to policies regarding sales, purchases, pricing and finances. In most of the firms, the information regarding the immediate future is necessary for forumulating a suitable production policy. This helps in avoiding both over production and under production. For this purpose, production schedules have to be tuned to expected sales. Short term is necessary to determine a suitable price policy. it helps the management to reduce cost of production, and controlling inventory. It helps in setting up sales targets and establishing controls and incentives. The sales targets must be set at a reasonable level. It should not be too high or too low. Demand forecasting helps in short term financial forecasting. It can be set up as a programme of cash requirements at different levels of sales. Neglect of demand forecasting will upset financial planning through its repercussions on production scheduling and inventory accumulations.

Most of the demand forecasting is concerned with short term projections for established products. Forecasting for the established products can be made with the information colleted from existing markets and past behaviour of sales. Forecast of new products is difficult.

Medium Term Forecasting: Medium term forecasting is intermediate between short-term and long term forecasting. This is usually followed by a firm which is subjected to the medium term variation of the trade cycle. If a firm is subjected to a trade cycle, then it has to assess its demand situations and plan its production activities accordingly. Firms such as garment manufacturers and engineering goods industries often faces such pattern of demand performance in the market.

Long Term Forecasting: Long term forecasting refers to a period beyond one year. The purposes of long term forecasting are: (i) Planning of a new unit or expansion of the existing unit. It requires an analysis of long term demand potential for the products in question. A multi-product firm must know not only the total demand situation, but also the demand for different items. (ii) Planning long term financial requirements is necessary for the firm to make necessary arrangements to secure fresh capital for investments. Issuing of new shares at premium, raising debentures, deposits, etc. (iii) Planning manpower needs – training and recruitment of personnel to meet the future growth of the firm.

Factors Involved in Demand Forecasting

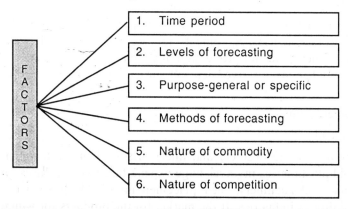

FACTORS
1. Time period
2. Levels of forecasting
3. Purpose-general or specific
4. Methods of forecasting
5. Nature of commodity
6. Nature of competition

1. **Time Period:** From the viewpoint of span of time, forecasting may be either short term or long term.

2. **Levels of Forecasting:** It is undertaken at different levels,

   (i) International level: International events like hike in petrol prices has worldwide implications.

   (ii) Macro level: It is concerned with the entire economy – the usual measure is GNP.

   (iii) Industry level: Industry sales volume is largely a consequence of impersonal economic forces over which a firm has no control. It is prepared by trade associations.

   (iv) Firm level: The firm estimates its sales and relates to industry's sales.

3. **Purpose-general or Specific:** Forecasting may be general or specific: A firm may find a general forecast useful to sell its product. Again, sales forecast may be done for specific products for specific areas.

4. **Methods of Forecasting:** Methods and problems of forecasting are different for new products from established products, past trends are known and these guide the future performance.

5. **Nature of Commodity:** While forecasting, the nature of the commodity should be known. Commodities are either producers' goods or customers' goods. The pattern of demand is different for different types of goods.

6. **Nature of Competition:** Nature of competition prevailing in the market and also sociological and psychological aspects have to be considered.

3. DETERMINANTS FOR DEMAND FORECASTING

Goods which are demanded may be classified into the following categories:

   (i) Capital goods,
   (ii) Durable consumer goods,
   (iii) Non-durable consumer goods

Demand forecasting for each type of goods is different. That is factors influencing demand for each of these categories are not the same. Factors influencing demand for durable, consumer goods are different from capital goods.

(i) Capital Goods

Capital goods are defined as goods which are required for further production of goods. They are various types of machineries, equipments, tools, etc. Capital goods are demanded when there is demand for consumer goods for production of which capital goods are needed. In other words, the demand for capital goods is derived demand. Further, the demand for capital goods is classified into two types:

(a) Replacement demand,

(b) New demand

Replacement of old and obsolete machinery arises when the maintenance cost goes high. Repairs of the old machineries involves huge expenditure. In such cases, the management takes a decision to replace old machinery. The replacement involves huge investment as such, it depends upon the profitability of industries. If the market for the products for which old machineries are to be replaced is sluggish and the future is bleak, scrapping of such machines is better than replacement of machineries. When modernisation is contemplated, existing machineries are completely scrapped and new machineries are installed in their places. For example, some factories like textile, cement, sugar are producing with old machineries, consequently the productivity is low and cost of production is high. In such cases, setting up of new factories based on modern technology is more profitable. Demand for capital goods depends upon – (1) their present uses and their capacity utilization, (2) scrapping rate, (3) the economics of their utilization and availability of internal finance and bank loans.

The following data are to be collected for establishing the demand for capital goods.

(i) The growth prospects of industries using capital goods.

(ii) The norm of consumption of capital goods per unit of installed capacity. It is assumed that norms of consumption would remain stable. But there might arise a situation of shortages of imported spare parts. For example, spare parts in the case of imported aeroplanes. If locally produced prototype spares can be used as against the shortage of imported parts owing to high cost of import or non-availability of foreign exchange. In such cases, norms of consumption would not remain stable.

(ii) Durable Consumer Goods

Durable consumer goods are those goods which are used continuously for a certain period of time. for example, residential buildings, personal motor cars, refrigerators, washing machines, T.V sets, furniture, etc. Like capital goods, the demand for durable goods is classified into new demand and replacement demand. Main aspects considered in estimating the demand for durable consumer goods are the following:

1. In the case of durable goods, demand consists of replacement demand (R) and new demand (N). The demand forecast for these two categories has to be made separately. When the consumers find that the existing durable goods such as old T.V set, refrigerator, automobiles are not serving satisfactorily, they think of replacing the old ones by new ones. When the consumers find latest models of durable goods, they think of selling the old goods and buying new goods. The choice depends on non-economic factors like

prestige, social status and economic factors like income or obsolescence. If the price of the new product is very high, then the consumers may think of using the old model with repairs for some more time.

In India, the rate of replacement of old durable goods is very low. If the consumers are very rich, then they are going to buy the new models, selling the old models. Majority of the consumers prefer to use the old model for a long time.

2. Consumer durable goods are generally used by households rather than individuals. It must be noted that for goods which are used by family together, the demand forecast should rely on household figures. A few durable goods like electric shavers are used individually and as such, demand forecast may be made on urban educated population figures.

3. The use of basic consumer durable goods such as electric appliances, automobiles, etc. depends upon the availability of infrastructures like regular supply of electricity, good roads respectively. The existence and growth of infrastructure facilities influence the demand for these durable goods.

4. Many durable goods are used by many members of family, the demand for them depends upon family characteristics, age, sex, distribution of the family, income of the family, etc.

5. In case of durable goods, the demand depends upon the growth of income and psychological factors. The social environment largely influences the demand for them. When once a person starts using a car, he will continue to use for a long time, no matter its servicing cost. In western countries, the demand for automobiles is so high, that a person replaces his car once in four or five years. This is due to enormous increase in the purchasing power of the people. The purchasing power, the number of households and the social status, etc. set up an upper limit to the maximum ownership level of durable goods.

6. The demand for durable goods also depends upon the availability of hire-purchase facility. In western countries, this facility is available in plenty and as such every householder thinks of owning a flat or a house and car, etc. in India, this facility is growing in all metropolitan cities. There are number of hire-purchase companies, specialised in selling durable goods on hire purchase basis. Some two-wheeler companies themselves are selling on hire-purchase basis. Demand for such durable goods is elastic.

Forecasting the demand for consumer durable goods poses some problems. Most of the costly durable goods are purchased after lengthy deliberation and thinking. They are not purchased instantaneously. It may take several months to take a decision on buying a house. Thus, durable goods are bought sporadically.

(iii) Non-durable Goods

Non-durable goods are those commodities which are used in a single act of consumption. They are food articles, beverages, tobacco, etc. Demand for such goods is influenced by three basic factors such as: (A) Disposable income of the people or purchasing power, (B) Price of the commodity, (C) Size and characteristics of population. The formula used for estimating the demand for non-durable goods is

$$d = f(Y.D.P)$$

where D is demand, Y is disposable income, D is size of the population and P is the price.

(a) Purchasing Power of the People: It depends upon the disposable income of the people of the country. The disposable income is obtained from personal income after making tax and other deductions. In a poor country like India, disposable income is very low and consequently the purchasing power of the people also is very low. Some people prefer to use a concept of discretionary income in place of disposable income. In the case of purchase of food articles, clothing, etc., there cannot be much discretion. Since they are necessities and comforts, everyone will have to buy them. Discretionary income will be an important factor in determining the demand for luxuries. If the disposable income is high, the demand for non-durable goods also will be high.

(b) Size of the Population and its Characteristics: This refers to total population, the different income groups, social status, age-sex composition, urban and rural population, geographical characteristics, level of education, etc. Demand for non-durable consumer goods depends upon all these factors. The demand for various goods can be estimated either for each market segment or for the total market with the help of these characteristics. For example, to determine the demand for toys, it is necessary to note the number of children studying in schools and the income of their parents. In the urban market, the demand for non-durable goods is very high, while it is low in the rural market. In the same way, to determine the demand for detergents and soaps, the size of population, the incomes of the people the mode of living etc. have to be taken into consideration. The demand for cloth is a function of price, the income of the people and the size of population. In the forties, fifties and sixties, there was a huge demand for coarse cotton cloth in India. But today, the demand for such cloth has fallen. The demand for blended cloth is increasing. This is mainly due to increase in income of the people and a little bit of education. The demand for fine cotton cloth is also a function of fashion. Thus, many factors influence the demand for non-durable goods.

4. OBJECTIVES OF DEMAND FORECASTING

Demand forecasting serves the main purpose of maintaining equilibrium in the economy. Some of the objectives are narrated below:

(i) Helping for Continuous Production: Demand forecasts help the producers to take up prodution planning so that the gap between demand and supply of goods is eliminated.

(ii) Regular Supply of Commodities: Demand forecasting induces the producers to maintain sufficient inventory of products, so that when supply falls and demand increases, the product may be released in the market to fill up the gap.

(iii) Formulation of Price Policy: Demand forecast helps the management to formulate appropriate price policies, so that the prices do not fluctuate over a period of time.

(iv) To Formulate Effective Sales Performance: One of the objectives of demand forecasting is to formulate effective sales performance. Since demand forecasting is made regionwise, movement of products may be arranged suitably. It helps the management to determine sales targets accordingly.

(v) Arrangement of Finance: Finance is indispensable for procuring materials and labour for production. On the basis of demand forecast, the management can prepare the budget for institutional finance.

(vi) To Determine the Production Capacity: The demand forecasting enables the companies to decide about the production capacity. If the demand forecast indicates that the demand for the product is elastic, then the Board Of Management can plan for a large sized plant. By studying the demand pattern for the products, the organisation can plan for a suitable plan and desire output.

(vii) Labour Requirement: Production of product requires skilled and trained labour force. If the demand forecasting indicates favourable trend, then the management can take up measures to train the labour force. This can ensure better labour supply and there will be no hinderance in the production process.

Thus, overall success of the enterprise mainly depends upon the quality and reliability of demand forecasting.

5. APPROACHES TO DEMAND FORECASTING

It should be noted that there is no easy method or simple formula for predicting the future demand. But demand forecasting is essential and hence some techniques have been tried in estimating the future demand. There are various techniques in forecasting demand, but too much emphasis on each technique is not desirable. The critical problem is to choose the most efficient technique subject to certain limitations. There are dangers in adopting any single technique and as such care must be taken in using the technique. Mathematical and statistical techniques are employed in forecasting future demand. Though statistical and mathematical techniques are essential in classifying relationships and providing techniques of analysis, they are not substitutes for judgement. Second danger is that sound judgement is no doubt an essential requirement but it needs to be supplemented by information and analysis. Thus, efficient forecast must depend on both sound judgement and rigorous analysis.

There are two approaches generally followed in demand forecasting.

   (i) To collect information regarding the intentions of the consumers by means of market research, survey and economic intelligence.

   (ii) To use past trends and taking them as a guide and by extrapolating past trends to estimate future demand. The first approach is followed to estimate short run forecasting while the second approach is resorted to long run forecasting. The following chart indicates different methods of demand forecasting.

Criteria of a Good Forecasting Method

Thus, there are a good many ways to make a guess about future. They show contrasts in cost, flexibility, and the necessary skills and sophistication. In order to make demand forecast realistic, the following criteria has to be remembered:

(i) Accuracy: It is necessary to check the accuracy of past forecasts against present performance and of present forecast against the future performances.

(ii) Plausibility: It means belief. The executives who use the forecasting results must be willing to believe in the market. Elaborate mathematical procedures become less desirable if the management does understand what the forecaster is doing.

(iii)Durability: Whenever a forecast is made, it should hold good for a certain period of time. It depends upon reasonableness and simplicity of the function fitted.

(iv) Availability: The technique employed should produce quick results and the data required by the management must be easily available.

(v) Economy: The cost of forecasting must be within limits.

6. METHODS OF DEMAND FORECASTING

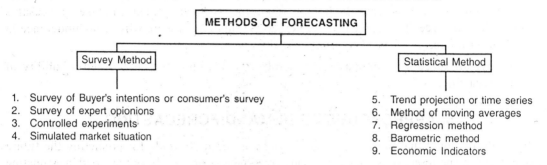

Statistical methods use past behaviour of sales as a guide and by extrapolating past statistical relationship and predict the future demand. The demand for established products can be forecast either by survey methods or statistical methods, but for new products, survey method is the only source.

(i) Survey Methods or Direct Methods

Forecasts are done both for established products and new products. Demand forecasting for the established products can be done in a routine manner with information drawn from the existing markets and past behaviour of sales.

Forecasts for new products are necessarily custom built jobs that involve more ingenuity and expense. Since the product has not been sold before, it is difficult to get any clue for demand forecasting. Therefore, forecasting for new products needs to be done by survey methods alone.

Forecasting of established products is based on personal judgement and experience while others are based on statistical methods. Both methods are frequently used to cross check each other with a view to make forecasting as accurate as possible.

a. Survey of Buyer's Intentions or Consumer's Survey

This is the least sophisticated method and the most direct method of estimating sales in the near future. In this method, customers are directly contacted in order to find out their intention to buy commodities in the near future. This method is known as *opinion survey* method.

Intentions of buyers are recorded through personal interviews, mail or post surveys and telephone interviews. Questionnaires are prepared to find out buyer's intentions. The work of consumer's surveys should be given to trained, reliable and experienced investigators.

In personal interveiw method, house to house survey is conducted. There is personal contract with the consumer but it is expensive and time consuming.

In the case of mail or post-surveys, more number of consumers can be covered within a short-period and it is less expensive. But there is no personal contact with the consumers and hence correct answers cannot be obtained.

In the case of telephone interviews, there is personal contact and are time and money saving. If telephone facilities are not available to all consumers, then this method cannot be relied on to a great extent. It is preferred only when quick information from consumers is desired.

There are two types of consumer's survey

    (i) **Complete Enumeration Method:** It covers all the potential consumers in the market and interviews are conducted to find out probable demand.

    (ii) **Sample Survey Method:** It covers only few consumers selected from total potential consumers interviewed and then the average demand is calculated on the basis of the consumer's interviewed.

Therefore, though consumer's survey method is direct and simple, it suffers from several shortcomings in forecasting, in that, according to Joel Dean, consumers' plans may be trigger-sensitive to short run economic changes while consumers' plans are fragile, capricious and expensive to collect.

b. Survey of Opinions of Experts

There are people who are experts in the field of selling goods like wholesalers and retailers. They will be in a position to tell what consumers would buy. Many companies get their basic forecasts directly from their salesmen who have the most intimate 'feel' of the market. The wholesalers and retailers by their experience are in a position to 'feel' about the probable sales in the coming year. In this kind of forecast, the total is built up by adding individual salesman's projections, then scaled down for errors of optimism by pooling the collective wisdom of top executives in second guessing and consolidating results. These people have been dealing in the products for a long period and are therefore in a position to predict the likely sales in the future period on the basis of experience. This work is simple and calculation also is very easy. This method may be used in place of opinion method. But there is one limitation in this method too. It is because the basis of forecast by the experts is difficult to identify for it may spring largely from hints and impulse under the pressure of enquiry. It is purely subjective for different experts may give different kinds of forecast or they may be biased for some reason. Despite this limitation, some companies use this method of forecasting for their products.

c. Controlled Experiments

Under this method, different determinants of demand are varied (price, advertising, packaging, etc.) and price-quantity relationships are established at different points of time in the same market or different markets. Only one determinant is varied and others are kept constant or controlled. In America, Parker Pen Co. used this method to find out the effect of price rise on the demand for Quick Ink. This method is relatively new. It is difficult to decide which variable is to be varied and what variables should be kept constant.

d. Simulated Market Situation

Under this method, an artificial market situation is created and participants are selected. These are called consumer clinics. Those participants are given some money and asked to spend the same in an artificial departmental store. Different prices are set up for different groups of buyers. The responses to price changes are observed and accordingly necessary decisions about price and promotional efforts are undertaken.

But this method is time consuming and a difficult job.

(ii) Statistical Methods or Indirect Methods

Demand forecasting also uses statistical methods. In this method, some statistical and mathematical techniques are used to predict the future demand. This method is useful for long run forecasting for the existing products. There are several ways of using statistical and mathematical data. They are:

(a) Trend projection method or Time series

(b) Method of moving averages,

(c) Regression method,

(d) Barometric methods,

(e) Other methods

(a) Trend Projection Method or Time Series

This method is based on analysis of past sales patterns. A firm which has been in existence for quite a long time will have accumulated considerable data regarding sales for a number of years. Such data is arranged chronologically with regular intervals of time. This type of data is called *Time Series*. The time series shows effective demand for the product during the period of past ten or fifteen years. On the basis of the data, a graph can be drawn and this is called a *sales curve*. The sales curve shows fluctuations and turning points in demand. If the turning points are few and their interval is widely spread over, firm forecasting becomes possible. Frequency of turning point indicates uncertain demand conditions. When a turning point occurs, the trend projection breaks down. If the turning points are few and spaced at long intervals, accurate forecast is possible. The real challenge is to point out the turning points.

Time series refer to the data over a period of time, during which time fluctuation may occur. Therefore, the time series has four types of components namely,

- **Secular trends:** Secular trend refers to the general tendency of the data and it is known as long period or secular trend. This can be upward or downward, depending upon the behaviour.

- **Seasonal Variations:** Seasonal variations refer to changes which occur during a climatic season or a festival season. It may be that of festival season like Deepavali or Dussherra etc. Normally, these changes which are repetitive in character are related to a 12 month period.

- **Cyclical variations:** Cyclical variations refer to the changes arising out of booms and depressions.

- **Random variations:** Random variations refer to changes which occur unnoticed like famines, floods, earthquake, etc. These cannot be predicted.

The real problem in forecasting is to separate and measure each of these four factors. When a forecast is made, the seasonal cyclical and random factors are eliminated from the data and only the secular trend is used. The trend in time series can be estimated by using any one of the following methods:

(i) the least square method,

(ii) the free hand method,

(iii) the moving average method,

(iv) the method of semi-averages

Illustration: In the time-series or trend projection analysis, past data of sales are taken to determine the nature of existing trend and then this trend is extrapolated into the future and thus a forecast is made.

Suppose a producer of toilet soap decides to forecast the next year's sales of his product using this method. The data for the last five years is as follows:

Sales of X Company

Years	Sales in Rs. Lakhs
1996	45
1997	52
1998	48
1999	55
2000	60

This data is plotted on a map which is shown in the following diagram:

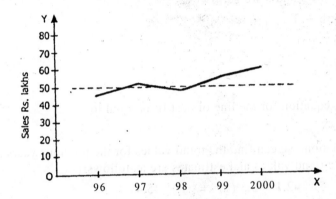

In the graph, it can be seen that sales have fallen in 1988 and then have increased. It shows that sales are fluctuatiing. But during the whole period, the sales trend is upward. The line so drawn is called *trend line.*

The trend line is filled by developing an equation giving the nature and magnitude of the trend. The common technique used in constructing the line of best fits is by the method of least squares. The trend is assumed to be linear. The equation for the straight line trend is: Y = a + bx, where a is the intercept and b shows the impact of the independent variable. Sales are dependent on variable Y. Since sales vary with time, the time periods will be the independent variable X. The Y intercept and the slope of the line are found by making appropriate substitutions in the following normal equations.

$$\Sigma Y = na + b\Sigma x \dots\dots\dots\dots\dots(i)$$

$$\Sigma XY = a\Sigma x + b\Sigma x^2 \dots\dots\dots\dots(ii)$$

Year	Sales Rs. in Lakhs (Y)	X	X²	XY
1996	45	1	1	45
1997	52	2	4	104
1998	48	3	9	144
1999	55	4	16	220
2000	60	5	25	300
N = 5	ΣY = 260	ΣX = 15	ΣX² = 55	ΣXY = 813

In the table below, we find the magnitudes of required quantities from the original data given above.

Substituting the above values in the two normal equations, we get the following:

$260 = 5a + 15b - 3$

Solving equations 3 and 4 we get $b = -3.3$

$813 = 15a + 55b - 4$

$260 = 5a + 15 \ (3.3)$

$260 = 5a + 49.5$

$a = 42.1$

Therefore, the equation for the line of best fit is equal to:

$Y = 42.1 + 3.3X$

Using this equation, we can find the trend values for the previous years and estimates of the sales for 2001. The trend values and estimates are as follows:

Y	1996	=	42.1 + 3.3 (1) =	45.4
Y	1997	=	42.1 + 3.3 (2) =	48.7
Y	1998	=	42.1 + 3.3 (3) =	52.0
Y	1999	=	42.1 + 3.3 (4) =	55.3
Y	2000	=	42.1 + 3.3 (5) =	58.6
Y	2001	=	42.1 + 3.3 (6) =	61.9

Based on the trend projection equation illustrated above, the forecast sales for the year 2001 is Rs.61.9 Lakhs.

(b) Method of Moving Averages

The trend projection method is very popular in business circles on account of simplicity and lesser cost. The basic idea in this method is that past data serves as the guide for future sales. But this method is inadequate for prediction whenever there are turning points in the trend itself. Moreover, while irregular factors such as storms and strikes can be averaged out and contained into the equation, it is desirable to know how valuable such an exercise could be.

The calculations depends upon whether the period should be odd or even.

In the case of odd periods like (5, 7, 9), the average of the observations is calculated for a given period and the calculated value is written in front of central valuable of the period, say 5 years. The average of the values of five years is calculated and recorded against the third year. In the case of five yearly moving averages, the first two years and the last two years of the data will not have any average value.

If the period of observation is even, say four years, then the average of the four yearly observations is written between second and third year values. After this, centering is done by finding the average of paired values. Let us take up the following illustrations:

The following are the annual sales of dresses during the period of 1993-2003. We have to find out the trend of the sales using (1) 3 yearly moving averages, (2) 4 yearly moving averages and forecast the value for 2005.

Year	Sales in Rs. Lakhs
1993	12
1994	15
1995	14
1996	16
1997	18
1998	17
1999	19
2000	20
2001	22
2002	25
2003	24

Solution: 3 yearly period:

e.g: The value of 1993 + value of 1994 + 1995

12 + 15 + 14 = 41 − written at the capital period 1994 of the years 1993, 94 and 95

Year	Sales in Rs. Lakhs	4 Yearly moving total	4 Yearly moving average trend values
1993	12	(−)	−
1994	15	41	41/3 = 13.7
1995	14	45	45/3 = 15
1996	16	48	48/3 = 16
1997	18	51	51/3 = 17
1998	17	54	54/3 = 18
1999	19	56	56/3 = 18.7
2000	20	61	61/3 = 20.2
2001	22	67	67/3 = 22.3
2002	25	71	71/3 = 23.7
2003	24	−	−

Four yearly moving averages

Year	Sales in Rs. Lakhs	3 Yearly moving total	Moving total of pairs of yearly total	3 Yearly moving average trend values
1993	12	–	–	–
1994	15	–	–	–
1995	14	57	–	–
1996	16	63	120	120/8 = 15
1997	18	65	128	128/8 = 16
1998	17	70	135	135/8 = 16.9
1999	19	74	144	144/8 = 18
2000	20	78	152	152/8 = 19
2001	22	86	164	164/8 = 20.5
2002	25	91	177	177/8 = 22.1
2003	24	–	–	–

57 = the value of 1993 + value of 1994 + value of 1995 + value of 1996

= 12 + 15 + 14 + 16

= 57 written between 1993 and 1996

120 = 57 + 63, 128 = 16 + 65.... written in the centre of 1994, 1995, 1996 i.e., 1994, 1995, 1996, 1997 and so on. 120 is the total of 8 years, so average is calculated by dividing 120 by 8.

Forecast for the year 2005

The trend values from the previous tables can be plotted on graph which is as shown below:

Trend line for 3 yearly and 4 yearly moving averages is same.

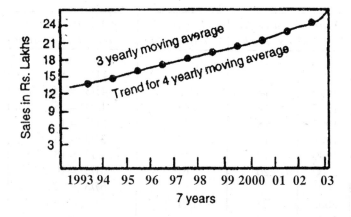

Advantages of this Method: This method is simple and can be applied easily. Secondly, it is based on mathematical calculations and finally this is more accurate.

Disadvantages of this Method: The disadvantage of moving average method is that it gives equal weightage to the data related to the different periods in the past. It cannot be applied if some observations are missing.

(c) Regression Method

The sales of any commodity does not depend on time only. It may be associated with competitors, advertising, one's own advertising, change in population, income and size of the family, environmental factors, etc. The nature of relationship between these factors can be used and future sales can be forecast. Regression analysis denotes methods by which the relationship between quantity demanded and one or more independent variables (income price of the commodity, prices of related commodities advertisement expenses, etc.) can be estimated. It includes measurement of errors that are inherent in the estimation process. Simple regression is used when the quantity demanded is estimated as a function of single independent variable. Multiple regression analysis can be used to estimate demand as a function of two or more independent variables.

Trend Projection by Regrestion Method

This is a mathematical tool, with this, adapting "Method of Least Squares" a trend line can be fixed to know the relationship between time and demand/sales. Based on this trend line sales/demand can be projected for future years.

This is an inexpensive method of forecasting. The data will be available with the organisation and based on this data, demand or sales can be projected for subsequence years. Following illustrations will give an idea as to how demand can be projected under 'Least Square Method".

Illustration 1:

Year:	1998·	1999	2000	2001	2002
Sales (Rs.in crores)	240	280	240 ·	300	340

From this data project the sales for 2003, 2004, 2005.

Solution:

First we have to calculate required values. They are (i) Time Deviation, (ii) Deviation Squares, (iii) Product of time deviation and sales.

Year	Sales (Rs.in crores)	Time deviation from middle year 2000	TD squared	Product of Time Deviation and sales	
n	(y)	(x)	(x^2)	(xy)	
1998	240	-2	4	-480	$\left.\begin{array}{c}\end{array}\right\}$ -760
1999	280	-1	1	-280	
2000	240	0	0	0	
2001	300	$+1$	1	$+300$	$\left.\begin{array}{c}\end{array}\right\}$ $+980$
2002	340	$+2$	4	$+680$	
x=5	$\Sigma y=1400$	$\Sigma x=0$	$\Sigma x^2=10$	$\Sigma xy=220$	

The equation is y = a + bx.

In this equation "a" is an independent variable and "b" exhibits rate of growth.

Now, we have to find out the value of "a" and "b".

$$a = \frac{\Sigma y}{n} = \frac{1400}{5} = 280$$

$$b = \frac{\Sigma xy}{\Sigma x^2} = \frac{220}{10} = 22$$

Now applying values to regression equation, the equation will be y = 280 + 22x.

From this we can ascertain sales projection from 2003, 2004 and 2005.

For the year 2003 = 280 + 22(3) = Rs. 346 crores.

2004 = 280 + 22(4) = Rs. 368 crores.

2005 = 280 + 22(5) = Rs. 390 crores.

Illustration 2:

Forecast the demand for the years 2003, 2004 and 2005 from the following data.

Years	1997	1998	1999	2000	2001	2002
Sales (Rs.in crores)	90	100	110	130	150	160

Year	Sales (Rs.in crores)	Time deviation from the middle of 1999-2000	Time deviation squared	Product of Deviation and sales
n	*(y)*	*(x)*	*(x²)*	*(xy)*
1997	90	−5	25	−450
1998	100	−3	9	−300 } −860
1999	110	−1	1	−110
2000	130	+1	1	+130
2001	150	+3	9	+450 } +1380
2002	160	+5	25	+800
n = 6	Σy = 740	Σx = 0	Σx² = 70	Σxy = 520

y = a + bx

$$a = \frac{\Sigma y}{n} = \frac{740}{6} = 123.33$$

$$b = \frac{\Sigma xy}{\Sigma x^2} = \frac{520}{70} = 74.28$$

Now Projections

Year 2003 = 123.33 + 74.28(7) = Rs.643.29 crores

Year 2004 = 123.33 + 74.28(9) = Rs.791.85 crores

Year 2005 = 123.33 + 74.28(11) = Rs.940.41 crores

Certain vital variables are considered in demand forecasting.

(a) Price of different brands in the market.

(b) Number of consumers interested in purchasing the brand in question.

(c) Average or annual household income.

(d) Annual advertising expenditure of the brand in question.

Considering these variables one equation is developed (Truett and Truett-1980).

$Q_A = f(P_A, P_B, P_C, y, A)$

Where: P_A=Price of A brand

             P_B=Price of B brand

             P_C=Number of consumers interested in product A

             y=Mean annual household income

             A=Advertising expenditure of product A per annum.

Demand projection can also be made adopting this equation.

Simple Linear Regression

In case of linear trend in the dependent variable, a straight line to the data can be fit in, whose general form would be: Sales = a + b price.

The straight line regression equation can be fit in either graphically or least square method. In the graphical method, the sets of data of two variables (sales and income) on a graph are plotted and a scatter diagram can be obtained.

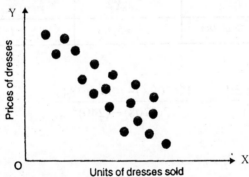

The regression in line can be approximated by sketching it free hand in such a manner that the line passes through the middle of the scatter.

In the least square method of estimating the regression line, S = a + bP, the value of the constants, a and b can be with the help of a following formula:

$$b = \frac{n\Sigma S_i P_i - (\Sigma S_i)(\Sigma P_i)}{n\Sigma P_i^2 - (\Sigma P_i)^2} \text{ and}$$

$$a = \frac{\Sigma S_i - b\Sigma P_i}{n}$$

Example

Fit a linear regression line to the following data and estimate the demand at price Rs.30.

Year	1981	82	83	84	85	86	87	88	89	90	91	92
Price Pi	15	15	12	26	18	12	8	38	26	19	29	22
Sales Si in 1000 Units	52	46	38	37	37	37	34	25	22	22	20	14

Solution:

Find the values of a and b and then the following table is constituted:

P_i	S_i		S_i^2	$S_i P_i$
15	52	225	2704	780
15	46	225	2116	690
12	38	144	1444	456
26	37	676	1369	962
18	37	324	1369	666
12	37	144	1369	444
8	34	64	1156	272
38	25	1444	625	950
26	22	676	484	572
19	22	361	484	418
29	20	841	400	580
22	14	484	196	308
$P_i = 240$	$S_i = 384$	$P^2 = 5708$	$S_i^2 = 13716$	$\Sigma S_i P_i = 7098$

Then we will have

$$b = \frac{n\Sigma S_i P_i - (\Sigma S_i)(\Sigma P_i)}{n\Sigma P_i^2 - (\Sigma P_i)^2} = \frac{12(7098) - (240)(384)}{12(5708) - (240)^2}$$

$$= \frac{-6984}{10896} = 0.641$$

$$a = \frac{\Sigma S_i - b\Sigma P_i}{n} = \frac{[384 - (240)(-0.641)]}{12} = 44.82$$

$\therefore$ The equation of the regression line is as:

$S = 44.82 - 0.641 \, P$

By assigning value 30 to P in the equation, the corresponding sales level is:

S (when P is Rs.30) $= 44.82 - 0.641 \quad 30 = 25.29$ thousand units.

(d) Barometric Method

Barometric method is an improvement over trend projection method. In the trend projection method, the future is some sort of an extension of the past, while in the barometric method, events of the present are used to predict the future demand. This is done by using certain economic and statistical indicators. The barometric techniques use time series to predict variables. The barometric techniques using time series, which when combined in certain ways, provide direction of change in the economy or in industries. These are called *barometers* of a market change.

This method may also be called "Economic Indicator" method. The economic indicators will help in estimating the demand for product at a future date. There are three types in this,

Leading Indicators

There are leading indicators which serve as useful guide for forecasting the demand for some products. The sales of baby milk can be forecast with the help of birth of children in the past five years. There is a correlation between the demand for baby milk and the birth rate of children. If the indicator is known, the sale forecast may be made on that basis.

Coincident Indicators

There are certain indicators which coincide with the rise or fall of general economic activity. The coinciding indicators are the gross national product index of industrial production, retail sales and labour force in the economy.

Diffusion Indices

These indices help the forecasters in relying on the leading indicators used. These indices move up and down behind some other series.

The following indicators are used in assessing the future demand for certain products:

Indicator	Demand for the Product
Construction Contracts	Demand for building materials
Increased prices of agricultural commodities	Demand for agricultural inputs
A rise in disposable income	Demand for consumer goods
Automobile registration	Demand for petrol

In the barometric method, it is necessary to find out the existence of any relation between the indicator and the demand for the product. after establishing the relationship through the method of least squares, we have to derive the regression equation.

If the relationships is linear, the equation will be $Y = a + bx$. Once the equation is derived, the demand for the product can be estimated.

The demand forecasting can be computed by adopting the Simultaneous Equation Method.

Example:

A refrigerator manufacturing company observes that there is a relationship between the consumer's disposable personal income index and purchase of refrigerators by them.

Year	Consumer DPI Index(x)	Refrigerator Sold (y)
1994	100	100
1995	120	140
1996	150	150
1997	160	170
1998	220	200

The following data is available to the firm:

From this data, compute the possible demand for the year 1999, if the index would be 250

Solution:

Regression equation of y on x

$y = a + bx$ Adopting simultaneous equations, find out the value of 'a' and 'b'

$\Sigma y = na + b\Sigma x$....................(i)

$\Sigma xy = a\Sigma x + b\Sigma x^2$..............(ii)

Year	DPI Index (x)	Sales of Refrigerator	Square of DP II (X^2)	Product of DPII and Sales(xy)
1994	100	100	10,000	10,000
1995	120	140	14,400	16,800
1996	150	150	22,500	22,500
1997	160	170	25,600	27,000
1998	220	200	48,400	44,000
N = 5	$\Sigma x = 750$	$\Sigma y = 760$	$\Sigma x^2 = 1,20,900$	$\Sigma xy = 1,20,500$

Computation of Values

By attributing values to the above equations

760	= 5a + 750b	(iii)
120, 500	= 750a + 120,900 b	(iv)

To bring equation (iii) to common base multiply it by 150

114000	= 750a + 112500 b	(v)
120500	= 750a + 120900 b	(vi)
−6500	= −8400 b	

$\therefore b = 6500 \div 8400 = 0.77$

Substituting the value of b in equation (iii)

760 = 5a + 750 (0.77)

760 = 5a + 577.5

5a = 182.5

a = 182.5   5

a = 36.5

If the index would be 250 for 1999 the number of refrigerators sold would be : $(y = a + bx)$

y 1999 $= 36.5 + 0.77 \, (250)$

            $= 36.5 + 192.5 = 229$

(iii) Other Methods of Demand Forecasting

Simultaneous Equation Method

In this method, all variables are considered simultaneously, for every variable influences other variables. It is a system of 'n' equations with 'n' unknowns. The advantage of this method is that an estimate of future demand for the product can be made with pre-determined variables.

Market Research Method

In all big industrial enterprises, there are market research cells. This cell is entrusted with collecting required information for sales forecasting. Or, there are independent market research. Organisation which can collect data for the customer industries. They conduct field surveys to collect information directly from the users of commodities. The collected information is then analysed and with the help of the data, the sales department make future estimates of demand for the product.

Exponential Smoothing Method

This is an improvement version of moving average method of forecasting. In this method, the past data is not used very much. All irregularities in the demand pattern are screened out. This method allows for trend and takes it into consideration the short term fluctuations in the determination of the forecast. In this method, new demand forecast is made from latest actual demand plus old estimate. The formula used in this method is

$F_t = (aD_t + 1 - a) \, F_t + 1$

Where F_t is the forecast at time t, D_t is the actual demand at time t, $F_t - I$ is the forecast at time $(t-1)$ a is the smoothing coefficient.

It is necessary to determine the value of smoothing coefficient 'a'. The size of 'a' reaction of response to real changes in demand. The value of 'a' lies between 0 and t. It is also observed that larger a's do not necessarily contribute to better forecasts. A high value of 'a' gives more weight to current values than to past ones.

Simulation Method

Every day life experiences cannot be mathematically explained. Sometimes the model may become complicated and its solution will become difficult. In such a situation, simulation method will be helpful.

The simulation method is associated with the name of Monte-Carlo. Pioneers in this field are Von Neumann, Ulam and Fermi. The simulation method is used to solve the problem by trial and error approach. It is defined as a device for studying an artificial stochastic model of a physical or, mathematical process. This method combines probability and sampling method to solve complicated problem. This method is useful in a situation where practical experience cannot be used as a guide.

"General simulation method is based on the selection of random numbers from random number tables and these numbers are considered to be probabilities of desired characteristic under study drawn from present population."

In this method, some preliminary survey is conducted to study the past behaviour of the system. Then an appropriate model is formulated with the help of sample observation. This model is used to determine the probability distribution of the characteristics under study. The probability distribution can be easily changed into cumulative distribution functions. Random numbers are chosen from the random tables and are then used to find the sequence values of the variable interest. Then some mathematical functions is filled to obtain the values.

7. FORECASTING DEMAND FOR NEW PRODUCTS

Joel Dean observes that methods of forecasting demand for new products are quite different from those for established products. For new products which are new to the economy and new to the company, an intensive study of the economic and competitive characteristics of products provide a guide to projections of demand. Forecasting techniques have to be tailored to the particular product. Possible approaches of forecasting demand for new products are as follows:

(i) Evolutionary Approach: Project the demand for the new product as an outgrowth and evolution of the existing old product. For example, it may be assumed that colour T.V picks up where black and white T.V. sets are off. This approach is useful only when the new product is very close to the old product. Scooter is an improvement of motor cycle. Mopeds are the improvement to the bicycles. The demand can be very much a projection of potential demand of the existing product.

(ii) Substitute Approach: According to this approach, the new product is to be considered as a substitute for the old product. For example, the new Foto Setter substitutes photographic composition for the established type-setting equipment (Linotype) or linoleum as a substitute for carpets or polythene bags as substitutes for cloth bags or ball pens for fountain pens. Since most of the new products are substitutes for old products and an improved one, the demand will have to be studied very scientifically.

(iii) Growth Curve Approach: The rlate of growth and the ultimate level of demand for new products can be estimated on the basis of the pattern of growth of the old products. For example, analyse the growth curve of the all household appliances and establish an empirical law of market development applicable to a new appliance.

(iv) Opinion Polling Approach: Estimate the demand by direct inquiry of the ultimate purchasers, then blow up the sample to full scale. Sending an engineer with drawing and specifications for new industrial products to a sample company is an example, opinion polling is widely used to explore the demand for new products.

(v) Sales Experience Approach: The new product is offered for sale in a sample market and then demand may be estimated for a fully developed market. The sample market has to be identified first. If Bombay or Calcutta is selected, and the results are applied to small towns, it becomes a failure. Therefore, selection of a sample has to be carefully done from middle sized cities to large cities.

(vi) Vicarious Approach: The consumers' reactions are indirectly studied in this approach. Specialized dealers are contacted because they have an intimate 'feel' of the customers. Dealers' opinions are very much solicited regarding the demand for new products. This approach is easy

but difficult to quantify. Bias on the part of the dealers cannot be ruled out completely. Care must be taken against undue enthusiasm of some dealers and undue pessimism of some others.

These methods are not usually exclusive. It would be desirable to combine all and then an estimate may be arrived at. The evolutionary approach is useful only when the new product is very close to the existing product. Its demand can be projected on the basis of the demand pattern of the old product.

Most of the new products are substitutes, though not exactly. For example, air travel is a substitute for land transport. Many a time, an upper limit of substitution is framed but what is important is the penetration of the new product and how this would replace the old product (ball pen).

8. SOME OF THE DIFFICULTIES IN FORECASTING OF CONSUMER DURABLES

The demand for consumer durables has certain peculiarities. Each durable product requires special study and distinct technique is to be adopted. Consumer durables fall into two categories, one is the new demand and the other is the replacement demand. Forecasting for these two categories has to be made separately. Some of the peculiarities found in forecasting consumer durables are as follows:

(i) Changes in the size and characteristics of population: Demand for consumer goods is related to the demographic characteristics like changes in size, growth rate, age-sex composition of population, etc. For example, the demand for tinned milk and toys depends upon the population of children. In fact, durable goods like T.V., washing machines, etc. depends upon household income.

(ii) Saturation limit of the market: There are durable goods which are going to reach saturation point. They are cars and electrical appliance, furniture, etc. Once the people have these commodities, they are not going to buy the new one.

(iii) Existing stock of goods: The size and age of the consumer durables determine the time of replacement. Longer the stock, greater is the replacement, shorter the life of the goods, earlier will be the replacement.

The replacement demand for consumer durables is conditioned by psychology, income and social status of the consumer. Most of the consumer durables are status symbols. It is only the rich peole who want to maintain their social status. Naturally, when they see new models with better service, they think of replacing the old ones. It is believed that higher the disposable income, higher is the demand for durable goods. There is one incentive which induces high income groups to buy a durable goods, that is credit facilities available. Wherever instalment credit system is prevailing, demand for some consumer goods also rises.

Thus, the forecaster of consumer durables uses different techniques to forecast the future sales. The forecaster uses barometer method in order to study the effect on demand of changes in size and characteristics of population, of income level of the consumers, etc. He takes up consumer's survey plan in order to study the consumer attitudes towards replacement of the old stocks. Once these difficulties are known, these changes can be incorporated in the model.

Constraints of the Firm

Before any firm can arrive at a decision it has to keep in mind the restrictions that it has to contend with. These restrictions can arise in two ways. Sometimes they may come from within the organisation i.e they are internal to the firm. For example, a firm which has very capital at its disposal need not explore all alternative possibilities of good and services that it can produce. Knowing that it has limited capital, it may explore only a few possibilities and decide to produce one of the goods. Here, capital is the constraint which has to be kept in mind before arriving at the decision of what to produce.

9. IMPORTANCE OF DEMAND FORECASTING

Demand forecasting play a significant role in decision-making of modern business. It is useful to management in the following ways.

1. It is very useful for planning of production in a firm. Firm can expand or contract its capacity accordingly and reduce the wastage of its capacity.

2. Sales forecasting depends on demand forecasting.

3. Demand forecasting helps in well planned budgeting of costs and sales revenue and thereby to have proper control over business.

4. Useful for controlling inventories.

5. Useful for policy making regarding long-term investment programmes.

6. To stabilise production and employment within the firm, demand forecasting is very useful.

7. Helps in achieving the targets of the firm.

SUMMARY

1. Demand forecasting means estimate of expected future demand conditions.

2. Demand forecasting serves the main purpose of maintaining equilibrium in the economy.

3. Survey method and statistical methods are the two approaches generally followed in demand forecasting.

QUESTIONS

1. Explain the factors which are involved in demand forecasting.

2. What is the utility of demand forecasting.

3. How is the demand for new products estimated.

4. Explain briefly different methods of demand forecasting.

5. State the general approach to demand forecasting.

6. Discuss the various methods of demand forecasting of established and new products.

7. What is demand forecasting? Explain the various techniques of forecasting demand.

8. What are different methods of forecasting of demand?

6 Chapter

Revenue Analysis and Linear Programming

CHAPTER OBJECTIVES

After reading this chapter you will be able to answer the following:

1. Concepts of Revenue
2. Relationship Between Average Revenue and Marginal Revenue
3. Relationship between Elasticity of Demand, Average Revenue and Marginal Revenue
4. Linear Programming

1. CONCEPTS OF REVENUE

The producer or seller of a commodity is very much concerned with the demand for goods, because revenue obtained by him from selling the product depends mainly on the demand for that product. The producer or seller is therefore, very much interested in knowing what sort of demand curve is facing him. The demand curve of the buyers for the product is the average revenue curve from the standpoint of view of sellers, since the price paid by the buyers is revenue for the sellers.

Therefore, revenue refers to the receipts obtained by a firm from selling various quantities of its products.

There are three concepts of revenue. They are as follows:

(i) Total Revenue

(ii) Average Revenue

(iii) Marginal Revenue

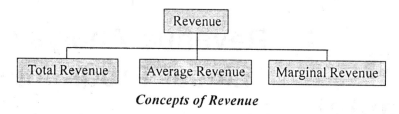

Concepts of Revenue

I. Total Revenue

Price paid by the consumer for the product forms revenue or income to the seller. The whole income received by the seller from selling various units of the commodity either at the same or at different prices is called total revenue.

Total Revenue = Price × Quantity Sold

i.e., TR = P × Q

> *The whole income received by selling various quantities of goods is called as total revenue.*

For example, if a seller sells 100 units of a product at Rs.15 then Rs.1500 is the total revenue.

II. Average Revenue

> *Average revenue is the revenue per unit*

On the other hand, *'average revenue'* is revenue earned by per unit of the product sold. It is found by dividing total revenue by the number of units of the product sold. If different units are sold at different prices, then the average revenue is also different. Average revenue equals prices at which the units of the product are available at the same price, then average revenue would be the same as price. If he sells different units of product at different prices, then the average revenue will not be equal to price. For example, a seller sells two units of product at Rs.10, then the average revenue is 20/2 = Rs.10. Here average revenue is equal to price. Hence, average revenue curve of the firm is the same thing as the demand curve for the consumers.

$$\therefore AR = \frac{TR}{\text{Quantity Sold(Q)}}$$

III. Marginal Revenue

Marginal revenue is the net revenue earned by selling an additional unit of the product.

> *Marginal revenue is the addition made to the total revenue by selling one more unit of the commodity.*

Expressing it in algebraic terminology, marginal revenue is the addition made to the total revenue by selling *n* units of a product instead of *n-1* where *n* is any given number. For example, if a producer sells 10 units of a product at Rs.15, then the total revenue is Rs.150. If he increases the sales by 11 units, suppose the price falls of Rs.14.50, then the total revenue is Rs.159.50 for 11 units. This means that the 11th units of the product sold added Rs.9.50 to the total revenue. Hence Rs.9.50 is the marginal revenue.

$$\therefore MR = TR_n - TR_{n-1}$$

Total revenue for 10 units (Rs.15) = 150

Total revenue for 11 units (Rs.14.5) = 159.50

Marginal revenue = 159.50 − 150 = 9.50

From the above example, it can be inferred that marginal revenue is less than the price at which the additional unit is sold.

Marginal revenue can be found either by taking out differences between total revenue, before and after selling the additional units or it can be obtained by subtracting the loss in revenue on previous units due to the fall in the price at which the additional unit is sold.

It follows from the above that, when the price falls as additional units are sold, marginal revenue is less than the price. When the price remains the same, as additional unit is sold, as under perfect competition, marginal revenue is the same as average revenue.

2. RELATIONSHIP BETWEEN AVERAGE REVENUE AND MARGINAL REVENUE

The concepts of total revenue, average revenue and marginal revenue are explained in the following table:

No. of units of a product sold	Price or Average Revenue	Total Revenue (Average Revenue × Quantity sold)	Marginal Revenue (Aditional made to the Total Revenue)
1	20	20	20
2	18	36	16
3	16	48	12
4	14	56	8
5	12	60	4
6	10	60	0
7	8	56	−4

The above table shows that when average revenue is falling, marginal revenue is less than average revenue. Marginal Revenue is positive so long as total revenue is increasing. Marginal Revenue becomes negative when total revenue declines.

In all forms of imperfect competition, i.e., monopolistic competition, oligopoly, monopoly, the average revenue curve facing the individual firm slopes downwards. This is because, the firm lowers the prices of the product if it wants to increase their sales. In the adjacent diagram, this aspect is explained.

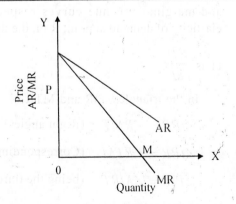

Under perfect competition, the price or the average revenue remains the same throughout sale of the output. Hence, marginal revenue will be equal to average revenue.

The average revenue and the marginal revenue of the firm is a horizontal straight line under perfect competition. This is because the firm under perfect competition cannot influence the price. He has to sell the product at the ruling market price. As such, the marginal revenue and average revenue curves merge with one another.

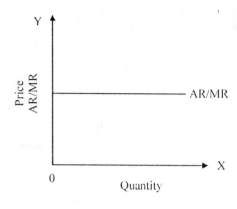

Incremental Revenue and Marginal Revenue

Incremental revenue is the difference between the existing total revenue and new total revenue. Incremental revenue is the change in total revenue, irrespective of change in sales, whereas marginal revenue is the change in total revenue per unit of change in sales.

Incremental revenue is not confined to the effects of price change. It rather measures the effect of any kind of managerial decision on total revenue.

3. RELATIONSHIP BETWEEN ELASTICITY OF DEMAND, AVERAGE REVENUE AND MARGINAL REVENUE

The concept of elasticity of demand is very much useful in determining the prices of products in different market conditions. Elasticity of demand can be measured in a straight line demand curve at any point. The point method helps to measure the elasticity of demand at any point on the demand curve. Let us study this aspect with the help of the adjacent diagram.

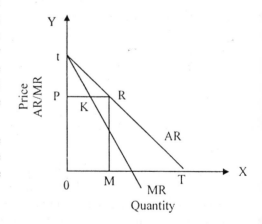

In this diagram AR and MR are average revenue and marginal revenue curves respectively. The elasticity of demand at point R on the demand curve tT is $\dfrac{RT}{Rt}$

In the triangles, PtR and MTR,

$\angle tPR = \angle RMT$ (Right angles)

$\angle tPR = \angle RTM$ (Corresponding angles)

$\angle PtR = \angle MRT$ (being the third angle)

Therefore, triangles PtR and MTR are equiangular

Hence $\dfrac{RT}{Rt} = \dfrac{RM}{tP}$

In the triangles of PtK and KRQ,

PK = RK

$\angle PKt = \angle RKQ$ (Vertically opposite)

$\angle tPK = \angle KRQ$ (Right angles)

Therefore, triangles PtK and KRQ are equal in all respects.

Hence Pt = RQ

From 1 and 2, we get,

Elasticity at R = $\dfrac{RT}{Rt} = \dfrac{RM}{tP} = \dfrac{RM}{RQ}$

Now it is obvious from the above diagram that:

$$\frac{RM}{RQ} = \frac{RM}{RM - RQ}$$

Hence, elasticity at $R = \dfrac{RM}{RM - QM}$

For OM output, RM is average revenue, OM is marginal revenue.

Elasticity at $R = \dfrac{AR}{AR - MR}$

Elasticity at the point R is half average revenue.

Prof. Joan Robinson's formula for measuring the relationship between marginal revenue, average revenue and price elasticity of demand is as follows:

At any output:

Average revenue = Marginal revenue $\times \dfrac{e}{e - 1}$

Marginal revenue = Average revenue $\times \dfrac{e - 1}{e}$

Where e is the price elasticity of demand.

The relationship between them can be summed up as follows:

(i) When price elasticity of demand is greater than one, the marginal revenue is positive and total revenue rises as price falls.

(ii) When the price elasticity of demand is unity, the marginal revenue is zero and a change in the price will not change the total revenue.

(iii) When the price elasticity of demand is less than one, the marginal revenue is negative and the total falls as price falls.

4. LINEAR PROGRAMMING

Introduction

Linear Programming is a new branch of mathematics developed for solving constrained optimization problems. This new technique was developed during 1950's. The problems of constrained optimization arise because of the limited resources available to maximize or minimize a certain objective. The main objective of linear programming is to find the permissible allotment of resources so as to yield maximum profit, turnover etc and to minimize the production cost, labour cost etc.

Definition

Linear Programming is a Mathematical technique developed for determining the optimal use or allocation of available limited resources to obtain the desired objectives.

The desired objective is expressed as a linear function of individual allocation (in terms of basic variables of the type $2x + 3y = 5$) and the limitations or restrictions imposed on the use of resources are expressed as linear inequalities involving the decision variables (of the type $2x - y \leq 1$; $x + 2y \leq 3$; $x \geq 0$; $y \geq 0$). These restrictions are called Constraints.

Mathematical formulation of Linear Programming Problem:

Given a linear programming problem it is very important to recognise the objective function to form the linear inequalities, involving the limited resources, subject to the given constraints. The method of formulation is explained in the following examples.

Example 1

A boy wants to buy some pants and shirts. A pant costs Rs.150/- and shirt Rs.90/-. The boy wants to buy at least 2 pants and 3 shirts, but he is allowed to spend not more than Rs.1000/- on clothes. How many pants and shirts should he buy so that he buys maximum number of clothes.

In the above example, let x and y be the number of trousers and shirts respectively purchased by the boy. Then the total cost of the purchase will be $150x + 90y$. Since the boy wants at least 2 trousers and 3 shirts, we have $x \geq 2$ and $y \geq 3$. Further, he is not allowed to spend more than Rs.1000/- on clothes.

This can be put in the form

$150x + 90y \leq 1000$

Here we have to maximise the function p = x+y subjet to constraints.

$150x + 90y \leq 1000$

$x \geq 2$ and $y \geq 3$.

Example 2

A manufacturer produces two types of products M and N. The product M gives per unit profit of Rs.8/- while the product N gives Rs.10/-. Both the products pass through two machines, machine 1 and machine 2. The processing of one unit of product M takes 2 hours of machine 1 and three hours of machine 2 time. The processing of one unit of product N takes three hours of machine 1 and two hours of machine 2 time. The total machine time per week available with machine 1 is ninety hours and with machine 2 is one hundred and twenty hours. Find out the product mix giving the maximum profit.

Objective: Maximise the weekly profit by the products M and N

Constraints: Machine 1 time - 90 hours per week

Machine 2 time - 120 hours per week.

Let 'x' be the number of units of product M and 'y' be number of units of product N. If p is the total profit of both the products, then the weekly profit of both the machines is given by

$p = 8x + 10y$

Constraints: $2x + 3y \leq 90$ (Machine time of Machine 1 per week)

$3x + 2y \leq 120$ (Machine time of Machine 2 per week) and $x \geq 0$ and $y \geq 0$

(Because number of units produced cannot be less than zero)

Example 3

A multivitamin tablet has to be manufactured by using a mixture of two products 'x' and 'y'. The quantity of each vitamin available per gram in 'x' and 'y', the minimum requirements and the cost of manufacture are given in the following table:

	No. of units of each vitamin content in one gram of product			Cost
	V_1	V_2	V_3	
Product x	6	2	4	20P
Product y	2	2	12	16P
Minimum requirement of each vitamin	12	8	24	

Find the least expensive combination which provides the minimum requirements of the three vitamins.

Let 'a' and 'b' be the number of units of produts 'x' and 'y' respectively in the mixture. Then the total cost of the manufacture is 20a + 16 b.

i.e., *Objective Function* P = 20a + 16b

Constraints: Since the mixture has to contain at least 12 units of vitamin 1.

We have 6a + 2b ≥ 12

Similarly, other constraints are

$$2a + 2b \geq 8$$

and   4a + 12b ≥ 24

Hence, the formulation of linear programming for the above problem is as follows:

Minimise: P = 20a + 16b

Constraints: 6a + 2b ≥ 12

                              2a + 2b ≥ 8

                              4a + 12b ≥ 24

Solution of Linear Programming Problems

Graphical Method: We observe from the formulation of simple linear programming problem, as explained in earlier pages, that the objective function is a linear function of two variables. Also, the available limited resources known as *constraints* are expressed as linear inequalities involving the decision variables. In the graphical method, we consider the given constraints as linear equations (of two variables) to draw straight lines in the OX and OY plane and then identify the common region represented by the inequalities under non-negativity restriction x ≥ 0; y ≥ 0. The point of intersection of these lines with the coordinate axes and their own intersection are called the *corner points*. The region bounded by the lines joining the corner points in the first quadrant is known as *feasible* region. The corner points of this feasible region, optimizes (maximize or minimize) the objective function. The feasible region, will be bounded region in the case of maximization and unbounded in the case of minimization.

Outlines of Graphical Methods are as follows:

Identify the decision variables.

Formulate the objective functions.

Consider each inequality constraints as equations.

Since each equation is linear, it represents a straight line. Draw the straight lines to represent the given equation.

Identify the corner points, and hence the feasible region.

Determine the set of ordered pairs (x,y) which satisfy the constraints and optimizes the objective function.

The method of solving linear programming problem by graphical method is illustrated in the following examples.

Example 1 Maximize: P = 4x + 3y

Subject to the constraints: $2x + y \leq 10$

$x + y \leq 6$

$x \geq 0 ; y \geq 0$

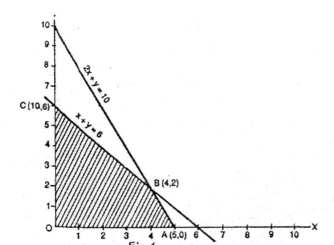

Fig.1.

Solution

Let OX and OY be the co-ordinate axes. The non negativity condition that $x \geq 0 ; y \geq 0$ implies that the feasible region of permissible values of the variables x and y lies in the first quadrant. Draw the line $2x + y = 10$ as shown in the figure 1.

Putting x = 0 we get y = 10

Putting y = 0, we get x = 5

Hence, (0, 10) and (5, 0) are the points on the line $2x + y = 10$.

Putting x = 0; y = 6

Putting y = 0; x = 6

Hence (0, 6) and (6, 0) are the points on the line $x + y = 6$.

The two lines intersect at (4,2)

Thus, the feasible region is the shaded area of the polygon OABC, whose vertices are 0(0,0), A(5,0), B(4, 2) and C (0, 6).

Substituting these values of (x, y) in the equation P = 4x + 3y, we get

$P_A = 4(5) + 3(0) = 20$

$P_B = 4(4) + 3(2) = 22$

$P_C = 4(0) + 3(6) = 18$

Clearly, the maximum value of P is 22 at x = 4 and y = 2.

Example 2: A farmer is going to grow rice and wheat. He estimates that rice needs four men per hectare and wheat needs six men. He has 26 men available. Rice costs Rs.240/- per hectare, wheat Rs.160/- per hectare. He is prepared to spend upto Rs.960/- find the maximum area of land in which he can grow.

Solution

Let x be the area of land required for rice. Let y be the area of land required for wheat (in hectares).

Requirement

Crop	Man Power	Cost
Rice	4	Rs.240
Wheat	6	Rs.160
Max man power available		Rs. 26
Max cost		Rs.960

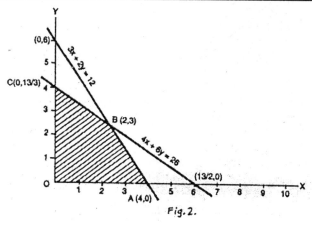

Fig. 2.

Mathematical Formulation

Constraints: $4x + 6y = 26$

$240x + 160 y = 960$

or $3x + 2y = 12$

Objective function $P = x = y$

We have to maximize $P = x + y$

Constraints: $2x + 6y = 26$

$3x + 2y = 12$

$x \geq 0; y \geq 0$

Let OX and OY be the co-ordinate axes

Consider $4x + 6y = 26$

Putting $x = 0$, $y = 13/3$

Putting $y = 0$, $x = 13/2$

Hence, $(0, 13/3)$ and $(13/2, 0)$ are the points on the line $4x + 6y = 26$

Similarly, consider $3x + 2y = 12$.

Putting x = 0, y = 6

Putting y = 0, x = 4

Hence (0, 6) and (4 0) are the points on the line 3x + 2y = 12.

From the figure, we observe that the two lines intersect at (2, 3). Thus, the feasible region is the ara OABC, with the corner points O(0, 0). A(4, 0), B (2, 3) and C(0, 13/3)

Substituting these values in P = x = y

We have $P_A = 4 + 0 = 4$

$P_B = 2 + 3 = 5$

$P_C = 0 + 13/3 = 1313$

Clearly, the maximum value of P is 5 at B (2, 3). Hence, the maximum area of land he can crop is 5 hectares.

Example 3:   *Minimise P* = 4x + 2y

Constraints: x = 2y ≥ 2

3x = y ≥ 3

4x + 3y ≥ 6

x ≥ 0; y ≥ 0.

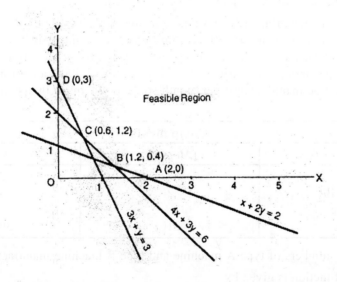

Solution

Consider the coordinate axes OX and OY.

Consider x + 2y = 2

Putting x = 0, we have y = 1

Putting y = 0 we have x = 2

hence, (0, 1) and (2, 0) are the points on the line x + 2y = 2. Draw the line x + 2y = 2 as shown in the figure 3.

Now consider $3x + y = 3$

Putting $x = 0$, we have $y = 3$

Putting $y = 0$ we have $x = I$

Therefore, $(0, 3)$ and $(1, 0)$ are the points on the line $3x + y = 3$. Draw the line $3x + y = 3$ as shown in figure 3.

Finally, consider $4x + 3y = 6$

Putting $x = 0$, We get $y = 2$

Putting $y = 0$, we get $x = 3/2$

Hence, $(0,2)$ and $(3/2, 0)$ are the points on the line $4x + 3y = 6$ Draw the line $4x + 3y = 6$ as shown in the fig.3 From the fig.3, we observe that the feasible region (shaded area) is an unbounded region with corner points $A(2,0)$, $B(1.2, 0.4)$, $C(0.6, 1.2)$ and $D(0, 3)$

Substituting these values of x and y in $P = 4x + 2y$, we have

$P_A = 4(2) + 2(0) = 8$

$P_B = 4(1.2) = 2(0.4) = 4.8 + 0.8 = 5.6$

$P_C = 4(0.6) + 2(1.2) = 2.4 + 2.4 = 4.8$

$P_D = 4(0) + 2(3) = 6$

From the above, we infer that P_{min}, is at the point C $(0.6, 1.2)$

Hence minimum value of the objective function $P = 4x + 2y$ is 4.8 at $x = 0.6$ and $y = 12$.

Example 4: A factory manufactures two types of electronic machines, A and B and earns a profit of Rs.20/- per unit of A and Rs.30/- per unit of B. Each unit A requires three motors and two transformers and each unit of B requires two motors and four transformers. The total supply of the components per month is restricted to 210 motors and 300 transformers. How many of each machine should be manufactured per month so as to maximise the profit?

Solution

Components		
Machine Type	*Motors*	*Transformers*
A	3	2
B	2	4
Max available Components	210	300

Let x and y be numbers of type A machine and type B machine manufactured per month.

The objective function is given by

$P = 20x + 30y$

$3x + 2y \leq 210$

$2x = 4y \leq 300$

$x \geq 0; y \geq 0$

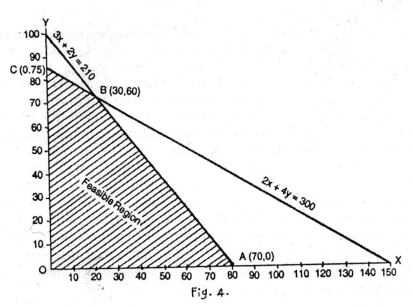

Fig. 4.

Consider the coordinate axes OX and OY. x ≥ 0; y ≥ 0 implies that the feasible region lines in the first quadrant

Consider $3x + 2y = 210$

Putting $x = 0$; $y = 105$

Putting $y = 0$; $x = 70$

Hence, (0, 105) and (70, 0) are the points on the line $3x + 2y = 210$ Draw the line $3x + 2y$ as shown in the Figure 4.

Now consider $2x + 4y = 300$

or $x + 2y = 150$

Putting $x = 0$, we have $y = 75$

Putting $y = 0$, we have $x = 150$

Hence, (0, 75) and (150, 0) are the points on the line $x + 2y = 150$

The two lines $3x + 2y = 210$ and $x + 2y = 150$ intersect at (30, 60). Hence, from the fig.4, we observe that OABC is the feasible region. The corner points are A (70,0), B(30,60) and C(0,75).

Substituting these values of x and y in the object function

$P = 20x = 30y$

we have $\quad P_A = 20(70) + 30 \, (0) = 1400$

$\qquad P_B = 20(30) + 30(60) = 600 + 1800 = 2400$

$\qquad P_C = 20(0) + 30(5) = 2250$

Hence, the maximum value of P is 2400 at B (30, 60)

Hence to maximise the profit the factory should manufacture 30 units of type A and 60 units of type B machines.

The Simplex Method

With the help of the graphical method, it was possible for us to solve simple linear programming problems. But if the linear programming problem is a little complicated involving more than two variables in the constraints, then it is possible to solve such problems using Simple Method. This method is also known as 'Simplex Algorithm Method'. The simplex algorithm was developed by George B. Dantzig, in the year 1947. The method of solving a linear programming problem by the simplex method is explained below, taking an example to maximise the object function subject to 'less than or equal to'constraints. The same method with modification can be applied to minimisation problems having equality constraints and 'greater than or equal to'constraints.

Stock Variables

We cannot use the Simplex Method unless all the constraints are stated as equations. The given inequalities are converted into equations by the device of adding what are known as *slack variables*. A slack variable represents unused machine time (as in case of machine time constraints), or unemployed capacity (as in the case of warehouse capacity) etc.

We add the slack variable, to the left hand side of the inequalities, while we replace the 'less than or equal to'sign by équality'sign.

The Simplex Method of solving an LP problem is explained in the following example.

Maximise   : $P = 300x + 200y$ subject to

Constraints : $5x + 2y \leq 180$

$3x + 3y \leq 135$

$x \geq 0 ; y \geq 0$

The given constraints can be re-written as

$5x + 2y \leq 180$

$x + y < 45$

$x \geq 0; y \geq 0$

Let S_1 and S_2 be the slack variables. The two inequalities can be converted into equalities by adding the slack variables S_1 and S_2 to the left hand side of the inequalities. Then the resulting equations will be given as:

$5x + 2y + S_1 = 180$

$x + y + S_2 = 45$ (1)

$x \geq 0, y \geq 0$

We shall minimise $P = 300 x - 200 y$ subject constraints given in (1)

The initial Simplex Tableau is set up as follows

Initial Simple Tableau:

	x	y	S_1	S_2	
S_1	5	2	1	0	180
S_2	1	1	0	1	45
	300	200	0	0	P=0

The entries in the first row and the second row are the co-efficients of the variables of (1) and the entry in the last row are called the *indicators*.

As we proceed with the Simplex Computation - the value of p will appear at the right hand bottom corner of the table where P = 0 is written.

Putting x = 0 and y = 0, we get P = 0. The other variables S_1 and S_2 which are not zero are called *basic* variables.

Step 1

We observe from the Initial Simplex Tableau that indicators are negative in sign. We observe that the solution obtained is not optimum solution and that we can improve the solution.

Since both the coefficients are negative in P, we can decrease the value of p, by making either of the coefficient positive. In the place of a basic variable, we can put either x or y. Since -3000 is less than -200, we choose to put x in the place of S_1.

We try the following alternatives:

1. Putting y = 0, S_2 = 0, we get x = 45 and S_1 = 45, which is negative. Therefore, the solution is not a feasible solution.

2. Putting y = 0 and S_1 = 0, we get x = 36 and S_2 = 9. Thus this is a feasible solution.

From the above, we find a simple rule to replace S1. The rule is: Find the ratios of the numbers in the last column to the coefficient of x, i.e., $\dfrac{180}{5}$ and $\dfrac{45}{1}$. Choose the least of these

i.e., $\dfrac{180}{5}$ which corresponds to S_1.

The column headed by x in this problem is called *pivotal* column. In general, the column which contains the smallest indicator is the pivotal column. The row containing S_1 is the pivotal row. The entry at the intersection of the pivotal row and pivotal column is called the *pivot*. Here, in this problem, 5 is the pivot. We shall make the pivot unity and the other number in this column zero, by applying suitable row transformation.

In this example, we apply

1. $1/5 \ R_1$
2. $R_2 - R_1$
3. $R_3 + 300 \ R_1$

With this, we can write down the first simplex tableau

	x	y	S_1	S_2	
x	1	2/5	1/5	0	36
S_2	0	3/5	-1/5	1	9
	0	-80	60	0	P=10800

Step 2

From the first simplex table, we observe that there is a negative indicator -80 in the third row. Hence the solution obtained above is not the optimum solution. The column containing -80 is now the pivotal column. Now calculate the ratio $\dfrac{36}{2/5}$ and $\dfrac{9}{3/5}$ which gives 90 and 15 respectively.

The second one being the least, the second row is the pivotal row and the pivot is 3/5. Now we have to replace S_2 by y in the next simplex tableau.

Now we shall make the pivot unity and the other elements in the column are made zero, by the following row transformation.

1. $5/3\ R_2$

2. $R_1 - 2/5\ R_2$

3. $R3 + 80\ R_2$

With the help of these row transformations, we can write down the second simplex tableau.

Second Survey Tableau

	x	y	S_1	S_2	
x	1	0	1/3	-2/3	30
y	0	1	-1/3	5/3	15
	0	0	100/3	400/3	P=12000

We observe from the second simplex tableau that there are no negative indicators in the third row. Hence the solution obtained is the optimum solution. The second simplex tableau in this case is called the *canonical* form of (1).

The elements in the last column of the second simplex tableau gives the solution of linear programming problem. Hence the solution of the LP problem is

x = 30; y = 15 and P_{max} = 12000

The method of solving linear programming problem may be summed up in the following steps:

Step 1

Express the constraints as equations by introducing slack variables. Write down the initial simplex tableau, the entries being the coefficients of x, y, S_1 and S_2 of constraint equations and the entries in the last row are the coefficients of x and y in p with their signs changed. Take P = 0.

Step 2

Observe the indicators. If there is no negative indicator, then the current solution P = 0 is the optimum solution. If there are negative indicators in the third row, choose the least among them. The column containing the least is the pivotal column.

Step 3

Calculate the ratios of the elements in the last column to the elements of the pivotal column. The least of the ratios is the pivot, and the row containing this is the pivotal row.

Step 4

By elementary row transformations, convert the pivot to unity and make the other entries in the pivotal column zero.

Step 5

Replace the variable corresonding pivotal row, determined in Step 3 by the variable in the pivotal column. Now we get the new set of basic variables. With this, write down the First Simple Tableau.

Step 6

Examine the indicators again. If there are negative indicators, repeat steps 2 to 5 and construct second simplex tableau, third simplex tableau, etc. If there are no negative indicators, then the process stops and the maximum value of p has been attained.

Duality

Every linear programming problem is associated with an intimately related linear programming problem called its 'dual'. The original problem is called the 'primal'. By working either of the problems, 'primal' or its 'dual' one can obtain the desired answer. The dual has the same optimum solution as the primal but is obtained by an alternative method. If the original linear programming problem called the primal is a maximizing problem, its dual will be a minimixing problem. The dual is formed by rearranging the coefficients of the object function and constraints.

Constructing the Dual Problem

We shall take a simple maximizing problem (primal) to form its dual.

Original Problem (primal problem)

Maximize: $Z = 5a + 6b$

subject to $2a + 3b \le 90$

$3a + 2b \le 120$

$a \ge 0; b \ge 0$

Dual problem

Minimise $Z_t = 90 a_1 + 120 b_1$

$2a_1 + 3b_1 > 5$

Subject to $3a_1 + 2b_1 > 6$

$a_1 > 0; b_1 > 0$

To write the dual linear programming problem, we follow the following steps:

The dual will also have an objective function. Let the objective function be Z_1 instead of Z.

Let a_1 and b_1 be the new set of variables which appear in the dual:

90 and 120 as appearing in the right hand side of the constraints are made coefficients of the variables a_1 and b_1 in the objective function of the dual. Since the dual problem is to be the opposite of the primal problem, we shall minimise this objective function instead of maximizing it.

Thus, the objective function of the dual problem is:

Minimize: $Z_1 = 90a_1 + 120b_1$

Interchange the coefficients in the rows of the constraints with the coefficients in the columns.

Reverse all the inequalities in the constraints.

Thus, the dual of the given primal is given by:

Minimize: $Z_1 = 90a_1 + 120b_1$.

Subject to $2a_1 + 3b_1 \geq 5$

$3a_1 + 2b_1 \geq 6$

$a_1 > 0, b_1 > 0$

Properties of Duality

The dual of the dual is the primal

The optimum value of the primal, if it exists, is equal to the optimum value of the dual.

Example 1

Primal: Minimise: $P = 2a_1 + 9a_2 + 5a_3$, subject to constraints

$a_1 + a_2 - a_3 \geq 1$

$- 2a_1 + a_3 \geq 2$

$a_1 \geq 0; a_2 \geq 0; a_3 \geq 0$

Dual: Maximise: $P_1 = b_1 + 2b_2$

Subject to constraints

$b_1 - 2b_2 \leq 2$

$b_1 \geq 9$

$-b_1 + b_2 \leq 5$

$b_1 \geq 0; b_2 \geq 0$

The above primal and dual problems have the same optimum solution.

Example 2

Primal Maximize $Z = 30x + 23y$

Subject to $x + 0.6y \leq 28$

$9x + 2y \leq 400$

$0.8x + 0.7y \leq 20$

$x \geq 0; y \geq 0$

Dual problem:

Minimize: $C = 28a + 400b + 20c$

Subject to $a + 9b + 0.8c \geq 30$

$0.6a + 2b + 0.7c \geq 23$

and $a \geq 0; b \geq 0; c \geq 0$

EXERCISE

1. (i) Maximize $Z = 3x + 4y$

    Subject to constraints

    $x + y \le 450$

    $2x + y \le 600$

    $x \ge 0; y \ge 0$

    Ans: $x = 0$

    $Y = 450$

    $Z \max = 1800$

    (ii) Maximize: $P = 3x + 2y$

    Subject to constraints

    $2x - y \le 1$

    $x + 2y \le 3$

    $x \ge 0; y \ge 0$

    Ans: $x = 1$

    $y = 1$

    $P \max = 5$

2. (i) Minimise: $P = 20x + 16y$

    Subject to constraints

    $6x + 2y \ge 12$

    $2x + 2y \ge 8$

    $4x + 12y \ge 24$

    $x \ge 0; y \ge 0$

    Ans: $P \min = 68$ at $(1, 3)$

    (ii) Minimise $Z = 40x + 50y$

    Subject to constraints

    $8x + 12y \ge 32$

    $10x + 6y \ge 22$

    $x \ge 0; y \ge 0$

    Ans: $x = 1, y = 2$

3. A manufacturer produces two types of products A and B which must be processed through two types of machines. The product A requires two hours of machine 1 time and 1 hour of machine 2 time. The product A earns a profit of Rs.4/- per unit and the product B earns a profit of Rs.3/- per unit. The total machine time available is 30 hours on machine 1 and 24 hours on machine 2. How many of each type of products should be manufactured so as to maximize the profit?

    Ans: type A = 12 units. Type B = 6 units

4. A factory manufactures two types of products X and Y, using the ftm machines A, B and C. The following table gives the time required and time available on each machines. The product X earns a profit of Rs.50/- and product Y earns a profit of Rs.30/-. How many of each type should be manufactured so as to maximize the profit.

Machine	Time in Hours		Max. time available
	X	Y	
A	6	8	380 hrs.
B	8	4	300 hrs.
C	12	4	404 hrs.

Ans: Product X : 22; Product Y : 31; P_{max} = Rs.2030

5. A dealer is going to buy some readymade shirts and trousers. He plans to buy a total of 100 units. The cost of each shirt and trouser is Rs.80/- and Rs.240/- respectively. He is prepared to spend Rs.20,800. The profit on shirt is Rs.32/- and trouser is Rs.64/-. Find the maximum profit he can make.

Ans: Rs.5760/-

6. A dietician has to prepare a mixture of two foods X and Y that provides at least 600 grams of proteins and 800 grams of carbohydrates. Each unit of X contains 20 gms. of protein and 30 gms. of carbohydrates and costs 40 paise. Each unit of Y contains 25 grams of proteins and 20 gms of carbohydrates and costs 60 paise. Find the minimum cost mixture of X and Y which provides the specified requirements.

Ans: 30 and 0, (C_{min} = Rs.12)

7. The number of units of vitamin A and B per kg of two breakfast cereals M and N are shown in the following table:

	Vitamin A	Vitamin B
M	16	8
N	18	4

The minimum daily intake required is 60 units of A and 40 units of B. What is the least total weight of breakfast cereal one must eat to have enough of these vitamins? Ans: 7 Kg

8. A drug manufacturer wants to make a vitamin tablet containing vitamins A, B and C using two types of natural resources x and y. Each tablet has to contain at least 10 units of vitamin A, 42 of B and 14 units of C. Further one gram of x contains 2 units of vitamin A, 15 units of B and 2 units of C. One gram of Y contains 3 units at A, 6 units of B and 7 units of C. If the cost of the source 'x' is 30 paise and that of 'y' is 20 paise per gram, how many units of x and y must be used as to make the cost minimum.

Ans: x=2; y=2; p_{min}=Re 1.

SUMMARY

1. Price paid by the consumer forms the revenue or income to the seller.
2. The whole income received by selling various goods is called total revenue.
3. The income received by per unit of the product sold is called average revenue.

4. Marginal revenue is the net revenue earned by selling additional unit of the product.

5. Linear programming is a mathematical technique developed for determining the optimal use or allocation of available limited resources to obtain the desired objectives. Linear programming problems can be solved either using graphical Method or simplex method.

QUESTIONS

1. What is marginal revenue?

2. Distinguish between incremental revenue and marginal revenue.

3. Draw average and marginal revenue curves both in perfect competition and monopoly.

4. Explain how elasticity of demand is useful in determining the price.

5. Explain the relationship between average and marginal revenue.

6. Discuss the relationship between marginal revenue and price elasticity.

7 Chapter

Production Analysis

Organising production of goods and services is an important managerial function. After ascertaining the nature of demand for goods and services, manufacturers arrange for producing them. Business managers keep their objective of maximum profits, while undertaking production of goods. In production, the business managers are involved in incurring expenditure in order to buy raw-material, fuel and power, pay wages to employees, etc. These expenditures are costs. After producing the products, they offer them for sale where they get revenue. The difference between the costs and revenues is the profit for the firm. The managers are required to keep the total cost of production within manageable limits. To do this, the managers try to produce optimum level of output and use the least cost combination of factors of production. Since the cost of production is an important determining factor in production, the managers try to find out a level of product in which the cost is minimum.

The purpose of understanding the costs is two fold; one is which helps to determine the price of the product manufactured in the factory. It provides a basis of decision making regarding the price to be fixed for the product. It also provides him an understanding whether to continue to produce the old product or to produce a new product. Cost analysis helps the managers to arrive at a correct decision. Secondly, this analysis helps him to control costs. They always attempt to keep the cost of production at the lowest level possible.

Production and cost analysis together determine the supply of the product to the market. Production is calculated in physical terms, while the costs are determined in financial terms.

Production analysis shows the relationship between physical inputs of the factors of production and the output of the product and studies the least cost combination of factor inputs and returns to scale, while costs analysis deals with various types of costs and their role in decision making.

1. MEANING OF PRODUCTION

The term production is a very broad concept. It includes all those activities direclty or indirectly connected to production process.

Production in economic terms is generally understood as the transformation of inputs into outputs. The inputs are what the firm buys namely productive resources and outputs are (goods and services produced) which it sells. Production is not the creation of matter, but it is the creation of value. It means that it is the transformation of raw product into consumable product. Apart from physical transformation of matter, it includes services like buying and selling, transporting and financing. In our study, the term *production* is used to mean the production of products for which we require the services of various factors of production. The factors of production are generally known as land resources, labour, capital and entrepreneurship. These factors of production are termed as *inputs*. The firm buys inputs and sells outputs. Inputs are those things that firms buy to produce goods. Outputs are those produced goods. The theory of production centres round the concept of production function.

> *Production refers to the creation of value or wealth*

Production Function

Production function is defined as the functional relationship between physical inputs (factors of production) and physical outputs (i.e the quantity of goods produced). As Stigler puts it, 'the production function is the name given to the relationship between the rates of input of productive services and the rate of output of the product. It is the economist's summary of technical knowledge.'

> *Thus, the production function expresses the technological relationship between the quantity of output and the quantities of inputs used in production.*

More precisely, it can be stated that how maximum output is produced from a given input in the existing state technology. Like demand, production refers to a period of time. Accordingly, it refers to a flow of inputs resulting in a flow of outputs over a period of time leaving prices aside.

Production function depends on:

   (i) quantities of resources (raw-materials, labourers, capital, machinery, etc.),

   (ii) state of technology,

   (iii) possible processes,

   (iv) size of the firms,

   (v) nature of firm's organization and

   (vi) relative price of inputs and the manner in which the inputs are combined.

As these change, the production function also changes. Output can be increased by increasing the quantities of inputs used in production. Production function depicts the whole set of choices open to the producer. The adoption of new technology will also change the combination of inputs. These will materialize in the long period.

Since production function is the job of the technologist, he has to specify what quantity of inputs are to be used in order to produce a given output. A production function is expressed as under:

O = f (a, b, c, d.............)

where O stands for output, a to d stand for input such as land, labour, capital and organisation and f stands for function.

The equation shows that a given quantity of output depends upon the quantities of inputs.

Every management has to make a choice of a production function, depending not only on industrial knowledge and the prices of various factors of production, but also on its own capacity to manage. The management has to select the various inputs and knit them together in economical combinations. These two choices are interlinked. The overriding consideration is to select a combination which gives him the minimum average cost and the maximum aggregate profit.

Definitions of Production Function

Different economists have defined production function in different manner. Few definitions are stated below.

Prof. Koutsoyiannis has defined as, "The production function is purely technical relation which connects factor inputs and output."

In the words of Prof. George J.Stigler, "Production function is the relationship between inputs of productive services per unit of time and outputs of product per unit of time."

According to Prof. L.R.Klein, "The production function is a technical or engineering relation between input and output. As long as the natural laws of technology remains unchanged, the production function remains unchanged."

In the words of Prof. Evans Douglas, "Production function is a technical specification of the relationship that exists between the inputs and the output in the production process."

According to McGuigan and Moyer, "A production function relates the maximum quantity of output that can be produced from given amounts of various inputs for a given technology."

Thus, from the above definitions, it is clear that production function shows the technical relation between the physical quantities of inputs and outputs produced out of it.

The Nature of Production Functions

1. The production function is purely technological – i.e., the knowledge of engineering is essential. That is why the production function is executed by engineers or production managers. This aspect of production function has nothing to do with the price.

2. Production function is a continuous function: The output is the result of joint use of the factor inputs. If the quantity of one factor is changed, keeping the other factors constant, then output also changes. Production function is determined by the state of technology used. For example, labour productivity depends upon the high quality of labour used in production, which depends upon their technological education and training. Again, the productivity of machine depends on technical advances embodied in them. It is on the basis of technological knowledge that labour, machinery and other inputs are combined. A change in technology means a shift to another production function. It will alter the cost of production. Improvement in technology will result in large output from a given combination of factors of production. Further, it is assumed that firms utilize their inputs at maximum levels of efficiency.

3. Production function has economic importance: Production function helps the producer to maximise the output with the minimum possible input. It is a statement of technical facts with which the producer can obtain the least-cost combination of inputs required to produce the output.

4. Production function differ from firm to firm and industry to industry: It is so because each firm produces different products and their input requirement will be different. Production function also shows that the firm can substitute one output for another without altering its total average of inputs used.

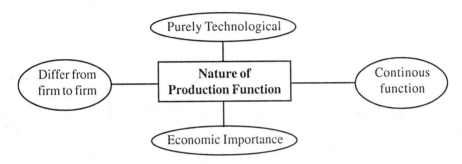

Nature of Production Function

2. TYPES OF PRODUCTION FUNCTION

There are three types of production function:

(i) Fixed proportion and Variable proportion production function.

(ii) Short period and Long period production function.

(iii) Cobb-Douglas Production Function.

(i) Fixed proportion and Variable proportion production function: Types of production function may take several forms. One is the relation where quantities of inputs used are fixed. In this case of fixed proportions of production function, the factors of inputs are used in fixed proportion. For example, a fixed number of workers are employed to produce a given unit of output. This is the second type of production function, where the proportion of factor inputs are varied. The behaviour of production, when all factors are varied, is the subject matter of law of returns.

In order to produce a given amount of output, several factors of inputs have to be used. Suppose to produce 200 units of output, 10 workers are required, this amount of labour is fixed. If the management wants to increase the output to 400 units, then 20 workers will be employed. In this state of technology, there is no scope for substituting labour for other factors. This is the case of *Fixed Proportion Production Function* in which the proportion of labour and capital used are fixed. The fixed proportion production function can be shown in the following diagram.

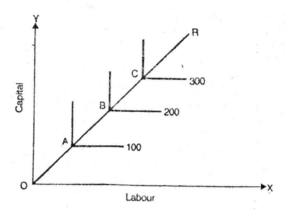

Fig: Fixed Proportion Production Function

In this diagram, OR represents the fixed capital labour ratio and two units of capital and three units of labour produce 100 units of output. In order to produce 200 units of output, the factor units have to be doubled. In other words, four units of capital and six units of labour are required. A – B – C are isoquant curves. An *isoquant* is defined as the curve representing different combination of inputs which will yield a certain amount of output. In the above diagram, the isoquant is right angled.

If one input is substituted for another input to produce the same amount of output, then the isoquant curve moves from upwards to the downwards as shown in the following diagram. This is called as variable proportion production function.

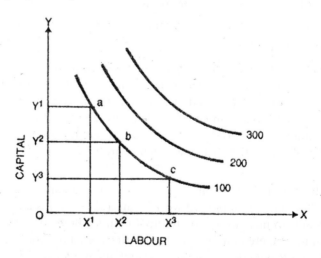

Fig: Variable Proportion Production Function

In order to produce 100 units of output, either OY^1 and OX^1 or OX^3 or OY^3 combinations of inputs can be used. If the quantities of one input is decreased, the quantities of other inputs have to be increased, to produce a given output.

(ii) Short period and Long period production function: The production function differs between short period and long period. In the short period, one or more inputs are fixed. In order to produce more units of output, the management has to increase the variable factor. For example, machinery is fixed and labour input is variable. In this case, the quantity of machinery cannot be increased in the short period. Then the only possibility is to increase labour inputs. This is called variable proportion of production function. Diagram 2 refers to variable proportion of production function. In this case, the ratio in which the factor inputs are used is not fixed but it is variable.

In the long period, all factor inputs can be varied. In the long period, the management can choose between increasing production through the use of more labour or through plant expansion, depending upon which the combination of labour and plant size is more efficient in producing a given output.

(iii) Cobb-Douglas Production Function: Economists have examined several production functions and have used statistical analysis to measure the relation between changes in physical inputs and outputs. One such statistical production function is Cobb-Douglas Production function. In its original form, this concept was applied to the whole of manufacturing in U.S.A. In Cobb-Douglas production function, the output is goods produced by the manufacturing industries. The inputs are labour and capital. The Cobb-Douglas formula says that labour contributes about 75 per cent increase in manufacturing production, while capital contributes only 25 per cent. The formula is as follows:

$P = bL^aC^{1-a}$

Where P = Total output,

L = Index of employment of labour in manufacturing

C = Index of employment of capital in manufacturing

a and 1-a = exponents of elasticities of production

i.e., a and 1-a measure percentage response of output to percentage change in labour and capital respectively.

$P = 1.01 \, L^{.75} \, C^{.25}, R^2 = 0.9499$

The production function shows 1 per cent change in labour, the capital remaining constant, is associated with 0.75 per cent change in output. Similarly, one per cent change in capital, labour remaining constant, is associated with a 0.25 per cent change in output. Returns to scale is associated with a 0.25 per cent change in output. R^2 means that 94 per cent of the variations on the dependent variable (P) were accounted for by the variations in independent variables (L and C).

According to Cobb-douglas production function Returns to scale are constant. That is, if factors of production are increased, each by 10 per cent, then the output also increase by 10 per cent.

3. PRODUCTION FUNCTION THROUGH ISO-QUANT ANALYSIS

The production function so far discussed is concerned with physical or technological aspects. It does not tell us about optimal combination of inputs. Further, the management has to incur expenditure in buying inputs.

Iso-Quant Curve

Iso-Quant is a concept which tells that the quantity produced will be same inspite of variation in production inputs. There may be different combinations of inputs. Each combination is called a scale of preference. Each scale when applied will produce the same quantity of output. Thus, "Iso-Quant" (which means equal quantity) curve indicates that each curve will have different scales of preference of input which can produce the same quantity of out.

An Iso quant is also known as Iso-Product curve or equal product curve or a production Indifference curve.

> *Thus, Iso-quant curve is that curve which shows the different combinations of two factors yielding the same level of output.*

Definitions

According to Prof. Samuelson, "Iso-product curve shows the different input combinations that will produce a given output."

In the words of Ferguson, "An Iso-quant is a curve showing all possible combinations of inputs physically capable of producing a given level of output."

Iso-Product Schedule

An iso-product schedule shows the differnet combination of 2 inputs namely labour and capital which yield the same level of output.

Following are the combinations or scales which give the same output.

Scale I		Scale II	
10 capital + 5 labour 6 capital + 10 labour 2 capital + 15 labour	100 units of output	15C + 8L 10C + 12L 8C + 15L	200 units of output

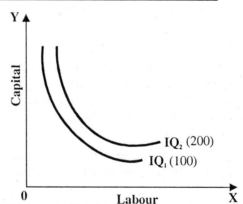

In this diagram, we present two IQ curves representing two output levels viz. 100 units and 200 units. IQ_1 represents 100 units of output and IQ_2 represents 200 units of output. In IQ_1 we see 3 scales of preference given in scale-1. In this scale there are three combinations of capital and labour. Producer can select any combination or scale of preference and adopt to get same output of 100 units.

Iso-Quant curve is also called "Production Iso-Quant." This is similar to indifference curve. This clearly tells that different combinations of factor inputs would produce a given quantity of product. Iso-Quants describe production functioon of a firm. It also suggests a least-cost combination of factor inputs with the help of another concept "Iso-Cost curves".

Iso-Quants like indifference curves have the following properties:

(i) They are convex to the origin of axis.

(ii) They slope downwards from left to right.

(iii) They never intersect each other.

(iv) Sometimes it will have a oval shape.

Marginal Rate of Technical Substitution (MRTS)

The producers substitute are input in the place of other in the production process. The substituting of one input for another without changing the level of output is called as maginal rate of technical substitution. The scope of iso-quant curve is measured in terms of MRTS. The MRTS of factor x (labour) for a unit of factor y (capital) may be defined as the amount of factor y which can be substituted or replaced for a unit of factor x without changing the level of output.

Thus, in terms of inputs of capital (K) and labour (L)

$$MRTS = \frac{\Delta L}{\Delta K}$$

MRTS is similar to MRS $i.e.$, marginal rate of substitution in indifference curve analysis. MRTS dimnishes always.

ISO-Cost Curves

The management has to buy many kinds of labour, raw-material, machinery, etc. In order to buy them, the manager is expected to know the prices of the inputs. In other words, the manager has to know what it costs to produce a given output. He wants to minimize the cost of any output he produces. He is required to draw ISO cost curves. An ISO cost curve is a curve or line representing equal cost. An ISO cost line is so called because, it shows all combinations of inputs having equal total cost. The ISO cost lines are straight lines which means that the firm has no control over the prices of the inputs and the prices are the same irrespective of the units of inputs bought by the firm. Let us study the following diagram:

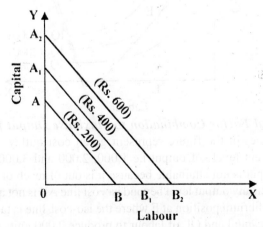

The prices of factor inputs are given. Say, the price of factor X is Rs.4 and that of factor Y is Rs.5. With outlay of Rs.200, we can buy 50 units of X or 40 units of Y. The straight line AB is the ISO cost line. If the outlay increases, then the ISO cost line moves upward. The ISO cost line will change if the prices of factors change. Outlay will be remaining the same.

Let us suppose the prices of inputs such as labour and machinery are fixed. One ISO cost curve represents the quantities of labour and machinery, which may be obtained at a fixed amount. For example ISO cost curve AB shows that quantities of X and Y inputs can be bought by Rs.200. ISO cost curve A_1B_1 shows that quantities of X and Y can be bought by Rs.400 and so on.

4. EQUILIBRIUM OF THE FIRM OR PRODUCER'S EQUILIBRIUM - CHOICE OF OPTIMAL COMBINATION OF FACTORS OF PRODUCTION ('ISO-QUANTS')

A producer or a firm is said to be in equilibrium, when it is able to produce more (highest) output with the given outlay and given factors of production or inputs of production. A rational producer may attain equilibrium either by maximising output for a given cost or minimising cost subject to a given level of output.

In order to determine the producer's equilibrium, we should integrate an iso-quant map with an iso cost line. An iso-quant is the locus of all the combinations of two factors of production that yield the same level of output. Isoquant map refers a group of isoquants, each representing different levels of output. An isocost line represents various combinations of two inputs that may be purchased for a given amount of expenditure.

Maximisation of output for a given cost

A rational producer will always try to maximise his output for a given cost. This can be explained with the help of a diagram. Suppose the producer's cost outlay is C and the prices of capital and labour are 'i' and 'w' respectively. Subject to these cost conditions, the producer would attempt to attain the maximum output level.

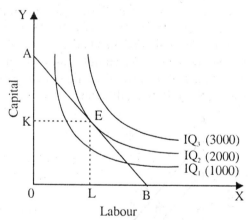

Fig. Optional Factor Combination to Maximise Output for a given Cost

Let AB (iso cost line) in the figure represent given cost outlay. IQ_1, IQ_2, IQ_3 are isoquants representing three different levels of output i.e 1,000, 2,000 and 3,000 units respectively. IQ_3 i.e, 3,000 units levels of output is not attainable because it is out of reach of the producer (the given cost outlay is only AB). In fact, any output level beyond isocost line AB is not attainable. Now the producers the firm reaches the equilibrium position at E where the iso-cost-line is tangent to IQ_2. At this stage he employs OK amount of capital and OL of labour to produce 2,000 units of output. Though the points F and G also lie on the same isocost line, they lie on the lesser isoquant IQ_1. Since the aim of the producer is to maximize his output with the given cost outlay, he will prefer only point E and not any other point on the isocost line. Therefore, by using OK of capital and OL of labour, the producer reaches the highest level of production possible given the cost conditions.

Minimisation of Cost for a Given Level of Output

Alternatively, the producer or the firm may seek to minimize the cost of producing a given amount of output. In both the cases (maximization of output and minimization of cost) the condition of equilibrium remains the same. That is the marginal rate of technical substitution must be equal to the factor price ratio.

i.e $MRTS_{LK} = \dfrac{w}{i} = \dfrac{P_L}{P_K}$

w = wages (price for labour)
i = interest (price for capital)
P_L = price of labour
P_K = price of capital

Cost minimisation can be explained with the help of a diagram.

Here, we have one isoquant representing given level of output (i.e 2,000 units) and a set of isocost lines representing various levels of total cost outlay (A_1B_1, A_2B_2, A_3B_3). The isocost lines are parallel, and thus have the same scope because they have been drawn on the assumption of constant prices of factors.

The iso-cost line, AB is not relevant because the output level represented by the iso-quant IQ_2 (i.e 2,000 units) is not producible by any factor combination available on this iso-cost line. The same level of output can be produced by factor combination 'F' and 'G' on A_3B_3 isocost line. But he can also produce the same level of output at point 'E' (equilibrium) on A_2B_2 isocost line at a lower cost. Since the producer's aim is to minimize the cost, he will choose the point 'E' rather

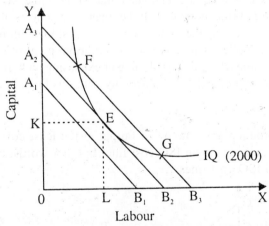

Fig. Cost Minimisation

than 'F' and 'G' because these two points lie on the higher cost outlay. Therefore, the producer by employing OK of capital and OL of labour can reach the equilibrium 'E' by minimizing the cost for a stipulated output (2,000 units).

Expansion Path: (Choice of Optimal Expansion path)

When the financial resources of a firm increases, it would like to increase its output. The output can be increased if there is no increase in the cost of the factors. In other words, the output produced by a firm increases with increase in its financial resources. By using different combinations of factors (inputs) a firm can produce different levels of output. Among these, the combination of factors which is optimum will be used by the firm and it is called as 'Expansion path'. It is also called as 'scale-line'. According to Stonier and Hague "Expansion path is that line which reflects least cost method of producing different levels of output."

Expansion path can be explained with the help of a diagram.

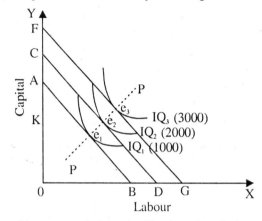

Units of labour employed is measured along the X axis and capital employed is measured along the Y axis. The first iso-cost line of the firm is AB. It is tangent to IQ at point e, which is the initial equilibrium of the firm. Supposing the price per unit of labour and capital remains unchanged and the financial resources of the firm increases, the firm's new iso-cost line shifts to right as CD. In this situation new iso-cost line CD will be parallel to the initial iso-cost line AB and tangent to IQ_2 at point e_2 which will be the new equilibrium point now. If the financial resources of the firm further increases, but the price of the factors remaining the same, the new iso-cost line will be FG. It will be tangent to the iso-quant IQ_3 at point e_3 which will be the new equilibrium point of the firm. By joining all the equilibrium points we get a line (PP) called scale-line or expansion path. It is called so because a firm expands its output or scale of production in conformity with this line.

Cost Minimisation

The firm wants to produce any amount of output at the least cost. This is obtained by the point of tangency of the isoquant to an ISO cost line. In other words, minimum costs mean that isoquants are tangents to ISO cost lines.

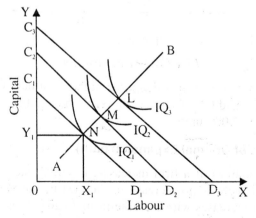

In the above diagram, the maximum output is obtained at a point of tangency between isoquant and ISO cost lines. N, M, L are the points of tangency. The firm expands output along the line AB. At the point of N output, the firm buys OX^1 of labour and OY^1 of capital inputs. This is the optimal combination of inputs. At this point, the marginal rate of substitution between inputs is equal to the ratio between the prices of the inputs. The minimum cost is represented by the point of tangency between the isoquant and ISO cost line.

5. MANAGERIAL USES OF PRODUCTION FUNCTION

The production functions developed in economic theory is a micro-economic concept. But the production function developed by Cobb-Douglas is a macro-economic concept. Anyway, production function is concerned with explaining how maximum quantity of output can be produced from the minimum quantities of inputs.

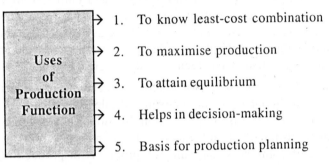

Uses of Production Function	→ 1. To know least-cost combination
	→ 2. To maximise production
	→ 3. To attain equilibrium
	→ 4. Helps in decision-making
	→ 5. Basis for production planning

1. It clearly states how much of inputs are required to produce a given quantity of output. The knowledge of production function though technological, has immense managerial use. Though the combining of inputs in the production function is purely technological, its direction is to be secured from management. The production function analysis mentions how some factor inputs have to be kept constant and some others are varied in order to produce a given amount of output. But there are certain indivisible inputs like machinery, technical skill, etc. which have to be used to the maximum extent. Therefore, the variable factors must be made suitable to the indivisible fixed factors. As such, the knowledge of the characteristics of various inputs is necessary in order to given managerial direction for their uses.

2. The knowledge of production function is very much necessary to managers whenever they want to maximize production from given inputs. In this regard, they use the isoquant and ISO cost curve concepts in order to choose the optimum combination of factor inputs. The ISO cost line plays a crucial role in determining the combinations of factor inputs in the production of a chosen commodity.

3. The producer like a consumer has to function in equilibrium. It is the responsibility of the management to produce a given quantity of output at a minimum cost. The management, in order to do so, has to equate the marginal rate of technical substitution with the price ratio of the two inputs. Its practical usefulness can be explained with the help of an example: Supposing the price of one input rises while the other input remaining constant, then he substitutes one with the other. How this can be done is known by drawing an ISO cost line and thereby equating this with the minimum cost. It buys the

inputs and uses them in a certain proportion. The production function analysis suggests that the optimal ratio of factor inputs is obtained at a point where the ISO cost line is tangent to isoquant curve. The position of tangency between these two curves is the point of least cost combination of inputs. In this analysis, it is assumed that the prices of inputs remain unchanged. Supposing the price of one input rises, while the other is unchanged, then the firm substitutes the input, the price of which has risen to the input for which the price has not risen. In such cases, he would recast the ISO cost curve and change the combination of inputs. Managements can use this analysis for increasing the output from their expenditure on inputs.

4.   The production function is not just theoretical, but very much practical. The production function is now being used in decision making. This analysis helps us to solve two important issues, namely, (i) how to obtain maximum and output from a given set of inputs and (ii) how to obtain a given output from the minimum aggregation of inputs. But in some complex situations where several inputs are to be used to produce a large quantity of output, then mathematical equations are being used. With the development of linear programming, complex problems have been solved to a great extent.

5.   Production function, serves as the basis of programming technique in production planning. Very recently, Earl Heady and his associates developed a device called *Pork Costulator* to solve complex problems which arise in production function. They developed this device to determine the most profitable ration for feeding hogs under different price conditions. With the application of computers, the complex problems in production function are being solved to the satisfaction of the manager.

Multiple products

A firm or an organisation which produces a single-product may find it difficult to cater to the needs of the consumers' which keeps changing over time. A firm producing multiple products, on one hand, has a better chance of satisfying consumers' needs. Firms, therefore, prefer to diversify and produce a variety of products.

A firm producing multiple products can produce similar products or it may produce entirely distinct and different products. A talcum powder manufacturing firm can produce baby foods or detergent powders.

Opportunities for Multiple Products

Opportunities for producing multiple – products may arise due to several reasons, such as:

(a) To make better use of the existing marketing facilities

(b) To cater to customers' demands.

(c) To consolidate on the reputation already enjoyed by the firm.

(d) To improve the sales of existing products of the firm.

(e) To utilize technological development in the production process in a better manner

(f) To identify new markets.

(g) To achieve full utilization of installed capacity.

Thus, to increase its competitive strength and earn more profits, a company aims at adding new products to its product line. Only when there is excess capacity, firms think of diversifying their product line by adding new products. Excess capacity can be interpreted as the type of idleness which can be exploited profitably by manufacturing some more products. This excess capacity may be the result of over-optimism, seasonal variations, cyclical fluctuations, secular shifts in the markets, research, etc.

Policy on Adding New Products

Before adding a new product, it is necessary for the firm to compare the incremental costs with incremental returns. Only when the net returns from adding a new product is greater than net return from other alternative investments, the firm can think of producing the new product.

In addition to this, the decision-makers, before adding a new product must first identify potential product additions. They must further evaluate the proposals and select the right ones. Most important of all, they must introduce the new product in a manner profitable to the company.

The several stages involved in introducing a new product are discussed below:

(i) *Generation of ideas:* The first step in the development of a new product is getting an idea. Ideas may be generated from various sources both internal and external. From within the organisation, ideas may be put forward by the executives, managers, technical personnel, research personnel, or even the company's sales force who are in close contact with the market. From external sources, ideas may come through competitors, customers, etc.

(ii) *Examining the ideas:* It is importable for any firm to accept all ideas that have been generated. Moreover, no firm can afford to pursue many product ideas at the same time. Careful evaluation and selection of the most economically viable product ideas is a must for the firm. In addition to this, the firm must take into consideration, availability of raw materials, technical know-how, finance, market potential and profitability before accepting a new product idea.

(iii) *Product concept and Analysis:* A product concept refers to the clear presentation of the product which the firm is offering to its customers. This requires giving information about the specific needs of consumers which the firm aims to satisfy, the way in which it is to be satisfied, the benefits which the consumer are going to receive and the price the consumers are expected to pay, etc.

The product concept must also be evaluated in terms of utilization of existing capacity, profit expectations, etc. Further, some important considerations relating to future sales, investment, costs, etc., have to be thoroughly analysed.

(iv) *Development of Product:* This is the stage where in abstract idea of developing a product, takes concrete shape. It is in this stage that the management takes the final decision regarding developing the new product on commercial basis. Once the firm decides to implement the idea, the process of building the product and releasing it for testing is carried out.

(v) *Testing of the Product:* This is a very crucial and important stage, where the acceptability of the product is tested. In the first place, testing the concept is done by evaluating the reactions and responses of the consumers. For this, the product must be made available in its finished form including packaging, price range, etc. Secondly, testing of the product is done by assessing the acceptability of its form, size, shape, colour, etc. This enables the firm to identify the consumers' tastes and preferences. Lastly, testing the market is undertaken by releasing the product in selected markets to determine how successful it is. This helps the firm in modifying the product, devising better advertising campaigns and dealing with competition more effectively.

(vi) Commercialise the Product: This stage involves introducing the product to a wider market and this can be done either in a phased manner or simultaneously. It is always advantageous for the firm to launch the new products in different phases in different regions. This ensures that there is no difficulty in meeting the demand of the consumers.

Policy on dropping old Products

Firms sometimes may have to face situations where it becomes necessary for them to drop certain products or a product from their product line. Such situations may arise due to the following reasons:

(i) A fall in the effectiveness of the product may force the firm to delete the product.

(ii) The entry of a substitute product which is superior to the existing product may force it out of the market.

(iii) Reduction in sales trend may slowly eliminate the product.

(iv) A downward trend in prices and profits may result in the removal of the product.

The decision-maker must therefore assume the responsibility of selecting the products for elimination after carefully examining the entire product line, analyzing the results and considering the opportunities for future profit possibilities before deleting a product.

The most important reason for product deletion is a falling trend in profits. It is necessary to find out the reason for declining profits before a decision to discontinue the product is arrived at.

6. THE LAW OF VARIABLE PROPORTIONS

The law of variable proportions occupies an important place in businss economics, for it examines the production function with one variable input, keeping the quantities of other inputs fixed. It refers to input-output relation, when the output is increased by increasing the quantity of one input. When the quantities of one input is varied, keeping the other inputs constant, the proportion between the fixed factor and the variable factor is altered. When the combination of inputs are thus altered, the resulting output also changes. The effect of output of variations in factor proportions is called the *law of variable proportions.* The law examines the production function with one factor input variable, while other factor inputs remain unchanged. The law of variable proportions is defined as follows, 'As the quantity of one input is increased, keeping the quantity of other inputs fixed, the output increase in the beginning and afterwards decreases.' Alfred Marshal defined it as 'An increase in labour and capital applied in the cultivation of land causes in general a less than proportionate increase in the amount of produce raised unless it happens to coincide with an improvement in the arts of agriculture.'

Samuelson defined it as 'An increase in some inputs relative to other fixed inputs will, in a given state of technology, cause output to increase; but after a point, the extra output resulting from the same additions of extra inputs will become less and less.'

Assumptions of the Law of Variable Proportions: The law of variable proportion refers to the behaviour of the output as the quantity of one factor is increased, keeping the quantity of other factors fixed and further, it states that the marginal product and the average product will eventually decline. The law of variable proportions as stated above holds good under the following conditions:

(i) The state of technology of production remains unchanged. If there is an improvement in the technology of production, the marginal and average product may increase instead of diminishing.

(ii) Some inputs are kept fixed during the process of production. It is only in this way that factor proportions are altered to know its effect on output. The law does not apply if all factor inputs are proportionately varied.

(iii) The law is based on the possibility of varying the proportions in which various factors can be combined to produce a product. This law does not apply to cases where the factor inputs have to be used in fixed proportions to yield a product.

Illustration of the Law

The production function can be expressed in the form of the schedule. In the following illustration, the amount of capital equipment employed is fixed and only the labour input is varied.

No. of Workers	(x) Output (O)	Average Product O÷Y	Marginal Product OY	Stages
1	8	8	8	Increasing
2	17	8.5	9	Returns - I
3	27	9	10	
4	36	9	9	Decreasing
5	43	8.6	7	Returns - II
6	48	8	5	
7	48	6.8	0	
8	46	5.7	-2	Negative Returns - III

From the total output, average and marginal output can be derived. Marginal product is the addition to total product which can be produced by addition of more units of the variable input. Average output is the ratio of total output to the amount of the variable input. The behaviour of the total average and marginal output is shown in the diagram below:

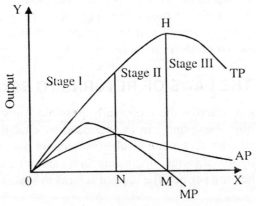

Amount of Variable Factor (Labour)

The behaviour of total product, average product and marginal product curves is shown in the above diagram.

In the stage I, total product increases at an increasing rate. Two men produce more than twice as much as one man. In this stage, both marginal product (MP) and average product (AP) are rising. Because MP is greater than AP, MP pulls up the average product. The boundary line of the I stage is reached when average product and marginal product are equal. This takes place at the point N in the diagram. The first stage is known as the stage of increasing returns, because the average product of the variable factor is increasing the throughout this period. It may be seen that the marginal product also is rising but later, it starts declining.

In the stage II, the total product continues to increase, but at a diminishing rate. When the marginal product is zero, the total product is the maximum. In this stage, both AP and MP are declining. MP being below the average product, pulls the average product down. At the end of the second stage at the point M, the marginal product to the variable factor inputs becomes zero, while the total point reaches the highest point. This stage is called the stage of diminishing returns as both the average and marginal products of the variable factor continuously fall.

In the stage III, total product declines and therefore the total product curve slopes downward. As a result, the marginal product is negative and the MP curve goes below OX axis. The average product decreases still further. It shows that the variable factor is too much to mixed factor. This stage is called the stage for negative returns.

It may be noted that stage I and III are completely symmetrical. In the stage I, fixed factor is too much relative to the variable factor. In this stage marginal product of the fixed factor is negative. On the other hand, in the stage III, variable factor is too much relative to the fixed factor. Therefore, marginal product of the variable factor is negative.

The Stage of Operation: The question is which stage of operation is rational to production. A rational producer will not choose to produce in the stage III. At the end of stage II at the point M, the marginal product and thus will be making the maximum use of the variable factor. In the stage I, the producer will not be making maximum use of fixed factor and he will not be utilizing fully the opportunities of increasing production by increasing the quantity of variable product, whose average product continues to rise throughout the stage I. Thus, a rational producer will not stop in the stage I, but will expand further. At the point N, the marginal product to the variable factor is the maximum and at the end point N of the stage I, he will be making maximum use of the fixed factor. So long as the average product, marginal product and total product are rising, the entrepreneur will not stop producing. Therefore, he goes to stage II, where both marginal product and the average product of the variable factor are diminishing. The stage II represents the range of rational production decisions.

7. THE LAWS OF RETURNS TO SCALE

The laws of production describe the technically possible ways of increasing the level of production. These show how the output can be increased by changing the quantities of factor inputs. In the short run, only one factor can be altered, keeping the other factor unchanged. It is because, in the short period, fixed factors like machinery, cannot be altered. But it is possible to alter the fixed factors in the long period. The laws of returns to scale refer to long run analysis of production.

The laws of returns to scale are entirely different from the laws of variable proportion. In the laws of returns to scale, all productive factors or inputs are increased or decreased in the same proportion simultaneously. In returns to scale, we analyses the effect of doubling or trebling, quadrupling and so on of all inputs on the output of the product. The study of changes in the output as a consequence of changes in the scale, forms the subject matter of 'Returns to Scale'.

The Three Phases of Returns to Scale: Producers who have not studied economic analysis think that output can be doubled by doubling all the inputs or treble the output by trebling all the productive inputs. But actually, this is not so. In other words, actually the output or returns do not increase/decrease strictly according to the change in the scale.

If the increase in output is proportional to increase in the quantities of input, returns to scale are said to be constant. It means that a doubling of inputs causes a doubling of output. If the increase in output is more than proportional, returns to scale are increasing and if the increase in output is less than proportional, returns to scale are diminishing.

Returns to Scale

Sl.No.	Scale of Inputs	Total Product	Marginal Product or Returns	Stage
1	1 Worker + 3 acres of land	2	2	Increasing Returns - I
2	2 Workers + 6 acres of land	5	3	
3	3 Workers + 9 acres of land	9	4	
4	4 Worker + 12 acres	14	5	
5	5 Worker + 15 acres	19	5	Constant Returns - II
6	6 Worker + 18 acres	24	5	
7	7 Worker + 21 acres	28	4	Diminishing Returns - III
8	8 Worker + 24 acres	31	3	
9	9 Worker + 27 acres	33	2	

Let us take up an illustration:

In the table, it can be seen that as all the factor inputs are together increased to the same extent, the marginal product or returns increases first up to a point, then constant for some further increase in the scale and ultimately starts declining. At the scale of 1 workers + 30 acres of land, the total product is 2 quintals. To increase the output, the scale is doubled, the total increases to more than double (5 quintals instead of 2 quintals). When the output is trebled, the total output increases to 9 quintals, the increase this time being 4 quintals instead of 3 quintals. In other words, the return to scale is increasing. If the scale of production is further increased, the marginal product remains constant up to a certain point and beyond it, it starts diminishing. This is illustrated in the following diagram.

Increasing Returns to Scale: Increasing returns to scale means that output increases in a great proportion than the increase in inputs. If, for example, all inputs are increased by 25 per cent, the output increases by 40 per cent, then the increasing returns to scale is prevailing. When the firm is expanding, increasing returns to scale are obtained in the beginning. One chief reason for this increase is the effect of technical and managerial indivisibility. Indivisibility means that

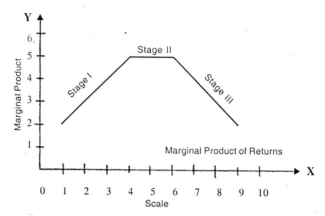

equipment is available only in minimum sizes and the firm has to start producing from the minimum size of equipment. In the beginning, the firm will not be in a position to use the equipment to its optimum capacity. In other words, the equipments are under-utilised in the beginning. When the scale of operations are increased, they are put into maximum use and hence the output or return increases more than proportionately.

Another cause for increasing lies in dimensional relations. Prof.Baumol gives an interesting example. A wooden box 3 ft cube contains 9 times greater wood than the wooden box of 1 ft. cube, i.e., 3 ft cube wooden box is 27 times greater than that of 1 ft cube. In the same way, if the diameter of a pipe is doubled, the flow through it is more than double.

Lastly increasing returns to scale comes from higher degree of specialisation.

Constant Returns to Scale: If the scale of inputs are increased in a given proportion and the output increases in the same proportion, returns to scale are said to be constant, i.e., doubling of all inputs, doubles the output. In mathematics, the case of constant returns to scale is called linear and homogeneous production function or homogeneous production function of the first degree. In some industries, expansion of output produces no net economies or diseconomies and the cost of production remains the same. Such industries are said to be governed by the law of constant returns.

Diminishing Returns to Scale: When the output increases in smaller proportion than the increase in all inputs, decreasing returns to scale is said to prevail. When a firm goes on expanding by increasing all its inputs, then eventually diminishing returns to scale occurs. Economists give different causes for diminishing returns. Some economists view that the entrepreneur is one fixed factor, while all other inputs are variable factors. But the entrepreneur factor cannot be increased. On this view, they say that the law of diminishing returns is the special case of the law of variable proportions. In this case, they say that we get diminishing returns beyond a point, because varying quantities of all other inputs are combined with the entrepreneur as a fixed factor. Other economists do not subscribe to this view, but they say that diminishing returns to scale occur because of increasing difficulties of management, coordination and control. When the firm becomes gigantic, it is difficult to manage it with the same efficiency as before.

Importance of the Diminishing Returns

Prof.Cairnnes observed that in the absence of diminishing returns, the science of political economy would be as completely revolutionised as if human nature itself were altered. Such is the importance of the law of diminishing returns. Whenever some factors of production are fixed and cannot be varied and other factors are varied, then the techniques of production remaining the same, diminishing returns are bound to follow sooner or later. There is no escape.

The validity of the law of diminishing returns is not merely based on theoretical reasoning, but it has been supported by empirical evidence. It has been remarked that if there is no possibility of diminishing return. Then it is possible to grow sufficient food grains in a flower pot by simple increasing the doses of labour and capital. But experience has shown that it is not so. Prof. Lipsey remarked, *'Indeed were the hypothesis of diminishing returns incorrect, there would be no fear that the present population explosion will bring with it a food crisis'*. It is because that the law of diminishing returns is bound to operate, enlightened thinkers are trying to prevent the occurrence of the law. With the application of science and technology, it is possible to keep the operation of diminishing returns in check.

8. ECONOMIES OF SCALE

Scale of production means the size of the plant which has an important bearing on cost of production. It is the manufacturers' experience that larger the scale of production, lower is the average cost of production. That is why entrepreneurs are tempted to enlarge the sale of production so that they may earn maximum profit.

In the scale of production, all factor inputs are increased simultaneously. The proportion of factor inputs is increased in the same manner to get higher output.

When a firm decides to produce the product on a large scale, it has to increase all inputs. The large scale production refers to the production of a commodity on a big scale, i.e., by enlarging the size of the plant and using higher quantities of raw materials, labour etc. Large scale production covers many advantages.

> *Economies of scale refers to those advantages enjoyed by a firm when its production size expands.*

Prof. Marshall classified economies of scale into *(i)* Internal Economies of Scale *(ii)* External Economies of Scale.

9. INTERNAL ECONOMIES OF SCALE

Internal economies are defined as those economies in production, those reduction in production costs, which accrue to the firm itself when it expands its output or enlarges its scale of production. The internal economies arise within a firm as a result of its own expansion independent of the size of an expansion of the industry. The internal economies arise when a firm increases the scale of production. From the managerial economies point of view, internal economies are more important as they can be effected by managerial decision of an individual firm to change its size or to increases of scale of production.

10. EXTERNAL ECONOMIES OF SCALE

External economies are those advantages common and general for all the firms and arise witht the expansion of the industry as a whole. They are enjoyed by all the firms irrespective of their size and scale of production. External economies are the function and the size of the industry and hence it cannot be monoploised by any one firm in an industry. When an industry is localised, it usually gets better facility which can be shared by all the firms and this is the main reason for external economies.

11. TYPES OF INTERNAL ECONOMIES

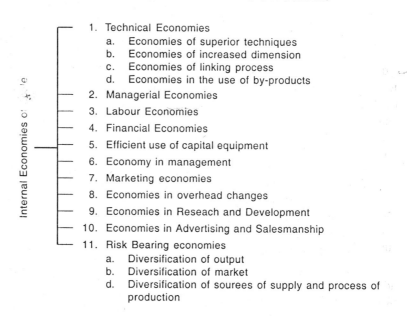

Internal Economies of scale

1. Technical Economies
   a. Economies of superior techniques
   b. Economies of increased dimension
   c. Economies of linking process
   d. Economies in the use of by-products
2. Managerial Economies
3. Labour Economies
4. Financial Economies
5. Efficient use of capital equipment
6. Economy in management
7. Marketing economies
8. Economies in overhead changes
9. Economies in Reseach and Development
10. Economies in Advertising and Salesmanship
11. Risk Bearing economies
    a. Diversification of output
    b. Diversification of market
    d. Diversification of sourees of supply and process of production

(i) *Technical economies:* Technical economies pertain not to the size of the firm but to the size of the factory. A firm may own and operate several factories at different places. The size of the factory depends upon the nature of the industry. If it is agriculture or diary, large plants can be duplicated in several establishments. In such industries, the size of the establishment is small. But in the case of mining, manufacturing of steel, automobiles, etc., the size of the factory is invariably big. It is because, it is economical to have such a large size.

Prof. Cairncross classifies technical economies into three types, (a) economies of superior techniques, (b) economies of increased dimension, (c) economies of linking process, (d) economies in the use of by products.

Economies of superior techniques arise when the firm uses machines representing superior techniques, for example, N.C.Machines. When large machines with superior technology are used, the firm can make use of the economies of increased dimension. For example, double decker bus is more economical than a single decker. What it means is that without using additional man power and other inputs, big sized machines can be operated and a larger quantity of output can be produced. A large plant can enjoy the economies of linking process. For example, the sugar factory having its own cane farm. Paper making and pulp making may be combined in the factory itself. Such linking saves transport costs.

There is another technical economy derived from a big factory which is that of using by-products. For example, molasses is used to manufacture liquor in a sugar factory. In large factories, it is possible to derive considerable technical internal economies.

(ii) *Managerial Economies:* Managerial economies refer to the advantages that a firm derives from efficient management. These economies arise from the creation of functional department and thereby several functions may be entrusted to these departments. For example, Personnel Department looks after recruitment, training and welfare, etc. This is possible only for a big firm. The management expenses can be reduced by means of rationalisation of administration. In a big firm, it is possible to make the fullest use of the services of the experts. Delegations of responsibility to subordinate officers will increase efficiency.

(iii) *Labour Economies:* Labour economies arise due to an increase in division of labour. When the output increases as the labour force grows may lead to specialisation and hence better prospects is possible. There will be overall development (both in efficiency and productivity of labour) which will result in reducing costs.

(iv) *Financial Economies:* When compared to the smaller firms, longer funds are available to the large firms and hence they reap financial economies. They can borrow from banks or any other financial institution. They can also raise capital through the sale of shares and debentures to the public.

(v) *Efficient Use of Capital Equipment:* In the large scale production, the producer installs most modern machinery and enlarges the scope of division of labour. Consequently, output increases and costs become minimum.

(vi) *Economy in Management:* In a big organisation, there is plenty of scope for division of labour. Specialised labour produces a larger output, keeping in mind the quality of the product. It is only in large scale business, that every person can be put on the job which he can perform most efficiently. The management can be better utilized in the large scale production. The entrepreneur is able to translate his ideas into practice in a large scale organisation. He can direct the organisation functioning most efficiently.

(vii) *Economies of Buying and Selling or Marketing Economies:* A big organisation can arrange for the purchase of raw materials and spares on favourable terms. Bulk purchase of raw-materials is always economical. While selling goods, it can attract customers by offering a greater variety of concessions and by ensuring prompt supply. A lower rate of profit results in larger sales and higher net profits in a larger scale business.

(viii) *Economics on Overhead Charges:* The expenses on administration and distribution are very much controlled in a big business. Interest, pay bill and other overhead charges are the same whether production is undertaken either in the medium scale or big scale. The same amount of expenditure is being distributed over a large output and as such becomes lower per unit of output.

(ix) *Economies in Research and Development:* A large organisation can set apart a certain sum of money for research and development from the total gross profit, which will not be burden to the organisation. It is well known that in the long run, these expenses more than repay. Successful research may lead to simplification of productive processes which may bring large profit to the firm.

(x) *Economies in Advertisement and Salesmanship:* A big concern can spend sufficient money on advertisement and salesmanship. Ultimately, they bear fruit. A big business can challenge the competitors by means of maintaining frequent advertisement and capture the market of the rivals.

(xi) *Risk Bearing Economies:* A large firm with its economically stronger position and better management can eliminate or minimise the business risks by spereading them over. A large firm can avoid risk by:

(a) *Diversification of output:* They can produce more varieties and multiple goods

(b) *Diversification of market:* They can sell goods in a wider market and can extend the market throughout the country

(c) *Divestification in the source of supply and also the process of production:* They can buy from different sources. They also follow different methods of manufacturing.

External Economies

The firms enjoy a number of external economies from the growth of the industry. When the industry grows a number of economies become available to the firms. They are listed below.

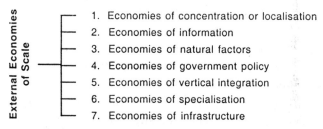

- Economies of localisation refers to the the mutual advantages enjoyed by all the firms through the tranining of skilled labour, provision of better transport facilities etc. Subsidiary industries also develop the same area to supply raw material and tools.

- Economies of information refers to the benefits shared by all the firms through establishment of research laboratories by an industry. Producers thus save expenditure on independent research which is very costly. Firms can share the informations.

- Economies of natural factors refers to the advantages enjoyed due to natural factors like climate, weather fertility of soil etc. This would help all firms and reduce their cost of production.

- Economic of Government policy are in the form of concessions, tax-holiday, subsidies, tax concessions etc. announced by the Government for the development of the industry.

- Economics of vertical integration refers to the benefits from integration of the several stages of production (i.e., vertical integration) and this results in the reduction of costs of production.

• Specialisation in the result of increase in scale of production. Firms start specialising in different processes and this helps in reducing costs.

These are the various internal and external economies of scale enjoyed by the firms when their scale of production increases.

12. DISECONOMIES OF LARGE SCALE PRODUCTION

Though there are a good number of advantages in the large scale production, it is not free from some diseconomies. Some of the weaknesses of the large scale production are:

(a) Over-worked Management: When a business grows very big, management becomes impersonal and consequently tells on the efficiency and honesty of the employees. Owing to delegation of responsibilities to the different cadres in the organisation, supervision becomes formal and laxity enters the field which causes higher expenditure. The management becomes overworked. Lack of personal contact and increase in impersonal relationship between top level officers and the lower level employees results in clashes and conflicts. This is positively harmful to the business.

(b) Over – Production: There is every possibility in big business that production may exceed the requirements, resulting in over production. It is very difficult to dispose off a large output profitably.

(c) Difficulties in Decision-Making: A larger firm may find it very difficult to make a quick and correct decision.

(d) Difficulties in Coordination: As the firm grows, it is very difficult to coordinate various departments and more over individual problem cannot be given attention by the management.

(e) Scarcity of Input Supplies: This may force the firm to reduce the scale of production. And moreover, due to competition among firms the factor prices may go up.

(f) Financial difficulties may also arise as the firm grows bigger and bigger.

(g) Labour Diseconomies may also arise with the growing scale of output. It may result in lack of initiative and industrial disputes leading to increase in cost of production.

Inspite of these weakness, large scale production offers several economies in production. The advantages outweigh the disadvantages. The scale of production is to be enlarged till the firm reaches the optimum size. At this scale of production, the total profit is the maximum and the average cost is the minimum. If the size of the firm goes beyond the optimum size, diminishing returns steps in and marginal cost will be more than marginal revenue. Differences in efficiency between firms will show themselves not in differences in marginal costs, but differences in output. The more efficient firm will produce larger output than inefficient firms.

13. SIZE OF THE UNIT

Size here refers to the size of the business unit. An entrepreneur has to first decide the size of the business unit, he wants to establish. Size of the unit means the scale of operation of the firm that is adopted at the time of the promotion. Size actually determines the profitability and quality of operation of the enterprise. Two vital aspects connected with the problem of size are "Laws of Returns" and the principle of "Division of Labour". Because of these two factors, economists were more worried about the concept of 'Optimum Firm'. Several factors determine the size of the business unit. Every size - big or small - should reach the optimum production by utilising the inputs to the full capacity. Even before determining the size, let us examine the factors influencing the size of the business unit.

Factors Influencing Size

Following are the factors which influence the size of business unit.

(i) Capital outlay.

(ii) Workers employed.

(iii) Size of output.

(iv) Output value.

(v) Management Structure

(vi) Raw material consumption

(i) **Capital Outlay:** One of the factors which determine the size of the unit is the total capital employed in the business. Although the total outlay is not properly disclosed by financial statements (certain financial resources are concealed), it is one of the factors which determines the size of the business unit. There are capital intensive units where more capital is employed. Normally, the size of such unit is considered as a big one. These are managed under the form of Joint Stock companies. If the capital outlay is small, they are managed by small forms like partnership firm and sole trading concerns. Thus, volume of capital determines the size of the business unit.

(ii) **Workers Employed:** This is one of the indicators of the size of the business unit. Prior to introduction of mechanisation in business units, labour employed in the unit was considered for determining the size. With the introduction of information technology in business operations, labour force is reduced even in big business houses. However, human factor cannot be ignored in an enterprise. It is one of the parameters considered to determine the size of the business unit.

(iii) **Output size:** Another factor which determines the size is the volume of output. Large volume of output can be produced by adopting economics in operation in big units. Smaller units cannot enjoy the economics of large-scale operations. The output of a firm also determines the size. If a unit producers more units or on a large-scale, it is considered as a big unit. Lesser output unit will be considered as a small unit. The size of the plant also determines the size.

(iv) **Output value:** Value of output is another indicator of the size of the business unit. But it is not a good factor to determine the size, when conditions in the economy are abnormal. For example, in an inflationary period, the value of output will be high. But in real terms, it may be less. Only under stable economic conditions, this factor can be considered for determining the size of the unit.

(v) **Management Structure:** Peter Drucker, considered to be the father of modern management thought, opines that "management structure is the ideal criteria or indicator of the size. The complexity of management structure is a more reliable indicator". More the levels of management, bigger will be the size of the unit. But this indicator cannot measure the size statistically.

(vi) **Raw Material Consumption:** This aspect is also considered in determining the size. The units which are self-sufficient and the output of these units are uniform or having little difference, the volume of consumption of raw material in these units can be taken as a parameter to determine the size of the unit.

These factors can be considered to measure the size of the business unit. However in real business situations, there is a blending of the factors like (i) Labour employed (ii) Capital employed and (iii) volume of output to measure the size of the business unit.

14. ECONOMICS OF SIZE AND CAPACITY UTILIZATION

Economics of size refers to the type and degree of economy a firm would enjoy due to the size of operation it possesses. In the previous paragraphs, the various types of economics a large firm would enjoy have been discussed. Diseconomies has also been briefly explained. In the whole analysis, it is observed that large firms have a definite edge over small and medium sized firms in availing benefits of operation and thereby reduce cost of labour/management per unit of output. Inspite of these economies that a large firm enjoys, they fail at times in their operations. On the other hand, many small firms with no or less economies in operation also exist side by side and get a firm footing in business operations and they gradually diversify and grow into big units.

Small firms survive, create large employment opportunities, can bring about balanced and diversified economic development, can ensure equitable distribution of wealth and power. They exist on a big scale because of the following reasons:

    (i) Widely fluctuating demand.

    (ii) Standardisation of components by ancillary firms.

    (iii) Shorter gestation period.

    (iv) Promotion by government by providing facilities like industrial estates, venture capital, soft loans, etc.

    (v) Small units have a greater support with employees and they are motivated by employers. As the units are small, personal care will be taken by the employers.

    (vi) Manufacturing process will be simple.

    (vii) Changing taste, fashion and preferences of consumers.

Whether it is big or small, enterprises operate with understanding and they are complementary to each other. The only aspect under full consideration in all these units of varying nature is that how they utilise the full capacity of production. Capacity utilisation is a task stage. Hence in the process of getting optimum output which will be the best in the existing conditions, managers cannot ignore the cost of production. Increasing cost will reduce the revenue. Therefore, the firms should not produce anything beyond optimum level. Optimum level is the maximum size indicating the most profitable combination of resources.

E.A.G.Robinson states that "By the optimum firm, we must mean a firm operating that scale at which in existing condition of techniques and organising ability, it has the lowest average cost of production per unit, when all these costs which must be covered in the long run are included". The following figure indicates the optimum capacity of a firm:

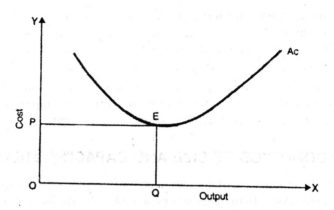

From the above diagram, it may be observed that firm produces OQ output to reach the optimum level. At point E, Average cost is lowest and beyond this point, the production cost raises before the managers and the promoters have to co-ordinate activities to achieve full production. Even at the time of promoting the enterprise, the promoters have to think of a viable business unit and plan accordingly. Thinking and establishing an Optimum unit is a dynamic concept and it changes in accordance with the change in technology. When once an unit is established, it has to work to the full capacity. Reaching full capacity of production needs good co-ordination of various factor services like managerial, market, financial and technical forces. Only then can the firm produce to the optimum.

The firm becomes optimum when further growth is not possible under the existing conditions of technology and managerial ability. When the firms are promoted, they have to think of a size below which it is not profitable to operate. After establishing the firm, they start growing and a point will reach where cost will be equal to revenue. Since the law of diminishing returns is bound to occur at a later stage, the cost will be more than revenue at this. Therefore, the firm produces only optimum output and if it has to raise the production beyond this level, it has to change or increase the production facilities like installing a new plant, appointing more labour, etc.

The conditions of optimum level are:

(i) All resources or factor services employed in production process have equi-marginal returns;

(ii) There will be rational allocation of resources and the inputs will be best combined to secure maximum output.

(iii) The size of production should yield maximum profit to the firm.

If all these conditions are fulfilled, the firm is said to be working at an optimum level and has fully utilised the capacity.

Capacity utilisation is governed by the factors or forces like (i) Technical forces (ii) Managerial forces (iii) Marketing forces (iv) Financial forces and (v) Forces of Risks and Fluctuations.

However, capacity utilisation can be achieved by conscious planning. But there should be a healthy market condition which provides constant demand for the product and firms playing in the market should maintain healthy competition.

15. SUPPLY

The concept supply occupies a significant place in economic theory. Supply analysis is related to the behaviour of the producer. Supply of a commodity like its demand also influence its price.

Meaning of Supply

Supply means the amount of a commodity offered for sale at a given price or at different prices. Supply refers to a schedule of quantities of commodities that will be offered for sale at different prices.

16. DEFINITION

Mc Connell defines supply as follows "Supply may be defined as a schedule which shows the various amounts of a product which a producer is willing and able to produce and make available for sale in the market at each specific price in a set of possible prices during some given period."

In the words of Prof. Bach, "Supply is a schedule of amounts that will be offered for sale at different prices during any given time period, other factors remaining unchanged."

> *Therefore supply can be summed up as the amount of commodity or service that producers are willing and able to offer for sale at a given price at a particular period of time or at any period of time.*

Mayers has defined "Supply as a schedule of amount of a commodity that would be offered for sale at all possible prices, at any one instant of time or during any one period of time, for example a day, a week and so on in which the conditions of supply remain the same."

Difference between Supply and Stock

Supply is different from the stock of a commodity. Stock is the total volume of a commodity brought into market for sale. Supply means the quantity which is actually brought to the market for sale. If the price of a product in the market is high, larger quantities are offered for sale from their stock. If the price is low, only small quantities are offered for sale, while the remaining is kept in the godown. In short, stock is potential supply.

17. LAW OF SUPPLY

Supply is the function of price. The law of supply states that "other things remaining the same, as the price of a commodity rises, its supply is extended and as the price falls, its supply is contracted." The quantity offered for sale directly varies with price—higher the price, larger is the supply and vice-versa.

Supply schedule represents the relation between prices and the quantities that the producers are willing to manufacture and sell. The following is the supply schedule of Firms A, B, & C.

It can be seen from the above schedule, if the price is Rs.2, no firm is willing to produce and sell. As the price rises, the quantity offered for sale by the firms also increase.

Supply Schedule of Firms A, B and C

Price	Commodity is identical			Aggregate of
	A Firm	B Firm	C Firm	A, B and C
Rs.2	Zero	Zero	Zero	Zero
Rs.4	300	400	50	450
Rs.6	400	200	150	750
Rs.8	500	400	300	1200
Rs.10	600	500	400	1500
Rs.12	700	600	500	1800
Rs.14	900	800	750	2450

Supply Curve

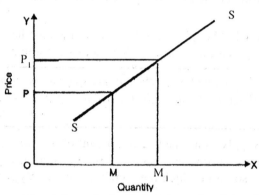

At OP price, quantity offered for sale is OM. Prices rise from OP to OP₁ and the quantity offered for sale also increases to MM₁. Supply curves slope left to right upwards. If the price falls too much, supply may dry up altogether. The price below which the producer refuses to sell is called the *reserve price*.

Assumptions of the Law of the Supply

The law of supply is based on certain assumptions. They are

1. The number of firms in the market remains the same and so is the case of technology.

2. The speed of production do not change.

3. Market prices of related goods remains constant over a period of time.

4. Cost of production does not change.

5. Climatic conditions and taste and preferences of the consumers also remains unchanged.

6. No other inputs are available in the market.

The law of supply will hold good only when the above mentioned assumptions or conditions remain the same. If any change occurs, it will give rise to a new supply curve.

The causes for upward sloping supply curve are as follows:

(i) An increase in price implies higher profits leading the producers to produce more and offer increasing quantities for sale.

(ii) This may cause incentive to new producers entering into the industry and setting up firms and produce more or the existing firms may install new plants and produce more. All these factors result in higher quantity of products for sale.

Features of the Law of the Supply

- There is a direct relationship between quantity supplied and price.
- Among the two variables price and supply, supply is the dependent variable and price is an independent variable.
- This law is not universal in nature because it is conditioned by a phrase "other things remaining constant."
- Supply curve usually slopes upward from left to right.

Exceptions to the Law of Supply

According to law of supply, the supply of a commodity expands at a higher price and contracts with a fall in price. But under certain instances, though the price rises, supply may not expand or even at a lower price same or more quantity may be sold. This happens in exceptional cases. In this case, the supply curve supply curve slopes backwards. The best example for this is the subsistence farming in developing countries. Though the price rises, the farmers cannot supply more of foodgrains because the agricultural farms are in subsistence level.

Other Exceptions are:

- When the seller badly needs money he will sell all his goods even at a lower price.
- When the sellers are not interested in maximising their profits.
- If a further fall in the price is expected, then he may try to sell more at a current price.
- Auction sale is an exception to law of supply because the price is determined by the bidders.
- When the seller wants to get rid of his goods, then will be forced to sell at lower prices.

18. DETERMINANTS OF SUPPLY

There are various factors which determine the quantity of supply of a commodity in the market. They are given as follows:

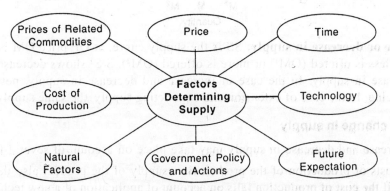

Factore Determining Supply

- Supply always depends upon the price of the commodity.
- Supply is also influenced by time period. In case of certain commodities the supply can be increased only in the long period, though there is a rise in the price (e.g.) the supply of labour.
- With the improvement of technology over time, the supply of individual goods are bound to change.
- Supply of a commodity is influenced by expectations of future prices by the seller.
- Taxation policy, subsidy scheme etc. of the government also influence the supply.
- Natural calamities like flood, drought etc., affect the supply of agricultural goods.
- When there is a change in factor prices, automatically cost of production also changes. If it is not accompanied by a price rise of the commodity then seller may reduce the quantum of production.
- Supply of a commodity is mostly influenced by the prices of its related commodities i.e., its substitutes and complementary goods.

Thus, the supply of a commodity is determined by many factors like price, cost of production, technology, natural factors etc.

19. CHANGES IN SUPPLY

Supply is said to increase when at the same price, more is offered for sale or the same quantity is offered at a lower price. The supply is said to decrease, when, at the same price, less is offered for sale or the same quantity is offered at a higher price. This is shown in the following diagram.

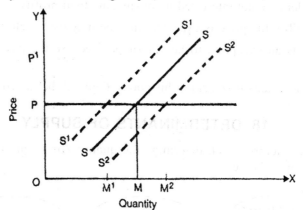

Increase or decrease in supply: SS is the supply curve, at OP price OM is offered. At the same price, less is offered (OM^1) or more is offered (OM^2). S^{1}S^1 shows decrease in supply, S^{2}S^2 shows increase in supply. In the case of increase and decrease in supply, new supply curves come into being. In the case of extension and contracting supply, the same supply curve prevails.

Causes for change in supply

The increase and decrease in supply may take place on account of several factors.

If the costs of production of the product rise, supply of the product also decreases. On the other hand, if the cost of production falls on account of application of a new technology, with the discovery of a new resource, the supply of the product rises.

In the case of agricultural commodities, good rainfall, application of improved seeds, fertilisers and new methods of production will cause increase in supply. If the rains fail, supply of the commodities falls.

Introduction of new technique of production will cause an increase in supply. The cost of production also will be lower in such cases. Political disturbances like war and other disturbances (man-made and natural) create scarcity for products and hence supply is reduced. Supply may be decreased by cartel agreements among the producers.

Finally, the supply of the commodity depends upon the prices of the product. Higher the price, higher is the supply and vice-versa.

The Supply Function

The supply function is determined mathematically as follows:

$$Q_x = F(P_x : P_y : P_i.T.MT.)$$

The quantity supplied of X varies with the price of that good (X), the prices of other goods (Y), the prices of factor inputs (P_i), technology (T), and time periods (MT).

Thus, the supply of commodities is very much influenced apart from price, by factors like availability of raw materials and other inputs at reasonable prices, technology, favourable political environment, etc.

According to Prof.Hirschman, the economic inter-dependence governs the supply of goods. He says that with dependent relationship in supply, it can be of two types - one is horizontal and the other is vertical. There is horizontal relationship between goods when they are used at the same stage of production. In this case, the two goods compete with each for the buyer's choice. Consequently, there is a unique pecuniary linkage relationship between the two that is essentially a demand cross elasticity relationship.

In the case of vertical relationship, one good is an input to another. A good has forward linkage relationship when it is used as an input for another, the good produced has a backward linkage relationship. In this case, there is functional relationship between the price of one good and the supply of another.

When the relationship is horizontal, it is almost an inverse relationship. If the price of one good rises, the demand for another good also rises. The coefficient cross elasticity is negative.

In the case of forward vertical relationship, an increase in the price of the final product will induce a rise in the price of the factor input.

Thus, the supply of a product depends apart from the price, on other factors like technology etc.

20. ELASTICITY OF SUPPLY

Elasticity of supply explains the response to any change in the price of the commodity. It is a measure of the case with which an industry can be expanded and of the behaviour of the marginal costs. If slight increase in price is followed by an increase in supply followed by the entry of new firms having minimum average, cost is equal to price and the marginal cost does not rise, then the supply is said to be perfectly elastic. In case the increased output can be obtained only by an infinite increase in price and no new firms enter into the industry, the supply will be inelastic. In between these two extremes, there will be a different degree of elasticity.

Prof. Boulding gives a beautiful simile to explain the elasticity of supply. The relation between the price and the quantity supplied is rather like the relation between a whistle and a dog - the louder the whistle, the faster comes the dog — raise the price, the quantity supplied increases. If the dog is responsive — in economic terminology elastic—quite a small sound in the whistle will send him bounding along. If the dog is unresponsive or inelastic, we may have to whistle very loudly before he comes along at all.

> *Elasticity of supply refer to the response of supply to a change in the price of a commodity.*

Measurement of Elasticity

If the supply curve is a vertical straight line, the supply is absolutely inelastic and if the supply curve is a horizontal straight line, the supply is an infinitely elastic supply. In between the two extremes, there will be varying degree of elasticity. A straight supply curve drawn through the origin has a unit elasticity. The following formula is a general measure of elasticity of supply.

$$\text{Price elasticity of supply} = \frac{\text{Proportionate change in the quantity supplied}}{\text{Proportionate change in price}}$$

The following diagrams explain the different types of elasticity.

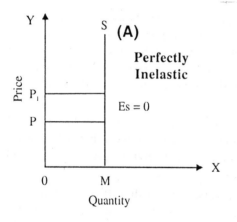

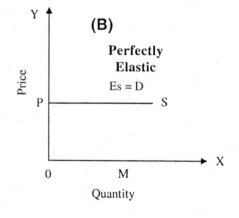

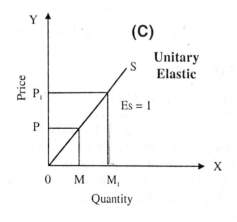

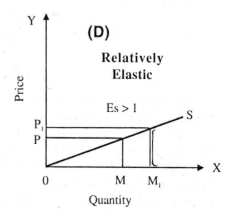

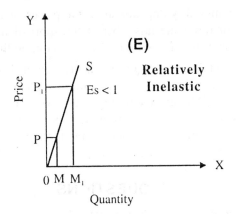

In figure A, there is no change in the supply and hence the supply curve is perfectly inelastic and Es=0

In figure B, even for a small change in price there will infinite change in supply and hence it is perfectly elastic and Es=D

In figure C, the change in price is equal to change in quantity supplied and hence it is unitary elastic and hence, Es=1

In figure D, the change in price is smaller than change in quantity supplied and hence it is relatively elastic and Es>1

In figure E, the change in quantity supplied is lesser than the change in price and hence it is relatively inelastic and Es<1

These are the five different types of elasticity of supply.

Factors influencing Elasticity of Supply

In the short period, the supply of a commodity is inelastic but in the long period, it is elastic.

In the case of agricultural commodities, supply is inelastic but in the case of industrial goods, it is elastic.

The factors influencing supply are the following:

(a) Generally, the firms aim at producing the goods to the maximum extent. If the cost of production rises, they are not sure that they can sell the entire output at higher prices. At higher prices, the demand for the products are elastic. Therefore, the producers have to take risk and produce the commodity. If they are not prepared to take risk, the production will suffer. If they expect that the price of that product would rise in future, they would withhold the supply and vice-versa.

(b) The supply of a commodity depends upon the prices of that commodity. Higher the price, higher is the profit from the sale of the commodity, as such the supply also would rise.

(c) The supply of a commodity depends upon the prices of all other commodities. An increase in the price of other commodities will make the production of that commodity, whose price does not rise, this would be less attractive and as such, the supply of that commodity falls, when the prices of other commodities rise.

(d) The supply of a commodity depends upon the prices of factors of production and their availability. If the prices of raw-materials, cost of transport of minerals from the mines to the production centres rises, then the production of a final commodity is very much affected.

(e) Technology is the catalytic agent in increasing output. It reduces the cost of production and at the same time, contributes to an increase in output. Technology is changing fast on account of inventions and discoveries. Modern technology has revolutionised the process of production. Consequently, host of new goods are coming into the market almost every month. Thus, technology's contribution is tremendous in increasing output and reducing the cost of production. This will be possible only through strategic planning.

QUESTIONS

1. Define production function. Explain the isoquant and IO cost curves.
2. Explain the nature and managerial use of production function.
3. What is the production function? Explain various types of production function.
4. What are the laws of variable proportions? Explain the three laws of production.
5. Explain the concept of 'Returns to Scale'.
6. Discuss the advantages and disadvantages of large scale production.
7. Distinguish between internal and external economies.
8. Discuss the properties of short and long term production functions.
9. Explain with the help of diagram the law of variable proportions.
10. Explain the law of diminishing returns with suitable illustration.
11. What is exspansion path?
12. What shape do the isoquants take when
    (a)   inputs are perfect substitutes.
    (b)   inputs are compliments?
13. Explain with diagram the law of variable proportions.
14. Explain the law of variable proportions.
15. Define (a) Marginal Rate of Technical Substitution and (b) Elasticity of Substitution.
16. Explain the three stages of production.
17. What are isoquant curves?
18. Distinguish between isoquants and ISO cost curves.
19. Distinguish between return to a factor and returns to scale.
20. Explain economies of scale.
21. What are managerial uses of production function?
22. Distinguish between returns to scale and returns to proportion.
23. What are iso-quants?
24. What is an expansion path?
25. What is a linear production function?
26. What are internal economies to scale?
27. Production function.
28. Distinguish between production and productivity.

Cost Analysis

8 Chapter

The knowledge of various cost concepts are very useful to business economists. There is a lot of difference between the approach of an accountant and that of an economist. The business economist does not consider the accounting aspect, but considers the costs. Many policy decisions are framed in terms of profitability calculations which are estimate of changes in the amount of future expenses and future revenues. The only expenses and revenues that need to be included in such calculations are those that will differ. The unchanged quantities cancel out in the comparison.

1. MEANING OF COSTS

The term 'Cost' means different things to different persons. For business executives, the use of cost figures is very important in the determination of profit. For the managerial economist, cost analysis has a specific purpose, namely to solve managerial problems. This calls for an economic analysis of the data about which costs are appropriate for different decisions.

The managers use the cost data for future planning and to choose an appropriate production pattern form among alternative plans. As Joel Dean says, 'It should be recognized at the onset. The only costs that matter for business decision are future costs, actual costs, i.e., current or historical costs'. In estimating profits, the manager is required to compare costs with revenue. While information regarding the future demand for a product is difficult to obtain, but it is not so with regard to information about costs.

Cost is the expense incurred in producing a commodity.

The cost of production of a product is the most important force governing the supply of a product. The cost of producing a unit of product is determined by the price of factor inputs used in the production of a product. If the prices of the factor inputs are high, the cost of production also will be high. While determining the profit, the cost is compared with revenue. The revenue depends upon the price of the product in the market. The business manager cannot control the price prevailing in the market, but he can control the cost by restricting the output.

2. COST CONCEPTS

It is necessary for the proper understanding of cost analysis, to know various cost concepts that are often employed. When an entrepreneur decides to produce a commodity, he has to pay prices for inputs, which he uses in production. When he employs labourers, he pays wages to them and pays money when he buys raw-material, fuel and power, rent for the factory building and so on. All these are included in the cost of production. The kind of cost concept used in a particular situation depends upon the business decisions that the management makes. An accountant will take into account only the payments and charges made by the manager to the suppliers of various productive inputs. But the business economist views the cost in a somewhat different form. The cost estimates made by conventional financial accounting are not appropriate for all managerial uses. Further, different business problems call for different kinds of costs. Therefore, it is necessary to have a complete understanding of different cost concepts for clear business thinking. One way of getting clear-cut distinctions among different notions of cost is to up the several alternative basis of classifying costs and show the relevant set of each for different kinds of problems. The very purpose of defining and distinguishing concepts of cost is to scout the fallacy that cost estimates produced by conventional financial accounting are appropriate for all managerial uses. Actually, they serve only the purpose of financial accounting. There is another purpose, namely different business problems call for different kinds of costs.

Cost concepts differ because of differences in view point. Different combinations of cost ingredients are important for various kinds of management problems. Disparities occur from deletions, from additions, from recombination of elements, from price level adjustments and from the introduction of measurements which do not appear anywhere in the accounting records. Different cost concepts explained in our study are:

a. Real cost and Money cost

b. Actual cost and Opportunity cost

c. Past and Future costs

    d. Short run and Long run costs

    e. Variable and Constant costs or fixed costs.

    f. Incremental costs and Sunk costs.

    g. Traceable and Common costs (direct and indirect cost)

    h. Replacement and Historical costs

a. Real Cost and Money Cost

Real Cost: Real cost includes the trouble, commotion and sacrifices involved in producing a product. The efforts and sacrifice of the factors or its owners is the real cost. Alfred Marshall defined the real cost of a product as follows. "The exertions of all the different kinds of labour that are directly or indirectly involved in making it together with the abstinence or rather waitings required for saving the capital used in making it."

The effort and sacrifice implicit in real cost of production are purely subjective and beyond accurate measurement.

Money Cost: Money cost refers to the total money expenditure incurred by a firm on the various items which it uses for production. It includes wages for labourers, prices for raw materials, fuel rent for buildings, power and light, transport, advertising, money spent on machines etc. All these are included in the cost of production.

The total money cost can be further divided into two:

    (i) Explicit cost.

    (ii) Implicit cost.

(i) Explicit cost: It includes those costs which are made by the firm to those factors of production not belonging to it. The payments for wages and salaries, materials, licence fee, insurance premium, depreciation charges are the examples of explicit costs. These costs involve cash payments and are entered in books of records.

(ii) Implicit cost: Implicit cost refers to those costs which do not take the form of cash outlay or appear in the accounting system. It arise in the case of those factors which are possessed and supplied by the employer himself. Example, an employer can contribute his own buildings, his own capital, computer and may even work himself as the clerk of the firm. He foregoes his salary and other costs for the sake of his business. Therefore, implicit costs may be defined as the earnings expected from the second best alternaive use of resources.

Thus, implicit costs refers to those costs which are hidden and do not appear in the accounting records of a firm. Such costs are known as implicit or imputed costs.

The explicit cost and implicit cost together make the economic cost.

b. Actual Cost and Opportunity Cost

Actual costs are those that involve financial expenditure incurred for acquiring inputs for producing a commodity. These expenditures are recorded in the books of accounts of the firm. The expenditure are wages paid, payment made for the purchase of raw materials, machinery, etc. These costs are called *actual costs* or outlay costs.

Opportunity cost is not the actual expenditure, but it is the revenue that would be earned by employing that good or service in some other alternative uses. Opportunity cost is the cost of producing any commodity which is the next best alternative good that is sacrificed. Opportunity cost may also be called alternative cost. For example, the inputs which are used for manufacturing a car may also be used in the production of a military equipment. Therefore, the opportunity cost of the production of a car is the output of the military equipment foregone or sacrificed, which could have been produced with the same amount of inputs, that have gone into making a car. Let us take another example. A farmer who is producing paddy can also produce sugarcane with the same factors. Therefore, the opportunity cost of one quintal of paddy is the amount of sugarcane given up.

Two points must be noted in the definition of opportunity cost. Firstly, the opportunity cost of any commodity is only the next best alternative foregone. Secondly, the next best alternative commodity could be produced with the same value of the factors, which are more or less the same.

In business decision making, opportunity cost concept is very important. It helps in determining the remuneration to service. For example, a mechanical engineer is drawing a salary of Rs.10,000 in a steel factory. It helps the manager to decide what he should produce in the factory. He can produce electric motors and telephone equipment. The opportunity cost of one electric motor is 20 telephones. The market price of one electric motor is Rs.5,000 and the price of telephone is Rs.200. Then it is profitable to produce electric motors.

Importance of the Concept of Opportunity Cost: When the company, with its limited resources, wants to make a choice between another layer of advertising in the established markets or some basic changes in the product line, it has to examine the opportunity costs of these two proposals. The profit that could be otherwise earned in these alternatives is the opportunity cost of using the funds. If the prospective earning from the expansion is less than the alternative earnings, there is a real loss. But the alternative earnings or opportunity costs can only be determined by comparing projected cash outlay costs and revenues which are thus the basic data for decision.

c. Past and Future Costs

Past costs are actual costs incurred in the past. These costs are mentioned in the financial accounts. Future costs are those costs which are to be incurred in the near future. This is only a forecast. Future costs matter for managerial decisions because, the management can evaluate the desirability of that expenditure. Since the past costs are costs that have already been incurred, there is no scope for managerial decision. If the management finds out that the past costs are excessive, it cannot do anything to rectify it now. In the case of future costs, if the management considers them very high, it can either reduce them or postpone the use of them.

For price policy, it is the future cost than the past cost that is needed. To the extent that costs are relevant at all, it is expectations that govern policy decisions and that should also guide the determination of specific prices. Though the future is uncertain, it is necessary to make explicit forecast of future costs.

d. Short Run and Long Run Costs

Short run costs are those associated with variation in the utilization of fixed plant or other facilities, whereas long run costs encompass changes in the size and kind of plant. Short run cost is relevant when a firm has to decide whether or not to produce more or less with the given plant and equipment. If the firm decides to expand the capacity of the plant, it must examine the long run cost. Long run cost is useful in making investment decisions.

e. Fixed and Variable Costs

There are some inputs which can be readily adjusted to the changes in the level of the output. Thus, a firm can readily employ labour and raw-material inputs without any delay if it wants to expand the output. Thus, labour, raw materials are the inputs which can be readily varied which change the quantity of the output. Such factors are called *variable* factors.

On the other hand, there are factors such as capital equipment, factor buildings, and top management cannot be readily varied, with the change in output. It requires more time to make variations in them. It takes time to expand the factory building. Similarly, it takes more time to manufacture the machinery. These factors are called *fixed* factors.

The distinction between fixed and variable costs is not a watertight one. It is very difficult to decide which is fixed and which is variable at a situation. Again, it may be noted that the variability of costs is in relation to output and not to the time factor though in the long run, all costs tend to be variable. What is fixed at one level of output may vary at another level of output.

In between the fixed and variable costs, there are semi-variable costs which vary but not at the same rate by which production increases or decreases. For example, a salesman may get a monthly salary as well as commission. Monthly salary is treated as fixed while commission is treated as variable cost, for it varies with the output.

The distinction between fixed and variable costs is important in forecasting the effect of short run changes in the volume upon costs and profits.

f. Incremental Cost and Sunk Cost

Incremental costs are the added costs of a change in the level of production or the nature of activity. It may be adding a new product, or changing distribution channel, or adding new machinery, etc. It appears to be similar to marginal cost, but it is not marginal cost. Marginal cost refers to the cost on the added unit of output.

Sunk costs are costs which cannot be altered in any way. Sunk costs are costs which have already been incurred. For example, cost incurred in constructing a factory. When the factory building is constructed, cost has already been incurred. The building has to be used for which originally envisaged. It cannot be altered when operations are increased or decreased. Investment on machinery is an example of sunk scost.

The distinction between the sunk cost and the incremental cost is very important in evaluation the alternatives. Incremental cost will be different in the case of different alternatives. Hence, incremental cost is relevant to the management in decision making. Sunk costs will remain the same irrespective of the alternative selected. The only costs that matter for the decision are the added costs.

g. Traceable and Common Costs (direct and indirect costs)

A traceable or direct cost is that cost which can be easily identified and traced. On the other hand common or indirect costs are those costs which cannot be easily identified and traced to any plant, machinery, department or to any product. For example, the salary of a Divisional Manager (if division is a costing unit) will be a Direct Cost. On the other hand, the salary of General Manager of a firm is an indirect cost or common cost because the General Manager is head of all the divisions.

h. Replacement and Historical Cost

Historical cost is the actual cost incurred at the time of the purchase of machinery while replacement cost is the cost which will have to be incurred if machinery is purchased in place of the old machinery. The two costs differ because of the differences in prices during that period.

For example, a machine purchased in 1985 for Rs.5 lakhs was Rs.7 lakhs in 1990. For this, it may be concluded that replacement cost was higher than historical cost. During the period of substantial price changes, historical cost is a poor indicator of actual cost.

Classification of Cost Distinctions

There are some cost distinctions as variable costs, constant costs, incremental costs, sunk costs and accounting costs. Some other cost restrictions such as opportunity cost, outlay costs, etc. are economic costs. The various cost distinctions are classified as follows:

Dichotomy		Basis of distinction
Opportunity	Outlay Cost	Nature of the sacrifice — Economic Concept
Past Costs	Future Costs	Degree of anticipation — Computation
Short run Costs	Long run Costs	Degree of adaptation of present output
Variable Costs	Constant Costs	Degree of variation with output rate
Increment Costs	Sunk Costs	Relation to added activity
Replacement Costs	Historical Costs	Timing of valuation
Marginal Costs	Incremental Costs	Economic concept

3. COST-OUTPUT RELATIONSHIP

Costs play a key role in determining theoretically optimum level of production. The accepted economic doctrine has been that marginal costs rise continuously as output increases above a given level. The average cost has a U shaped relation to output.

In the cost output relationship analysis, several cost concepts are studied. They are fixed cost, variable cost, total cost and the marginal cost. The cost-output relationship in different periods is very important for various kinds of managerial problems such as expense control, profit prediction, pricing promotion etc. Cost−output relationship can be discussed under two time periods. (1) Short Run (2) Long Run.

Short Run and Long Run: Traditional theory distinguishes between short run and long run. *Short run* is defined as a period in which the firm can vary its output by varying only the amount of variable factors such as labour and raw-materials. In the short run, the quantities of fixed factors like capital equipment, buildings, top management cannot be varied. In other words, in the short run, the firm cannot build a new plant or abandon an old plant. If the firm wants to increase production, it can do so only by increasing labour and raw material inputs. It has to overwork the existing capital equipment. It cannot increase output in the short run by enlarging the size of the existing plant or building a new plant of the large size. Thus, short run is a period of time in which only quantities of the variable factors can be increased while fixed factors remain constant.

Long run is defined as a period in which quantities of all factors can be increased. It means that the firm can increase the quantities of both fixed and variable factors in order to increase the output. In the long run, capital equipment can be increased or the size of which can be changed or a new plant may be set up. In the long run, there are no fixed costs, but all costs are variable.

Short run becomes relevant when a firm has to decide whether or not to produce more in the immediate future. In this case, there is no need for setting up of a new plant. The firm manages with the given plant itself. Long run costs become relevant when the firm has to decide whether to set up a new plant. Long run costs help the businessman in running the best scale of plant or best size of the firm for his purposes.

Cost and Output Relationship in the Short Run (Total Cost Curve): The cost of production may be analysed from another point of view. Some costs vary more or less proportionately with the output while others are fixed and do not vary with the output. The former is called *prime* costs while the latter is called *supplementary* costs. The supplemented fixed costs are incurred even though production has been stopped temporarily. For example, rent of the factory building, interests on capital invested on machinery, salary to the essential staff, etc. The prime costs, on the other hand, are variable costs. Variable costs vary with the output. They are incurred only when the factor is at work. Total cost is obtained by adding total fixed cost and total variable cost.

Thus, TC = TFC + TVC

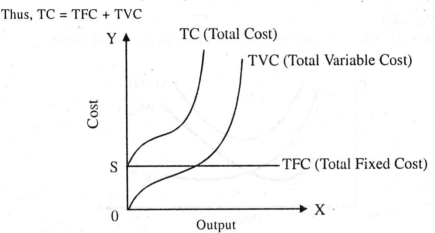

Short run cost curves are shown in the above diagram.

In the diagram output is measured on the x-axis and cost is measured on the y-axis. Since the total fixed cost remains constant whatever the level of output; the total fixed cost curve (TFC) is parallel to x-axis. It will start from y-axis, indicating that TFC will be incurred even if the output is zero.

The total variable cost curve (TVC) rises upward showing thereby, as the output is increased, the TVC curve also rises. TVC starts from the origin which shows that when the output is zero, the TVC is also zero.

Total cost curve (TC) has been obtained by summing up the total fixed cost curve and total variable cost curve because TC indicates total fixed cost and total variable cost. When the output is zero, the total cost is OS (i.e., when the output is zero, total variable cost is also zero). The TC curve starts at the point where TFC curve starts. The shape of the total cost curve (TC) is exactly the same as that of total variable cost curve (TVC) because the same vertical distance always separate the two curves.

Average Total Cost and Marginal Cost: The average total cost or what is called average cost is, total cost divided by the number of units of the product. Average total cost is obtained by adding average fixed cost and average variable cost. This can be proved as follows:

$$ATC = \frac{TC}{Q} \quad \text{Since TC + TVC + TFC}$$

Therefore, $ATC = \dfrac{TVC + TFC}{q}$

$$= \frac{TVC}{q} + \frac{TFC}{q} = AVC + AFC$$

∴ ATC = AVC + AFC

Average cost is also known as *unit cost*, since it is the cost per unit of output.

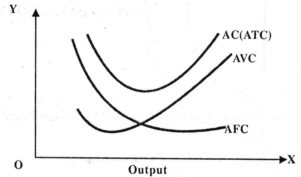

it follows from the above that the behaviour of ATC depends upon the behaviour of AFC and AVC curves. In the beginning, both the AVC and AFC curves fall. Then, the ATC curve also falls sharply in the beginning. When AVC curve begins rising, though AFC curve is falling, the ATC curve begins to rise. Afterwards, ATC rises steeply. Therefore, ATC curve falls first, reaches the minimum and rises afterwards. The ATC curve is thus U shaped. The U shape of both AVC and AFC reflects the law of variable proportions.

Average Fixed Cost and Average Variable Cost: Average fixed cost is the total fixed costs divided by the number of units of output produced. Graphically, total fixed cost is shown by a straight line parallel to OX axis. As output rises, the average fixed cost also decreases. AFC falls steadily as output rises. AFC curve slopes downwards throughout the length. For example, a firm starts with a fixed cost of Rs.50,000. When the output includes 100 units, AFC will be Rs.500. When the output rises to 200 units, the AFC will be Rs.250. When the output rises to 400 units, the AFC will be Rs.125. Since the total fixed cost is a constant quantity, the average fixed cost will steadily fall as otput rises.

Average variable cost is the total variable cost divided by the number of units of output produced. The average variable cost is the variable cost per unit of output. The average variable cost will generally fall as output rises from zero to normal capacity output due to increasing returns. But, beyond the normal capacity output, the average cost will rise steeply because of the operation of diminishing returns.

The average fixed cost and average variable cost curve are shown above.

Marginal Cost: The concept of marginal cost is very important in economic analysis. Marginal cost is the addition to the total cost caused by producing one more unit of the output. In other words, marginal cost is the addition to the total cost of producing n units instead of n-1 units (i.e., one less) where n is any given number. In symbolic language, it is stated as

$$MC_n = TC_n - TC_{n-1}.$$

Suppose the production of 100 units of a product costs Rs.2,000. If the increase in production to 101 units raises the total cost to Rs.2,025, then the marginal cost of 101th unit of output is Rs.25 (2025 – 2000 = 25). Marginal cost is derived from the total costs of two successive units. Marginal cost of any product closely follows the average cost of the product. When the average cost is falling, marginal cost is below it. When the average cost is rising, marginal cost rises above it more sharply than the average variable cost. The average cost and marginal cost curves diagram is shown below.

Marginal cost is independent of the fixed cost. Since fixed cost does not change with output, it then follows the average variable cost. It should be noted that the marginal cost of production is intimately related to the marginal product of the variable factor. Marginal cost varies inversely with the marginal product of the variable factor. The shape of the marginal cost is determined by the law of variable proportion, i.e., the behaviour of the marginal product of the variable factor.

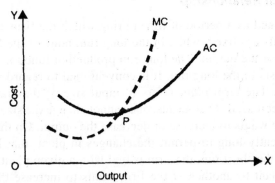

Marginal cost concept, when taken with marginal revenue concept, helps the management in rational decision taking.

Diagrammatic Illustration (Relationship between AC and MC)

The relationship between AC and MC can be explained through the illustration of the following diagram:

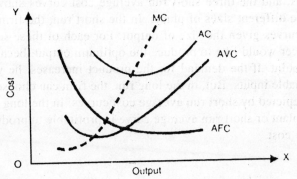

The AFC curve shows the average fixed cost. The total fixed cost is constant for the amount of output, while the average fixed cost falls as output rises. The shape of the AFC is a rectangular hyperbola. The average variable cost curve (AVC) first slopes downwards and then rises slowly as output rises. The ATC curve shows the average total cost. Since ATC is the sum total of average fixed cost and the average variable cost, it is related to downward sloping of ATC and upward rising of the AVC. The MC curve shows that the marginal cost curve intersects both AVC and AC curves at their lowest points. If marginal cost is less than average cost, it pulls average cost down. If MC is greater than AC, it will push up AC. If MC is equal to AC, equilibrium is restored. Therefore, MC will intersect AC at its lowest point.

Relationship between AC & MC can be explained as follows.

- Initially both AC & MC slopes downwards.

- After a certain level of output MC starts rising while AC continues to fall.

- MC intersects AC only at its (AC's) minimum point.

- Before intersection AC was greater than MC, but after intersection MC is greater than AC.

Long–Run Cost Output Relationship

The *long run* is defined as a period of time during which the firm can vary all its inputs. In the short run, some inputs are fixed, while in the long run, none of the factors are fixed. All are varied in order to increase the output. The long run production function has no fixed factors and the firm has no fixed costs in the long run. It is conventional to regard the size or scale of plant as a typical fixed input. The term *plant* refers to input size of the plant which is fixed and it cannot be increased or decreased. That means, one cannot change the size of the capital equipment in the short period if one wants to increase or decrease the output. On the other hand, long run is a period of time sufficiently long to permit the changes in plant, that is, in capital equipment, machinery, land, etc. In the short run, the firm is tied with a given plant, but in the long run, the firm moves from one plant to another. If the firm wants to increase the output, it can make a large plant. The long run cost of production is the least possible cost of combination of producing any given level of output when all inputs are variable including of course the size of the plant.

The *long run* average cost is the long run total cost divided by the level of output. The long run average cost curve depicts the least possible average cost for producing all possible level of output. To derive the long run average cost curve, we have to take three short run average cost curves as shown in the following diagram. The three short run average cost curves are also called *plant* curves, and the three short run average cost curves show three different scales of production or three different sizes of plants. In the short run, the firm is operating on any short run average cost curves given the size of output. For each of these scales, there is an optimum output. The producer would like to produce the optimum output, because his average cost is the least cost at that point. If the demand for the product increases, he wants to produce more by increasing the variable inputs. But, in the long run, the firm can choose among the three possible sizes of plant as depicted by short run average cost curves. In the long run, the firm will examine which size of the plant or short run average curve is profitable to produce the given output at the minimum possible cost.

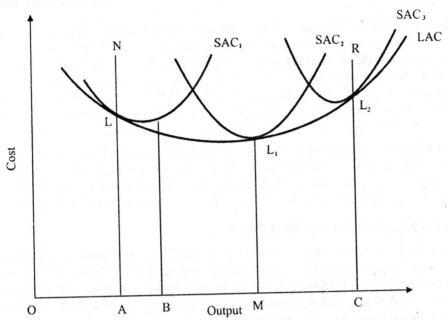

In the above diagram, SAC_1, SAC_2, SAC_3 are short run average cost curves depicting three different plant sizes or scale of production. When the firm is producing under short run average cost curve SAC_1 it produces OB output at lower cost. If it produces OA output, the average cost is AL. If it produces the same output under SAC_2 curve, it costs AN. Since AL is smaller than AN, the firm will produce with SAC_1 curve. Similarly, all other output levels up to OB can be produced with the smaller plant size of SAC_1 rather than SAC_2. In the long run, the firm will be producing OB output in the SAC_1 size of the plant. It will be seen that if more output could be produced in SAC_2, the average cost will be lower than SAC_1. If the output OM is produced, the average cost will be OL_1, which is taken to be the lowest in the SAC_2 plant size. If the firm wants to increase output up to OC, it incurs CR cost which is higher than the cost of SAC_3 size. If it produces OC output, at SAC_3 plant size, the average cost CL_2 is lower than CR on the SAC_3 size. Therefore, for output larger than OM, the firm will employ a plant size corresponding to the short run average cost curve SAC_3. If the tangents of all the short run cost curves are added, a long run average cost is derived. This will be the LAC. It is also U shaped and it will be flatter than the short run average cost curves. The longer the period to which the curve relates, the less pronounced will be the U shape of LAC curve. Economists generally call this curve as envelope since it envelopes all the short run average cost curves. It is also called the *planning curve* of the firm.

The tendency for the long run average cost to fall as the firm expands its scale of operations is a reflection of cost economies available with the increase in size, while the ultimate rise in the long run cost curve is largely due to the setting up of the diseconomies of scale.

It is to be noted that the long run average cost curve (LAC) is not tangent to the minimum points of the short run average cost curves. when the long run average cost curve is declining that is for the output less than OM, it is tangent to the falling portion of the short run average cost curve. This means that if there is any output small than OM, it will not pay to operate the plant at the minimum average cost. If the output is produced at the lowest point of the short run cost curve, it means the average cost is higher in the short run than in the long run. If the firm expands the size to SAC$_2$, then the LAC is tangent to its lowest point.

When the long run average cost is rising, it will be tangent to the rising portion of the short run average cost curve (SAC$_3$). This implies that the output larger than OM is produced more cheaply by constructing a plant with a given optimal capacity and operating it to produce larger than its capacity, i.e., using it to produce at more than its minimum unit cost of production.

Usefulness of Long–Run Average Cost Curve

Long run average cost curve often called *'the planning curve'*. It is because it helps a firm to plan to produce any output by choosing a plant on the long run average cost curve. The long run average cost curve reveals to the firm how large a plant should be for producing a certain output at the least cost. Thus, while making decisions regarding the choice of a plant, the firm has to look at its long run average cost curve enveloping a family of plant curve (short run cost curves). The long run average cost curve thus helps the firm to select the best size of the plant.

Features of LAC Curve

(a) LAC curve is called as an **envelope curve** because it envelopes all the short run average cost curves.

(b) LAC curve is also called as **tangent because** it is drawn by joining the loci of various plant curves relating to different operational short run periods.

(c) LAC curve is also called as **planning curve** of the firm. It indicates the least unit cost of producing each possible level of output.

(d) LAC curve is **flatter U-shaped**. Initially it slopes downwards and then after reaching a certain point, it gradually begins to slope upwards.

(e) LAC curve represents minimum cost combinations for each level of output in the long run.

Long Run Marginal Cost Curve (LMC)

The long run marginal cost curve (LMC) can be derived from the short run marginal cost curve *i.e.*, from SMCs. To derive LMC, the tangency points between SACs and LAC, the tangency points between SACs and LAC shouel be considered, because in the long run production planning there points determine the output levels at the different levels of production.

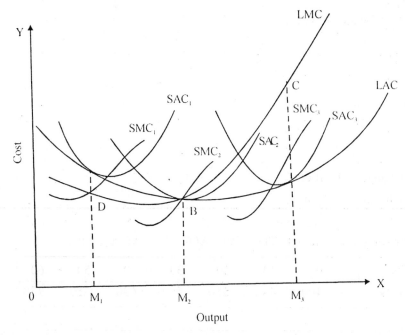

Output

In the diagram output is measured along the x axis and cost is measured along the y axis. When the firm produces OM_1 level of output, LMC is equal to M_1D. If output increase to OM_2 LMC decereases to BM_2. It starts rising if the output is produced beyond OM_2. Similarly CM_3 measures LMC at output OM_3. The LMC curve is also a fiatter U-shape like LAC. It shows the trends in the marginal cost in response to the changes in the scale of productions. The shape of LMC cruve is also a flattu U-shape indicating that initially as output expands in the long run with the increasing scale of production.

The relationship between LML & LAC is as follows:

- When LAC decearses LMC also decereses.
- After a certain level and output LMC tends to rise, through LAC continues to fall.
- When LAC is minimum, LMC intersection LAC and hence LAC = LMC.
- After the intersection both slope upwards and LMC becomes greater than LAC. Till intersection LMC is less than LAC

Cost of Production – Formulae
1. TC = Cost per unit × Total quantity produced
TC = TFC + TVC
2. TFC = TC − TVC or AFC × Q
3. TVC = TC − TFC or AVC × Q or addition of MC
4. $AC = \dfrac{TC}{Q}$ or AFC + AVC

5. $AFC = \dfrac{TFC}{Q}$ or $AC - AVC$

6. $AVC = \dfrac{TVC}{Q}$ or $AC - AFC$

7. $MC = TC_n - TC_{n-1}$ or $\dfrac{\Delta TC}{\Delta TQ}$

where

ΔTC = Change in total cost

ΔTQ = Change in output.

Illustration:

Using the following data calculate TFC, TVC, AFC, AVC, AC and MC.

Output in units	0	10	20	30	40	50	60
Total cost (in Rs.)	400	480	550	590	620	650	730

Solution:

Output	TC	TFC	TVC	AC	AFC	AVC	MC
0	400	400	–	–	–	–	–
10	480	400	80	48.0	40.0	8.0	80
20	550	400	150	27.5	20.0	7.5	70
30	590	400	190	19.6	13.3	6.3	40
40	620	400	220	15.5	10.0	5.5	30
50	650	400	250	13.0	8.0	5.0	30
60	730	400	330	12.2	6.7	5.5	80

4. COST ESTIMATION

There are three methods of estimating cost of production. They are the Statistical method, the Engineering method and the Accounting method.

In the statistical method of cost estimation, statistical techniques are used. The objective is to find a functional relationship between changes in costs and the factors upon which the costs depend such as output, rates, sales quantity, etc. Statistical method has the advantage of isolating fixed cost elements from the total cost.

The Engineering method of cost estimation depends upon the knowledge of physical relationships. Usually, the engineering estimate is built up in terms of physical units, such as man-hours, and quantity of materials.

The Accounting method is based on historical data found in the account books of the firm. Its objective is to find the relationship between output levels and cost for similar cases to that for which the present estimate is needed. In this method, costs are classified into fixed, variable and semi-variable cost. Fixed costs are those which the accounts show to be the same in the monthly total regardless of the output rate. Variable costs are those which are accounts show to vary in direct proportion to the level of output. Semi-variable costs are neither perfectly variable nor absolutely fixed in relation to output. They change in the same direction as volume but not in direct proportion thereto. For example, electricity bills often include both a fixed charge and a charge based on consumption.

The advantage of accounting method is that it is very simple. It must be noted that the future may not be like the past records of the firm. Therefore, this method is used in cost estimation.

Cost Awareness

The long run prosperity of the firm depends upon the ability of the firm to earn sustained profits. The profit depend upon the selling price of the product and the cost of production of the product. Very often, the firm is not in a position to dictate the price of the product to the market. But, it has all the possibility of controlling the cost. The firm is required to aim at doing at the minimum cost. If the firm wants to produce a certain amount of output during a given period, control must be exerted to ensure that the given output is produced at the minimum cost. This aspect of management is called *cost awareness*. Cost awareness by management is a search for a better and efficient way of completing the production of the product. It means bringing down the cost of production as much as possible.

There are two ways of minimising cost:

(1) Reduction in specific expenses. (2) Efficient use of the money spent. Cost control involves keeping the cost down than bringing the cost down. There is more profit in cost control when the business is good than when business is bad.

Cost control helps a firm to improve its profitability and competitiveness. In the absence of control, despite large and increasing business, profits are bound to be reduced. A big sale will not indicate big profit. An increase in sales may create a false sense of prosperity while behind the scene increasing costs will eat up profits. Therefore, cost management is indispensable for stability of a firm.

5. TOOLS OF COST MANAGEMENT

A control of any type depends upon comparing actual performance with some pre-determined criterion. The two criteria which are in use today are: (1) Standard cost and (2) Budgets.

(i) *Standard Costs:* The techniques of standard costing has been developed to establish standards of performance for producing goods and services. These standards serve as a goal for attainment and basis of comparison with actual cost. The standard cost is a pre-determined cost which determines what each product or service should cost under given situations. Standard costing starts with an estimate of what a product ought to cost during a future period, given reasonably efficient working. Once the standard costs have been worked out, then actual costs for the products have to be compared with them. If there is any adverse difference, cost control could be enforced. Standard costing makes it possible to isolate the causes which have contributed to high costs.

Standard cost need not be ideal cost or the best cost under ideal conditions, but a cost could be reached if it were operated efficiently. Standard cost is not rigid but can be revised from time to time.

Standard costs provide a yard stick against what actual costs may be measured. Since standard cost is calculated under efficient operating situations, it is a good yardstick for measuring efficiency. If the standard cost is below the actual cost, there is a need for immediate investigation. Standard costs provide a valuable aid to management in determining pricing policies.

(ii) Budgets: A budget is a pre-determined statement of management policy during a given period which provides a standard for comparison with the results actually achieved. Budgetary Control is a system of controlling costs which includes the preparation of budgets, coordinating the departments and establishing responsibilities and comparing actual performance with the budgeted one.

Estimated cost of future operations is used as standard against which actual costs are compared. Estimated future costs are determined from the past experience. Estimated costs are better than historical costs for it takes into consideration future development. In a business of rapidly changing situations, estimated costs are feasible for cost control purposes. Intangible operations such as research and development, public relations, morale building etc., are not subject to control by any other standard except estimated cost.

Cost control even with budgets and standard cost remains unconvincing because they are not cent per cent accurate. If the standards are set, they have to be adhered strictly. But normally, such adherence is not to be seen anywhere. However, a realistic standard has to be set up and managers must be encouraged to achieve them.

For decision taking purposes, cost information is necessary. If the cost information is given in an arbitary way, then this misleads the managers. Therefore, realistic cost information is to be supplied to the managers to take timely action. (A detailed study follows).

Cost Benefit Analysis

Cost-benefit analysis is a method for assessing the desirability of projects when it is necessary to take both a long and a wide view of the repercussions of a particular programme expenditure or policy change. Cost benefit analysis is being used in government undertakings in order to study the economic consequence of a product. It seeks to measure all economic imports of the project, direct as well as the side effects.

As in the case of collective goods like defence, public health measures, educational facilities, it is not possible to use market price to evaluate their benefits. These are not quantifiable and hence cannot be valued in any market sense.

Cost Effectiveness

It is not possible to apply cost benefit analysis in those governmental activities like defence, environmental protection, income distribution, etc. Cost effectiveness analysis may be used as an alternative strategy. Cost benefit analysis ask the question: What is the money value of programme costs and benefits and do the benefits exceed the costs to justify undertaking the programme? Cost effectiveness asks the question: Given that some prespecified objective is to be reached, what are the costs of various alternative means for reaching that objective?

Cost effectiveness analysis is similar to cost benefit analysis. But the former is used in defence programmes while the latter is used in the civilian sector.

There are many programmes where the output is abstract and hence difficult to evaluate in money terms. One such programme is pollution control. It is not difficult to measure the pollutions being emitted in but factories and by motor vehicles, but it is difficult to evaluate the social benefit derivable from various levels of discharge reduction.

In evaluating the programme, the most important task to do is to find out whether the goal has been achieved. If the goal is achieved from the cost incurred for running the project, then it is considered to be beneficial.

While selecting projects for investments out of a number of technically feasible alternatives, the most important consideration is to weigh their costs and benefits and to select those which maximise the differences between costs and benefits. The costs include capital cost, cost of raw-material, rent, salaries, wages, etc. and benefits refer to returns obtained from the sale proceeds of the output. The aim is to maximise the present value of all benefits less that of all costs.

The purpose of cost-benefit analysis is to indicate whether a particular industrial project is worth starting. If there are alternative projects for investment, a correct choice is to be made for this purpose. The cost benefit analysis is thus useful.

The alternative projects differ in type and also require a number of labourers, raw-materials and their quantity and capital equipment, the period required for completion and also the resultant revenue from such investments. The differences affect costs and benefits of these projects. A selection of a project requires valuation of costs and benefits.

The general principles of cost benefit analysis involve the following issues. They are:

(i)   What costs and benefits are to be considered?

(ii) The ways of evaluating the costs benefits of the projects.

(iii) The rate of interest to be charged for the gestation period.

(iv) The constraints that are to be faced.

In this connection, it is necessary to distinguish between social costs - social returns and private costs-private returns. *Social cost* means the opportunity cost. Social costs and benefits are different from accounting costs and returns. '*The costs and the benefits of a project are the time streams of consumption foregone and provided by that project.*' It is necessary to find out the opportunity cost of various alternative investment opportunities when benefits of a project are reinvested. Some of the funds used for the project would otherwise have been invested or it has been rendered impossible to invest these funds in some other mutually exclusive investment projects, because the cost has been used here in the sense of opportunity cost.

Costs and Benefits

In this cost-benefit analysis, generally direct and supplementary costs and benefits are to be considered. When an investment is made, there will be production of a commodity and the investing firm gets the revenue. Apart from it, society also derives benefit. For example, when an investment is made on road building, apart from the total tax revenue the organisation gets; which is the primary benefit, others like road side restaurants, gas refuelling stations generate individual incomes. These are *secondary* benefits. The total benefit is to be imputed. The benefit which causes in the form of changes in land value and rents to land-lords also count in the calculation of benefit.

Valuation of Costs and Benefits

In the valuation of costs and benefits, if they are expressed in money terms, we have to make adjustments to the expected prices of future inputs and outputs in order to make allowance for the anticipated changes in the relative prices of the concerned items, but not for the expected in the general price level. The expected change in the level of output are also to be noted. Some corrections will be needed for the distortion resulting from the market imperfetions.

Social costs of materials, machinery and equipment should be calculated like labour. In the case of a material like sand, stones, the only social cost of labour is the use of labour for collecting and digging etc. In the case of imported machinery, social cost is higher than the private accounting cost.

Rate of Discount

There is the question of ascertaining the present value of the future costs and benefits. This is called *discounting* process. The rate of discount is very important, because a higher rate may completely switch investment priorities. Baumol has preferred the opportunity cost criterion for estimating social discount rate. This approach is based on the fact that resources invested in one sector might be withdrawn from that sector and invested elsewhere, which yields a higher return. For example, if the resource can earn 10 per cent in one sector, it should not be transferred to another sector unless it earns more than 10 per cent.

6. RELEVANT CONSTRAINTS

The constraints are classified as physical, legal, distributional and budgetary constraints. The most common physical constraint is the production function which relates to physical inputs and outputs of a project. This directly enters into the calculation of cost and benefits. If the supply of one input is inelastic, regulated pricing is to be made. There are administrative and distributional constraints such as constraints in the income distribution, etc. It is not possible to make the gainers compensates the losers. The budgetary constraint is that the project should be completed within the budget allotment.

The main purpose of the cost-benefit analysis is to select the project for investment or lay down the investment criteria. Where no projects are inter-dependent or mutually exclusive and where there are no constraints, the project which maximise the present value of total benefits less total costs are to be selected.

In those projects where the present value of the benefits exceed the present value of costs, they are supposed to be good projects. Further, in those projects where the rate of return exceeds the chosen rate of discount, they are considered to be good.

7. COST CONTROL

The business organisations aim at producing the product at the minimum cost. This is necessary in order to achieve the goal of profit maximisation. The success of financial management is judged by the action of the executive in controlling cost. Modern business is not only highly complex but also competitive. The business organisations are incurring a large number of costs, all of which go to the production cost. If the cost of production is increasing, the firm has to sell the product at a higher price. It is then that the competitive capacity of the firm comes into existence. If the firm fails to take note of cost control, its very survival is threatened.

What is Cost Control?

Cost Control is referred to as a programme, but it is not something that the executive sets out to achieve apart from his other activities. In fact, it is a programme of effective management. Cost control does not mean mechanical cost reduction. It means better management of material purchases, effective organisation of factors of production, etc. Cost control aims at keeping the cost of production at a manageable limit.

Cost control is defined as the regulation by the executive action of the costs operating in an undertaking. Cost control means a search for better and more economical ways of completing each operation. In other words, it is a device of reduction in a percentage of costs and in turn increase in the percentage of profits. By controlling costs, the competitive strength of the firm increases. It also means how a firm is making the best use of every rupee spent in producing a commodity. If the costs are unmanagable, the profits of the firm decline and in course of time, it is called an *inefficient* firm.

Cost control is a function of better management. What it means is the better operation of the units. By so doing, unnecessary costs are avoided and the unit is run under optimum level. Thus, cost control is an integral part of the operations of the firm.

Difference between Cost Control and Cost Reduction

Cost control does not mean cost reduction. It is cost management. Cost reduction refers to bringing down the cost of production. In a competitive situation, bringing down the price poses severe problems. If the price goes below the average cost, the firm is sure to incur loss. Therefore, in order to maximise profit, certain costs will have to be lowered. Cost reduction is possible only when the firm makes the optimum utilisation of resources. It is again possible by incorporating internal and external economies. That means by economising the cost of manufacture, adminsitration, selling and distribution, average cost reduction may be achieved. It is in this respect, that cost reduction holds good. Thus, cost reduction is stated as the real and permanent reduction in unit costs of goods manufactured or services rendered without impairing their suitability for the intended use.

Cost control is not cost reduction. It is an efficient tool of management. Cost control and cost reduction aim at the same thing, though an application, their scope is diferent. Cost control aims at achieving the target of sales. While costs reduction aims at bringing down the average costs, cost control involves setting the standards. The firm is expected to adhere to the standards. Any deviation from the established standards is not preferred. While cost reduction has nothing to do with standards, cost control makes an emphasis on past and present. While cost reduction considers the present and future only, cost control are applied to things which have standards. Cost reduction is applied to all departments of business. Cost control is a preventive function while cost reduction is a corrective function.

Aspects of Cost Control

Cost controls is exercised through many techniques such as Standard Costing, Budgetary Control, Inventory Control, Quality Control, Performance Evaluation etc. Cost control has to be brought in the following manner:

(a) Initially, a plan of action in the form of determining production targets, upholding the quality of the produce, etc.

(b) The plan of action is to be communicated to concerned persons.

(c) After the plans is into action, the evaluation of performance has to be undertaken. It is here that costs are compared at different levels of production.

(d) Comparison has to be made with the predetermined targets and actual performance. Deficiencies are noted and discussion is started to overcome deficiencies.

(e) Corrective action and remedial measures are followed and the goal is realised.

Effective cost control is possible only when it is exercised by the executive who spend money on resources like material and labour. Since it is a management action, it should be borne in mind what exactly is cost control. It means keeping the costs down rather than bringing the costs downwards. This aspect of cost control has been earlier mentioned in the book. It is further stated that the amount of effort put into cost control tends to increase when the business is bad and decrease when the business is good. There is more profit in cost control when business is good. Therefore, the management must be alert as regards expenditure when the business is good.

Advantages of Cost Control

Cost control has several advantages:

(a) It improves the performance of the firm by means of getting good profit and ensuring competitiveness.

(b) In the absence of cost control, even though the firm is increasing the sales, the profitability may be drastically reduced.

(c) Cost control is indispensable in achieving great productivity.

(d) Cost control enables the firm to restrain cost escalation and maintain the price of its product stable and reasonable.

(e) If the price of the product is stable and reasonable, it can maintain higher sales and thus the employment of work force.

8. TECHNIQUES OF COST CONTROL

There are two distinct but inter-related techniques of cost control. They are: (1) Budgetary Control and (2) Standard Costing.

1. Budgetary Control

A *budget* is defined as a financial statement prepared to achieve an objective of cost control. It is a comprehensive statement which includes separate statements for different work centres of a firm. A budget is both a device for planning and coordination as well as for control. Budget control is a system which uses budgets as a means of planning and controlling. It involves constant evaluation of results with the original budget objectives.

Budget control involves planning, coordination and control. Planning is a device in which future action is very well defined. In planning, details are given as regarding production schedules, material requirement, labour force requirement, inventory management, and sales targets. Then comes coordination of all executive action. It is concerned with establishing coordination between production department, materials department and sales department. This coordination is done through budget control. Thirdly, there is an operational performance which controls action, is resorted to ensure that objectives are achieved. Budgetary control makes the control effetive by comparing actual performance with that of budgetary goods and the gap is filled up by suitable adminsitrative action.

Advantages of Budgetary Control: Budgetary control provides a norm in which actual performance can be compared with the budgetary details. It provides a clean enunciation of objectives and policies and with the help of budget control, these policies are scrutinised. It provides for sufficient funds for the execution of activities. Budget control enables the management to safeguard the finances of the company by means of effective utilisation of allotted funds. Since budget represents the company's overall functions, it helps in promoting coordination between different departments. Budget control directs the spending departments to be accountable for every rupee spent. Since detailed expenditure items are given in the budget, the persons responsible for expenditure are given greater responsibility which in turn helps them to work efficiently. Budget control indirectly performs the function of internal audit and thereby ensures continuous appraisal of performances.

Essentials of Budgetary Control: The traditional accounting system gives a picture of expenditure made in the past. Under the system of budget control, the accounting system is required to peep into the future also. That is why the system of budget is adopted. The budget is a plan for the future and as such it is a base for cost control in the long run. The management may take up several cost reduction measures, in the course of day to day functioning, but without budgetary control, there can be no long range processes. It is now felt that though budgetary controls require time and money, it is effective in bringing about cost improvement.

In order to get the best results from budgetary control, it is necessary that there must be cooperation among the top executives of the firm. It is equally necessary that highly placed executives should prepare the budget estimates. As far as possible, any deviation from the budget is minimum and resorted only when there is the sign of unfavourable performance. It is very important that periodic reports should be prepared to compare the actual performance with the targets.

2. Fixed and Flexible Budgets

Cost budgets form the kingpin of the expected level of economic activity of any company. Other budgets are prepared on the basis of (1) selling and distribution costs, detailed and planned marketing personnel, advertising and transport costs, (2) administration costs, personnel department costs, accounting department costs, (3) production costs which include material costs, labour costs and factory overhead costs.

Cost budget also indicates detailed expenditures on plant and machinery. All these budgets influence the company's cash position and to trace out these efforts, a cash budget may also be prepared for the whole organisation.

All major departments are required to prepare their budgets and these are aggregated to the Company's Master Budget.

A budget may be flexible or fixed. A fixed budget is prepared for a specific output level and it has no concern with the changes in the level of activity of the firm. Fixed budgets are called *short period* budgets in which there is no possibility of change in the output pattern.

A Flexible budgets are also called *variable* budgets. In the flexible budget, provision is made for change in the production level of the firm. Flexible budget is adaptable to change in operating conditions. It provides a flexible standard of comparing the costs of an actual volume of activity with the cost that should be or should have been. The variance can then be analysed and necessary action taken in the matter. Flexible budget is thus more realistic and useful.

Flexible budgets are necessary to have an effective cost control. It is possible to compare the performance of a manager about his actual achievement with that of anticipated achievement. In a system of flexible budgets, a series of fixed budgets are prepared for each manufacturing budget centre, so that within limits, whatever the level of output achieved, it is possible to compare the achievement with an appropriate budget. In the flexible budget, all items of anticipated expenditure are classified into fixed, variable and semi-variable groups. In the fixed cost group, costs remain the same for all levels of activity. In the variable and semi-variable group, the costs vary. Let us take an example.

XYZ Biscuit Company

	Standard Hours of Direct Labour		
	25,000 Rs.	30,000 Rs.	35,000 Rs.
Labour Cost at Rs.5 per hour	1,25,000	1,50,000	1,65,000
Other variable cost	25,000	30,000	35,000
Semi-variable costs	10,000	12,250	13,000
Fixed cost	1,00,000	1,00,000	1,00,000
	2,60,000	2,92,250	3,13,000

In the above table, there are three budgets, one each for 25,000; 30,000 and 35,000 standard hours of work. In practice, there might be many cost items in the budget.

Limitations: In the budgets, the future expenditure is shown and as such there remains a certain amount of uncertainty regarding reality. In the budget estimates generally, accuracy is not possible beause there is no guarantee that material prices remain constant throughout the period of the budget.

Whenever there are changes, the budgetary programme also is to be changed to fit into changed circumstances. It takes a long time to develop a reasonably good system of budgetary control.

Its success depends upon operational efficiency. The executives must be trained suitably to use the budgetary tools effectively. Further, budgeting also to be reviewed as a tool of management. Its effectiveness depends largely on the dedication and coordination of top management.

Performance Budgeting: To make budgetary control effective and realistic, its dimension is extended. One such dimension is *performance budgeting*. In the performance budget, each item of expenditure is related to a specific performance. Each executive in charge of an expenditure is required to be responsible for effectiveness of an expenditure. The conventional budget is not effective because the concerned department does not like expenditure with performance. The performance aspect is side-tracked in all government or public sector industries department. It is therefore necessary to have performance budgeting. To make performance budgeting successful, it is neessary to establish a programme of target performance for each centre. It should be followed by the evaluation of performance.

Zero Base Budgeting: The USA was the first country to introduce Zero Base budgeting in 1969. In the conventional budget, the previous years figures are extrapolated to become the basis of next year's budget. In zero-base budgeting, it is assumed that the budget for the next year is zero and starts the demand for the project. The burden of execution shifts on each manager and he has to justify the demand for money. Such an analysis indicates which activities are important and which are not important. Unimportant activities are eliminated or made productive and profitable. Thus, zero base budgeting helps in choosing those activities which are essential and important.

In the case of manufacturing industries, costs cannot be zero and as such the executives in charge of production are asked to state the basic requirements of their departments, while over and above that, the requirements are reviewed and justified. However, zero based budgeting may be adopted in areas where discretionary costs are incurred such as marketing and administration.

3. Standard Costing

Standard Costing is defined as the preparation and use of standard costs, their comparison with actual costs, and the measurement and analysis of variances to their causes and points of incidence. Standard costs are the costs that should be obtained under efficient operations. They are pre-determined costs and represent targets that are considered important for cost control. Standard costing starts with an estimate of what a product ought to cost during a future period given reasonable efficiency. Standard costs are established by bringing together information collected from various sources within the company. For example, material costs are compiled from the product specifications indicating quantities of materials used in producing a given unit of commodity.

In the standard costing, the first requisite is to establish standard of performance for producing goods and services. For example, the actual cost of producing a commodity is Rs.180 while the standard material input of a unit of the commodity is Rs.200, then the variance of Rs.20 measures the performance. This shows that actual performance is better than standard performance. This comparison of actual costs with standard cost will help in fixing responsibility for non-standard performance and will focus attention on areas in which cost improvement should be sought by showing the source of loss and inefficiency.

Advantages of Standard Costing

(i) Standard costing will help in establishing a yard stick with which the efficiency of performance is measured that helps to exercise control.

(ii) It suggests how the goal is to be achieved by providing incentives and motivation.

(iii) Standard costs provide the management the basic information to fix the selling price, transfer pricing, etc.

(iv) It helps in fixing responsibility and suggests delegation of authority.

(v) It provides means for cost reduction. It helps in achieving optimum utilization of plant capacity.

Limitations: Even though this method confirms several benefits, there are difficulties in formulating standard costs and apply it in practice.

Secondly standards many a times becomes rigid, outdated, loose, inaccurate and unrealisable and as such they become unhelpful in application.

Thirdly, if standards set are higher than reasonable, they act as discouraging factors.

Fourthly, when there are random factors, it is difficult to explain variance properly. However, for cost control, the authorities must concentrate on significant variances from the standard. If effective action is to be taken, the case and responsibility of a variance, as well as its amount must be established.

Basis of Setting Standards Costs: The standard costs are to be established by collecting all information pertaining to material cost, labour cost, production cost, overhead cost and so on. The main basis of setting standard costs are technical and engineering aspects. A major issue in standard costing is the determination of tightness of standards, which may range from a desire for engineering perfection to very slack practices. The other basis of setting standards are: (1) time of use, (2) performance level, (3) price level and (4) output level.

Normal Standards: The *normal standards* represent the maximum level of efficiency i.e., using minimum resources to complete the goal without any loss of time. Since the objective of setting standards is to motivate individuals towards achievement, it is very difficult to use ideal standards. Hence, a certain amount of waste is permitted and the ideal standard is so modified that it may be possible for application.

Basic Standards: Basic standards are those standards which are at their initial level. Since the basic standards emphasise the past instead of the future, its effectiveness is very little in situations of change in production methods, range of products and prices.

However, it is necessary to arrive at a standard cost taking into consideration material costs, labour costs, other production costs and overhead costs. After preparing the standard costs for the products, actual costs can be obtained from the finance department and comparison can be made. Adverse difference or variances arise due to (a) excess use of material, (b) higher material prices, (c) lower labour efficiency, (d) greater expenditure on overhead items, etc., and in such cases reappriasal of standard costs has to be made. It should be noted that deviation should not go beyond tolerance limits. The standard must not be very tight and at the same time it should not be very loose. Therefore, it is necessary to establish currently attainable standard costs. Standard costing helps to isolate the causes which have contributed to higher costs and identifies the person responsible for such a thing.

Variance Analysis

There are four broad kinds of variance, namely,

    (i) Material cost variance,

    (ii) Labour cost variance,

    (iii) Sales variance and

    (iv) Overhead variance.

Material cost variance is the difference between the standard cost of materials and actual cost of materials. Material cost variance arises due to change in prices of the materials used in the production of a commodity. Material cost variance may arise due to price changes, usage of materials and mixing of materials and finally the yield.

Labour cost variance is the difference between standard wages and actual wages paid. If the wages rise, variation rises. There is also labour efficiency variance due to the operating efficiency of labour.

Sales variance is the difference between specified standard cost of sales and actual sales cost. In the same way, as that of material variance, sales variable arises due to sales mix, quantity of the product sold and price variance.

Overhead variance is the difference between the standard cost of overhead absorbed and the actual overhead cost. If the overhead expenditure rises, efficiency changes and variations arise.

Illustration

Standard Price	Material A	Rs.5 per kg
	Material B	Rs.10 per kg

Standard mix   A - 75%

B - 25%

Standard yield weight of the final product to the weight of the materials used, 80%

Actual usage	5000 kg of A costing Rs.25,000
	2500 kg of B costing Rs.25,000

Actual output   7200 kg of product

Budgeted output   8000 kg

Solution

Standard yeild   6000 kg of final product

Standard Mix   A = 75% of 7500 kg

= 5625 kg at Rs.5 =   Rs.28125

B = 7500 ÷ 25%

= 1875 kg at Rs.10 = Rs.18750

Rs.46875

Less loss   20% of 7500 kg

1500 kg

Standard output   6000 kg

Standard cost for actual output

$$\frac{7200kg \times Rs.468751}{6000kg} = Rs.56250$$

Actual cost

A 5000 kg at Rs.5

= 25000

B 2500 kg at Rs.10

= 25000

A + B = Rs.50000

Less: Loss

7500 kg

$$\frac{300}{7200} = 5000 \ Rs.50000$$

Variance Analysis

(a) Material variance = Actual cost – Standard cost

   50000 – 56250 = 6250 (Favourable variance)

(b) Price variance

   Material A 25000 – 23800 = 1200 (Unfavourable variance)

   Material B 25000 – 26000 = 1000 (Favourable variance)

(c) Mix variance

   Material A 28125 – 23800 = 4325 (Favourable variance)

   Material B 25270 – 26000 = 7250 (Unfavourable variance)

(d) Yield variance: $\dfrac{\text{Rs.}46875}{6000\text{kg}} \times 7200\text{kg} - 6000\text{kg} = 9375$ Favourable variance.

Ratio Analysis

Ratio analysis is used to exercise cost control. Ratio is a statistical yard stick which measures the relationship between two figures. The ratios may be expressed as a rate i.e. costs per unit of sales as a per cent (cost of sales as a percentage of sales or as a quotient, sales as a certain number of time the inventory). Since the use of absolute figures mislead, ratios are used commonly in the operation analysis.

Ratio can be used for comparing the performance of the firm over time. In the ratio analysis, an acceptable ratio is determined first and then it is compared with actual performance and then corrective measures can be resorted to. The most significant aspect in this analysis is that the management can take a greater interest in relative as opposed to absolute figures. Ratio analysis is mainly used as an external standard i.e., for comparing performance with the other organisations in the industry.

Ratio analysis is used as an instrument of cost control. It is used in two ways:

   (i) Ratios can be used to compare the performance of a business firm between two periods. Such a comparison helps it to identify areas which require its immediate attention.

   (ii) Then standard ratios are used to compare actual ratios. Standard ratios are average of the results achieved by several firms in the same line of business.

With the help of these comparisons, the management can analyse the causes for differences and then take necessary action to control increase in costs. Some of the commonly used ratios are:

   (i) Net profit and sales,

   (ii) Gross profit and sales,

   (iii) Net profit and sales,

   (iv) Sales and total assets,

   (v) Production costs and of sales,

   (vi) Selling costs and cost of sales,

   (vii) Administration costs and cost of sales,

(viii) Sales and inventory or inventory turnover,

(ix) Material costs and production costs,

(x) Labour costs and production costs,

(xi) Overheads and production costs.

Some Other Techniques of Cost Control

There are two other tools used in control. They are *value analysis* and *method study*.

Value Analysis: Value analysis is a technique which studies cost in relation to product design. Normally, a study of a utility of the machine or an equipment is made before making its purchase. This study would reveal whether the machine or the material would serve the purpose for which it is purchased. Either, there are other designs available at lower costs or is it possible to obtain an alternative at lesser cost. Can scrap be used by changing the design or the type of raw materials or is there any product design which is cheaper, or is there any less expensive process design? Thus, value analysis helps the management to establish the appropirate costs and determine the alternatives which are effective in performance.

The objectives of value analysis are to identify the areas of alternative processes of production design of the product, which is available at reduced costs. It is a process of reducing costs of production without sacrificing the required standard of performance. The emphasis is on the identification of the required function and then on the way in which the function is performed at lower cost.

Value analysis is closely related to value engineering. It is very useful in industries where production is done on a large scale and in such cases even a fraction of savings in cost would help the firm significantly. Some of the areas where savings are gained through value analysis are:

(i) Discarding tailored products where standard components can do.

(ii) Dispensing of facilities not required by customer.

(iii) Use of newly developed materials in place of traditional meterials.

(iv) To examine the use of alternatives which are available at a lower price, for example, plastic cabinets as against wooden cabinets in the case of TVs, radios, etc. In the same way, decision can be taken on effective alternatives easily available at reduced prices.

Method Study: It is systematic study of work data and critical evaluation of the existing and proposed ways of undertaking the work. This technique is known as *work study* and organisation method.

Work study helps to investigate all factors which enable the management to get the work done efficiently and economically. The primary object of work study is to analyse all factors which effect the performance of a task, to develop and install work methods which make optimum use of human and material resources available and to establish suitable standards by which the performance of the work can be measured.

Method study is the creative aspect of work study. It suggests improved methods of doing existing jobs or efficient methods of doing new jobs in order to achieve the optimum use of human and material resurces. It also involves standardisation through which cost reduction of capital equipments can be brought about.

Area of Cost Control

Cost control can be affected in the following main areas:

(i) Materials, (2) Labour, (3) Overheads, (4) Sales

Materials: There are many ways of reducing material costs. If purchasing of materials is done properly, the firm can get various types of discounts. As such, the sources where materials are available will have to be identified. Along with that, the cost of freight also has to be examined. For example, iron ore may be available at cheaper prices in some placed but to transport coal and other materials, costs much. Consequently, the advantage of lower iron prices is not available to the firm. While buying the product, it is necessary to examine carefully whether there are any alternatives to the product. It is very necessary to have a suitable product design so that the firm can derive the benefit of reduction in material usage. It is indispensable to concentrate on items where saving potential is the highet.

At the same time, alternative processes of production have to be examined, namely, whether it is advantageous to buy a component or to produce it in one's own factory. In many cases, buying the components from outside is cheaper than producing in one's own factory. Suppliers deliver them at low cost. Many automobile firms purchase components from outside.

Better utilisation of materials will result in preventing wastes. The use of standard parts and components and utilisation of waste and by products may lead to a significant reduction in costs.

There are many areas in which materials costs can be reduce. They are inventory management, improved prodution planning, elimination of slow-moving stock and the improved flow of parts and materials.

Labour: Labour costs also contribute to high reduction costs. Reducing wages in any factory is not a solution to reduce labour costs. It is only through proper utilisation of labour that saving in this field can be achieved. It is by increasing labour productivity, improving the working conditions and by means of proper training, that production of optimum output becomes possible. Labour productivity is a function of motivation, working conditions and coordination. Therefore, the firm should have a benevolent labour policy. A proper recruitment and training policy, incentive and penalty system, reducing absenteeism and coordination among different sections of the firm, improved methods of production, proper scheduling of work and materials and efforts to boost labour morale will go towards increasing labour productivity.

Overheads: Overhead costs are fixed costs which are incurred at the commencement of production. Factory overheads may be better utilised by the proper selection of equipment and effective utilisation of space and equipment. Proper maintenance of equipments will reduce costs to a considerable extent. Lighting costs can be reduced by flourescent lighting. Faulty designs result in excessive use of power and materials. It is stated that in India, there is no economy in the use of power. It is also stated that fuel wastage in the Indian industry is as high as 25 per cent. This can be redued by means of effective planning and implementation. Transport costs may be reduced by means of better utilisation of time and space. Proper training of sales personnel and by good designing of sales programme, extra selling costs can be reduced. There is enormous wastage in advertisements too. There is considerable scope in reducing the wastages in advertisements. There are strategic ways of reducing wasteful expenditure which should be considered.

Sales: Sales is another area which needs monitoring of costs. In appointing sales personnel, only persons talented in sales are to be recruited and suitable training is to be given in effective selling of goods and services. Sales costs can be controlled by rearranging market segments on the basis of demand. Advertising also has to be done accordingly. Sales campaign must be planned properly and thereby wastage in advertisement can be brought down.

All these are areas where there is plenty of scope for the reduction in costs.

Cost Reduction in Practice

Cost reduction is more practical than theoretical. It is purely a management function. The most important thing to remember is to see that the output is produced according to its full production capacity. If the production capacity is under-utilised, then the cost per unit is bound to be high. There are many ways in which cost reduction can be accomplished. Cost reduction is a continuous process extending to all departments of a company. Every responsible executive must take up this matter seriously. Cost reduction requires cooperation of all spending departments. With better office automation, administrative expenses can be controlled.

The most important aspect in cost reduction is that the top management must be sincere in cost reduction programme. If the expenditure on directors is not controlled and any attempt to control costs at the lower levels fails, the very objective of cost control gets defeated. Therefore, every individual from the managing director to supervisor and to the labourer should recognise the need for cost reduction. There is a need for a committee to suggest cost reduction in areas where it is possible. The committee also should examine the practical difficulties in executing this assignment. Cost reduction does not mean stoppage of any activity, but it is better management of the activity. Cost reduction does not mean mere money cost reduction but also the reduction in real costs.

A programme of cost reduction should consist of the following:

(i) Cost centres must be identified and grouped department wise.

(ii) All the cost centres must be subject to the scheme of value analysis and they must see whether the performance is of optimum efficiency.

(iii) Suitable corrective measures and techniques are to be followed.

(iv) Employees should be convinced about the need for cost reduction.

(v) It should be a continuous programme in which the management should have sustained interest.

Factors Inhibiting Cost Control Programme

Cost control programme is not seriously viewed in India, especially in government departments and public sector industries. Costs of raw materials and other intermediate products are very high. Transport costs also are very high. When the public sector enterprises producing goods and services are incurring losses, the losses are covered by increasing their prices. As a consequence, cost of raw materials, steel and other intermediate goods rise higher than international prices. Though overheads have been provided fully, due to under-utilisation of production capacity, overhead costs per unit of output are very high. Huge working capital is locked up in inventories and as a result of this, cost reduction has become an utopia in India.

Indian Industries want to live in protected markets. They, to a certain extent, hesitate to face competition from other countries. They are not cost-conscious. With the promulgation of the new economic policy, namely liberalisation and free competition, the Indian industries are now strategically working towards paying great attention to cost consciousness.

Cost of Multiple products

For a single - product firm, it is easy to determine the cost of production per unit. But for a multi-product firm, the problems that arise become difficult to deal with for instance, if a firm produces three commodities X, Y and Z, then the cost of raw materials and cost of labour employed on each of these products can be easily calculated. This is the variable cost. But the total cost of production includes not only variable costs, but also fixed costs. For example the electricity bill for a big firm producing three different kinds of products cannot be easily distributed. When a decision has been taken by the management, the conventional full costs are of no relevance because the fixed costs may have been distributed arbitrarily.

Some costs are traceable to individual products while other costs are common to several products, for example, the cost of a factor building is common to all the products produced by the firm. The problem of product costing arises in identifying parts of common costs with particular products.

Joint Products and Alternative Products

When an increase in the output of one product leads to an increase in the products, they are called joint products. In principle, two joint cost situations can be distinguished. First, when the proportions of the end product can be altered; second, when these proportions are fixed. The case of fixed proportions, presumably, cannot exist in the long-run, due to changes in technology etc. Even in the short run, it may be assumed that in all cases of joint products, it is possible to vary the proportions in some degree so that there is no instance of the absolutely invariable proportion of end products.

For joint products of both fixed and variable proportion, cost problems relate more commonly to the incremental effect of an increase in output levels, in order to meet new demands for one of the joint products. Such an increase results in higher output of all the products and may therefore cause a reduction in prices of joint products in order to get rid of them. Thus, the added revenue from one joint product must cover not only the marginal cost of the whole products package, but also loss of revenue resulting from lowered prices of the other joint products as well.

When an increase in the output of one product is accompanied by a reduction in the output of other products, it is a case of what may be called alternative products. The existence of alternative products is generally the direct result of incomplete adaption. The cost of an alternative product can always be computed in turns of the foregone profits from the other product. This is nothing but opportunity cost. So, for decision making, opportunity cost analysis is useful in respect of laternative products.

Cost and Profit Forecasting

Profit forecasting forms the basics for planning cash and capital expenditures, pricing policy etc.

Three approaches to profit forecasting may be distinguished:

(i) Spot projections,

(ii) Break even analysis

(iii) Environmental analysis

These aspects are discussed elsewhere in this book.

9. COST FUNCTION

The theory of production consists of vital elements like optimiation of resource, equilibrium of firm, costs, revenue, economics in production (both internal and external) etc. All these concepts are examined to take a sound production decision. A firm irrespective of size lays emphasis on good return on investment to enhance the value of capital employed in the long-run and pay regularly the reward to owners of the firm in the form of profit. If an unsound production decision is taken, the operation of the firm will be affected and the two objectives of the firm - steady growth of profit and wealth will not be fulfilled.

Normally, the production takes place in accordance with the market demand. The demand for new goods or services is also created by aggressive sales promotion activities. Producers develop consumer awareness for the new product through different channels of promotion. The producers have to focus on two aspects of demand to maximise profit and to maximise wealth. First one is to maintain and expand demand for the product or service for which the brand is already created and secondly to promote the new product and create a brand image for it. In both the cases, the firm cannot ignore the two vital aspects of profit earning namely cost of production and revenue earning. It is understood that a "firm will be at equilibrium when MC = MR in short-run and when AC = AR in the long run".

It is also understood that total revenue (TR) will be maximum when marginal revenue (MR) is zero. This is one aspect of profit maximisation. Similarly cost of production also plays a vital role in profit maximistion. Hence cost function is a major aspect of production function and requires detailed analysis of this function. Cost reduction and resource optimisation are the two vital aspect of profit maximisation. The 'Cost' concept we analyse here is called 'Private Cost' or 'cost of production'. 'Social Cost' which is incurred by firms to discharge the social responsibility of business is not relevant in the theory of production.

As said so far, cost function is the key factor in production function. Number of cost concepts of different nature have been evolved in prodution process. The concepts like 'fixed cost', 'variable cost', 'opportunity cost', 'sunk cost', 'money cost' etc have been evolved ever since the production function took place. These cost functions are the derivatives of production function. The cost function and its elements are changing from time to time and new cost concepts have emerged in the theory of firm and production process. Therefore, for clear understanding of cost concepts and their involvement in production process some opinions otherwise called theories are evolved.

For better understanding of these theories we should know the concept of 'cost function'.

> *Cost function is a term used to show the relationship between product and costs.*

Cost function is governed by two elements (i) production function and (ii) price of factor service used in production process. Cost function, when presented in the form of diagram is also called 'cost curve'.

10. COST THEORIES

Cost theories viz., (i) Traditional theory and (ii) Modern theories are evolved considering the movement of cost or behaviour of different costs in different points of time. Therefore 'time' element plays a vital role in the theory of cost. The cost theories show the shapes of the cost curves at different points of time. Time element has four stages such as:

(i) Market period/Very Short period

(ii) Short period

(iii) Long period

(iv) Secular period/Very Long period

But in economic analysis, economists use only two periods viz., short period (popularly called short-run) and long period otherwise called long-run. These two terms may be used for weeks, months and years. But in economic analysis, these periods indicate production position and do not have reference to the specific calander period. For ex: market period is a term used to explain the time period in which the producer has no time to produce additional units to meet the market demand. Here calander period has no relevance.

Traditional theory explains the cost output relationship in the short run and long run. The same is dicussed in the first part of this chapter.

11. MODERN THEORY

Several cost concepts have been discussed so far, highlighting the importance of cost function in production function. Some recent thoughts on cost behaviour under different time periods have been subjected for discussion. In this discussion, the shape of short-run cost curve as propounded by traditional writers that it is a strict "U" shaped curve has been questioned. The assumptions on which "U" shaped curve is developed are also criticised. The studies have also revealed that diseconomies which creep in due to large scale production or production beyond optimum production level are not natural occurence. Because of these factors, both short-run average cost curve (SAVC) and long-run average cost (LAVC) curves are not strict "U" shaped curves. Empirical studies have revealed the following aspects which are considered to be the theme of modern theory of cost.

The Theme

1. Traditional theory of cost highlights two types of cost in short period viz fixed cost and variable cost and states that the shape of Average Fixed Cost (AFC) in short run will be a rectangular hyperbola. Modern theory also accepts this distinction between fixed cost and variable cost. But it doubts the shape of AFC.

2. Further, modern theory emphasizes that short-run average variable cost (SAVC) has a flat base and not strict "U" shape. The shape of SAVC will be like a saucer.   SAC

12. MODERN THEORY - ANALYSIS

Short Run Costs

In short run the distinction between AFC and AVC is accepted by modern writers. But they are of the opinion that cost behaviour is nor strict "U" shaped in case of AVC and rectangular hyperbola in case of AFC. The arguments based on empirical studies are as follows:

- Production is planned as per the projected sales. The size of the plant is determined by the capacity to produce the output efficiently considering the seasonal and cyclical fluctuations in demand for the product. This means that there should be a high degree of flexibility in production.

- Flexibility involves the maintenance of inventory at a higher level than required for planned output and the equipment will facilitate expanded production in response to changing demand.

- Therefore, the firm possesses a reserve capacity both in inputs and size of the plant to produce planned output without any break. This means the time gap for break down of plant or suspending production due to natural or unnatural reasons, or expanding production in times of unusual demand will be convered by "*The Reserve Capacity.*" Therefore, modern firms will have two or more production levels of production capacity equipment.

Average Fixed Cost (AFC)

AFC in short period will be as follows. As every producing firm will have the reserve capacity or two or more production levels in the same plant or equipment.

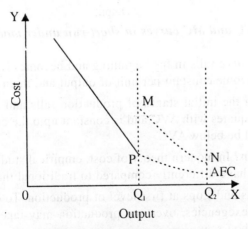

Fig. '*L*' *Shaped LAC curve*

In this diagram, cost is exhibited on OY axis and output on OX axis. OX_1 sets the limit for short-term production and OX_2 exhibits the maximum production capacity of the equipment with reserve capacity. In the initial stages of production AFC declines and stops at P or OQ_1 (the first level of production) as the production has to catch the market demand. This means the product has to be popularised in short run. AFC curve moves upwards (PM) in short period, if the firm has to expand production for meeting additional seasonal demand and working overtime employing labour for longer hours. Afterwords - AFC curve declines reaching the full capacity of the plant (MN). Then the shape of AFC curve will be |_{AFC} (Opinion of modern cost theory).

- Alternatively, the firm will expand production upto full capacity (OQ_2) in normal circumstances in short-run depending upon market demand. Then AFC curve slopes downwards as usual. (|_{AFC} Traditional Theory concept).

Average Variable Cost (AVC)

AVC in short run as per modern theory involving reserve capacity of production, will also behave differently. It is opined (based on empirical studies) that AVC curve falls in accordance with the production of each unit and will have a flat stretch before it rises. Therefore the shape of the curve will be like a bowl with a flat bottom and not exactly "U" shaped. Observe the following diagram:

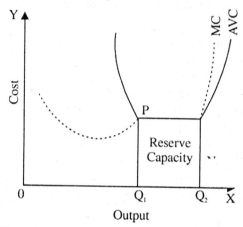

Fig. Movement AVC and MC curves in short-run under modern theory of cost

In this diagram, AVC curve falls in the beginning and becomes flat after range of output. At this point AVC and MC become constant per unit of output and them AVC rises.

Marginal cost curve in the initial stages of production falls and is below AVC and reserve capacity and at point P it equates with AVC and is constant upto the crossing of reserve capacity level. After it rises and will be below AVC.

What does all this mean? In modern theory of cost, empirical studies have revealed that both fixed and variable costs behave differently compared to traditional theory.

AFC slopes downwards and stops at first level of production. To expand production beyond this level to meet market exegencies, overtime production may take place asking the existing labour to work for longer hours.

This exhibits the vertical rise of AFC curve at the point of exhaust of first level production capacity. Then again falls upto the point of maximum or absolute production level.

AVC curve, as per modern theory, falling and rising will be same as in case of traditional theory. Falling AVC denotes efficient use of fixed factors. Rising trend explains the disturbing situations in efficient use of fixed factors. The disturbance may be in the form of defective production process or frequent trouble caused by equipment or monotony caused to workers due to long hours of work or over payment to workers or production waste.

Marginal cost curve will slope downwards and goes below the reserve capacity, then equates with AVC and finally rises below AVC.

ATC or popularly called AC (AFC + AVC = Average Cost) will also move in a different way compared to the movement as explained in traditional theory. As AFC falls and AVC remains constant when they move in reserve capacity domain, AC also falls upto the last tip of reserve capacity. Beyond this point AC rises. Because AFC, after this point will not match with AVC as AFC will be insufficient to neutralise the increase in AVC. Observe the following figure:

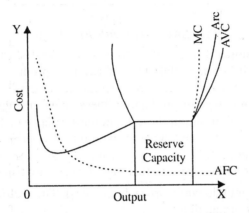

Fig. Short-run cost curves as per modern theory

In this diagram, the movement of AFC, AVC, MC and AC curves in short-run are exhibited. This is a comprehensive picture of cost behaviour based on empirical studies of modern thinkers on economic laws. On this AFC curve slopes downwards as usual in accordance with production and stops at point where reserve capacity exhausts. AVC first slopes downwards, then becomes flat in the region of reserve capacity and then rises. ATC or AC which is the composition of AFC and AVC moves downwards upto the last tip of reserve capacity and then raises as AFC exhausts at this point. But it rises above AVC.

All these four curves (AFC, AVC, MC and AC) behave as said in previous paragraphs, because the modern production units will have production capacity little more than planned capacity to achieve efficiency in prodution. This extra or reserve capacity of plant and equipment provides flexibility in production.

The point of distinction between traditional and modern theory is that "Cost Reduction" (no reserve capacity) was the central theme in traditional theory and modern theory, evolved on the basis of empirical studies, tells that "Reserve Capacity" is planned and "is to be distinguished from the involuntary or unplanned excess capacity."

Long-run Cost Curve (LAC)

As per the traditional theory LAC will be an enveloped curve showing "U" shape. But the modern theory, (as per empirical studies) reveals that LAC will have "L" shape. This is analysed in terms of "smoothly falling production costs which generally more than offset small increases in managerial costs at very large scales of output". Observe the following figure.

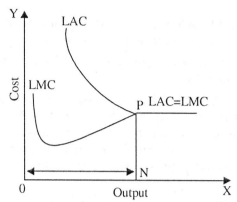

Fig. LAC curve with Flat Region

In this diagram LAC slopes downwards upto point P indicating steep fall in production costs in the initial stages, then it becomes flat. The reduction in production cost has occured due to technical economies of large scale production or economies of expanded production (optimal use of equipment). But at a later stage of production, these economies gradually start declining and after reaching particular level of output these economies disappear. This can be observed, in the diagram at point 'P'. At point 'P', the firm reaches 'minimum optimal scale of production'. With a given technology. After point 'P' LMC merges with LAC for higher levels of output and hence it exhibits a flat region. To reduce cost further, new technology has to be added.

The region of ON output (shown in arrow both sides). The region of ON output exhibits the minimum optimal scale of production.

Therefore the long-run average cost curve is not a "U" shaped as propounded by classical theory. The movement of LAC in "L" shaped because *all modern firms have reserve capacity for planned production.*

Administrative expenses associated with production is also a key factor in cost-effectiveness. Small-sized plants will have less administrative expenses and its impact on total cost or average cost will be less. But in large-scale production, managing the plant and equipment becomes more complex and administrative expenses increase. However, the quantum increase in administrative expenses will be neutralised by reduction in cost of production.

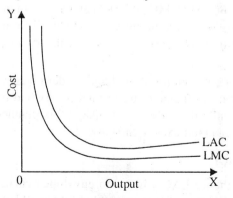

Fig. 'L' Shaped LAC curve

In some cases, LAC curve will not have flat region as shown in previous figure. It slopes towards right and LMC curve will not merge with LAC curve.

In this figure LAC slopes gently towards right side. Even LMC curve also moves in similar way.

Modern theory explains both the types of LAC curves - flat at later stage and gently sloping downwards to right - with the same reason that they are broadly "L" shaped one. Costs are broadly distinguished between production and managerial. Both are variable in the long period.

13. ENGINEERING COSTS

The concept of engineering cost was brought to lime light by H.Chenery in his article in "Engineering Production Function" in Journal of Economics, in 1949. According to him engineering costs can be obtained from production.

He says that each production process is having number of activities or methods regarding different technical processes. Supposing the sugar production process will have sub-activities like crushing, boiling the cane juice, converting it into crystal and packing. These subactivities need factor services of varied degrees in each level. Therefore the cost of production of each level also varies. The total of costs of each phase constitutes the total cost of production. In our example of sugar prodution, we have identified 4 phases of production. The break-up of cost in each subactivity level is given in the following table. The quantity taken for production is 100 tons or 10,000 kgs.

	Raw material (Rs.)	Labour (Rs.)	Production Overheads (Rs.)	Total (Rs.)
Crushing	20,000	10,000	10,000	40,000
Boiling	10,000	10,000	10,000	30,000
Crystal	5000	10,000	5000	20,000
Packing	5000	2500	2500	10,000
Total	40,000	32,500	27,500	1,00,000

In this table we can observe that each production phase will have cost distribution in varied proportions. The ratio or cost of each phase is different. In first phase it is Rs.40,000, in second it is Rs.30,000. Like this the ratio is 4:3:2:1 in the total cost of Rs.10 per kg of sugar production. The price of each factor input also varies in each phase. The calculation made for each technical process of different plant size is called "Engineering cost".

In each level or size of production, technology of one or more sub-activity can also be varied. Here the cost of each technology used in production process is called 'Engineering Cost.' For example sugar, instead of manufacturing from cane, if jaggery is used as raw material, then also whole production technology changes. This technology cost is called "Engineering Cost".

Therefore "Engineering Cost" may be understood as the cost of technology adopted in each phase of one production process (different phases of production of sugar by using sugar cane) or the cost of technology involved in different sizes of production or different production processes using different raw materials (ex: conversion of jaggery into sugar).

Technical aspects of production in each sub-level of the whole production process will be limited. This means the technology or engineering aspects adapted in a production method will be a specific one and cannot be frequently changed as it involves huge capital. Only little change can be made in some phase of production to reduce cost of production. In a competitive market, producer should think of a technology which reduces cost of production and he cannot change it frequently. There is a limitation in technology adoption. Therefore the factor inputs applied in the production process cannot be frequently substituted. Factor services vary only when there is change in technology. Hence the production isoquants (equal quantity production adapting any scale of factor inputs) will be kinks in character. This means, the technical processes will change, if needed, and it will be at the point of kinks of isoquants. Observe the following figure.

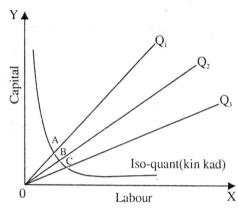

In this figure, there are three scales or combinations of technology OQ_1, OQ_2, OQ_3 which give the same output. The isoquant curve is drawn which crosses all the three scales. Isoquant passes through OQ_1 at point A, OQ_2 at point B and OQ_3 at point C. Whenever the technology changes from one scale to another to reduce cost, the isoquant will be kinky. Observe points A, B and C. At each point it is kinky.

> "Factors cannot be changed for each other except by changing the levels at which entire technical processes are used beause, each process uses factors in fixed characteristic ratios" –
> [R.Dorman in "Mathematical or Linear Programming - A Non-Mathematical Exposition" -
> American Economic Review (1953)].

It is clear from this analysis that engineering costs will be incurred whenever there is change in technology. But it cannot frequently take place. It is said that "Engineering production functions are the basis of linear programming".

Engineering cost curves, as in case of other cost curves, move in different directions in short-run and in the long run.

Engineering Cost-Short Run

The modern theory of cost developed on the basis of empirical studies has questioned the shape of cost curves both in long-run and short-run. As discussed earlier, the shape of short-run average cost cure or LAC will be "L" shaped and not "U" shaped. This is because of planned reserve capacity maintained by firms. Similarly the engineering cost also move in the same direction as it is part of LSC or LAC.

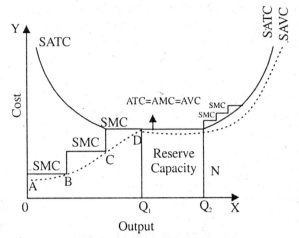

Output

In this figure, SAC falls over the output range ABCD. SMC increases step-wise upto this point of production (OQ). Planned reserve capacity is OQ_1. It can also be observed that the slope of the ATC, AVC and SMC are equal in this output range (QQ_1). Planned reserve capacity of the firm exhausts at point OQ_1 and the firm can produce additional output by employing factor inputs on overtime basis and not by changing technology in this period. After planned reserve capacity the average variable cost increases continuously, but it will be lower than SMC.

Engineering Cost - Long Period

It is now understood that engineering costs refer normally to technical cost of production. Managerial cost is not associated with this cost. As it is assumed that each production process will have minimum optimal size of the plant and production process being limited, cost curves in the long-run will be "L" shaped. In the long period, engineering costs do not move upwards. Observe the figure on next page:

In this figure, LAC is not moving upwards after it merges qwith LMC. It slopes downwards first and then becomes flat. It is L shaped because there are only limited technical processes available in a plant size adopted for production.

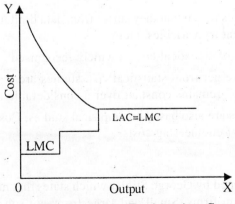

Fig. Long-run Engineering Cost

Thus engineering costs are the ones incurred on technology of production. Empirical studies reveal that cost curves are not "U" shaped as noted in traditional theory, but they are "L" shaped in real production activity. In short period TVC (Total Variable Cost) curve is linear with a positive slope. This means both MC and VC will be constant over a fairly wide range of output.

In the long period AC falls steeply over low level of output and then continue almost constantly with the increase in scale of production.

Though empirical studies suffer from number of limitations and their validity is continuously questioned, the real movement of cost curves is not "U" shaped as in traditional theory. "The fact that so many diverse sources of evidence point in general to the same direction (that is, lead to broadly similar conditions) regarding the shape of costs in practice, surely suggests that the strictly U-shaped cost curves of traditional theory do not adequately represent reality". (A.Koutsoyiannis - "Modern Micro Economics").

14. STATISTICAL COST

This cost is concerned with the application of statistical tools like regression analysis or time series to estimate cost of production of firms producing different levels of output or of a single firm over a period with given plant capacity.

Inferences drawn from statistical cost studies are:

(i) Regression analysis can be adopted to estimate cost function from cross section data drawn from firms of the same plant capacity, each of them producing different levels of output.

(ii) Time series can be adopted for a single firm to estimate cost over a period during which the firm utilises its given plant capacity at different levels.

(iii) As there is difficulty in obtaining data from cross section, of the firms of the same plant capacity, short-run costs are estimated by adopting time series tool for a single firm with a given plant capacity with varying output level.

(iv) Time series cannot be adopted to estimate long period cost and technology changes in the long-run. Therefore, cross-sectional data can be used to estimate long-run statistical cost functions.

(v) Statistical cost studies reveal that they suffer from data limitations, inadequate treatment of important explanatory variables, etc.,

(vi) However the utility of statistical cost is widely recognised.

(vii) Vital information we get from statistical cost studies are that LAC curve generally is "L" shaped and SAC remains constant over a considerable range of output.

Statistical cost estimations are also based on empirical studies. Cost curves behave and move in similar manner as in case of engineering costs.

Survivor Technique

This is a technique developed by George Stigler which states that medium sized firms survive long and they are the optimum firms. Small and large firms are sub-optimal firms and cannot survive because of inefficiency due to higher costs. This is an inference drawn by him studying the steel industry for two decades, taking market share of steel manufacturers.

Firms were grouped into seven categories on the basis of market share and the study revealed that small and big firms could not sustain the cost over runs and the market share of these two category firms declined. The hypothesis of the study was that "Firms with lowest costs survive over time". This was proved to a greater extent. Medium sized firms could survive for long due to cost effectiveness over the period of time. "Survivor Technique" is the concept emerged out of twin study way back in 1958. Based on this study, LAC curve of firm will have saucer type shape "_/". The base of the curve will be flat stretched. But the limitation of this shape is that it only gives broad shape and it will not explain the extent of economies or diseconomies of scale.

Cost Behaviour-Decision Making

Decision making is a very tough task. The decision maker will have to prepare alternative decision plans for a particular task and examine the viability of each decision plan and adopt the best one which suits the concerned task in a given environment.

The shape of cost curves of different types of costs in different time periods will be behaving as per the production schedule. Cost reduction or cost optimisation is one of the main activities of a firm to have economic gain-profit. The shape of the cost curves projects the behaviour of cost in the production process. The historical cost data of a firm will give the movement of cost of the firm for a given production level. Based on this cost behaviour, the producer can take cost decisions to produce the required output. The firm will understand the cost variations of different types of costs in a given business environment and accordingly prepare a cost schedule for a given output.

Supposing the firm has to produce 1000 tons of a product for the current year. Besides finding the source for total cost, the firm has to decide as to how much cost is incurred for producing 1000 tons. Following steps are taken to prepare the cost sheet.

- Study the cost data for previous years. The shape of cost curves will give the information about the cost behaviour for a given production.

- Analyse the movement of different types of cost considering the shape of cost curves which are the projections of money costs incurred on different types of cost elements like, raw material, labour and overheads. These types of costs are termed as variable costs.

- To decide about the technology, adaptation, equipment, and other infrastructural facilities to produce the required output and to have some reserve capacity to meet emergency production (i.e to produce beyond the scheduled output) the shape of fixed cost and its movement over a period of time will have to be analysed.

- Based on this shape of historical cost curves, the firm has to prepare the project report for its projected output.

- Three to four alternative project reports have to be prepared considering the disturbing factors known and unknown – which may come in the way of production.

- Examine these alternates looking at them from different production and environmental angles.

- Adopt a project report out of the alternates prepared (with or without modifications) which suits the projected production plan.

- Fixing the outlay for projected output is governed by business environment in the target market, economic conditions in the society, government's attitude towards business consumer behaviour, etc.

- The basic economic principle of distinguishing between fixed cost and variable cost in the short-run and considering all costs are variable costs in the long-run will hold good while taking costing decisions.

- While adopting technology for production and installing equipment, reserve capacity over and above the actual requirement for production is also installed to have flexibility in production. This is the modern trend and it is revealed by empirical studies.

- The decision maker regarding production plan of a firm should look into all the issues analysed so far, prepare a production plan and implement it.

SUMMARY

1. Cost is the expense incurred in producing a commodity.

2. There are various cost concepts like actual, opportunity cost, past and future cost, short run - long run costs, incremental cost, sunk cost, etc.

3. Opportunity cost is not the actual expenditure but it is the revenue that would be earned by employing that goods or service in some other alternative uses.

4. Marginal cost is the addition to the total cost caused by producing one more unit of the output.

5. Cost control is a programme of effective management. It means better management of material purchases, effective organisation of factors of production etc. It aims at keeping the cost of production at a manageable limit.

6. The traditional cost theory assumes perfect 'U' shape for average cost curve. But the modern theory assumes that short-run average cost curve has a flat base and not strict 'U' shape and this is due to the existence of excess capacity of the firms.

7. Engineering cost refers to the cost of technology adopted in each phase of production process.

8. Statistical cost is concerned with the application of statistical tools like regression analysis or time series to estimate cost of production of firms producing different levels of output or of a single firm over a period with the given plant capacity.

9. Survivor technique which was developed by George Stigler states that medium sized firms could survive for long due to cost effectiveness over a period of time. Small and large firms are sub optimal firms and cannot survive because of inefficiency due to higher costs.

QUESTIONS

1. Discuss briefly different concepts relevant to managerial decision making.

2. Define short-term and long-term costs. What are the practical uses of distinguishing between them.

3. Distinghish beween:

   a) Past Cost and Future Costs

   b) Direct costs and indirect costs

   c) Incremental costs and sunk costs

   d) Fixed costs and variable costs

4. Explain the "Opportunity Cost Principle".

5. Explain Cost-Output Relationship in the short run.

6. Explain the relationships between Average Fixed Cost and Output, Average Variable Cost and Output and Average Total Cost and Output in the short-run. How are short run cost curves derived.

7. State the features of the long period cost curve of a firm.

8. The long-run average cost curve though 'U' shaped will be flatter and less pronounced than the short-run average cost curves. Explain it with the help of a diagram.

9. "While marginal cost is essentially incremental cost, incremental cost is not so." Explain.

10. What is cost function? Explain how to derive cost function from the production function.

11. Explain the traditional theory of costs.

12. In what aspect the traditional theory of costs differs from modern theory of costs.

13. Explain Modern theory of costs.

14. Write short notes on:
    (i) Engineering costs
    (ii) Statistical costs
    (iii) Survivor Techniques

15. Explain how the cost behaviour influences the decision-making of a firm.

16. Why does the average cost curve take 'U' shape in the short-run?

17. Define opportunity cost and marginal cost.

18. Distinguish between out of pocket cost and book cost.

19. Define production function.

20. What are the internal and external economies of scale?

21. Fixed and Variable costs.

22. Explain cost-output relationship in the short run.

23. What are isoquants?

24. Distinguish between Fixed costs and Variable costs.

9 Chapter

Market Structure

CHAPTER OBJECTIVES

After reading this chapter you will be able to answer the following:
1. The Market - Meaning and Definitions
2. Classification of the Market
3. Perfect Competition
4. Features/Characteristics of Perfect Competition
5. Price Determination under Perfect Competition
6. The Role of Time in Determining the Price

The determination of prices of the products is an important managerial function. Price affects profits through its effect both on revenue and cost. Total profit is the difference between total revenue and total cost. Total revenue is the sale proceeds of the firm at a single price or at different prices. The quantity sold varies with the price and the total revenue depends upon the total volume of the output produced. If the producer sets a high price for the product, he cannot sell more of it and as such his profit also is reduced. If the producer sets a low price, he can sell more of it, but he cannot make much profit. Therefore pricing occupies an important place in economic analysis. However, all firms are not able to set prices for their products. There are some firms which are price takers while others are price makers, depending upon the market situations they face.

The knowledge of market structure in which a firm is to operate is useful in understanding the nature and extent of manouevreability which the firm has in deciding about the price and the quantity of the products.

1. THE MARKET – MEANING AND DEFINITIONS

Market structures are different. Market forms are based on the degree of competition prevailing in the market. Broadly, the market forms are classified into two types, (a) Perfectly competitive market. (b) Imperfectly competitive market. Before we begin to study the characteristics of market structure, let us understand what we mean by market.

Market in economics means, a meeting place of buyers and sellers directly or indirectly. Cournot, a French Economist, defines market as "Economists understand by the term market not any particular market place in which things are bought and sold, but the whole of any region in which buyers and sellers are in such a free intercourse with each other that the prices of the same goods tend to equality easily and quickly."

In the words of Jevons, "The word market has been generalised so as to mean any body of persons who are in intimate business relations and carry on extensive transactions in any commodity."

Stonier and Hague have explained the term market as "any organisation whereby buyers and sellers of goods are kept in close watch with each other .... There is no need for a market to be in single building......... The only essential for a market is that all buyers and sellers should be in constant touch with each other either because they are in the same building or beause they are able to talk to each other by telephone at a moment's notice."

Benham explains the term market as "any area which buyers and sellers of a commodity are in close touch with each other either directly or indirectly that the price obtainable in one part of the market affects the prices paid in other part. Ely observes, market "as the general field within which the forces determining the price of particular product operate."

If we study the above definitions, we find that a market comprises of the following components:

(a) *Consumers:* The buyers of the product are called consumers. The buyers of a product are identified by means of income, need etc. If there are high income groups and they are concerned with trade and commerce or higher government administration, they need luxuries like motor cars, VCRs etc.

(b) *Sellers:* There should be manufacturers of a product in the market. There must be industries manufacturing motor cars in a country. They form sellers in the market.

(c) *A Commodity:* A market means the buying and selling of a commodity. If there is no commodity, the market will not exist. Each commodity has a separate market, in the sense that every commodity has a separate set of buyers and sellers.

(d) *A Price:* If the commodity is to be bought and sold, there must be a price for the product. The exchange of the product between buyers and sellers occur at a particular place. Thus, all the four components form a market and it can be defined as:

> *Market is set of conditions in which buyers and sellers contact each other and conduct exchange transactions.*

2. CLASSIFICATION OF THE MARKET

Market is classified *on the basis of an area*, such as local market, regional markets, national markets and international markets.

On the basis of the nature of transactions, the market is classified into spot market and future market. Where goods are physically exchanged on the spot, the markets are called *spot markets*. In the case of transactions involving agreements of future exchange of goods, such markets are known as *future markets*.

Market is classified into wholesale market and retail market **on the basis of the volume of business.**

Market is classified **on the basis of time** as very short period market, long period market and very long period market or the secular market.

On the basis of status of sellers, the market is classified into primary, secondary and terminal markets. The primary market consists of manufacturers who produce and sell the product to the wholesalers. The wholesalers who sell the product to retailers comprise of the secondary market. The business involving the retailer who sells it to the ultimate consumers are called *terminal markets.*

Market is further classified into regulated market and unregulated market. If the government stipulates certain conditions and regulations for the sale and purchase of product - then that market is called *regulated markets.* These are absent in unregulated markets.

Market is further classified on the basis of competition as perfectly competitive market, monopoly market, duopoly market, oligopoly market, monopolistic competitive market, etc. If there is no competition for the product, then such a market is called *monopoly* market. In a competitive market, several producers are manufacturing the product. The product is homogeneous. There are large number of buyers and sellers in the market. Such a market is called perfectly competitive market.

Classification of Market Forms

	Form of market structure	Number of firms	Nature of product	Price elasticity of demand for an individual firm	Degree of control over price
1.	**Perfect competition**	Large No.of firms	Homogeneous product	Infinite	None
2.	**Imperfect compeition**				
a)	**Monopoly**	One	Unique product without close substitute	Very small	Considerable
b)	**Duopoly**	Two	Substitutes	Small	Some
c)	**Pure oligopoly**				
	(i) **Oligopoly without product differentiation**	Few firms	Homogeneous	Small	Some
	(ii) **Differentiated oligopoly**	Few firms	Differential product (Close substitutes)	Small	Some
d)	**Monopolistic competition**	Large no. of firms but less than perfect competition	Differential products but close substitutes	Large	Some

In the table given in the previous page, market forms are classified on the basis of number of firms producing the product and the nature of products produced by them.

(a) Perfect Competition

Perfect competiton comes into existence when there are a large number of firms producing homogeneous products. The maximum output that a firm produces is so small when compared to the industry output. And hence, a firm cannot affect the price by varying output. With a large number of firms and homogeneous products, no individual firm is in a position to influence the price. The demand curve of firms under perfect competition is horizontal straight line. That is the price elasticity of demand for a single firm is infinite. Joan Robinson says, 'Perfect competition prevails when the demand for the output for each producer is perfectly elastic. This entails first that the number of firms is large, so that the output of any one seller is negligibly small proportion of the total output of the commodity and second that the buyers are all alike in respect of their choice between rival sellers, so that the market is perfect.'

(b) Imperfect Competition

Since perfect competition is very rare, what actually prevails is imperfect competition. In imperfect competition, the number of firms exercising control is large since the product is differentiated. Imperfect competition has several sub-categories.

(i) **Monopoly:** Monopoly is a market form in which a single producer produes a single product which has no close substitute. This is an extreme case of imperfect competition. Since a monopoly firm wields a solid control over the supply of the product, which can have only remote substitutes, the expansion and contraction of output will affect the price. Contraction of output will raise its price while expansion of output will lower it. Therefore, the demand curve facing the monopoly is downward sloping but has steep slope. For monopoly, sometimes, the words absolute monopoly or pure monopoly, complete monopoly are used. But such a pure monopoly or absolute monopoly does not exist in the real world.

(ii) **Duopoly:** Duopoly is another type of imperfect market situation where there are only two sellers producing identical products or differenciated products. When there is product differentiation, each seller has his own set of clients and is not affected by his rival. But when the two sellers are dealing with identical products, both will be aware of each other's price and output policies. Suppose they have a good relationship and understanding, it is possible for them to avoid competition and enjoy monopoly in determining price and output.

(iii) **Oligopoly:** The second category of imperfect competition is oligopoly. There are two types of oligopoly - one without product differentiation and this is called pure oligopoly. Under this category, there exists competition among the few firms producing homogeneous product. The other one is differentiated oligopoly. The firms under this produce differentiated products. Since the number of firms is few, each of them exercises some control over the price. The demand curve facing the firms under oligopoly is downward sloping.

(iv) **Monopolistic Competition:** Prof.E.H.Chamberlin defines monopolistic competition as a market form characterised by a large number of firms with product differentiation. Demand curve facing the firms in monopolistic competition is highly elastic indicating that the firm enjoys control over the price.

(c) Monopsony

Monopsony refers to exclusive control over a particular product or service by one buyer in the market. In other words, monopsony is buyer's monopoly. The monopsonist as the only buyer, enjoys control over purchases so as to obtain the lowest possible price.

(d) Oligopsony

Oligopsony is the opposite of oligopoly. It is buyers' market. Simply speaking, there is the existence of only a few buyers in the market. It refers to selling of goods or service to a small number of buyers (oligopsonists).

Forms of Non-Price competition

Any attempt made by sellers to win more customers through means other lowering the price, is called as *non-price competition*. The seller may try to compete by resorting to product differentiation, advertising, packaging, special services, future payment plans etc.

In non-price competition, the sellers keep the prices stable and try to improve their market positions through other means. They make an attempt to chalk out other means. They make an attempt to shift the demand curve to the right by differentiating the product through some other promotional activities.

Suppose a producer can sell 40,000 shirts a year at Rs.250 per shirt on the basis of price competition alone, he can increase the sales to 50,000 shirts if he sells them at Rs.220 per shirt. However, the producer is interested in boosting sales without reducing the price. He resorts to a novel advertising strategy (a form of non-price competition) which persuades customers to buy at the original price of Rs.250 only.

In figure 1, change on shift in demand curve from DD to D'D' due to non-price competition has been represented graphically.

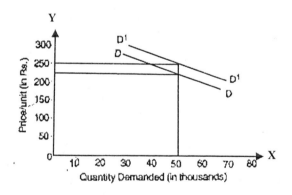

In the case of price-competition, there is danger of the customer preferring the brand only as long as its price is lowered. Customer loyalty is very weak, if price is the only feature differentiating the products. When it is resorted to for a long time, it may have dangerous effects on profits. However, with non-price competition, companies have more control over their sales. The best approach in non-price competition is to build a strong brand name for the company's product either by developing a unique, distinctive product or by creating a new promotional programme.

3. PERFECT COMPETITION

Meaning

Pure or perfect competition is said to exist when there are large number of buyers and sellers found in the market and the product sold is homogeneous. In perfect competition, in addition to the above two conditions of pure competition, there are some other conditions to be fulfilled. They are (1) free entry and exit of firms, (2) perfect mobility of factors of production, (3) perfect knowledge of the market and (4) a uniform price.

> *Perfect competition refers to the market situation where there are large number of buyers and sellers engaged in buying and selling homogeneous products, at uniform prices.*

4. FEATURES/CHARACTERISTICS OF PERFECT COMPETITION

Following are the various features of perfect competition.

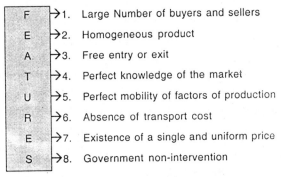

FEATURES	
→ 1.	Large Number of buyers and sellers
→ 2.	Homogeneous product
→ 3.	Free entry or exit
→ 4.	Perfect knowledge of the market
→ 5.	Perfect mobility of factors of production
→ 6.	Absence of transport cost
→ 7.	Existence of a single and uniform price
→ 8.	Government non-intervention

Features of Perfect Competition

1. Large Number of Buyers and Sellers: The first condition of pure competition is, there should be a large number of buyers and sellers operating in the market. The quantity bought or sold by the buyer or the seller respectively is so small that no single seller or buyer can influence the market price. The output of a single firm is only a small portion of the total output and the demand of the single buyer is only a small portion of the total demand. Hence, the market price has to be taken as given and unalterable by every purchaser and seller. Thus, no individual buyer can influence the market price by varying his own demand and no single firm is in a position to affect the market price by varying its own output. In perfect competition, the individual seller is only a price taker and not a price maker. If he charges a slightly higher price than the ruling price, no one will buy from him. If he sells at a lower price than the market price, every one will buy from him. If he sells at a lower price than the market price, every one will come to buy from him, but his stock is so limited that he cannot meet the rush of demand. Thereby he increases prices to the level of market price. This leads to the perfectly elastic demand curve of the perfectly competitive firm.

2. Homogeneous Product: The product produced and sold by producers is homogeneous. It is standardised and purely identical. It means that the products of various firms are indistinguishable from each other. They are perfect substitutes for one another. In the case of homogeneous products, the quality is the same and identical in size and everything that there is, leaves nothing to distinguish one from the other. In these circumstances, if the firm raises its price, it will lose all the customers. It can sell as much as it likes at the prevailing price. The firm enjoys complete freedom to operate in the potential market.

3. Free Entry or Exit: This is another essential characteristic of perfect competition. The firms under perfect competition enjoy full freedom either to start a strategic business venture or close their business. In this situation, all firms are earning normal profit. If the profit is more than normal profit, new firms will enter into production and extra profit earned by old firms will be shared by new firms. If on the other hand, profit is less, some firms will stop producing this product and consequently the profits of the remaining firms will rise. If there are restrictions on the entry of firms, some existing firms will earn super-normal profit. Only when there are no restrictions on entry or exit, the firm will earn only normal profits.

4. Perfect Knowledge of the Market: Another condition for the existence of perfect competitions is that both buyers and sellers are fully aware of the prices that are being offered and accepted. In perfect competition, all buyers are expected to know the market price of the product and as such, the seller cannot charge more than the market price. When the producers and customers have full knowledge of the prevailing price, nobody will offer more and none will accept less and the same price will rule throughout the market. The producers can sell at that price as much as they like and the buyers also can buy as much as they like.

5. Perfect Mobility of Factors of Production: The factors of production move from one place to another without any restriction. If the demand for factors of production increases more than the supply, then the additional factors move into the industry. Mobility of factors of production is very essential to enable the firms and the industry to achieve an equilibrium position.

6. Absence of Transport Costs: It is assumed that, under perfect competition all the firms work so close to each other and hence no cost is incurred on transport or there is equal transport cost faced by all. There will be price equalisation of both commodity and factors geographically and among alternative uses.

7. Existence of a Single and Uniform Price: The most important feature of perfect competition is the existence of single uniform price. All the participants are considered as price takers, i.e., both buyers and sellers cannot influence the price. They should accept the prevailing price in the market and hence the demand curve under perfect competition is perfectly elastic.

8. Government Non-Intervention: Since perfect competition is assumed to work under market economy, there is no Government intervention. There are no taxes, subsidies, tax holidays, rationing of goods, licensing policy or any other Government intervention.

Thus, perfect competition is marked by a large number of buyers and sellers all engaged in the purchase and sale of homogeneous commodity with perfect knowledge of market prices and quantities. Perfect competition is thus an extreme case and is not found in the real world. Actual competition departs form the ideal of perfection. Perfect competition is a mere concept and a standard by which to measure the varying degrees of imperfect competition.

Pure Vs. Perfect Competition

It is necessary to make a distinction between Pure and Perfect competition. For a market to be considered pure competition, three essential conditions have to be fulfilled. Firstly, there must be a relatively large number of buyers and sellers. Secondly, the product must be homogeneous. Thirdly, there must be no restriction either for entry or for exit of firms.

On the other hand, for a market to be called perfect, some more additional conditions have to be fulfilled viz (a) the buyers and sellers must have perfect knowledge of existing market conditions (b) the factors of production must be perfectly mobile between industries (c) the government should adopt the policy of laissez-faire (d) we must assume that there are no transportation costs.

Perfect competition is a myth and is non-existent in the practical world. On the other hand, pure competition tries to prove the ideal of perfect competition without actually accomplishing it.

5. PRICE DETERMINATION UNDER PERFECT COMPETITION

One main objective of a firm under perfect competition is to maximise its profit. The most important question which the management of the firm has to decide is how to determine output in such a way as to maximise its profit. In perfect competition, the firm is a price taker. That is, he has to accept a price which is determined by the forces of demand and supply. The price for the product is fixed at a point where demand is equal to supply. This is shown in the following diagram.

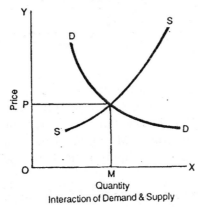

Interaction of Demand & Supply

DD is the demand curve and SS is the supply curve. A look at the diagram shows at higher price, demand is low, but supply is high. At lower price, demand is high and supply is low. At OP price, demand and supply are equal. As shown in the Table, at Rs.30 demand and supply are equal.

Price per metre	Quantity demanded	Quantity supplied million metres	Pressure on price million metres
Rs. 50	10	25	Falling
Rs. 40	15	23	Falling
Rs. 30	20	20	Neutral
Rs. 20	25	15	Rising
Rs. 10	30	10	Rising

From the above discussion, it is clear that the equilibrium between demand and supply or market equilibrium determines the price. Price comes to stay at the level where demand and supply are equal.

Interaction of Demand and Supply

Response to a change in demand and to a change in supply may be due to change in price or change in quantity. If the demand is highly elastic, consumers will respond to price changes. As a result, most of the adjustments to change in supply will take place. If the demand is inelastic, adjustment will take place in price. Sellers also are responsive to changes in price. If price falls, supply is restricted, if price rises, supply also rises. Let us study the following case.

Price rises on account of an increase in demand while supply remains the same.

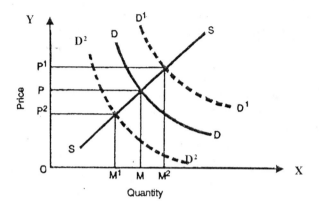

Increase in demand results in shift in the demand curve, upward to the right from DD to D^1D^1 whereas the supply remains the same. As a result, price goes up from OP to OP^1. Quantity supplied goes up from OM to OM^2. If demand falls, supply remains the same, price falls from OP to OP^2. Quantity supplied also falls from OM to OM^1. This is shown in the above diagram. In other words, when demand changes and supply remains the same, equilibrium position also changes.

In the below diagram, the demand remains the same, but supply changes. To begin with, the SS supply curve interacts with DD demand curve at the price OP. If supply increases from SS to S^1S^1, the equilibrium price falls from OP to OP^1. Price falls when supply increases from OM to OM^1. When supply decreases from OM to M^2, price rises to OP^2. Decrease in the supply is shown as S^2S^2. The equilibrium price becomes OP^2. Thus, changes either in demand or supply will change the equilibrium price.

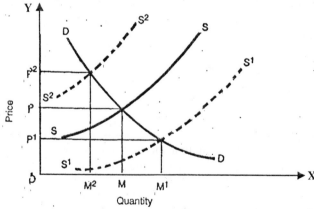

When the demand curve shifts, supply remaining the same, price changes. The rise or fall depends upon the elasticity of supply curve. If the supply curve is elastic, the demand curve being inelastic, price will be less. If the supply curve is steep, price will rise.

Given the shifts in supply curve, the price will rise or fall if the demand curve is elastic. If both demand and supply are inelastic, the price will rise more or fall more. If both demand and supply increase, sales are bound to increase, but price may rise or may not rise. An increase in demand with a simultaneous decrease in supply will raise price and increase in sales if the new demand price for the old equilibrium amount is higher than its new supply price. Similarly, price will rise and sales will diminish, if the new supply price for the old amount is higher than its new demand price.

Limitations of Demand and Supply in Determining Price .

The above analysis shows how price is determined by the interaction of demand and supply under perfect competition. Demand and supply are not independent identities. They in turn are governed by a host of other factors. It is stated that 'supply and demand' is only a superficial formula. Prof.Samuelson has remarked that, *'Supply and demand are not ultimate explanations of price. They are simply useful catch-all categories for analysing and describing the multitude of forces causes and factors impinging on price. Rather than being final answers supply and demand simply represent initial questions. Our work is not over but just begun.'*

The role of cost of production in determining the price cannot be ignored. A change in the cost of production will change the supply curve, and will thus change the equilibrium price. In the same way, market demand may change because of change in the incomes of the people, resulting in an increase in the number of consumers owing to increase in population.

Thus, the factors like cost of production and income of the consumer and the size of the population influence in determining the price. But all of them work through either supply or demand.

6. THE ROLE OF TIME IN DETERMINING THE PRICE

Supply of any commodity is the result of production. Production of any commodity whether agricultural or industrial, takes considerable amount of time. To decide what to produce and how to produce takes considerable planning and formulation of policies of implementation. This aspect was not examined thoroughly by economists earlier to Alfred Marshall. Marshall suggested four periods of time, i.e. market period, short period, long period and secular period.

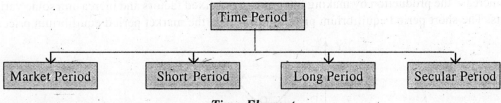

Time Element

Market Period: Marshall defined market period to be so short a period in which supply of a product is fixed or limited to existing stock. In other words, supply curve in the market period is absolutely inelastic. Graphically, it is a vertical straight line. The supply remains fixed for whatever the price may be. Market period supply curve differs between perishable goods and non-perishable goods. In the case of perishable goods like fish, flowers and vegetables and other agricultural commodities, which is also limited by the quantity available and other agricultural commodities, the supply is limited by the quantity available in a day and which cannot be kept back for the next period. In such cases, a sudden shift in demand will result in the increase in price. In the case of non-perishable goods, the supply curve cannot be a vertical straight line, but it is inelastic for the supply may be slightly increased by bringing from the stock. The stock is so limited and as such, the price is bound to rise in the market period if there is a sudden spurt in demand. This is shown in following diagram.

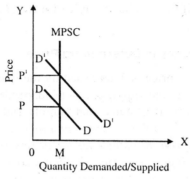

I. Market period

As shown in the above diagram, though there is increase in demand from DD to D'D', since the supply being constant (vertical straight line), the price increases from OP to OP'. The quantity supplied remains the same at OM.

Short Period: Marshall defines short period as a period long enough for the supplies of the commodity which can be altered by increase or decrease in the current output. But not enough for the fixed equipment to be changed to produce a larger or a smaller one. In other words, short run average curve remains the same. It means that the size of the plant remains unchanged in the short period. Thus, short period is a period sufficient only to make a limited output adjustment with the existing equipment by expanding output along the short run marginal cost curves. The output in the short period is greater than the market period output. Here, the supply curve would be a sloping line moving upward from left to right, thereby indicating that as price goes up, supply also goes up.

The determination of short period price is again at the point of intersection between the short period supply curve and the new demand curve. Under the stimulus of demand, the producers will increase the production by making intensive use of fixed factors and increasing some variable inputs. The short period equilibrium price is lower than the market period equilibrium price.

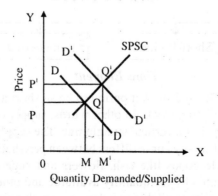

II. Short period

It is very clearly shown in the above diagram that supply can be adjusted to certain extent when there is an increase in demand. When the demand increases from DD to D^1D^1, the price also increases from OP to OP^1 resulting in increase in supply from OM to OM^1.

Long Period: Long Period is defined as a period in which there is plenty of time for the firms to change the size of their plants or build new plants. New firms may also start producing this commodity by installing more modern plants. As a result of expansion of the firms, the output rises considerably. The long period supply curve will be more elastic and the supply curve will lie flat. In certain cases it may be a horizontal straight line. The long period equilibrium price is determined at a point of intersection between long period supply curve and the new demand curve. In the long period, a larger output is supplied and sold at lower prices. Thus, in the long run, larger supplies of the product will be forthcoming at reduced prices.

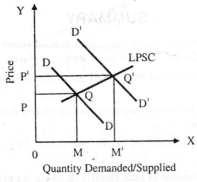

III. Long Period

In the above diagram long run LPSC refers to long run supply curve. When the demand increases from DD to D^1D^1, the price also increases from OP to OP^1. But at the same time supply also increases, it increases from OM to OM^1. The increase in supply is greater than the increase in price in the long run.

Comparative Analysis

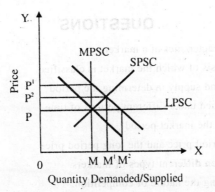

Above diagram shows that when the increase in demand occurs, it results in changes in supply rather than increase in price. The degree or percentage of increase in price differs in different time period depending on the supply.

As the demand increases, the market price rises from OP to OP^1. The short period price OP^2 is slightly lesser than the market price (OP^1) because of adjustments in supply. The supply increases from OM to OM^1. In the long period, the price falls to the original level OP and the supply also increases to OM^2.

Secular Period: Secular period refers to very long period. It includes all those changes in demand and supply which require a very long period of time such as size of population, supplies of raw materials, supply of capital etc. Since the time period is very long no generalisation can be made about it.

Marshall's introduction of time element was most significant in determination of price and it very clearly gives a solution that demand for a commodity and its supply in the market determines the price.

SUMMARY

1. Market refers to a situation where the buyers and sellers contact either directly or indirectly and conduct exchange transactions. Market need not be a particular area, or a place.

2. Market can be classified on the basis of an area, the nature of business transactions, the volume of business and time.

3. Market can also be classified on the basis of competition as perfectly competitive market, monopoly market and imperfectly competitive market.

4. Under perfect competition price is determined by the interaction of two market forces namely the demand for the supply of a product.

5. Alfred Marshall stressed the importance of time element in fixing the price of a product.

   In the market period, since the supply is inelastic if demand increases suddenly the price also increases and the supply curve will be vertical straight line.

   In the short period, supply can be altered to certain extent if when there is a change in demand and hence price will be determined by interaction of demand for and supply of a product in the market.

   The long period equilibrium price is determined at a point of intersection between long period supply curve and the new demand curve.

QUESTIONS

1. Discuss the meaning and characteristics of a market.
2. Discuss the criteria on the basis of which the market is classified.
3. What is the role of demand and supply in determing the period?
4. Explain how price is determined under different periods of time.
5. What is the role of supply in the market period?
6. Distinguish between short period price and the long period price.
7. Write a comprehensive note on different types of markets.
8. Discuss the factors determining the nature of competition.

Chapter 10

Equilibrium of a Firm Under Perfect Competition

CHAPTER OBJECTIVES

After reading this chapter you will be able to answer the following:

1. Conditions of Equilibrium
2. Short-run and Long-run Equilibrium of Firm
3. Industry Equilibrium

Under perfect competition a large number of firms are producing and selling homogeneous commodity to a large nubmer of buyers. The firms which are producing the commodity under perfect competition enjoy perfect freedom either to start producing or stop producing. Under perfect competition no buyer has a preference to buy from a particular seller and no seller has a preference to sell the products to a particular buyer.

1. CONDITIONS OF EQUILIBRIUM

Under perfect competition, price for the individual firm is given. The industry is the price maker and the firm is the price taker. The firm cannot influence the price by its own action. The firm works under the assumption that it can sell as much as it likes at the prevailing price. The demand curve facing the firm under perfect competition is a horizontal straight line. It shows perfect elasticity of demand.

The firm, under perfect competition, aims at maximising profit. The most important question is how to determine the output in such a way as to obtain maximum possible net revenue. At the same time the firm has to attain equilibrium. Equilibrium is a state of business in which the firm is earning maximum money profits. When a firm attains equilibrium, it has no tendency either to expand or contract its output. Since its aim is to earn maximum net revenue from a level of output, it goes on producing the output when its total revenue is equal to total cost. Total revenue is the amount realised by output, the expenditure incurred is the total cost. It includes the total fixed cost and the variable cost. An increase in output means an increase in revenue and cost. A firm is in equilibrium when it does not change the amount of output produced. The output that maximises net revenue of a firm is the best profit output of a firm.

There are two approaches to determine equilibrium.

(i) Total cost and total revenue approach

(ii) Marginal cost and marginal revenue approach

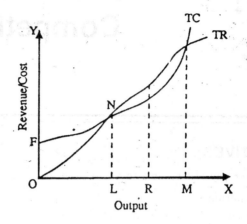

(i) Total Revenue and Total Cost Approach

The equality between total revenue and total cost at a point of output is called the equilibrium output. In the following diagram, the equilibrium position of the firm is illustrated.

In the following diagram TC represents total cost and TR represents total revenue. Total cost curve starts at the height of OF. This is because that even if the firm produces nothing, it has to bear certain costs of prodution due to fixed factors. These are the fixed costs. At the output less than OL, the cost is higher than the revenue and hence the firm is incurring losses. At OL, the total revenue is equal to total cost but the firm is neither getting profits nor incurring losses. This point N and the output OL is called Breakeven point. At the output larger than OM, the total costs are higher than total revenue and hence the firm is incurring losses. The point P is the break-even point. Between OL and OM will lie the optimum point of maximum profit.

The maximum profit will be where revenue cost spread is the largest or where the vertical distance between the total revenue and the total cost curve is the greatest. The maximum profit is determined where the tangents to the total revenue and total cost curve are parallel as shown in the above diagram. At OR output the firm attains equilibrium and earn maximum period.

Though this method of finding out the maximum profit is reasonable, yet it suffers from some diffculties. This method uses total revenue and total costs concepts, and to find out the total revenue, it is necessary to sell all the units of output. At the same time, when some costs have been incurred, all the inputs must have been used full and nothing remains in stock. Such a situation is difficult to come across in any industry and therefore another way of finding equilibrium has been used. This is called marginal revenue and marginal cost equality.

(ii) Marginal Revenue and Marginal Cost Approach

Marginal revenue and marginal cost concepts are readily available for the management to examine whether the firm is moving on desirable path. The marginal revenue and the average revenue curves are one and the same under perfect competition. The firm under perfect competition cannot influence the price by its individual action. As a result of this, the demand curve or the average revenue curve of the firm is a horizontal straight line (perfectly elastic) at the prevailing price level. Since additional output is sold at the same price, marginal revenue coincides with average revenue curve. Marginal cost is U shaped like average cost curve. In order to decide about the equilibrium level of output, the firm will compare marginal cost with marginal revenue. It will be in equilibrium when the marginal cost is equal to marginal revenue at the level of output. At this level of output, marginal cost curve cuts marginal revenue curve from below. At this level, it will be maximising profits. Since the marginal revenue is the same as price or average revenue, the firm will be in equilibrium when the marginal cost is equal to price. The level of output where marginal cost and marginal revenue are equal is the point of maximum profit. The diagram shows in the next page how a firm attains equilibrium and earns maximum profit.

The firm attains equilibrium at a point where marginal cost is equal to marginal revenue. In the diagram the MR and AR show the marginal revenue curve and the average revenue curve. MC is the marginal cost curve. MC cuts MR line (curve) at two points L and T. At both these places, the marginal revenue is equal to marginal cost. But the equilibrium output is OM but not ON. At

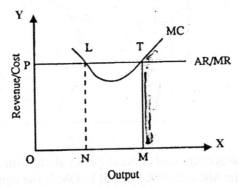

Output

ON output, the firm's marginal cost is equal to marginal revenue but it is not the equilibrium point, for at this level, the marginal cost curve cuts the marginal revenue curve from above. At the same time, any increase in output after ON is more profitable for Marginal Cost is lower than marginal revenue. But beyond the level of output OM, the marginal cost is greater than price. Hence OM is the equilibrium output and the company is making maximum money profit.

Thus, there are two conditions which must be followed if the firms want to attain equilibrium undr perfect competition.

1. MC = MR = Price

2. MC must cut MR from below and MC must be rising after the point of equilibrium

If these conditions are fulfilled, the firm is said to have attained equilibrium. But, it is not possible to know whether the firm is making profit or not from this analysis. To make the analysis complete, one more aspect is to be added. That is, average cost concept. As already known, average cost curve is a U shaped curve. After drawing the average cost curve, it must be compared with average revenue curve. If the average cost equals average revenue, the firm is making normal profit while attaining equilibrium. It may also be possible where average cost is lower than average revenue. If that is the situation then the firm is making supernormal profit. In the following diagram, the profit aspect is shown:

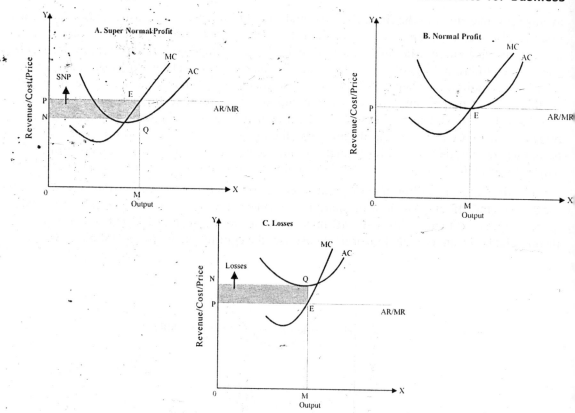

In the diagram 'A' the average cost curve is drawn along with average revenue, marginal cost and marginal revenue. The MC cuts MR/Price at E. OM is the equilibrium output. The firm sells the product OM at the price OP. It costs ON or MQ to produce this output. The average cost is lower than price. Hence the firm is making supernormal profit. The shaded portion in the diagram is the supernormal profit. NQEP indicates supernormal profit. Because the normal profit is included in the average cost, NEQP indicates supernormal profit. In the diagram 'B', the firm is making normal profit and in the diagram 'C', the firm is making losses because its costs are greater than its revenue and it is clearly shown in the diagram. The shaded portion NQEP in the diagram is the loss incurred by the firm.

2. SHORT-RUN AND LONG-RUN EQUILIBRIUM OF FIRM

Short–run Equilibrium

Short run, as already defined, is a period in which output can be increased by the existing plant. Each short run average cost curve indicates the plant size. If the firm produces more with the existing size of the plant, the average cost rises. In perfect competition, there are a large number of firms producing the output. Since all firms are not alike, cost differs. But the firms have to accept the price given by the interaction of demand and supply. And as such, profit earning also differs. What happens in perfect competition is that when the firms are making supernormal profits (AR is greater than AC), some more firms enter into industry to share the supernormal profits earned by some firms. On the other hand, it may be that circumstances are so unfavourable that some firms are going to incur losses. With the entry of some firms, more output is produced. This causes the price to fall. If the price is greater than average cost, firms earn supernormal profits. If the price is equal to average cost, the firms earn only normal profit. If the price is lower than the average cost, then the firms experience losses. The loss making firms leave the industry, which means they stop producing the output. As a result of these changes, the industry will not be in equilibrium. In the short run, the industry will be in disequilibrium which is due to the fact that supernormal profit-making firms attract new firms to the industry and losses making firms leave the industry and those firms making supernormal profit will now be making only normal profit. The output is changing and the price also is changing.

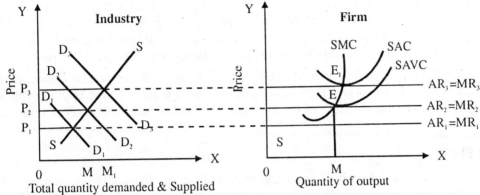

Total quantity demanded & Supplied   Quantity of output

The short run equlibrium of the firm can be explained with the help of a diagram.

The above left hand side diagram shows that price is determined (by the interaction of total demand and total supply) by the industry and the firms accepts the same. It is represented by horizontal lines $P_1P_2P_3$. Suppose in the short period, if price is OP_1, then the firm will not produce because the price does not cover the cost. If price increases to OP_2, it may start producing, but even then it will not make profits. Price will cover only variable cost. Though the firm reaches equilibrium at E where MC=MR, it prefers to produce more at E_1 because the firm may like to produce at higher price (OP_3) which will give extra income.

Thus in the short period, the firms tries to earn maximum profits.

Long–run Equilibrium

The industry will be in equilibrium only in the long period. In the long period there will be no entry or exit of firms. All firms are attaining equilibrium and earning only normal profit, which is shown in the following diagram.

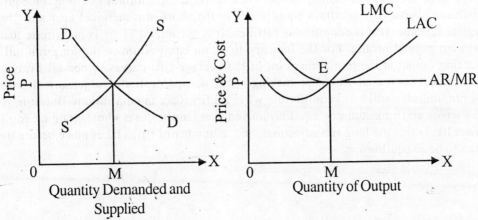

Quantity Demanded and   Quantity of Output
Supplied

The long period is a period of time which is long enough to allow the firms to buy all the inputs including plant and machinery. In the long run all costs will be variable. In the long run, no firm will be making supernormal profit. In fact all firms are making only normal profit. In the long run, the average cost will be equal to price. If the price exceeds average cost, there arises supernormal profit, which is an incentive for some more firms to enter into industry and increase the output. When supply rises, prices fall to the equilibrium level. In the long run all firms will have identical costs and price will be equal to average cost.

The industry will be in equilibrium when the following conditions are fulfilled. There should be equality between long period demand and supply of the industry's product. All firms in the industry must be in equilibrium and all firms are making normal profit equating AC and AR. There should be no incentive for new firms to enter the industry and old firms to leave the industry. In other words, all firms are in equilibrium and hence the industry is also in equilibrium.

From the diagram it is clear that, in the long run, the firms under perfect competitions are earing only normal profit. The firm reaches equilibrium at point E where both the conditions necessary for equilibrium are met. In the long run the firm produces OM level of output at OP price.

Normal Profit

The concept of normal profit is important in describing equilibrium of the industry. Normal profit is a fixed amount (independent of the level of output) which the firms must earn if they are to remain in the industry. Normal profit is included in the average cost itself. As normal profit is considered as a fixed amount, when output rises, normal profits calculated per unit of output falls. If the firms want to stay on in the industry, they must cover at least average total cost. If, on the other hand, some firms in the industry are running below normal (i.e., when they are having loss) profit they will leave the industry and search for normal profits elsewhere. Then the number of firms in the industry will diminish and consequently output also decreases. With a decrease in supply, price rises to equilibrium level. In conclusion, it can be said that equilibrium of the industry or full equilibrium, as it is sometimes called would be attained when the number of firms in the industry is in equilibrium (i.e., no movement into or out of the industry) and also all the individual firms are in equilibrium. At the point, all the firms are equating average cost, average revenue and marginal cost and marginal revenue with one another.

3. INDUSTRY EQUILIBRIUM

It is here necessary to distinguish between short run equilibrium and long run equilibrium of an industry. For a firm to attain equilibrium in the short run, marginal cost must be equal to marginal revenue. If this condition is fulfilled, it is sufficient. There is no criteria that all firms must earn normal profits. For the industry to attain equilibrium in the long run, all firms are producing output at the minimum point of the average cost curves. When all firms are having identical cost curves all would be making either normal profits or supernormal profits. In the long run, industry will be in equilibrium when all firms are in equilibrium. But, it is very rare to come across all firms attaining equilibrium and also industry as a whole attaining equilibrium. It is more likely that the long run adjustment in the number of firms takes place before the industry comes to be in equilibrium.

Therefore in the long run, when industry expands, several adjustments take palce such as number of firms may increase, the existing firms may expand by adopting new technology, etc. It is possible also that firms derive benefits of internal and external economies. Consequently, costs may decline. The firms will be in a position to sell the output at lower price. The price will settle at a point where marginal revenue is equal to marginal cost. All firms are selling at that price and achieve equilibrium.

SUMMARY

1. Under perfect competition the industry is the price maker and the firm is the price taker.

2. The two conditions which the firm should satisfy to attain equilibrium under perfect competition are

   (i) MC = MR = Price

   (ii) MC must cut MR curve from below or from left and it should raise after the point of equilibrium

3. The firm may earn super normal profit or normal profit or even incur with losses in the short run.

4. In the long run all the firms will be in equilibrium and earn only normal profit. The industry will also be in equilibrium in the long period. There will be no entry or exit of firms. All firms are selling at that price where MR = MC and thereby achieve equilibrium.

QUESTIONS

1. What is equilibrium of a firm? Under what conditions a firm is in equilibrium under perfect competition?

2. Distinguish between the equilibrium of a firm and industry undr perfect competition.

3. Distinguish between short run and long run equilibrium.

4. Why is short run equilibrium called unstable equilibrium?

5. Why is long run equilibrium stable equilibrium.

6. What do you mean by equilibrium of the firm and industry? How can it be achieved?

7. Explain the features of 'optimum firm' concept.

8. Distinguish between perfect competition and monopolistic competition.

9. Explain how price is determined under perfect competition.

10. What is general price level?

11. Distinguish between firm and industry.

12. Distinguish between firm's equilibrium and industry's equilibrium.

Chapter 11

Pricing Under Monopoly and Monopolistic Competition

Monopoly is another important market structure which prevails extensively in the capitalist economies of the world. It is found in India also with slight variations. In fact, the monopoly form of business is found in public utility services. We shall study the output and price determination under monopoly.

1. MEANING OF MONOPOLY

Monopoly is defined as that market form in which a single producer controls the whole supply of a single commodity which has no close substitute. Three points should be noted in regard to this definition. Firstly, there must be a single produer, a seller or a product. This single producer may be a joint stock company or a proprietary firm. If there are many producers producing a product, either perfect competition or monopolistic competition will prevail depending on whether the product is homogeneous or heterogeneous. If there are few producers, this will be oligopoly. If there is to be monopoly, there must be one firm producing the commodity. This firm itself becomes the industry in the essence of monopoly. In monopoly, there is no distinction between firm and industry.

A second condition which is essential for a firm to be called a monopoly is that there must be only one commodity produced by the firm for which there is no substitute. This means that there is no rival for the monopoly firm. Monopoly implies absence of competition as such. If the product produced by a firm has close substitutes, it cannot be called a monopoly. The second condition of monopoly can be expressed in terms of gross elasticity of demand. The cross elastiity of demand for the monopoly product and the produt of another producer is zero.

Thirdly, there are strong barriers for the firms to enter into the industry. It means other firms for one reason or other are prohibited from entering the monopoly industry. The barriers may be economic or else institutional and artificial in nature.

The above conditions ensure that the monopolist can set any price for his product and can follow an independent price policy. Since the monopolist is producing a commodity for which there is not even a distant substitute, he can dictate price, as well as the quantity of the product sold in the market. Though he has got absolute power to determine price and the output, he cannot do both. He can do one of these things only - either he can fix the price and, leave the amount sold in the market or he can fix the quantity of output produced and leave the price to be determined by demand. Joel Dean has called a monopolised product *a product of lasting distinctiveness*. Such a product has no acceptable substitutes and its distinctiveness lasts for several years.

2. DEFINITIONS OF MONOPOLY

According to Koutsoyiannis, "Monopoly is a market situation in which there is a single seller. There are no close substitutes of the commodity it produces, there are barriers to entry."

In the words of Ferguson, "A pure monopoly exists when there is only one producer in the market. There are no dire competitions."

According to A.J.Braff, "under pure monopoly there is a single seller in the market. The monopolists' is market's demand. The monopolist is the price maker. Pure monopoly suggests a non-substitute situation."

Lerner defines monopoly as any seller who is confronted with a falling demand curve for his product.

> *Thus, monopoly can be defined as that market form in which a signle producer controls the whole supply of a single commodity which has no close substitute.*

3. FEATURES OF MONOPOLY

The characteristic features of monopoly firm are as follows:

FEATURES		
F	→1.	Single seller in the market
E	→2.	No close substitutes
A	→3.	No competition
T	→4.	Price Maker
U	→5.	Monopoly is also an industry
R	→6.	Difficult entry of new firms
E	→7.	Can fix both price and output by himself
S		

Features of Monopoly

1.   The monopoly is a sole producer with large number of buyers.

2.   There is no close substitute for a product produced by monopoly and hence buyers have no alternative or choice.

3.   Under monopoly, there is complete absence of competition.

4.   Monopolist is a price maker. Since there is no rival, he can fix the price for his product as he likes. He also charges different prices to different customers.

5.   Under monopoly there is only one firm which constitutes the industry i.e., there is no difference between firm and industry under monopoly.

6.   Monopolist has no immediate rivals due to either natural or artificial restrictions on the entry of the firms into the industry.

7.   Monopolist has complete control over the market supply and hence he can fix the price and quantity output to be sold in the market.

4. CAUSES OF MONOPOLY

Monopoly is formed by domineering producers by means of engulfing the small firms through cut-throat competition. A producer may possess certain raw materials, patent rights and the secret methods of production or specialised skill might give a monopoly power. Wherever a huge amount of money is required for investment, which for the other it might not be possible, then such a company becomes a monopoly naturally. The public utility services like water supply and electricity are state monopolies everywhere. In some industries, economies of scale are so particularly pronounced that competition is impracticable, inconvenient or simply unworkable. Such industries are called *natural monopolies*. The public utilities are given exclusive rights by the governments to run as monopolies.

5. OUTPUT AND PRICE DETERMINATION UNDER MONOPOLY

Monopolists are price makers and not price takers as under perfect competition.

The AR curve for the monopolist is a downward sloping curve. If a monopolist reduces the price of his product, he can sell more. If he raises the prices, naturally the demand for his produce decreases. When he decreases the price to sell additional units of his product, then the price for his total output goes down. Since his output affects the price at which he can sell, price is not a given factor for him, as it is for the firm producing under perfect competition.

A monopolist like the firm under perfect competition wants to maximise the profit. At the same time, he has to attain equilibrium. In order to maximise the profit, he has to raise the price. If he raises the price, he cannot sell more. Therefore, in determining the price, the monopolist has to look into the market forces. The question is how the monopolist is going to determine price and the output of the product. It again depends upon the demand and the cost consideration.

As said earlier, the demand curve or Average Revenue curve is a downward sloping curve. The marginal revenue curve falls below average revenue curve. The cost curves do not undergo any change in imperfect competition. They are the same everywhere where output is produced. The average cost is U shaped and the marginal cost curve cuts the average revenue curve at its minimum point.

Equating marginal cost and marginal revenue curve is an important condition for the monopoly firm to attain equilibrium. It is only by equating these two concepts, that the monopoly firm maximises its total money profits. Therefore, the firm will produce upto a point and charges a price which brings its maximum money profits. In other words, the firm will be in equilibrium at the price-output level at which its profits are maximum. The firm will go on producing so long as marginal revenue is equal to cost. It does so because, as long as marginal revenue exceeds marginal cost, the firm will be increasing its total profits. At the point where the marginal revenue is equal to marginal cost, the profits are maximised and here the firm stops producing further. If the production is continued after this point, the firm experiences loss for every additional unit produced.

In the following diagram, the price-output determination by the monopoly firm is shown. AR is the demand curve. MR is the marginal revenue curve. AC and MC are average cost and marginal cost curves respectively. The MC and MR are equal at the point Q. The firm produces OM output and sells the OM output at OP price. For this output, OT is the average cost and since the AR is higher than OT, the firm is earning monopoly profits as shown in the shaded area PRTS.

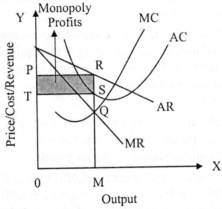

Note: In the short run there are two possibilities for a monopoly firm.

(i) It may earn super normal profits provided its price is greater than AC.

(ii) It may also incur with loss, if its price is lesser than its cost (i.e., AC).

But it may continue because the monopolist aim is to maximise profits and hence he will take all necessary measures to overcome the loss and to earn maximum profits even in the long run.

Monopoly and Elasticity of Demand

One important point about the equilibrium of the monopolist is that the equilibrium of the monopolist will lie at the level of output where the elasticity of demand for his product is greater than one. It means that the monopolist will never be in equilibrium at a point on the demand curve or average revenue curve at which elasticity of demand is less than one. If he wants to fix the output, where the elasticity of his average revenue curve is less than one, he can not equate marginal cost with marginal revenue. Therefore, no sensible monopolist will produce on that portion of the demand curve which gives him negative marginal revenue.

Monopolist's sole consideration is to maximise his profit. He is not interested in the production for social welfare. Therefore, it is the total profit that guides the monopolist in the price and output determination.

Long Run Consideration

For the monopolist, long run considerations also influence in determining price and output.

A monopolist wants to make monopoly profit even in long run too. The price determined by him depends upon the elasticity of demand. If the demand for his product is elastic, the monopoly power becomes weak. It happens when he finds a competitor for his product. The more inelastic the demand, the stronger is the position of the monopolist.

In the long run, the monopolist changes the size of the plant in response to a change in demand. In the long run too, he has to equate marginal revenue with marginal cost. In the long run too, he is maximising profit by producing the equilibrium output.

Monopoly and Perfect Competition Compared

1. Under perfect competition, price is determined by the intersection of demand and supply and the individual producer has no control over the price. Whereas under monopoly, the producer has control over the price.

2. Under perfect competition, the demand curve or the average revenue curve is perfectly elastic and is a horizontal line. Under monopoly at the equilibrium level, marginal revenue curve is a downward sloping curve and the marginal revenue is less than average revenue at all levels of output. In the equilibrium position, average revenue is greater than marginal revenue under monopoly.

3. The monopolist will always sell the product at a price higher than average cost and marginal cost. But, under perfect competition, the price is higher than average cost only in the short period but both are equal in the long period.

4. Under perfect competition, a firm is attaining equilibrium at the lowest point of the average cost curve. But under monopoly, the firm is attaining equilibrium at the highest point on the left side of the average cost curve. The chief reason, if the monopolist stops producing at the lowest point of the average cost curve, implies that he cannot equate marginal revenue and marginal cost and attain an equilibrium.

5. Under perfect competition, there may be supernormal profits in the short run but they will be competed away in the long run. In monopoly however, supernormal profit persists even in the long run.

6. In monopoly, the price is higher and output is less than in perfect condition and conditions of cost and demand remain unchanged.

7. Competitive industry implies more efficient utilisation of resources and provides the consumers a product at a lower price while the monopoly restricting the output sells it at a higher price ignoring the interest of the consumers.

8. It is a common saying that monopoly means exploitation. Therefore, the governments consider it necessary to curb the tendency of monopolistic growth. There is no government intervention under perfect competition.

9. Joan Robinson viewed that perfect competition would bring about all economies, which monopoly could introduce. She observed that cost curve will not shift downward, as a result of the establishment of a monopoly in place of large number of firms working under perfect competition. Thus, according to her, monopoly price is higher and monopoly output always is smaller than perfect competition.

10. There is another significant difference that is monopoly can discriminate prices for the same product, while firms under perfect competition cannot do. By discriminating price, monopolist increase his profits.

6. DISCRIMINATING MONOPOLY (PRICE DISCRIMINATION)

Monopoly firms have the sole objective of earning maximum profits. They may charge uniform price for their products to all the consumers or they may charge different prices for their product to different consumers.

> *Charging different prices to different consumers of their product is called price discrimination.*

Price discrimination refers to the practice of a seller selling the same product at different prices to different buyers. Joan Robinson defines price discrimination as charging different prices for the same product or same price for differential products. Product may be differentiated by time, appearance or place, so that the purchasers are not able to shift to the low price commodity. The concept of price discrimination may be broadened to include the sale of various varieties of the same product at different prices. When a seller sells different varieties of the same product at different prices, such an act of the seller implies this discrimination. For example, a bookseller selling the same edition of a book in an ordinary cover at Rs.25 and with deluxe cover at Rs.50, then he is said to be discriminating prices — those who want deluxe cover pay Rs.50 and others pay Rs.25 for the ordinary cover of the same book.

7. TYPES OF PRICE DISCRIMINATION

There are various forms of price discrimination. They are (a) personal discrimination (b) local discrimination (c) discrimination according to use or trade (d) product (e) age (f) sex.

(a) Personal: Price discrimination becomes personal when a seller charges different prices for different customers. This depends upon the ability of the buyers to pay. This type of price discrimination is made openly but in a disguised manner. For example, a publisher may sell a book as a deluxe edition at a high price. It will cater to rich consumers. he may sell the ordinary editions to middle class consumers. This principle is also followed by public utility concerns. Passengers travelling in air-conditioned carriages pay more than the cost of providing extra facilities.

(b) Local Discrimination: Then there is local discrimination where different prices are charged from different localities or places. Prices in fashionable shops are higher than ordinary shops. Only rich persons go to fashionable shops and buy the same product at a higher price. Dumping is an example of local discrimination. The monopolist charges higher prices in the home market and a lower price in the foreign market.

(c) Discrimination According to use or Trade: Thirdly, there is price discrimination according to use. Different prices are charged for a commodity according to the uses to which the commodity is put. For example, electricity is sold to agriculturists at lower prices and to households in cities at higher prices. Many a time, the producers make product discrimination by means of special labels and charge different prices for the same product packed in different covers.

(d) Product discrimination: Monopolists introduces product differentiation by means of special names, labels, packages etc. giving him a chance to charge different prices for the

differentiated products. For example, Surf Excel and Surf Excelmatic may be sold at a higher price than Surf, even though there may be no real difference between the two.

(e) Age discrimination: Under this type of discrimination the buyers are usually grouped into children and adults. In the case of transport services, it is very common to see that children below 12 years of age are charged at half rates.

(f) Sex discrimination: Some producers may discriminate between male and female buyers. They may charge low price to females when compared to males. For instance, ladies are provided certain services at concessional rates (e.g. Internet connection is provided at concessional rates for ladies by DSNL

(g) Size discrimination: On the basis of the quantity purchased or size of the product, different prices may be charge. Usually higher prices are charged for smaller size product than the larger sizes. For example, an economy size shampoo, toothpaste, soap etc. are relatively cheaper than a small size.

(h) Quality variation discrimination: Different prices may be charged based on the quality differences in the product. Quality variation may be in the form of material used, the nature of packing, colour, style etc.

Price discrimination may also be practised on other basis also. Different prices may be charged based on the special services or comforts provided (e.g. Railways), based on the use to which the commodities or product is put into (e.g. Electricity), based on the time of services (e.g. Autorickshaw fares).

The types of price discrimination practised by monopolists are summarised in the table below:

Types	Basis of Dicrimination	Examples
1. Personal Group	Income of the buyers Age Status of buyers	Doctor's fees Children are charged at half price in transport organisations Higher discount to bulk buyers
2. Product	Quality of the product Labels on products Size of products Season	Higher rate to deluxe models Lower price to unbranded Relatively lower prices to economy size Lower prices in slack season and higher price in busy season
3. Local	Fashionable shops Ordinary shops	Higher prices for all branded ones Lower price
4. Use	Necessary or priority	Price is less (Electricity for agriculture) is charged less
	Luxury	For commercial purpose electricity is charged more

8. DEGREE OF PRICE DISCRIMINATION

Prof.A.C.Pigou has distinguished between the three types of price discrimination.

(i) Price discrimination of the *first degree* is also known as *perfect price discrimination*, where the buyers are fully exploited. Under this, monopolist charges the maximum that each buyer is willing to pay, rather than go without the goods.

(ii) Price discrimination of the *second degree* would occur if a monopolist was able to classify buyers into different groups and from each group, a different price is charged which is the lowest demand price for that group. This is explained below with a diagram.

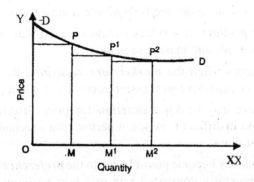

DD is the market demand curve. Mth unit of a product has a demand price MP and earlier units have a demand price (greater MP) as indicated in the slope of demand curve. All OM units of output are sold at MP price. On Mth unit of output, buyers do not enjoy consumer surplus but buyers of earlier units enjoy consumer surplus. Similarly, for M^{1}th unit, the demand price is M^{1}P^1. For units between M and M^1 demand price is greater M^{1}P^1, but all units from M to M^1 enjoy consumer surplus. In this way, price discrimination of the second degree is made.

(iii) Price discrimination of the third degree occurs when the monopolist divides the buyers into different groups and then charges different prices to different groups. The price charged in a sub-market need not be the lowest demand price of the sub-market or group. The price charged in each sub-market depends upon the output sold in the sub-market. Price discrimination of the third degree is most common. A common example of such price discrimination is found in the practice of a manufacturer who sells his goods at a higher price at home and at a lower price abroad. Another example may be mentioned here. Where the electricity company sells electric power at a higher price to households, it charges lower prices to industrial users. Price disrimination of the third degree is more commonly found in the real world.

9. WHEN IS PRICE DISCRIMINATION POSSIBLE?
(conditions necessary for price discrimination)

Monopolists practice price discrimination provided that it is profitable. If price discrimination is to be practiced, the monopolist has to fulfil the following conditions:

The sub-markets so classified by the monopolist must maintain a separate identity. It should not be possible to transfer any unit of a commodity from one market to another market. The classification of a sub-market is based upon the elasticity of demand for the product. Price discrimination is possible only if the elasticity of demand in one submarket is different from another market. Supposing he classifies his buyers into two markets, a market with an elastic demand and a market with an inelastic demand, he sells at a lower price in the former market and at a higher price in the latter. If the buyers in the elastic market were to sell the product in the inelastic market to make the advantage of higher prices, the monopolist will not stand to gain anything from price discrimination.

Secondly, it should not be possible for the buyers in the dearer market to transfer themselves into cheaper markets to buy the product at cheaper price. For example, if a doctor is charging a smaller price from poor patients than from the rich patients, then his price discrimination would fail if the rich patients assume themselves to be poor.

Price discrimination is possible under the following circumstances:

(i) The *nature of the product* or services should be such that there is no possibility of transfer of product from one market to another.

(ii) Discrimination occurs when the *markets are separated* by large distance or tariff barriers, so that it is expensive to transfer goods from one market to another market.

(iii) In some cases, there may be *legal sanction* for price discrimination. For example, travelling in railways in different classes. A person with a second class ticket is forbidden to travel in the first class.

(iv) Price discrimination may become possible due to the *preference or prejudices of buyers*. A commodity is generally converted into different varieties by providing different packings, different names or labels etc., in order to convince the buyers that certain varieties are superior to others. Different prices are charged for different varieties though they only differ in name or label. In this way, the producers are usually able to break-up their market and sell the so called superior varieties to the rich people at higher prices and the so called ordinary varieties to the poor people at lower prices. This is a clear case of price discrimination based on the preference or prejudices of various buyers of the product. Joan Robinson puts this aspect of price discrimination in a very clear manner: *"Various brands of a certain article under names and labels which induce rich and snobbish buyers to divide themselves from poor buyers and this way the market is split up and the monopolist can sell what is substantially the same thing at several prices. In posh localities the prices of the same goods are different from congested and ugly localities"*.

(v) Price discrimination occurs when buyers have *let go attitude.* If the price differences between two markets are very small, consumers may not consider such discrimination.

(vi) As long as buyers have an *illusion* that high-priced goods are always of high quality, a monopolist can practice price discrimination.

(vii) If a monopolist is able to *prevent re-exchange of goods* between buyers of a low priced market and a high priced market, then he can resort to price discrimination.

Price discrimination is being practised all over the world by producers. As said earlier, price discrimination is found only under imperfect competition, especially in monopoly and not in perfect competition.

Is Price Discrimination Profitable?

Monopolists practice price discrimination with a view to make monopoly profits. If it is to be profitable, the elasticity of demand in one market must be different from the elasticity of demand in a different market. If different elasticities of demand are there in two markets, the monopolist can discriminate prices and make profits. If the demand curves in the two markets, are isoelastic, at every price, elasticity of demand is the same. Then, it will not pay the monopolist to charge different prices. If the elasticity of demand is the same in the two markets, marginal revenue in the two markets at every price of the product will also be same. If marginal revenues at every price of the product are same in the two markets, it will not be profitable for the monopolist to transfer any amount of goods from one market to another market and thus charge different prices of the product in the two markets.

Let us study how a discriminating monopolist is going to attain equilibrium and earn profit through monopoly.

10. EQUILIBRIUM UNDER PRICE DISCRIMINATION (THIRD DEGREE DISCRIMINATION

Under simple monopoly, the firm charges uniform price for the whole output. But under price discrimination, different prices are charged for the same product. In order to do price discrimination, the monopolist has to divide his total market into two sub-markets on the basis of differences in elasticities of demand.

In order to reach an equilibrium, the discriminating monopolist has to take two decisions: (i) How much total output he should produce and (ii) How should he distribute the total output between the two markets and what prices he should charge in these two markets.

The following diagram presents the technique adopted by the discriminating monopolist in order to attain equilibrium.

In order to determine equilibrium, the discriminating monopolist has to equate marginal revenue with marginal cost. Since he has to sell the output in two markets at different prices, he has separate demand and marginal revenue curves. He has to add the marginal revenues in two markets and then compare this to the marginal cost of the total output. The third diagram shows the equality between marginal revenue and the marginal cost. AMR is the aggeregate marginal revenue. The AMR curve cuts the marginal cost curve at E (Diagram iii) and the total output produced is OM. The output is to be distributed to the two markets.

The monopolist will distribute OM output in the two markets in such a way that marginal revenues are equal. Marginal revenues in the two markets must be equal if the profits are to be maximised. If the marginal revenue is high in one market and low in another market, it will pay him to transfer some amount from a market where marginal revenue is less to the market where it is more. Therefore, marginal revenues must be the same in the two markets. Then it will be unprofitable for him to shift any amount from one market to another.

In order to attain equilibrium, it is essential, that not only the marginal revenues must be same but also they should be equal to the marginal cost of the whole output. As shown in the diagram (iii), at the equilibrium output OM, marginal cost is ME. Now the output OM is to be distributed in the two markets in such a way that marginal revenue in them should be equal to marginal cost of the whole output.

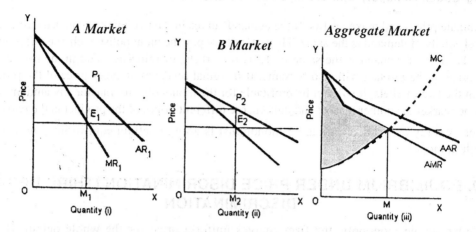

It is now clear that in diagram (i), OM_1 output is to be sold in A market, because marginal revenue M_1E_1 at the OM_1 output is equal to marginal cost ME. Similarly OM_2 output is sold in B market, since marginal revenue M_2E_2 is equal to marginal cost ME of the whole output. Thus, the discriminating monopolist produces OM output and sells OM_1 output in Market A at M_1P_1 price and OM_2 output in market B at M_2P_2 price. The total output is now equal to $OM_1 + OM_2$. As shown in the diagram he sells at a higher price in the A market and at a lower price in the B market and finally makes profits as shown in the shaded area in the diagram (iii) *i.e.,* ABE.

Is Price Discrimination Justified?

It is rather difficult to say whether price discrimination is beneficial from the social point of view. Sometimes, price discrimination may be beneficial to society. Discrimination in consultation practiced by the physicians and surgeons is considered beneficial to poor patients who are charged low fees. This extends the basic medical services to them. It is not economically objectionable to make the rich pay more for the same service. The rich people have greater ability to pay and the society does not stand to lose if money is transferred from rich people to the monopolist. Another example may be given to justify the policy of price discrimination. If there is a uniform fare for rail travel, the railways cannot provide the service and make some profit. It has been observed by many that if railway authorities are not permitted to charge higher fare from the rich people who travel in upper classes, then it may not be profitable for the authorities to run the railways on a single uniform fare from the two economic strata of the society.

From the social welfare point of view too, since discriminating monopoly produces more output than a simple monopoly, it is desirable. Under price discrimination, when price is raised for the rich and is lowered for the poor, it has a redistributive effect, the poor are benefitted at the expense of the rich. From the point of view of reducing inequalities of personal real income, price discrimination is justified. If the price discrimination increases the production of the output and more is provided for the poor, then it is desirable. In those cases in which discrimination will decrease the output, it is undesirable on both counts.

Joan Robinson has observed from the point of view of society as a whole, that it is impossible to say whether price discrimination is desirable or not. From one point of view, price discrimination may be held superior to simple monopoly when there is increase in output. If price discrimination results in maldistribution of resources between different uses, it is not desirable.

11. PRICE DISCRIMINATION UNDER DUMPING

A monopolist may have monopoly power in domestic market but not in the international market due to lot of competition in the world market. He faces perfect competition in the world market. The monopolist charges prices in the world market on the basis of perfect competition and within his country he can fix the price at the higher level. If the monopolist or any producer charges a lower price in the world market and a higher price in the home market, it is said to be dumping in the world market.

> _Therefore dumping can be defined as a special case of price discrimination in which a monopolist fixes a higher price for his product in the home market where he is a monopolist and a lower price for the same product in the foreign market where he is facing perfect competition._

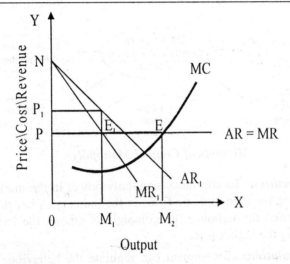

Output

MC = Marginal Cost Curve

AR = Average Revenue Curve of the world market

MR = Marginal Revenue Curve of the world market

AR_1 and MR_1 = Average and Marginal revenue of home market.

This can be explained with the help of a diagram.

The producer is a monopolist in the home market. MR_1 and AR_1 are the marginal and average revenue curves in the home market and both are sloping downward becuse he is a monopolist in his home country. His world market average revenue (AR) and marginal revenue are represented by horizontal straight line where he is facing perfect competition. For finding out equilibrium under dumping first we must find out combined marginal revenue curve. The aggregate marginal revenue curve is NE_1E which is the summation of MR_1 and MR. This agggregate MR intersects the MC at E which is equilibrium position and the output is OM_2 units. E_1 is the eqquilibrium position for home market. He sells OM_1 units of output at OP_1 price in the home market. He sells M_1M_2 units of output in the world market at OP price where he faces perfect competition.

Hence, the monopolist sells OM_1 output at OP_1 price in the home market and M_1M_2 output at OP price in the world market which is less than the price charged at home market. This action of monopolist is called dumping.

12. MONOPOLY CONTROL

Monopoly always fixes a higher price than other markets. His aim is to earn the maximum profits. Sometime he may even earn maximum profit in the long run. This may result in social unjustice. Many large monopoly houses tend to influence political parties and may spread economic corruption.

Hence, monopoly power need to be regulated.

Methods to Control Monopoly

There are several ways to control monopoly power.

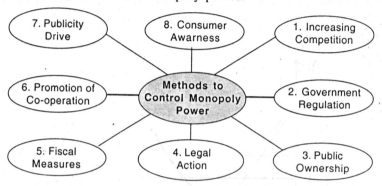

Methods of Control Monopoly

1. *Increasing Competition:* To eliminate monopoly power in the market, competition can be promoted among the monopolistic firms in the industry. A fair degree of competition has to be maintained throughout. The competition among the firms will prevent the monopoly in fixing the higher price.

2. *Government Regulation:* Government can regulate the behaviour of monopolists. To protect the interest of the consumers and to reduce the expoiltation by the monopolist firms, the Government may fix the maximum statutory prices for the goods supplied by the monopolist beyond that he cannot fix the price.

3. *Public Ownership:* To protect the interest of the consumers, the government can run the monopoly by itself. This solution is common in many countries. In India, the Government runs the Raiwlays. This may eliminate the competition among the firms and it protects the interest of the consumers.

4. *Legal Action:* The government can enforce and enact laws to prevent the emergence and growth of monopolies. It can restrict the entry of new firms and encourage competitions in different fields. Thereby it can reduce or eliminate monopoly power.

5. *Fiscal Measures:* To control the excess profits earned by monopolist, Government can impose heavy taxes on monopoly profits. This may discourage the monopoly from fixing the high price for his product.

6. *Promotion of Co-operation:* Encouragement for promoting co-operative movement or organisations should be given by the government. Co-operative societies are useful in reducing the expoiltation, excessive profits, restricted output etc. thereby monopoly power can be controlled.

7. *Publicity Drive:* All the facts regarding monopoly practice should be made known to the public. When monopoly depends on the goodwill and the consumers, publicity can adversely affect him.

8. *Consumer Awareness:* Consumer awareness programmes should be launched by government or by consumers themselves. Through buyer's association competition among the firms can be eliminated and the buyers can get the goods at reasonable prices.

Case Let – Price Discrimination

Concept: *Price discrimination maximises the profit of monopolists and raises economic welfare of people.*

Price discrimination is market power tool in the hands of monopolist. This can be examined by analysing this example.

Ram Enterprises, Bangalore, manufacturers of Gas Stoves, have two markets - Bangalore and Hyderabad. The production cost (marginal cost) of the stove is Rs.600 per piece. There is a brand loyalty in Hyderabad for the product and 1000 consumers want this make only. They are willing to pay Rs.2000 per piece. Marketing and other expenditures will be Rs.1000 per peice at Hyderabad. On the other hand, Bangalore is a competitive market. But still the firm has brand preference (less enthusiastic customers) and the potential is for 1500 pieces. The potential price (willing to pay) is Rs.1200.

What is the price to be fixed by the firm to maximise profit?

In this example, there are two prices to consider. (i) Rs.2200 is the maximum price that can be charged to customers at Hyderabad who have brand loyalty and (ii) Rs.1200 as the highest price and still get entire customers of 2500.

At a price of Rs.2200 (Maximum price), the firm sells 1000 pieces and makes a profit of Rs.12 lakhs considering a market expense of Rs.400 per piece foregoing the opportunity to sell 1500 peices to less enthusiastic customers at Bangalore.

This decision of selling only 1000 pieces at Hyderabad causes dead weight loss. There are less enthusiastic customers who are prepared to pay Rs.1200 per piece. If this opportunity is not ceased the firm will lose Rs.10 lakhs of additional surplus.

Thus "Dead Weight Loss" is the inefficiency of monopolist when he charges a price above MC.

The marketing department of Ram Enterprises has already identified two markets one at Hyderabad which has brand loyalty for the product and another at Bangalore which has less enthusiastic consumers.

If the firm adopts discriminating price policies for two markets as said it can make a total profit of Rs.15 lakhs (Rs.12 lakhs + Rs.3 lakhs). In this case, the firm may sell only 1000 pieces in Hyderabad at Rs.2200 and ignore Bangalore market as risk of selling is high and profit realisation will be slow.

Three important aspects to be considered before making price decision are:

(i) Whether a price close to willing to pay by customers is to be charged in brand loyalty market and avoid selling the product in high risk market where the product moves slowly and still makes profit.

(ii) Whether to charge different prices in different markets and maximise profit; In this case, monopolist has to identify customers as per their ability to pay. This ends up in market segmentation on the basis of risk involved in selling in different regions.

(iii) Whether the customers in low priced market (LPM) can purchase the product in LPM and sell it in high priced market (HPM) conveniently. This can reduce monopolist's profit as in our example, consumers of Bangalore market can be competitors in Hyderabad market with some product selling at low price of Rs.1900 and still making profit.

But still price discrimination by monopolist eliminate inefficiency inherent in monopoly pricing and increase welfare as the product is available to willing consumer in every segment.

13. MONOPOLISTIC COMPETITION

We have already seen how price and output are determined under perfect competition and monopoly. But pure or perfect competition and perfect monopoly are rarely found in the real world. In the real world, we do not find commodities which are perfect substitutes. What we find in the real world is that commodities have close substitutes. Therefore, firms which are producing close substitutes come under imperfect competition. Monopolistic competition is another form of imperfect competition.

Theory of monopolistic competition was propounded by Prof.E.H.Chamberlin while the theory of imperfect competition was developed by Prof.Joan Robinson. Though the theory of imperfect competition propounded by the latter is similar in various ways, it differs in some important respects. The nutshell of these theories is that pure or perfect competition and pure monopoly are the two opposite limiting cases, lying in between in a market structure where there is imperfection in competitive elements.

14. MEANING AND NATURE

Monopolistic competition refers to a market situation in which there are either many producers producing goods which are close substitutes to one another or the product is differentiated.

Chamberlin's concept of monopolistic competititon is a strategic blending of monopoly and competition. The distinguishing feature of monopolism produced by various producers are not homogeneous but different, though they are closely related to each other. When there is differentiation between the products produced by many producers, the monopoly element comes in. These monopolies are competing with each other. Since each producer is a monopolist and yet has competitors, a market situation comes into existence which is described as *monopolistic* competition.

It is thus clear that products produced by firms in monopolistic competition are not identical as in perfect competition, but they are close substitutes. The important distinguishing features of monopolistic competition are (i) existence of large number of firms, (ii) differentiated products and (iii) products are close substitutes.

Product differentiation is an important characteristic of monopolistic competition. The product of various sellers are fairly (but not the same) similar and serve as a close substitute to each other. Product differentiation means that the products are different in some ways, but not altogether so. The producers differentiate the product in such a way that each one has a monopoly of his own product. Many examples of monopolistic competition can be given from the Indian market scene. Many firms in India produce toothpaste, brush, soap, etc., and the product of each one is different from its rivals in one way or the other. Different toothpastes like Colgate, Binaca, Forhans, Kolynos, McClean; soaps like Lux, Hamam, Rexona, Breeze, etc., tooth brushes like Colgate, Binaca, Dr.Wests', Wisdom etc., are strategic examples of monopoly. Thus, monopolistic competition corresponds more to the real world than pure competition or monopoly.

Product differentiation is made in several ways. Firstly, differentiation is made in the product itself. It may be a patent, trademark, package, use of wrapper, differentiation in quality design, colour or style of the product, or attractive packets etc. Secondly, differentiation is made with regard to conditions of sale. This means that a product is differentiated if the services rendered in the process of selling the product by one seller is not identical with those of other firms. Product is differentiated through fair dealing, market courtesy and efficiency. Thus, in the case of differentiated products, we find the existence of the characteristics of both monopoly and pure competition.

15. DEFINITIONS

According to Joe S.Bain, "Monopolistic competition is found in the industry where there are a large number of small sellers selling differentiated but close substitute products."

In the words of Leftwitch, "Monopolistic competition is a market situation in which there are many sellers of a particular product; but the product of each seller is in some way differentiated in the minds of consumers from the product of every other seller."

According to A.L.Meyers, "Monopolistic competition is a situation where there maybe many sellers, but with differentiated products so that competition is no longer on price basis."

In the words of Stonier and Hague, "there is competition which is keen, though not perfect, between many firms making similar products."

16. FEATURES OF MONOPOLISTIC COMPETITION

The main characteristic features of monopolistic competition are as follows:

F	→1.	Many firms
E	→2.	Independent price policy
A	→3.	Product differentiation
T	→4.	Free entry and exist
U	→5.	Selling cost
R	→6.	Lack of perfect knowledge
E	→7.	Lack of mobility of factors
S	→8.	More elastic demand

Features of Monopolistic Competition

1. Under monopolistic competition there are *many firms* producing the products. But the number is not as large as perfect competitions. Each firm contributes only a small portion of the total output and has a limited control over the price of the product.

2. *Independent price policy* is followed by firms under monopolistic competition. The firms are producing differentiated products which are close substitutes and as such, each determines the price taking into consideration only his cost of production and demand.

3. Firms under monopolistic competition are producing products which are similar but not identical. This is called as *product differentiation* i.e., each firm tries to differentiate its product from that of other rival firms in one way or other.

4. Like the perfect competition, the *firms can enter or exit the market freely* under monopolistic competition. If the existing firm earn super normal profit it will attract the entry of other firms into the market resulting in increase in supply and fall in price. On the other hand, if the existing firm incur losses then it will leave the market. This may lead to reduction in supply and increase in price. In both the cases, the result is, under monopolistic competition the firm can earn only normal profits.

5. *Selling cost* is an important feature under monopolistic competition. The expenses incurred for advertisements and other selling mediums are called selling costs. Most important form of selling cost is advertisement cost. This is undertaken by the firm in order to popularise his brand in the market.

6. Both the *buyers and sellers do not have perfect knowledge of the market*. There are a large number of products each being close substitute of the other. Therefore, he may be able to choose the right product. Similarly, the seller does not know the exact perference of the buyers and hence he cannot get any added advantage out of the situation.

7. It is assumed that both *factors of production* and goods and services *are not perfectly mobile* under monopolistic competition.

8. The firms under monopolistic competition have *more elastic demand curve i.e.,* if the firm wants to sell more, it must reduce its price.

17. EQUILIBRIUM OF A FIRM UNDER MONOPOLISTIC COMPETITION

(a) Short Run Equilibrium

Individual equilibrium refers to the equilibrium of the individual firm. Every firm is required to attain equilibrium if it wants to continue in business. Equilibrium of a firm requires equality of marginal revenue with marginal cost. Marginal revenue of a firm closely follows the average revenue of the firm. Average revenue curve or the demand curve for the product of an individual firm is shown downward sloping. Since various firms under monopolistic competition produce products which are close substitutes of each other, the position and the elasticity of the demand curve depends upon the availability to competing substitutes and their prices. Therefore, equilibrium adjustment of an individual firm cannot be attained in isolation from the group of which a firm is only a part.

The demand curve of the firm under monopolistic competition is more elastic since there are several substitutes available in the market. Even though the firm under monopolistic competition has monopolistic control over its product, but its control is restricted with the availability of close substitutes and if it sets too high a price for his product, many customers will shift to the rival products.

The individual equilibrium in the short run is graphically shown below:

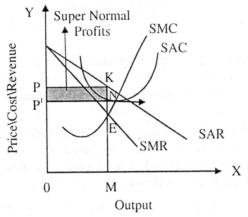

AR is the demand curve for the product of an individual firm, the nature and prices of substitutes are assumed as given, MR the marginal revenue curve follows the average revenue curve. AC and MC are the average cost and marginal cost curves respectively. MR and MC intersect each other at E and OM is the output produced. OP or MK is the price because K is a point on the average revenue curve. The firm is making a supernormal profit equivalent to the area known in the diagram P'PKN. KN is the supernormal profit per unit of output. Since the demand and cost are very favourable, the firm is earning supernormal profit and also attaining equilibrium.

If the demand and cost conditions are less favourable, then a monopolistically competitive firm experiences losses. This is shown in the diagram in the next page.

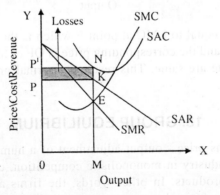

The firm is in equilibrium equating marginal revenue with MC. But average cost is greater than average revenue OE. Price OP is less than the cost MK per unit of output. The loss is shown as the area KNP'P. In such circumstances, there is no alternative for the firm except to make the best of the bargain.

Thus, a firm is in equilibrium but may be earning supernormal profit or making loss depending upon the position of the demand curve relative to the position of the cost curve. It is also possible for a firm making normal profit in the short run if the demand curve happens to be tangent to the average cost curve.

When once a firm fixes the price, it will not deviate from the price anymore. If it varies its price upwards, the loss due to fall in the quantity demanded will be more than made up by the higher price. If it cuts down the price, the gain due to increase in sales will be less than the loss due to the lower price. Hence, the price will remain stable.

(b) Long Run Equilibrium

In the long run, each firm can change its production capacity by changing the fixed as well as variable factors. New firms may enter into the industry and the old ones may exit. Even in the long run the price-output policy of an individual firm is determined by the same general principle of equality of MR and MC as in the short period.

In the long period, the firm can't make super normal profit as it will be competed away by the new firms which enter the industry. On the other hand, if a firm incur losses, it will leave the industry. Firms in the long run will earn only normal profit. The long run equilibrium of a firm is explained graphically with the help of following diagram.

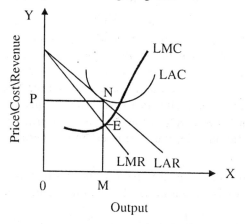

Output

In the diagram, LMR is equal to LMC at point E which is the equilibrium point. OM is the long run equilibrium output and the corresponding price is OP or MN. At this point both average cost and the average revenue are same. This results in normal profit, which forms part of the cost of production.

18. GROUP EQUILIBRIUM

Group equilibrium means price - output adjustment of a number of firms, whose products are close substitutes. The industry in monopolistic competition, consists of a number of firms producing differentiated products. In other words, the firms are producing heterogeneous products. Hence, the firms producing heterogeneous products cannot be added to form the market demand and supply schedule. Hence, Prof.Chamberlin uses the concept of *'product group'* for the industry. In modern parlance, though the firms are producing heterogeneous products, they are brought under the concept of industry. For example, though there are six or seven car manufacturers in the country, though each is different from the other, they are all clubbed to be called the *motor car industry*. But the costs and revenue structures vary between firms. In Prof.Chamberlin's anslysis, the product group includes products which are closely related, i.e., they are technological and economic substitutes. Technological substitutes are products which can technically cover the same want and economic substitutes refer to products which cover the same want and have similar prices.

> *The 'group' is defined as 'the demand for each single product which is highly elastic and that it shifts appreciably when the price of other products in the group changes,' i.e., products forming the group or industry should have high costs and price elasticities. Product differentiation enables each firm to charge a different price.*

Each firm in the group is a monopoly. Yet, there is competition among those firms which are producing closely related products. The price-output determination of one firm will affect the decision of other firms. There is not much qualitative difference between the products of the firms. Yet, there is price and cost difference between the firms. The demand curves and cost curves vary between firms. As a result, there are differences in prices, including output and profits of the various firms in the group.

Assumptions: In order to develop the theory of 'group equilibrium' Prof.Chamberlin makes certain assumptions.

(i) He makes uniformity assumptions. It means that the demand and cost curves of all the products in the group are uniform.

(ii) He assumes that consumers' preferences are evenly distributed among different varieties and differences among them are not such as to give rise to differences in costs.

(iii) Prof.Chamberlin has introduced another assumption, namely symmetry assumption. It means that the number of firms under monopolistic competition are large enough to ensure that individual decision regarding price and output adjustment has little influence on the rivals. This means that there is no possibility of retaliation.

Keeping the above assumption in mind, the *'concept of group equilibrium'* is illustrated in the diagram shown in the next page.

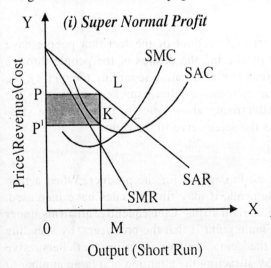
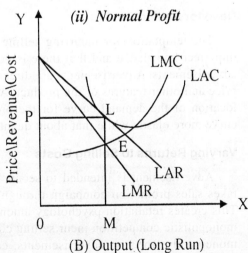

The diagram A represents short run equilibrium and diagram B represents long run equilibrium. In the short run, the firms earn supernormal profits. In the long run, all firms make only normal profits. The situation is similar to one prevailing under perfect competition. But there is a great difference. Under perfect competition, the demand curve is a horizontal straight line. The firms attain equilibrium at the lowest point of the average cost curve. While in monopolistic competition, the demand curve is downward sloping and it is in tangent to long run average cost curve at the higher slope of the long run with average cost curve at its left side. It indicates that equilibrium occurs at a smaller output than perfect competition.

19. SELLING COSTS

The firms under monopolistic competition manufacture and sell closely related products in the potential market. As such, the firms are required to incur expenses in order to advertise in papers and other media. The expenses incurred for advertisements and other selling mediums are called selling costs. Prof.Chamberlin defines selling costs as 'costs incurred in order to alter the position or shape of the demand curve for a product'. As examples, he mentions, advertising of all varieties, salesmen's salaries and the expenses of sales department, margins granted to dealers in order to increase their efforts in favour of particular goods, widow displays, demonstrations of new goods, etc.

> *Thus, selling costs represent the costs on all those selling activities which are directed to persuade the buyers to change their preferences, so as to raise the demand for a given article.*

Selling costs are distinguished from production costs. Production costs are those costs which include the cost of raw-materials, cost of manufacture and labour used in production. Cost of production includes all expenses connected with the manufacture of a commodity, its transportation to the market etc., while the selling costs include all expenses incurred in order to secure a demand for the product. Chamberlin distinguishes the two costs as follows: Production costs adopt commodity to the demand, while selling costs adopt demand to the commodity. This is to say that production costs create utilities which will satisfy demand, while selling costs create and shift the demand itself.

Need for Selling Costs

The temptation for incurring selling costs arises on account of the fact that people have imperfect knowledge and that there is possibility of altering the desires of the people through advertisements. Advertisements are directed to spread the information regarding the quality, the price and other features of the product. Advertising increases a seller's market and changes the location of the demand curve for the product. Advertising about price offer makes the sales curve more elastic while that about quantity, shifts the sales curve to the right.

Varying Returns to Selling Costs

Advertisement is intended to secure an increase in demand for the product. When a firm takes sales promotion compaign through advertisements, it may find its sales have increased. This creates retaliation psychology among the other rival firms. Consequently, all firms under monopolistic competition incur selling costs. The main point is that the producers, by spending money and efforts on advertisements, can alter the demand curve for a product. Persuasive advertisement usually results in increase in sales, by attracting the attention of a large number of prospective buyers. The aim is to increase the sales of one firm at the expense of the other.

At first, selling costs may not yield increasing returns because of the built up habits of the consumers. As advertisements are prolonged, it becomes easier to attack more customers. A point is reached where additional or increased advertisements would not increase the sales. That is after the optimum is reached, any additional expenditure on advertisements would result in diminishing returns.

Selling cost is considered as a variable cost required to dispose the output at the same price. When the selling costs are added to the production cost, then the cost curve moves up. The diagram illustrates the effect of selling cost of price.

In the below diagram, AR is the average revenue or demand curve. MR is the marginal revenue curve. PC is the production cost curve and the shaded area B is the selling cost. By adding these two we get average total cost (ATUV = PC + SC). RS is the net return per unit while RM is the price. The price minus RS we get the average total unit cost and OM is the level of output. The total revenue OPRM minus the total cost OTSM is the net return PRST.

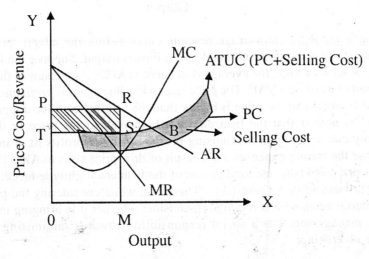

If the firm incurs selling cost, its average cost is bound to rise. As a result of selling costs, if the demand curve shifts, then it can sell more. When the firm is selling more, its sales expenses rise and consequently its total average cost also rises. The firm considers whether it is making maximum profit by selling more at a higher price. If the profits rise, its sales expenses also rise. This cannot go on for ever. The firm has to stop producing more when the marginal revenue equals marginal cost. Beyond this, further expenditure on advertisements will reduce profit, since it will add more to the cost than to revenue. Thus, for a firm under monopolistic competition, corresponding to different levels of selling costs, there are a series of average revenue curves and average cost curves. The producer has to select that set of cost and revenue curves where the profits are maximum. The following diagram illustrates this:

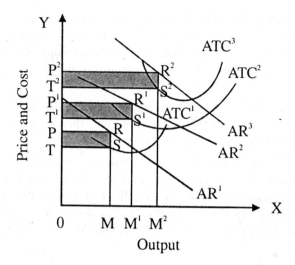

In this diagram, AR, is the average revenue curve before the advertisement. ATC¹ is the average cost curve. OP is the price. OM is the equilibrium output. Suppose the firm incurs selling expenditure of about Rs.1 lakh, the average cost curve is ATC². As a result of this sales expenses, the firm sells more output i.e., MM¹. The price rise to P¹. This again is *profit maximising position.* Here the output is larger and the price is higher than the original equilibrium price. But the most important point to note is that the firm does not bother about the price or the volume of the output. It is only concerned with maximising profit. Since the profits have increased, the firm wants to increase the selling expenses. As a result of this, price rises to AR³. The ATC also rises to ATC₃. In this price and cost, the total profits of the firm are slightly reduced. Beyond this, any increase in advertisement is not profitable. Therefore, while considering the problem of selling cost, the managerial economist is required to consider whether it is bringing maximum profit or not. However, management has a social responsibility towards minimising the undersirable implications of advertising.

20. WASTES IN MONOPOLISTIC COMPETITION

Under monopolistic competition, output is slightly less and prices are higher than perfect competition. According to Prof. Chamberlain and Joan Robinson, firms under monopolistic competition or imperfect competition produce less than socially optimum or ideal output. In other words, the firms do not produce that level of output at which the long run average cost is the minimum. This will happen when the firms operate at a point on the falling portion of the long run average cost curve. A firm under monopolistic competition will attain equilibrium when the demand curve is tangent to the falling position of the long run average cost curve. If the firm produces at the minimum level of the long run average cost curve, it cannot attain equilibrium. Since the demand curve is a sloping curve, the equilibrium is attained at a falling portion of the long run average cost curve. It means to say that the productive resources of the company are not fully utilised. This gives the measure of excess of capacity which lies unutilised under imperfect competition. This is also called *waste.*

Under monopolistic competition, the consumers can buy any product which satisfies them, since there are many close substitutes. The firms engage in high pressure salesmanship, which directly influence the buyers to have preference of a product over another product.

All these have resulted in the restriction of output and higher prices for the products. The consumers have to pay a price higher than the marginal cost. This excess of price causes additional burden on the consumers. It is not the total amount of profit that pinches, but selling too high a price is the greatest evil of imperfect or monopolistic competition.

Expenditure on competitive advertisements is considered as a waste of financial resource. If competition is perfect, there is homogeneous product and as such there is no need for advertisement. Since competition is imperfect, the expenses on advertisements are unavoidable. Every firm in the group is required to set apart a certain percentage of revenue for this expenditure. Under imperfect competition, much larger redution in price will be necessary to prevent consumer from shifting their preferences to other products. They spend money on advertisements to persuade the consumers to buy the product which has been concentrated upon by the advertising firm. Such expenditure is a waste from the point of view of social welfare of the community.

Another similar waste is expenditure on cross transport. A firm in South India is selling the product in North India. At the same time, the same commodity is being sold by a firm located in North India. This state of affairs is due to the absence of perfect competition. Since the firm in South India makes advertisement of its product in the whole of India, a sort of preference is created in the minds of the buyers in North India. Then the product will have to be transported to other regions. The firm considers it worthwhile spending money on advertisement and transport rather than reducing the price sufficiently to attack the neighbouring consumers with irrational preference.

Wastes in imperfect competition arises from the non-utilisation of opportunities for specialisation by each firm. Under perfect competition, the firms specialise for which they are best suited. Consequently, they enjoy various economies in operation. While under monopolistic competition, since each firm has to spend a considerable sum of money on advertisements, they do not resort to improvements of the product.

Thus, under imperfect competition, firms incur losses. Valuable resources of the country are wasted and consumers are considered to be victim of very high prices.

SUMMARY

1. Monopoly is defined as, that market form in which a single producer controls the whole supply of a single commodity which has no close substitute

2. To attain equilibrium the monopoly firm has to equate marginal cost and marginal revenue curve. By equating these two, the firm can maximise its total money profits.

3. Both in the short run and in the long run the monopoly firm will earn super normal profits.

4. Price discrimination refers to the practice of a seller selling the same product at different prices to different buyers.

5. Price discrimination is possible and profitable only under certain circumstances and not always.

6. Monopolistic competition refers to a market situation in which there are either many producers producing goods which are close substitutes to one another or the product is differentiated.

7. Product differentation means that the products are different in some ways. i.e the producers differentiate their product in such a way that each one has a monopoly of his own product.

8. Firms under monopolistic competition may either earn super normal profit or they may even incur with losses also if the cost conditions are less favourable in the short run.

9. In the long run almost all the firms under monopolistic competition will earn normal profit.

10. Selling costs are those costs which are incurred by the firms to persuade the buyers to change their preferences, so as to raise the demand for a given product. The firms under monopolistic competition incur a huge expenditure on this due to competition in the market. (Eg) for selling costs - expenditure incurred on advertisement, window display, salaries to sales executives, free sample etc.

QUESTIONS

1. Define monopoly. State factors which give rise to monopoly.

2. Explain the difference between perfect competition and monopoly.

3. Is monopoly price higher than competitive price. Explain.

4. Could long run profit ever exist in a monopoly.

5. What do you mean by degrees of monopoly? Analyse them.

6. How does a monopolist fix the price and output. Explain with diagram.

7. What is price discrimination? What are different types of price discrimination?

8. What is discriminating monopoly? Under what conditions is price discrimunation possible and profitable?

9. Illustrate how price discrimination is done by a monopolist.

10. Illustrate how price discrimination is done under world market and home markets.

11. What is meant by monopolistic competition?

12. Distinguish between price discrimination and product differentiation.

13. Explain what do you mean by non-price competition

14. What is meant by monopolistic competition? Is product differentiation an outcome of monopolistic competition?

15. Explain how a firm attains equilibrium under monopolistic competition.

16. What are selling costs? How do selling costs influence in shifting the average revenue curve of a firm under monopolistic completion?

17. Price is higher and scale of output is smaller under monopolistic competition than under perfect competition. Explain.

18. Discuss the main features of monopolistic competition.

19. Distinguish between production cost and selling cost.

20. Distinguish between industry equilibrium and group equilibrium.

21. What are the pre-requisties of price discrimination?

22. What is Price Discrimination?

23. Explain the salient features of monopolistic market situation.

24. Explain the salient features of monopoly.

25. Distinguish between perfect competition and monopolistic competition.

26. Monopolistic competition.

27. Briefly discuss how the equilibrium of the firm is attained with new firms entering the industry under monopolistic competition.

28. "A Monopolist cannot obtain equilibrium in the short as well as in the long run". Substantiate this statement.

29. Explain the determination of equilibrium output and price of a product in case of a monopoly using revenue and cost curves.

12 Chapter

Pricing Under Oligopoly

CHAPTER OBJECTIVES

After reading this chapter you will be able to answer the following:

1. Meaning
2. Characteristics of Oligopoly
3. Importance of Advertisement and Selling Costs Under Oligopoly
4. Objectives of Firms Under Oligopoly
5. Pricing Under Oligopoly
6. Effects of Oligopoly
7. Empirical Evidence Regarding Oligopolistic Behaviour
8. Duopoly
9. Features of Duopoly
10. Types of duopoly

---

1. MEANING

Oligopoly is an important form of imperfect competition. Oligopoly is said to prevail when there are few firms or sellers in the market, producing or selling a product. In other words, when there are four or five firms producing and selling a product oligopoly comes into existence.

Oligopoly is defined as competition among the few.

When there are only two firms producing the product in the market, duopoly prevails. When there are a few firms but not more than eight or ten, then oligopoly comes to prevail. In this market form a large portion of output is produced by a small number of large firms.

Firms under oligopoly are classified into pure oligopoly and differentiated oligopoly. In pure oligopoly, the product produced by firms is homogeneous. While in differentiated oligopoly, the products produced by the firms are close substitutes. But in the present day world, only differentiated oligopoly is found.

2. CHARACTERISTICS OF OLIGOPOLY

In oligopoly sellers are few in number. The firms are interdependent. It means the competition among them is less important than firms under monopolistic competition. If a firm were to reduce its price, it affects the prices and the output production of rivals. Therefore, every seller can exert influence on the price and output of rivals. Every seller is so influential that his rivals cannot ignore the adverse effects on their price and output policies. It is therefore necessary for the oligopolistic firm to consider not only the entire demand for the product and also the likely effect of other firms in their price and output policies.

Following are the salient features of oligopolistic market.

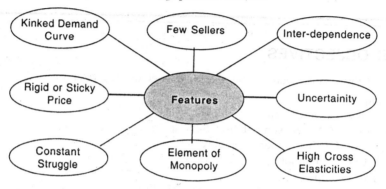

Features of an Oligopolistic Market

1. *Few Sellers:* There are only few sellers selling either homogeneous or differentiated products.

2. *Inter-dependence:* The firms under oligopolistic market depend on each other in fixing the prices and determination of output.

3. *Uncertainity:* Interdependence of firms creates uncertainty for all firms, i.e., the demand or revenue curve of each firm is indeterminate. Because any action taken by a firm may or may not be responded by other firms in the market.

4. *High Cross Elasticities:* The products produced by the firms under oligopolistic market have a high cross elasticities. Hence there is always a fear of retaliation by rivals.

5. *Element of Monopoly:* Under oligopoly each firm controls a large share of the market and produces a differentiated product it enjoys monopoly power in determining price to that extent of differentiation.

6. *Constant Struggle:* The firms under oligopoly are subjected to constant struggle of rivals against rivals.

7. *Rigid or Sticky Price:* The firms under oligopoly sticks to its own price, oligopoly prices tend to be rigid or 'sticky'. If a firm resort to a price cut in the market, it will be followed by other firm in the market resulting in 'price war'. To avoid that, the firms stick to their own prices.

8. *Kinked Demand Curve:* A firm under oligopoly will have a kinky demand curve because of price rigidity.

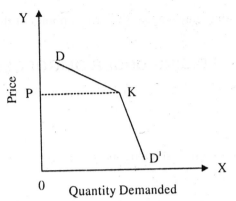

At price OP, there is a kink on the demand curve DD'. The segment DK is elastic and KD' is inelastic. Hence, the kink (k) on the demand curve represents an abrupt change in the slope of the demand curve.

3. IMPORTANCE OF ADVERTISEMENT AND SELLING COSTS UNDER OLIGOPOLY

The firms are so few that each one wants to sell as much as possible. In order to do so, they incur enormous expenditure on advertisement and other modes of selling campaigns. They resort to aggressive and defensive marketing weapons to gain a greater share in the market and to prevent a fall in the price of the product. Baumol in his book 'Economic Theory and Operations Analysis' says that is only in oligopoly that advertising comes fully into its own. Under perfect competition and monopoly, advertising is not required. Under monopolistic competition, advertising plays an important role because of product differentiation. But in oligopoly it is a matter of life and death, if a firm fails to keep up with the advertising budget of its competitors, it may find that its customers are drifting away to a new product. True competition is found only in oligopoly which involves corporate struggle, a rival against rival.

4. OBJECTIVES OF FIRMS UNDER OLIGOPOLY

It is natural for a firm to achieve profit maximisation. This objective has been refuted by several economists. According to Prof.Rothschild, oligopolists aim at maximizing their security of achieving reasonable amount of stable profits over a long period of time. On the other hand, Prof.Baumol thinks that it is sales maximisation as a objective of an oligopoly firm. Some other economists say that it is maximizing the utility function. Prof.R.L.Morris thinks that firms try to maximise their growth rate. Thus, there is lot of controversy about the most probable objective of the oligopolistis. This controversy has led to the indeterminancy in the price and output policies. Indeterminancy means the non-availability of a single solution to the problem of price and output determination. If an acceptable solution is to be offered, then the concept of inter-dependence is to be ignored. If this is assumed, then we can have a determinate demand curve. With this, the standard analysis of the theory of the firm can be applied to provide a determinate solution to the price and the output problem of oligopoly.

Economists have accepted the *Cournot model* of an oligopoly firm. In this model, the assumption of interdependence is ignored. Here, the demand curve is downward sloping curve of a monopolist. It is assumed that the firm would fix the price for the output on the belief that other firms keep their price and output unchanged. But critics point out that ignoring interdependence is a mistaken approach.

5. PRICING UNDER OLIGOPOLY

Important forms of price fixation under oligopoly are as follows:

(a) Kinky demand curve.

(b) Price Leadership.

(c) Pricing under collusion. [Collusive oligopoly]

(d) Independent pricing.

(a) Kinky Demand Curve

The demand curve facing the oligopolist is indeterminate. The demand curve shows what amounts of the product a firm can sell at different prices. Under perfect competition, the demand curve is given as definite. A firm knows the price and the amount of output that it can sell. Since the firm under perfect competition is producing an identical product, it is incapable of influencing the prices by its own individual action. Even the demand curve of the monopolist is definite. He knows at what price he can sell the amount of a product. Under monopolistic competition too, the demand curve is somewhat definite and is given by the buyer's preference for its product.

But under oligopoly, the situation is different and the firms are interdependent. Under oligopoly, a firm cannot change its price assuming that rivals do not take any retaliatory action. As a result of this, the demand curve facing the oligopoly firm loses its definiteness.

There is one particular shape of demand under oligopoly that is called Kinky Demand Curve. There is a kink in the demand cure. The kink is always at the ruling price. Assuming a ruling price as given, a rise in price on the part of a given oligopoly firm will not invite retaliation from the rivals. It means that rivals will not resort to increase in their prices to neutralise the effects of price increase by the first producer. Since the firm increased the price, he is sure to lose its customers. So the upper part of the curve is more elastic while the downward part of the curve is less elastic. This is because, a price cut will invite retaliation from the rivals, they also cut the prices with a view to protect their own sales. The result will be, if a firm lowers its price, it can increase the sales. The demand curve of a firm under oligopoly is shown in the diagram clearly.

MR is the marginal revenue curve. Since it follows AR, there is discontinuity in the marginal revenue curve below the point corresponding to the kink. The marginal cost cuts the marginal revenue curve between the points T and S. Hence the equilibrium output and price do not undergo any change. The firm will be in equilibrium producing ON level of output at OP price. This is one of the ways of pricing a product under oligopoly.

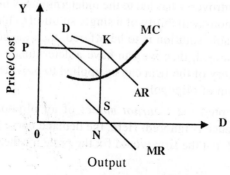

(b) Price Leadership

The price determination under oligopoly is not an easy task. The practical solution is that of the formation of a collusion, formal or tacit and thereby work out an agreed pattern of price and output determination. The firms under oligopoly collectively come to an agreement on price and output. A variant approach is that dominant firms or low cost firms exist as their leader. Other firms follow their leader in the fixation of price and output.

Generally, there is a tacit agreement among the oligopolists. Under tacit agreement, without any fact to fact contact, consultation or discussion, they come to have some understandings between themselves and pursue a uniform policy with regard to the price and output. An example to tacit agreement is found in price leadership, but informally, the firms follow the instrutions of the leader. Experience is that this type of price leadership does not violate anti - trust laws. Sometimes, price leadership emerges from a formal agreement among the oligopoly firms.

Types of Price Leadership

There are several types of price leadership. The main types of price leadership are as follows:

(i) **Price leadership of a dominant firm:** Under this, one of the few firms in the industry, which produces a large portion of the product is selected as the leader. This is a dominant firm which wields a great influence in the market. It sets the price and makes other firms to accept this price. The other firms being small are hence not capable of exercising any influence on the price. The dominant firm estimates its own demand for the product and fixes a price which maximises its own profits. The other firms which are small, having no individual influence on the price, follow the dominant firm and accept the price set by the dominant firm and adjust their outputs accordingly.

(ii) **Barometric Price Leadership:** Under this type of price leadership, an old experience, largest or most respected firm assumes the role of a custodian and thus protects the interests of all. This firm, instead of promoting its own interest, acts as a custodian of all firms. It assesses the market conditions with regard to demand for the product, costs of production, competition from the related products etc. and fixes the price which is suitable to all firms in the industry, since the interest of all firms is suitable to all firms in the industry. All firms are protected by the dominant firm and all firms follow the leader willingly. The barometric price leader may change from time to time.

(iii) **Exploitative or Aggressive Price Leadership:** In this case, one big firm comes to establish its leadership and follows aggressive price policies and thus compels other firms to follow this leader and accept the price fixed by it. If a firm shows any independence, it is threatened with dire consequences and hence it is also forced to accept the price.

Price and Output Determination Under Price Leadership

Economists have developed various models concerning price and output determination under price leadership, taking different assumptions about the behaviour of the price leader and his followers. Let us take up a simple case here to show price - output determination under dominant price leadership on the following assumptions:

(a) There are only two firms A and B. The firm A has lower cost of production than B.

(b) The product produced by the two firms is homogeneous so that the consumers have no preference between them.

(c) Both A and B firms have equal share in the market. In other words, they are facing the same demand curve which will be half of the total market demand curve.

The diagram given in below illustrates the price output determination subject to the assumptions stated above:

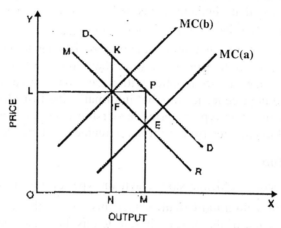

In the diagram, DD is the demand curve facing each firm which is half of the total market demand curve for the product. MR is the marginal revenue curve of each firm. MC(a) and MC(b) are the marginal cost curves of A and B firms respectively. Firm A will be maximizing its profits by selling OM output MP price. Since at OM, its marginal cost is equal to marginal revenue. For firm B, the profits will be maximum when it sells ON output at NK price, because at this output, its marginal cost is equal to the marginal revenue. It will be seen from the above diagram that profit maximizing price MP of A firm is lower than the profit maximizing price NK of B firm. Since the two firms are producing homogeneous products, they cannot charge two different prices. They have to sell the product at a uniform price because the product is homogeneous. Because the profit maximizing price MP of a firm A is lower than the profit maximizing price NK of firm B, firm A will dictate its price to firm B. In case the firm B refuses to fall in line, it can be ousted by firm A which is charging a low price. Thus, firm A will be the price leader and firm B will be the price follower.

It can also be seen that although the firm B is compelled to sell at the price MP, the firm B will produce OM output like firm A, since the demand curve DD facing each firm is the same. Thus, both firms will charge the same price and sell the same amount of output, while in the case of firm A, the price leader will be maximizing its profit by selling OM output at MP price. But at this price and output, the firm B will not be maximising its profit It is because that firm B by selling OM output at MP price will be smaller than firm A, because its costs are higher.

When the products of the price leader and his followers are differentiated, then the price charged by them will be different, but the prices charged by the followers will be only slightly different either way from that of the price leader and they will conform to a definite pattern of differentials.

Difficulties of Price Leadership

In the real world, price leadership does not operate smoothly, because it involves some practical difficulties:

(a) One such difficulty is that the price leader cannot assess correctly the reactions of his followers. If his estimate about the reactions of the rivals to price changes proves to be incorrect, then not only the success of his price policy, but also his leadership in the market will be jeopardized.

(b) When a price leader fixes a higher price than the followers would prefer, there is a strong tendency on the part of the followers to make hidden price cuts in order to increase their share in the market, without openly challenging the price leader. The manufacturers use a good number of devices which amount to secret price cutting such as rebates, favourable credit terms, 'money-back' guarantees, after-delivery free services, sale on the payment of price in easy instalment with low rates of interest, etc. Price leaders are generally fed up with the increasing number of concessions granted by their rivals and they make an open price cut to prevent further fall in their share of the market. In such circumstances, price leadership becomes infructuous.

Oligopoly and Non-Price Competition

The price leader has to face another difficulty, when he finds that the rival firms are indulging in non-price competition. Non-price competition is a device used by rival firms to capture a higher share of the market. The device is viewed with far more equanimity than price cutting and is frequently quite unrestrained. The devices used under non-price competition are advertising, personal selling, product improvement, better quality packing and appearance, easier credit items, improvement of the quality of the product and so on. While changing the same price, the rivals try to increase their share of the market by resorting to non-price competition. As a result of non-price competition, the price leader has also to adopt similar devices to prevent the fall in its sales or has to make an outright cut in price in order to achieve his objective. In view of these facts, the price leader may not be able to maintain his leadership.

There is a great limitation on the price leader to fix a high price. It is because, if he fixes a high price, it will induce the rivals to make secret price cuts, which will adversely affect the price leader. Moreover, a higher price fixed by the price leader will attract new competitors into the industry which may not accept his price leadership. Lastly, differences in costs also post a problem. If the cost of production of the price leader is higher on account of which he fixes a high price and the rival producers with lower costs of production, they will have no problem in under cutting the price. On the other hand, if the price leader has lower costs than the rivals, then he will set a low price which will antagonise his rivals who will try to break his price leadership.

3. Pricing under collusion (Collusive Oligopoly)

There is another development witnessed in oligopolic industries and that is of collusion. Under this situation, the Oligopolists arrive at a tacit or formal agreement on a common policy to be followed by them. These firms may reach an agreement after indulging in price-war. Otherwise, cut-throat competition is harmful to all of them. Alternatively, they may show foresight and enter into collusion with each other believing that they can promote their interests best if they pull together to survive in the market.

When the various oligopolists of an industry enter into a formal agreement, they are said to form a *Cartel*. originally, the term cartel was used for the agreement in which there existed a common sales agency which alone undertook the selling operations of all firms which were party to the agreement. Nowdays, all types of formal agreements reached by oligopolists are known as cartels. Since these cartels restrain competition among the member firms, their formations, have been made illegal in some countries by the government passing laws against them. For example, for formation of a cartel is illegal in United States of America. However, inspite of the illegality of cartels, they are still formed in USA through secret devices.

There is an extreme form of collusion in which the firms entering into an agreement, surrender completely their right of price-output determination to a central agency, so as to secure maximum joint profits for them. Formation of such a formal collusion is called *perfect cartel*. Under this perfect cartel type of collusive oligopoly, the price and output are determined for the whole industry as well as for each member firm by the central agency. The total profits are distributed among the member firms in agreed proportions which may not be necessarily in proportion to the output quota assigned to each firm. The total cost is sought to be minimised by asking the firms of the cartel to produce such separate outputs as to make their output costs equal.

But the formation of perfect cartels is not very common in the real world, even when their formation is not illegal. In the actual collusion, the agreement is only on the price which is generally the joint profit maximizing price and member firms are free to produce and sell the outputs which will maximise their individual profits given the fixed agreed price. Each firm in this case will earn profits depending on the output produced and sold by it. If a firm produces and sells a small output, its profit also is small.

4. Independent Pricing

Under differentiated oligopoly, the firms may follow an independent price and output policy which is similar to monopoly price. This is possible because, each firm produces differentiated products. Due to competition among the firms, they may face "price war" in the market. It may result in competitive price. The upper limit is the monopoly price fixed by them. In reality the firm may fix a price between the two limits depending upon the condition prevailing in the market. This may lead to price instability in the market or price may settle at an indeterminate level. Sometimes, the firm may also accept the long run price prevailing in the market and adjust its price accordingly. Since independent pricing under oligopoly leads to uncertainity and insecurity in the market, it cannot last long.

6. EFFECTS OF OLIGOPOLY

The economic effets of oligopoly are briefly described as follows:

(*i*) *Small output and higher prices:* Under oligopoly, the total output is restricted while the prices are high.

(*ii*) *The prices exceed the average costs:* Owing to restriction on the entry of new firms, the prices are fixed and such prices are higher than costs. The consumers have to pay more than what is necessary to restrain the resources in the industry. The resources of the economy cannot move into the making of products desired by the consumers from those where they are desired less. In other words, the productive capacity of the economy is under-utilised in oligopoly.

(*iii*) *Lower Efficiency:* There is no tendency for the firms under oligopoly to build plant of optimum scale and consequently they cannot attain maximum potential economic efficiency. This is because the prodution of the output is dependent on the quota fixed by the industry.

(iv) *Selling costs:* The firms under oligopoly have to spend a considerable sum of money on advertisements. The firms engage in aggressive and extensive sales promotion effort by means of advertisement and by changing the design of the product and by improving the quality of the product.

(v) *Welfare Effect:* Under oligopoly, since output does not generally correspond to the minimum long run average cost, more units of resources per unit of output are used than it is necessary. And also the price is higher than average and marginal cost. Huge sums of money are spent on sales promotion and hence from the welfare point of view, oligopoly fares very badly. The oligopolists push non-price competition beyond socially desirable limits.

7. EMPIRICAL EVIDENCE REGARDING OLIGOPOLISTIC BEHAVIOUR

On the basis of empirical evidence, the following conclusions have been made regarding the behaviour of oligopoly business:

When the pricing decisions are centralised in the case of stores with branches spread all over the country, the prices are set by the central office and the branches are to face competition from rivals, then price cuts are resorted by branch managers only for a short duration. Stores managers felt that they would retaliate if they thought that the price cut was permanent. In Australia, the stores announce weekly specials, making price cuts lasting not more than a week and this is too temporary to call for retaliatory price changes by competitors.

At times, the oligopolist may fail to obtain proper information regarding the possible reactions of the competitors, since many firms would like to keep their decisions very secret.

Safeguarding Competition and Anti-Trust Laws

In several countries, the governments have enacted legislations to prevent the formation of monopolies and oligopolies. The objective of those governments in curbing the formation of monopolies is to encourage the spirit of competition. The US Attorney General's Committee on Anti-Trust laws mentions that where there is workable competition, rival sellers whether existing competitors or new or potential entrants into the field, would keep this power in check by offering or threatening to offer effective inducements, so long as the profits to be anticipated in the industry are sufficiently attractive in comparison with those in other employment when all risks and other determinants are taken into account.

Many economists have upheld the economic benefits of competition on the following grounds:

(i) Firms do not make agreements as to prices, output, investment or the allocation of markets.

(ii) A very wide and ever-increasing range of goods and services are offered to the consumers at reasonable price and competition is what increases the alternatives for the consumer and monopoly is what narrows the choice.

(iii) Increasingly close substitutes for most products tend to make their appearance in competition. The closer the substitutes for most products, the less important it is whether there is one producer or more than one for each of the substitutable products.

(iv) The consumer is exercising actively the function of directing the production towards those suppliers who make the best offer. The best offer would be decided in terms of price, quality and service in the mixture preferred by the consumer.

Though there are several advantages in competition, obstructions to it have been found since times immemorial. Many producers by means of forming combinations and conspiracies have been making competition unfair and unworkable. Competitive functions of the trade industry are undermined through various concerted acts of minimum prices to be charged on resale, exclusive dealings, exclusive areas to be served, typing up arrangements etc. Such practices are required to be curbed by means of enactment and enforcement of anti-monopoly and trade restrictive acts.

The governments in a good number of countries have enacted a number of legislations to declare the monopoly formation as illegal. Some of the important legislations enacted in several countries are worth examination. The Monopolies and Trade Restrictive Practices (Industry and Control Act) 1948 was the first legislation enacted in England to deal with the problems of monopoly and restrictive practices. In the USA, the government enacted several Anti-Trust laws between 1885 and 1891 to declare the formation of monopolies anti-national. One such famous legislation is the Sherman Act which declares illegal every contract, combination in the form of Trust or otherwise or conspiracies in the restraint of trade and commerce. The Federal Trade Commission Act of 1914 prohibits unfair methods of competition in commerce.

In Australia also, the government enacted a comprehensive legislation in 1997 to prohibit the monopolisation and restraint of trade and commerce.

In India also, Monopolies and Restrictive Trade Practice Act (MRTP Act) was enacted in 1969 to prevent the concentration of economic power in the hands of few persons. The Government of India constituted a commiossion to implement the MRTP Act.

8. DUOPOLY

Meaning

The word 'duo' means two and 'pollein' means "to sell". Thus, the word duopoly refers to that form of imperfect competition where there will be only two sellers producing and selling either identical products or differentiated products. Each seller is a monopolist. Each one tries to guess the rivals actions and motives and they may either resort to competition or collusion. They may compete with each other to eliminate the rival and become a monopolist. Otherwise the two-firms may agree to co-operate and fix the price and output (i.e., they may fix the same price if products are identical).

Economists like Augustin Cournot, Edgeworth, Chamberlin in Paul Sweezy and Stackelberg have contributed for the development of the theory of duopoly.

9. FEATURES

1. It is a form of imperfect competition.
2. Two sellers selling goods in the market.
3. The firms produce and sells either identical products or differentiated products.
4. The two firms may either resort to competition or collusion.
5. It is a simple form of oligopoly.

Therefore we can define duopoly as:

> *Duopoly is a market situation in which there are only two sellers producing and selling either identical products or differentiated ones.*

10. TYPES OF DUOPOLY

There are 2 types of duopoly.

They are: (i) Duopoly without product differentiation.

(ii) Duopoly with product differentiation.

(i) Duopoly without Product Differentiation

In this type of market, there are two monopolies selling identical or homogeneous products. In this case, they may enter into agreement and divide the market among themselves. They may determine the prices based on their cost conditions and degree of competition in the market. If there is unity among them they may try to avoid competition and they may establish a monopoly situation in the market. On the other hand, if there is no agreement or unity among them, then each seller tries to eliminate the other and there arises a 'price-war' or 'cut-throat competition.'

In this situation, the price fixed by them may fall to the level of competitive price where it equals the cost of production and the firm may earn only normal profits. Sometimes the price may fall even below the average cost resulting in losses. But in the long run, competition is eliminated and better conditions are revived and they may fix a higher price and earn profit.

Therefore under duopoly, if there is competition between the two firms competitive price will prevail on the other hand if there is no competition monopoly price will prevail in the market.

(ii) Duopoly with Product Differentiation

When there is product differentiation, each seller may have his own customers for his products in the market and need not be afraid of his rival. Each firm becomes a monopoly and can have its own price-output policy. In this situation a firm which is able to produce and sell a better quality product can earn more profit than the other firm both in the short-run as well as in the long-run.

SUMMARY

1. Oligopoly refers to a market situation where there are few sellers or firms producing or selling a product.

2. The sellers are few in number and they are interdependent

3. The firms incur enormous expenditure on advertisement and other modes of selling campaign.

4. A firm under oligopoly has a kinky demand curve. The demand curve is made of two segments (due to kink). The kink always prevails at the ruling price.

5. A dominant firm or a low cost firm fixes the price and the same is followed by other firm under oligopoly. This is called a price leadership.

6. All the firms may enter into agreement in fixing the price and a common policy will be followed by them. This is called collusive oligopoly.

7. Under oligopoly market, the prices are higher but output is small. The prices exceed the average costs. The efficiency of the firms is low and they spend a considerable sum of money on advertisements.

QUESTIONS

1. What are the striking features of a oligopoly market?
2. Diagrammatically show price determination under oligopoly.
3. Explain price rigidity under oligopoly.
4. What is price leadership? Explain the conditions necessary for price leadership nd advantages of price leadership.
5. Industrial structure of India is characterised by oligopoly. Comment.
6. What is a Kinked Demand Curve?
7. 'If the firms under oligopoly collide, they earn only normal profit, if they collude, they earn supernormal profit'. Comment.
8. Write short notes on:
   (a) Barometric price leadership
   (b) Collusive price leadership
   (c) Need for anti-trust laws.
   (d) Aggressive price leadership.
9. Examine the price and output. Determination under oligopoly.
10. Critically examine the price and output determination under collusive oligopoly.
11. What are the main features of Oligopoly?
12. Explain the concept of oligopoly and the kinked demand curve hypothesis.
13. Give the meaning of Duopoly. What are its features.
14. Explain the types of duopoly.

13 Chapter

Neoclassical Theory of Firm

CHAPTER OBJECTIVES

After reading this chapter you will be able to answer the following:

1. The Neoclassical Theory of the Firm
2. The Marginalist Controversy
3. Gordon's Attack on Marginalism
4. Defence of Marginalism

---

1. THE NEOCLASSICAL THEORY OF THE FIRM

The neoclassical theory based on the marginalistic behavioural rules was in use till 1938. But in 1939. Reprinted in P.W.S Andrews and T.Wilson (eds) Oxford Studies in Price Mechanism (oxford University Press 1952). and C.I.Hitch[1] criticised the marginalist approach of the traditional Neo-classical theory by providing empirical evidence concerning the behaviour of firms. But their findings were also not accepted without criticism.' During 1940's few economists, namely R.A.Lester and R.A.Gorden expressed serious doubts about the validity of the marginalist approach. M.Friedman and F.Machlup defended the Marginalism in their writings.

Assumptions: The important assumptions of the neoclassical theory of the firm are as follows:

(i) This theory assumes that entrepreneur is the owner of the firm.

(ii) The main goal of the firm is profit maximisation.

(iii) The decisions are made using the marginalist principle.

(iv) The firm's demand and cost functions are known with certainty.

(v) According to the type of market structure the entry conditions differ.

(vi) The firm acts with a certain time-horizon.

(1) Entrepreneur is the owner of the firm: This theory considers entrepreneur as the owner of the firm. But modern corporate enterprises are different. There is separate existence of

shareholding owners and the decision making managers. But this is not recognised by the neoclassical theory and it also assumes that the entrepreneur-owner has all the information that he needs. He also possesses the capability for decision making at the firm level. So, this assumption will not suit the modern firms where it is characterised by the separation of ownership and management.

(2) The firm's main goal is profit maximisation: The neoclassical theory considers profit maximisation a the main goal of a business firm. But many economists have criticised it and they say that, modern business firm no longer aim at maximisation of profit, instead they have several other goals to be achieved. According to them profit maximisation is one of the multiplicity of goal which a firm has to be achieved in the long run. Critics of this theory have suggested some alternative goods of a modern corporate firm which are given as follows:

    (a) *Maximisation of the Managerial Utility Function:* In modern corporate enterprises managers attempt to maximise their own utility function. But William J.Baumol says that to maximise managerial utility, growth of sales revenue has to be maximised. R.Manis says that a modern corporate firm aims at maximisation of the balanced rate of growth of firm's sales and its capital supply.

    (b) *Satisficing:* Cyert and March are of the opinion that due to uncertainty in the real world, information constraint, limited time, manager's limited ability to analyse information, etc., no firm can aspire to maximise profits. Instead they try to achieve satisfactory profits, satisfactory sales, and satisfactory growth. This is called as satisficing behaviour of the firm.

    (c) *Long Run survival and retention of a constant market share goals:* According to K.W. Rothschild, the entrepreneurs give more priority to long run survival. In present day market set up, retention of market share has become the primary goal of the corporate firms. Though this objective is not contradictory to marginalist principle it may not lead to maximisation of long run profit.

    (d) *Entry Prevention:* Modern corporate firms are more interested in entry prevention. They set the price at such a level that the potential entrants have no incentive to enter the market. They considered entry prevention goal is more important because it is considered necessary for long-run profit maximisation, long-run survival and to avoid risk associated with the behaviour of new entrants into the market.

    Though many economists have suggested alternative goals to profit maximisation, yet the controversy is not completely resolved. Many economists still believe that managers cannot deviate from profit maximisation goal. They have a rather limited discretion in goal setting and modern corporate enterprise usually have multiplicity of goals.

(3) The Marginalist Principle: The important assumption of the neoclassical theory is that, the firms follow the marginalist principle while making any decision.

The marginalist principle implies that in each period a firm attempts to maximise its profits by determining its price and output at the level where its marginal cost (additional cost incurred to produce additional product) is equal to its marginal revenue (additional revenue earned from additional product).

$$\therefore MC = MR.$$

(4) The Certainty Assumption: This theory assumes that the firm not only has complete information about its past and present conditions but also has full knowledge about the future happenings in the business world. Later this assumption was modified. In the modern day world, it is not possible to predict about the future course of actions in the business world. So, this theory adopted a probabilistic approach which meant that firms do not have perfect knowledge. This modified approach made this theory more realistic and convincing. But at the same time it is criticised also.

(5) Entry Considerations: This theory assumes that entry takes place in the long run. Potential entry and its implications, though at times significant, have been completely ignored.[2]

Neoclassical theory suggests that entry under different market structures, purely depend on their specific characteristics. Under perfect competition, entry and exit are free by definition. Under monopolistic competition entry is assumed to be free because firms do not have any policy to prevent entry of new firms. Oligopoly traditional models are silent on the question of entry. The classical duopoly models being closed, rule out the entry. Even in the theory of cartels, entry is possible.

(6) The Static Nature of the Firm: The neoclassial theory does not give importance for different time periods. It is essentially static in nature. It ignores interdependence of decision taken in different periods. This theory considers time aspects in three respects. (a) The neoclassical theory of the firm makes a distinction between the short run and long run in decision-making process of the firm. (b) The theory assumes that each firm has its own time - horizon over which it wishes to maximise its profits. (c) It also deals with the timing of demand relative to the production flows and also considers gestation period of investment. All these clearly shows that Neo-classical theory has given consideration to time element to a certain extent.

Despite its time considerations, this theory is static in nature.

2. THE MARGINALIST CONTROVERSY

Chamberlin's Theory of monopolistic competition and Joan Robinson's theory of imperfect competition enjoyed wide acceptability till 1939. According to these theories the firms were considered to be pursuing the goal of profit maximisation both in the short run and long run and it was realised by following the marginalist principle, that is MC = MR. In 1939, 'The Oxford Economists Research Group' carried out a study on pricing behaviour of business firms and submitted a report which is also called as Hall and Hitch Report and it was based on an empirical study of 38 firms. The findings of the Oxford Economists Research Group given by Hall and Hitch may be summarised as follows:

(a) Hall and Hitch pointed out that firms do not act automatically. They observe the behaviour of their competitors and react accordingly. Hall and Hitch found that oligopoly was for more prevalent than monopolistic competition.

(b) Empirical studies undertaken by them revealed that firms tries to maximise long run profits rather than short run profits. Hence they have concluded that the firms do not follow the marginalist principle (MC = MR) to determine price and output in the short run. Hall and Hitch pointed out that, the firms generally follow the *full cost pricing principle*. This principle implies that the firms set the price (P) to cover the average variable cost (AVC), the average fixed cost (AFC) and a normal profit margin.

∴ P = AVC + AFC + NPM

Hall and Hitch in their report points out that, the firms generally follow full-cost principle and abandon marginalist principle for two reasons:

(i) The marginalist principle can be used in price setting only when the marginal costs and the demand schedule is known to the firms. If these information are not available then the firms cannot use the marginalist principle.

(ii) Full cost pricing principle is considered appropriate principle because it ensures a fair amount of profit margin besides covering the cost of production.

(c) Hall and Hitch in their report mentioned that the firm's main pre-occupation is price and not output as assumed by the traditional neoclassical theory. Hall and Hitch further say that: the firms set the price in accordance with the average cost principle. However, the firm may deviate this in two circumstances; one is when they get big order, they may fix a price lower than average cost plus profit margin. Secondly, to avoid competition they may deviate from this principle and set a lower price.

(d) Hall and Hitch found out that despite changes in demand and costs, the prices of industrial products did not change and they explained this phenomenon with the help of 'kinked demand curve'. The kink in the demand curve of the firms implies that, when a firm increases its price it may not be followed by competitors but at the same time if it lowers the price, the competitors may also follow the same and thus increase in the sales will be a negligible amount. Hall and Hitch points out in their study that firms will set their prices in accordance with the average cost principle and kink occurred at the price where it would be equal to average cost and they also set the price without any illusion. Therefore the study made by Hall and Hitch clearly indicates that the firms operating in oligopolistic markets determines price by applying average cost principle and tends to be sticky (stable). Hence we can conclude that Hall and Hitch did not develop a determinate theory of pricing in oligopoly markets.

3. GORDON'S ATTACK ON MARGINALISM

R.A. Gordan has criticised the neoclassical marginalist principle by questioning the assumptions and postulates of the theory of the firm in his work, 'Short-period Price Determination in Theory and Practice', American Economic Review (1948). The important criticisms of the marginalist principle made by him are as follows:

(i) *The changes in Economic environment of business and Real World Complexity:* The neoclassical theory of the firm does not take into account the real happenings (complexities) of the business world. The determinants of demand and costs keep on changing with the time and hence while fixing the price the manager cannot equate MC and MR. Hence the possibility of following marginalist principle is ruled out. Instead he suggests that, under these changing environment, it is better to set the prices according to average cost principle which is a rationalistic approach.

(ii) *Uncertainty:* The element of uncertainty is not given much importance in the neoclassical theory of the firm which is more important in the estimation of costs and future demand. It is not possible to collect the adequate information required for setting the price as assumed by the neo classical theory. Businessmen always want to avoid uncertainty and may think that they can do it by setting some other goals besides maximisation of profits. According to Gordan, all these cannot be dealt satisfactorily with the help of marginalist principle.

(iii) *Average Cost Pricing:* Gordon supports average cost pricing principle and the empirical studies also shows that firms adopt the average cost rule for setting their prices. When the managers of the firm are preoccupied with various kinds of problems, they will never follow marginalistic principles and profit maximisation. It is not possible to know the marginal costs of various products. In such circumstances, their choice will be average cost pricing principle.

(iv) *Multiplicity of goods:* The modern firms pursue a multiplicity of goals. It include firm's growth, goodwill, and non-conflicting labour relations and empirical studies also provide evidence to prove this. These goals are definitely related to profit but it is not clear that such goals are consistent or competing with the profit maximising goal. If these goals are incompatible with profit maximisation, then the marginalist principle will not be followed by the firms.

(v) *Subjectively conceived demand and costs:* If the demand and cost curves are not known objectively, the marginalist principle cannot be followed. F.Machlup believes that if business firms estimate demand and costs subjectively, then marginalist principle become a mere tautology (i.e. a necessarily true statement) because any observed behaviour of firms could be treated as an attempt towards profit maximisation goal.

Tautological Predictions

The neoclassical theory of the firm allows additional goals into costs and revenue functions before attempting application of the marginalist principle. According to Gordon it leads to tautological predictions. In his opinion, a dyanmic multi-period analysis should be used to avoid tautology. In dynamic multi-period model, cost and revenue functions are postulated in each period within the firm's time horizon and then the firm managers attempt maximisation of the present value of future profits. The marginalist principle avoids the expectations and time element and by passes the problem of uncertainty.

4. DEFENCE OF MARGINALISM

The neoclassical theory of the firm, which uses marginalist principle, is supported by many economists now. They are arguing in favour of marginalism. Their arguments in defence of this theory are so strong that it is not easy to abandon it. Their arguments in defence of marginalist principle are as follows:

(i) *Provided empirical evidence to support their argument:* J.S.Early conducted empirical studies to analyse the pricing behaviour of business firms in USA.[3] His example constituted of 110 companies and found out that those firms adopted marginalistic rules in their pricing decisions. He has concluded on the basis of his studies that modern accounting methods provide required information on marginal costs and marginal revenues and this information can be used for determining price and output. His studies contradict with Hall and Hitch study which was based on 33 will organised firms in UK. According to R.Barback, all the firms may not adopt marginalist principle in the short run because they think that this may adversely affect their long-run profits.[4]

(ii) *Validity on the basis of predictions:* Milton Friedman defends this theory on the basis of its predictions. According to him, the theory should be judged on the basis of its predictions rather than the realism of its assumptions. Though no evidence is available to prove his defence, yet he asserts that the neoclassical theory and the firm has produced reasonably good predictions and this should be considered satisfactory.

(iii) *Only profit maximising firms can survive:* A. Alchian Edith Penrose have defended the neoclassical marginalist approach on the basis of the principle of survival of the fittest.[5]

According to them only those firms which maximises their profit can manage to build up assets and can grow faster. Whereas the non-profit maximisation firm would feel resource constraint and are likely to stagnate.

(iv) *Assumptions of the marginalist theory are fairly realistic:* F. Machlup defends the neoclassical marginalist principle's assumptions. He asserts that they are fairly elastic. However he agrees that MC and MR may not be objectively known to the business firms. He does not consider this as serious problem. According to him, what is relevant is the belief of the firms, as to what their MC and MR are. The objective values of MC and MR are not required for the firm to adopt marginalist principle.

(v) *Limitations of 'evidence' against marginalism:* F. Machlup is not satisfied in the empherical evidence provided by Hall and Hitch and he also rejects R.A.Lester's criticism of marginalist approach. He rejects them for three reasons.[6] They are not familiar with the concept of marginal cost, marginal revenue and elasticities, hence they would say that, they determine the prices equal to average cost which is not inconsistent with the marginalistic rule which economists follow. The firm is said to be in equilibrium when MC = MR. If the industry is in equilibrium along with the firms, then each firm's price will also be equal to average cost.

(vi) Machlup (F. Machlup, 'Marginal Analysis and Empirical Managerialist Behavioural", American Economic Review, 1946 and 1967) says that elasticity of demand is also considered in their pricing methods. Even the average cost pricing also requires estimates of elasticity of demand. Under these conditions both the rules i.e marginalist sales and the average cost principle lead to determination of same price.

(vii) Businessmen do not admit that profit maximisation is their goal. So the modern firms discretely state that they adopt average cost principle for setting the price.

(viii) *Profit maximisation is the goal:* F. Machlup says that, firms proceed along the goal of long-run profit maximisation. They do not consider any other goal along with the profit maximisation. To attain this, they make use of their long run costs and long run demand curves which incorporate changes in business environment as well as expectations of future conditions.

Conclusions

It is very clear from the above arguments, that the controversy on the validity of the marginalist approach is not completely explained. So we may conclude that, marginalist principle is not followed in the short run due to the fact that prices are often sticky despite continuous changes in the firm's environment. More over, it is not very clear that; the pricing policies followed by the firms covered under various studies are inconsistent with marginalism. Therefore, it is not possible to conclude that average cost pricing theory is an alternative to the marginalist theory.

SUMMARY

1. The neoclassical theory of firm assumes the entrepreneur is the owner of the firm and profit maximisation is the goal of the firm.

2. This theory gave more importance to marginalist principle.

3. The certainty approach of this theory is not correct because the probabilities of future events are influenced by the risk attitude, time-horizon and the changes in the business environment.

4. The neo-classical theory of the firm takes note of actual entry in the long run and ignores the potential entry and its implications.

5. This theory though gives consideration for time factor, is static in nature.

6. The Oxford Economists Research Group Report also known as Hall and Hitch Report says that firms do not act automatically and do not follow the marginalist principle and their main preoccupation is price.

7. According to them firms generally follow the full cost pricing principle. It also includes a normal profit margin.

8. Hall and Hitch found that the prices of industrial products did not change despite changes in demand and costs. They have explained this phenomenon with the help of the kinked demand curve.

9. R.A. Gorden has criticised the neoclassical marginalist principle by questioning the assumptions and postulates of the theory.

10. He criticises that: the neoclassical theory does not take into account the business world's complexities.

11. According to him, the marginalist principle is not relevant for price and output determination where as he supports average cost pricing principle.

12. He further says that profit maximisation is not the only goal of a business firm. They pursue a multitude of goals, including growth of goodwill and non-conflicting labour relations.

13. Though the marginalist theory (neo-classical) was criticised, even now it finds many supporters and they have even provided empirical evidence to support their argument.

QUESTIONS

1. Discuss the marginalist theory of the firm or neo-classical theory of the firm.

2. Briefly explain Hall and Hitch report.

3. Average-cost principle of pricing or full cost principle is generally followed by the firm in fixing the price. Is this statement correct? If so, give answer to support you view.

4. Write a short note on Gordon's attack on marginalism.

5. What are the various criticisms levelled against marginalist principle by R.A. Gordan?

6. Explain how the supporters of marginalist theory of the firm defend the theory.

REFERENCES

1. R.L. Hall and C.I. Hitch, '*Price, Theory and Business Behaviour*', Oxford Economic Papers, 1939.

2. P.W.S. Andrews, '*On Competition in Economic Theory*', London, Macmillan, 1964.

3. S. Earley, '*Recent Developments in Cost Accounting and the Marginal Analysis*', Journal of Political Economy (1955) and '*Marginal Policies of Excellently Managed Companies*', American Economic Review, 1956.

4. Barback, '*The Pricing of Manufactures*', p. 36, Milton Friedman, '*The Methodology of Positive Economics*', in Essays in Positive Economics.

5. A. Alchian, "*Uncertainty, Evolution and Economic Theory*", - Journal of Political Economy, 1950, pp. 211-21.

6. Edith Penrose, "*Biological Analogies in the Theory of the Firm*", American Economic Review, 1952, pp. 804-19.

14 Chapter

Pricing Theories - Various Models

CHAPTER OBJECTIVES

After reading this chapter you will be able to answer the following:

1. Bain's traditional theory of Limit Pricing
2. Bain's Version of Competition and Entry
3. Bain's Theory of Limit Pricing (Revised Version)
4. Bain's Models
5. Sylos-Labini's Model of Limit Pricing
6. Franco Modigliani's Model of Limit Pricing
7. Bhagwati's Model of Limit Pricing
8. Pashigian's Model of Limit Pricing (Mixed Strategy)

Introduction

J.S.Bain developed his theory of limit pricing in an article published in 1949. In 1956, he revised his theory in his book "Barriers to New Competition". Bain's article "Oligopoly and Entry Prevention" has provided the basis for limit pricing theory history. In his article, he has explained why firms did not charge the price that would maximise their profits. According to him the firms set their prices at a level of demand where the elascticity was below unity.

1. BAIN'S TRADITIONAL THEORY OF LIMIT PRICING

Bain's traditional theory did not consider the threat of potential entry. It took note of only the actual entry which resulted in the long-run equilibrium of both firm and industry at a point where price would be equal to long-run average cost. He say a that in reality this was not a correct postion. In the long run price did not fall to the level of long run average cost due to barriers to entry. At the same time firms did not charge the price that would maximise their profits because of their idea about potential entry.

> *According to J.S.Bain the firms determine price at a level below short run profit maximising monopoly price and above the long-run average cost which equals the pure competition price. This price is rightly called the limit price because the existing firms' believe that they can charge it without attracting entry.*

The firms make certain assumptions while setting the price like (a) threat of potential entry is real and it cannot be ignored (b) there are barriers to entry which will prevent the prices from falling to the level of LAC.

Bain has developed two models of limit pricing in oligopolistic markets in his article of 1949. The model one is about *collusion* with the new entrant and second is *no collusion* with the new entrant.

In the first model, where there is collusion with the new entrant the established i.e., existing firms estimate the limit price correctly and it will charge the price which will maximise their profit. In this case the limit price may be higher than monopoly price. But by charging monopoly price both firm's as well as industry's profit can be maximised. But by changing monopoly price, if they expect more risk then the existing firm will charge the limit price. In this case the entry may be prevented but profits cannot be maximised.

In the second model the established firm decides to have no collusion with the new entrant. In this case the established firms may go in for charging a price which will maximise their profits. So, they may either set a price equal to limit price or below the limit price and there by prevent the entry. Some times they may charge a price above the limit price and attract entry into the industry. The established firms may go in for charging the price above the limit price, when they find the limit price lower than their LAC.

Whatever the situation is, if it is a rational firm, it will choose a price which will maximise their profits.

To conclude, we can say that, the limit price is generally chosen by the established (i.e existing firms) firms to prevent the entry and this is done in order to maximise thier long run profits.

2. BAIN'S VERSION OF COMPETITION AND ENTRY

In 1956, Bain published his book "Barriers to New Competition." He has given a new approach to limit price in this book. In this book he has explained why firms actually charge a price above the competitive price, that is, the price equal to long-run average cost. He says that, because of barriers to entry, the actual price which is the limit price is set above the competitive price. So Bain has attempted to develop a theory of pricing to prevent entry.

Concepts of Competition and Entry

Bain makes distinction between the actual competition and potential competition in his new book. According to him the actual competition (which is mentioned in his traditional theory) refers to competition among the existing firms in the industry where as potential competition refers to the competition from outside the industry that is from new entrants into the industry. However the potential competition is not considered to a greater extent by Bain. According to him, the actual competition in the long run leads to price becoming equal to LAC and LMC. Under monopolistic competition the actual competition leads to the price equal to LAC but higher than

LMC. In oligopolistic markets the firms are interdependent with their actual competitors in fixing their price.

Even R.L.Hall and C.J.Hitch and P.W.S.Andrews did not give much importance to potential competition. It was W.Fellner who was the first economist argued that firms under oligopoly do not charge monopoly price due to threat of potential entry.[1]

According to Bain, entry refers to setting up of a new firm which creates new productive capacity which was not in the industry before setting up of the new firm. He does not include the following in his concept of entry.

(1) Expansion of capacity by an established firm.

(2) Takeover of an existing firm by some other firm leading to a change in ownership.

(3) Entry by a firm already existed in some other industry.

So according to Bain, entry involves addition of new capacity by a newly established firm. In his book Bain has developed the concept of the condition of entry. He defines the condition of entry as a margin by which the limit price is higher than the long-run competitive price. Symbolically the condition of entry is stated as follows:

$$E = \frac{P_L - P_C}{P_L}$$

where   E = Condition of entry

P_L = limit price

P_C = long run competitive price

Entry in Bain's theory is long term phenomenon because for him entry refers to building of capacity only by the new firms which is invariably a time consuming process. He excludes expansion of capacity by the existing firms, take-overs and cross-entry from his concept of entry. The time period implied in the concept of condition of entry is "long enough to encompass a typical range of varying conditions of demand, factor prices and the like. This period normally might be thought of as 5 to 10 years."[2]

Bain considers lag of entry is main determinant of the barriers of entry. The lag of entry differs from industry to industry. The lag of entry refers to the time required for setting up a new firm in a given line of production, depends on the number of factors. The lag of entry may be four to six months in ready made garments industry, one to two years in beverages and 5 to 6 years in iron and steel industry and other heavy industries. The threat of entry is less when the lag of entry is long.

According to Bain, there are four kinds of barriers which determine the time span of the entry lag. They are:

(i)   Product-differentiation barrier or preference barrier.

(ii) Absolute cost advantage barrier

(iii) Initial capital requirements barrier

(iv) Economies of scale barrier.

(i) **Product Differentiation or Preference Barrier:** In general buyers have preference for certain existing brands and they will not be attracted by the new brands launched by the newly established firms in the market. In this situation the entrant is at disadvantage because he has to spend a lot on advertising his products so that he can popularise his brand and influence the customers in favour of his own brand and he should also set a lower price to catch up the demand in the market. So, the entrant finds himself in a double disadvantage as his costs are higher due to heavier advertising expenditure, while the price he can charge for his product is lower. These factors naturally act as barriers to entry and they are called as product differentiation or preference barrier.

(ii) **Absolute Cost Advantage Barrier:** An already established firm often enjoys absolute cost advantage over a new entrant. The absolute cost advantage may arise due to various reasons like:

(a) Control over the supply of raw materials by the established firms or getting them at lower prices.

(b) They can have the advantage of having the services of expert managerial personal at a lower cost.

(c) They may find it easier to raise capital and also have the advantage of internal financing.

(d) Patents and superior techniques are available to the existing firms at a lower cost.

(e) The established firms enjoy the advantage of lower costs due to vertical integration of production processes.

Because of all these advantages, the cost of production is less and the established firms can also maximise their profits which is not possible for the new entrants.

(iii) **Initial Capital Requirements Barrier:** To set up a new firm a large initial capital is required due to sophistication of technology. Volume of capital needed depends on the size and nature of the plant and other equipment. The new firms usually face difficulties in obtaining the required initial capital. Financial institutions and banks may be reluctant to finance new firms and due to their lacking goodwill they may find it difficult to raise capital from the capital market also. Though they succeed in getting the capital, they may be forced to pay a higher rate of interest. Sometimes, though they are ready to pay a high rate of interest, yet they may find it difficult to raise capital. In these circumstances the initial capital requirement becomes an entry barrier.

(iv) **Economies of Scale Barrier:** According to Bain economies of scale are of two types (a) single plant economies and (b) multiplant economies. But he found through his studies that economies arise from both the types are same. Economies of scale refers to advantages enjoyed by the firm when its production size expands. It may arise in the form of technical managerial labour economies. etc. These economies helps in reducing the cost and increasing the output. So these economies constitute an important barrier to entry because, those economies cannot be enjoyed by the new firms initially and more over the established firms operating at optimal scale of plant set a price at which potential entrants do not consider it worthwhile to enter the industry.

3. BAIN'S THEORY OF LIMIT PRICING (REVISED VERSION)

The Revised Version of Bain's theory of limit pricing is given in the form of models. He has given three models to explain his theory.

Bain's Models are based on the following assumptions.

(1) Each industry has a minimum size of plant and the economies of scale are fully realised and this is called as the minimum optimal scale of plant.

(2) All the firms and entrants are the same technology and hence LAC is same for all. The existing firms have already reached the output larger than the minimum optimal and the new firms will reach the same in course of time.

(3) In the long run price cannot remain lower than the LAC and the flat part of the LAC curve determines longrun competitive price.

(4) Both the established firms and the new entrants know the market demand curve.

(5) All firms produce very similar products and have equal market shares.

(6) At all price levels, the share of each firm is a constant proportion of the market demand. Thus each individual firm shares the market demand curve.

To explain the equilibrium of the firm Bain uses individual LAC and dd curves and aggregate LAC and the aggregate demand curve DD to derive competitive output and price.

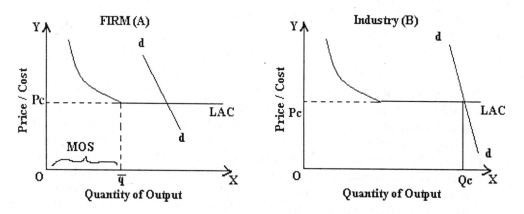

Equilibrium of the firm: In the above diagram two graphs have been drawn to show the quantity produced by the individual firm and industry. Figure A represents individual firm while figure B represents industry. $O\bar{q}$ is the minimum optimal output produed by the firm. OPc is the competitive price and OQc is competitive output.

4. BAIN'S MODELS

Model I. Constant Price at the Pre-Entry Level

In this Bain's model, the potential entrant expects that the existing firms will maintain the price at the pre-entry level and allow it to secure any market share it can earn at this price. Thus given the market demand curve, the market share of the existing firms will be reduced by the amount of the market share earned by the entrant (new firm).

The existing firms (established ones) will set the price at a level which will not attract the potential entrants. The limit price i.e the entry preventing price is expressed symbolically as follows:

$$P_L = P_C = (1 + E)$$

P_L = Limit Price

P_C = Competitive Price

E = (Premium E) the amount by which the limit price P_L exceeds the competitive price Pc and it depends on the following factors.

(1) The initial share of the entrant relative to the minimum optimal scale.

(2) The number of already existing firms.

(3) The steepness of the LAC curve.

(4) The elasticity of demand.

1. **The initial share of the entrant relative to minimum optimal scale:** The existing firms can do nothing, when the share of the entrant is equal to or greater than the minimum optimal size of the plant. In this situation the existing firms will have to set the competitive price at which there is no barrier to entry.

2. **The number of already existing firms in the industry:** The number of existing firms will normally decide whether each firm will produe at optimal scale or not when the entry occurs, the share of the entrant and every existing firm will be lesser than minimum optimum size of the plant. Therefore, greater the number of existing firms, the higher the entry preventing price (limit price) will be. This implies that the number of existing firms and the premium E are positively related.

3. **Steepness of the long-run average cost curve (LAC):** The another determinant of the premium E is the steepness of the long run average cost curve. It shows the rate at which LAC increase when the plant is used at a sub-optimal level. The steeper the LAC curve, the higher the premium will be. The flatter the LAC curve lower will be the premium. This indicates that steepness of the LAC curve and the premium are positively related.

4. **Elasticity of the industry demand curve:** It is assumed that elasticity of the market demand curve is the same as the elasticity of the individual firm's share-demand curve. If individual share-demand curve is more elastic both premium and entry preventing price will be higher. So, it can be generalised that greater the elasticity of demand higher will be the premium price and the entry preventing price.

To conclude, the potential entrant expects the price to remain constant and his market share is equal to or greater than the minimum optimal plant size, there is barrier to entry and the existing firm will set a competitive price. If the entrants share is lesser than minimum optimal plant size output then the existing firms will set a limit price. When more number of firms exist the entry gap will be higher. The steeper the LAC curve and greater the elasticity of demand, higher will be the premium.

Model 2: Constant quantity at the Pre-Entry Level

In contrast to the previous model, in this model the entrant assumes that existing firms will not change their level of output when entry occurs. Due to entry of the new firms however the industry output will increase and result is fall in the price. The existing firms expect that entry will not take place when the price falls below the minimum long run average cost and entry occurs only at the minimum optimal plant size.

In these circumstances entry is not possible due to scale barrier. The existing firms will set a limit price above the competitive price in order to prevent entry.

The factors which will determine the premium, E that is the amount by which the limit price P_L exceeds the competitive price P_c are as follows:

(a) The size of the market at the competitive price

(b) The minimum optimal scale

(c) The number of firms already existing in the industry

(d) The elasticity of market demand.

The premium is positively related with minimum optimum scale and negatively related to the market size. There is a positive relationship between the number of established firms and the limit price. This is very similar to what has been discussed in the context of the previous model. The limit price and the premium are negatively related to the price elasticity of demand. Among these four factors except the third, all others behave just in opposite direction to that of the previous model.

Model 3: Price and output change at Post-Entry

According to this model, the new firm expects that the existing firms will accept it partially by reducing their output and price will also decrease in the meanwhile. This model is the intermediate case between the above mentioned two models. According to Bain this is more realistic. However the output reduction by the existing firms is less than the output of the new firm and hence there will be a fall in the price. Therefore in this case, scale barriers to entry will be operative and will lie between the entry barriers of the above two models of limiting cases.

5. SYLOS-LABINI'S MODEL OF LIMIT PRICING

P.Sylos-Labini has developed a model of limit pricing in his book "Oligopoly and Technical Progress", Harvard University Press, 1957. His model is more refined than Bain's model. His model is based on economies of scale barriers to entry to certain restrictive assumptions. Franco Modigliani relaxed restrictive assumptions and presented a model of limit pricing which is a generalised model of Sylos-Labini's limit pricing model.

Sylos-Labini has chosen a case of oligopoly using the same technolgy which has two characteristic features. (i) technical discontinuities and (ii) economies of scale.

Sylos-Labini's model of limit pricing is based on the following assumptions.

1. The market demand is given and its price elasticity is unitary.

2. Technology used by the firms consists of three types of plants with different capacities.

3. The product is homogeneous and a single equilibrium price will be determined.

4. The price is set by the leader (largest firm) which has also the lowest cost.

5. All the firms want to earn at least normal profit

6. The price leader knows the market demand and the cost structure of all plant sizes.

7. The new firms entering the industry has smallest plant size.

8. The entrant expects that the established firms will maintain their level of output in post-entry period at the level of output in the pre-entry period.

9. The existing firms expect that the new firms will join industry only if he thinks that the post-entry price will not lower than its long-run average cost.

Franco Modigliani calls the last two assumptions as "Sylos's Postulate".

Price Determination

According to Sylos-Labini, there are four factors which determine the limit price. They are:

1. The price elasticity of market demand.

2. The size of the market.

3. The technology determining the plant sizes in the industry.

4. Factor prices which together with plant sizes determine the TAC of firms.

In the model of Sylos-Labini the price is determined by the leader which is the largest and most efficient firm. The price fixed is called as equilibrium price and it fulfils two conditions i.e., one, it is acceptable to all the firms in the industry and secondly it would prevent the entry.

In an industry, since different firms use different plant sizes, their costs vary accordingly. Moreover in an industry there are many minimum acceptable prices and it is computed according to average cost principle.

$$P_n = TAC_n + (1+r)$$

where P_n = the minimum acceptable price for the nth plant size

TAC_n = total average cost of the nth plant size.

r = the rate of normal profit of the industry.

So, the price fixed as per this model includes TAC of the plant and the normal profit rate of the industry and it is uniform for all plant sizes. The price set by the leader is accepted even by the least efficient firms which carry out production with the help of the smallest plant. The price set by the leader is low enough and will prevent the further entry into the industry. In this case, the least efficient firms earn normal profit while the medium and large scale firm earn super normal profits due to their lower costs. For the new entrants the price fixed by the leader is not very attrative and hence it may not induce him to venture entry.

To conclude we can say that in Sylos-Labini's model, the long run equilibrium price which is set by the leader is not only acceptable to all the firms including the least efficient, but also prevents entry.

6. FRANCO MODIGLIANI'S MODEL OF LIMIT PRICING

Franco Modigliani has developed a model of limit pricing in his work "New Developments on the Oligopoly Front" Journal of Political Economy, (1958). In his model he does not include the restrictive assumptions considered by Sylos-Labini. He has relaxed his assumptions but retained the assumption of economies of scale barriers and the behavioural pattern of what he calls Sylos's postulate. The model developed by Modigliani is considered as a generalisation of Sylos-Labini's Model.

The assumptions based on which Modigliani has built his model are as follows.

1. The same technology is used by all the firms in the industry and the size of the plant is same for all the firms. At this plant size firms fully exploit all the economies of scale. Therefore once the minimum scale is reached, the LAC stops falling and becomes a straight line parallel to X axis which implies L shaped LAC curve and is same for all the firms in the industry.

2. Only new firms enter the industry. A firm makes entry with the minimum optimal plant size.

3. The products produced by all the firms is homogeneous and they know the market demand. In the long run, the competitive price will be set taking into consideration, the flat LAC and market demand curve and the competitive output will be the quantity that can sell at competitive price.

4. The market leader which is the largest firm will set the price at a level that entry is prevented.

5. The behaviour of the existing and new firms is in accordance with the Sylos's postulate. This implies that the existing firms expect the new entrant to join industry with the plant of the minimum optimal scale.

6. He assumes that post-entry price will not be lower than flat segment of LAC.

7. The entrant (new firms) expects that the existing firms will continue the same level of production and is not expected to fall in response to entry.

Price Determination

In Modigliani's model of limit pricing the scale barrier is reflected in the minimum optimal plant size. ($O\overline{M}$) in the following figure.

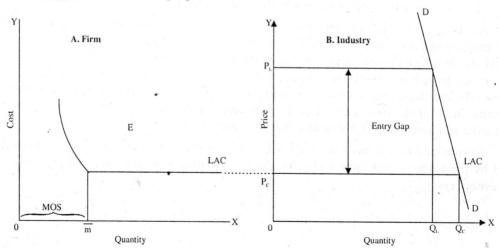

The existing firms, as per the assumptions stated will set the price OP_L and earn super normal profit, because that is greater than competitive price. OP_C and the price set by the firms will prevent the entry. The limit price is OP_L is determined by knowing the total output that all the firms including the entrant can sell at the competitive price OP_C. The difference between limit price and competitive price is called as "entry gap". From the figure it is clear that the existing firms will OQ_L output at OP_L price and the entry is not attracted at this price because, if the new firm joins the output in the market will exceed automatically resulting a fall in the price, i.e below OP_C. This price will not be high enough to cover the longrun average cost.

Franco Modigliani considers certain factors which determine the entry gap and the limit price. They are as follows:

(1) The minimum optimal scale

(2) The size of the market

(3) The competitive price

(4) The price elasticity of demand.

> *According to Franco Modigliani, the limit price has a positive relationship with the minimum optimal plant size and the competitive price which equals LAC. It is negatively related with the size of the market and the price elasticity of demand.*

Therefore Modigliani summarises the relationships of determinants and limit price as follows:

$$P_L = P_C\left[1 + \frac{\overline{m}}{Q_C \bullet e}\right]$$

where

P_L = limit price

$\overline{m}$ = minimum optimal plant size

e = price elasticity of demand

     = competitive price

Q_C = size of the market.

To conclude we can say that, according to Modigliani, the scale barriers are responsible for a higher limit price than the competitive price. The difference between the two is called as entry gap or premium and it measures the amount by which the price can exceed the long-run average cost without attracting entry into the industry.

7. BHAGWATI'S MODEL OF LIMIT PRICING

J.N.Bhagwati has extended Franco Modigliani's model of limit pricing. This he has done in two respects.[3] Firstly he has added two more determinants of limit price to Modigliani's set of determinants. They are (i) the number of firms in the industry and (ii) switch over of customers of the existing firms to the new firms due to their dissatisfaction with the former. Secondly he has introduced a term to make the limit pricing dynamic which implies that prediction of changes in limit price occuring on account of market growth becomes possible.

Bhagawati in his model states that "The premium obtainable in an industry will vary directly with (i) the minimum size of scale of most efficient production $(\bar{x})$ and (ii) the number of existing firms (N); and inversely with (1) the size of the total market (X_c), (2) price elasticity of industry and (3) the extent to which existing buyers will transfer custom to the entrant consequent upon entry." He further extends his theory to cover dynamic changes in market demand. If demand increases by an amount λ and out of this increase in the new entrants' share of demand is K per cent, the limit price will be defined as follows:

$$P_L = P_C \left[1 + \frac{\bar{x} - k\lambda}{X_C \left(\dfrac{e}{N+1} + \beta \right)} \right]$$

where

P_L = limit price

P_C = Competitive price in the market

X_C = aggregate demand at the competitive price after growth

$\bar{x}$ = minimum size of scale of the most efficient production

e = price elasticity of demand

λ = increase in demand

k = percentage of increased demand accruing to the entrant

N = number of existing firms

β = Proportionate decrease in the sales of existing firms in response to entry of new firms.

From the above definition it is clear that k is inversely related to P_L which indicates that an expanding market entry is easier. If $(k\lambda)$ is greater than $\bar{x}$, then entry cannot be prevented beause P_L will be lower than P_C =LAC. In this situation the market growth will be very fast and the existing firms cannot depend on price policy alone to prevent entry. In dynamic markets such firms must try to maximise their demand and look for factors other than price to discourage the entrants (new firms) from entering the industry.

8. PASHIGIAN'S MODEL OF LIMIT PRICING (MIXED STRATEGY)

The limit pricing theories given by J.S.Bain, Sylos-Labini, Franco Modigliani and J.N.Bhagawati considers, scale barriers to entry lead to fixation of limit price which is usually higher than competitive price which equals LAC. Thus the existing firms in the industry manage to earn super normal profits without any risk. However, Bhagawati states that in certain situations the firms may adopt a mixed strategy. That is they may charge the monopoly price which is higher than limit price over a certain period of time. This will not attract entry into the industry. When it starts attracting entry, the existing firms reduce the price to prevent entry. In this situation entry preventing or limit price will be set.

The mixed strategy will be adopted depending on the length of the two periods: One, the period in which the entry is not expected and the second where entry will occur if the price is not brought down to the level of entry preventing price. If the first period is longer, then the existing firms obtain more profits by adopting mixed strategy. If the second period is longer, then the existing firms will maximise their profits by following the limit price from the beginning.

B.P.Pashigian, in a systematic manner has examined the implicationsof the mixed strategy.[4] According to him, during that period T the existing firm may abandon the monopoly price and may start charging the limit price or competitive price whichever is more profitable among these two. He makes a simple assumption that there is just one firm in the industry. So, the firm enjoys monopoly power, but expects new firms to join industry if monopoly price is continued forever. So the firm has to decide whether and for how long it can charge monopoly price to maximise its short-run profits. Suppose, if the existing firm sets the price at monopoly level, it will attract entry sooner or later. Therefore, the important element is the number of periods in which the price remains higher than the limit price.

For simplicity sake Pashigian considers just two alternatives available to the existing firms. He assumes that over a period T, the firm may set a price equal to monopoly level, but it may result in entry. He further assumes that new entrants operate in collusion with the established firms and charge the same monopoly price which prevail during the period T.

After period T, the existing firm which acted as monopoly initially has two options: Either it can charge the limit price and earn excess profits that this price allows or it can continue charging the monopoly price even in period TT' as a result of which more entry occurs and the price falls to the competitive level. The choice between these two alternatives depends on the comparison of the discounted flow of profits.

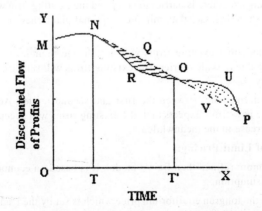

Alternatives Open to the Existing Firms

If the existing firm adopts first strategy of charging limit price after the period T, then the discounted profits is shown by the area NQOR. But on the other hand if it continues to charge monopoly price and allows further entry, then the discounted profits is indicated by the area below the dotted line. (i.e TNQOT), so the existing firm finds that by charging the limit price, though it forego the profit represented by the shaded area NQOR, it will earn additional profit represented by the shaded area OUPV during the time period TT'. Since OUPV is greater than

NQOR, the firm will prefer to set the limit price after the time period T because this strategy maximises the profits.

So, to conclude we can say that Pashigian's time period analysis while treating time explicity justifies the setting up of limit price which is the entry preventing price on the grounds of maximum profitability.

SUMMARY

I. Bain's Theory of Limit Pricing

1. According to Bain the firms determine price at a level below short-run profit maximising monopoly price and above the LAC which equals the pure competition price.

2. This price is called as 'limit price' because the established firms believe that without inducing entry they can charge that price.

3. Bain makes distinction between the actual competition and potential competition. Actual competition - competition among the existing firms in the industry. Potential competition - competition from outside the industry.

4. According to Bain entry refers to setting up of a new firm which creates new productive capacity which was not in the industry before setting up of the new firm.

5. He further says that, there are four barriers to entry and they also determine the timespan of the entry. Barriers are -

    (i) Product Differentiation

    (ii) Absolute cost advantage

    (iii) Initial capital requirement

    (iv) Economies of scale

6. Bain in his revised version of limit pricing has given three models to explain his theory.

Model I - The potential entrant expects the price to remain constant and his market share is equal to or greater than the minimum optimal plant size, there is barrier to entry and the existing firm will set a competitive price. On the other hand if the entrants share is lesser than minimum optimal plant, then the existing firms will set a limit price.

Model II - The entrant assumes that existing firms will not change their level of output when entry occurs. Moreover entry is not possible due to scale barrier. The existing firms will set a limit price above the competitive price in order to prevent entry.

Model III - This model is intermediate between the first and second model. According to Bain this is more realistic. As per this model the new firms expects that, the existing firms will accept it partially by reducing their output and price will also decrease in the meanwhile.

II. Sylos - Labini's Model of Limit Pricing:

1. Sylos-Labini's model is more refined than Bain's model. It is based on economies of scale barriers to entry and certain restrictive assumption.

2. In Sylos-Labini's model, the longrun equilibrium price which is set by the leader is not only acceptable to all the firms including the least efficient, but also prevents entry.

III. Franco Modigliani's Model of Limit Pricing:

1. The Model developed by Modigliani is considered as a generalisation of Sylos-Labini's Model.

2. According to Modigliani, the scale barriers are responsible for a higher limit price than the competitive price. The difference between the two is called as entry gap or premium. It measures the amount by which the price can exceed LAC without attracting entry into the industry.

IV. Bhagwati's Model of Limit Pricing:

1. J.N. Bhagwati has extended Franco Modigliani's model of limit pricing.

2. He has added two determinants namely (i) the number of firms in the industry and (ii) switch over of customers of the existing firms to the new firms due to the dissatisfaction with the former.

3. He further extends his theory to cover dynamic changes in market demand. In dynamic markets, the firms should try to maximise their demand and look for other factors to discourage the entrants from entering the industry.

V. Pashigian's Model of Limit Pricing:

1. Pashigian has adopted Mixed strategy in his theory.

2. According to him, during a particular time period the existing firm may abandon the monopoly price and may start charging the limit price or competitive price which is more profitable among these two.

3. Pashigian's theory explicitly justifies the setting up of limit price which is the entry preventing price on the grounds of maximum profitability.

QUESTIONS

1. What is limit pricing?
2. Explain Bain's traditional theory of limit pricing.
3. Briefly discuss Bain's version of competition and entry.
4. Compare and contrast Bain's traditional theory and his revised version.
5. Explain all the three models of Bain's revised version.
6. Why Sylos-Labini's Model of limit pricing is considered as more refined than Bain's Model?
7. Explain Modigliani's model of limit pricing.
8. Explain briefly Bhagwati's extension of Modigliani's model.
9. Discuss the mixed strategy version of limit pricing given by Pashigian.
10. What is Bain's limit pricing theory?

REFERENCES

1. W. Fellner, 'Competition Among the Few', 1949.
2. J.S. Bain, "Barriers to New Competition", Harvard University Press, 1956, p.7.
3. J.N. Bhagwati, "Oligopoly Theory, Entry Prevention and Growth", Oxford Economic Papers, 1970.
4. B.P. Pashigian, "Limit Price and the Market Share of the Leading Firm", Journal of Industrial Economics, 1968.

15 Chapter

Managerial Theories of a Firm

Managerial theories of a firm can be considered as a part of behavioural theory. A firm is a coalition of managers, workers, shareholders customers, suppliers, collectors etc., who have conflicting goals which have to be considered, so that the firm can survive. In practice, the management has more power and it tries to pursue goals which maximises their utility, subject to a minimum profit constraint.

In this chapter we shall present the important theories of managerialism.

1. Baumol's theory of Sales Revenue Maximisation.
2. Manis Model of the Managerial Enterprises
3. William's Model of Managerial Discretion.
4. The Behavioural Model of Cyert and March.

All these theories are alternatives to profit maximisation.

1. BAUMOL'S THEORY OF SALES REVENUE MAXIMISATION

W.J.Baumol, in his work 'Business Behaviour, Value and Growth' suggests that sales maximisation as an alternative to profit maximisation. He has given two basic models. The first one is a static single period model and the second is a multi period dynamic model. Both the models have two versions - one without advertisement expenditure and the other with advertisement expenditure. To verify Baumol's theory of sales maximisation and examine thereby the predictions of his model few empirical evidences are also available.

Static Models

Baumol's static models have the following assumptions.

  (i) A firm's decision making is subjected to a single period.

 (ii) The firm's objective is to maximise sales revenue rather than volume of sales during this period.

(iii) The sales revenue maximisation goal is related to minimum profit constraint and the critical minimum profit is exogenously determined by the demands and expectations of the share holders (owners) and other members of the firm.

(iv) Conventional cost and average revenue functions are assumed which implies U shaped cost curves and negative sloping demand curve.

Price and Output determination under single product firm without advertisement

The firm will try to maximise total revenue than physical volume of output. The conventional cost and revenue functions are assumed and accordingly curves are drawn and same is shown in the following figure.

As per the diagram, the sales revenue maximising output is OQ_2 because at this level of output the total revenue is maximum (i.e BQ_2). This output level is fixed according to the rule that the maximum total revenue will be obtained only at that output level at which the elasticity of demand is unity. Profit is represented by the difference between total cost (TC) and total revenue (TR) curve. At this level of output profit is not maximum. The curve TP is drawn by taking into the account the difference between total cost (TC) and the total revenue (TR).

The firm's total profit is maximum when the difference betwen the TC and TR is maximum and at this situation the output produced by the firm is OQ_1. But at this level total sales revenue is not maximised because $AQ_1 \angle BQ_2$.

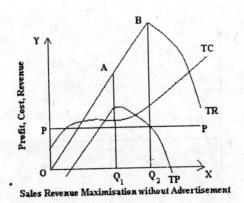

Sales Revenue Maximisation without Advertisement

But, according to Baumol's model, the firm is interested only in maximising its sales revenue and not profit. This model also takes into account profit constraint, which is represented by PP. If OQ_2 level of output is not satisfying the minimum profit represented by PP then the firm has to change its level of output. In this diagram the profit constraint is met when the firm produce sales maximising output OQ_2, this level of profit will satisfy even the share holders. The firm fixes the price equal to BQ_2.

If not necessary the firm changes its profit constraint (minimum required profit) level, then it may also change its level of outut to be produced accordingly.

Model with Advertising

In this model also the firm assumes sales revenue maximisation, subject to a minimum profit constraint which is exogenously determined. In the present day world, advertisement plays a crucial role in the sales of a firm. So advertisement is considered as an important tool of the firm. This model also assumes that advertisement expenditure will result in increase in demand and thereby the firm can sell more and can increase its total revenue. In this model Baumol assumes two things - one is that price remains constant and the other, the production costs are not affected due to advertising. advertisement is considered as a means of sales promotion.

In the imperfect market where competition is more and when the firms' product is differentiated from other's product and where the firm is a price maker, advertisement plays a crucial role. The decision amount of money to be spent on advertisement is an important decision. The firm should decide on optimum advertisement by examining its effect on sales revenue.

The same logic is used as before to find out sales revenue maximising output subjected to profit constraint.

In the following figure advertising cost is measured along the x axis and cost, revenue and profit level on the y axis. Baumol assumes that increased advertisement expenditure will always result in increased volume of sales, though it may decline after a certain point. He says that: in the case of price reduction the total sales revenue may or may not increase, but it is sure to increase with the increased advertising expenditure. In the previous case the total sales revenue depends on elasticity of demand for the product.

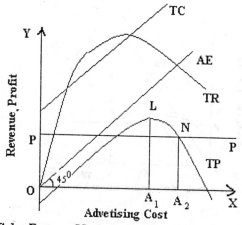

Sales Revenue Maximisation with Advertisement

In the diagram 45^0 line drawn represents advertisement expenditure. (AE). Baumol assumes that total costs i.e TC is independent of cost of advertising and so according TC curve is drawn. TP cure (i.e total profit) is drawn by plotting the difference between TC and TR^1.

The profit maximising advertising expenditure is OA_1. The total profits TP reaches its maximum A_1L at this point. But it is less than profit constraint level. So the firm can increase its expenditure on advertisement i.e OA_2, so that it can reach the profit constrained sales maximising level.

So, it can be concluded that the advertisement expenditure incurred by the firm will always result in inreasing the sales of a firm.

It will thus "always pay the sales maximiser to increase his advertising outlay until he stopped by the profit constraint - unit profits have been reduced to the minimum acceptable level."

2. DYNAMIC MODEL - MULTI PRODUCT FIRM

Choice of Output Combinations

In a modern economy an oligopolistic firm is not a single product enterprise. It generally produces a large number of different items. Therefore, Baumol examines the effects of sales revenue maximisation on the amounts and allocation of the firm's various outputs. Hence Baumol says that "Given the level of expenditure, the sales maximising firm will produce the same quantity of each output, and market it in the same ways as does the profit maximiser"[2].

By this statement, Baumol explains that both profit maximising firm and sales revenue maximising firm produce the same quantity of output and market it in the same way.

Baumol has used the following figure to illustrate his results.

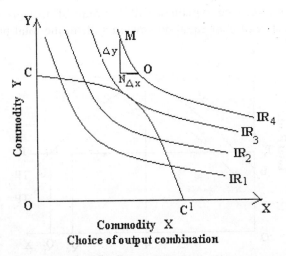

Commodity X
Choice of output combination

The two commodities sold by the firm commodity X and commodity Y are measured along the X axis and Y axis respectively. The curves IR_1, IR_2, IR_3 and IR_4 are iso-revenue curves, which shows different levels of revenues. Each curve is the locus of various combinations of the two commodities, which will yield the same level of revenue. The prices of X and Y are assumed to be fixed and hence the revenue curves are linear. These curves are convex to the origin depicting the diminishing marginal revenues from the sale of commodities X and Y as their quantitiy sold increases in response to their falling price. In the same manner, given the total outlay (total cost) various combinations of commodities X and Y can be produced. The curve CC^1 represents the total outlay and all the combinations that can be produced. The equilibrium is reached at point E where the curve CC^1 is tangent to IR_3 which is the point of profit maximisation. Moreover, the point 'E' is also the point of revenue maximisation because it is on the highest iso-revenue cure that is attainable with the given outlay.

This clearly proves the Baumol's generalisation, that is given the amount of expenditure the sales maximising firms will produce and sell the same quantity of output as the profit maximising firm.

Changes in Overhead Costs and Sales Revenue Maximisation

The overhead costs are not considered relevant for determining equilibrium price and output in the traditional theory of firm. As long as these costs do not vary with the level of output, and the changes do not lead the firm to close down altogether, changes in over head costs will not induce profit maximising firm to change either price or output. According to Baumol "This piece of received doctrine is certainly at variance with business practice where an increase in fixed costs is usually the occasion for serious consideration of price increase.[3]"

As stated in Baumol's revenue maximisation model, since a firm treats its profits ad a consttraint rather than as an ultimate objective, an increase in overhead costs leads to a price increase.

Since the aim of the firm is to earn a reasonable profit (profit constraint) rise in the overhead costs will reduce their earnings below acceptable minimum. So, the firm has no choice but to reduce the output and advertising expenditure or only the advertisement expenditure to retain the acceptable profits. Any decrease in output will increase the firm's selling price.

This model of Baumol can be explained with the help of a diagram. Baumol says that an increase in overhead costs cause an equal downward shift in the total profit curve.

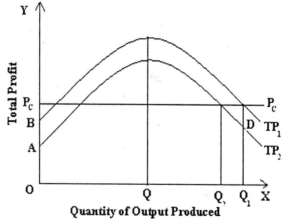

Changes in overhead cost and sales revenue maximisation

In the diagram total profit is measured along Y axis and quantity of output produed by the firm is measured along the X axis. The parallel line drawn to X axis represents the firms profit constraint and TP curves represents total profit curves of the firm. A rise in the overhead costs by the by the amount AB shifts the total profit curve TP_1 downwards and thus the new total profit curve is TP_2. The profit constraint is OP_C, and so the firm earlier produed OQ_1 level of output. But with the increase in the overhead costs by AB amount, the firm will not produce OQ_1 because the total profits falls to Q1D which is less than the minimum profit acceptable level OP_C. In this situation the firm will produce OQ_2 level of output which is less than earlier output level OQ_1. But, in contrast, the profit maximising firm will continue to produce OQ level of outupt even when overhead costs increases by AB amount.

Criticisms

Baumol's sales maximisation hypothesis is not easy to verify because the various data required are not generally available to researchers. The data required for measuring demand and cost function are not easily available. Hence his thesis is criticised by economists on the following grounds:

(i) In the long run, both the objectives of sales maximisation and profit maximisation results in same solutions. After all, in the long run the firms can earn only normal profit due to competition in the market and therefore the maximum profit constraint automatically coincides with it.

(ii) The theory does not deal with the difference between the firm and the industry and also does not explain how a change in firm's sales maximisation will affect the industry's equilibrium.

(iii) This theory is unrealistic in the sense, it ignores the actual competition and the threat of potential competition. But in oligopolistic market; if the firm wants to capture the rival's market, then it cannot maximise its sales, because of the reaction by his rivals in the market.

(iv) Increased outlay on advertisement will not always yield desired result of increase in sales, as assumed by Baumol. Sometimes, excessive advertising is repelling and hence it may not increase the sales; it may be counter produtivities.

3. MARRIS MODEL OF THE MANAGERIAL ENTERPRISES

Marris model is found in two of his celebrated works (i) An article: "A Model of the Managerial Enterprise" in Journal of Economics, 1963. (ii) A book: Theory of Managerial Capitalism (Macmillan) 1964.

Marris does not consider that a modern corporate firm is a profit maximiser. According to him "The goal of the firm is the maximisation of the balanced rate of growth of the firm." Marris recognises the dichotomy between owner's and manager's interest. Accordingly, he assumes that the owners being interested in the growth of the firm want maximisation of growth of the supply of capital, which is assumed to maximise their utility. The owner's utility function may be written as follows:

$U_0 = f(g_c)$

where U_0 = utility of owners

g_c = growth rate of capital

Managers believe that growth of the firm depends on the growth of demand for the products of the firm. Further salaries, status and power are strongly correlated with the growth of demand. Hence managerial utility function can be written as follows:

$$U_M = f(g_D, S)$$

where U_M = utility of managers

            g_D = growth rate of demand for the products of the firm

            S = a measure of job security

In pursuing this balanced growth objective, the firm faces two constraints (a) managerial constraint and (b) financial constraint. The '*managerial constraint*' is set by skill and efficiency of available manager's team. The '*Financial Constraint*' is set by the desire of managers to attain the maximisation of their own utility function and their owner's utility function. The managers can do so because most of the variables (e.g status, salaries, job securities, power, etc) appearing in their own utility function and those appearing in the utility function of the owners (e.g profit, capital, market share, output, public esteem, etc) are positively and strongly correlated with a single variable i.e size of firm.

In modern organisation though ownership is separated from management, their interest may coincide because, if the firm does not have balanced growth, both manager's job and owner's capital will be at stake. Thus the goals of managers may coincide with the goals of owners. In other words, despite ownership being separated from management, owners and managers work together for a common cause or concern, namely "balanced growth of the firm". Therefore, they seek to maximise a steady growth rate for their firm.

A Critique of Marris Model

Marris model clearly presents a picture regarding modern organisation of a firm. He suggests that although the managers and owners have different goals, it is possible to find a solution, which maximises utility of both. He also says that growth and profits are competing goals. Marris correctly says that owners of the corporate firms do prefer the maximisation of the rate of growth and for this they are ready to sacrifice some of thier profits.

But Marris' theory fails to deal with oligopolistic interdependence, as rightly pointed by A. Koutsoyiannis. Apart from that, he does not explain determination of costs or prices, which is the main concern of profit maximisation hypothesis. Marris' model too does not seriously challenge the profit maximisation hypothesis.

4. THE BEHAVIOURAL MODEL OF CYERT AND MARCH

The model given by Cyert-March is an extension of Simon's hypothesis of firms "satisfying behaviour". Simon in his model argued that: the real business world is full of unertainty; accurate and adequate data are not readily available, though it is available the managers have little time and ability to process them and they work under number of constraints. When such conditions are present, it is not possible for the firms to act in terms of rationality postulated under profit maximisation hypothesis. The firms cannot maximise sales, growth or anything else. Instead they can earn "satisfactory profit", "satisfactory growth" etc. This kind of behaviour of firms is termed as "satisfaction behaviour."

Added to this, Cyert and March says that, apart from dealing with uncertain business world, managers have to satisfy a variety of group of people - managerial staff, labour, shareholders, customers, financers, raw material suppliers, accountants, government authorities, lawyers, etc. All these people have their interest in the firms - but often conflicting. It is manager's responsibility to satisfy them all. Therefore, according to the "Behavioural Theory of Firms" firm's behaviour is "Satisfying Behaviour". The important assumption of "Satisfying Behaviour" of firms is that a firm is a coalition of different groups of people connected with the various activities of the firms, (e.g) shareholders, workers, raw material suppliers, customers, managers, bankers, government authorities, etc., All these people have some kind of expectations high and low from the firm. The firm should seek to satisfy all of them in one way or another by sacrificing some of its interests.

To reconcile between the conflicting interests and goals or objectives of the firm, managers form an "aspiration level of the firm" combining the following goals:

(i) Production goal

(ii) Sales and market share goal,

(iii) Profit goal and

(iv) Inventory goal

All the above said goals and aspiration level are set on the basis of the past experience of the manager's and their assessment of the future market conditions. The aspiration levels are modified and revised on the basis of achievements and changing business conditions.

Criticism

(a) This model cannot explain the firm's behaviour under dynamic conditions in the long run, though it deals realistically with the firm's activity.

(b) It cannot be used to predict exactly the future course of firm's activities.

(c) This model does not deal with equilibrium of the industry.

(d) Like other models, this model also fails to deal with interdependence and interaction of the firms.

5. WILLIAMSON'S MODEL OF MANAGERIAL DISCRETION

In his article "Managerial Discretion and Business Behaviour" in American Economic Review (1963) Williamson has developed his theory and later extended in the book entitled "The Economics of Discretionary Behaviour" published in 1964.

According to this theory, managers have discretion in pursuing policies which maximise their own utility rather than maximising the profits, which result in maximisation of the utility of the owners, i.e shareholders. Instead, they assure a certain minimum amount of profit to shareholders in the form of dividend. Therefore, profit works as a constraint to the "managers" discretion. Managerial Utility function depends on variables such as salary, job security, power prestige, status, job satisfaction and professional excellence. Among these variables except salary, others are non measurable. But these can be measured in terms of other variables. For example, manager's prestige and position is reflected in terms of the amount of emoluments they receive in the form of expense accounts, luxury offices, company car, etc. Staff expenses is an indication of manager's power and position. The level of discretionary investment gives satisfaction to managers. Considering all these, the utility function of the managers may be written as follows.

U = f (S, M, I$_D$)

where   S = Staff expenditure (includes manager's salary)

         M = Managerial emoluments

         I$_D$ = Discretionary investment.

Definitions and Relations

(i) The demand for the firm X

The firm's demand curve is downward sloping and is defined by the function.

X = f (P, S, E)

where   X = Output

         P = Price per unit

         S = Staff Expenditure

         E = a demand shift parameter.

The demand is negatively related to price and positively related to staff expenditure and to the shift factor.

(ii) The production costs: C

Costs depends on the level of output and assumed to be increasing function of output.

C = f (X)

where $\dfrac{\partial C}{\partial X} > 0$

(iii) Various concepts of profits

(a) Actual profit; π_a:

Actual profit is sales revenue minus total cost and staff expenditure.

$\pi \, a = R - C - S$

(b) Reported profit π_r

Reported profit is the actual profit less managerial emoluments which is reported to the tax authority (M)

$\pi_r = \pi_a - M$ i.e. $R - C - S - M$

(c) Minimum Profit: π_0

This is the minimum level of profit to be earned to satisfy the shareholders. If this minimum amount of dividend is not given to the shareholders, they may sell the shares or change the top management. This will adversely affect the job security of the managers.

$\pi_a \leq \pi_r - T$

where T = tax

(d) Discretionary profit π_D

It is the amount of profit left after deducting the minimum profit (π_0) and the tax (T) from the actual profit.

$\pi_D = \pi_a - \pi_0 - T$

(iv) Discretionary investment I_D:

It is the amount remaining from the reported profit after deducting the minimum profit (π_0) and the tax (T) from the reported profit (π_r).

$I_D = \pi_r - \pi_0 - T$

The Model of Managerial Discretion

The managerial emoluments are assumed to be zero (M = 0) in Williamson's simplified model and thus the actual profit is the same as the reported profit. The simplified model is given as follows:

Maximise U = f (S, M I_D)

subject to $\pi_a \geq \pi_0 + T$

All the discretionary profit (π_D) gets absorbed in discretionary investment (I_D) because it is assumed that there are no managerial emoluments (M=O). Therefore the managerial utility function may be written as:

$u = f[S, (\pi_a - \pi_0 - T)]$

For simplicity reason it is assumed that there is no lumpsum tax so that T = $t\pi$.

Therefore the managerial utility function assumes the form

$$u = f[S, (I - t)\pi_a - \pi_0]$$

where $(I - t)\pi_a - \pi_0 = \pi_D$ i.e discretionary profit

Equilibrium of the Firm: (Diagramatic explanation)

Williamson's Model can be explained with the help of diagram. In order to know the equilibrium of the firm, we need to integrate indifference curves map of the managers and the discretionary profit - staff curve. The indifference curves map of the managers represents different combinations of staff expenditures and discretionary profit (π_D) providing certain level of utility.

In the diagram IC_m curves represents indifference curves of managers and the curve PS represents profit - staff curve. Staff expenditure is measured on the X axis and discretionary profit is measured along the Y axis.

The indifference curves are convex to the origin implying diminishing marginal rate of substitution of S for π_D. As per their property, indifference curves do not intersect the axes and hence the manager choose the positive value of S and π_D in their utility function. The relationship between S and π_D is determined by the profit function i.e profit is the function of output.

$$\therefore \pi = f(X) = f(P, S, E)$$

All other factors like π_0 and T are given by the shareholders, demand for dividends and tax laws. The behaviour of the PS curve shows that, till the firm reaches the maximum level of profit both discretionary profits and staff expenditure increases. If the firm continues production beyond this i.e SN, the discretionary profits falls and the staff expenditure increases.

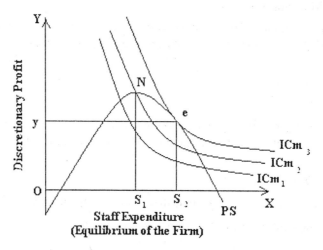

(Equilibrium of the Firm)

In the diagram, the equilibrium of the firm is determined by the point of tangency of the profit staff curve (PS) and the highest possible managerial indifference curve (ICm_3) i.e at point 'e' in the diagram. At the equilibrium point the discretionary profit is S_2e and the staff expenditure is OS_2. But at this stage the profit (S_2e) is lesser than the (OS_2) maximum profit i.e S_1N and staff expenditure is also greater than that of a profit maximiser (OS_1).

Thus Williamson's Model proves that corporate managers tries to maximise their own utility using their power of discretion rather than maximising the profits.

Critical Appraisal

Williamson's Model is a realistic one. He has tested the hypothesis that managerial discretion influences the expenditures for which managers have a strong "expense preference" which includes staff expenditure, emoluments, discretionary investment. But like other managerial theories, this theory also fails to explain oligopolistic interdependence in non-collusive markets. This model or theory is applicable in market where competition is not strong or firms who have some advantage over their rivals.

SUMMARY

I. Baumol's Theory of Sales Revenue Maximisation

Static Models

1. In Baumol's sales revenue maximisation model, a firm produces at the level of output at which its sales revenue is maximised subject to profit constraint.

2. In his model with advertisement, he concludes that the firm by increasing expenditure on advertisement it can increase its sale.

Dynamic Models

1. Baumol says that both profit maximising and sales revenue maximising firm produce the same quantity of output and market it in the same way.

2. According to Baumol, since a firm treats its profits as a constraint rather than as an ultimate objective, an increase in overhead costs leads to a price increase. So, to avoid a price increase the firm may reduce the output and advertising expenditure or only the advertisement expenditure to retain the acceptable profits.

II. Marris Model of Managerial Enterprises

1. According to Marris, the goal of the firm is the maximisation of the balanced rate of growth of the firm.

2. The goals of the managers and owners may coincide and they work together for a common cause or concern, namely "balanced growth" of the firm and thereby seek to maximise a steady growth rate for their firm.

III. The Behavioural Model of Cyert and March

1. The model given by Cyert and March is an extension of Simon's hypothesis of firms 'satisfying behaviour'.

2. Apart from dealing with uncertainities of the business world, managers have to satisfy a variety of group of people like shareholders, workers, customers, managers, bankers, government authorities, etc.

3. The firm should seek to satisfy all of them in one way or another by sacrificing some of its interests.

IV. Williamson's Model of Managerial Discretion

1. According to Williamson managers have discretion in pursuing policies which maximise their own utility rather than maximising the profits. The profit works as a constraint to the 'managers' discretion.

2. The managerial emoluments are assumed to be zero in Williamson's simplified model and thus the actual profit is the same as the reported profit.

QUESTIONS

1. Explain the static models of theory of sales revenue maximisation given by Baumol.

2. Explain the role of advertisement in increasing the sales of a business firm.

3. How far do changes in over head costs affects the sales revenue maximisation?

4. Critically examine Marris Model of Managerial enterprises.

5. State and explain the behavioural model of Cyert and March.

6. Why do managers have discretion in pursuing policies? How does Williamson's model explain this situation?

7. State and explain some of the basic propositions underlying the managerial theories of the firm.

8. Discuss decision making process in Cyert and March model.

REFERENCES

1. W.J. Baumol, "*On the Theory of Oligopoly*", Economica, New Series, Vol. 25, 1958 (ed.) pp. - 187-98, reprinted in G.C. Archibald (ed.). *The Theory of the Firm*, Harmondsworth; Penguin 1973, p.262.

2. *Ibid.*

3. *Ibid.*

16 Chapter

Pricing Methods, Policies and Practices

1. THE MEANING PRICING POLICY

Managerial decision making involves two important things, one is the formulation of rational price policy and secondly, the setting up of prices which are remunerative to the producers. All businessmen have a fundamental objective in business, i.e., to make maximum profits not only at a particular point of time but also during the whole period of existence. It is possible only when the producers set a price for the product which is greater than the cost. The businessmen use the pricing device for the purpose of maximising profits. At what price the product is to be sold depends upon a number of factors. Many problems come in the way of determining a price for the product. The price theory points out that the *equilibrium price is determined at a point where marginal revenue is equal to the marginal cost*. Some economists like Hall and Hitch of the Oxford University, rejected the assumption of profit maximisation as unrealistic and inapplicable to actual business conditions. Business firms do not determine price and output at the point of equality between MR and MC. Besides, businessmen are reluctant to charge a high price for the product, because this might result in bringing more producers into the industry. In other words, in real life, the firms want to prevent the entry of rivals and therefore they prefer to charge a high price which would bring supernormal profit. Often firms with a view to get a higher share in the market charge a right price.

Two factors which influence in determining prices are classified into internal and external factors. Internal factors are costs and the management policy. The external factors are the elasticity of supply and demand, the goodwill of the company, the extent of competitions in the market, the purchasing power of the buyers and the government policy towards prices.

2. GENERAL CONSIDERATIONS INVOLVED IN THE FORMULATION OF PRICING POLICY

General considerations involved in the formulation of pricing policy. Following are the general considerations.

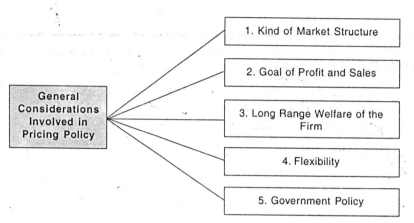

(i) Kind of Market Structure: Pricing policy is to be set in the light of the competitive situations in the market. We have to know whether the firm is facing perfect competition or imperfect competition. In perfect competition, the producers or sellers have no control over the price. It is because that they have to sell the homogeneous product at a price determined by the market demand and supply. They have no pricing discretion. Pricing policy has special significance only under imperfect competition. Under the present competitive market situation, the producers are forced to sell the best product at a reasonable price. Joel Deal says that the following market conditions influence in determining the price.

(a) The number, relative size and product line of competitors, (b) the likelihood of potential competition, (c) the stage of consumer's acceptance of the product, (d) the degree of product differentiation adopted by firms in the market, (e) the richness of the mixture of service, advertisement and sales propaganda and the reputation of the firm and the qualitative improvement in the product bundle.

(ii) Goal of Profit and Sales: Pricing should normally aim at stimulating profitable combination sales. Sometimes, the firms seek profit maximisation and at some other times maximisation of sales. In any case, the sales should bring more profit to the firm.

(iii) Long Range Welfare of the Firm: Pricing should take care of the long run welfare of the company and at the same time should discourage entry of new firms into the industry considering the market essence of the existing firms.

(iv) Flexibility: The prices determined should be flexible enough to meet the changes in the demand pattern and the market situation. Prices should also be flexible to take care of cyclical variations. If a firm is selling its product in a highly competitive market, it will have little scope for pricing discretion.

(v) **Government Policy:** It is also possible that the Government may prevent the firms in forming combinations to set a high price. Very often, the government prefers to control the prices of essential commodities with a view to prevent the exploitation of the consumers. The entry of the government into the pricing process, in the alliance with farmers and trade unions, tend to inject politics into price determination.

Other Considerations in Pricing and Price Forecasting

Pricing of a product is a complex problem and there is no readymade formula which can be immediately applied to solve the problem. However, several general considerations have been suggested to serve as guidelines in the pricing of products. Some of them are stated as follows:

(i) **Nature of Corporate Objectives:** Before taking up the technical function of the pricing of a product, it is absolutely necessary to know the objectives of the firm. These objectives might be the maximisation of profit, maximisation of sales to get a large share in the market etc. Every firm has fixed a target rate of profits and the concerned authorities have to achieve this objective in the manner of pricing of the product. While fixing the price, it is also necessary to examine the impact of pricing on other policies and the growth of the firm.

(ii) **Nature of competition:** This is another consideration which the management of the firm has to bear in mind, namely whether the firm is facing perfect competition, imperfect competition like monopoly, monopolistic competition, etc. In the case of perfect competition, the firm has to accept the price and the firm has no option in this. The pricing of the product becomes very important when the firm is facing imperfect market. Since the product is not homogeneous, the pricing of the product is to be related to its utility. Thus, pricing policy must be governed more by this relative aspect than by its absolute price.

(iii) **Promotional Policies:** Pricing of the product is also governed by the promotional efforts of the company. The sales campaign plays a very important role in the sale of the product. The pricing of the product should also take care of the promotional policy of the company.

(iv) **Co-ordination in Product Line:** There are many channels in the sales of the product and the pricing should establish proper co-ordination among producers, distributors and retailers. The interests of the producers and the distributors must be identical, otherwise, the purpose of pricing will be defeated. The price fixed by the producers must be accepted by sales channels.

(v) **Pricing Routine Function:** Pricing of product is no doubt based on some systematic studies. Generally, it is not done arbitrarily. Yet, it becomes a routine function in the sense, that instead of following its own independent policy, it may mechanically follow the prices fixed by its competitors. If there is a wide difference between the prices of alternate product, firms with higher price find it difficult to sell the products in the market. Therefore, firms fix the prices as it is prevailing for similar products in the market.

3. OBJECTIVES OF PRICING POLICY

Pricing is a very difficult process. There is no infallible formula in determining a right place for a product. Every pricing situation is unique and therefore, the management has to use discretionary powers in determining a just price. In fact, pricing is a matter of judgement. The judgement should be based on sound principles in order to be effective. Pricing is not an end in itself. It is a means to an end. Therefore, while determining a price, the following objectives have to be borne in mind.

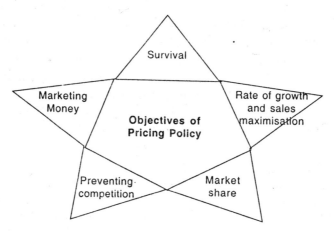

(a) Survival: In these days of severe competition and business uncertainties, the firm must set a price which would safeguard the welfare of the firm. A firm is always interested in its survival. For the sake of its continued existence, it must tolerate all kinds of obstacles and challenges from rivals.

(b) Rate of Growth and Sales Maximisation: A firm has to set a price which assures maximum sales of the product. Only then, it can achieve growth. As Kotler says that the firms should set prices which would increase the sales of the product's line, rather than yield a profit on one product.

(c) Market Share: The firm can secure a large share in the market by means of following a suitable price policy. It can also acquire a dominating leadership position in the market.

(d) Preventing Competition: By adopting a suitable price policy, the firm wants to restrict the entry of rivals. It would try to fix up a price which would avoid competitors.

(e) Making Money: Some firms want to use their special position in the industry by selling the product at premium and thus making quick profit as much as possible.

Other Objectives of a Pricing Policy

The objectives of pricing of products are many. While fixing the price of the products, the firms have to look into objectives. These broad objectives are as follows:

    (i) To achieve a given rate of return for the entire product line,

    (ii) To maintain price stability at a desired level,

    (iii) To follow a price policy which meets all market conditions and

    (iv) To prevent new firms from entering into the industry

There are no doubt certain advantages and disadvantages in achieving each objective. However, the firms have to make a compromise between the two extremes. If the firms aim at maximising profits, they have to keep a high price to the products. If the prices are high, the sales of the products might be affected and the firms cannot maximise profits. If the price is high, it is impossible for the firm to get a greater market share. If the price of the product of a firm is high, it encourages the rival firms to complete this product. All these are conflicting objectives. Therefore, it is better to follow the suggestions given by Kotler in pursuing a pricing policy.

(i) A firm may not fix a price which achieves the maximum returns, but would rather fix a price which gives it a smaller but satisfactory rate of return.

(ii) Often, firms are found to fix a price which gives maximum profit on the entire range of products rather than price on one product and very low profit on the rest of the product line.

(iii) The firms which face the problem of liquidity, fix prices at a level which would ensure rapid cash recovery.

(iv) Some firms fix prices in such a manner that they can capture a larger share of the market and

(v) The product which has a high value for some of the buyers is sometimes sold at a high initial price to take advantage of the situation known as *market skimming*.

Apart from what has been stated above; there are managers who want to avert risk by following safe-pricing policies. There are some others who love to take risk, follow unorthodox pricing policies. Some managers follow old techniques of determining prices. All these peculiarities can be seen in the manufacturing unit.

Price-profit Stabilisation

The firms are interested in keeping their prices stable within a certain period of time irrespective of changes in demand and costs, so that they may get the expected profit.

Phillip Kotler has mentioned the following objectives in his book 'Marketing Management'.

(i) *Market Penetration:* Here the firm sets a low price to stimulate the demand and capture the market.

(ii) *Market Skimming:* In the beginning, the firm charges a high price to take advantage of some buyers who are willing to pay that price and afterwards charge a low price to enable the less fortunate buyers to buy the product.

(iii) *Early Cash Recovery:* Some firms set a price which will create a mad rush for the product and recover cash early. They may also set a low price as a caution against uncertainty of the future.

(iv) *Satisfaction:* In order to achieve a satisfactory rate of return, the firms set a price which will result in higher sales.

However, the survival of the firm is the main objective in pricing. At the same time, the firms bear in mind the following objectives while pricing the product:

(i) to fulfil a good rate of return on investment,

(ii) to seek anticipated rate of growth,

(iii) to improve the market share,

(iv) to stabilise prices and profit margin.

4. FACTORS INVOLVED IN PRICING POLICY

The pricing of the products involves consideration of the following factors:

(a) Costs, (b) demand and psychology of consumers, (c) competition, (d) profit, (e) government policy.

(a) Cost Factor in Pricing: Cost data occupy an important place in the price setting processes. There are different types of costs incurred in the production and marketing of the product. There are production costs, promotional expenses like advertising or personal selling as well as taxation, etc. They may necessitate an upward fixing of price. The prices of petrol and gas are rising due to a rise in the cost of raw materials such as crude, transportation, refining etc. If the costs rise, the price of the product also rises. For setting prices, apart from costs, there are other things which cannot be turned down. They are the demand and competition. Costs are of two types: fixed costs and the variable costs. In the short period, i.e., the period in which a firm wants to establish itself, the firm may not cover the fixed costs but it must cover the variable costs. But in the long run, all costs must be covered. If the entire costs are not covered, the producer stops production Consequently, the supply is reduced which in turn may lead to higher prices.

Regarding the role of cost in pricing, Nickerson has observed that costs may be regarded only as an indicator of demand and price. He further says that the cost at any given time represents a resistance point to the lowering of price. Again, costs determine the profit margins at various levels of output. Cost calculations may also help in determining whether the product whose price is determined by its demand is to be included in the product line or not. 'What costs determine is not the price but whether the production can be profitably produced or not' is very important. If the price in the short run is lower than the cost, then the question arises, whether this price covers the variable cost. If it runs, the firm cannot sell at a price lower than the cost. Product pricing decision should therefore be made with a view to maximise the company's profits in the long run.

(b) Demand Factor and Psychology of Consumers: In the pricing of a product, demand occupies a very important place. In fact, demand is more important for effective sales. The elasticity of demand is to be recognised in determining the price of the product. If the demand for the product is inelastic, the firm can fix a high price. On the other hand, if the demand is elastic, it has to fix a lower price.

Demand for the product depends upon the behaviour of the consumers. There are consumers who buy a product provided its quality is high. In fact, product quality, product image, customer service and promotion activity influence many consumers more than the price. Supposing the consumers want to buy durable goods such as television set, refrigerator, car etc., they go in for quality than price. If the price of the product is too low, the product is regarded as of poor quality and hence the demand may not rise. Manufacturers of durable goods always set a high price, even though the sales are affected. If the price is too high, it may also affect the demand for the product. They wait for the arrival of a rival product with a competitive price. Therefore, the demand for a product is so sensitive to price changes. With an increase in personal income, the consumers become quality conscious. This may also lead to an increase in the demand for durable goods. People of high incomes buy products even though their prices are high. In the affluent societies, price is the indicator of quality. Advertisement and sales promotion also contribute very much in increasing the demand for advertised products. It is because, the consumers think that the advertised products are of good quality. To conclude, income of the consumers, the standard of living and the price factor influence the demand for various products in the society. In determining the price, the income elasticity and the price elasticity will have to be taken into consideration.

(c) **Competition Factor:** The market situation plays an effective role in pricing. In perfect competition, the individual producers have no discretion in pricing. They have to accept the price fixed by demand and supply. In monopoly, the producer fixes a high price for his product. In other market situations like oligopoly and monopolistic competition, the individual producers take the prices of the rival products in determining their price.

(d) **Profits:** In setting the price for products, the manufacturers consider primarily the profit aspect. Each producer has his aim of profit maximisation. Usually, the pricing policy is based on the goal of obtaining a reasonable profit.

Most of the businessmen want to hold the price at constant level. They do not desire frequent price fluctuations.

The price rigidity is the practice of many producers. Rigidity does not mean inflexibility. It means that prices are stable over a given period, say a year.

(e) **Government Policy:** In the capitalist societies, the government generally does not interfere in the economic decisions of the economy. It is only in planned economies and socialist states that the government's interference is very much. In a mixed economy like India, the government resorts to price control. The firms have to adopt the government's price policies. Within the maximum parameters fixed by the government, the individual firms have to determine the price. In the case of agricultural commodities, to protect farmers. The government announces the support prices. In the case of essential commodities and services, the government determines the prices with the view to safe guard the consumers. All others have to accept this price.

External Factors

The external factors which influence the pricing policies of firms are the elasticity of demand and supply of a product, the trend in the market, purchasing power of the people of the country, the inflationary or deflationary position prevailing in the country.

5. PRICING METHODS

There are **five** important methods of pricing: (i) Cost-plus or full cost pricing. (ii) Pricing for a rate of return. (iii) Marginal cost pricing. (iv) Administered pricing and (v) Going-rate policy.

(i) Full Cost Pricing Method or cost Plus Pricing

Cost-plus or full cost pricing is a method commonly adopted by the businessmen to fix a price of the product. He calculates the cost of production per unit and adds a margin of profit to it. In other words, the producer adds a certain percentage of profit which he considers as fair to his cost in order to arrive at a price which is acceptable to the consumers. This procedure is known as cost-plus pricing.

> *Full cost or cost plus pricing is calculating by adding a certain percentage of profit to the average total cost of prodcution.*

Cost-plus pricing means the addition of a certain percentage of profit to the cost of production to arrive at a price. For example, the cost of production of a product is Rs.10. If the management decides to have a mark of 100 per cent, then Rs.10 is the addition to the cost. Hence, the price is Rs.20 per unit of the product. Here two elements make up the price: one is the average cost or cost per unit and the other is the mark-up (profit). These two components are found in the cost-plus pricing.

A clear analysis of profit is known only from the cost analysis. Moreover, cost is the base on which is grounded the percentage of profit which the manufacturer wants to arrive to the price of the product. The computation of cost of production of a commodity is a difficult thing. There are three different methods of computing cost. According to Joel Dean, there are three different concepts of cost components used in cost-plus pricing. They are: (a) the actual cost, (b) the expected cost and (c) the standard cost.

(a) Actual costs are those costs which are actually incurred by the firm in order to produce a given commodity. They are also called *historical cost*. Actual costs include wage bill, raw-material costs and overhead charges at the current output rate. The prices of these materials prevailing in the latest periods will be taken into consideration to determine actual costs.

(b) The expected cost is a forecast of the actual expenses for the pricing period. Suppose the company wants to introduce a new product six months from today, the company first determines the cost at the prevailing prices. Then the prices of various products are projected for the next six months and thus the expected cost is calculated.

(c) Standard cost refers to a normal cost determination at some normal rate of output at a given level of capacity utilisation. To calculate the standard cost, the capacity of the plant is considered. Supposing the plant is running at 60 per cent capacity - if the plant works at 80 per cent of the capacity, then the cost may be normal or optimum. This optimum is taken into consideration in calculating the standard cost.

Though these three methods are available to calculate cost, each company follows one of the methods. Again, a firm may first arrive at costs based on the three methods and then decide upon the one which suits it best. Each method gives a different figure and as such different prices emerge.

The firm, after arriving at a cost, records a fair rate of profit which is added to it and determines the price. What is fair rate is difficult to say. But a fair rate of profit is assumed to be between 10 and 15 per cent of the cost.

Limitations

(i) The cost-plus pricing ignores the demand side of the problem. This method takes into account only the costs and a certain rate of profit. When a firm starts producing a new product, it should take into account the willingness of the consumers to buy it.

(ii) It fails to consider the importance of competition and as such, it ignores the existence of competitors completely. In fact, any pricing of product should take into consideration the price of the products of the rival.

(iii) When a firm manufactures and sells multiple products, there is bound to be some common costs. These costs are allocated arbitrarily. When costs are not allocated precisely, then the method cannot become valid.

(iv) This method is totally based on conventional accounting system. It ignores the future costs in the pricing decision. It considers only the past and the present costs. Moreover, opportunity cost is very important in determining the price. Thus, the cost-plus pricing method does not make use of economic tools altogether.

(i) It helps in selling fair and plausible prices.

(ii) It is easy for all forms to calculate this price and apply.

(iii) Cost-plus safe guards the interest of the firm against risks when the demand is uncertain.

(iv) It is economical for decision-making by the firm.

(v) It may help the firms in protecting against price-wars or competition.

(vi) Cost-plus pricing is more useful specially in public-utility pricing.

(ii) Rate of Return Pricing or Target Pricing

The cost-plus pricing method has led to a controversy with regard to fair rate of return. Some businessmen argue that the decent percent of return on investment is fair, but some others do not accept this conclusion. Therefore, the word *'fair'* is an ambiguous word.

> *Under the method of rate of return pricing, the price is determined based on the pre-determined target rate of return on capital invested by the manufacturer.*

Under this method, the price is determined by the planned rate of return on investment which is expected to be converted into a percentage of the mark up. The profit margin is determined on the basis of the rate of production and the total cost of a year's normal production. Then, the capital turnover is computed by taking the ratio of invested capital to the annual standard cost. Then the mark up percentage of profit is obtained by multiplying capital turnover by the goal rate of return. Let us take the following example:

Say, the capital turnover is Rs.0.9 lakh. The desired rate of return is 27 per cent. Now -

% mark up = Capital turnover x desired rate of return

= 0.9 x 27 = 24 per cent

Now, 24 per cent is the mark up. Or it may also be found out by this method:

American firms start with a rate of return which they consider satisfactory and then fix a price that will allow them to earn that return when their plant is running at 80 per cent utilisation. They determine the standard costs as standard volume and add the margin necessary to return the target rate of profit over the long run.

While defining the rate of return, it is held that it should cut across business cycles and should be determined on the basis of standards of reasonableness. This method is essentially the cost-plus pricing method but an improved one. Since it builds price on cost which is standardised, it develops a profit mark up related to a rate of return.

(iii) Marginal Cost Pricing

Under cost-plus pricing and rate of return pricing, the prices of products are determined on the basis of total costs. (variable + fixed costs). Under marginal cost pricing, fixed costs are ignored and pricing is determined on the basis of marginal costs. Marginal cost means cost of producing additional units of the product. The firm uses only those costs which are directly attributable to the output of the specific period. The price so determined must cover the marginal cost and the total cost will have to be covered in the long run. Price based on marginal costs will be much more aggressive than the one based on total costs. Further, when a firm has a large unused capacity, it should explore the possibility of producing and selling more - it should cover the marginal cost. The real difficulty is to know the marginal cost.

> *Marginal cost pricing refers to the method of determining the price on the basis of marginal or variable cost.*

Advantages of Marginal Cost Pricing

(i) Under marginal cost pricing, prices are never rendered uncompetitive merely because of higher fixed overhead costs. If the variable costs are higher, the prices also will be higher, but they can be controlled in the short period and thus make the price competitive.

$$\text{Percentage Markup} = \frac{\text{Capital Employed}}{\text{Total Annual Cost}} \times \text{Planned Rate of Return}$$

(ii) Marginal costs reflect more accurately the future as distinct from the present cost structure.

(iii) Marginal cost pricing permits a producer to resort to aggressive price policy than is possible under full cost pricing. An aggressive pricing would lead to higher sales and by increased marginal physical productivity and lower input factor prices, marginal cost can be reduced.

(iv) Marginal cost pricing is very much useful over the life cycle of a product.

(v) Marginal cost pricing is more effective than full cost pricing because it helps in solving short run problems. That is, under the conditions of change, marginal cost is the most suitable method of short run pricing. In the short run pricing, only marginal costs are covered and fixed costs are completely ignored.

The only difficulty in marginal cost pricing is ignorance of the marginal cost technique. In a period of business recession, the firms using marginal cost pricing can overcome the recession by lowering the pries and thereby allowing the sales to increase. With the existence of idle capacity and the pressure of fixed costs, firms successfully cut down prices to a point equivalent to marginal cost and earn a fair rate of return in the period of crisis.

(iv) Going Rate Pricing

The going rate pricing is opposite of full cost or cost-plus pricing. The going rate policy means, adjusting its own price policy to the general price structure in the industry. This policy is adopted where it is difficult to measure the costs. Though the firm has complete freedom to fix its own price, it will not do so, but instead, it tries to adjust its own price policy with the price prevailing in the market. The going rate pricing is adopted when the price leadership is very well established. When firms want to avoid the tension of price rivalry in the market, they adopt the going rate pricing. This is very easy and there is no need for a firm to take the trouble of calculating costs and demand.

It is also called as acceptance princing.

> *Going rate pricing means fixing price for a firm's product which is the same as the one which was already set by a competitor firm for a similar product.*

Advantages

1. It helps to avoid competition among the firms.
2. It can be adopted even when costs are difficult to measure.
3. It is economical.
4. It is suitable to avoid price hazards in.

Limitations

1. It is relevant only for well established and well-known product.
2. It is not possible to find out going rate for a new product.
3. It is not suitable for those products whose marketing is fading away.

(Many big firms in America have adopted this policy of price leadership.)

(v) Administered Prices

The Government may adopt administered prices for essential commodities like steel, cement, fertilizers and petroleum products etc. in the case of petrol, the Government has fixed the price and the retailers have to sell it at that price only. In the case of the other commodities, the government has reserved the right of allotment to users and the products are sold at the administered prices.

> *Administered prices are the prices of commodities fixed by the government to prevent price escalation, black-marketing and shortages in supply.*

The objective of administering the prices of some essential commodities is to prevent any sudden rise in their prices and to ensure reasonable prices to the users. It is because of the importance of raw materials like steel, cement, fertilizers etc., and their prices must be stabilised at a reasonable level. If the prices of these commodities are allowed to rise or fall, the production of final commodities is affected. Administered prices denote a pool price while the production units are given an assured price called *retention price*. These retention prices may be the same for all units or may be different to different units. The administered prices are fixed on the basis of the cost of production plus a certain amount of profit. Administered prices are advantageous both to the users and to the producers. When there is a change in cost of production, the administered prices are also changed. The cost of many articles like steel, cement, etc., are worked out by the Bureau of Industrial Costs and Prices in India.

Need for Administrative Pricing

1. To correct the imperfections in the market mechanism.
2. To arrest the undue price rise of scarce essential consumption goods and raw materials, when there is supply is less than their demand.
3. To provide a relatively stable and assured income to the farmers.
4. To protect the consumers from greedy monopolists.
5. To provide the items of mass consumption at low subsidised prices to the poor sectors of the society.

Advantages

1. Administered prices protects the interests of the weaker section of the society by discouraging and encouraging the consumption of certain commodities.
2. It also mitigate inflation or prevent strongflation.
3. It increases the public revenue.
4. It ensures efficient allocation of scarce resources.
5. It also helps in promoting egalitarian goal.

Limitations

1. Sometime, administered prices may discourage the production of certain goods.

    e.g. fertilizer, cement, steel, electricity, generation and railways.

2. Changes should be introduced when there is change in the cost of production. Otherwise, it will lead to reduction in the supply of certain goods (which comes under administered prices) in the economy.

6. DUAL PRICING

Dual pricing is a system in which two types of prices are prevailing for a product. Under this system, one price is fixed and controlled by the government and the other price is to be determined by market forces. The price fixed by the government is fairly static while the other price is fluctuating. In this system, a certain percentage of output is brought under government pricing and the balance is allowed for private pricing. In the dural pricing system, both socialist pricing and capitalist pricing co-exist. Government of India introduced this system in the case of products like sugar, cement, etc. The dual pricing is still being practised in the sale of sugar in India. Fifty or sixty percent of the output is brought under public distribution system through fixed prices, while the balance is sold at market prices. The Government's fixed price is always less than the market price.

The price fixed by the Government under the dual price system covers the cost of production and allows a reasonable amount of profit. Since there is another price which is higher than the controlled price, the manufacturers get a higher amount of profit. The dual system is practised so as to protect the weaker section of the society from higher price for the essential commodity. All consumers are assured of minimum requirements at the controlled price. If the consumers require more than the minimum, they have to pay a higher price for the product. The demand under the dual system is regulated by two prices. Under the controlled price system, demand is regulated while under the open market price system, price establishes the equilibrium between the demand and supply.

7. GUIDELINES FOR PRICE FIXATION

Some guidelines for price fixation have been given by Bates and Parkinson in the book *'Business Economics'*.

(1) It is necessary to know the costs incurred in relation to output and also to distinguish between prime costs and overhead costs.

(2) In the beginning, prices should cover prime costs and later on the price should cover the entire costs.

(3) The firms must know the prices of the products sold by other firms. The costs incurred must be comparable to the costs of the other firms for the same amount of output.

(4) If the demand for the product of a firm is sluggish, then it will have to reduce the price a bit in order to improve its position.

(5) If the costs of raw-materials and labour rise, the firm is compelled to increase the price.

(6) If the costs are rising and the sales are sluggish, then the firm must be able to refrain from raising the price.

(7) The capacity of the plant must be used to the optimum extent. Production should be concentrated on those products whose demand is high.

(8) The firm by improving sales campaign, must build the image of the firm.

(9) As far as possible, prices should cover the costs. Further, if the costs are higher than the costs of rivals, the firm in question is required to reduce the costs by means of better management.

(10) If the prices set by the firm are bringing good profits, then the firm should resort to expansion of production.

(11) Prices should not go against the public interest.

(12) If the company is making high profits by selling at a price, the rivals are sure to enter into the industry and compete away the profits.

8. SOME PRICING PROBLEMS

The life period and its distinctiveness - pricing of a new product

In the production of a product, a distinction is made between perishable and non-perishable products. a perishable product does not last for a long period, whereas a non-perishable product has two characteristics, namely its life period and its distinctiveness. In a real situation, the life of a product does not extend beyond a particular period of time. In this case, non-perishability refers to the period of time for which a particular product lasts. This period of life lasts as long as the product is distinctive. A manufacturer introduces a new product into the market, which is substantially distinct from the existing product. This newness is its distinctiveness which lasts over a period of time, for the rivals try to bring the products which are identical to the company's products, so that they might serve as its substitutes. In this sense, the so called distinctiveness is completely lost. That distinctiveness of a product lasts only for a short time.

There are five stages in the lifecycle of a product. They are: (i) Introduction of a product through innovation, (ii) Growth of sales, (iii) Maturity, (iv) Saturation and (v) Decline.

When a new product is introduced in the market, which is distinctive in many respects, but owing to the lack of consumer awareness, the sales are minimum. In order to create interest in the product, a huge advertisement budget is necessary. There are high promotional costs while the volume of sales is low and the profit also is less and in fact, the firm may incur losses. These are the characteristics of the product in the first stage.

Then the product begins to make gradual progress and the sales increase. The firm starts making profits also. In order to maintain high sales, the firm is required to improve the quality of the product. This is the second stage of the product.

In the third stage, it gets maturity. Though the sales rise, the rate of growth is slow, because of the entry of rivals. Profit margin also diminishes inspite of good sales.

The next stage in the lifecycle of the product is the saturation stage. Sales reach a particular level here and it remains there for long. When the substitutes emerge in the market with better quality and price, the sales of the existing product starts declining.

The life cycle of a product is always short. It is due to several factors like continuous research for product development, improvement of the product made by several companies and the emergence of competitors. If one company offers a better product, the rivals also imitate the product strategy and try to produce much better products than the previous company. If a competitor makes better improvement, the sales of his product increases and thus makes good profits.

When the distinctiveness of the product fades, the pricing discretion enjoyed by the firm no longer holds essence.

Perishable Product: When a product is perishable, it means that its distinctiveness is lost. This is so when new products develop a distinctiveness and protect themselves from the attack of the substitutes. This results in *product degeneration*. Viewed from this angle, every product has a degeneration cycle. When a new product is launched in the market, the distinctiveness of the existing product starts declining. At this stage, it itself becomes a target of competitive encroachment. New rivals enter the field and their innovations reduce the extent of distinctiveness between the first product and the product of the rivals. As a result of this, the distinctive product gradually degenerates and becomes a footpath product. In such cases, the pricing policy needs to be carefully determined to take care of the cyclical changes.

Degeneration: A pricing policy should also take into consideration the degeneration aspect of the product. The degeneration of a product arises as a result of the negligence of technical and economic factors. The technical factors relate to the improvement of the quality and design of the product. The economic factors relate to the market acceptance and the entry of rival firms. Market acceptance is conditioned by cultural lags. For example, when power based mixies were introduced for the first time in the city market, the housewives accepted them on the ground that it relieved them from physical torture they experienced from conventional grinders. When more competitors entered into this market with better performance and price concessions, the mixies became *'footpath'* products. The problem that arose then was how to price those products.

9. PRICING OF A NEW PRODUCT

If the new product is with high distinctiveness among the existing products, then the fixation of the price should be based on the demand, the market target and the promotional strategy.

In the case of pioneer products, the estimation of their demand is very difficult. The estimate of demand for such products should be studied in the following manner:

(i) Whether the new product is accepted by the consumers.

(ii) At what price it is acceptable.

(iii) If three or four prices are fixed, what would be the volume of sales at each price and

(iv) What would be the reaction of the manufacturers of the substitutes.

(i) **Product Acceptability:** It is based on the willingness of the consumers to buy the product. The willingness to buy depends upon a factor that is whether it would meet their requirements. If it does not meet the needs and requirements of the consumers, the product should be improved to serve the purpose. Supposing the new product is a strategic alternative, then it should be found out how many consumers would buy the new one in place of the old one.

(ii) **Range of Prices:** It is very important to assess the action of the consumers at different prices. For this, a market research will have to be undertaken. There are specialised market research institutions which can undertake this survey. The core question that arises is at what prices different quantities of the product are demanded. There are some practical difficulties as regards the price that consumers are willing to pay for the product. It is possible to find out the reaction of the consumers at different prices at different places through substantial market research.

(iii) **Expected Volume of Sales:** The next important task is to determine the anticipated volume of sales at different prices. This depends upon demand elasticity and cross elasticity. If the product introduced is a pioneer, it is very difficult to estimate the demand. If the consumers refuse to accept the product when it is brought into the market, then the whole exercise of determining the expected volume of sales is a waste. If the product is going to be accepted, it would be worthwhile to assess price as well as cross elasticity. Supposing a company introduces a new product which satisfies the consumers, the demand would naturally rise and the company which introduced the product would also makes profits. Even other companies start producing and selling similar products with sufficient sales campaign, with the product being distinct, the sales of it will not be affected.

(iv) **Reaction of Price:** The assessment of the reaction of the consumers to the price is a very tricky task. The company which introduces a new product will have to monitor the activities of the rivals in order to find out the marketing strategies that they are going to adopt.

Product Testing

The acceptance of a new product by the consumer depends upon product testing and test marketing. It is the experience of trade and commerce that more than 80 per cent of the new products fail to click in the market. In order to make it acceptable, product testing is essential.

Product testing refers to the various methods which are employed to assess the acceptance of products by the consumers. It is necessary to know from the consumers whether they are satisfied with the product. Therefore, some samples of a new product is to be released at different centres of the country to assess the reaction of the consumers. It is generally said that most of the new products are given a blind test. In this blind test, if the brand name is concealed and the reaction is known, the brand name might influence the consumers. When a new product is put to test with an established image and reputation, it becomes all the more necessary to find out whether the product is acceptable and whether it lives up to the image of the brand name of the concerned company.

Test Marketing

Market research is indispensable when a company wishes to produce a new product. The test market research may not guarantee the success of a new product, but it will reveal the actual position. The usefulness of test marketing has been upheld by E.J.Devis as follows:

"Test marketing is a complex operation. Its foundation in statistical theory is not popularly sound, but practical difficulties may prevent much improvement in this direction. Many of the prediction made on the basis of test marketing are too facile a basis and far more need to be done to investigate the possibilities of improved predictive techniques. In general test marketing is under-researched, with far too many organisations being content to measure one aspect of the end result through retail outlets and ignoring the possibilities of and the need for collecting other types of data as the test proceeds. Against all this, with the ever-increasing expense of marketing, there may be even less willingness on the part of a manufacturer to jump directly from pre-testing to the national launch. Consequently, test marketing is likely to remain. Test marketing can provide a great deal of knowledge and experience of a new product and it should give atleast a clear indication of a plan which is failing to meet its objectives."

The pricing policy of a new product involves apart from the cost of production, the study of prices of the alternative products of the group to which the new product belongs. For example, if the new product is an household appliance, the prices of household appliances should be studied. The prices of the substitute products and their usage have to be known before pricing a new product. Let us take the following example:

Household Product (Pressure Cooker)

Product	Price Rs.	Weightage	Weighted Price Rs.
A	800	15	12,000
B	1000	20	20,000
C	1200	20	24,000
D	1500	30	45,000
E	2000	15	30,000
		100	1,31,000

$$\text{Suggested Price is} = \frac{131000}{100} = \text{Rs.}1,310$$

Weightage is given on the basis of the usage of the appliance. If, in a house only a bachelor lives, its usage is limited and therefore less weightage is given. In a big family, its usage is high therefore high weightage is given. Thus, taking the total weightage price and dividing it by the weightage, the suggested price is arrived.

High Skimming Price: A skimming price is that where the initial price is high. Whenever a company introduces a new product, it spends a huge sum of money on advertisements. The company may put the product in attractive packages. Therefore, to cover all these costs, the company fixes a high price. If the new product which has no substitute also has a good usage, the product can be sold at a high price. The company is quite sure that in course of time, the substitutes are going to enter into the market. When it has no rivals, a high price is fixed for the product. When the substitutes enter into the market, then the price is reduced and thereby the challenge is posed. However, by the time the substitutes enter the market, it is not certain that this product will command a market value. It may lose to the product of the competitors. Therefore, an initial high price is suggested for a new product when it is introduced for the first time.

When a new product with a high skimming price is introduced, the demand may not increase all of a sudden. Therefore, promotion expenditure of a high magnitude will have to be incurred. Further, if the price is very high, many consumers may not buy it. Therefore, a potential market will have to be decided on the basis of elasticity of demand. If the demand is inelastic, a high price may be fixed. When this segment of the market is exhausted, then the second segment of the market will have to be tapped at a lesser price. For example, in the case of the publication of a text book, it is priced high. But the next paper back edition is priced low.

A high initial price may be useful if the production of the product requires high technical skill and it is difficult and time consuming for competitors to enter on an economical scale.

A Low Penetration Price: A low penetration price pertains to charging a low price in the beginning itself. If the price is low, it can penetrate into the market quickly. It is due to the fact that the consumers may buy the product at a low price. Before fixing the low price for the new product, a market research is necessary. In the high skimming price situation, the firm gets profit which may arise in the short run quickly but in the case of low penetration price, profits may arise in the long run. One way this is advantageous, for it is possible for the product to establish itself firmly in the market. If the price is raised afterwards, the demand is not going to fall.

The objective of low penetrating pricing is to keep the rivals away from entering into the market with substitute products. The low price of the products prevents competition. If the price is set low, the margin of profit also is low and thereby new - comers are not going to venture into the production of this product. A low penetration price is advantageous when the productive capacity of the plant is high. A low price is sure to capture the entire market and production price is profitable because large quantity can be sold. In the case of a multi-product firm, it is not the margin of profit that matters. If the potential market is large, the big companies by selling the product at a low price, drive away many small companies.

10. PRICING CONCEPTS

Pricing is an important element in marketing mix. Determination of a right place for a product is very essential in a sound marketing mix. Right price can be determined either by research or by test marketing. A study of pricing involves a study of pricing concepts which serves as a guide for executive decision making and control. The various concepts of pricing which helps in decision making are:

(i) Peak load pricing,

(ii) Pricing over life cycle of a product,

(iii) Pricing and public utility and services,

(iv) Product line pricing,

(v) Transfer pricing.

(vi) Multi-product pricing

(i) Peak Load Pricing: There are certain products which cannot be stored and demand for them varies over time. For example, demand for electricity is high during the day time and low during night time. It is high in a cold country and low in a hot country. But, it is high in desert countries for electricity is needed for airconditioning and cooling. In cold countries, it is needed for room heating. There is some exception in demand for some commodities as mentioned above. In the same manner, demand for telephone is more during day time and low during night time. If electricity and telephone are offered at a constant price, it would result in great pressure on demand during one time phase and excess capacity during the other time phases. Since these services are not storable, the capacity to be installed should depend upon that maximum demand, i.e., peak load demand. In the case of electricity and telephone and some postal services, the prices are high for the peak load period and low for the low demand period. During the nights, the demand is low and charges are also low. Such price differences change the demand from peak period to non-peak period.

In view of the high peak load demand, the installed capacity of the machines are put into maximum use and cost is covered. Any loss in the non-peak period is covered by excess of earnings earned during the peak period. The prices are determined for both the demand functions in such a way that the entire costs are covered, i.e. both variable and fixed costs. The peak load pricing involves flexible pricing over time, thereby an optimum combination of prices for the peak as well as non-peak is determined.

(ii) Pricing over the Life Cycle of a Product: There are some products which are constantly changing owing to strategic innovation. If a new product, an instrument or a process of production technique is developed, it will not be for a long period. In the course of a year or two, a new product is developed making the old one unpopular. Therefore, it can be said that most products have something of a perishable distinctiveness, whereby these products become ordinary commodities over a period of time. Joel Dean calls this a *'cycle of competitive degeneration'*. With the development of a new product followed by an innovation, the existing product loses its

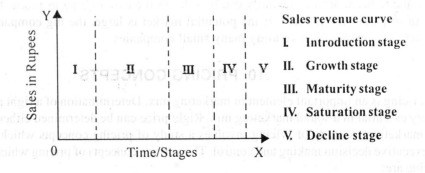

Sales revenue curve

I.   Introduction stage

II. Growth stage

III. Maturity stage

IV. Saturation stage

V. Decline stage

distinctiveness. At this stage, competitors enter the market with innovations and substitutes, making the original product disappear from the market. The following figure shows different stage of a product, life cycle. It is stated that there are five different stages in the life cycle f a product. The innovation of a new product and its degeneration into a common product is kn wn as life cycle of a product.

When the product enjoys distinctiveness, the producer enjoys monopoly power and it could be vice versa, under certain situations proving detrimental to the producer. In this stage, he can withstand competition. As the product moves from one stage to another stage, there is improvement in the beginning and after reaching the maximum, the product becomes insignificant. In order to save itself from the stage of insignificance, he also takes up innovation. Either he improves the old product or he produces a new product.

Introductory Stage: In this stage, the firm develops a new product through and advertisements innovation. The product is put into the market with all necessary propaganda. But the demand for the new product in the beginning is very slow. At this stage, the firm incurs higher promotional costs, but the sales revenue is so low, and eventually it cannot cover any costs fully.

Growth Stage: In this stage, there is rapid expansion of sales because of the effect of sales promotion undertaken in the introductory stages. In view of increased sales, the company earns good profits after covering the entire costs.

Maturity Stage: When the product enters the maturity stage of growth, the volume of sales goes on increasing, but the rate of growth is rather slow. This is because all those who need the product, have already purchased it and the number of new customers for the product is low. The firm spends considerable amount on sales promotion to boost its sales. But there is only a replacement demand in the market as against new demand. Maturity stage is a stage of optimum growth. It cannot go on forever. During this period, there emerges an innovation. This innovation results in the development of a better product. Consequently the demand for the old product starts declining. Then the product enters the fourth stage called *saturation*.

Saturation Stage: Saturation point is defined as the declining posture after reaching the zenith in the demand for the product. At this point, the firm is producing the product at a higher cost in view of high promotional expenditure. Since the sales are declining, the firm is not in a position to cover any costs. On the other hand, it starts incurring losses. Finally it enters the stage of decline.

Decline: Decline is the last stage of the life-cycle of the product. The sales of the product falls significantly in view of the emergence of the rival product with better quality and appearance. When the competitors enter the market with limitations, then the existing product loses its distinctiveness.

Causes for Growth Cycle of the Product: There are many reasons for the rise and fall in the growth of a product. Where there is no competition for the product, a new product commands a great demand, sales and profit. When the alternatives emerge as a result of innovation, with better image and prices, the original product loses its distinctiveness.

When the distinctiveness of the product fades, the prices of the product decline. Throughout the life cycle of a product, we find change in demand, price, promotion expenses, cost of production and distribution. Therefore, the pricing policy of such products must also be suitably modified to adjust the various phases of the product.

Pricing of the Product at the Maturity Stage: In the introduction stage, the price of the product is generally low. But when the product experiences growth, the price also rises. When it reaches the maturity stage, the price of the product must also be stable. When the demand for the product starts declining and the replacement demand also is more than the new demand, the technology for the production of the product is the same for all firms and finally with the emergence of substitutes and imitations, the distinctiveness of the product is eroding, the price of the product also has to be altered. In the later maturity stage, the firm is required to take stock of the situation and change the price policy. In other words, the firm is required to bring down the price to the extent the demand elasticity of the product permits.

(iii) Pricing of Public Utility Product and Services: Pricing of public utility products and services like electricity, railways, telephones, etc. poses some special problems. These undertakings are natural monopolies and they are not meant for making monopoly profit. Since enormous investment are made for generating and supplying electricity, it must earn sufficient revenue to meet all costs of production and distribution. Technology of production and distribution enable the undertakings to achieve economies of scale, so that large firms can produce at much lower costs than small units.

Generally, full-cost pricing is followed in the case of public utility products. Further, the enterprises are also required to pay a certain agreed dividend to the government for providing investment capital. Hence, they have to fix a price which assures fair returns for the investments made.

(iv) Product Line Pricing: Product line pricing refers to pricing of a group of products which are related either as substitutes or complements. The cross elasticity of demand is the important factor in determining the price of product line.

Substitute Goods: Supposing the company is producing substitute goods, then the market is segregated on the basis of elasticity of demand. Each product in the product line competes 'in house' with each other. There are a good number of firms producing substitute goods and competing internally and externally. If the price of a substance good is favourable, it pushes the sales of that product as against the sales of another product.

The pricing of substitute products is generally determined by two methods. One is the mark-up methods in which the producers use a margin i.e., pricing in the proportion to costs. The second method is to price the product varying the size of the margin with the level of costs. If the product is costlier, the margin also is higher and hence the price also is high.

The weakness of these two methods is that, they do not take demand and competition into consideration. The decision of costs among the products is done arbitrarily and hence the pricing also reflects the arbitrariness.

Complementary Goods: In the case of complementary products or joint products, the demand inter-relationship is complementary. The degree of complement takes two forms:

   (i) Fixed proportions - for example, cotton and cotton seeds or hides and meat.

   (ii) Variable proportions - for example, passenger and freight services in the case of railway services.

In the case of complementary goods, a fall in the price of one results in an increase in the demand for other goods. In such cases, cross elasticity is negative. Generally, the sellers lower the price of one (hide) in the hope of selling the complementary product (meat) at a higher price.

In the case of joint products, since the costs are common to both, their allocation to each item is difficult.

In the case of joint products, of fixed proportion and group of products, they are one package so far as production is concerned, but they are priced separately. For example, cotton is priced higher than cotton seeds. The allocation of cost is not made to each individual product but priced differently with a view to earn maximum profits.

In the case of joint products with varying proportions, the total cost is apportioned to each product. The optimal price-output combination for the joint products would require simultaneous cost-revenue relationships.

The allocation of costs to joint products is done arbitrarily, resulting in prices which reflect the arbitrary allocation of common costs. The main consideration in pricing of these products is that the firm should get a higher margin of profit after covering all costs. The cost structure of the product line is a follows. For example, supposing a biscuit manufacturer produces two types of biscuits - the first category needs more labour but less material cost per packet while the other brand needs more materials than the first one. The cost structure for these two varieties of biscuits is as follows:

		Biscuit 'A'	Biscuit 'B'
Material cost		4	2
Labour cost		2	3
Over cost		1	2
Full cost 1 + 2 + 3		7	7
Incremental costs (1+2)		6	5
Conversion cost (2+3)		3	5
The pricing can be worked out as follows:			
Full cost pricing	10%	7.70	7.70
Incremental cost pricing	10%	6.60	5.50
Conversion cost Pricing (2+3)	90%	5.70	4.50

Some Problems in Product Line Pricing: There are some problems in pricing of the products in product line. There are two approaches to tackle the problem:

(i) There is a practice of charging a uniform price irrespective of size differences. For example, products of the same quality are priced uniformly. The shoe manufacturing companies fix a uniform price for the shoes of same quality. In such cases, the sizes are not taken into consideration.

(ii) There is another approach namely charging prices on the basis of sizes. In such cases, quality of material, labour used is the same, but prices vary according to the size. For example, jute sack manufacturers fix a lower price to cement bags and higher price for sugar bags. But it is not so in the case of products like toothpastes and other packed products like oil and tooth paste. Groundnut oil of five kgs is cheaper per kilogram than smaller tins, The same thing is found in advertising also. If a producer takes one full page advertisement, it is cheaper than a small space advertisement.

Price of Multi-Products — General Considerations   ·

Pricing in multi-product firms is not an easy job, because in the production of several products in a firm, there are facilities which are commonly used in all such cases. There is a greater amount of interdependence between the production of different products. The following considerations are used in the pricing of products.

(i) Pricing in the case of products which are different widely and have no element of inter-dependence, is done separately on the basis of cost and demand functions. It is like the pricing of a single product.

(ii) In the case of joint products, the basic consideration of pricing is the total cost is recovered by selling the main product and the by-product. The joint products are of two kinds: (a) where proportion of main products and by-products can be varied, (b) where the proportions cannot be varied. In case of the former, the producer manipulates the share favourable to him. In the fixed proportion case, the prices are determined on the basis of demand. One product (for example, raw cotton) commands a high price and the seeds are sold at a lower price. In all, the total price should cover the total cost.

(iii) In the other case of goods, the production is done using some common facilities. The price and output determination in case of such products depend on the contribution of each product to the fixed costs.

(v) Transfer Pricing: In a large sized firm, several products are produced using different processes of production. In such business organisations, the work is divided among several sections or departments. For all practical purposes, each section is an independent unit. This results in the transfer of goods, services and even money from one section to another section or from one unit to another unit. Many large sized companies have this inter-company transfer of goods. For example, in a huge automobile company, production and marketing of trucks, cars, two-wheelers, engines and so on are organised in a separate manner. The managerial decisions taken are also different. In other words, each unit enjoys considerable autonomy. The units transfer goods among themselves. The prices that units change affect the performance of the other units. If transfer prices understate or overstate the values of costs, the decisions of the units would go counter to the company's corporate objectives. The price and output decisions of other departments are influenced by the transfer price. It affects profitability also. The rules observed in such pricing are as follows:

(i) Each division must be treated as an autonomous unit.

(ii) Intra-company transfers should be priced at their marginal costs

(iii) The inter-transfer of goods are meant for meeting the requirements of inter-dependent divisions of a big company.

For example, pig iron produced in one division is meant for the steel making division of the same company. In such cases, the marginal costs of the product of a division is determined by its own cost.

For calculating the transfer price, one of the following three methods are followed: (i) Market price method, (ii) Cost basis and (iii) Cost-plus basis.

Market Price Basis: In the case of transferred products, the appropriate price is the market price. This is the most suitable system of the pricing of transfer goods. If the market price is preferred, it makes the inefficient division to be alert and efficient. If the product is homogeneous, it is easy to ascertain the market price. But there are differences in the quality of the product or services, and then the market prices is required to be adjusted to cover all such factors.

Cost Basis: Cost consideration is made in the case of products produced by one division and meant for sale to another division of the company. For example, if there is a separate maintenance department, then the cost of service or maintenance is assessed on the basis of costs incurred by the department in keeping the assets of other departments in good condition. In other words, the goods meant for inter-divisional transfer should be priced at the level of the marginal cost of production. This pricing policy will maximise group profits.

Cost-plus Basis: Under this method, the pricing is based on the actual cost plus some percentage of profit. The transferring division adds a certain percentage of profit just to inflate the profits of the company. Normally, this division incurs the cost, so that the amount of profit added to it will cover the unexpected losses which may occur in future. Thus, transfer pricing by helping the individual divisions to maximise the profits, also maximises the profits of the company.

(vi) Multi-Product Pricing: Modern industrial concerns are producing many products. They are called multi-product producers. The multi-product firm is classified into several types:

(a) A joint product firm: A firm manufacturing soaps can easily produce various by-products. Soap is the main product, glycerine is another product, and cosmetics are also produced in such firms.

(b) Firm producing related products: A shoe manufacturing company produces various kinds of shoes for ladies, for children and gents. Since the product is raised from the same plant and uses the same labour and raw materials, there exists some sort of inter-dependence.

(c) Firm producing unrelated products: A firm manufacturing refrigerators also produces washing machines, vacuum cleaners, etc. A company producing steel almirahs, produces refrigerator, watches, etc. These products use different facilities, raw-material and manpower. These firms diversify into different unrelated products mainly to take advantage of goodwill and sales network.

Pricing of the products of a multi-product firm requires the study of the following relationships:

Demand Relationships: If the different products are either substitutes or complements, a change in the price of one product affects the demand for a related product, according to their cross elasticity.

Cost-Relationships: When the multiple products are produced with the help of the same production facilities, some costs are directly chargeable to the products and some costs are common to all. For example, if the raw-material is different, its price is charged to the product while the space, the rent, the administration and the sales services are common to all the products.

Production Relationships: If the multiple products of a single production process are available then a primary product along with several by-products can be produced either through fixed or variable proportions.

Capacity Relationship: If a firm has excess capacity or idle capacity, this can be used to produce one or more additional products. The cost of fixed factors can be shared between other products.

11. PRICE DISCOUNTS AND PRICE DIFFERENTIALS

Price discounting is a normal practice found in large-scale marketing of the products, may be agricultural raw materials or finished products. The discounts are given generally to buyers of goods who are called *distributors*. Such discounts are called distributor's discounts. They are price reductions given by manufacturers to wholesale buyers. Wholesalers in turn, offer discounts to retailers. The discounts which are given to dealers and retailers and distributors are called *trade channel discounts*. The discounts result in differential pricing, which has become an accepted practice in price policy.

Kinds of Discounts: There are different types of distributor's discounts determined on the basis of experience. Generally, there are three kinds of price discounts shown to the distributors:

(i) On the basis of position of the buyer,

(ii) A price list drawn to show discounts to different types of distributors and

(iii) A single discount combined with supplementary discounts.

Discounts are offered to the distributors on their market position. For example, if a distributor commands a large portion of a country's market like the whole of South India commencing business from Deccan, the discount is generally higher than the regional distributor. The discount pattern followed in practice is five percent to retailers, three percent to local distributors and two percent to regional distributors. The net prices are shown on the package of products. This includes the discounts at different trade levels.

Determination of Distributors Discounts: Distributors are direct buyers of products from manufactures. They perform some important functions such as offering the product to the retailers on credit with a view to clear the product from the godowns. They maintain an organisation with men and equipments in order to deliver goods and offering free services whenever required. For example, the distributors of TVs, refrigerators and other durable household equipments maintain technicians to provide free servicing, which is one of the conditions of sale. This free servicing for a specific period forms a sort of discount.

Trade discounts cover the operating costs and the normal profits of the distributors. These distributors undertake sales promotion and get higher discounts. The rate of discounts depend upon the type of services offered by the distributor. The discount must be such that, it should cover the entire operating costs, and also bring a certain amount of profits to the firm.

Most of the manufacturers, either by custom or practice have been following a fixed discount structure. In the case of high priced luxury goods which are slow moving, the rate of discount is high. But those companies which face stiff competition offer discounts twice as high as those given by market leaders. Apart from a discount, the dealers also get price advantage.

Trade channel discounts are used to achieve profitable market segmentation. In order to make effective sales of certain products, the market has been divided into sub-markets. If there is a main distributor in a region, he provides for sub-markets. If there is a main distributor in a region, he provides for sub-dealership in different places of his region. These sub-dealers in turn may appoint local dealers who supply the product to the retailers.

Since demand elasticities in these sub-markets are different, the prices are also different. The discount structure is arranged in such a manner, that it becomes possible to have different prices suitable for each sub-markets. For example, in the case of components, prices would not influence demand. The demand for a car type does not depend upon the price, but it depends upon the need. If the need persists, the owner has to buy the product even at a high price. But the dealers have to maintain adequate stock at the local level for which an attractive discount is required to be given. The bulk buyers of the components are the manufacturers and the producers are required to offer higher discounts. The quantum of discounts given to distributors and dealers depend upon the price elasticity of demand for goods. In the case of replacement goods such as types for cars and other automobiles, the manufacturers have to give huge discounts to dealers. Here, the consumers prefer to buy a product for which they have preference and price has no effect to them. In order to shift the demand from one preferred product to an alternative product, the dealers also have to offer discounts. The dealers in such cases discriminate prices between the old customers and new customers. They charge somewhat higher prices to the old customers and lower prices to the new customers.

The discount facility has given rise to several problems in the pricing of products. The main problem is whether to fix a high price and produce products of high quality or to fix a low price and produce goods of low quality. Whenever the discounts are offered, they become the item of cost and as such the price will be naturally high. Discounts are indispensable until the product becomes popular. When the product becomes popular, its demand increases sufficiently, making it possible for the company to reach an optimum capacity.

The manufacturers often depend upon the goodwill of the distributors. If the distributors do not show any interest in the brand product, the manufacturers are put into difficulties. The distributors have, by experience, the capacity to judge whether the quality of the product and its price are favourable or not. Therefore, the manufacturers have to satisfy the distributors and dealers more than the consumers, as consumers are guided by the dealers. If the dealers say that the product 'X' is better than product 'B', then the consumers prefer 'X' product. It is therefore, very important for the manufacturers to secure the goodwill of the distributors. This can be done by not only supplying the products of good quality with reasonable price, but also offering substantial discounts. If the product is a highly advertised one, then the dealer's influence on the consumers is limited. In such cases, the dealers have to be content with a small percentage of discount.

Quantity Discounts: Quantity discounts are price concessions offered to the distributors on the basis of the quantity of the product purchased. Quantity discounts are related to the size of a single purchase. The size of the lot purchased may be measured either in terms of physical quantity or the value of the product. In case of homogeneous products such as refrigerators, scooters or cars etc., it is the physical quantity considered. In the case of heterogeneous products, which are difficult to add, like furniture and scientific instruments, the money value of these products is preferred. Therefore, the quantity discounts are related to either physical units of the products or the money value of the products. High discount is offered if the dealer buys a bigger lot size. The main objective of quantity discounts is to encourage the dealers to buy the product in large amounts, thereby the manufacturers can reduce their cost of selling, packaging, delivery etc.

It is stated that quantity discounts was examined by Monopolies and Restrictive Trade Practices Commission. Initially, the MRTPC Commission agreed with the grant of high discounts to large orders in many cases referred to it. But later on, the Commission came to the conclusion that this practice distinguishes between larger buyers and small buyers ultimately coming to the conclusion that this practice is unsound.

Cash Discounts: Cash discounts are price concessions offered when the payment is made promptly. For example, if the dealers make the full payment within the specified period, a discount of two percent is allowed. Firms offer cash discounts with a view to improve the liquidity position and to minimise bank borrowing.

Cash discount is a very good device. It eliminates the accumulation of credit. If the buyers make payment on receipt of the consignment, the manufacturers are also willing to offer higher discounts. If the buyers decide to purchase the product on credit, they have to forego the discount also.

It is necessary to compare the benefit of cash discount with that of the cost of cash discount. The rate of cash discount must be lower than the benefits which the firm gets by offering these discounts.

12. PRICE DIFFERENTIALS

An important aspect of price differential is price discrimination. In open price discrimination, the producer divides the market into several sub markets and charges different prices in each market, depending upon the elasticity of demand for the product. If the demand for the product is inelastic, he charges a higher price.

Time Differentials: There are different ways of discrimination of prices. One such discrimination is that of *time differentials*. The producers take the advantage of change in demand elasticities over a period of time. The demand for a product may be high in a particular season, for example, the demand for woollen goods is high in winter, while the demand for cotton cloth is high during summer. Let us take up another example. Demand for telephones is higher during day time than during the night. There are two cases of time differentials. (i) Clock time price differential and (ii) Calendar time price differential.

Clock Time Price Differential: Suppose demand elasticities change during a day, sellers can charge different prices at different points of timed during the 24 hours period. Such a price differential is known as *clock time price differential*. Its object is to charge a higher price when the demand for the product is inelastic and a lower price when the demand for the product is elastic. The common examples are telephone services and the differences between morning shows and afternoon shows in cinema houses. In the case of telephone services, day time charges are higher than night time charges. It is due to its inelastic demand during day time, that the charges are high and at night time, the demand is elastic and hence the rates are low.

The following conditions are to be fulfilled if the clock time differentials are to become profitable:

(i) Buyers must have a definite preference for buying a product at a particular time.

(ii) The seller must be in a position to offer his product at a lower price in the slack period.

(iii) The product offered for sale is not a storable item either wholly or in parts. If the product is a storable one, the buyers buy it when its price is low and use it whenever it is required.

Calendar Time Price Differentials: In the calendar price differentials, the period of sale of a product or a service is more than 24 hours like days, weeks, months, etc. For example, swimming pool charges and charges for hotel accommodation on hill stations differ on the basis of seasons.

During winter, the charges are low and in spring, they are higher. The seller of these services charge higher prices in spring in view of its inelastic demand. Taking this opportunity, the sellers of the services exploit the consumers.

The economics of pricing points out that the pricing of product or services must be related to cost. The prices are differentiated during a whole period of a year or so in such a manner that higher cost of maintenance must be overcome by charging a higher price during seasons.

Use-price Differentials: Price discrimination is made by the public utility organisations like electricity organisation, railways etc. on the basis of use of the services. Railways are used to transporting different commodities and they can be used not only for long distance travel but also short distance travel. Charges for these uses are different. The sellers of these services divide the market into different segments and charge prices according to the demand.

In order to make use of price differential effective, the demand elasticities for the product or services must be different.

Geographical Price Differential: Price discrimination is practised by sellers on the basis of buyer's location. Such discrimination is called *geographical price differential*. For example, at the place of production of a commodity the price of the product is low, while at different centres of the nation, the price is high. The price of the product at the point of production is known as FOB Price (i.e free on board), while the latter is a delivered price. The delivered price includes the cost of shipping goods.

13. OTHER PRICING CONCEPTS

FOB Pricing

It indicates that the buyers have to pay the transport and handling charges and they are responsible for any loss of goods during the transport. Sellers charge uniform price to all categories of buyers at the point of production. The sellers do not make any discrimination between a buyer of large quantity and small quantity. But they have to bear the entire transport cost. It is the responsibility of the buyers to arrange for their own mode of transportation. If the sellers take up the responsibility of transportation, then include the transport charges in the price of the commodity.

In order to practice FOB Pricing, the sellers have to fulfil the following conditions:

(i) If the transport cost is small when compared to the production cost of the commodity, the sellers will sell outside the place of production or local market.

(ii) The fixed cost must not be very high to force the sellers to go out searching for customers in distant markets.

(iii) If the firm sets up plants at different demand centres, it can cater to the regional market needs easily without bothering about excess production.

Uniform Delivered Pricing or Postage Stamp Pricing

It implies that the seller charging uniform price for his product without looking into destination of the product, is called 'Postage Stamp Pricing'. In the case of postage stamp pricing, the seller sells the product at a uniform price at all centres of a country. The quoted price includes the transport cost also.

Postage price is quoted in two ways: (i) the seller sells the product at a single price all over the country and (ii) secondly, a uniform FOB Price is quoted and the buyers are allowed to deduct a certain percentage from the price towards the freight charges. In these two cases, there is a certain amount of discrimination.

Postage pricing is commonly practiced by sellers in selling popular brand products and having wide national markets. For example, most of the soap manufacturing firms sells their brand soaps at a uniform price all over the country. They advertise the prices of their products in newspapers. For example, the Bata Shoe Company sells its different brand shoes at a uniform price all over the country. Most durable goods are sold like this.

Postage stamp prices are very suitable when the transport cost is insignificant to their actual cost of production. Goods like clothes, cosmetics, soft drinks, electrical and electronic equipments, radios, typewriters are some examples for postage pricing. This pricing gives the producer easy access to all markets regardless of the location.

Zonal Pricing

Many a time, the producers, instead of charging a uniform price in all regions of the country, differentiate between zones. They divide the country into several zones and the price in each zone is different from the other zone. This is known as *zone pricing*. This is done with a view to cover transport charges. Zonal pricing is referred when the transport cost on goods is too high. If the transport cost is high, the producers fix different prices for different zones.

Base Point Pricing

A major production centre for a particular product is chosen for pricing, which consists of a factory price and transportation price. This is called *base point pricing*. A delivered price is quoted on the basis of base point. In other words, a base point price includes mill price of ex-factory price and transportation costs. The transportation cost, which is taken into consideration, is not the actual freight charge, but transportation charge from a designated centre.

A seller of the product may use single base point pricing or multiple base point pricing. Under the single base point, all sellers quote a uniform price irrespective of their locations. In the case of multiple base point pricing, two or more producing centres are chosen as base points. The seller then quotes a delivered price which includes mill price and transportation charge from the base point to the buyer's nearest point. Base point pricing is used extensively by heavy machinery manufacturers.

Special Order Pricing

In the pricing of products produced specially for a consumer, the produced takes into consideration the full cost of producing this. The full cost includes a certain percentage of profits also. In special order pricing, the producer, though he enjoys monopoly, cannot exploit the consumer. If the producer quotes a high price, he may lose the order. If the producer has idle capacity of plant and machinery, he may be forced to accept the lowest price. If the alternative is idleness, he may charge a price equal to incremental costs. The incremental revenue must exceed the incremental cost of producing the special order product. If the plant is not idle, then he quotes a price which covers his full costs plus a certain percentage of profit.

Pricing of Spare Parts

Every producer of durable goods produces spareparts for replacing the wornout parts. When the capital good is to be repaired, then the broken parts will have to be replaced. In such circumstances, prices of spare parts pose some problems. Pricing of spare parts involves the considerations of the following aspects:

In case of parts produced by the original manufacturer of capital goods, he enjoys a monopoly and he charges a high price. If there are alternative spare parts almost similar to original products, then the original producer of spares cannot charge a monopoly price. If the prices of the spares of original producer are very high, the buyers may not buy them from him. They may go in for alternatives. In the case of manufacturers, they may start producing the spare parts. For example, large manufacturing companies have their own workshops and research departments. They may fabricate the spares. Now many ancillary industries have specialised in producing components to machineries. In fact, the producers of capital goods buy the components from the ancillary industries. In such cases, the prices of the spares are lower than the prices of original spares manufactures. Therefore, the prices of spares are generally kept at reasonable level. However, the manufactures of these spares follow certain thumb rules to fix the prices for the spares:

    (i) Full cost of producing the spares plus a reasonable profit will be the basis of pricing the spare parts.

    (ii) Spare parts are priced sometimes according to their weight after making adjustment for the complexity.

    (iii) The sum of the price of all the parts taken individually should not exceed twice the price of the equipment as a whole.

    (iv) The prices of different spare parts should have consistency among themselves.

Normally, the prices of the spare parts which are available in plenty are low and further those spares can be produced easily and will be priced low. Japan by producing and exporting spare parts of their capital equipments at lower prices is making large amount of profits. Many automobile manufacturers are also selling parts at lower prices and thus making good profits.

Pricing Leases and Licences

There are companies leasing the equipments on lease rent to the manufacturers. If the manufacturers find that obtaining an equipment on lease is profitable, they are not going to buy a new machine the lease rent is charged on the basis of the capacity of the user. That is perfect price discrimination followed in all such cases. If the equipment is used for different purposes, the benefits accruing to the users also differ. A person is going to make a high profit from using it. He is naturally charged a higher lease rent. The minimum rent is fixed by the leaser on the basis of cost of the equipment, its servicing charges, depreciation etc.

Royalty is levied when a patent is given for use. The loyalty and licence charges are determined, keeping in mind various considerations:

    (i) The expenses incurred in developing a patented product are basically sunk cost. They cannot be used for any other purpose. Hence they are not relevant in determining the patent fee.

    (ii) The minimum rent is determined on the basis of incremental cost of operating the licensed patents.

(iii) The upper limit of the royalty takes into account the benefit of the product to the license and

(iv) In between these two limits, royalty is determined taking into account the possible competition, infringement of the patents and the intervention of the government in the high royalties fixed.

For example, in the case of patents offered for copying, the incremental cost of producing is taken into consideration in determining the royalty.

14. PRODUCT LINE BALANCING

Producing multiple products is the order of the day. Prof.Nickerson in his book 'Managerial Cost Accounting and Analysis' said that it is like a family in which all children are not born with same facility and aptitude. In the same way, the products produced by a firm are unrelated, the production of which is done with a view to make high profit. There are some more profit-intensive products and some others are less profit-intensive products. In pricing the whole range of products, the producer takes into account the whole range of products. The producer takes into account several considerations.

(i) In the case of widely different products which have no interdependence, pricing for each product is done separately on the basis of its cost and demand. The firm may give up producing loss making products and concentrate on products which are giving good profit.

(ii) In the case of a joint product firm, the basic consideration is to recover the total cost by the sale of the main product and the by product.

(iii) In the case of products which are inter-dependent, the output and price determination depend on the contribution of each product to the fixed costs.

15. PRODUCT LINE DIVERSIFICATION

Product line diversification arises whenever there is excess production capacity in a firm. In such cases, the firm thinks of adding a new product to the existing products. If it adds a new product, no additional cost is involved and it can sell the product at a reasonable price and thereby remove the unutilised capacity of production.

Excess capacity may occur for several reasons. It may occur whenever the firm makes over optimistic demand for its product. If the firm cannot sell that much of production, then there exists excess capacity. Excess capacity may arise due to seasonal variations in the demand for product. Companies producing goods which meet seasonal demand, find excess capacity in out of seasons. In such cases, companies producing goods which meet seasonal demand start producing a new product. Excess capacity may also occur due to cyclical fluctuating in sales. It may occur when there is change in demand for the product. In such cases, the companies produce new products to make use of the unutilised capacity of the plant and machinery.

Diversification: Many companies are adding new products to their existing product line. For example, a company manufacturing sugar production machinery may take up producing earth moving equipments or textile yarn or cloth making machinery, etc. Diversification is considered to be profitable in such circumstances. The main goal of such diversification is to make maximum profit from the present investments. If the net return from the new product covers the incremental costs, the companies are highly satisfied.

There are many examples found in the present industrial set up to justify the diversification. For example, a company which commenced as a sales organisation, after some time, took up the production of that product. The Godrej company which was producing almirahs, subsequently took up the production of typewriters. In all such cases, the objective of diversification was to maximise profits.

Consideration for Diversification: Diversifications mean producing one or more products to the existing products in the same plant. Diversification is taken up when the existing products are facing stiff competition and their future prospects are not good. Many companies take up diversification owing to political, social and economic compulsions. It may also be taken up to avoid the various restrictive regulations of the government. The Indian Tobacco Company (ITC), a cigarette producing company in course of time, diversified its activities into hotel business, paper boards manufacturing, marine products, etc. In fact, many companies have diversified their activities and are earning enormous profits.

Diversification is undertaken to make the best use of the existing marketing network. For example, Indian Express was publishing only English language newspapers and now it is publishing many regional language newspapers, weeklies, film newspapers, business newspaper, etc.

A company may take up diversification with a view to derive advantage of the concessions offered by the government.

Companies, while taking diversification, must justify their action by showing economic advantages. It is not desirable to launch diversification for the sake of adding a new product. The management has to examine all possible advantages and disadvantages before adding a new product to the product line. If the diversification does not involve additional investment and additional capital expenditure, it is sound. Otherwise, diversification tends to result in additional costs.

Scope of Diversification: Any company can diversify its activities. But the scope of diversification is limited to companies which have excess of production and marketing capacity. There are certain factors which restrict the scope of diversification.

    (i) The Costs: The costs play an important place in the diversification of the company. If the diversification does not result in additional costs, it is permitted. If a company producing sugar can diversify to make use of the by products available in the factory, it does not require additional costs.

    (ii) Demand: Demand for the product is very essential for diversification. A firm having earned reputation for safeguarding and maintaining the quality of products may take up adding another product to the existing products. It will be easy for that firm to sell the new products without any difficulty. Sometimes, manufacturers of high quality goods start producing a new product using the byproduct produced in the company. When the quality product is sold in the company's name, the company can sell the new product in its own name and can thus sell the product easily. If companies producing similar goods under different brand names amalgamate themselves, even then the products can be sold under the same brand names. The firms producing consumer goods will have to study the consumer's preferences before undertaking the production of them. Their preferences are so very uncertain because they are choosy and buy different types of goods. The firms have to spend a considerable sum of money on advertisements in order to attract the consumers and to retain the loyalty of the consumers.

Need for Market Research

Market research is very necessary in order to assess the potential demand for the products. It is one of the ways of forecasting demand. If the company adds a product without considerable market research, it may have to incur heavy losses.

The consumer's social and economic background play a decisive role in consumer's demand. Most of the consumers in India, even in urban areas do not use foreign system of eating foods. If an Indian company takes up producing households appliances which are being used in foreign countries, they may find lack of demand and finally incur heavy losses. It is because that the Indian consumers have very little need for them. Even the price does not influence them to buy the products. For example, there are packaged fast foods being produced by several firms. Demand for these products may be found in metropolitan cities like Mumbai, Delhi, Chennai, etc. but it is very low in many urban places. As such, a through market research is to be undertaken before embarking on the large scale production of new products. With strategic market research, the consumers are accepting these products in a big way.

Alternative Approach

There are three alternatives for the firms which are facing uncertain demand for new products. They are improve, buy or drop. If the firm finds that the demand for its product is very low and not picking up even after heavy advertisement and publicity campaign, then it has to decide any one of the three alternatives mentioned above. Improvement means redesigning the shape of the product and introducing improvements to please the consumers. When the existing product is obselete or out of fashion, the firm is required to change the shape and appearance of the product. This can be seen in many consumer durable goods like refrigerators, washing machines, television sets or automobiles, etc. For example, Godrej has improved the refrigerators in order to accommodate more things. This improvement may satisfy the consumers and the demand may pick up.

Then, there is another alternative, namely buying a product. It means, that the companies buy the product if the price of the product is low. The advantage in buying is that it will help in large scale production. The third alternative is to drop the product from production. If the production of a new product does not assure a reasonable profit, then it is better for the firm in stopping its production. In relation to the production of a new product, if the demand is uncertain, it is better for the firm to stop producing the product. Many a time, producers are reluctant to eliminate the product on the ground of sentiment. And care must be taken to produce an attractive and user friendly commodity which satisfies the consumers. If the company finds it unable to sell the product, then it is better to drop the product instead of incurring more loses.

Retail Pricing

Generally, price determination is made by the producers of products. Retailers have very little say in the matter. However, retailers also incur some costs and they also add their costs to the pricing of the products. The costs that are incurred by retailers are storage and handling etc. Sometimes retailers, while selling a particular product, influence the buyers to buy other products also. In the case of many products, the retailers have no chance of adding anything to the price marked on the product. Many manufacturers of brand products fix the retail price. Further, the producers suggest a price and this appears in the form of 'price not to exceed...........' and as such, the retailers sell at the price marked on the product. Nowadays, the governments are fixing the retail prices of certain commodities like sugar, vanaspathi, etc. Alternatively, the trade associations may fix the prices of certain products. There is what is called what the traffic will bear in terms of pricing. It means charging the consumer as high a price he is prepared to pay. Sometimes retailers also fix the price on these basis.

There is another method of pricing by retailers namely, pricing in accordance with terms of sale. In this case, the actual price is higher than the invoice price. If the retailers provide some services like home delivery and credit facility, then an additional price is added to the retail price. Sometimes, old stocks are sold at reduced rates.

The retailers generally are satisfied with low margin in view of high turnover. But it is not so in the case of departmental stores. The percentage of margin in such stores varies between 10-per cent and 15 per cent. If there is stiff competition in the market, then the percentage of margin is within five percent.

The Package Commodities Regulations Order 1975

This order maintains that no person shall pre-pack for retail sale or cause to be pre-packed for retail sale any commodity, unless each retail package in which such commodity is prepared, bears thereon a label securely affixed, a declaration as to the name of the commodity, the quantity, the date of package and the price. The producer may state ex-factory price plus central excise and further states that it excludes States taxes. Sometimes the maximum price at which the commodity is sold may be mentioned on the package, which includes all taxes, transport charges, commissions, etc. Thus, the manufacturers have several options such as ex-factory price, FOR, destination price, sales price exclusive of all taxes and retail sale price inclusive of all taxes, etc. If the retail price is mentioned on the package of the product, the retailer has to sell at the price itself. The authority to fix the retail price is the manufacturer of the product. The price that is mentioned on the package is the maximum price and not the minimum price. Supposing the price falls owing to various factors, the retailers are required to sell at the reduced price if they want to sell more.

Re-sale Price Maintenance

Prof.G.C.Allan defines resale price maintenance as the stipulation by a supplier so that his retailers shall resell particular goods at prices fixed by him or for not less than those prices.

Resale price maintenance means selling the branded products at a uniform price. The manufacturers of branded products fix and stipulate the price of the products at which the product is to be sold by the individual retailer. This is done to maintain a uniform selling price of branded products at different outlets. Since such a price is handed down from the producer to the retailer, it becomes a kind of vertical price control.

There are two types of resale price maintenance. One is called collective resale price maintenance and the other is individual retail sale price maintenance. Under the collective resale price-maintenance, the manufacturers of different brand products collectively fix a resale price and notify it as a condition to all traders who buy products from them. Any retailer who reduces the price of the branded product, is removed from the manufacturer who maintains control over his own resale price. The resale price of manufacturers of similar products may differ. Retailers can search for alternative sources of supply of the product. Collective price maintenance is highly effective in the sense, it controls at the very source of the supply of alternative products.

Resale prices maintained, whether individual or collective, does not allow competition to exist among the distributors and the price is stabilised which attracts the consumers. If a dealer reduces the price of a product, it does not increase sales and on the contrary, the consumers may feel that the quality of the product is not good.

Advantages: Resale price maintenance has several advantages. It enhances the reputation of the firm keeping the price uniform and stable. It does not allow indiscriminate selling of high priced products. It maintains the quality of the product. It eliminates unfair competition. It prevents excessive profiteering. It safeguards the interests of the consumers by enforcing the stability of the price of the product. It promotes fair trade practices. It enables the manufacturer to maintain his reputation in the market.

Disadvantages: The resale price maintenance has the following disadvantages too. The practice of resale price maintenance prevents competition and supports the formation of monopolies. In India, under Section 39 of the MRTP Act, all kinds of resale price maintenance are considered as void *ab initio. If* the manufacturers keep the high price and by withholding the supply of the product or products, it results in the exploitation of the consumers. That is why resale price maintenance is not allowed in India under the MRTP Act. It encourages inefficient dealers to survive for long periods. The resale prices are set generally at a higher level and as such prevent the efficient distributions with lower overheads to sell at lower prices. The policy of resale maintenance is being debated seriously in Western Countries like USA, West Germany and Great Britain.

16. PRICING IN PUBLIC UTILITIES

The term public utilities refers to services provided by the Railways, water supply, electricity, telephone and Posts and Telegraphs (P&T), etc. All forms of transport are also included in the term public utilities. Public utilities are run either by the government department or government formed corporations. They render services in the interest of safeguarding the public from private sector exploitation. The commodity or service rendered by such industries is so essential to the economic life of the people and hence these services are considered as necessities.

The product of public utilities are different from the product of other industries. The products of public utilities are services rather than tangible commodities. The transport services provided to the city commuters by the Government Road Transport System, the Railway facility, water supply, telephones, etc. are all services which are meant for the entire community. In all these cases, the services are punctual and effective and they have more value than products. Constant and reliable supplies of these are the criterion. Since the public utilities are in the nature of rendering essential services, these products cannot be stored. Water and gas supply, telephone services, P&T services cannot be stored to render stability in production and distribution. The nature of public utility services can be stated as follows:

(i) *Monopoly in nature:* They are monopolistic in nature. Monopolies are created by the act of the government and competition is prevented with a view to avoid wastage. Even if competition is allowed, it may last for some time in the beginning but later on it may become a monopoly by means of amalgamation and integration. If the monopoly is allowed in the private sector, it will exploit the consumers and therefore, the government takes the monopoly of these services.

(ii) *Large sale operation:* Public utility services are nationwide in character. They operate on a large scale which in turn, enables the company the device internal and external economies. Consequently, the average cost falls and the service can be rendered at no loss and no profit basis.

(iii) *Inelastic demand:* The demand is inelastic for the public utility services. If the prices of the services are increased by limiting the supply, it results in the exploitation of the consumer. The services are so important that the consumers will not reduce demand, even if the prices of these services are high. For example, the railway travel, telephone services etc. These essential services enjoy the inelasticity of demand.

(iv) *Large Fixed Investments:* Huge investments will have to be made in the case of public utility service industries. The cost of construction and maintenance of different transport services are very high. Huge investments are required in the railways. Providing track, construction of bridges, tunnels, installation of signals, rolling stock etc. cost enormous sums of money. In the case of supply of electricity, main costs relate to the construction of transmission lines. Further, in all public utility services, some unused plant capacity will be maintained in order to meet unforeseeable contingencies. This involves huge investments in plants and equipments.

(v) *Decreasing Cost:* In such public utilities, in view of the surplus capacity of plants, it is possible to increase the output at a decreasing average cost. When the output is increased, the cost per unit also falls. But when the plant is over utilised, then the averaged cost is bound to rise.

(vi) *Price discrimination:* In most of the public utility services, price discrimination is practised. The utilised can charge different prices to different types of consumers. Electricity Boards, Water Supply Boards are charging high rates to industrial users and low rates to domestic users. In the case of bulk consumers, the rates are lower than small consumers. The railways too are following price discrimination. High rates are charged for short distances and the low rate for long distances.

(vii) *Welfare Principle:* The main objective of public utility services is to provide services on - profit and no - loss basis. Their main consideration is to promote the welfare of the community. Since the goal of public utilities is to promote community welfare, they charge low prices to poor people. Utility services are available to the people at cheaper rates. In fact, water supply to the people is done without any price. Water Boards provide public taps for this purpose itself. In times of scarcity, these services are owned by government. Electricity supply, water supply are provided by the state governments, while posts and telegraphs and railways are provided by the Union Government. In foreign countries like the United States of America, utility services are provided by private companies but they are all controlled by statutory regulations.

Pricing Policy: Since the main objective of public utilities is to promote social welfare, it cannot adopt maximum profit principle. Further, the pricing policy of public utilities is based on the principle of no profit and no loss. As such, in practice, they follow one of the following principles: (i) Fair rate principle, (ii) Average cost pricing and (iii) Marginal cost pricing.

(i) *Fair Rate Principle:* The fair rate principle states that public utilities must get a fair rate or reasonable rate of return for the investments made. A return of six to nine percent or around 10 per cent is considered as a fair rate. This principle is adopted in order to make the utility concern cost-conscious and to make it work efficiently. The capital investment is first assessed and the expected returns to be obtained is calculated. The fair rate is decided on the basis of the following grounds:

(i) Original cost less depreciation

(ii) Current replacement or reproduction cost less depreciation,

(iii) Capitalised market value of firm's assets.

If there is no change in the price level, the utility concern follows the first two methods. If the prices rise, then the firm follows the second principle and accordingly, the rates are also increased with every rise in price. The principle of capitalised market value of the firm's assets is not practised in most of the cases. The best method practised in all countries is that of the principle of replacement costs.

(ii) *Marginal cost pricing:* Marginal cost pricing method is advocated by Professor Montgomery and Professor Lerner to the Pricing of the public utility services. In competitive conditions, the firms follow marginal cost pricing to determine the prices. According to marginal cost pricing, the price of the products should be equal to marginal cost. The utility company produces maximum output when it equates the marginal cost to the prices of services. The prices of service is not uniform for all the users. What is followed generally in a monopoly utility organisation is that marginal cost is equal to average price and not the marginal revenue. In the case of a private monopoly, which is not utility organisation, is that the marginal cost is equal to the average price and not the marginal revenue. In the case of a private monopoly, which is not utility organisation, is that the marginal cost is equal to the average price and not the marginal revenue. When MC is equal to MR, the firm maximises its monopoly profits. The public utility is not concerned with monopoly gain. If the cost is equal to the revenue, the organisation is highly satisfied. Hence, the monopoly utility organisation fixes the prices of the service in such a way that marginal cost is equal to the price.

The principle of marginal cost pricing is severely criticised by economists on the following grounds:

Firstly, this principle does not recognise the importance of long period problem. This principle holds good when the problem is of a short period only. But, public utility services are not short period phenomenon. Its importance in the long period is more than short period. Secondly, in a large utility monopoly company, the marginal cost is negligible when it produces on a large scale. On this ground, no public utility service can be supplied free of cost as the marginal cost is very low. Calculation of marginal cost in a large public utility monopoly is also very difficult in view of many where the overall cost is not ignored, even though they form a significant proportion of the total cost. Hence the marginal cost principle is not accepted in the pricing of service of a monopoly public utility firm. Further, when the public utility firm produces a product or service under deficits, it is covered by public taxation. Price is not going to be increased to cover the losses.

(iii) *Average cost principle:* In the average cost principle, the firm is equating price with the average cost. When the utility firm is working under increasing costs, the equality of

AC with price is beneficial to the firm. When the firm is working under decreasing cost, equality of AC with AR will result in lesser output. If this principle is practiced, the concept of public welfare has to be abandoned.

17. ACTUAL PRICING

Actual pricing practice followed in most of the public utilities firm in that of what the traffic can bear. This principle is known as *value of service principle*. Each category of consumers is charged a price that it is able to pay according to its demand for service. The consumers are divided on the basis of the elasticity of demand. If the demand is inelastic, higher rates are charged. Lower prices are charged where the demand is highly elastic. Thus, the public utility organisation practices the discriminatory pricing and thus renders useful service to the community.

The commissions and tribunals of public utilities take various factors such as the production cost, the administration cost, fair return on capital in determining the prices for services. More than that, they also look into promotional aspects namely the social services that each firm renders. Sometimes, the authorities may fix the price of a utility concern arbitrarily without • looking into cost aspects.

18. IMPORTANT DETERMINANTS IN PRICING

Role of Costing in Pricing

While determining the prices of the product, the importance of cost cannot be ignored. Producers add some percentages of profit to the average cost and thus determine the price. This gives the impression that the price is determined by cost. But this is clear contradiction of the equilibrium rule of the firm, namely MC = MR. Actually in practical life, costs play a minor role in determining the price. The managers have to see apart from costs, other things such as market situations, demand factors and finally the determining factor, then there will be different prices for the same product since different costs prevail for many firms.

Some managers take note of market conditions, demand for the product and the cost in determining the price. If the demand for the product is inelastic, the producers may increase the price, even though there is no change in the cost. Sometimes, the prices remain the same even if there is change in cost of production. It is because that the managers are guided by the market situations.

It is seen in the business world that given the price, the producers 'tailor' their products in accordance with the preference and purchasing power of the buyers. In order to do this tailoring, the producers find out ways for selling the product at a price which gives profit. It has been observed that the producers instead of increasing the price when the costs rise, change the quality of the product. In conclusion, it can be said that if the price is determined on the basis of costs, the firm definitely gets a profit. But we have seen that a good number of firms are being wiped out from the business world, which is entirely due to continued losses. If the price fixed by the firm is lower than the cost, then the firm is sure to incur losses. Whatever may be the other factors, the costs cannot be ignored. It is absolutely necessary that the price should be higher than the cost. At what percentage it should be higher is determined by the other factors such as market situations and the demands.

Yet, costs play decisive roles in determining the products. It prevents the managers to lower the price in the hope of selling more and also it determines whether or not a product is worth including in the product line on the basis of its profitability rate.

Costs no doubt are an important factor in determining the price. Among the several types of costs, there is a question to be answered here as to which type of cost the managers have to cover. In the case of short-periods, if the firms cover all the variable costs, it is sufficient. Short period is so small a period that the firm should not think of covering the fixed costs. While in the long run, the firm must not only cover all costs but costs should also earn a target rate of profits.

Price	Effect of Price Reduction	
	Product X Elastic Demand	Produt Y Inelastic Demand
Initial price Rs. 20		
(a) Units sold	2,000	2,000
(b) Sales Revenue	Rs.40,000	Rs.40,000
(c) Cost	30,000	30,000
(d) Profit	Rs.10,000	Rs.10,000
Change in Price to Rs.18		
(a) Units sold	3,100	2,100
(b) Sales Revenue	Rs.55,000	Rs.37,800
(c) Cost	45,000	31,500
(d) Profit	Rs.10,800	Rs.6,300

Price	Effect of Increase in Price	
Initial price Rs. 20		
(a) Units sold	2,000	2,000
(b) Sales Revenue	Rs.40,000	Rs.40,000
(c) Cost	30,000	30,000
(d) Profit	Rs.10,000	Rs.10,000
Change in Price to Rs.22		
(a) Units sold	1,400	1,900
(b) Sales Revenue	Rs.30,000	Rs.41,800
(c) Cost	21,000	28,000
(d) Profit	Rs.9,800	Rs.13,300

Elasticity of Demand

The price elasticity of demand plays an equally important role in pricing of a product. If the demand for the product is inelastic, the firms can increase the price and earn a target profit. If the firm, with a view to increase sales, reduces the price, the result will be utterly defeating. This is because quantity demanded of inelastic product remains the same after price reduction.

When the demand for the product is elastic, a fall in the price will result in the increase in sales. If the firm rises the price, the sales are sure to fall. The loss of sales is more significant than the benefits of rise in price. The above table explains the effect of change in price when the demand for the product is elastic and inelastic.

If the demand for the product is elastic, the firm should not increase the price. If the demand for the product is inelastic, it can increase the price. According to the above table, the effect of change in price, when the demand is elastic is that sales and profit fall. On the other hand, when the demand is inelastic, the sales fall marginally but profit is more than the normal profit.

Price Forecasting

A manufacturing unit generally comes across some problems regarding the change in prices of raw materials and other factors of production and the prices of finished products. A change in the price of the product may be due to the change in the economic conditions of the country, but at times, prices of certain commodities change even though there is economic stability in the country. Whatever may be the reason for a change in price, the firm must be in a position to foresee these changes in prices, then it will not be possible to it to adjust its prices to cost changes and it may also experience losses. Therefore, the producers and sellers and these persons involved in the commodity markets must make price forecasts if they want to grow in business.

Impact of the Nature of Commodity and its Market

The dealers in products are required to know the nature of the commodity and its market for the forecasting of prices. It is because prices of different commodities fluctuate differently, depending on the demand and supply conditions. McNair and Meriam say that an understanding of supply and demand conditions of the commodities is essential for price forecasting.

The main reason for price fluctuations is the differences in the nature of commodities and their markets. The understanding of the nature of the commodity is necessary in price forecasting. The main things to be known in this context are as follows:

(a) It is necessary to know whether the product is the main one or the by product. If it is a byproduct, its supply depends upon the main products. Therefore, a byproduct is linked with the main product and byproducts are not produced for their own sake. For example, the production of oil cake depends upon the production of oil. Therefore, in making the price forecast of a byproduct, the cost aspect need not be taken, because they are products for their own sake. If the supply does not respond to price changes, then prices of the byproducts will automatically fluctuate.

(b) The price forecasting must take into account the changes in the price of the related commodity. For example, the prices of manufactured goods depend upon the current prices of raw materials. If the prices of raw materials rise, the manufacturers can forecast the rise of the manufactured goods.

(c) If the supply of a commodity is unpredictable, the price forecasting is uncertain. If there is striking of oil in the Kaveri delta, then the supply can be predictable and price forecasting may also be made with certainty.

(d) The extent of competition in the market also determines the extent to which price forecasting can be successfully made. If there is a dominant firm in the industry, its price policy will become the base for price forecasts. If there is severe competition in the market, the price forecast is not easy.

(e) The price setting of some products is made not only by domestic users but also international users. For example, the prices of some raw materials like rubber are set in the world markets. In such cases, forecasting the prices for domestic raw materials will be very difficult. The prices of minerals and metals generally fall in this category.

(f) If there are tariffs and other barriers for the free flow of international trade, the firm has to take into account the import duties in forecasting the price of internationally traded goods.

(g) The nature of the elasticity of demand is to be understood in forecasting the prices. If the demand for a commodity is elastic, any change in supply does not matter much on the price. If the demand for the commodity is inelastic, the supply of goods will have an impact on its price.

(h) The influence of supply on the price of a product is to be studied in price forecasting. There are many agricultural commodities whose supply depends upon climatic factors. The supply of these commodities cannot be changed because their prices have risen. For such commodities, the price forecaster has to analyse the supply position. In the case of manufactured products, the supply can be adjusted to the demand. The basis of price forecasting for such commodities is the demand.

Importance of data on the Commodity Markets

Commodity data regarding the actual production of the year, the previous year's stocks and the demand for the commodities are all necessary for price forecasting. There are some commodities the demand for which is only seasonal. Therefore, business, firms have to maintain sufficient stocks to meet an increasing demand whenever it arises. In the case of agricultural commodities, it is necessary to maintain sufficient stocks to meet unforeseen situations. While in the case of capital and durable goods, heavy inventory is not necessary. So, seasonal variations have limited impact on price in the case of manufactured articles. Therefore, the maintenance of data is necessary for price forecasts.

Normal Stocks: Normal stocks are stocks which are maintained by the businessmen to meet immediate demand. Stocks maintained for three or four weeks are considered normal stocks. These stocks are necessary and would be useful whenever the supply channels experience set backs. Supposing there is transport bottle-neck owing to floods or strike or transport workers, normal stocks become insufficient and the prices tend to rise. But, it becomes sometimes difficult to quantify normal stocks.

Consumer Stocks: Data on commodity stocks are obtained from producers, wholesale dealers, retailers, stockists, etc., But they do not say anything maintained by consumers. Consumers too generally maintain stock of some goods of importance. They maintain a stock of grains of one month's requirements at home. The manufacturers also maintain stocks of raw-materials of two to three weeks of requirements. These stocks also influence price forecasting and hence they should also be taken into consideration.

Seasonal Stock Variations: In the case of agricultural commodities like wheat, millets, pulses, oil seeds, cotton and jute, production is seasonal while consumption is throughout the year and as such the seasonal stock varies. In the harvest season, the stock increases while in the sowing season it diminishes. As such, prices fall during the harvest season, while prices rise during sowing and growing seasons. In the same way, there are commodities, the consumption of which is seasonal while the production goes on throughout the year like woollen cloth. The price variations between the seasonal and non-seasonal stocks depend upon the cost of maintaining the stocks.

Demand and Supply Conditions of Commodities

The knowledge of future demand and supply conditions of the commodities is essential in forecasting of prices. While estimating the demand and supply of commodities prevailing at the time of making pricing forecast, it is also essential to estimate future demand and supply of commodities for a specific period, say three months, six months, one year, etc. If the forecast is being made for six months, then the probable supply and demand conditions during the coming six months have to be estimated carefully.

While making estimates of future demand for commodities, the following factors have to be noted:

(a) The consumption of commodities in the past three or four years has to be obtained, for this would give an idea of future consumption. In the case of durable commodities, past consumption is not a guide. In the case of non-durable commodities, past consumption will be a reliable guide. In the case of durable goods, past consumption is not a guide. In the case of durable goods, low demands in the past often indicates a high demand in the future.

(b) In order to assess the demand for consumption of goods, the purchasing power of the people has to be known. In addition to the purchasing power of the people, the employment situation in the country also must be taken note of. If the disposable income of the people is high, then the demand for consumption of goods will also be high. As regards the industrial commodities, the liquidity position of industrial buyers and the conditions in the capital market have to be studied.

(c) In order to forecast the price of the products, it is necessary to take into consideration, the propensity to consume by the people. It is also necessary to study whether the willingness to buy depends upon the price or not. If the price of the product is low, the consumers may not buy. Even if the price is high, the consumers may not buy. If the buyers come to know that the prices of the products would come down, they may not be willing to buy at low prices. Thus, willingness to buy has to be intensified in order to induce the consumers to buy the commodities. This is possible only when the employment increases and good payments are made.

While estimating the prospective demand, the forecaster is required to look into the past behaviour of demand, the purchasing power of the people and the propensity to consume.

Prospective Supply

The following factors have to be considered in estimating the prospective supply:

(a) It is necessary to compare the actual production with the productive capacity in the industry in order to assess the excessive capacity. If there is any additional demand for the product, it can be met by using the excessive capacity which can be done at lower costs and such a rise in price can be checked. Therefore, the firm must ascertain any excess capacity in the industry before any forecasting.

(b) The supply of a product is always determined by the price of the product. If some firms are producing the product at higher costs than others, a low price of the product will make those firms to suspend production. As a result of this, the supply of the product falls. The high cost firms compare the price with the variable cost of production. If they find that the price is higher than the variable cost of production, then they start producing and as a result, total supply would again rise.

(c) The production forecasts of agricultural commodities made by the Department of Agriculture and Statistics has an impact on market prices. Good crop reports lead to a decline in price and vice-versa.

Thus, a sound knowledge of supply and demand of product helps the forecaster in estimating a realistic price structure.

The Typical Price Changes

Prices of products change, i.e., the rise or fall according to certain situations. The changes in prices over a period of time are due to economic and non-economic factors. The non-economical factors are also called seasonal price fluctuations. The economical factors are *cyclical* changes.

Seasonal changes

Demand for certain commodities will only be seasonal. For example, umbrellas are required during rainy season. Ice-creams are used only in summer seasons. Woollen clothes are used only in winter. These are seasonal commodities. Fruits of certain types are grown only in certain seasons. Normally in seasons, when the supply is more than the demand, price falls. Or it may also be possible that the demand may rise during the seasons and consequently, the prices may also rise. These fluctuations are common in agricultural commodities where they cannot be stored for longer periods. In the case of manufactured articles, seasonal variations have a limited impact on prices for they can be stored.

Cyclical Changes

During business cycles, prices of all commodities fluctuate. In the boom period, prices of all commodities rise very significantly, while during the period of depression, prices of manufactured articles, shares and stocks fall more steeply than agricultural commodities. During the periods of business cycles, prices fluctuate, but the intensity of fluctuations differ between products. If the supply of the products cannot be adjusted to demand, the prices fluctuate violently. Thus, in order to make reliable forecasts, it is necessary to study the nature of economic conditions prevailing at a period.

Further, the prices of certain products fluctuate with products in the same way but the prices of some of the products fluctuate earlier or later than for the products in the economy. In other words, some products are early movers while some others are late movers. While making price forecasts, the knowledge of fluctuations of general economic conditions and their impact on the economic scene is quite useful.

SUMMARY

1. The price theory points out that the equilibrium price is determined at a point where marginal revenue is equal to the marginal cost.

2. The objectives of pricing policy includes survival of the firm, sales maximisation; securing a large market share, preventing competition, making money etc.

3. The important factors involved in pricing policy of a firm are costs, demand and psychology of consumers, competition, profit and government policy.

4. Full cost pricing or cost-plus pricing means the addition of a certain percentage of profit to the cost of production to arrive at a price.

5. Under, rate of return pricing, the price is determined by the planned rate of return of investment which is expected to be converted into a percentage of the mark up.

6. Under marginal cost pricing, fixed costs are ignored and pricing is determined on the basis of marginal costs.

7. Going rate pricing means, adjusting its own price policy to the general price structure in the industry.

8. The new products can be priced based on its demand, the market target and the promotional strategy.

9. There are various other pricing concepts such as peak load pricing, pricing over life cycle of a product, pioneer pricing, product line pricing, and transfer pricing.

10. Dual pricing is a system in which two types of prices are prevailing for a product. One price is fixed and controlled by the government and the other is to be determined by market forces.

11. Administered prices are the prices fixed by the government to prevent price escalation, black marketing and shortages in supply.

12. Pricing in public sector is based on fair rate principle or average cost pricing or marginal cost pricing.

QUESTIONS

1. What is meant by 'Pricing policy'?
2. What are the objectives of pricing of a product.
3. What is the utility of cost-plus pricing.
4. What are the advantages and disadvantages of marginal cost pricing
5. What do you mean by 'transfer pricing'?. How is transfer price determined.
6. Explain the pricing policies of a life cycle of a product.
7. What are the unique problems in multi-product pricing.
8. Distinguish between skimming price and penetration pricing.
9. What is product line pricing. What is peak load pricing.
10. What are the general considerations of the Pricing Policy.
11. Describe the factors which help price forecasting.
12. Discuss the problems that the management faces while pricing of new products.
13. What is cyclical pricing?
14. Write a short note on product life cycle.

17 Chapter

Circular Flow of Income

CHAPTER OBJECTIVES

After reading this chapter you will be able to answer the following:
1. Two Sector Model
2. Introduction of Savings
3. C and S Relationship
4. Three Sector Model

In the present day world, production is carried out mainly for the purpose of sale in the market. To produce a wide variety of goods the business firms combine various factors of production and try to sell those goods in the market. In the economy, the sales made by the business firm generate a flow of money incomes which are used to make payments to the factors of production for their services.

In a modern capitalist economy the process of production and exchange generate two kinds of circular flows:

(i) The households supply various factors of production which are demanded by the business firms. Once the goods and services are produced they are sent to the market for disposal and sold to the households. This process indicates that there is a circular flow of goods and services between the households and the business firms. It is called as real flow by the economists.

(ii) The business firm pay rewards in cash for the factor services which are supplied by the households. With that money income that households purchase goods and services from the business firms. This process results in circular flow of money between the households and the business firms. In short, there is a continuous flow of money and income between the households and the firms, and vice versa.

Whatever may be the nature of the economy there will be circular flow of money and goods and services. In the case of a closed economy there are only two sectors - households and firms, hence it is known as two sector model. If we include government, then it becomes three-sector closed economy. If international sector is included it is known as four-sector open economy.

Money expenditure on foreign goods i.e., on imports cause an outflow of income. The exports cause an inflow of income into the circular flow of income.

1. TWO SECTOR MODEL

In current day world producers produce goods and services mainly to sell in the market. Today wide variety of fast moving consumer goods (FMCGS) are produced by manufacturers employing various factors of producion in different proportions. The FMCGs are sold in different markets for different prices to get as much profit as possible. The revenue so flown into the hands of producers in the market will not fully stay in their hands. Only residue will be used by producers as profit after giving the share of revenue to the owners of factors of producion for the service rendered by them. Therefore, in an economy, production processes and markets generate two types of flows:

(i) Supply of factor servies by the households to the production process of firms.

(ii) After production, goods and services are sent to the market by firms for selling to the households.

When we observe these two types of flows, we understand that some type of flow, which is CIRCULAR in nature takes place. This is called by economists as 'REAL FLOW'.

Another type of 'flow' takes place in this process which may be called 'MONEY FLOW'. There will be circular flow of money. Production firms pay in cash for goods or services they get from households for producing finished produts money so received by households will be spent on required goods and services produed by the firms.

These two situations tell us that there is a continuous flow of money and income between the households and firms and vice-a-versa.

In the whole analysis only two main sectors are considered. They are (i) Households and (ii) Firms. In every economy, irrespective of size of population, this flow takes for ever. This is called 'Circular Flow of income in a two sector model'. This model acts as a base for measuring national income and national expenditure. These two are assumed to be equal.

In this two-sector model *savings* is not taken into account. Even before adding 'savings' sector into our discussion, we have to understand certain other aspects that prevail in this model.

(i) Households cannot be isolated economic units as they cannot produce themselves all their consumption requirements.

(ii) Firms supply the requirements of households for consideration which may be in the form of money or in kind.

(iii) No saving aspect is included in this situation.

This thinking is based on the definition of national accounting system which tells that National Income is equal to National Expenditure. (NI = NE). The implication of NI = NE is that in a two sector model of an economy total expenditure of the household is exactly same as the total factor earnings of the households. What is two-sector model?

In the analysis we have made so far, we have perceived the following:

• There will be circular flow of money, goods and services in an economy.

• Only two sectors are considered for analysis viz Households and Firms.

- Savings aspect is ignored for the time-being.

- Households spend all their income on consumer goods and services produced by firms.

- Goods and services produced by the firms just cover the market requirement, because of this, level of inventory of the firm remains unchanged.

- The amount of money or revenue received by the firms on sale of products to households will be distributed to factor services in the form of rent, wage, interest and profit (loss). Nothing is retained in the firm as undistributed profit. (This is an assumption for the time being.).

All these aspects when presented in circular flow form becomes a two-secor model of national accounting system.

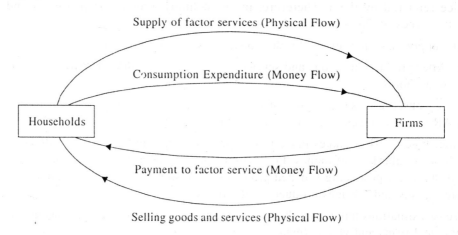

Fig. Two-sector Model without Savings

In this chart it is observed that factor services are provided by the households (physical flow) to the producers and producer produces goods required by households and supplys through market to households when factor services are paid monetary considerations to houeholds as rewards for factor services in the form of rent, wage, interest and profit. This becomes an income for factor owners. The whole process is called 'two sector model' in national income analysis. In this it is assumed and evident that factors of production receive rewards which will be equal to the value of current output. It is also true that Gross National Income (GNI) will be equal to Total Disposable Income (TDI).

It can also be said that money paid to households by the firms as factor payments comes back to the firm in the form of consumption expenditure of households. This simple example indicates that irregular flow of money and incomes will continue till infinity. It is fully assumed so far that no other element disturbs this model in any manner.

2. INTRODUCTION OF SAVINGS

We now introduce another element of savings. In any economy circular flow of income cannot be constant as discussed in previous paragraphs. The income received by households will have two channels (i) Consumption Expenditure and (ii) savings

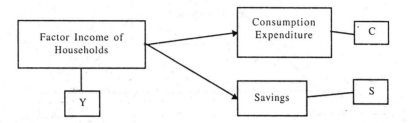

In a two-sector model it is understood that y = c+s or S = y-c. Where 'y' is income, 'c' is consumption and 's' is savings.

Even before we go into the analysis of this equation, it should also be understood that in a circular flow two situations can occur. (i) withdrawal of money out of income flow (This is technically called 'leakage') and (ii) introduction of income into circular flow (This is termed as 'injection').

Leakage ocurs because of savings of the households, tax paid to government and payments for imports.

Whereas 'injection' may be in the form of investment, government spending and exports.

In this backdrop, the equation y = c + s can be analysed.

3. C AND S RELATIONSHIP

The relationship between savings and consumption implies that every household does not spend all money received from firms towards consumption and a portion will be saved. The savings will have its impact on circular flow of money and income. Both decline due to savings. If household keep savings for liquidity purposes, the leakage occurs. However, if savings is kept in a bank or any other financial institution it becomes productive. This means these banks would advance money to producers which will be used for productive purposes. Thus money withdrawn from circular flow will be coming back to the firms in different circuit. In this process another concept viz "Investment" emerges.

"Investment" is a term referred to capital expenditure made by firms. This expenditure will be in the form of capital goods like, land, building, plant machinery etc without which firms cannot produce goods for households. Investment comes from two sources, viz borrowings and retained earnings. Investment will be an addition to circular flow of income. Circular flow of income in a "Two-sector model" is shown in the following picture.

Savings vary from economy to economy. In advanced economies savings will be more say upto 20 per cent and 80 per cent will be consumption expenditure. But in developing economies voluntary savings will be less and forced savings may constitute 10 per cent of household income.

Savings and investment in any economy need not be necessarily equal as investment takes place by firms and savings by the people. Savings may exceed investment.

(S > I) or vice-versa (I > S)

Therefore Y will not be in equilibrium if S and I are not equal in a given point of time.

Normally, investment will be more than savings. It is also common that there will be leakage in circular flows of income due to savings. This leakage will be more than neutralised by injection

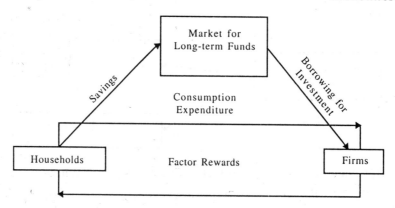

Fig. Circular flow of income in a Two-Sector model with savings and Investment

in the form of investment. This raises the level of income. After certain time S and I become equal at a higher level of income.

In the beginning of this analysis we have assumed that whatever money income earned by the firms will be paid to households in the form of reward for factor services without retaining anything. But, in real business operations that too current day corporates retain some undistributed profits for gaining liquidity and investment in some form to increase the value of share holdings. In advanced countries retained earnings will be substantial and in developing countries like India, very few companies will have considerable savings.

4. THREE SECTOR MODEL

In a three-sector model of circular flow of money, besides households and firms, another institution, namely government, will be functioning. In government operations, we observe many economic functions. The impact of these economic functions on the circular flow of income should be examined. The revenue for government comes from different sources. Tax is the main source of revenue. Besides tax, grants from foreign sources, export earnings, subsidies etc constitute the source of government revenue.

However, tax is assumed as only the source of revenue. Government levies many types of taxes (T) on households and firms. Direct and indirect taxes constitute the main tax revenue from households to the government. Symbolically, we express this sources as "T_1". Corporate tax is the main source of income for government from firms. This is symbolically expressed as T_2. Therefore, total revenue of the government from taxes will be $T_1 + T_2$ or $T_R = T_1 + T_2$.

On the other hand government expenditure will be on various heads. It may be broadly classified as current or revenue expenditure and capital expenditure. Various types of expenditure takes place in these two domains. Following is the list of expenditure a government does.

1. Development expenditure under plans and other approved expenditure on specific develomental activities outside the plans (GE_1).

2. Current expenditure on services rendered by the households to defence and civil administration. (GE_2).

3. Government consumption expenditure on a range of goods and services purchased from firms and other business enterprises (GE_3).

4. Various types of social security expenditure like pension, unemployment relief, accidental relief, transfer payments (Expenditure on welfare schemes are called transfer payments), etc. (GE_4) and

5. Subsidies to farm sector and business firm to develop new industries (GE_5).

Therefore $GE = GE_1 + GE_2 + GE_3 + GE_4 + GE_5$

The government was following the classical approach in its budget preparations upto to the turn of twentieth century. That is presenting a balanced budget as propounded by classical economists. This means that government expenditure should be equal to government revenue. But modern governments are following the deficit budget concept. The gap in revenue is covered by loans from households and capital market. If a surplus budget is presented, there will be a net leakage from the circular flow of income to the extent of surplus. The following picture exhibits three-sector model economy and circular flow of income in this model.

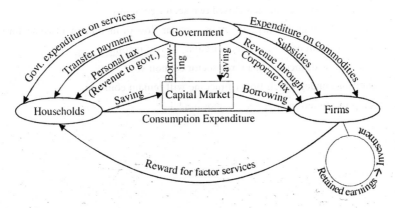

Three Sector Model

The above diagram clearly shows that the income flow between households, firms and the government. There are two main points to be noted in this model. Firstly, the firms do not distribute all the profits earned by them. It results in lower income to the households than the net national income of the country. The firm use the undistributed profits for their future investment. Secondly, if the government budget is not balanced, there may be a flow of income between the capital market and the government. If government expenditure is greater than its tax revenue (GE > TR), then the government will have to borrow from the money market. It will result in a flow of money from capital market to the government. On the other hand if government expenditure is lesser than its tax revenue (GE < TR), there may be a flow of money from the government to the capital market. This will happen only when the government spends the surplus revenue otherwise the circular flow of income will decline.

SUMMARY

1. Real flow and money flow are the two flows which are present in a modern economy.

2. Income flows from firms to households in the form of factor payments, in turn income from households goes back to the firms in the form of price paid by them when they buy the consumer goods.

3. Income received in the form of factor payments is either spent on consumption or saved.

4. In the case of two sector model, there is circular flow of income between the households and the firms in the form of factor payments and the price.

5. Any leakages may reduce the circular flow of income whereas injections may increase it.

6. In the case of three sector model, where government is included, its activities affect circular flow of income.

7. When the government's budget is balanced, the amount of income taken in the form of taxes is replaced through government expenditure in the circular flow.

8. In the case of an open economy, the imports cause an outflow while the exports cause an inflow of income into the circular flow of income.

QUESTIONS

1. Give the meaning of circular flow of income.

2. Explain the circular flow of income in a closed two sector economy.

3. Discuss the effects of savings and investment on circular flow of income in a two sector economy.

4. In what way do government activities affect circular flow of income?

5. Explain the circular flow of income in a three sector economy.

6. Discuss the conditions under which flow of income will remain constant.

7. Examine consumption function under two sector model.

18 Chapter

National Income Analysis

CHAPTER OBJECTIVES

After reading this chapter, you will be able to answer the following:

1. Meaning and definition of National Income
2. Concepts of National Income
3. Measurement of National Income
4. Relation of GNP, NI, PI and savings
5. Significance of NI estimates
6. Difficulties in the estimation of National Income

The study of National Income Analysis has gained greater importance since the outbreak of the 'Great Depression' in the thirties and in this century. Keynes *"General Theory of Employment, Interest and Money"* was a pioneering work in this direction. The subject further gained importance as a result of quest for rapid economic development in under-developed countries. The factors on which employment in a country depends upon includes investments on various activities. Investment in turn depends upon the aggregate demand for goods and services. Investment is also the function for the future rates of profit.

The main problem that is required to be investigated is that, what determines the level of output in a given period. The volume of output of employment in a country depends upon National Income.

1. MEANING AND DEFINITIONS

National Inome is generally defined as income of the nation. The national income reveals the nature of economic activity in a country. National Income data provides an idea of a country's aggregate economic activity.

Alfred Marshall, defines National Income as: "The labour and capital of a country acting on its natural resources, produced annually a certain 'net' aggregate of commodities, material and immaterial including services of all kinds." The word 'net' means that from the gross volume of the output, the depreciation must be deducted.

Pigou has defined National Income as "that part of the objective income of the community including income derived from abroad which can be measured in money." Prof. Fisher says that "National income refers solely to services received by ultimate consumers, whether from the material or human environment."

Thus, the concept of national income has three interpretations. It represents the income, consumption and saving of the people of the community.

Keynes concept of national income is entirely different. According to him, the Gross National Product refers to the total value of the output produced in a year. If the user's cost or depreciation value of capital equipment is deducted, we get Net National Produt (NNP).

National Income is also defined as the aggregate factor income which arises from current production of goods and services of a country. The nation's economy refers to the factors of production supplied by the people of that country.

> *Thus, National Income is the sum of all incomes in cash and kind accruing to factors of production in a given time. It is also the values of net outputs arising in several sectors of the nation's production. It is also the sum total of all consumer's expenditure, government expenditure on goods and services and net expenditure on capital goods.*

National Income is expressed with reference to a period of time, namely a year. This is because National Income is a flow and not a stock, i.e., income generated every year and at different rates and their period is mentioned during which income is generated. It is measured and shown with reference to a year as a *annual flow.*

2. CONCEPTS OF NATIONAL INCOME

The different concepts of NI are as follows:

  (i) Gross National Product.

  (ii) Gross Domestic Product.

  (iii) Net National Product.

  (iv) National Income at Market Price.

  (v) National Income at Factor Cost.

  (vi) Personal Income.

  (vii) Disposable Income.

  Other Concepts.

  (a) Corporate Income, (b) Private Income, (c) Real Income and (d) Per capita Income.

(i) Gross National Product (GNP)

> *GNP is defined as the total market value of final goods and services produced in a year.*

The Gross National Product is the basic social accounting measure. It includes all economic productions in the economy during a year.

Two points must be noted in calculating GNP. Firstly, it is a monetary measure. There is no other way of adding up the different sorts of goods and services produced in a year except with their money prices. But, in order to know accurately the changes in physical output, the figure of Gross National Product is adjusted for price changes by comparing to a base year.

We must take into account the money value of the final goods (and services) produced in the economy to avoid double or multiple counting, since most of the goods pass through several stages in production before reaching the market. Many parts and components are sold by potential companies which are used in a final product. These goods are called *intermediate goods*, which enter into the production of other goods. For example, bread is a final good, flour is an intermediate product. Motor car is a final product. Steel and its components used therein are intermediate goods. Thus intermediate goods are to be excluded and only the value of final goods alone should be taken into the calculation of GNP.

Secondly, the money value of currently produced goods must be taken into the calculation of GNP, because it is a measure of country's productivity during a year. If certain goods produced in 1991 are not sold till 1992, they would be part of the GNP of 1991 and not 1992.

Another important thing to be noted in this connection is that the non-productive transactions should be excluded. The non-productive transactions are transfer payments such as old age pensions, unemployment compensations, grants or gifts, etc.

In the gross national product, the depreciation or replacement value of the used capital goods is not deducted.

(ii) Gross Domestic Product (GDP)

Gross Domestic Product is the aggregate values of output of goods and services produced in a country, without adding net factor incomes received from abroad.

GDP is measured at market prices.

GDP = GNP − Income received from abroad.

(iii) Net National Product (NNP)

In the net national product concept, the net value of goods and services produced in a country in a year is considered. It means that in the production of goods and services, there is the consumption of capital goods such as equipment and machinery. The capital goods like machinery wear out or depreciate in value as a result of its consumption or use in production process. This consumption of fixed capital or fall in the value of capital due to wear and tear is called depreciation. In order to get Net National Product, the value of depreciation has to be reduced from gross national product.

> *Net National Product means the market value of all final goods and services after providing for depreciations.*

NNP is also referred to as National Income at market prices. it is a better concept than GNP, because it makes proper allowance for depreciation, NNP is helpful in the analysis of long run problems of maintaining and increasing the supply of physical capital in the country.

Net National Product = Gross National Product − Depreciation

(iv) National Income at Factor Cost and Market Prices

National income is also called National Income at Factor Cost. There is also a concept called national income at market prices. National income at factor cost means the sum of all incomes earned by the suppliers of resources for their contribution of land, labour, capital and entrepreneurial ability which go into the year's net production. In other words, national income at factor cost shows how much it costs to society in terms of economic resources to produce the net output. The term national income refers to national income at factor cost. The difference between the national income and national income at market prices is that indirect tax and subsidies cause market prices of the products to be different from the factors resulting from it.

NI at Factor Cost = NI at Market Prices (GNP) − Taxes − Depreciation + Subsidies

NI at Market Price = NI at Factor Cost + Taxes − Subsidies + Depreciation

For example, a motor car costs Rs.2 lakhs which includes excise duty of Rs.20,000. The market price of the car is Rs.2 lakhs while the factors engaged in production get Rs.1.80 lakhs. Thus, the value of national income at factor cost would be equal to the market prices minus the indirect taxes plus subsidies. The concept of national income is very important in economics for it throws light on the distribution side of the national output. It tells us how the national income is distributed among the four factors of production in lieu of the services rendered by them. As such, it is closely related to economic justice.

(v) Personal Income (PI)

Personal income is that income actually received by the individuals or households in a country during the year, from all sources.

Actually, the whole national income earned by factors of production in a year is not available to them. For example, the companies have to pay corporate taxes before the distribution among shareholders. Further, a part of the corporate profits is retained by the companies. Further, the workers and salaried employees have to make social security contributions out of their wages and salaries. To the extent of these deductions, the amount available to them is reduced. Further, the government may give some social security benefits such as old age pensions, unemployment etc. to the people. Such payments are not given for any productive work. They are known as *transfer payments*.

In order to derive personal income, the following three types of incomes namely social security contributions, corporate income taxes and undistributed corporate profits have to be deducted from national income. Transfer payments have to be added.

Personal income = National Income − Social Security contribution, corporate income taxes and undistributed corporate profits + Transfer payments.

The concept of personal income is a very useful concept. It indicates the potential purchasing power of households in an economy. It enables us to measure the welfare of the whole body of consumers in the country. The weakness of this concept is that it does not tell us clearly the actual amount of income available for the consumers to spend on consumption and services. To know this, we have to study another concept called *disposable income* of the household.

(vi) Disposable Personal Income (DPI)

The whole personal income is not available for the consumers to spend on consumption. The reason is that, out of the income received, the individuals have to pay personal income taxes. When this amount is paid, the available income is very much reduced.

That part of income which is left behind after the payment of direct taxes is called Disposable Personal Income.

It is the disposable personal income which is spent by the individuals on consumption. At the same time, there is also saving. Out of the disposable income, the individuals save a part of the income for their security in future. Disposable income can either be consumed or saved. Therefore Disposable Personal Income = Consumption + Savings

DPI = PI − Taxes

Other Concepts

(a) Corporate Income: The term corporate income refers to the incomes and profits of companies or firms or public utilities. We should deduct the income tax and profit tax from their income to get corporate income.

(b) Private Income: The term private income refers to the income received by private individuals from any source whether productive or unproductive.

Private Income − NI (at factor cost) + Transfer payments + Interest on public debt − Social security contributions − Profits and surpluses of Public Undertakings.

(c) Real Income and National Income: National Income of a country is expressed in terms of money. But the value of money goes on changing over a period of time. This creates difficulties in comparing the national income over the years. To overcome these difficulties, the economists have introduced another concept called *real income*. The country's income of a particular year when measured at current prices, it is called national income. The national income of a particular year, when compared with the nominal income of a base year, it will include the effect of two changes. (i) The change in the production of goods and services (ii) change in the price level. When price level changes, the national income of a particular year reflects the change in the price level, while the price level of the base year is constant. To make the comparison clear, the national income will have to be deflated. This deflating is done in the following manner. Supposing 1980 is kept as a base year in which price level is equal to 100. We have to calculate the real national income of the year 2002. The price level of 2002 will have to be deflated to the price level of 1980.

Thus, when the country's income is expressed in terms of current prices it is called *national income*. When it is expressed in terms of constant prices or prices prevailing in the base year, it is called real income.

(d) Per Capita Income (PCI): The concept of per capita income is used in economic writings and discussions as an index of changes in the standard of living of the people of a country. The per capita income indicates the changes in economic progress in terms of goods and services available per head of the population. The formula for calculating per capita income is as follows:

$$\text{Per Capita Income} = \frac{\text{National income at constant prices}}{\text{Population}}$$

3. MEASUREMENT OF NATIONAL INCOME

There are three methods of measuring national income or an economy's output or national product. They are

1. The Product Method

2. The Income Method

3. The Expenditure Method

1. The Product Method: Under product method, production of all types of goods is estimated and they are valued at market prices. The net production of all the industries in the country are added up (like agriculture, industry, trade and commerce, etc.). There are two approaches to calculate NI under product method. They are

  (i) Value added approach

  (ii) Final goods approach

According to value added approach, a summation of the increase in value at each separate production stage, which results in output in final form, gives the value of GNP(NI).

According to the final goods approaches only the final values of goods and services are added ignoring all intermediate transactions. Since the value of intermediate goods (raw materials, fuel etc.) are included in the value of final product, its value should not be considered, so that double counting can be avoided. If the value of intermediate goods are also added, then it would inflate the figure of national income. To avoid this, the value of only the final product has been considered.

The calculation of GNP(NI) by the value added method is not popular because it is a tedious procedure. Instead final goods method or approach is preferred. The data for the value of production can be had from the various statistical organisations.

Under product method, the following categories of production are added in order to findout GNP(NI).

  (a) *Product of agricultural sector:* This includes the total value of foodgrains produced by the farmers in the country during a year.

  (b) *Product of industrial sector:* This includes the total market value of all goods produced in various industries like electronics, cement, steel etc. in a country during a year.

  (c) *Products of trade:* This induces income resulting from various activities which are connected to internal trade.

  (d) *Service sector incomes:* This includes the total value of the proceeds of the service sector namely, the services of government servants, doctors, lawyers, soldiers, singers, players etc.

  (e) *Foreign trade:* The value of exports or the income earned abroad should be added and the value of imports or payments made abroad should be deducted.

(f) *Indirect Taxes and Subsidies:* The indirect taxes which are included in the price should be deducted to get exact market value of the goods. Similarly subsidies given by government to certain products should be added to calculate the exact value of the product.

2. The Expenditure Method: Expenditure approach method involves in calculating the value of the final goods consumed. Most of the goods produced in a country are consumed. But there are some goods which remain unsold. If unsold stocks are regarded as having been bought by the producers who hold them as inventories, then the monetary value of the total national production would be equal to the national expenditure.

Under this expenditure approach, the following categories of expenditures are added in order to find out the GNP.

(a) *Personal Consumption Expenditure:* This includes those expenditures made on durable and non-durable goods produced in a country during a year. This also includes the expenditure on services, such as transport, education and medical. Expenditures made on houses are treated as investment rather than consumption expenditure. Expenditure on household equipment such as motor car, refrigerator, television, etc. forms the consumption expenditure on durable goods.

(b) *Gross Domestic Private Investment:* This includes private investment on capital goods such as buildings, machinery, plant, equipment, etc. Such investments are made by business firms. Houses are also included in this category of expenditure, because they are durable and that they represent capital goods. If a business firm purchases a second hand machinery, it is not investment. In the same way, if a person purchases already constructed houses, this is not investment. Purchase of existing shares and stocks also is not investment for purposes of national income accounting.

(c) *Government Purchase of Goods and Services:* The governments both at the centre and states purchase from the market consumer goods such as paper, stationary, machinery, equipment, etc. for their enterprises. In addition, the government incurs expenditure on payment of salaries to Military Personnel, Police and Administration etc. Government also pays old age pension, unemployment dodles, etc. If the payments are not made for currently produced services, they are not included in GNP.

(d) *Net foreign investment* - arises from international transactions like imports and exports. If there is positive surplus, it is added to GNP. If there is negative deficit, it is deducted from GNP.

It is thus clear that if the entire production of a country is purchased at market prices, the amount so spent will represent the gross national product of a country. If the expenditures of the above four categories are added, we get the GNP *i.e.,* NI.

3. The Income Method: The expenditure made by the people of a country on goods and services produced in a country during a year becomes the income of the various factors, which are collaborated in the production of these goods and services. The factor income is grouped into following categories:

(a) Wages and salaries

(b) Income of company business

(c) Rental incomes of persons

(d) Corporate profits

(e) Income from net interest

The wages and salaries received by the employees, both government and private sector firms during a year plus certain contributions such as provident fund contribution made by the employers. This includes the income earned by self-employed persons, rental income earned by individuals on agricultural and non-agricultural property, corporate profits earned by joint stock companies before the payment of taxes and dividends to shareholders. The net interest earned by individuals from sources other than the organs of the government are to be added to get national product.

An aggregate of all the given categories of incomes will not be equal to the GNP as estimated by the expenditure method. The reason is that it is part of the total expenditure incurred by the community does not become available to the factors of production in the form of incomes. There are two such leakages - one is that of indirect taxes levied on goods and services by the government, second is the depreciation on plant and machinery, buildings etc. The expenditure by households on goods and services includes indirect taxes levied by the government. The income from indirect taxes goes to the government. In the same way, depreciation is not the income of any factor of production. While calculating GNP by Income Method, we have to add indirect taxes and depreciation.

The three approaches are shown in the following table:

Product Method	**Expenditure Method**	*Income Method*
(i) Product of agricultural sector **plus**	(i) Personal consumption expenditure **plus**	(i) Wages and salaries of employees **plus**
(ii) Product of industrial sector **plus**	(ii) Gross domestic private investment **plus**	(ii) Incomes of non-company business **plus**
(iii) Product of trade **plus**	(iii) Government purchases of goods and services **plus**	(iii) Rental incomes of persons **plus**
(iv) Service sector incomes **plus**	(iv) Net foreign investment.	(iv) Corporate profits **plus**
(v) Income from foreign trade **plus**		(v) Income from net interest **plus**
(vi) Subsidies **minus**		(vi) Indirect taxes **plus**
(vii) Indirect Taxes.		(vii) Depreciation of capital goods
Total = Gross National Product (GNP)		

Merits of the Three Methods

Gross National Product is the most frequently used concept. Whatever may be the approach used, the result is the same. But some allowance will have to be made for all errors and omissions. Hence, in actual practice these three methods are used in combination with one another in order to get accurate figures.

GNP is a better index of the country's actual production and employment. It is also statistically simple for it does not take into account the problem of depreciation. But it is not a net measure of the nation's economic performance. It is only a gross measure. In order to get net measure, we have to examine another concept called *net national product*.

4. RELATION OF GNP, NI, PERSONAL INCOME AND SAVINGS

	Rs. Crores
GNP	50,000
Depreciation	−5,000
Net National Product	45,000
Indirect Taxes	−6,000
	39,000
Subsidies	+1,000
National income	40,000
Corporate profits	−7,000
Dividends	+1,500
Government and Business transfers	÷2,500
Personal Income	37,000
Personal Direct taxes	−7,000
Disposable Income [DPI]	30,000
Personal Consumption Expenditure	27,500
Savings	2,500

Illustration

Estimate of National Income of a Country in a Given Year:

A : Income Method	Rs. Crores
Income: Wages, salaries, etc.	10,000
Profits (Public & Private)	5,000
Rent	2,000
Interest	1,000
Total Domestic Income	18,000
Less: Stock appreciation	−2,500
Residual error	−500
Net Property Income from abroad	1,000
GNP	16,000
Less: Depreciation	−1,500
National Income	**14,500**

B : Expenditure Method	Rs. Crores
Consumer's Expenditure	11,000
Public Authorities current expenditure on goods and services	6,000
Gross Capital formation investment	5,000
Domestic Expenditure at market prices	22,000
Plus Exports and Income from abroad	6,000
Imports and Income paid abroad	−2,500
Taxes on Expenditure	−10,000
Plus subsidies	+500
	16,000
Less: Depreciation	1,500
National Income	**14,500**

5. SIGNIFICANCE OF NATIONAL INCOME ESTIMATES

1. The National Income of a country reveals the true picture of the economy. A rise in national income indicates a rise in standard of living of the people of a country. It also reveals the improvement of economic welfare.

2. The national income estimate reveals the overall production in each year and thereby we can compare the real growth of the economy. If the growth is stagnant, measures can be adopted to increase the national income.

3. Of the national income concepts, the per capita income occupies a very important place in comparative economics. It measures the average standard of living of the people. Economic welfare depends to a considerable degree on the level of national income and the average standard of living of the people. Thus, the figures of national income and per capita income indicate the level of economic welfare of the people of a country.

4. By comparing the national accounts of various periods, we will be in a position to know the nature of the economy. This is very important when the government of a country launches planning for economic development. Supposing national income is stagnant in a year or a period of two or three years, the government can initiate development through investments.

5. National income estimates show the contribution made by different sectors of the economy such as agriculture, industry, trade and commerce etc. According to National Income figures of India, we will come to know that about 27 per cent of the national income comes from agriculture. This shows that agriculture is very important from the point of view of the economy.

6. National income estimate also throws light on the distribution side. This means how far the different categories of income such as wages, profits, rents and interest are contributing to national income. If the contribution of wages is higher than the profits, it indicates that the labour class are contributing more than the proprietor class.

7. National Income estimate also throws light on the three major aspects of the economy namely, consumption, savings and investment. Information regarding these things is necessary for promoting suitable economic policies. It is the rate of saving and investment that determines the rate of economic growth. Further, consumption plus investment constitutes the level of aggregate demand on which the level of employment and income depends.

8. The National Income figures are used to measure the economic welfare in different countries. A country is declared as a developed country or an under-developed country on the basis of the per capita income.

9. The formulation of planning for different sectors of the economy is based on the national income figures. By looking at the national income figures of various sectors, various states and we can say which sector needs more emphasis for develoment. From the national income estimates, we can also see the part played by the government in the national economy.

10. In fact, no development planning is possible without the complete study of national income estimates. National income estimates are very useful in formulating plans for the

development of agriculture, industry and infrastructure, etc. Preparation of the Five Year Plans depends very much on the availability of data regarding national income, consumption, savings and investment, which are all provided by the national income estimates. Further, we can evaluate the achievements of the development targets laid down in the Plans from the changes in national income and various components.

6. DIFFICULTIES IN THE MEASUREMENT OF NATIONAL INCOME

Measurement of national income is not an easy task and is invariable full of guess work and arbitrary discussions. Basically there are two types of difficulties in the calculation of national income.

(i) Conceptual difficulties.

(ii) Statistical difficulties.

Following are the difficulties involved in the calculation of NI.

1. Difficulty in defining the 'Nation': National income includes not only the income produced within the country, but also income earned in other countries. Hence, the definition of nation goes beyond the political boundaries.

2. Lack of reliable information and data: Adequate, reliable and up-to-date datas regarding production, income and other variables are generally not available. Hence, it is very difficult to measure the national income accurately.

3. The error of double counting: Another difficulty in calculating the national income is that of double counting, which arises from the failure to differentiate final and intermediate goods.

4. Non-Monetary transactions: The national income is always measured in terms of money value, but there are goods and services which may have no corresponding flow of money payments. Example, the food grains consumed by the farmers instead of selling after production.

5. Unpaid Services: Services performed for love, kindness and mercy and not for money have no money value but have only economic value. These are excluded from national income figures and leads to the under estimation of the national income.

6. Inapplicability of any one method: Which method to use to calculate NI is a difficult question. It is better to use the three methods simultaneously depending upon the availability of satistics.

7. Changing price levels: Due to change in prices, it is not easy to estimate the national income accurately. This is because when the general prices rise, the national income in money terms rises even though the national output remains the same.

8. Income from illegal activities: The income obtained from illegal activities such as black marketing, gambling, smuggling etc. is not included in the national income thus reducing the real value of the national income.

9. The Co-existence of monetised and non-monetised sectors: In UDCs a large non-monetised sector exists along side of the monetised sector. The goods in non-monetised sector are not exchanged for money. Hence, these goods do not enter into monetary transactions and thus pose a problem in calculating.

10. The Co-operation of the people: A major part of the population are illiterate and hence may not co-operate in providing the informations needed for the estimation of national income.

The people should not be indifferent to the government requirement. This may mislead the official and estimates will become a mere guess work.

SUMMARY

1. National Income is the aggregate annual income of the country derived from the production of goods and services.

2. There are five concepts of NI namely (i) Gross National Product, (ii) Net National Product, (iii) National Income, (iv) Personal Income and (v) Disposable Income

3. In the calculation of GNP, generally two methods are employed: (a) expenditure or output approach method; (b) income approach method.

4. Under the first method, personal consumption expenditure, gross domestic private investment, government purchase of goods and services, net foreign investment are added to get GNP or NI.

5. According to the second approach all the factor incomes are added together.

6. National Income Estimates are very useful in formulating plans for all the sectors of the economy and it also helps in evaluating the achievements of the development targets laid down in the plans from the changes in national income and various components.

QUESTIONS

1. Explain the concept of National Income.
2. What are the different methods of measuring national income?
3. Explain the following concepts:
    (i) Gross National Product,
    (ii) National Income,
    (iii) Disposable Personal Income,
    (iv) Real Income and National Income.
4. Explain the importance of National Income Analysis to business people.
5. Explain the various concepts of National Income.
6. What are the various methods of meaning National Income. Explain.
7. What are the difficulties involved in measurement of National Income.
5. Define Personal Disposable Income.
6. Explain different methods of measurement of national income.
7. Gross National Product.
8. State the practical difficulties involved in the measurement of national income.
9. Define: (a) GDP, (b) GNP and (c) National Income.

19 Chapter

Macro Economic Policies and Balance of Payments

Macro economics deals with the economy as a whole in terms of total consumption, total production, growth and other aggregate aspects. In this chapter, concepts like fiscal policy and monetary policy are discussed.

1. FISCAL POLICY

Meaning and Importance

Fiscal policy refers to the policy of the government regarding public revenue, public expenditure and public debt. Fiscal policy tells the methods adopted by the government to earn revenue, to spend it and manage the deficit. It engulfs the field of public finance, money and banking.

Prior to the Great Depression of the 1930s, governments all over the world (particularly in capitalist countries) played a passive role in economic activities. This concept of *'laissez-faire'* (non-interference of the government in economic activities) proved to be disastrous and had to be given up. The notion of 'Welfare State' was accepted by most governments. It was realised that the governments should actively involve themselves in economic activities to bring about economic growth and equality, through the adoption of appropriate fiscal policies. Today, fiscal policies of the government are used as powerful tools of public policy to achieve the goal of welfare state.

The popularity of the fiscal policy since 1930s, according to Edward Shapiro, was due to the following factors:

(i) The failure of monetary policy in dealing with severe unemployment resulting from the Great Depression.

(ii) The influence of Keynes' 'new economics' with its emphasis on aggregate demand.

(iii) The increasing importance of public expenditure and taxation on the economy's total income and output.

Economists became increasingly aware of the growing disparities in economic conditions and maladjustments between consumption, production and distribution. The realised that the government should adopt appropriate policies to change, shape and direct the economic activities. Keynes believed that the government could raise or lower aggregate demand through appropriately designed policies relating to government spending, taxes and purchases.

Modern economists believe that the fiscal policy can be used to change aggregate demand in a such way and to such an extent that contributes to economic stabilization, especially in a developing economy. Where there is chronic unemployment of human resources and low rates of investment, fiscal policy can play a very important role. Its aim should be to promote the highest possible rate of capital formation without inflation.

> *Fiscal policy refers to a policy under which government uses its expenditure and revenue programmes to produce desirable effects and avoid underrirable effects on the national income, production and employment.*

2. OBJECTIVES OF FISCAL POLICY

The main objectives of fiscal policy in developed economies are, attainment of full employment and maintenance of economic stability. However, in developing economies, fiscal policy aims at increasing the rate of investment, reducing inequalities in income and wealth, reducing the levels of unemployment and controlling inflationary tendencies.

The above mentioned objectives are discussed in detail in the following paragraphs.

(i) Attaining Full Employment

An increase in government expenditure pushes up aggregate demand and through the multiplier effect, there would be multiple increase in national income and employment. The objective of full employment is achievable given a sufficient increase in aggregate demand. The fiscal policy should be designed so as to increase aggregate demand by increasing public expenditure and reducing taxes.

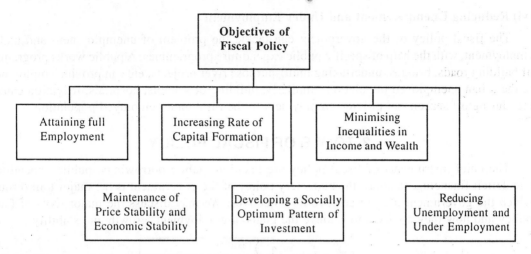

(ii) Maintenance of Price Stability and Economic Stability

Fiscal policies of the government should be framed in a such a manner as to counteract the cyclical fluctuations i.e., booms and depressions. During a depression, the appropriate fiscal policy would be to increase public expenditure and decrease tax rates. On the contrary, if there are inflationary pressures in the economy, the appropriate policy would be to reduce public expenditure and increase taxes, thereby reducing purchasing power in the hands of the people. This will help in achieving price and economic stability.

(iii) Increasing the Rate of Capital Formation

In a developing country where the level of income and employment are very low, the fiscal policy must aim at increasing the rate of investment. This can be done by restricting consumption and pushing up the incremental having ratio. The government tries to achieve this through taxation and public borrowing.

But in a developing economy where incomes are low, raising revenue through direct taxes is very low. The government may have to resort to indirect taxes.

The second measure of raising resources through public borrowings has earned increasing importance in recent times. This is because both institutions as well as people who invest in government securities hope to receive incomes while their savings remain secure.

(iv) Developing a Socially Optimum Pattern of Investment

A socially optimum pattern of investment varies from country to country. In some countries, fiscal policy may have to aim at producing investment in social and economic overheads like transport, communication, power plants etc. In some other countries, investment in basic and heavy industries may come under the category of socially optimum investment.

(v) Minimising Inequalities in Income and Wealth

In order to reduce disparities in distribution of income and wealth, the government may design a tax structure which is progressive in nature. The indirect taxes should be heavy on luxury goods and light on necessary goods. As regards public expenditure, the government can undertake welfare activities like free medical, education, housing facilities, etc. to the poorer section of the population. Thus, by a sensible blend of tax policies and public expenditure policies, the government can minimise the inequalities of income and wealth.

(vi) Reducing Unemployment and Under Employment

The fiscal policy of the government can tackle the problem of unemployment and under-employment, with the help of specific public expenditure programmes. A public works programme of building roads, bridges, undertaking multi-purpose river projects, etc can provide employment to the urban unemployed population. Similarly, building of schools, hospitals, irrigation canals, etc. during off season can provide employment to the rural under employed population.

3. TOOLS OF FISCAL POLICY

The chief instruments of fiscal policy are taxation, public borrowings, public expenditure and deficit financing. In short, the budgetary policy of the government is the major tool through which the government tries to achieve its objectives. We may discuss the major tools of fiscal policy and how they are used to achieve the goals of employment, growth and stability.

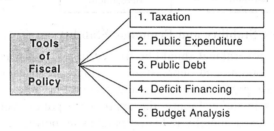

(i) Taxation

A suitable tax policy can act as an important tool in bringing about economic stability. Changes in tax rates bring about changes in the disposable incomes and levels of consumption of the people. During inflation, an increase in the rates of existing taxes and introduction of new taxes will reduce purchasing power and demand and thereby prices in the economy. During depression, a reduction in the tax burden will stimulate consumption and investment.

(ii) Public Expenditure

Public spending is another major tool of fiscal policy, which has far-reaching effects on income, output and employment in the economy. Whenever private investment is insufficient, the government should spend enough to fill the deflationary gap and restore full employment. On the other hand, if private investment is inflationary, the government should spend less so as to wipe out the inflationary gap. Thus, public expenditure can bring about an equilibrium between savings and actual investment.

Public spending is specially important in those areas where private sector is neither willing nor has the resources to invest. Therefore, the responsibility of building necessary infrastructure such as power generation, development of transport and communication, investment in basic and heavy industries etc. has to be borne by the government. This requires huge public expenditure and is called 'compensatory spending.'

Sometimes, public expenditure is necessary to correct temporary mal-adjustments in the economy and to make it work smoothly. This helps the economy to have a continuous flow of economic activity and is called 'pump priming' method of public expenditure.

In modern times, the state has to fulfil certain social obligations such as free public health services, educational facilities, old age pensions, subsidies to the farming sector, etc. Therefore, additional public expenditure has to be incurred towards the provision of these facilities.

(iii) Public Debt

Public borrowing is another important tool of fiscal policy through which the government raises loans from the public either in the form of voluntary loan or compulsory loan. Public borrowing and repayment can be used as an effective scheme to fight inflation and depression respectively. The government has to keep two things in mind while borrowing. The burden of public debt should be kept low and it should be done in those sections of the community who keep idle funds. The necessity to raise public loans arises often to help the government in the development process and build up the repaying capacity of public authorities.

(iv) Deficit Financing (forced saving)

Forced saving or deficit financing is a new weapon in the armoury of fiscal policy. In advanced countries, deficit financing occurs whenever there is an excess of public expenditure over revenues receipts. In other words, it involves the filling of budgetary gaps through loans. In developing countries, deficit financing literally means printing of more currency by the central bank and putting it into circulation.

During times of depression, deficit financing could be used by the government to increase its public expenditure by initiating public works programmes. This would lead to an expansion in employment, consumption and investment and would in turn lead to further rise in employment income and consumption. In modern times, it is being increasingly realised that deficit financing can be used to reduce the intensity of business cycles and to deal with the problem of secular stagnation. These two tasks come within the purview of the 'compensatory fiscal policy.'

(v) Budget Analysis

Budget is an important fiscal tool which helps the government to fight inflation and depression and stabilise the economy. Various budgetary principles have been advocated from time to time. The 'managed compensatory budget policy' is considered to be the best fiscal policy in modern times. This policy consists in deliberately managing the budget to adjust public revenues, expenditure and debts in such a way so as to achieve full employment without inflation. According to this principle, if the economy shows signs of stagnation, the budget should take up compensatory spending and it should be a deficit budget. On the other hand, if there is inflation, a surplus budget is welcome. We should forget about balancing the budget as a separate goal.

4. LIMITATIONS OF FISCAL POLICY

Implementing the fiscal policies effectively has certain limitations and practical problems.

(i) Whenever legislative sanctions are required to bring about changes in tax structure, there may be administrative delays in implementing fiscal policies.

(ii) Effective implementation of fiscal policy involves accurately forecasting the future course of business cycles which is extremely difficult.

(iii) Existence of time lags between the initiation of the fiscal measure and realization of its impact reduces the effectiveness.

(iv) An increase in public investment may be followed by a decline in private investment.

(v) The fiscal policies may be inadequate in dealing with run away inflations and deep depressions.

5. MONETARY POLICY

Monetary policy refers to the measures adopted by the central bank of a country to control the money supply to achieve the objectives of general economic policy. According to R.P.Kent, monetary policy is *'the management of the expansion and contraction of the volume of money in circulation for the explicit purpose of attaining a specific objective such as full employment.'* In other words, monetary policy refers to those measures adopted by the central banking authorities to manipulate the various instruments of credit control which are at its disposal generally and both monetary and credit policies and clubbed together under th heading of 'monetary policy.'

Monetary policy can be defined as *"all monetary decisions and measures irrespective of whether their aims are monetary or non monetary, and all non-monetary decisions and measures that aim at affecting the monetary system"*

6. OBJECTIVES OF MONETARY POLICY

There have been changes in the objectives of monetary policy from time to time and they also vary from country to country. Sometimes, the monetary policy adopted by a country may have different objectives which are conflicting. In such cases, the country may have to compromise by setting definite priorities.

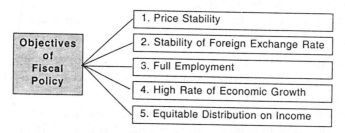

Some of the major objectives of monetary policy may be discussed below:

(i) Price Stability

The 'Great Depression' of 1930s made all countries of the world realize the importance of price stability as the primary objective of monetary policy. When prices rise, the fixed income group gets adversely affected and when prices fall, the producers and businessmen get affected. It is now argued that price stability ensures steady growth in production and employment.

But price stability should not be confused with constant price level. There is a general consensus among economists that a mild inflation is consistent with price stability and that the slowly rising price level is really conducive for economic growth. The problem is to determine the rate of inflation that is 'safe'.

(ii) Stability of Foreign Exchange Rate

This is one of the traditional objectives of the monetary policy. When countries were on the gold standard, the aim of the monetary authorities was to regulate credit in such a way as to minimise fluctuations in foreign receipts and payments and thereby protect gold reserves. With the fall of the gold standard exchange rate, stability no more remains an important objective of monetary policy.

Today, most countries aim at maintaining a reasonable balance in their balance of payments. Accordingly, deliberate changes in exchange rates are now often resorted to in an effort to correct disequilibrtium in the balance of payments.

(iii) Full Employment

Since the Great Depression and after the publication of Keynes 'General Theory', the objective of full employment has gained importance. The monetary policy should aim at solving the unemployment problem by expanding consumption and investment expenditure. In order to increase the volume of investment, borrowings have to be stimulated by following the cheap money policy. This will increase the level of employment through the multiplier-acceleration effect. Once the level of full employment level, by equating savings and investment. If at any time, investment exceeds savings, there is the danger of inflation setting in. On the contrary, if investment falls short of saving, the economy may experience deflation and therefore, maintenance of full employment automatically ensures price stability.

In developing countries like India, since there is an imbalance between the supply of labour and supply of other resources like land capital etc., full employment of labour is unfeasible. Therefore, such countries have to aim at 'optimum employment' instead of full employment in order to ensure highest national income.

(iv) High Rate of Economic Growth

The concept of economic growth implies a qualitative and quantitative increase in the volume of goods and services produced in the economy. For this purpose, the government in developing countries through their monetary policy are trying to ensure adequate provision of credit for productive purposes. A large number of branches of commercial banks have been set up in the rural areas, and special institutions for providing credit to industries have been started in the urban areas.

The monetary policy in these countries allows money supply to slightly exceed the demand for money so that there is a small increase in price which is conducive for economic growth. However, this policy carries the inherent danger of giving rise to inflationary pressure in the economy.

(v) Equitable Distribution of Income

As regards this objective of achieving a more equitable distribution on income and wealth, fisal policy is supposed to be more effective. But in recent times, the monetary policy is playing a 'supportive role' to fisal policy in this respect. The credit policy can be organised in such a way as to provide more credit to the poor and needy, to help them purchase produtive assets. Such a policy will also help in tackling the problems of unemployment and poverty.

7. TOOLS OF MONETARY POLICY

In order to regulate credit in the economy, the central bank uses certain well known weapons which can be generally classified into:

    (i) General or Quantitative and

    (ii) Selective or Qualitative Methods of Credit Control

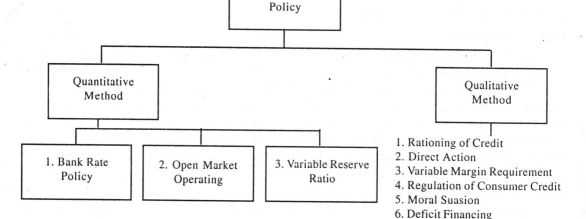

(i) General or Quantitative Methods of Credit Control

General methods are used to control the quantum of credit in general throughout the economy rather than the use of credit. The effects of general methods are all pervading and affect the whole economy indiscriminately, as a result of which even the productive investments would be hard-hit whenever there is credit contraction.

The three important general methods are discussed below:

(a) Bank Rate Policy

This is the oldest method of credit control first used by the Bank of England in 1839.

Bank rate refers to the rate of interest at which the Central Bank rediscounts approved bills of exchange. This policy works under the assumption that all other interest rates in the market invariably respond to changes in the bank rate. In a developed money market, this kind of relationship between bank rate and other market rates exist. Therefore whenever the Central Bank raises the bank rate (also known as dear money policy), all other interest rates rise and borrowings become less attractive and this results in contraction attractive and this results in the contraction of credits. A reduction in bank rate (also known as cheap money policy) on the other hand, reduces all other market rates of interest, thereby making borrowings more attractive and resulting in the expansion of credit.

Limitations of Bank Rate Policy:

(1) The effectiveness of bank rate policy depends on how far the commercial banks rely on the Central Bank for obtaining financial accommodation. Since most of the modern commercial banks have succeeded in becoming financially self-reliant, this method has failed to exercise the necessary control over the lending policy of commercial banks.

(2) In modern times, the required flexibility in the money market is lacking. As such, not only savings and investment but also the quantity of money and credit do not show adequate responses to bank rate.

(3) In most countries, a large, private market for reserve loans has emerged, which has succeeded in acquiring control over massive financial resources.

(4) Development of alternative and more effetive methods of credit control have emerged in recent years, rendering the bank rate policy ineffective.

(b) Open Market operations

Open market operations refer to the buying and selling of government and other securities (in which it deals) by the Central Bank. This method exercises direct influence on the supply of money in circulation and the cash reserves of the commercial banks. Whenever the central bank sells securities, it intends to contract the quantity of money and credit by absorbing the purchasing power in the hands of the public. At the same time, it manages to reduce the cash reserves of the commercial banks and thereby reduce their capacity to create credit. On the other hand, whenever the central banks want to expand credit, it purchases securities. This will immediately put money into circulation, the cash reserves of the commercial banks will also go up thereby increasing their power to create credit.

Limitations of Open Market Operations

Although open market operations are one of the most widely used methods, it suffers from certain limitations:

(i) The effectiveness of this method depends to a great extent on the demand for and supply of government securities through which these operations are done. Many times, it so happens that when the central bank sells securities, the demand for them may be very less or non-existent. Under such circumstances, the Central Bank fails to exert the necessary influence on bank reserves and thus on their capacity to create credit. Conversely, when the central bank wants to purchase securities, it may find the supply of securities inadequate. Consequently, it cannot improve the supply of money and credit in the economy.

(ii) Open market operations become ineffective during times of depression when there is very little demand for credit by the borrowers for purposes of investment. During such times when the Central Bank purchases securities, only the liquidity position of commercial banks will improve without leading to expansion of credit in the economy.

(iii) Sometimes, this method may be rendered ineffective when people use hoarded money or income received from abroad, to purchase the securities. In such cases, the necessary impact on the reserves of commercial banks may not occur.

(iv) Lastly, the success of this method depends on the existence of a well developed money and capital markets in the economy. In many developing countries, the securities market is relatively underdeveloped. thus the Central Banks of these countries do not have sufficient securities with them to conduct open market operations.

(c) Variable Statutory Reserve Ratio

The Central Bank of a country enjoys the power to determine the statutory cash reserve requirements of the commercial banks. Under this policy, the Central Bank requires the commercial banks to maintain a certain percentage of their demand and time deposits as reserves.

An increase in the reserve requirements, implies that banks will be able to support lesser amounts of demand deposits. This will reduce the funds available for loans and hence lead to a reduction in credit. For example, if the banking system has Rs.6,000 crores in total reserves and the legal reserve requirement is 8%, then the banking system can support Rs.5,520 crores of demand deposits. Let us suppose that legal reserve requirement is raised to 9%. Now the banking system will be able to support only Rs.5,460 crores.

Conversely, a decline in reserve requirements will imply that banks are now required to hold less reserves to support the existing amount of demand deposits. This means that the banks will now have excess reserves and this will help them to create more credit.

(ii) Selective or Qualitative Methods of Credit control

The selective methods of credit control as distinguished from general methods are directed towards particular users of credit. They operate by means of official regulations issued and enforced by the Central Bank. They aim at curtailing the flow of credit into unproductive channels and diverting them into productive channels of the economy.

Some of the important methods of selective credit control are:

(a) Rationing of Credit

The Central Bank may issue directions to commercial banks to restrict (ration) credit to certain sectors or sections of the population. This method is particularly useful in controlling inflationary pressures.

(b) Direct Action

This refers to forceful measures adopted against those commercial banks which have committed errors. The puritive measures used here are denial of re-discounting facility, charging penalty, fixation of quantitative credit ceiling etc.

(c) Variable Margin Requirements

This measure is used to thwart speculation and hoarding activities by traders. For instance, if traders hoard necessary commodities like foodgrains in an attempt to create artificial scarcity and thereby push up prices, then the Central Bank can raise margin requirements with respect to such goods. If the margin requirement is 50%, then the trader can get a loan of only Rs.10 lakhs against a security of Rs.20 lakhs. If the margin requirements is raised to 75%, he can get a loan of only Rs.5 lakhs against the same security.

(d) Regulation of Consumer Credit

This measure is resorted to only under severe inflationary conditions in an effort to restrict consumer demand for credit. For example, credit given for the purchase of consumer durables may be charged very high rates of interest to discourage borrowing for this purpose by the consumer. This results in a fall in demand and thereby a fall in the prices of these goods.

(e) Moral Suasion

This is a measure used by the Central Bank to put pressure upon the lending activities of commercial banks by urging them to voluntarily adopt certain restrictive practices.

(f) Deficit Financing

Deficit financing is a method adopted to cover the budgetary gap by resorting to loans from the banks in developed countries. However, in developing countries, resort is made to the Central Bank which merely prints more notes to cover the deficit.

In whatever way it is defined, deficit financing results in an increase in the level of expenditure of the community because it involves an increase in total money supply. Since there is creation of new money, it almost invariably results in inflation and as a result of deficit financing, the purchasing power in the hands of the people increases, but the production of goods does not increase simultaneously.

8. LIMITATIONS OF MONETARY POLICY

As pointed out by Anthony S.Campagna, 'untimeliness is one of the risks of the operation of monetary policy, and that risk is increased, the longer the lag between policy and response.'

(i) There is usually a noticeable time lag between recognition of the 'need' for action, which is by way of monetary policy, and actual implementation of the policy decision. Such lags occur due to the simple reason that monetary authorities can only alter the money market conditions, but it is the other economic units like firms, consumers, government etc. that must alter their plans keeping in view the changed money market conditions. Adding to this is the unreliability of forecasts, generally at a particular point of time, some sectors of the economy will be expanding while others may be contracting. Thus, it is very difficult to determine just where the economy is operating.

(ii) In recent years, the participation of a large number of financial intermediaries in money and capital markets and over which the Central Bank has no control, has rendered the monetary policies ineffective.

(iii) Sometimes, the Central Bank is faced with contradictory objectives particularly in the case of developing countries - for instance, attainment of economic growth and stability are the twin objectives of monetary policy. but the attainment of one may be possible only at the cost of the other. Economic growth requires a continuous but low rate of rise in price-level in the order to keept he inducement to invest active.

But, often mild inflationary trends tend to develop into severe inflationary pressures and thus may come in the way of economic stability.

(iv) The most serious limitations of monetary policy arises from the fact that the money and capital markets are under-developed and unorganised. This makes it very difficult for the government to expand or contract money supply or to raise or lower the costs of borrowing in the private sector.

(v) Lastly, the ineffectiveness of the instruments of credit control which have already been discussed, limit the success of monetary policies.

9. BALANCE OF PAYMENTS

Meaning

The balance of payments of a country is a systematic record of all international economic transactions of that country during a given period, usually a year.

Balance of payments accounting of any country uses a double entry system of recording accounts with the rest of the world. Thus, the balance of payments account is divided into transactions giving rise to payments (or debit) and receipts (or credit). In the accounting sense, thus, the balance of payments of a country must always be in balance. In other words, the balance of payments as a whole must necessarily balance. This means the total receipts of a country are necessarily equal to its total payments, if receipts include not only the volume of goods exported but also the volume of gold or other monetary reserves exported in order to obtain purchasing power over that part of imports which is not covered by normal commercial exports.

In other words, debit or payment side of the balance of payments account of a country represents the total of all the uses made out of the total foreign exchange acquired by the country during a given period, while the credit or receipts side represents the sources from which this foreign exchange was acquired by this country in the same period. The two sides as such necessarily balance. If in the actual balance of payments account the credits and debits do not balance, the balance is usually achieved by adding an item called error and omissions.

> *The balance of payment refers to the relation between the payments of all kinds made by a country to the rest of the world and its receipts from all other countries. BOP includes both visible and invisible items and it consists of two accounts-current account and capital account.*

10. STRUCTURE OF BALANCE OF PAYMENTS

A balance of payments statement is tabulated to summarise a nation's total economic transactions undertaken on the international trade account. It is usually composed of two sections: (i) the current account and (ii) the capital account.

(i) Current account mainly consists of two sub-groups: merchandise or the trade account and the invisible account.

In the trade or merchandise account, only the transaction relating to goods are entered. That is, all goods exported and imported are recorded in the trade account.

The invisible account usually compirses the services account and the gifts or charities account. The services account records all the services rendered and received by residents of the nation. It consists of such item as banking and insurance charges, interest on loans, tourist expenditure, transport charges etc. Simiarly, the gifts or charities account consists of all those items which are received or given away free by residents of the nation. It may be in kind or in cash. It goes without saying that these are all referred to as invisible transactions in the balance of payments theory and therefore recorded in the invisible account. It is interesting to note here that the International Monetary Fund (IMF) includes the following items as invisible transaction:

(i) International transportation of goods, including warehousing while in transit and other transit expenses.

(ii) Travel for reasons of business, education, health, international conventions or pleasure.

(iii) Insurance premiums and payments of claims.

(iv) Investment income, including interest, rents, dividends and profits.

(v) Miscellaneous service items such as advertising, commissions, film rental, pensions, patent fees, royalties, subscription to periodicals and membership fees.

(vi) Donations, migrant remittances legacies.

(vii) Repayment of commercial credits.

(viii) Contractual amortisation and depreciation of direct investments.

(ii) Capital account, on the other hand, deals with payments of debts and claims. It consists of all such items as may be employed in financing both imports and exports, namely, private balances, assistance by the international institutional agencies and specie flow, and balances held on government account. Accordingly, we shall have private capital account, international institutional capital account, species account, and government capital account. Balances in these accounts may rise or fall from year to year, depending upon the movements or fluctuations in other items on capital account.

Items of balance of payments account may thus be summarised in Table 1.

It should be noted that the two accounts - current and capital - in the balance of payments should necessarily balance. The surplus in the trade or current account must be equal to the deficit in the capital account or the deficit in the current account.

For instance, if India is importing more goods than its exports of goods and services to the foreigners, it will have a deficit in its current balance of payments. This she will have to pay either by gold and other assets or by borrowing from other countries. These are credit items in the capital account of the balance of payments. Therefore, the current and capital accounts together will balance each other.

Current Account	Capital Accounts

1. Merchandise - Exports and Imports
  (a) Private
  (b) Government
2. Non-monetary gold movement
3. Foreign travel
4. Transportation
5. Insurance
6. Government, not included elsewhere
7. Investment income
8. Miscellaneous
9. Transfer payment
  (a) Official
  (b) Private
Total Current Transactions
Error and Omissions
	1. Private (non-banking) loan
	  (a) Long - term
	  (b) Short - term
	2. Banking (excluding Central Bank)
	3. Official (including Central Bank)
	  (a) Loans
	  (b) Amortisation
	  (c) Miscellaneous
	  (d) Reserves (including changes in the foreign
	      exchange assets of the Central Bank)
	
	Total Capital and Monetary Gold

Balance of Payments and Balance of Trade

There is a marked distinction between the concepts of balance of trade and balance of payments. Balance of payments is a wider concept than the balance of trade. In fact, balance of payment includes in its structure, the notion of balance of trade.

As we know, a country may export and import many items, both visible and invisible. Balance of trade refers only to the value of imports and exports of goods, i.e., visible items because it is an open trade between the countries and can be easily certified by the customs official. On the other hand, balance of trade is only a partial study of the balance of payments. It simply refers to the difference between the value of visible exports and visible imports.

This is what is represented in the trade or merchandise account section of the current account in the balance of payments statement. Thus, balance of trade is nothing but a major component of the balance of trade or merchandise account. The invisible account which is again composed of services sector and gifts and charities account comprising varieties of invisible items, plus the record of capital account.

Balance of Payments Always Balances

Since the balance of payments statement is drawn up in terms of debits and credits based on a system of double-entry book-keeping, if all the entries are made correctly, total debits must equal total credits. This is because two aspects (debits and credits) of each transaction recorded are equal in amount but appear on the opposite sides of the balance of payments account. In this account sense, balance of payments of a country must always balance.

In other words, debit or payment side of the balance of payments account of a country represents the total of all uses made out of the total foreign exchange acquired by the country during a given period, while the credit or receipts side represents the sources from which this foreign exchange was acquired by this country in the same period. The sides as such necessarily balance.

It should be noted that the two accounts - current and capital - in the balance of payments should necessarily balance. The surplus of the trade or current account must be equal to the deficit in the capital account or the deficit in the current account must be equal to the surplus in the capital accounts. Thus, the balance of current account need not be equal but can show a surplus or a deficit. There is, however, a corresponding surplus in the balance of capital account. As a result, the credit and debit sides of the balance of payments are exactly balanced.

To illustrate the point, an imaginary account of a country's balance of payments is represented in the following table:

Country's Balance of Payments Account			
Credit (Receipts)		**Debit (Payments)**	
I) Current Transactions			
	Rs. Crores		Rs. Crores
1. Merchandise trade (goods exported)	2000	1. Merchandise trade (goods imported)	4000
2. Services exported	1000	2. Services imported	1000
3. Income from foreign investment	3000	3. Foreign income from investment at home	1500
4. Unilateral receipts	500	4. Unilateral payment	500
Sub Total	*6500*	*Sub Total*	*7000*
II Capital Transactions			
5. Long-term borrowings	1500	5. Long term lending	1000
6. Short term borrowings	1000	6. Short term lending	500
7. Sale of gold / assets	1000	7. Purchase of gold / assets	1400
Sub Total	*3500*	*Sub Total*	*2900*
		Errors and omissions	100
Grand Total	**10000**	**Grand Total**	**10000**

As already stated, the balance of the current account need not be equal but can show a surplus or a deficit. In the table, the balance of current account shows a deficit of Rs.500 crores. However, there is a corresponding surplus of Rs.500 crores in the balance of capital account. As a result, the credit and debit sides of the Balance of Payments Account are balanced.

11. DISEQUILIBRIUM IN THE BALANCE OF PAYMENTS

Although in the accounting sense, the balance of payments accounts must balance, it need not be in equilibrium. Suppose a country's balance of payments shows a deficit in the current account, its credit balance in the capital account must be large enough so that total debits equal total credits. In other words, when a country is facing a deficit in the current account, it has to either borrow capital on a short term as long term, or it has to export gold or receive donations from foreigners so that its credit in the capital account is equal to the extent of its deficit in the current account.

Hence, we may simply consider the balance of payments as the difference between receipts from the payments to foreigners by the residents of the country. A country's balance of payments is said to be in disequilibrium when there is either a 'surplus' (favourable) or 'deficit' (unfavourable) in the balance of payment. A country enjoys a 'surplus' balance of payments when total receipts exceeds total payments. Conversely, a country's balance of payments is said to be unfavourable when total payments exceeds total receipts in a particular year.

Causes of Disequilibrium

A country may experience a disequilibrium (either surplus or deficit) in its balance of payments either for a short period or for a long period. The nature and intensity of disequilibrium vary from country to country. The following are some of the important causes producing a disequilibrium in a country's balance of payments:

(i) Business cycles or trade cycles may cause cyclical disequilibrium.

(ii) Structural disequilibrium may be caused when heavy investment programmes are undertaken by developing countries. Three countries tend to import capital goods for rapid industrialization while they may not be in a position to export much because they are basically primary producing countries and also because domestic requirements may increase.

(iii) Structural disequilibrium may also be caused due to increasing self reliance on the part of both advanced countries and also poor nations. The advanced countries have become self-reliant in food stuffs, raw materials etc., thus, affecting the export of poor agrarian countries. Similarly, the advanced countries are also experiencing a decline in their export due to the tendency of poor countries to become self-reliant in manufactured goods.

(iv) Rapid growth of population leading to inrease in imports and decrease in the capacity to export may cause disequilibrium in the balance of payments, especially of developing countries.

12. CAUSES FOR DISEQUILIBRIUM IN INDIA'S BOP

Since the inception of economic planning era in 1951, India has been facing the problem of BOP deficits. The major factors which are responsible for the disequilibrium in the BOP are as follows:

1. Sharp increase in the imports is the major cause for deficit in the balance of payments. The value of total imports in 2003-2004 stood at $58233 million. This was mainly due to import of machinery on a large scale.

2. Slow growth rate of Exports when compared with the growth rate of imports is another reason for the deficit in India's BOP.

3. Rapid growth of population has reduced the exportable surplus of our country and also resulted in more imports.

4. Introduction of substitute products in the International market by the developed nations like synthetic jute, rubber, fibres etc., has reduced our exports.

5. The International **oil crisis** has led to increase in the price of crude oil, petroleum and its products. On an average the price of oil has increased by about 300% which has resulted in a phenomenal rise in India's import hill.

6. Increased expenditure on servicing of foreign loans is another major cause for the deficit in India's BOP.

7. Due to demonstration effect, the people in India tend to initiate the consumption pattern of the developed countries resulting in disequilibrium in BOP.

8. The terms of trade for Indian goods have sharply reduced in recent years. The decline in net terms of trade was about 25% during the last 2 decades.

9. Due to unfavourable climatic conditions, India is forced to import to meet the acute shortage in the foodgrain production.

Apart from the above mentioned factors, other factors like political conditions prevailing in the country, international capital movements, changes in foreign exchange rates, etc. also cause disequilibrium in India's Balance of Payments.

Measures for Correcting Disequilibrium

Disequilibrium in the balance of payments may be corrected either through monetary or through non-monetary measures.

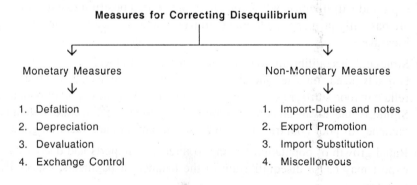

Measures for Correcting Disequilibrium

Monetary Measures	Non-Monetary Measures
1. Defaltion	1. Import-Duties and notes
2. Depreciation	2. Export Promotion
3. Devaluation	3. Import Substitution
4. Exchange Control	4. Miscelloneous

(a) The following **monetary measures** may be used:

(i) Deflation

Deflation refers to the contraction in the volume of the home currency which would result in a fall in prices, and rise in the value of the home currency. When prices fall, exports become cheaper and imports become costlier. Thus, the volume of exports increase and volume of imports decrease and the disequilibrium (deficit) would be set right.

(ii) Depreciation

When the rate of exchanges of one country falls in terms of another country, it is called 'exchange depreciation.' suppose 1 Re = 60 pence and India experiences an adverse balance of payments with regard to British pounds, then the demand for the British pound will rise. This results in a rise in the value of pound in terms of the rupee. To correct the disequilibrium, the rate of exchange of the Indian rupee in terms of pound has to be depreciated from 1 Re = 60 pence to 1 Re = 40 pence. This makes Indian goods cheaper for Britain and British goods become costlier for India. This encourages India clearing the deficit in the Balance of Payments (BoP).

This method works automatically and is suitable to correct a mild disequilibrium. This method can be successful only through the co-operation of foreign countries, which should not retaliate by depreciating their currencies as well. Moreover, depreciation may initiate inflationary pressures due to an increase in money incomes and rise in domestic prices.

(iii) Devaluation

Devaluation refers to the deliberate reduction in the external value of a country's currency in relation to the currencies of all countries or in terms of gold or in relation to the currencies of selected countries.

This is an extreme measure resorted to by the government to correct a serious and fundamental disequilibrium in the balance of payments. The direct and immediate effect of devaluation is stimulation of exports and reduction in imports. The distinction between devaluation and depreciation is that the former implies an official and deliberate reduction in external value of the currency announced by the government whereas the latter stands for automatic reduction in the external value of the country's currency brought about by market forces.

Devaluation will be successful only if the demand for imports and exports is fairly elastic. There should also be no change in the cost price structure in the devaluing country. Again, the foreign countries have to fully co-operate with the devaluing country by not raising their import duties or giving export concessions or by devaluing their own currency so as to multiply the favourable effects of devaluation to the country under consideration.

(iv) Exchange Control

Another effective method of correcting disequilibrium used by governments is exchange control.

According to this method, the foreign exchange earned by the exporters have to be surrendered to the Central Bank, which will in turn be distributed among the licensed importers. This helps in controlling the volume of imports and keeping it within the limits of export earnings.

But exchange control is only a temporary measure and not a permanent solution to correct a basic disequilibrium in the balance of payments.

The Non-Monetary Measures

(i) Import Duties and Quotas

In order to discourage imports, heavy import duties may be imposed especially on selected items of conspicuous consumption.

The government may sometimes fix quotas and thereby restrict the quantity of imports. This method can be used to eliminate or reduce the deficit in the balance of payments.

(ii) Export Promotion

The government may introduce policies and programmes which encourage exports, whenever the country is facing a deficit. Duties on exports may be reduced and incentives as well as subsidies may be given to exporting industries.

(iii) Import Substitution

It refers to the growing substitution of imported goods by encouraging indigenous production. By doing this the country can save its precious foreign exchange. For this purpose tax concessions and tax holidays shculd be provided to such industries.

(iv) Miscellaneous

(a) Government by promoting tourism particularly foreign tourists to visit the country, it can earn foreign exchange and thereby reduce the deficit in the balance of payments.

(b) Government can encourage the production and sale of handicrafts, particularly to foreigners.

(c) Government can attract investment from Non-Resident Indians.

(d) Government can also borrow loans from foreign banks or foreign governments to reduce the deficit in the balance of payments.

(e) Government can also sell or pledge its gold and silver in international market to meet its deficit in the BOP.

13. INDIA'S BALANCE OF PAYMENTS SINCE 1990s

India witnessed some major changes in its Balance of payments position since 1990. The 1990 decade started with the crisis BOP and it continued for next 2 years. India faced severe crisis in its BOP only during 1991-92 and 1992-93. Then its BOP started recovering.

By the beginning of 1990s India's BOP was vulnerable to external shocks. The foreign exchange reserve decreased. But deficit in the trade was offset by a rising surplus on the invisible items. The earnings from tourism and remittances from NRIs helped to solve the problem to a little extent. The oil crisis of 1990s due to Gulf war and subsequent rise in crude oil price and petroleum products. The balance of payments condition became deteriorated. Following the Gulf crisis, Government of India resorted to substantial with drawals from the IMF from 1990-91 onwards under one or other schemes. India withdrew Rs.3,394 crore from the Fund in 1990-91 to meet its deficit under compensatory and contingency financing facility (CCFF). In 1991-92, the withdrawal was Rs.3,205 crore. Under the standby arrangement with the Fund, India received Rs.2,077 crore in 1991-92 and Rs.3,363 crore in 1992-93.

Added to the oil crisis, India also faced the problem of large outflows during the same period. This happened during 1990-1992 as the international confidence in India's abilities was shaken leading to a downgrading of India's credit rating. Dr.BimalJalan then Governor RBI, has estimated that there was a net erosion of Rs.6,000 crore in receipts from NRI deposits and commercial banks during the 18 month period from July 1990 to December 1991. During this period the government also resorted to a policy of import liberalisation and industrial liberalisation. This resulted in sharp growth of imports which could not be supported by our own exports, other receipts and normal aid flows. In turn they had to be financed by commercial borrowings or other borrowings on stiffer terms. Jalan has correctly pointed out in this juncture that, even this could be sustained only as long as the commercial borrowings were available. The Indian economy was plunged into a crisis as soon as these resources were dried up.

There was a decline in foreign exchange reserves to a low of $0.9 billion in January 1991. To overcome this situation cash margins were imposed by Government of India. It was raised to 133% in March 1991 and further to 200% in April 1991. Added to this RBI also imposed 25% surcharge on interest on bank advances for imports. Due to this imports dropped during 1991-92. India also had to pledge gold to overcome the crisis to the tune of 67 tons during May-July 1991.

The new government which was formed in June 1991 had taken initiative to overcome this crisis. it devalued India's currency twice in July 1991. After this, slowly the situation improved with the introduction of new economic policy announced by the government. There had been marked improvement in BOP with the introduction of liberalisation policy since 1991-92.

India's Balance of Payments: 1990-91 to 2002-03

						(US $ million)
Years	Trade Balance	Invisibles (Net)	Current Account (Net)	Capital Account Total (Net)	BOP as % GDP	Exports/ Imports (%)
1990-91	-9438	-242	-9680	8402	-3.1	66.2
1991-92	-2798	1620	-11.78	4754	0.3	86.7
1992-93	-5447	1921	-3526	4254	1.7	77.6
1993-94	-4056	2896	-1158	9882	0.4	84.8
1994-95	-9049	5680	-3369	8013	-1.0	74.8
1995-96	-11359	5449	-5910	2974	-1.7	74.0
1996-97	-14815	10196	-4619	10437	-1.2	69.7
1997-98	-15507	10007	-5500	9393	-1.4	69.7
1998-99	-13246	9208	-4038	7867	-1.0	72.1
1999-00	-17841	13143	-4698	10840	-1.1	69.1
2000-01	-14370	10780	-3590	9420	-0.5	75.8
2001-02	-12703	13485	782	10976	0.2	77.96
2002-03	-12910	17047	4137	12843	0.8	80.3

(**Source**: Government of India, Economic Survey, 2003-2004 (Delhi 2004) Table 6.2, p.101 and Table 6.3, p.102.)

BOP as percentage of GDP, India's current account deficit fell from the high of 3.1 per cent in 1990-91 to surplus of 0.8 per cent in 2002-2003. Balance of payments position improved considerably from 1993-94 onwards. During this year current account deficit was only 0.4 per cent of GDP and foreign exchange reserves were sufficient to cover the imports. There was an improvement even in the export sector during the same period. The exports recorded a growth of

20.2% on balance of payments while the imports increased only by 10.0%. Heading to a marked turn around in the balance of payments situation in 1993-94.

The situation in 1994-95 was also satisfactory. The foreign exchange reserve was sufficient to meet its 8.4 months imports. Current account deficit was only 1.0% of GDP. The balance of payment position situation in 1995-96 reflected a renewal of economic growth with an increase in current account deficit as a percentage of GDP to 1.7% from 1.0% in 1994-95. However from 1996-97 onwards balance of payments position of India is showing some improvement due to increase in exports by 4.01% and imports 5.99% when compared to that of 21.58% and 25.74% of exports and imports of the previous year. Steadily after that there was an improvement in the balance of payment position of India. It was verify comfortable in 1997-98. Both export and import growth rate slowed down. There was a good increase in the amount of net inflows due to sustained growth of software exports. Though capital account showed a surplus of $9393 million, the overall trade deficit on BOP basis increased from 3.7% of GDP in 1996-97 to 3.9% in 1997-98.

India's balance of payments position is gradually improving in recent years. The current account deficit was only 0.9% during 1999-2000 despite unfavourable international trade. This was possible because of increase in the growth of exports and net inflow of invisibles. In 2000-2001 India's balance of payments position remained comfortable. The current account deficit was brought down to 0.5% of GDP from 1.1% of HDP in 1999-2000. This was made possible due to improvement in the export performance and sustained buoyancy in invisible receipts.

In 2001-02 India's balance of payments experienced a mixed developments. The exports remained stagnant, while imports declined by 2.8%. This has lead to a decline in merchandise trade deficit from 3.1% GDP in 2000-01 to 2.6 per cent in 2001-02. After 24 years India experienced a surplus in balance of payments. Mainly due to increase in earnings from invisibles.

In 2002-2003 the exports incurred by 18% while imports increase only by 13.6% on BOP basis. Though there was a trade deficit to the tune of $12910 million, there was a strong positive earnings from invisible which has finally resulted in current account surplus of 0.8%.

Current Balance of Payments Position (2003-2004)

In recent years, India's balance of payments has been characterized by surplus in both the current and capital accounts. The current account surpluses in India's balance of payments in recent years are attributable to the expending invisibles surpluses. In the first three quarters of 2003-04, the trade deficit estimated at around US $15 billion was more than compensated by an invisible surplus of US $18.2 billion resulting in a positive current account balance of US $3.2 billion. The size of the invisibles surplus has increased by 60 per cent over the period 2000-01 to 2002-03. This was mainly due to high level of private transfers which exceeded the trade deficit in 2002-03 and fully financed it during April-December 2003-04. Even the contribution of non-factor services to the invisible amount has been steadily increasing since 2001-02 and it enhanced further in 2002-03. India's BOP is witnessing a growing trend (surplus) in recent years due to increase in net inflows software services, travel transportation etc. There is also a growth in the non-resident deposits, external commercial borrowings and foreign investment in India. All these enabled India to reduce its trade deficit and an improvement in balance of payments position.

SUMMARY

1. Fiscal policy refers to the policy of the government regarding public revenue, public expenditure and public debt. It tells the methods adopted by the government to earn revenue, to spend it and manage the deficit.

2. Objectives of fiscal Policy includes attaining full employment, maintenance of price stability and Economic stability, increasing the rate of capital formation, developing a socially optimum pattern of investment, minimising inequalities in income and wealth, and reducing unemployment and under employment.

3. Tools of Fiscal Policy includes taxation, public expenditure, public debt, deficit financing and budget.

4. Monetary policy refers to those measures adopted by the Central Banking authorities to manipulate the various instruments of credit control which are at its disposal.

5. Major objectives of monetary policy are: price stability, stability of foreign exchange rate, full employment, high rate of economic growth and equitable distribution of income.

6. Monetary policy uses 2 weapons namely (i) Quantitative methods or general (ii) Qualitative credit control methods or selective method.

7. Quantitative methods include bank rate policy, open market operations and variable reerve ratio.

8. Selective or qualitative methods include rationing of credit, direct action, variable margin requirements, regulation of consumer credit, moral suasion and deficit financing.

9. The balance of payments of a country is a systematic record of all international economic transactions of that country during a given period, usually a year.

10. Balance of payments is composed of two accounts: (i) the current account, and (ii) the capital account.

11. Balance of trade includes only visible items of export and import while balance of payment includes both visible and invisible items of export and import.

12. When there is disequilibrium in the balance of payments, it can be corrected either through monetary or through non-monetary measures.

QUESTIONS

1. What do you mean by Fiscal Policy? Distinguish between fiscal policy and Monetary Policy.
2. What are the objectives of fiscal policy?
3. Give an explanatory note on tools of fiscal policy.
4. What do you mean by monetary policy? Briefly explain the various objectives of monetary policy.
5. Distinguish between balance of trade and balance of payments. What information do you hope to get about the economic position of a country from its balance of payments?
6. Give an explanatory note on structure and components of balance of payments.
7. Explain the causes for disequilibrium on the balance of payments.
8. Explain the remedial measures adopted to correct the disequilibrium in balance of payments.
9. Explain the concept of Fiscal Discipline.
10. Differentiate between Balance of trade and Balance of payment.
11. List the usefulness of fiscal instruments.
12. What are the objectives of monetary policy?
13. What are the objectives of fiscal policy?
14. What is disinvestment scheme of Government?
15. Balance of payments.
16. What are the objectives of monetary policy?
17. What are the objectives and limitations of fiscal policy?

20 Chapter

Inflation

Inflation refers to a situation when there is a general rise in prices and a corresponding fall in the value of money. However, every increase in prices cannot be treated as inflation. Inflation is a persistent upward rise in the general prices level at a substantial rate that continues for a prolonged period of time. It results in deterioration in the value of money over a period of time.

Inflation occurs when the volume of money in circulation increases faster than the volume of goods and serives. When there is excess purchasing power in the hands of the people, it leads to persistent rise in demand for goods and services. If such an increase in demand cannot be met by an increase in production, prices begin to rise. Prices may also rise due to other factors such as rise in wages and profits.

Inflation is a monetary phenomenon. It is a major economic problem affecting both the developed and undeveloped countries of the world.

> *Inflation refers to a rise in the general level of prices and rate of inflation is the rate of change of general price level. Thus, inflation is not just high prices, it is rising prices; that is inflation is a process and not a state of prices.*

1. DEFINITIONS

Crowther defines inflation as "a state in which the value of money is falling. i.e., prices are rising.'

Prof. Coulbourn defines inflation as "... too much of money chasing too few goods."

Pigou states that , "Inflation is a situation in which the community's money income increases faster than its real income."

According to Prof. Samuelson, "Inflation occurs when the general level of prices and costs are rising."

According to Hawtrey, inflation is the "... issue of too much of currency."

It is clear from above definitions that inflation is a sustained rise in the general price level due to high rates of expansion in the aggregate money supply. Inflation occurs in a situation where increased demand is not met by corresponding increase in production or supply. The increase in the supply of money is the cause and rise in the price level is the effect.

Characteristics of Inflation

The following are the main characteristics of inflation:

 (i) Inflation is a long term operating dynamic process.

 (ii) It is a process of persistently rising price level.

 (iii) Inflation is a rising trend in the price level and not a cyclical movement.

 (iv) Inflation is endogenous to the economic system.

 (v) Inflation in the real sense, is a post-full employment phenomenon.

 (vi) Inflation is also a monetary phenomenon. It is usually characterised by an overflow of money and credit.

2. TYPES OF INFLATION

Inflation occurs in the economy due to increase in the money incomes of certain sections of the population without any equalant increase in their produtivity, giving rise to an increase in the aggregate demand for goods and services which cannot be met at current prices by the total available supply of goods and services in the country.

Inflation can be categorised based on the severity of it into the following types:

Creeping Inflation

When the prices rise by about 2% per year, it may be called "creeping inflation". In this kind of inflation, the annual rise in price is almost inperceptible. If creeping inflation is not controlled at correct time it will prove disastrous for the economic and political stability of the economy.

Walking Inflation

It is a mild and tolerable form of inflation. When the rate of inflation is less than 10% annually, economists call it as walking inflation or moderate inflation. This kind of inflation is regarded as a stable inflation where people's expectations remain more or less stable.

Running Inflation

Running inflation emerges when the prices rise rapidly. When the price rise by more than 10% a year, running inflation occurs. (It ranges between 10 - 20 per cent). if it exceeds that figure, it may be called "galloping inflation".

According to Samuelson, when the prices are rising at double or triple digit rates i.e, 20, 100 or 200% a year the situation may be described as "galloping inflation". This kind of inflation is a serious problem and causes economic distortions and disturbances in the economy.

Hyper Inflation

When the prices rise every moment, and there is no limit to the height to which prices might rise, it is called as hyper-inflation. It is difficult to measure its magnitude, as prices rise by fits and starts.

During this situation prices may rise over 1000% per year. The purchasing power of the people reaches very low level, real wages fall and inequalities increases. Finally it may result in serious disruptions and distortions in the overall economic condition.

Above mentioned four types of inflation are presented diagramatically.

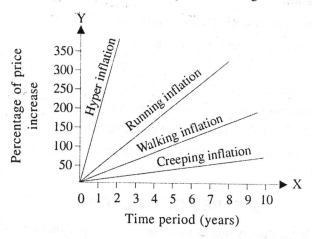

3. OTHER TYPES OF INFLATION

War-Time Inflation

This kind of inflation arises due to certain exigencies of war, on account of increased government expenditure on defence which is of an unproductive nature.

Post-war inflation

It is usually experienced immediately after the war. This is due to increase in the disposable income of the community, withdrawal of war time taxation or repayment of public debt in the post-war period.

Peace-time inflation

When the prices rise during the normal period of peace, it is called as peace time inflation. It may arise due to increased government out lays on capital projects having a long gestation period.

Comprehensive Inflation

When prices of almost all commodities throughout the economy rise, it is known as economy-wide inflation or comprehensive inflation.

Sporadic Inflation

It occurs in a particular section. It is also called as sectional inflation. This kind of inflation consists of cases in which the average of group of prices rise because of increases in individual prices due to abnormal shortage of specific goods.

Open Inflation

The inflation is said to be open when the government does not attempt to prevent a price rise. In this case, prices rise without any interruption. The post-war hyper-inflation during the twenties of 20th Century in Germany is a good example of open inflation

Repressed inflation

When the government intervenes in the price rise, there is a repressed or supressed inflation. Supressed inflation refers to those conditions in which price increases are prevented through adoption of price controls and rationing by the government. However the prices so controlled may rise on the removal of such controls and rationing.

4. TYPES OF INDUCED INFLATION

Credit Inflation

When the inflation occurs due to excessive expansion of bank credit or money supply, it is called as credit inflation.

Deficit Inflation

When the government resort to deficit financing, through creating new money, the purchasing power in the community increases and price rise. This results in deficit induced inflation.

Scarcity Inflation

Whenever scarcity of real goods occurs or artificaly created by hoarding activities of traders and speculators which may result in black-marketing, thereby leading to rise in prices. This type of inflation is called as scarcity inflation.

Profit Inflation

The concept of profit inflation was originally given by J.M.Keynes in his book 'Treatise on Money'. According to him the price level of consumption goods is a function of the investment exceeding savings. He says that, inflation is unjust in its distribution effect, because it redistributes income in favour of profiteers and against the labour class. During inflation the producer expects an increase in MEC and they are induced to invest more even by borrowing at higher interest rates. So investment exceeds savings and economy tends to reach a high level of money income equilibrium. At this juncture, if there are any bottlenecks of market imperfections, real output will not increase in the same proportion resulting in imbalance between money income and real income and is corrected through rising prices.

Foreign Trade - Induced Inflation

Inflation is an international phenomenon and beyond their control. It may be either export-boom inflation or import price-hike inflation.

Export boom inflation occurs when there is significant portion of export trade or continuous boom of export demand, causing terms of trade to be favourable all the time.

Import price-hike inflation arises due to rise in the prices of import components due to inflation abroad, the domestic costs and prices of goods using the imported parts will tend to rise. This kind of inflation is referred to as imported inflation.

Tax Inflation

When there is increase in commodity taxation every year such as excise duties and sales tax may lead to rise in prices of taxed goods. Such an inflation is called tax inflation.

Cost-push Inflation

Cost-push inflation occurs when prices rise due to an increase in the cost of production on account of rising wages, high profit margins and increase in commodity taxes. Due to rising costs of living, workers demand higher wages which will be compensated by the producer by increasing the prices of the products to a higher level.

Demand Pull Inflation

When the available aggregate supply of goods and services is lesser than the aggregate demand, prices tend to rise. This situation of disequilibrium can be corrected either by increase in prices or increase in output. Since full emloyment is assumed, no increase in output is possible. Finally prices rise sufficiently to bring about equilibrium between demand and supply. Forces like population growth, rising money income etc play a significant role in generating demand pull inflation.

5. CAUSES OF INFLATION

Inflation is a complex phenomenon which cannot be attributed to a single factor. It is caused and sustained by over-spending in the economy. Prices generally rise when the firms, households and governments spend more than the available goods in the economy over a period of time.

Inflation occurs when the total demand for goods and services exceeds their total supply at the current price level.

Prof. Kurihara has pointed out certain major factors which cause inflation on the demand side. They are as follows:

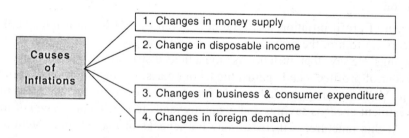

(i) Changes in money supply

  (a) Increase in money supply due to various reasons, such as wars and expansion of bank credit or deficit financing, causes a rise in the money income of people leading to a rise in demand for goods and services.

  (b) When deficit financing is resorted to by the government.

  (c) Increase in government expenditure on large development project.

  (d) Due to expansion of bank credit.

(ii) Disposable Income

(a) An increase in the disposable money income of the consumers leads to an increase in the demand for goods and services.

(b) Disposable income may increase due to a fall in the level of taxation, an increase in national income, a fall in the savings ratio, a rise in the income without corresponding increase in savings, etc.

(iii) Business and Consumer Expenditure

(a) when consumers spend more on goods and services the demand will also increase and also business outlay.

(b) consumer's expenditure may increase when their disposable income increases or when there is a reduction in current savings. It may also increase through the introduction of higher purchase and instalment schemes.

When business community increases their outlay it directly results in an increased demand for capital goods raw materials etc. It may results in inflationary pressures in the economy.

(iv) Foreign Demand

According to Kurihara, 'an additional factor in the increased monetary demand is foreign expenditure for domestic goods and services.'

Inflation may also be caused due to changes in supply of goods and services particularly when it does not keep pace with the increased demand for goods and services.

6. EFFECTS OF INFLATION

A period of prolonged persistent inflation results in the economic, political and moral disruption of society. Inflation affects different groups of individuals in different ways. Some are favourably affected and some are adversely affected.

Effect on Production and Employment

Mild inflation is actually beneficial for the economy beause it stimulates production, employment and income. When prices rise, costs do not rise immediately as a result profit increases and it encourages further investment. But, when inflation goes beyond a certain limit, it reduces production and increases unemployment. Due to a fall in the value of money, savings and capital formation are discouraged.

Effect on Distribution of National Income

Inflation affects all sections of society, either directly or indirectly. Some may gain and others may lose. Generally the rich becomes richer while the poor becomes poorer.

The effects of inflation on various groups are as follows:

(a) Effect on producers

Producers, traders and speculators gain during inflation. Prices rise much more than production cost because production cost remains more or less fixed in the short run and do not increase.

(b) Effect on wage and salary earners

People earning wages and regular salaries suffer during inflation because salaries and wages increase in a lesser proportion to the rise in price. There is also a time lapse between the rise in the price level and the rise in their incomes.

(c) Effect on fixed income groups

The worst affected group during inflation is this group because their income is fixed but the cost of living increases due to rising prices.

(d) Effect on debtors and creditors

Debtors gain and creditors lose because during inflation though debtors return the money to their creditors, they pay less in terms of goods and services when they repay loans. Creditors lose during inflation because they get less value for their money in terms of goods and services compared to the time when they had lent the money.

(e) Effect on farmers

Farmers gain during inflation because the price of farm products increases much faster than production costs leading to higher profits. Big farmers gain more than small farmers because the former have a considerable surplus to dispose off in the market.

Thus inflation is unjust because it transfers income from the poor to the rich. It harms the interests of economically weaker section, middle class and fixed income group and favours businessmen, traders, debtors and big farmers.

7. CONTROL OF INFLATION

Appropriate measures should be taken to control inflation in its initial stage, otherwise it may lead to hyper inflation which has harmful effects on the economy. Control of inflation should involve monetary and fiscal steps which aim at reducing the level of aggregate demand.

Following are the measures which can be taken to control inflation.

    (i) Direct Measures

    (ii) Fiscal Measures

    (iii) Monetary Measures

    (iv) Other Measures

(i) Direct Measures

It includes direct control on prices and rationing of scarce goods. Government can resort to ceiling on prices on certain goods and should not allow it to rise further. In the case of necessaries like food grains, the government can introduce rationing along with price control.

(ii) Fiscal Measures

Fiscal policy refers to the policies of the Government in relation to public expenditure, public borrowing and taxation. An increase in government's revenue and a decrease in its expenditure can successfully check inflationary pressures in the economy. Government should decide a suitable tax policy to restrict aggregate demand to equate the available supply.

Reducing government expenditure or postponing of it on unproductive public works will have a stabilising effect during inflationary periods.

Government can also resort to introducing voluntary schemes and appeal to the public to reduce their consumption. It can also introduce 'compulsory saving scheme' by deducting a certain amount from current wages and salaries to be credited to workers' saving accounts which can be released for spending after some time. Government should also reduce its borrowing externally. Instead, it can resort to internal borrowing.

(iii) Monetary Measures

These are measures adopted by the central bank of the country to control and regulate money supply in the economy. It usually uses monetary policy to control inflation. To control inflation, the central bank of the country reduces the volume of money supply by restricting bank credit. This can be achieved through measures such as selling government security in the open market and increasing the rate of interest to reduce borrowings. This helps in reducing aggregate demand and prices.

(iv) Other Measures

Inflation can be controlled by diverting resources towards the production of necessary commodities, instead of luxury items. Exports can be used to increase the domestic supply of goods which may help in reducing inflation. Similarly import restrictions can be relaxed, it may help to increase the supply of essential commodities and help to reduce inflationary pressures.

Government should also try to restrict the growth rate of population and at the same time increase production levels in the economy.

To curb inflation successfully, a combination of different methods should be judiciously used because any single measure may not be successful in controling inflation.

SUMMARY

1. Inflation refers to a situation when there is a general rise in prices and a corresponding fall in the value of money.
2. Inflation is a monetary phenomenon.
3. Inflation may be caused either by excess demand or cost-push in goods or factor markets.
4. Based on the severity of inflation it can be classified into creeping, walking, running and hyper inflation.
5. Cost-push inflation occurs when prices rise due to an increase in the cost of production on account of rising wages high profit margins and increase in commodity taxes.
6. When the available aggregate supply of goods and services is lesser than aggregate demand, prices tend rise and this is called as demand-pull inflation.
7. Inflation occurs when the total demand for goods and services exceeds their total supply at the existing price level.
8. Inflation affects all sections of the society either directly or in directly favouring some and affecting others.
9. Appropriate measures should be taken to control inflation. For this, government can resort to direct measures, fiscal meaures, monetary measures and other related measures.

QUESTIONS

1. Define inflation.
2. What is cost-push inflation?
3. Mention any four types of inflation.
4. Give the meaning of inflation. Illustrate the different degrees of inflation.
5. Explain the various monetary measures adopted by the central bank to control inflation.
6. Explain the major factors which cause inflation.
7. Explain the effects of inflation on different sections of the society.
8. Explain the various methods that can be adopted to control inflation.
9. "Inflation is a necessary evil". Discuss the implications of this statement by analysing different forms of inflation.
10. What are the implications of inflation on Indian economy?

21 Chapter

Unemployment

CHAPTER OBJETIVES

After reading this chapter, you will be able to answer the following:

1. Effects of Unemployment in the economy
2. Types of Unemployment
3. Causes for Unemployment
4. Measures to cure Unemployment

Unemployment poses a serious problem before any country in the world. Although this problem is very old, in the last few years it has assumed a serious proportions. Inspite of implementing different types of schemes and development programmes under economic planning, the problem of unemployment has not been solved. It may be considered the biggest social and economic misfortune of a country because it is a major obstacle to power, which otherwise, is a source of energy.

According to A.C. Pigou 'Unemployment means unemployment among the wage work only and excludes the idleness of those who are definitely incapacitated from wage earning work.'

According to Karl Pribram definition, 'Mass unemployment is a pecularity of modern capitalist economy with its extreme division of labour, its methods of production, distribution and income accumulation all conditioned by the mechanism of market and price and its complex credit system.'

In simple words, we may define the term unemployment as when a person who is capable of working both physically and mentally at the existing wage rate and who does not get prospective job is called unemployment.

Unemployment is a situation where every able bodied person willing to work is not engaged in proper work for the number of hours considered normal for a fully employed person at the ruling rate of wages.

1. EFFECTS OF UNEMPLOYMENT IN THE ECONOMY

The effects of unemployment are quite serious, not only in a developing country like India, but it also affect the developed nations like USA, UK etc of the world. The main adverse effects of unemployment are:

(i) Unemployment reduces the income and the standard of living of the workers. In turn it affects the savingts and investment in the country which is more essential for the development of a nation.

(ii) It even results in starvation of the workers and their families which in turn affect their efficiency and capacity to work.

(iii) It affects the morale of the workers adversely and undermines their self-confidence.

(iv) It makes the workers lose their skills initially and after sometime, makes them unemployable in any kind of work i.e they become unfit to join in any type of work.

(v) Unemployment results in inefficient utilisation and wastage of human resources.

The above mentioned ill effects of unemployment are applicable to all the economies of the world and if it is not tackled properly will be the biggest hindrance for the development of the respective economy.

2. TYPES OF UNEMPLOYMENT

There are many types of unemployment from the cause of view of unemployment. They are:

(i) *Cyclical Unemployment:* It refers to that unemployment which is caused by trade cycles or cyclical fluctuations in business activities, such as business depression, boom, etc. As trade cycle i.e the phases of trade cycle follow each other continuously in a cycle and if unemployment is caused due to that trade cycle it is called as cyclical unemployment. This kind of unemployment is unavoidable because the fluctuations in the business activities are unavoidable. More cyclical fluctuations occur during business depression, when there will be fall in business activities leading to fall in production which in turn results in reduction in employment or unemployment. This kind of unemployment is a necessary evil in a developed capitalist economy. Since it is a characteristic feature of a well developed capitalistic countries it is not found in less developed countries like India.

(ii) *Technological Unemployment:* Technological unemployment refers to that unemployment which results from technological development or changes like the invention of an improved model of machine, changes in techniques of production, etc. For instance when an improved model of machine is invented and installed in an industry, naturally there will be a reduction in employment or unemployment.

(iii) *Structural Unemployment:* Structural unemployment refers to that unemployment resulting from the structural changes or basic changes in the economic structure of an economy or a country, which affect the nature of the economy itself. For example, when there is a change from a backward system of production to an advanced system of production or from a backward transport system to an advanced system, these will be considerable decrease in demand for labour leading to unemployment. Similarly, if there is a sharp decline in the exports of a country, naturally there will be much decline in the production of exports industries which in turn results in a fall in employment or increase in unemployment.

Indian unemployment is structural unemployment and it arises due to the inadequacies of productive capacity to create enough jobs for all the able bodied and willing persons.

(iv) *Frictional Unemployment:* It refers to that unempoyment which is caued by the improper adjustment between the supply of and the demand for labour. This kind of unemployment arises either because of lack of adjustability of labour or because of immobility of labour.

(v) *Seasonal Unemployment:* Seasonal unemployment means unemployment which arises due to seasonal variations in economic activities. For example sugar industry is a seasonal industry, starting the production immediately after the harvest of sugarcane and closing the production within 3 or 4 months. So, for the remaining days in the year the labour remains unemployed i.e during off season. Similarly in agricultural sector during the period of agricultural operations the labourers are employed and they remain unemployed during the off season.

It is also concerned to a particular industry through seasonal variations in its activity brought about by unfavourable climatic condition or by the non-availability of raw materials, or by changes in fashion etc.

(vi) *Temporary Unemployment:* It refers to that unemployment which results from temporary changes in demand for labour. For instance, when there is a strike or lockout in an industry leading to suspension of workers, naturally the workers in that industry remain unemployed temporarily.

(vii) *Chronic Unemployment:* It refers to that kind of unemployment which occurs in backward economies or countries like India where sufficient number of industries do not exist to absorb the entire supply of available labour. This kind of unemployment is called chronic unemployment because it is more or less permanent.

(viii) *Disguised unemployment:* Disguised unemployment refers to a situation where the number of workers engaged in a given operation is much more than that which is actually needed for that operation. In such a situation though labour is apparently employed, there is some sort of unemployment which is disguised or concealed (i.e) in this case unemployment is not visible. It is also called as hidden unemployment when there is disguised unemployment, the contribution of the extra or surplus labour is nil and the total output does not increase.

(ix) *Open unemployment:* Open unemployment refers to a situation where in a large labour force does not get employment opportunity that may yield them regular income or it refers to a situation where the workers are totally unemployed (i.e, are unable to find any jobs). This type of unemployment is due to lack of complimentary resources, specially capital.

These are the various types of unemployment which prevails in an economy.

3. CAUSES FOR UNEMPLOYMENT

There are a number of causes for unemployment and they are complex in nature. Some of the important causes are briefly discussed below.

(i) Seasonal unemployment is due to the climatic conditions which vary from season to season. This causes variations in the demand for seasonal goods and hence the demand for labour also varies with the demand for goods.

(ii) The increased use of machinery and new techniques of production which replaces labour results in technological unemployment. Similarly schemes of rationalisation and scientific management will also reduce demand for labour.

(iii) The growth of new trade and the decline of old ones is also responsible for creating unemployment.

(iv) The cyclical recurrance of booms and depression which are beyond the control of human beings is responsible for cyclical unemployment in the country.

(v) It was believed by the classical economists that unemployment was due to maintenance of high wages by the trade unions. They argue that employers would find it very difficult to absorb the whole labour supply because of the high wage rate and therefore unemployment was bound to occur.

(vi) Lord Keynes, an eminent modern economist states that people remain unemployed because the current demand for goods and services is not sufficient to absorb all the available labour force.

Apart from the above mentioned causes, there are various other factors which are responsible for unemployment. They are:

(a) Rapid growth of population in the country.

(b) The economic under-development of the economy.

(c) The non-utilisation of economic resources due to politial and social factors.

(d) Destruction of small scale and cottage industries which are mainly labour intensive in nature.

(e) Very little importance to labour intensive technology in modern days.

(f) Economic planning was not at all employment oriented.

(g) Lack of proper man-power planning.

(h) The slowing down of agricultural and industrial production.

(i) The preference of people for jobs in factories and offices and not self employment projects.

All these causes are also responsible for growing unemployment in the countries.

4. MEASURES TO CURE UNEMPLOYMENT

Various measures have been suggested to cure unemployment. Some important measures are given below:

(i) *Industrialisation:* The development of various industries in the country provide a number of new employment opportunities to the people. Therefore, more and more industries should be started in different parts of the country. If the private capital is shy and is not forth-coming, the government itself should start new industries, which should also encourage the starting of new industries under private management. The encouragement should be given in the form of subsidies, grants, concessions in taxes or exemptions from the payment of taxes, supply of essential raw materials, etc.

(ii) *Seasonal unemployment:* It can be minimised by the diversification of trade and production. For example, the production of two or more commodities whose demand occurs alternatively should be undertaken, so that the factory keep on working throughout the year.

(iii) *Establishment of Employment Exchanges:* Employment exchanges should be set up for removing casual unemployment. They notify the vacancies existing in several factories, commercial concerns, Government and semi-government offices and arrange for appointment of the right person in the right job.

(iv) *Measures should be taken to increase the mobility of labour:* Spread of technical and general education, provision of better transport facilities, adequate wages, security of service, housing accomodation etc would increase the mobility of labour. If it is done so, then laboures will move from the depressed areas suffering from unemployment to the developed areas having wide employment opportunities.

(v) *Unemployment insurance schemes:* These schemes should be introduced in order to provide subsistence to workers who lose jobs in the middle and who are to be maintained until they get job somewhere else.

(vi) Effective man-power planning is essential to do away with frictional unemployment. It can be reduced by adopting efficient training methods for workers, by providing better transport facilities, housing accommodation, etc.

(vii) *Rationalisation:* Structural unemployment can be tackled by carefully adopting the programme of rationalisation. This means that, rationalisation must be introduced in stages and not at once. During each stage, some workers lose jobs, but since the number of such workers is small, they can be provided with employment elsewhere.

(viii) *Starting subsidiary industries:* Disguised unemployment which is commonly seen in agriculture can be reduced by starting various subsidiary industries in the rural areas. They will provide employment to the surplus labour existintg in the rural areas.

(ix) *Creating New demand:* Government should undertake several steps to increase the purchasing power of the people in order to create new demand for goods and services. For this purpose, government should under take public work programmes such as construction of roads, bridges, canals, etc. Government should also subsidise industries or introduce rebate system in those industries which have lost demand due to high prices of their product. Even J.M.Keynes advocated the concept of effective demand in the economy to curtail the problem of unemployment.

(x) *Service Sector:* Service sector has potentiality to solve unemployment services like, financial services, healthcare services, telecommunication, personal care services, tourism, hospitality (Hotel) services, etc., can provide remarkable solution for solving problem to a greater extent.

Thus, the measures stated above should be taken together in order to solve the problem of unemployment in the country.

SUMMARY

1. Unemployment is a situation where every able-bodied person willing to work is not engaged in proper work for the number of hours considered normal for a fully employed person at the ruling rate of wages.

2. The ill-effects of unemployment are applicable to all the economies of the world and if it is not tackled properly, it will be the biggest hindrance for the development of the respective economy.

3. Unemployment can be classified into many types based on the cause for it.

Types	Cause
(i) Cyclical unemployment	Due to Trade cycles
(ii) Technological unemployment	Due to Technological development
(iii) Structural unemployment	Due to structural or basic changes in the economy
(iv) Frictional unemployment and demand for labour	Due to improper adjustment between the supply of
(v) Seasonal unemployment	Due to seasonal variations in economic activities
(vi) Temporary unemployment	Due to strikes and lockouts
(vii) Chronic unemployment development.	Occurs in backward economies due to its under
(viii) Disguised unemployment	It refers to a situation where the number of workers engaged in a given operation is much more than that which is actually needed for that operation.
(ix) Open Unemployment	Where the workers are totally unemployed.

4. Generally unemployment arises due to seasonal variations, increased use of machinery, the growth of new trade and decline of old trade, cyclical fluctuations in economic activities etc.

5. Unemployment can be cured by rapid industrialisation, proper man-power planning, establishment of employment exchanges, increasing the mobility of labour, rationalisation, creating new demand etc.

QUESTIONS

1. What is unemployment?
2. Explain the various effects of unemployment in the economy.
3. Define unemployment. What are the various types of unemployment.
4. What are the various causes for unemployment?
5. Suggest your ideas to cure unemployment in an economy.
6. Differentiate between unemployment and underemployment.

22 Chapter

Consumption Function

CHAPTER OBJECTIVES

After reading this chapter, you will be able to answer the following:

1. Meaning of Consumption Function
2. Consumption Schedule
3. Factors Determining Consumption Function
4. Investment
5. Multiplier Concept
6. Money and Interest Rate
7. IS - LM Analysis

John Maynard Keynes' epoch-making book, *'General Theory of Employment Interest and Money'*, published in 1936, disproved the classical theories, particularly the doctrine of *Laissez-faire*. Keynes clearly pointed out that there is no automatic adjustment or *'invisible hand'* as the classicist called it, to guarantee full employment in the economy.

Keynes' general theory touches all spheres of the economy and hence may be called *Macro Economics*. The determiniation of income and employment in the economy forms the most important aspect of macro economics and Keynes has dealt with these two aspects in great detail.

According to Keynes, the level of national income depends on the level of employment, and they are directly related. So Keynes stressed the need for increasing the level of employment.

According to Keynes, national income is composed of national consumption, national investment and national expenditure which is given by the equation $Y = C + i + G$. He said that employment in the economy depends on *'effective demand'* which in turn depends on consumption expenditure. Consumption in the economy depends on income and propensity (willingness) to consume.

1. MEANING OF CONSUMPTION FUNCTION

Consumption is the aim and end of all economic activity. Income is the most important factor which determines consumption. A major part of our disposable income goes towards consumption. A major part of our disposable income goes towards consumption expenditure. It may be possible for investment expenditure to be zero in the economy, but consumption expenditure can never fall to zero, because of the simple fact that we have to exist. Generally, greater the disposable income, greater will be the consumption expenditure. But we cannot assume that consumption expenditure will be equal to income. According to Keynes, the psychology of the community is such that when aggregate real income is increased, aggregate consumption is increased, but not by so much as income. 'This observation of Keynes has come to be known as 'Consumption Function or Keynes' Psychological Law of Consumption.

Thus, Consumption Function is a brilliant tool in Keynesian analysis, which seeks to establish the relationship between income and expenditure. According him, as aggregate income increases, the expenditure also increases but in smaller proportions. Again, as income increases, the additional income is divided between spending and saving, more so on saving i.e., what is not spent, is saved. And lastly, as income increases, both saving and spending increases.

> *Consumption Function refers to the general income consumption relationship. It shows what expenditure consumers will wish to spend on consumer goods and services at different level of disposable income. Thus, consumption function shows the relationship between income and consumption.*

The consumption function can be expressed in the form of a function in the following manner:

$$C = f(Y)$$

where   C = consumption

Y = Income

At different levels of income, there will be different levels of consumption which can be measured by the average and marginal propensities to consume. These two concepts may be briefly explained as follows:

Average Propensity to Consume (APC)

Average Propensity to Consume (APC) refers to the total consumption expenditure out of the given total income during a particular period. It is the rate of aggregeate expenditure over the aggregate income. Thus,

$$APC = \frac{\text{Total consumption}}{\text{Total Income}} = \frac{C}{Y}$$

Suppose the economy's aggregate income is Rs.750 crores and its aggregate consumption expenditure is Rs.600 crores then,

$$APC = \frac{600}{750} = 80\%$$

Marginal Propensity to Consume (MPC)

Marginal Propensity to Consume refers to the change in consumption resulting from a given change in income. It is the additional consumption as a result of additional income. it is expressed as a ratio of change in consumption to change in income.

$$MPC = \frac{\text{Change in Consumption}}{\text{Change in Income}} = \frac{\Delta C}{\Delta y}$$

where, ΔC = incremental change in consumption

           Δy = incremental change in income

Suppose an economy earns an additional income Rs.250 crores, out of which Rs.200 crores is consumed and the rest is saved, then

$$MPC = \frac{200}{250} = 0.8$$

The total income of the economy is divided into consumption and savings i.e., Y = C + S (Income = Consumption + Savings). We thus have average and marginal propensities to save. Average propensity to save means the amount of savings out of a given income and can be expressed as

$$APS = \frac{\text{Total Saving}}{\text{Total Income}} = \frac{S}{Y}$$

Marginal Propensity to save implies the amount of additional savings out of additional income which can be expressed as

$$MPS = \frac{\text{Additional Saving}}{\text{Additional Income}} = \frac{\Delta S}{\Delta Y}$$

Since MPC and MPS taken together constitute one whole, we can find out one with the help of the other.

Thus, MPS = 1 − MPC

2. CONSUMPTION SCHEDULE

Assuming *Cetirus Paribus*, the consumption schedule represents the amount of consumption and savings at different levels of income.

The following is an imaginary schedule showing the division of income into consumption and savings, and the average and marginal propensities to consume:

From the following table, we can see that as income increases, the expenditure also rises but the propensity or willingness to consume is declining. When the income is only Rs.500, the Average Propensity to Consumer is 100 per cent, but as income rises to Rs.3000, the APC has declined to 61 per cent. The MPC also declines with increase in income.

Income (in Rs.)	Consumption	Savings	% APC	% of MPC
500	500	0	100	—
1000	800	200	86	.6
1500	1050	450	78	.5
2000	1250	750	72	.4
2500	1400	1100	66	.3
3000	1500	1500	61	.2

A graphical representation of the consumption can be shown by taking income on X axis and consumption on Y axis.

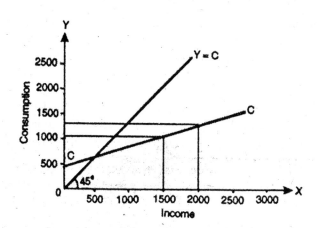

In the above figure Y = C, line is drawn at 45° angle denoting that it is a condition where the entire income is spent on consumption. The consumption function line CC is a straight line implying that as income increases, consumer demand also increases.

3. FACTORS DETERMINING CONSUMPTION FUNCTION

There are certain important factors which influence the propensity to consume. The factors governing the consumption function can be studied under two heads viz, subjective factors and objective factors.

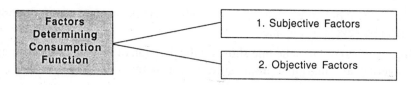

(a) Subjective Factors

Keynes has distinguished between several subjective motives which influence consumption:

(i) An individual's present consumption is influenced by his forethought regarding unforeseen emergencies in the future for which he has set aside some income at present. This may be called the *'motive of foresight'*.

(ii) Present consumption of the individual may be influenced by his desire to provide for future requirements in relation to old age, education of his children, maintenance of his family, etc. This can be called the *'precautionary motive.'*

(iii) Sometimes individuals may prefer to have smaller present consumption in order to enjoy and win appreciation for a larger consumption at a later data. This can be called *'calculation motive.'*

(iv) Sometimes, individuals may prefer to improve their standard of living gradually and this can be attributed to the *'motive of improvement.'*

(v) In order to enjoy the feeling of freedom and power to do anything one wishes, individuals may prefer to consume in lesser proportion to an increase in income. This can be called the *'motive of independence.'*

(vi) Consumption expenditure of individuals may be influenced by the needed to be able to carry out speculative or business activities. This is called the *'motive of enterprise.'*

(vii) In order to leave a fortune behind, consumption at present may be restricted by an individual. This is called the 'motive of pride.'

(viii) Lastly, consumption may be inhibited in order to satisfy the need for hoarding. This is the 'motive of avarice.'

According to Keynes, the subjective factors do not change in short run and thereby the consumption function remains stable.

(b) Objective Factors

There are several objective factors which influence consumption. Some important ones may be considered here:

(i) *Income:* Money incomes of the individuals is by far the important factor that influences consumption. The relation between income, consumption and savings has already been dealt with.

(ii) *Price Level:* According to Keynes, a change in the price level affects the real income of the individuals although money remains constant. This affects the purchasing power and also consumption.

(iii) *Distribution of Income:* A more equitable distribution of income will increase the average and marginal propensity to consume. This is due to the fact that the poor will have many unfulfilled needs clamouring for satisfaction and hence any additional income goes towards consumption expenditure.

(iv) *Fiscal Policy:* Progressive tax rates will reduce income inequalities which in turn help to increase the propensity to consume. At the same time, a reduction in indirect taxes will leave more disposable income which will help to increase consumption.

(v) *Rate of Interest:* According to Keynes, a rise in interest rates makes durable consumer goods more expensive especially when instalment purchases are made. This will discourage consumers from consuming more goods. A fall in interest rates will encourage consumption.

(vi) *Demographic Feature:* Generally, it is observed that large-sized families spend more than small-sized families. Again, urban-based families spend more than rural-based families. Professional people spend more than farmers and petty businessmen.

(vii) *Duesenberry Hypothesis:* According to Prof. Duesenberry, the consumption expenditure of individuals depends not only on the current incomes but also on past standards of living. This is because people find it difficult to adjust expenditure to changed conditions or incomes.

Again, 'individual's consumption depends not only on his absolute income but also on its size relative to other income'. It is natural for low income groups to follow the consumption pattern of richer sections. This will make the richer section go in search of better goods. Thus, the mutual reactions will push up consumption expenditure which Prof. Duesenberry called it the *'Demonstration Effect.'*

Measures to Increase Propensity to Consume

The following measures may be advocated to improve the average and marginal propensities to consume:

(i) Government through its fiscal policies must aim to bring about a more equitable distribution of income.

(ii) Introduction of social security schemes such as old-age pension, health insurance, etc. will help increase the purchasing power of the people.

(iii) An appropriate wage policy accompanied by a suitable productive policy would increase the propensity to consume. A mere rise in wages without improvement in productivity would lead to inflation.

(iv) Availability of easy and cheap credit facilities, encourage consumption. This is especially true in the case of consumer durable goods.

(v) Effective sales promotion techniques through advertisement and propaganda can influence the tastes and preference of the people. This may increase demand and the consumption function of the economy would increase.

4. INVESTMENT

Investment refers to the addition to capital assets like buildings, machinery, etc. and also addition to stocks like raw materials and finished goods. According to Heilbroner, 'Investment, as the economist's result, is an activity that uses the resources of the community to maintain or add to its stock of capital wealth'.

Types of Investment

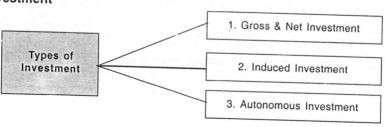

(i) Gross and Net Investment

Gross investment refers to the total real investment, but part of the new capital is nothing but the replacement of depreciated capital. Hence this part should be deducted from gross investment to give net investments. Net investment is that part of gross investment which represents the net addition to the total existing capital stock in the economy.

(ii) Induced Investment

Higher income levels of the people leads to greater effective demand, which in turn pushes up sales and profit margins. This induces entrepreneurs to invest more. Such a kind of investment which is income elastic is called as *'induced investment'*. It depends directly on income and given the marginal propensity to consume, an increase in income leads to an increae in investment and vice versa.

Normally induced investments are private investments since they are backed by profit motive. The following figure illustrates the direct relationship of income and induced investment:

The figure shown in the next page induced private investment at different income levels. When income is OY, investment is nil. As income increases to OY, investment also increases to T_1Y_1 and when income further increases to OY_2, investment also increases to T_2Y_2.

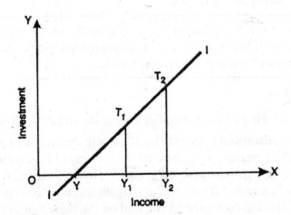

(iii) Autonomous Investment

Autonomous investment is independent of income levels and interest rates. Autonomous investments take the form of public expenditure by the government. It is dependent on factors like public policy, demographic composition, innovation, etc. Examples of autonomous investments would be government investments on roads, railways electric products, dams, etc.

The below figure indicates the autonomous investment curve which is horizontal to the x axis indicating that autonomous investment is income inelastic. It remains constant at various levels of income.

Aggregate investment at any given point of time will be the sum of induced and autonomous investments.

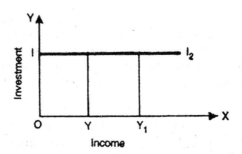

5. MULTIPLIER CONCEPT

'Multiplier' is an important concept developed by Keynes to analyse his theory of income and employment. Multiplier is defined as the ratio of change in income and changes in investment will lead to changes in consumption, which in turn will lead to changes in incomes. The multiplier tries to measure the final change in income due to a certain initial change in investment. According to Prof. Samuelson, 'Multiplier is the number by which the change in investment must be multiplied in order to present us with a resulting change in income.' Thus, the final effect of an increase in investment on income is called the multiplier.

> *Multiplier is the ratio of the final change in income to the initial change in investment. It expresses the quantitative relationship between the final increase in national income and the increase in investment which induces the rise in income.*

Working of the Multiplier

The process of the working of the multiplier can be illustrated with the help of an example.

Let us suppose that a businessman invests Rs.10 lakh in the course of expanding his business. This will result in an initial increase in income of those engaged in producing investment goods, by Rs.10 lakh. Let us further assume that MPC is 0.5. Hence Rs..5 lakh will be spent by these income recipients in the first round. This amount is again received as income by those engaged in consumer goods industries. This assumption is based on the logic that one person's consumption expenditure is another person's income. Those who have received Rs. 5 lakhs will spend 50 per cent of it i.e Rs.2.5 lakhs (since MPC is 0.5) in the second round. Again, the process continues and in the third round Rs.1.25 lakhs will be generated and so on.

Economists presume that each round takes about three months to materialise and this time interval between one round and the next is the multiplier period. As we move from one multiplier period to another, the initial expenditures give rise to gradually diminishing additions to income (when MPC > 0 but < 1). This process will continue till the total increase in income becomes so huge that it generates additional savings which is almost equal to original increment in investment.

The multiplier process may be illsutrated in the following table:

Multiplier Period (in years)	Initial Investment (in lakhs)	Increase in consumption (MPC=0.5)	Total increase in Income (in lakhs)
0	10		10
1	10	5	15
2	10	5+2.5	17.5
3	10	5+2.5+1.25	18.75
4	–	–	–
5	–	–	–
6	10	–	20.00

We can see from the above table that an initial investment of Rs.10 lakh leads to an increase in income by Rs.20 lakhs assuming MPC = 0.5.

The effect of the investment multiplier in generating income may be graphically represented.

In the figure, C represents the linear consumption function curve which has a constant MPC of 0.5. The effective demand is given by C + I cure. The 45^0 line indicates that Income = Consumption + Saving (Y = c + S). The original equilibrium is E, where C + I intersects the 45^0 line.

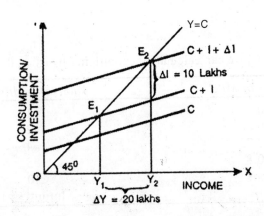

An increase in investment is shown by C + I curve to C + I + Δ I curve. The difference between these two curves shows the extent of new investment (in our example it is Rs.10 lakhs). This C + I   I interests the 45^0 line at E_2 which gives the new equilibrium level of income of OY_2. The difference in income is shown by Y_1Y_2 (which is equal to Rs.20 lakh, in our example). It is infact, twice the initial investment indication that the multiplier co-efficient is 2.

MPC and Multiplier

The value of the multiplier depends on the consumption function and MPC. Greater the volume of consumption expenditure, larger is the volume of aggregate income and greater is the value of the multiplier.

The formula for the multiplier is:

$$K = \frac{1}{1 - MPS}$$

where, K = multiplier

MPC = marginal propensity to consume.

Since marginal propensity to save is 1-MPC (as already explained in the earlier part of the chapter) the multiplier formula can also be written as:

$$K = \frac{1}{MPS}$$

In our example, we have assumed MPC = 0.5. Hence the value of the multiplier is

$$K = \frac{1}{1 - MPC} = \frac{1}{1 - \frac{1}{2}} = \frac{1}{\frac{1}{2}} = 2$$

Hence the value of the multiplier is 2, and we have shown that an investment of Rs.10 lakhs has led to Rs.20 lakhs of aggregate income over a period. Algebrically, this relationship can be expressed as,

$$\Delta y = K \cdot \Delta I$$

$$= 2.10 \text{ lakhs}$$

$$\Delta y = 20 \text{ lakhs}$$

Thus, given the MPC, we can calculate the multiplier by using the multiplier formula:

Value of MPC	Value of Multiplier
0	1
0.5	2
0.75	4
0.8	5
0.9	10
1.0	Infinity(∞)

Assumptions of Multiplier Concept

There are certain assumptions implicit in the Keynesian multiplier concept which may be stated as follows:

(i) It is assumed that MPC remains constant till increased investment results in increased aggregate income.

(ii) Only the original increase in investment is considered and subsequent induced investments (due to increase in consumption) have been ignored.

(iii) Fiscal and monetary policies are assumed to remain constant, so as not to influence the propensity to consume.

(iv) Multiplier effect is considered only when the economy is operating at less than full-employment level, when increase in investment leads to an increase in output, income and employment.

(v) The concept of multiplier is working under the assumption of a closed economy. The effect of international economic transactions on the domestic level of income and consumption is ruled out.

(vi) There is no significant time-interval between the receipts of income and its expenditure. Thus, the process of income propogation is assumed to be continuous.

(vii) Lastly it is assumed that the output of consumer goods should be responsive to changes in demand, if the multiplier is to work effectively. Otherwise, the propensity to consume would fall and this reduces the size of the multiplier.

Leakages in the Multiplier Process

Income, if it is not spent on consumption, is considered as leakage in the income propagation process. The operation of certain factors reduces the effect of the multiplier and these factors are called *'leakages.'* This leakage acts as a limitation to increase in national income. The following are some of the important leakages:

(i) *Savings:* Greater the volume of savings, lesser is the value of the multiplier.

(ii) *Debt Repayments:* When people use a part of their increased incomes to repay old debts, instead of spending it on consumption, that part of income is eliminated from the income stream.

(iii) *Hoarding:* If people prefer greater liquidity, then consumption expenditure falls and so also the value of the multiplier.

(iv) *Inflation:* With a rise in prices, the increase in income is lost on high prices. Consumption remains at the same level and hence value of the multiplier is less.

(v) *Import:* If imports exceed exports, the increased income resulting from increased investment, flows out of the country. This amount is not available for expenditure within the domestic economy.

(vi) *Taxation:* Heavy taxation reduces the multiplier effect by reducing the propensity to consume (of the people).

(vii) *Purchase of Stocks and Securities:* When people buy stocks and securities from their newly earned income, then to that extent their consumption expenditure falls, consequently value of the multiplier also falls.

To the extent that these above mentioned leakages can be avoided, the effect of the multiplier will be greater on the level of income and employment.

Limitations of the Multiplier Concept

(i) It fails to consider the effects of induced investments due to induced consumption and consider only the induced incomes.

(ii) It is a static phenomenon which shows how income gets propagated from one point of equilibrium to another. It does not tell about the actual sequence of events by which final increase in aggregate income is attained.

(iii) The assumption of MPC being constant is impractical. Practically speaking, MPC changes from person to person, place to place and time to time.

(iv) Keynesian Multiplier assumes a linear relation between consumption and income. But consumption is not the function of income alone but it influenced by a host of other factors.

(v) Keynes has given no empirical evidence of his multiplier concept. According to Haberler, 'Keynes offers no adequate proof, only a number of rather disconnected observations' Hazlitt branded it as a 'myth' and 'a worthless toy of monetary cranks.'

6. MONEY AND INTEREST RATE
(Keynes Liquidity Preference Theory of Interest)

Investment in any economy is determined by the marginal efficiency of capital (expected rate of return) and rate of interest. This topic deals with the determination of rate of interest.

According to the classicist, demand for and supply of savings determines the rate of interest. The rate of interest is determined by equality of and the interaction of saving and investment schedules.

But Keynes criticized the Classical theory saying that they had ignored the changes in income level and their effet on savings and investment due to the 'multiplier effect.'

In his 'General Theory of Employment, Interest and Money', Keynes put forward his celebrated, 'liquidity preference theory' of interest rate determination.

Keynes defined interest as 'reward for parting with liquidity.' According to him, money is the most liquid asset and to make a person part with his cash (liquid asset), a reward has to be paid, and this reward is called *'interest.'* Greater the desire for liquidity, higher shall be the rate of interest demanded for parting with liquidity. Thus, interest becomes a purely monetary phenomenon.

Demand for Money

Keynes put forward three motives for preferring liquid assets (money) and the demand for money arises due to these motives, which are discussed below:

(i) *The Transaction Motive:* People prefer to hold money to meet the expenses incurred in the time interval between expenditure (outlay) and income (receipts from sales). The amount of money held for this purpose depends on the level income and the volume of business done.

(ii) *The Precautionary Motive:* People sometimes hold money in order to meet unforeseen contingencies. The amount of money depends on the nature of the individuals, his business activities and how easily he can borrow credit etc.

(iii) *Speculation Motive:* Sometimes, people would like to hold cash in order to take advantage of changes in the rate of interest. If an individual anticipates that interest rates are going to rise in the future, he may hold more cash, to take advantage of the situation. On the other hand, if he expects interest rates to fall in the future, he may prefer to hold less cash. Hence, there is a close relation between rates of interest and money held for speculative purposes.

Supply of Money

The supply of money in an economy at any specific period is given by the sum - total of all money - holdings. The supply of money can be controlled (unlike the demand for money) because it is in the hands of a single monetary authority viz. the Central Bank of a country. The rate of interest can be influenced by the supply of money, which in its turn, influences the demand for money (liquidity preference). Assuming *cetirus paribus*, higher the supply of money, lower the rate of interest and vice-versa.

Determination of Rate of Interest

Rate of Interest is determined by the supply of money and demand for money. If the total demand for money is 'M' and the demand for transaction and precaution taken together is M_1 and demand of money for speculation is M_2 then, we get

$M = M_1 + M_2$

M_1 is not influenced by the rate of interest but by income levels. It is M_2 which directly depends on the rate of interest. So, it is M_2 which determines the actual changes in the demand for money at different rates of interest. On the supply side, the Central Bank fines the money supply and on the demand side, we have the liquidity preference. The rate of interest is given by the intersection of the two as shown in the following figure.

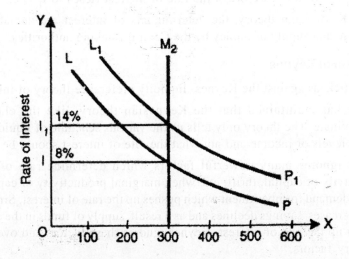

Suppose the Central Bank of a country creates a total amount of money (M) equal to Rs.1000 crores. Out of this total of Rs.1000 crores, an amount equal to Rs.700 crores is held for transaction and precautionary motive (M_1). The amount for speculative motive (M_2) would be Rs.300 crores indicated by the vertical line M_2 in the figure, showing the supply side of money, which is fixed. The demand for money to satisfy the speculative motive is shown by the Liquidity Preference curve, (LP) in the figure. Under given conditions, the demand for money (for speculative purposes) would fall if interest rate rises (they anticipate that it will fall in the future). The equilibrium rate of interest is shown by OI, i.e., 8 per cent as at this rate of interest, supply of and demand for money are equal. If supply of money remains constant and liquidity preference of the people rises, the rate of interest would go up to OI_1, i.e., 14 per cent.

Rate of Interest When the Supply of Money Changes

There is an inverse relationship between supply of money and rate of interest, holding the demand for money constant, as shown in the diagram given below:

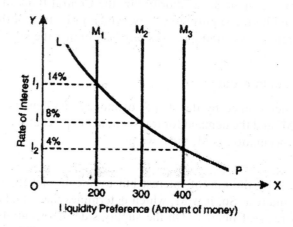

In the above figure, if supply of money increased from M_2 to M_3 (i.e., from Rs.300 crores to Rs.400 crores), the rate of interest falls from I to I_2 (i.e from 8% to 4%). Conversely, if supply of money falls to M_1 (i.e to Rs.200 crores), the rate of interest rieses to I_1 (i.e., 14%).

Thus, in the Keynessian theory, the determinants of interest are demand for money for speculative purpose and supply of money by the Central Banking authorities.

Critical Evaluation of Keynes

The major criticisms against the Keynes' liquidity preference theory of interest rate:

(i) Hansen has maintained that the Keynesian theory, like the classical theory, is indeterminate. The theory only tells us the various schedule of liquidity preferences at various levels of income and not what the rate of interest should be.

(ii) Keynes ignores many powerful factors which determine rate of interest such as productivity of capital, thrift, etc. when marginal productivity of capital rises, there is greater demand for investment which pushes up the rate of interest. Similarly, if people's MPC increases, savings declines and as a result, supply of funds in the economy declines, pushing up the rate of interest. Keynes ignores these factors and over-emphasized the monetary factors.

(iii) Keynes overlooked the fact that without savings, there would be nothing which could be parted for interested. According to Viner, '*Without savings, there can be no liquidity to surrender.*'

(iv) Keynes' theory does not hold good during a depression or a boom. Contrary to Keynes theory, the rate of interest is low during a depression and high during boom period.

(v) The term 'liquidity' used by Keynes is vague. For instance, a person having money in the form of time deposits or short-term treasury bills, will obtain interest on them and also enjoy liquidity.

(vi) Lastly, Keynes' theory concentrates on the short-term and ignores long-term rate of interest.

7. IS - LM ANALYSIS

(Modern Theory or Neo-Keynesian Theory of Interest)

The modern theory of interest, put forward by J.R.Hicks and Hansen, is an attempt to blend the Classical and Keynesian theories of interest. They took into consideration the real aspects of the classical theory and the 'monetary' aspects of the Keynesian theory and successfully combined the variables of savings, investment, liquidity preference and money supply.

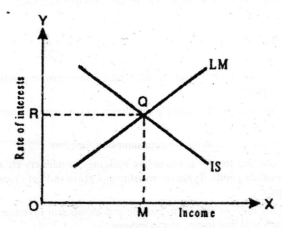

According to this theory, there are four determinants of the rate of interests, namely, savings function, investment function, liquidity preference function and the supply of money function. The Classical theory showed that the rate of interest is determined at that point where savings and investment are equal. Keynesian theory showed that the rate of interest is determined at that point where demand for money (liquidity preference) and supply of money are equal. All these four variables used by the classicists and Keynes, have been integrated with income to determine the rate of interest statisfactorily.

To arrive at the rate of interest, the modern theory uses two curves - the IL curve and the LM cure. The IS curve shows the equilibrium in the real sector (product market) and LM curve represents the equilibrium in the monetary sector (money market) the equilibrium of the real and monetary sectors give the equilibrium rate of interest. At this rate of interest, total savings will be equal to total investment, and total demand for money will be equal to total supply.

Criticisms

(i) Keynes's theory is too general to help us in analysing the entire economy where the conditions of production are varied and the markets are too wide.

(ii) The theory does not take into consideration the effects of government policies and production and prices of commodities.

(iii) It is wrong to assume that the productive resources are responsive in supply, till full employment level is reached. In an under-developed economy, this is not true, because there are several bottlenecks in production and therefore an increase in money supply may not lead to increased employment and output.

(iv) The Theory of money supply and price level, put forward by Keynes, holds good only when we assume that the determinants of income such as MEC and propensity to consume retain constant.

SUMMARY

1. Consumption function concept was introduced by John Maynard Keynes. According to him, consumption is directly related to income and it can be expressed in the form of a function:

$$C = f(Y)$$

   Where   C = consumption

   Y = income

2. Average Propensity to Consume (APC) refers to the total consumption expenditure out of the given total income during a particular period.

3. Marginal Propensity to Consume (MPC) refers to the change in consumption resulting from a given change in income.

4. Both subjective and objective factors determine consumption function.

5. Investment refers to the addition to capital assets like buildings, machinery etc and also addition to stocks like raw materials and finished goods. Types of investment - gross and net investment induced investment and autonomous investment.

6. Multiplier is defined as the ratio of change in income and changes in investment will lead to changes in consumption, which in turn will lead to changes in income.

$$K = \frac{1}{1 - MPC}$$

   where   K = multiplier

   MPC = Marginal Propensity to consume

7. According to J.M.Keynes, money is demanded for three motives namely: (i) Transaction motive; (ii) Precautionary motive; (iii) Speculative money.

8. Keynesian theory states that the demand for money (speculative purpose) and the supply of money by the central bank determine the rate of internet.

9. Accordingly to IS-LM analysis, the rate of internet is determined by savings function, investment function, liquidity preference function and the supply of money function.

QUESTIONS

1. Explain the concept of effective demand. Discuss the relevance to the theory of employment and income.
2. What do you mean by consumption function? What factors determine the consumption function?
3. What is Marginal Propensity to Consume? How is it related to the concept of 'Multiplier'?
4. Explain the changes in income responsible to changes in investment with the help of Multiplier.
5. Discuss the principle of Multiplier. What are its limitations?
6. Briefly explain the Liquidity Preference Theory of interest.
7. Explain the leakages of multiplier.
8. Define consumption function with suitable example.
9. What is marginal propensity to save? What is its importance in the determination of national income?
10. How are IS and LM curves derived? What are their main properties?

23 Chapter

Rational Expectations

CHAPTER OBJECTIVES

After reading this chapter, you will be able to answer the following:

1. Nature and Scope of Rational Expectations
2. Theories of Expectations Formation

Rational expectation is the main theme of the modern debate in Economic Theory. The new concept highlighted the defects of the old theories and concepts. The failure of the existing theories to explain about the bad economic performance during the seventies and eighties of the 20th Century all over the world, gave rise to the theory of "Rational Expectations". It is also called as the theory of Ratex.

During 1970s and 1980s, many countries in the world suffered from high inflation and high unemployment simultaneously, which is described as 'stagflation.' This was due to over optimism which prevailed during that time. To overcome this problem of stagflation, the existing theories (fiscal policy and monetary policy) did not have any tools, which led to the emergence of macro economic theories and a new set of theoretical propositions in economic which is called 'rational expectations.'

Expectations are necessary for three important reasons. They are

(i) They play an important role in determining the future value of economic variable like, price, demand supply, employment, output, etc.

(ii) Expectations exert a strong influence upon what happens today.

(iii) Expectations play a crucial role in the concept of equilibrium. All the schedules used in economies represent expected or anticipated or ex-ante values of the variables concerned. Equilibrium means is a state or condition in which actual and expected values coincide.

1. NATURE AND SCOPE OF RATIONAL EXPECTATIONS

During the 1960s, the governments were able to manage control and direct the economy towards the attainment of their objectives in the field of income and employment in the best possible manner. They were able to do this with the help of the then existed Keynesian theories. But everything changed with growing stagflation in the early seventies. The growth rates declined sharply and inflation and unemployment rates steadily increased.[1] The growth rate of the real GDP at market prices declined from 6% in 1965 to 0.2% in 1980s in USA; from 5.6% to 1.8% in Germany; from 2.3% to 1.8% in UK; from 6.8% to 0.1% in Canada and from 5.7% to 2.9% in Australia. In the same manner, the unemployment rate as percent of total labour force increased in all these countries.

No one country was able to find a suitable macro economic policy, which the government could implement and thereby to eliminate unemployment and inflation in the economy. Their fiscal and monetary policies utterly failed. Some economists considered that the stagflation in the countries was due to the policies of the activists group (they believed that the government can manage the economy and it can ensure an equilibrium in the economy). Because of all these reasons, a new theory called "rational expectations theory" emerged.

The rational expectationists gave more attention to the role of the government and they believed in the capability of the government. This has led to the sudden fall of Keynesian macro economics.

'Rational Expectations' theories concentrated upon the supply side rather than demand side. These theories also states that Government can do not much towards solving the problem of unempolyment and inflation. They insisted that the government give incentives to investors to expand the supply. They also maintain that benefits of expansion will pull the economy from stagflation, and growth will take place.

Definitions

"Rational expectation is the application of principle of rational behaviour to the acquisition and processing of information and to the formation of expectations."[2]

> *Rational Expectations are forecasts about the rate of change of some economic variables based on the available information. This approach implies that expectations are formed on the basis of all currently available information. These rational predictions or forecasts are based on economic model.*

In economics, expectations are essentially forecasts of the future values of economic variables, which are relevant to present decisions. For example, the firms have to forecast the demand and price for their products in the near future, so that they can decide about the amount of investment in the current period. Similarly, the farmers should also forecast the prices of their crops, so that they can determine which is the most profitable crop to grow. Therefore, expectations are nothing but decision makers forecast regarding uncertain economic variables which are relevant to his or her decision. Expectations are subjective in nature and differ from person to person, place to place and from time to time.

Origin of the Concept

The concept expectations is not a new concept in economics. It was used by various economists in their theories, which are used even now. Marshall (1920) and Gunnar Myrdal (1939) have used in their respective works.

The concept of rational expectations was first used by Muth (1961). He has used this concept in his managerial theories of the firm (in the context of decision-making process of the firm). Later on it was picked up by Lucas (1972) and Sargent (1973), Sargent and Wallace (1973, 1975, 1976), Barro (1976, 1977) and Mccallum (1976). These people have made original contributions to the development of the theory of Rational Expectations called "Ratex".

2. THEORIES OF EXPECTATIONS FORMATION

Exekial's study of 'Cobweb Theorem" (1938) was the first to make use of hypothesis of expectation formation. He stated that expectations are formed in a simple manner that is the expected price was equal to the most recently known price.

(i) Cobweb Model

This model explains about the behaviour of agricultural markets. This model is an example of dynamics and market stability. The important feature of this model is some delay between the formation of production plans and their realisation. This model states that farmers will make expectations regarding the future price for his crops and based on that he will allot the land for crop which will be harvested in the following season. His expectations will be based on the price prevailing at the time of planning of crops. Since all the farmers may think alike, it may finally lead to 'glut' in the market (i.e plenty of production) and this will be followed by a year of scarcity and again followed by another year plenty and it goes on like this in Cobweb fashion. The Cobweb model follows a particular fashion. i.e., over-supply, under-suply, over-supply-under-supply. But in reality we cannot learn anything from this model expect for the fact that it highlighted the use of expectations.

(ii) Extrapolative Expectations

To overcome the limitations of Cobweb Model, Metzler (1941) introduced the concept of "extrapolative expecations". In his, model he has stressed the importance of direction of change of economic variable. Therefore extrapolative expectations in any time period is equal to the price level in the previous period and some proportion of the change between the previous two periods.

A more refined version of this model was given by Hicks (1946) in his work. His model states that the expected rate of inflation equals the current inflation rate plus an adjustment factor which allows for the rate of change of inflation. It means that, people are forming their expectations not about the current rate of inflation, but also the rate of change of it.

(iii) Adaptive Expectations

This concept was put forward by Cagan (1956) and Nerlove (1958). This concept states that, people revise their expectations in each period according to the degree of error in their previous forecasting and hence this concept is called as adaptive expectations. An alternative name is also given to this concept i.e., the error learning hypothesis. The speed or the rate at which the expectations adjust to the past error is called the co-efficient of adaptations.

This concept of adaptive expectations was used on a large scale till the concept of rational expectations was introduced in economics. The adaptive expectations are effective only when the forecasted economic variable is reasonably stable but otherwise not.

(iv) Rational Expectations

The failure of Cobweb model of expectations, extrapolative expectations and adaptive expectations led to the introduction of rational expectations by John Muth in his publication in 1961 of a classic paper. According to John Muth "I would like to suggest that expectations, since they are formed predictions of future events, are essentially the same as the predictions of the relevant economic theory ... in particular the hypothesis asserts that the economy does not waste information and the expectations depend specifically on the structure of the entire system."

The hypothesis given by John Muth includes 3 things (a) information is scarce and the economic system generally does not waste it. (b) depending on the structure of the system decribing the economy, the expectations are formed specifically. (c) A 'public prediction' will have no substantial effect on the operation of the economic system.

Muth says that information should be considered as the resources available to be allocated to maximum advantage and the individuals should use the information informing their expectations. So, he concludes that rational economic agents would use their knowledge of the structure of the economic system informing their expectations. The development of rational expectations in economics is more useful in the areas of learning and expectations formation.

Criticisms

(a) The theory of rational expectations has been criticised on the ground that it is unrealistic. Because it assumes that individuals know the past history of relevant variables and also the structural parameters of the true economic model. But this is not possible in reality because information cannot be gathered as very easily as expected in this theory.

(b) This theory is based on the assumption that continuous market clearing mechanism (i.e demand is equal to supply) and flexible prices. And it is also assumes that the demand for labour is equal to supply of labour and hence there is no possibility of unemployment and this is done by adjusting wages accordingly. If unemployment exists even then, it is only voluntary unemployment. In practice it is not possible to equate the demand and the supply of labour by adjusting wages. Now almost all the economies suffer from the problem of unemployment.

(c) The rational expectations theory do not include assets, capital accumulation, inventories, taxes and money behaviour in the economy. When money and capital is introduced in the theory, its validity decreases in reality.

(d) If rational expectations theory has to hold good in reality, it should give room for the inclusion of not only empirical and statistical evidences but also empirical tests on a variety of level.

(e) The rational expectation's hypothesis states that expectations should have certain properties, unbiased and based on the best possible information available at the time of their formation. But in reality the expectations are not observable directly.

(f) The rational expectations models failed because they are not able to attract or provide much empirical evidence to support their propositions.

Conclusion

Rational Expectations though try to provide a solution to tackle inflation and unemployment have not provided any solid solution to tackle the problem of stagflation, which prevailed during the time when the concept was introduced. What the rational expectations theorists learnt about their models is not quite clear. Among the various types of expectations formation methods, the adaptive expectations method is most popular among the economists. Since it includes various assumptions which are not valid in reality, this theory has been challenged on various grounds.

SUMMARY

1. Rational Expectations theory is an important element of neo-classical economics.

2. This theory argues that all economic agents form expectations rationally.

3. They believe that any policy action on the part of the government will be ineffective unless the policy action is foreseen.

4. Rational expectationists believe that any policy action on the part of the government is unnecessary and cannot affect output, income, employment and price level.

5. Expectations are formed to understand the future values of economic variables.

6. Rational expectations was first put forward by Prof. Muth (1961) and he was supported by Lucas and Sargent etc.

7. Adaptive expectations method is most popular among the various types of expectations formation methods.

8. There are many implications of rational expectations theory.

9. Because of these implications and limitations, this theory has been challenged on various grounds.

QUESTIONS

1. Give the meaning of rational expectations. Explain its nature and scope.

2. Explain the various theories of Expectations Formation.

3. Why is the adaptive expectations method most popular among the various types of expectations formation methods?

4. How far will any policy action on the part of the government be effetive?

5. Critically examine Rational expectations theory or on what grounds has the rational expectations theory been criticised?

REFERENCES

1. Source OECD, Economic Outlook, No.29, July 1981, pp.132, 140, 142.

2. Journal of Economic Literature, March, 1982, Vol.XX, No.1, P.41.

24 Chapter

Supply Side Economics

CHAPTER OBJECTIVES

After reading this chapter, you will be able to answer the following:

1. Supply Side Economics
2. Features of SSE
3. Critical Evaluation of SSE

The failure of keynesianism to solve the problem of stagflation in 1980's was the main reason for the emergence of the new concept supply side economics. The attempt to deal with unemployment on the lines, recommended by Keynes, did not create more jobs; instead, it quickened the pace of inflation and led to deterioration of the balance of payments. Even developed countries were affected to a great extent with the result the dollar had to be devalued and then it became inconvertible into gold, and finally the major currencies of the world began to float.[1] This gave rise to the new supply side economics, which emerged in response to the growing imbalance between production and consumption. Many economists had contributed to this theory - including Roberts, Normen True, Arthur Laffer, Paul Craig, Alan Reynolds, George Gilder, Robert Mundell, Jude Wanniski, and Laffer's Bosewell.

Supply Side Economics (SSE) is a body of theoretical ideas. It does not constitute a coherent set of relationships like the Keynesian model, relationships which explain how the macro economy works. Supply side economics is based on two propositions - (i) full faith in the validity of Say's Law of Markets (i.e supply creates its own demand) and (ii) a belief that tax rates are the prime determinant of incentives, which in turn, are the prime determinant of production. Supply Side economists insist on the validity of Say's Law and had that law as the basic for their argument and they had given greater importance to aggregate supply rather than aggregate demand. SSE does not allow money to enter into motives or decisions - as it does in Keynesian Liquidity Preference Theory.

1. SUPPLY SIDE ECONOMICS

It only means manipulating the aggregate supply curve by modernisation, skill formation, rationalisation, liberal depreciation, re-organisation, cost manipulation, etc. SSE shifts the emphasis from aggregate demand management of the economy to micro-motivations for productivity. The importance is given to *"incentives"* for the supply of labour, improvements in productivity and removal of restraints on optimising activities. The important theme of SSE is the responsiveness of work, productivity, saving, investment and enterprise to 'after-tax' rewards. High tax rates are opposed because (a) they discourage economic activity; (b) divert resources to tax-shelter industries and tax exempt goods; (c) induces tax evasion and encourages smuggling and fraud; (d) people try to find loopholes in tax laws; and finally it also causes disintegration of the normal values of the nation.

> *In simple terms, SSE is the application of price theory to aggregate entities in the economy - nothing more, nothing less. It has its underlying philosophy the belief that the market is stable and if left to itself will lead to an efficient allocation of resources.*

Supply Side economists say that a producer should be given incentive rather than any money and they say that high tax rates are potential barriers to commerce. They agree that high tax rates collect very little revenues; Laffer's cure graphically proves that a 100% tax rate will collect no revenue and the same is illustrated in the diagram below:

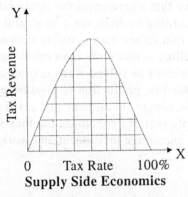

Supply Side Economics

According to Arthur Laffer, there is a close relationship between tax rates, revenues and productivity. When the tax rate is 100% the revenue is nil and people will not work for nothing. On the other hand, if the tax rate is zero, there is no revenue to government. Therefore, there is an optimum point on the curve where tax rates will produce the desired revenues and the desired national product. That point can be variable and need not be fixed. Dr. Laffer rightly says that point can be "where the electorate desires to be taxed." According to him, too much of tax burden will reduce the incentives to work which results in lower revenue and production. Lower taxes can increase both.

In the diagram, at the beginning on the left side of the scale, the government imposes no taxes on income and so gets no revenue. Moving right along the scale, as the tax rate increases, the revenue also increases. When the tax rate reaches 100 per cent, it yields zero revenue and people will not bother to earn taxable income if the government imposes higher taxes. Therefore, we can conclude that according to Supply Side economists government should impose a reasonable rate of tax, so that it will fetch high revenue to the government, at the same time not affecting the commerce i.e production in the country.

2. FEATURES OF SSE

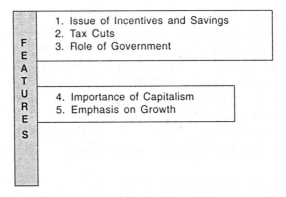

Features of SSE

(i) Issue of Incentives and Savings

SSE treats incentives as the main engine of growth and they energies the whole economic system. SSE states that people should work less hard but more productively and the Supply Side economists seek the removal of disincentives to saving and investment.

(ii) Tax Cuts

It is an important feature of SSE that supply siders believe that a permanent cut in tax rates will induce the people to produce more, save and invest. According to them, tax cuts should be designed in such a manner that, it should encourage production rather than boosting demand, particularly when there is stagflation. Entrepreneurs will be willing to take more risks encouraged by incentives. Supply side economists believe that stagflation can't be solved when tax rate are high in the economy. According to them, the main reason for low production is taxation and taxes are a disincentive to production. Taxes on capital discourage investment and taxes on people discourage work. This is the essential message of supply side of Economics. So, they say that government should introduce effective tax cuts that will encourage investment and work in the economy.

(iii) Role of Government

SSE does not assign a primary role to the government. Supply siders insist that government should do only the minimum necessary Acts, which are essential to maintain law and order in the society, including protecting it from enemies (external aggression) and that all other Acts are a waste. They consider government regulations as a necessary evil to be tolerated. According to them, to prevent the wasteful use of productive resources, the Acts of the Government should be minimum.

(iv) Importance of Capitalism

SSEs "believe in capitalism, in the enriching mysteries of inequality, the inexhaustible mines of division of labour, the multiplying miracles of the market economies, the compounding gains from trade and poverty."[2] They are the champions of capitalist order and prefer individualism. Their main idea is that "effort and enterprise must be unleashed from the shackles of governmental control and regulations and must be encouraged through incentives in the form of tax reductions in order to promote production."[3]

(v) Emphasis on Growth

SSEs have full faith in Adam Smith's wealth definition and they say that - The 'Wealth of Nations' - is still the best book to read. They say that Smith's ideas can solve the problems of developing and developed countries in the matter of industry and commerce. As such they give more emphasis on growth, not on redistribution. It aims at improving everyone's economic conditions over time but not in the same degree or in the same period of time.

3. CRITICAL EVALUATION OF SSE

SSE is far from being new or revolutionary. It is not a unified body of thought. It is more concerned with the policy of tax cuts on earned income, tax incentives to increase savings etc. It stresses that an economy policy must focus on the supply side of the economy - on the long term capacity to produce rather than stimulating aggregate demand which only aggravates inflation. No one has given any exact definition of the SSE; only Arthur Laffer had a definite view, "Supply side economics is nothing more than classical economics in modern dress." It is nothing but old wine in new bottle. SSE as such do not have any distinguishing feature.

Its main limitations are:

(a) SSE is not providing any solution to poverty and unemployment. This is based on capatilist model imposed by big business, international private capital, multinationals, IMF and IBRD. SSE suits the interests of the dominant classes and generate more exploitation instead of taking the problem of unemployment and poverty.

(b) SSE suggested a tax cut to encourage savings and revenue to the government. But it has not suggested any method to determine the optimum tax rate. Moreover the effects of tax cut may not be the same all the time. The effect of tax cut on savings, investment, output and tax revenues will vary between countries and also between different time period. The relationship between the human behaviour and economic variables over time is unpredictable. Hence, there is no assurance to the government that by reducing tax rate it can increase its revenue and improve the development in the economy.

(c) SSE favours "Trickle Down Effects" but they are not aware of the actual effect of that.

According to Tobin, Trickle Down Effects' are redistributions of income, wealth and power from government to private enterprises, from workers to capitalists from poor to rich." Such a redistribution will benefit the immediate losers and beneficiaries in the long run. But this is not that very easy to achieve this as said by supply siders.

The economists who has supported the trickledown effects once, is in doubt now. i.e whether really the redistribution will work or not because the richer section of any country being more powerful, redistribution will always favour them and not the poor. Hence, the rich will become more richer and poor will remain as poor which will further widen the inequalities among them and rise more unequal income distribution in the economy.

(d) This theory is not suitable for under developed countries. Supply siders assign neutral role for government, small size for public sector and support for the maintainence of the existing inequalities. According to them, the economic activities should be taken care by the private individuals and State's duty is just to act as referee and to maintain law and order in the economy. But this kind of notion is wrong, because for development of any economy particularly in underdeveloped countries where majority of the population live below the poverty line, government intervention is a must in the economic activities in the country. In not the weaker section of the society will be exploited by affluent section and hence it results in more inequalities in the economy.

(e) SSE has assigned less role for public sector. In those areas where private sector is unwilling to, or is incapable of, fulfilling the developing needs of the nation, as in the case of provision of social overhead capital, there is no other alternative except enlarging the public sector to achieve that goal. But the view is not accepted by the supply side economists.

Conclusion

Though SSE has been criticised on various grounds, yet it is useful. It has great applicability in developing economies because it gives stress on increasing the supply of goods and services; which is the main problem in dveloping economies. The idealogy of SSE very well suits the conditions of developing economies as it glorifies incentive, hard work, production and savings which are very very essential for the growth in developing economies.

SUMMARY

1.   Supply Side Economics is an important element of new classical economics.

2.   Failure of Keynesianism and the problem of stagflation led to the introduction of SSE.

3.   Chief Exponent of SSE is Prof. Arthur Laffer supported by G.Gilder, P.Craig, N.Ture, J.Wanniski etc.

4.   SSE means manipulating the aggregate supply curve by skill formation modernisation, rationalisation, tax cuts, incentives etc.

5.   The main features of SSE are encouragement to incentives and savings, tax cuts, less role of government, etc.

6.   It has many implications. It has not been accepted and is criticised on various grounds.

7.   SSE has more applicability in developing economies because it gives stress on increasing the supply of goods and services; which is the main problem in these countries.

8.   To cope up with the problems of stagflation, an integrated policy of demand and supply aspects of management is considered essential.

QUESTIONS

1.   Give the meaning of Supply Side Economics.

2.   What are the various features of SSE.

3.   Critically evaluate the SSE.

4.   Can we apply the concept of SSE to developing economies? or Discuss the role fo SSE in developing economies.

REFERENCES

1.   Gupta, R.D, "Supply Side Economics - An Illusion or Reality The Indian Journal of Economics, Allahabad, No.247, Vol.LXII, April 1982.

2.   Gilder George - Wealth and Poverty, Kalyani Publishers, New Delhi, 1982.

3.   Kreiger, R.A - Supply Side Economics, Choice, November, 1981.

Indian Economy - Planning Era

25 Chapter

CHAPTER OBJECTIVES

After reading this chapter you will be able to answer the following:

1. General Growth and Development Indicators
2. Human Resources
3. Planning Era

Back Drop

The economic development of any country is based on certain important factors like natural resources, topography of the country, political system, education, ethnic factors and so on. It is also based on the opinion of experts on economics expressed from time to time. Classical economist Adam Smith identified forces leading to economic progress. David Ricardo analysed the condition necessary for growth. Other great economists like Robert Mathus spoke about volume of output and other causes for the growth of wealth in a nation. By 1870, the concept of "Economic Development" was "Focusing on search for the conditions of efficiency in utilising existing resources in the economy." Economic growth as a policy objective was ignored for quite a long time. Post world war II period was one situation in which the concept of "economic development" attained importance throughout the world. There was keen competition between capitalist and socialist countries in the sphere of economic development. Political issues like disintigration of Soviet Union, liberalisation of Afro-Asian countries etc. also contributed for the strengthening the concept of economic growth.

Concept

The concept of economic growth cannot be precisely defined. As we are talking of "Indian Economy and Her Growth," we have to clearly understand the concept of economic growth and the parameters to be considered for growth. Many feel that economic growth is obvious and the time should not be wasted on the definition of a concept which definitely happens. But growth cannot be precisely analysed unless some workable meaning of the concept has to be given.

Otherwise it leads to ambiguity and waste of time in measuring the growth. This particularly happens in developing countries like ours. In this direction the concept of economic growth may be understood, as "a rate of expansion that can move an underdeveloped country from a near subsistence mode of living to substantially higher levels in a comparatively short period of time i.e., in decades rather than centuries."

To understand the economic growth of a nation, we have to examine certain economic variables. The growth concept in a developed economy is different from that of developing or underdeveloped economy. In a developed economy, the focus will be on maintenance and further growth, if possible, of the economy. But in a developing economy rulers look to the optimisation of economic resources for the growth of the system.

In this backdrop, we will examine the various economic variables which throw light on the economic growth of a nation. Important variables are:

(i) Gross National Product (GNP)

(ii) Gross Domestic Product (GDP)

(iii) Equitable Distribution of Economic Wealth

(iv) Growth of per capita income

(v) Quantitative as well as qualitative growth of economic variables.

Even before we discuss the growth of Indian Economy, we have to understand the difference between "Economic growth and economic development." "Economic growth" concept focuses its area on quantitative development of the economy, whereas the concept "economic development" besides focusing on quantity dimension, it also involves qualitative aspects of economic variables. "Economic development involves growth plus progressive changes in certain critical variables which determine the well-being of the people." Development considers the aspects like progressive reduction of poverty, gradual elimination of malnutrition, disease, illiteracy, inequality etc. Quantitative aspect like increase in per capita income, GDP etc. are the concepts involved in economic growth. Therefore, when we study the economic history of India, we should look into both economic growth and economic development issues.

1. GENERAL GROWTH AND DEVELOPMENT INDICATORS

As we have to discuss in future paragraphs the economic history and development of India, we have to decide as to what indicators we have to adopt for understanding the growth and development of the country. Although much discussion has undergone about the decision of indicators, for our analysis, we can adopt the following indicators.

(i) Occupational distribution

(ii) Per capita income

(iii) Development potential

(iv) Quality aspects like poverty, unemployment and inequalities of income.

(i) **Occupational Distribution:** India is basically an agricultural country and a developing country too. While deciding the development and growth of a nation, occupational distribution of population is one of the economic variables which is invariably considered. Undoubtedly it is an acceptable indicator, but it is not totally reliable. It is generally accepted that a country which provides employment to larger section of the people in agriculture, forestry, animal husbandry etc. (Primary Sector) is underdeveloped. Although some countries have established some industries, the impact is less on the socio-economic life of the people. India falls in this category. Other countries to follow the suit are China, Tanzania, Nepal, Bangladesh etc. There are certain other countries in Latin America such as Chile, Argentina, Venezula etc. which cannot be called agrarian countries, as more employment generation is in industrial sector, are also categorised as underdeveloped countries. Therefore, occupational distribution of the population cannot fully provide a base for assessing the growth of the economy. But it gives the direction in which the economy is changing. In this analysis, it may be observed that India is still in its initial stages of growth as agriculture is still the main occupation of the large majority of the population. We are in a transition period and are shifting towards service sector for larger employment.

(ii) Per Capita Income: Another parameter adopted to measure the growth of a nation is 'Per Capital' income. Low real income per capita in India compared to Western Europe, US, Australia, Canada etc. is one of the indicators to exhibit that India is a developing nation. India did not adapt for a long time or rather did not get latest technology and scientific research since independence to develop the country. Neither, India gave top priority for education as soon the country attained independence. Although, the country has wonderful natural resources, it could not exploit these resources for growth. These factors contributed for the slow growth of Indian economy. It is estimated that three-fourth of the world population have low real per capita income. Some countries may not have natural resources to exploit and develop their economy in terms of per capita. Natural resources becomes a disturbing factor for economic growth and increase in national income. But per capita income alone cannot indicate development or underdevelopment of a country or region. In India, technology transfer is taking place at greater rate compared to pre 1991 situation. Therefore, growth rate of per capita is marginally increasing.

(iii) Development Potential: This indicator may be a better one to measure the growth of an economy. This indicates that the country which has growth potential should exploit it for the improvement of standard of living in the country. Growth potentiality can be exploited by using more capital or more labour or more available natural resources. Indian economy has been doing this through Five Year Plans.

(iv) Quality Indicators: As already discussed earlier, economic growth focusses on quantitative growth of the economy and economic development concept looks into quality aspects. Elimination of poverty, reducing inequality in income, providing facility for education and reducing unemployment are vital issues involved in development concept. Indian economy has been concentrating on these issues and have implemented several programmes to improve qualitative growth. But the State governments failed in fixing up priorities for growth. Educational sector, which can contribute for qualitative growth was not given priority. That is why today Indian economy has still 28% illiteracy level. Awareness is now created and this may take little time to improve the literacy level and improvement of education in the country. Both economic and non-economic factors are involved in the quality development of the country.

Economic factors involved economic development are (i) Natural resources of the country (India has abundant natural resources and needs economic power to exploit this, (ii) capital generation, (iii) surplus in output of agriculture and other sectors, (iv) position of foreign trade and (v) economic system.

Non-economic factors that contribute for economic development are (i) Human resources, (ii) General education, (iii) Political freedom and (iv) People participation (Social Institutions).

All these factors contribute for the quality development of an economy. In India every one views the concept of economic development in the light of achievements made in the economic planning period including the current one. Planning, although contributed for the growth of Indian economy, some very disturbing factors emerged. Industries were monopolised. Economic power was concentrated in few hands. A new class of 'rich agriculturists' has emerged. This class has created a disparity in rural sector. Nature is disturbing the agricultural sector through pests and diseases, irregular monsoons etc. Inter-state water sharing disputes have increased. But this sort of disturbance is not a good augury. Because of these factors density of population on agriculture in India gradually started declining. Exodus started, Rural people have slowly started shifting to urban places for better living. Service sector is activated in a bigway and has started providing employment. This sector is very fertile in the country and can generate enormous employment.

2. HUMAN RESOURCES

Of various factors stated earlier, that are contributing for economic growth and development in India, human resources are plenty and capital formation is taking place at a slow pace. This mismatch is mainly due to the lop sided development of human resources.

Important components of human development have to be looked into very seriously to develop human resources. In India, after the introduction of New Economic Policy in 1991, service sector gained momentum. This sector is mainly contributing to GDP (52%). The role of human resources in service sector is very big. Today quality development of human resources is the major problem of the country. For this, people involved (Governments) should create more opportunities to utilise huge man power of the country. Population growth need not be a disturbing for economic growth or development. It is experienced that illiteracy, unskilled workers, disease ridden and superstitious people are the ones that are contributing for slow growth of our country. Had there been are properly utilised, could have made of positive contribution for the growth and development rather than to be a burden to the economy. The concept of over population is always viewed from this angle. Man power management is a vital factor for the quality development of our economy. The governments should give priority for the development of human resources in terms of (i) Equity (ii) Productivity (iii) Sustainability and (iv) Empowerment.

Human Development Index (HDI) formulated and defined by United Nations Development Programme (UNDP) published in HUman Development Report (HDR) in 1990 states that "concept of human development is much wider and richer than what can be caught in any index or set of indicators." GNP is one of the strong indicators of economic growth. But HDI of UNDP adds considerable aspects to understand the development of a nation in many respects. It focusses on nutrition, education, health etc. to measure the economic development. The issues on which HDI focuses are:

- Education for all sections of the society
- Health condition in whole economy
- Views of policy makers on development aspects

- Whole economy is considered for income and resource distribution
- Comparative analysis of all economic and social data of its member countries

In this back drop, the status of Indian economy is discussed with reference to (i) National Income Trends, (ii) Structural changes, (iii) Progress in financial sector, (iv) Development of infrastructure, (v) Growth in different sectors like industry, agriculture, service and business. All these issues are analysed in detail under "Planning Era."

3. PLANNING ERA

Free and independent growth of an economy or Laisdsez-faire economy concept conceived by classical economists, has now become the history of the past. Today capitalist economies do not strictly follow "planned economy" concept. But socialist economies (covering a fourth of the population of the world) are planned economies. These economies cannot think of their growth without State ownership. This is what happened in India. When the country got independence, state only had to take the lead in its ownership to develop the country. That is how, planning era emerged in India.

Meaning

The countries which have planned economic growth, have different economic systems. A country might be a "mixed economy" as ours or fully State owned economies as China or Russia of the past (Today they are opened to market). In this context it is difficult to understand the concept of "Economic planning" unless one understands the nature of the system, a country follows. Economic planning here refers to the estimation of expenditure to be made in different sectors of the economy, resource mobilisation, projecting the expected revenue from each sector, growth rate to be achieved in each sector, leveraging the disturbances that may occur during the period under operation, to take place in a time frame.

Indian economy is a mixed economy. Planning was introduced in 1950-51. We have completed nine "Five Year Plans." Tenth plan is in progress. Mixed economy denotes the coexistence of public and private sectors in the economy supporting each other for the growth. Indian private sector comprises (i) Farming and handicrafts (ii) Small Scale individual and family owned business (iii) Small scale industries (iv) Medium sized commercial enterprises in agriculture, trade and industry and to some extent large manufacturing enterprises, mining companies and plantations, in which production takes place for both domestic and foreign markets. Public sector concentrated on developing infrastructure and development of basic and heavy industries. In this mixed economy structure of India, two vital aspects of economic planning can be identified.

- Government plays the promotional role by providing infrastructure like railways, hydroelectric projects, irrigation system which will be in its priority sector. Besides these main activities, government worked for the development of basic and heavy industries in which private participation was impossible as it involved large finance and long gestation period. Government provided funds through certain economic policies like taxation, industrial licensing, tariffs, wages, prices, interest rates and from foreign finance.
- Besides its own direct participation, government motivated private sector to some extent with certain controls to harmonise the operations and behaviour of private enterprises with the social objectives of the government. However, government liberalised this in

1991 with the introduction of new economic policies. With this, today, private sector is liberalised and is being empowered to take up big projects in industry, infrastructure and other service activities.

Why Economic Planning?

There are very many reasons as to why the Government of India (GOI) went to economic planning for her growth since 1950-51. Some vital reasons are highlighted here.

(i) Overall Development: The country, after independence was in a bad shape due to colonial ruling. Resources were very limited and had to be used judiciously. Investment had to be made for growth of the economy and not for profitability. If private investment allowed to a greater extent, it would harm the growth in terms of long term benefits. Therefore, country had no choice except to resort to economic planning. With the state intervention, development projects should look for social gains rather than private profitability. Even the resource mobilisation for the projects was easier, as the government took lead in evolving plans. When the country was facing resource crunch, it was apt that government resorted to economic planning for overall development.

(ii) Concentration of Economic Power: Had the government allowed economy to grow on its own with its least intervention (this means allowing economy to develop in the hands of private people), then benefits of growth would not have trickle down. There would have been more concentration of economic power. This would have created more problems and economy would have been in the hands of few people like British Managing Agents who did not allow Indian entrepreneurs to grow in their regime in this country. In order to reduce economic inequality and unemployment, government resorted to economic planning, thinking that economic, social and other problems could be solved within the framework of development planning.

(iii) Adverse Effects of Market Mechanism: Socialists believe that market mechanism is opposed to working class. One of the important variables of human development index - Equity - would be ignored by market mechanism. In most of the economies economic planning has been adopted to overcome the limitations of market mechanism. When India got independence, the situation was unfavourable to adopt market economy, i.e., free open market economy. Only hope was that the country should adopt the Russian type of planning for economic growth which gave less scope for private investment and thus avoid wrong priorities of investment which would have hampered the growth of economy in real terms.

This was the rationale behind the adoption of economic planning as a growth tool in India. No doubt planning era has given the economy certain long term benefits. There are lapses too. In the following paragraphs, a brief analysis all Five Year Plans implemented and achieved is made. India has adopted a type of economic planning "with the objective of translating developmental promises into practice."

Features of Indian Plans

- Planning in a mixed economy, where government has no control on certain vital areas like agriculture. But sets the targets and facilities the owners to achieve targets.
- Indian plans have embraced all fields. They are comprehensive.
- IPs are socially oriented and are physical plans.

Broad Objectives of Economic Planning

Although objectives were laid down in the First Five Year Plan, each plan had emphasis on one or the other objectives well within the framework of broad objectives. Following are the broad objectives of economic planning laid down.

- **To increase the growth rate of the economy:** Growth during British regime was nil as they amassed massive wealth from India. Therefore "Economic Growth" became the main objective of Indian economic plans.

- **Self reliance:** This means overcoming the need for external assistance for implementing economic plans and other national activities. This has to be achieved through correction of macro-economic imbalances and implementing structural reforms. Although India has achieved self-sufficiency in food and notable development in manufacturing sector, self-reliance objective has to be achieved yet, as today global players are competing in the country with domestic producers. But India is in a fairly good position as far as foreign exchange resources are considered.

- **Reducing Unemployment:** This objective is high lighted in every plan of the country to reduce poverty. Every able bodied person who wants to work should be assured a job to have honest living. This objective was not achieved till today as government did not have any separate employment policy. It was jointly considered with investment. It was expected that investment could automatically reduce unemployment which did not happen. Separate employment plans have to be prepared considering the requirement of different regions, sectors and economic classes.

- **Reduction of Inequalities of Income:** This is one of the objectives of economic planning of the country. However, redistribution of wealth did not receive priority in the hands of planners. By the time the Seventh Plan document was prepared, not even a single passing reference was made regarding redistribution of wealth. Planners thought that economic growth will automatically reduce inequality in income. With the introduction liberalisation policy, inequality is growing. But government has to view this seriously.

- **Poverty Elimination:** Draft Fifth Five Year Plan categorically mentioned this objective. From the experience of previous four plans, government realised that poor had hardly benefited from plans and their life was as miserable as it was in 1947. Draft Fifth Plan, emphasised this and said in Sixth plan document "that the incidence of poverty in the country is still very high. Thus determined measures are necessary to combat poverty." Inspite of various measures adopted poverty has not been reduced, let alone elimination. Government estimates still stand at 26.1% in 1990s and private estimates say that 44.9 per cent of rural population 31.6 per cent of urban population was below the poverty line in 1998.

- **Modernisation:** Planners, although gave priority for technological and scientific growth in Five year plans, the concept of modernisation was explicitly mentioned in Sixth Plan document. Draft states that "The term modernisation connotes a variety of structural and institutional changes in the frame work of economic activity." "A shift in the sectoral composition of production, diversification of activities, an advancement of technology and institutional innovations so as to transform a feudal and colonial economy into a modern and independent economic activity." If this statement in the Sixth Plan document can be accepted, it may be said that there is modernisation in the economy in terms of improvement in manufacturing sector, agricultural sector, mining construction and infra structure. With the development of new sector viz., Information Technology (IT), export earnings have increased. National income has increased resulting in improved purchasing power in the hands of public. This has improved the standard of living of people. Priority of expenditure in households have changed giving raise to the development transport vehicles and other consumer durable goods manufacturing. Priority is gradually being given to education which is the vital element of economic growth. With the application of IT, use of new materials and developing fuel efficiency equipment, country is modernising. But there is a threat from automation in both manufacturing and farm sectors. However, service sector is growing and creates more employment opportunities to maintain the rate of modernisation.

Development in planning period is discussed in subsequent chapters.

SUMMARY

1. Economic growth concept focusses on quantitative development of an economy where as Economic development besides focussing on quantitative aspect, it also involves qualitative aspects of economic variables.

2. General growth and development of an economy depends on occupational distribution, per capita income, development potential, poverty, unemployment and inequalities of income in an economy.

3. Human resource development is very essential for the development of a nation.

4. Indian economy is fast developing in various fields under planning era. Five year plans including 10th FYP has sown the seed for the development of our country what we see today.

5. Economic planning is very essential to the objectives such as, to increase the growth rate of economy, to increase employment opportunities, national income, per capita income, reduction in inequalities of income, modernisation etc.

QUESTIONS

1. Distinguish the concept of economic growth and economic development.

2. Explain various general growth and development indicators of an economy.

3. Write a short note on occupational distribution pattern of Indian economy.

4. 'Human resource development is essential for the development of a nation' - Elucidate.

5. What is economic planning?

6. Explain the various objectives of economic planning in India.

26 Chapter

Characteristics of Indian Economy

CHAPTER OBJECTIVES

After reading this chapter you will be able to answer the following:

1. Characteristics of Indian Economy as an undeveloped Economy
2. India as a Developing Economy
3. India as a Dualistic Country
4. India as a Mixed Economy

An economy or economic system refers to the manner in which the various economic activities relating to production, distribution, exchange and consumption of goods and services are organised in a country and the way in which the people of a country earn their living. It comprises the factories, firms, mines, shops, banks, schools, offices, transport systems, theatres, hospitals, public administration, defence etc. which help in the production and distribution of goods and services in the country.

An economy of a country usually consists of three sectors, viz., (1) Primary sector (2) Secondary sector and (3) Tertiary sector.

The primary sector includes agriculture, forestry, mining, fishing etc. and it is generally called agricultural sector.

The secondary sector includes all kinds of industries both large as well as small and it is generally called industrial sector.

The tertiary sector includes services like transport, banking, insurance trade, public administration, defence etc. and it is usually called service sector.

Indian economy refers to the manner in which the various economic activities like farming, manufacturing mining, trade, transport, banking etc. and the various economic institutions such as farms, factories, mines, shops, transport systems, banks, offices, public administration, educational institutions, defence etc. connected with the production and distribution of goods and services are organised in India, It also shows the way in which the people of India earn their livelihood.

Indian Economy comprises three sectors, viz., like any other country agricultural sector, industrial sector and service sector.

Indian economy is presently characterised as an. underdeveloped economy. But it no longer suffers from stagnation. India has opted for a planned capitalist development, and accordingly built up a mixed economy. Due to the growth efforts taken by the country it has emerged as a dualistic country. So, Indian economy can be viewed as an underdeveloped economy, developing economy, a dualistic economy and a mixed economy.

1. CHARACTERISTICS OF INDIAN ECONOMY AS AN UNDEVELOPED ECONOMY

The important features of an underdeveloped economy were present in the Indian economy at the time of independence and it has not changed much since then. Indian Economy has several characteristics. The important features of the Indian economy are:

1. **Low Per capita Income:** The per capita income of the people (i.e.) the annual income per head of population in India is very low: As per the World Development Report, 2002, the per capita income in India in 2000 was $460 and it is much lower than that in many under developed countries. The rate of increase in per capita income over the years is very low.

2. **Low Standard of Living:** Due to low per capita income, most of the people of India do not have the basic necessities of life. The standard of living of the people is very low. Nearly 39% of the total population of the country live below the poverty line and there is mass chronic poverty.

3. **Rapid growth of Population and High Dependency Ratio:** According to 2001 Census the population of India is 1,025 million as against 439 million in 1961. Over these years population has increased at the rate of 2.14% per annum and it may not decline substantially in the near future. Indian economy at present passing through the second stage of demographic transition which is characterized by a falling death rate without a corresponding decline in birth rate. This has resulted in population explosion.

4. **Predominance of Agriculture:** About 64.9% of the working population depend on agriculture for their livelihood. It is still primitive and is gamble in the monsoons and it is still under-developed. In 2000 agriculture contributed 27% and the GDP and it is much less than the share of agriculture in GDP in 1950-51 (when it contributed more than 50%). Though we have adopted planning for about five decades we have not achieved much in agriculture.

5. **Industrial Backwardness:** India is industrially backward though industrialisation had started in the country as early as in 1850, India has not made much progress in industrial development. Only 10% of our population is engaged in industries as compared to 88% in the USA. In 2000 the contribution of industrial sector towards GDP was 27%.

6. **Deficiency of Capital:** There is shortage of capital and also low rate of capital formation in India.

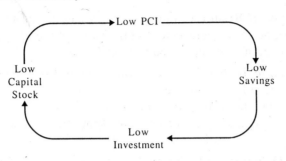

Figure

On account of poverty the people of India are not able to save much which results in low investment, low production and again low per capita income. Only 12%-15% of our national income is saved and invested as against 20% in USA and Great Britain and 30% in Japan. Ragnar Nurkse has rightly said that, "A country is poor because it is poor."

7. **Low level of Technology:** In India there is technical backwardness. In all the fields of production, the techniques of production are mostly old and obsolete. There is also lack of quality education and technical training to absorb the modern technology.

Modernisation in the industrial sector is quite limited. There is also a wide gap existing between the sophisticated production techniques of the developed countries and our technology. This will result in inefficient production and it causes in general poverty in our country.

8. **Inadequate Transport and Communications Systems:** There is lack of infrastructural facilities like transport and communication facilities, electricity facilities, power facilities, economic organisation etc. Even today many of our rural areas are not provided with well developed roadways.

9. **Existence of Dualistic or Dual Sector:** In India both ancient and modern sectors exist side by side. In agriculture, we find the ancient wooden ploughs as well as the modern tractors. In industries also we find old and obsolete machines and methods as well as modern sophisticated machines and methods, and small artisans and craftsmen along with giant multi-national firms.

10. **Unemployment:** On account of the rapid growth of population supply of labour is more than the demand for it in India. Due to this, all the working population are not provided with jobs. There is large-scale unemployment, under employment and disguised unemployment in the country. Disguised unemployment prevails especially in rural areas that too in agriculture. That is, in agriculture, the number of persons engaged is much more than that is actually needed due to lack of alternative employment opportunities.

11. **Poor quality of Indian Working Population:** The quality of Indian labour force is very poor and less efficient when compared to the labour in advanced countries. The poor quality of the Indian labour is due to the reason that the labourers of India are poor and under-fed, and so, do not have good health. Moreover, they are illiterate and do not have technical training. Human Development Index (HDI) is very low in India when compared to other UDCs like Srilanka, Brazil etc.

12. **Under Utilisation of Resource:** India is rich in natural resources like land, minerals, forests, wild life, power, fisheries etc. But they are not properly utilised due to shortage of capital, low level of technology and technical skill.

13. **Lack of Economic Institutions:** Economic institutions such as banks, insurance companies, co-operative credit societies, investment houses, etc. are not adequately developed in India. Because of this, the savings in rural areas are not mobilised for economic development. They are hoarded and kept idle in the form of gold ornaments or cash.

14. **Foreign Trade Orientation:** Indian economy is foreign trade oriented. Most of our raw materials are exported to foreign countries and are not used within the country. Finished goods and machines, chemicals, ete. are imported from foreign countries. This may check the growth of industries in the country, reduce employment opportunities and create deficit in the balance of payments.

15. **Social Backwardness:** In India there is social backwardness due to several factors like caste system, joint family system, illiteracy, ignorance, superstitious beliefs etc. The law of succession and inheritance has contributed to sub-division and fragmentation of land holdings. The social factors have prevented people from taking modern methods of production.

16. **Presence of Monopolistic Tendency and Lack of Entrepreneurs:** Most of the industries in our country are owned and controlled by a few business families. India also lack innovating entrepreneurs. They concentrate on quick, speculative profits rather than on the long-term industrial development of the country.

17. **Inequitable Distribution of Income:** In India there are gross or glaring inequalities in the distribution of income and wealth among the people. During the 1990s in equalities in household consumption expenditure have increased as a result of pro-rich liberalisation policies. The inequalities are found in both rural and urban areas.

18. **Lack of Clean and Efficient Administration by the Government:** The country lacks clean and efficient administration required for the exploitation of the natural and human resources of the nation for the betterment of the economic conditions of the people. There is inefficiency in all levels of administration. There is favouritism, nepotism and corruption are there every where.

When we look into the above mentioned characteristics which are present we can say that India is an under-developed economy.

2. INDIA AS A DEVELOPING ECONOMY

Indian Economy is no doubt, an underdeveloped economy. But it is not stagnant and it has started marching towards economic progress. With the help of the economic planning, during the last 52 years, the country has made much progress in agriculture, industry, science and technology, health and education and in various other fields. The following changes in the Indian economy over the last 52 years clearly prove that India is a developing economy.

• India's net national product (NNP) at factor cost (national income) was Rs.1,32,367 crore in 1950-51 and it has increased to 10,44,915 crore in 2000-2001 with the growth rate of 4.2% per annum.

- There is a rise in PCI from Rs.3,687.1 in 1950-51 to Rs.10,254.3 in 2000-2001.
- The share of tertiary sector (service sector) in the gross domestic product has increased from 27.5% in 1950-51 to 48.4% in 2000-01.
- There is continuous rise in agricultural production and India has achieved the stage of self-sufficiency in terms of foodgrains. It is also able to build up buffer stocks of foodgrains for lean periods.
- At present there is growth of basic capital goods industries. A large number of industries have been developed on large scale like iron and steel, heavy chemicals, nitrogenous fertilizers, heavy engineering, machine tools, aluminum petroleum products etc.
- There is progress of science and technology. Sophisticated machines and instruments are produced within the country with the indigenous scientific and technical know-how.
- There has been considerable improvement in the provision of infrastructural facilities and social security services.
- Transport and communication facilities have been extended and there has been a remarkable improvement in power supply.
- Banking and financial facilities have been expended.
- Over the last 52 years, the inequalities in the distribution of income and wealth have been reduced through progressive taxation, increased public expenditure social security measures etc.
- There have been desirable changes in the society over the last 52 years because of urbanisation and the spread of education. The caste system, untouchability and superstitious beliefs are on the decline.

So we can say that, though Indian economy is economically backward no longer it is an underdeveloped economy. The improvements which had taken place and taking place have changed the face of Indian economy. It has become a developing economy today.

3. INDIA AS A DUALISTIC COUNTRY

At present Indian economy is characterised by a dualistic economic structure i.e., a modern economy existing side by side with a traditional primitive economy. In India there is a clear evidence of technological dualism prevailing in all the sectors. India possesses the traditional rural sector (agriculture) and modern industrial sector.

Due to decline in the mortality rates and steady growth rate of population has resulted in population explosion in India. Industrial sector failed to absorb the increased labour force and hence they were diverted to agricultural sector resulting in disguised unemployment in the rural sector. This is mainly because technological progress favoured capital intensive sector.

Though there is spectacular technological development in industrial sector including mining and petroleum, the technological progress is slow in agriculture and handicrafts. Trade union movement and Government intervention have increased wage rates in organised industrial sector.

But this had no effect on real wages in the rural sector. This has contributed to the emergence of technological dualism.

4. INDIA AS A MIXED ECONOMY

Indian Economy is a mixed economy. Features of both capitalism and socialism are found in India. There is simultaneous existence of public sector and private sector. The share of public sector in the total national output is less than 25%. A greater percent of industrial sector is in private hands. Except some basic industries all other industries are in private sector. Railways is state owned whereas road transport is mostly in private hands. Agriculture which is the main economic activity is in the private sector. Their behaviuour is not responsive to market changes.

Market mechanism, though dominated by private sector, it is not completely free from state control. Licensing system and other controls were introduced by the Government. G.Thimmaiah has rightly said that, the license and control system has failed in controlling private sector. Due to the introduction of structural reforms in 1991-92 various physical controls have been withdrawn and market mechanism now operate more freely than past.

The presence of public sector alongwith free enterprise makes the character of the Indian as mixed economy. Though India has introduced economic planning like socialist country, yet it is basically capitalistic economic framework. The economic planning in India over the past five decades and the development of the public sector in this period were thus meant to move a static economy. Their aim was not to change the basic character of the country's economy. Therefore the character of Indian economy has not undergone any change since independence and it still continues to be a mixed economy.

SUMMARY

1. Indian economy can be viewed from four dimensions.
    (i)   As an underdeveloped economy
    (ii) As a developing economy
    (iii) As a dualistic economy
    (iv) As a mixed economy.

2. Since India possesses all the characteristic features of an UDC like low per capita income, low standard of living, rapid growth of population, predominance of agriculture, industrial backwardness, low level of technology, etc., it can be called as an underdeveloped country.

3. India has started marching towards economic progress with the help of economic planning. There is development both in quantitative terms and in structural changes.

4. There is significant rise in national income and PCI (per capita income) higher than the rate of population growth.

5. The structural changes which are taking place in India indicate the process of development which began in the early 1950s is still continuing.

6. Indian economy is also characterised by a dualistic economic structure. The modern industrial sector exist side by side with a traditional primitive economy. There is also technological dualism in our country.

7. The Indian Economy is also a mixed economy. There is the simultaneous existence of both large public sector and enlarged private sector. The existence of mixed economy framework has provided a feasible proposition for a developing country as it allows for a modest rate of growth.

QUESTIONS

1. Give the reasons for low per capita income in India.
2. Give the meaning of under-developed economy.
3. What are the main causes for deficiency of capital in India?
4. Explain the features of Indian economy as an under developed country.
5. Is India a developing economy?
6. Explain the features of Indian economy as a developing economy.
7. Give the meaning of dualistic economy.
8. Is India a dualistic economy. Discuss.
9. India possesses the features of a mixed economy. Do you agree? Explain.

27 Chapter

Development of Indian Economy (Sector Wise Analysis)

The position of Indian economy has changed radically after the World War II. Though India possess the features of an underdeveloped country, since it is not a stagnant economy, and also it has started marching towards economic progress we can call India as a developing economy. During the past 52 years, the country has made much progress in agriculture, industry, science and technology, health and education and in various other fields. All these improvements have changed the face of Indian economy. Indian economy which was almost stagnant for 100 years from 1850 to 1950, has become a developing economy today with the recent liberalisation of Indian economy. One can very confidently say that India will definitely catch up with the advanced countries of the world within a few years.

1. STRATEGY AND PLANNING IN INDIA

In 1951, economic planning was adopted as an instrument of development. India's independence in 1947 paved the way for the adoption of economic planning. Over the past five decades the country has completed nine five year plans. During these years the National income has increased and also considerable development has taken place in the various sectors.

The economic planning in India has been formulated on the basis of long term objectives of (a) economic growth (b) self-reliance (c) full employment (d) modernisation and (e) social justice.

Till 1970s growth was accorded priority in the plans. However, the emphasis was shifted to social justice in 1970s and 1980s. In 1990s liberalisation process was given importance by the decision makers at the government level. Lately, modernisation has received a high priority as it is considered as a pre-requisite for the acceleration of growth process.

The economic growth achieved by Indian economy can be reflected in its GDP growth rate. The national income rose as the rate of 3.6% per annum during the First plan period. National income started increasing steadily after that: During the eighth plan GDP increased at an impressive rate of 6.8% per annum but it has decreased to 5.4% (average annual growth rate) during the period of Ninth Five Year Plan (1992-2002).

India has achieved self-reliance in the field of agriculture and basic industries. Since 1977-78 India has managed to cut down its food imports and government has succeeded in building buffer stocks and it successfully handles any type of situation without recourse to large imports. Development of basic industries such as iron and steel, machine tools and heavy engineering has reduced the dependence on developed countries for capital equipment.

In 1991 Government of India adopted a new development strategy which is often known as Export-Led Growth (ELG) strategy. The new strategy assumed the trade as an engine for economic growth. The ELG strategy leads to globalisation of the economy. This new strategy under the Ninth Five Year Plan enabled India's broad based private sector to reach its full potential for raising production and income levels. The role of the Government in the new strategy is very limited as it will no longer be a controller of private enterprise. It may concentrate on social development and infrastructural development.

. 2. ECONOMIC REFORMS AND LIBERALISATION IN INDIA

Indian economy faced a major economic crisis in early 1991. To tackle this, since July 1991 comprehensive liberalisation measures have been undertaken to improve the supply side of the economy. The important reforms which are undertaken by the Indian Government are:

(1) Trade and capital flows reforms

(2) Industrial deregulation reforms

(3) Disinvestment and public enterprise reforms

(4) Financial sector reforms.

1. Trade and Capital Flows Reforms: The Government has introduced a series of reforms in the trade sector since July 1991. It will help in integration of the Indian economy with the rest of the world. Various measures taken towards this are:

(a) devaluation of rupee in July 1991.

(b) full convertibility of rupee on trade account was introduced in 1993-94.

(c) Import duty was reduced to 150% in 1991-92.

(d) It was further reduced to 50% in 1995-96 and to 30% in 2002-2003 budget.

(e) Decanalisation of imports and exports has been done in recent years. Besides these it has also established Exported Oriented Units, Export Promotion Capital Goods Scheme etc.

It has also introduced measures to accelerate the country's transition to a globally-oriented economy.

2. **Industrial Deregulation:** Many economists of India criticised the regulatory activity taken by the Government towards industrial sector. They have also criticised the MRTP Act. According to them regulatory device has led to widespread inefficiency in the industrial sector. So, the Government has relaxed some of the controls since 1991. The New Industrial Policy which was announced in July 1991 has relaxed various procedures and it has provided a gate for opening up a large number of industries to the private sector. Industrial licensing has been abolish except 6 product categories. The number of industries reserved for public sector has been reduced to 3 from 17. Core industries like iron and steel, electricity, air transport, ship building, heavy machine industry etc., and even defence production have been opened for private sector.

3. **Public Sector Reforms and Disinvestment:** Government has taken steps for encouraging the entry of private sector which was originally dominated by public sector. Now-a-days government has resorted to disinvestment in the form of transfer of a part of the ownership of state owned enterprises to the public.

Till March 2001, equity amounting to Rs.25,894 crore in select public sector undertakings was disinvested to public sector financial institutions, mutual funds, private corporates and general public. The union budget for 2001-2002 had proposed to raise Rs.12,000 crore through disinvestment. About 18 public sector undertakings (PSUs) are on the anvil for disinvestment. In India, there is a lack of enthusiasm for outright privatisation.

4. **Financial Sector Reforms:** The Government set up a committee on Financial System under the chairmanship of M.Narasimham and the committee submitted its report in December 1991. Since then it has been used as basis for financial sector reforms in the country. Meanwhile, major changes had taken place in the domestic economic and institutional scene. There was a movement towards global integration of financial services. So, the Government appointed a committee on Banking Sector Reforms under the Chairmanship of M.Narasimham. The committee submitted its report in April 1998. In its report the committee stressed on important measures like the increase in capital to Risk-Wrighted Assets Ratio, the introduction of market risk on government securities, the stricter Non-performing Assets (NPAs) norms and provisioning requirements and the introduction of asset-liability management guidelines and risk management guidelines.

As per the recommendations of the Second Narasimham Committee report, CRAR was raised to 9%. Commercial banks were asked to provide additional information in the 'Notes to Accounts' in the balance sheet to increase transparency.

3. AGRICULTURAL DEVELOPMENT DURING THE PLANNING PERIOD

Agricultural sector in India has reached the stage of development and maturity. The share of agriculture in NI is often taken as an indicator of economic development. At the time of First World War, agriculture contributed two-thirds of NI. But, after the initiation of planning in India, the share has come down drastically on account of the development of the secondary and tertiary sector of the economy. The share of agriculture in GDP at factor cost was 59.2% in 1950-51 and it has declined to 26.6% in 2000-01 (at 1993-94 prices). The percentage of working population depending on agriculture has come down to 60% in 1999. The share of agriculture in export earnings has also comedown. The share of agriculture in total exports was 44.2% in

1960-61 and it fell to 17.6% in 1992-93. In 1993-94 it increased to 18.7%. But its share has once again declined to 15.7% in 1998-99 and 14% in 2000-01. India has resorted to large scale imports of food grains during drought conditions. It also imports dairy products, vegetables, vegetable and animal oil, and raw materials.

There has been a continuous increase in agricultural production and productivity in India. The total production of good grains has increased from 50.8 million tonnes in 1950-51 to 155 million tonnes in the Seventh Plan period and further to 187 million tonnes in Eighth Plan (annual average). It reached the highest record level of 209.8 million tonnes in 1999-2000 but fell to 195.9 million tonnes in 2000-01.

There has been a considerable improvement in the production of non-foodgrains also. The production of oil seeds was impressive and it reached a record level of 24.7 million tonnes, though it fell to 20.7 million tonnes in 1999-2000 and further to 18.4 million tonnes in 2000-01. Production of cotton and sugarcane has registered a more or less a steady growth during the period 1950-51 to 2000-01.

The period of mid 1960s was very significant from the point of view of Indian agriculture. During that period India experienced "Green Revolution," due to the adoption of New Agricultural strategy. However, in 1990s the growth in agricultural sector has declined.

4. IMPORTANT POLICY MEASURES

The important policy measures introduced in the agricultural sector in India during the period of planning are as follows:

    (i) Technological measures.

    (ii) Land Reforms.

    (iii) Co-operation and Consolidation of holdings.

    (iv) Institutions involving people's participation in planning.

    (v) Procurement and support prices.

    (vi) Institutional credit.

    (vii) Input subsidies to agriculture.

    (viii) Food security system.

    (ix) Rural employment programme.

    (x) Provision of irrigation facilities.

    (xi) Promotion of agricultural Research and training.

    (xii) Provision and expansion of storage and warehousing facilities etc.

Apart from the above mentioned measures. New scheme titled 'National Agriculture Insurance Scheme' was introduced from Rabi 1999-2000. Through five year plans, agricultural sector of our country has made considerable progress during the last 52 years.

5. INDUSTRIAL DEVELOPMENT AND INDUSTRIAL POLICY

The industrial development in Indian economy can be divided in to four phases.

(i) I Phase (1951-1965): laid the foundation for industrial development in the country.

(ii) II Phase (1965-1980): industrial deceleration and structural retrogression.

(iii) III Phase (1980-1991): industrial recovery.

(iv) IV Phase (1991-92 - till date): post reform period.

During the I phase the basic industries like iron and steel, heavy engineering and machine building industry registered a significant increase in their growth.

Huge investments were made in their industries. The annual growth rate of industrial production increase from 5.7% in I Plan to 7.2% in II Plan and further to 9.0% in III Plan. This shows that a strong base for industrial development was laid during the first three plan periods.

During the II Phase there was a declining trend in the industrial growth. The industrial growth was mere 4.1% per annum during 1965-76. In 1976-77 it increased to 10.6%. In 1979-80 it recorded a negative rate of growth of industrial production of 1.6% over preceding year. There was a decline in the growth rate of capital goods industries and basic industries after the III Plan period reflecting structural retrogression. Consumer goods industry showed are improvement in its growth.

During the III Phase it was a period of industrial recovery. Industrial growth was 6.4% per annum during 1980-81 - 1984-85, 8.5% per annum during 1985-90 and 8.3% in 1990-91. This industrial recovery was noted by various economists. The important reason for industrial recovery during this phase was the liberalisation of industrial and trade policies by the Government.

During the IV Phase Indian Industry entered into a new era of economic liberalisation. This has affected the performance of industrial sector. Due to the liberalisation there is a steep fall in the rate of growth of capital goods sector. Even the basic goods sector also registered a decline with its rate from 7.4% to 5.9% in 1992-93 - 2000-01. Intermediate goods and consumer goods sector has shown improvement (particularly consumer durable's sector).

6. INDUSTRIAL POLICY

After independence Government of India, to seep up the industrial development in the country, announced its policy on 6th April, 1948 in the form of a resolution. Since the Government felt the need for change in the industrial policy, it announced a new industrial policy on 30th April, 1956. This policy was in force for nearly two decades and it had contributed to the industrial development of the country to a considerable extent. It was defective in some respects. To remove the defects, the Janata Government announced its industrial policy on 23rd December, 1977 in the form of a statement. In 1980, when the Congress-I Government replaced Janata Government, it felt a need for change in the Industrial policy and accordingly it announced a new industrial policy on 23rd July, 1980 in the form of a statement. This policy was based on the industrial policy of 1956. In line with the liberalisation measures announced during the 1980s the Government announced a New Industrial Policy on July 24, 1991.

New Industrial Policy, 1991

The new policy de-regulates the industrial sector in a substantial manner.

Objectives

(a) To build on the gains already made.

(b) To maintain sustained growth in production.

(c) To maintain gainful employment.

(d) To correct the distortions that might have crept in.

(e) To upgrade industrial technology and attain international competitiveness.

(f) To ensure that India grows as a part of the world economy.

Features

(i) This policy abolished all industrial licensing, irrespective of the level of investment, except for 18 industries. In due course these industries were also delicensed. At present only 6 items of health, strategic and security considerations, remain under the purview of industrial licensing.

(ii) Public sector's role is diluted. Only 3 industries (atomic energy, mineral specified to atomic energy and rail transport) exists in public sector.

(iii) The MRTP Act has been amended to give adequate protection to consumers.

(iv) In January 1997, the Government also announced new guidelines for foreign direct investment. Many concessions were announced in 2000-01 and 2001-02 to promote foreign investment. The Government has also allowed 26% foreign direct investment in defence production.

(v) Industrial location policy was liberalised. A major amendment was effected during 1997-98.

(vi) The industrial policy of 1991 removed the mandatory convertibility clause from the term loans that would be granted by the public sector institutions for new projects.

Evaluation

The changes brought out by the policy will reduce the project cost. The changes in respect of foreign investment and foreign technology agreements will raise the availability of scarce resources and also improve the efficiency of production. Amendment of MRTP Act will promote healthy competition and efficiency. Though there is brighter side for industrial development through this policy, this policy has been strongly criticised by economists.

They say that there is no evidence of positive impact on industrial growth. Due to liberalisation, there is threat from foreign competition. MNCs penetrate through foreign direct investment and this may push the Indian businessman to subordinate position or simply oust him.

The industrial policy of the Government of India has not been static. It has undergone changes in the political, industrial and economic scenes in the country.

7. INDIA'S FOREIGN TRADE

Indian economy is foreign trade oriented. Government of India has announced Massive Trade Policy in 1991 to open up the economy to foreign trade and to integrate the Indian economy into the global economy.

The value of India's exports and imports has increased considerably over the planning period. In 1950-51 the value of export was $1,269 million and it rose to $2,031 million in 1920-71 and to $8,486 million in 1980-81 and further to $44,560 million in 2000-01. The imports during the same period has increased from $1,273 in 1950-51 to $50,536 million in 2000-01. The study of statement 7.1 (B), P.S.82 of Economic Survey 2000-01 reveals that Indian trade balance was positive during the period 1949-50 to 1999-2000. i.e., during 1972-73 and 1976-77 it recorded surpluses of $!34 million and $77 million respectively. In all other years only deficits in balance of trade were recorded.

Indian economy has undergone changes both in its composition and direction of foreign trade. Before the economic planning was started in India, main exports were primary goods and imports consisted of manufactured goods. But after the planning, there has been a total change in its composition. In recent years India started exporting various kinds of manufactured goods like engineering goods, ready made garments, chemicals and allied products, software, leather and leather products etc. Similarly the imports of our country has undergone a change. Now major position of import expenditure goes to POL (Petroleum, Oil and Lubricants).

Regarding India's direction of Foreign trade, major changes had taken place. OECD dominated in India's import (78.8%) in 1960-61 and it has come down to 39.9% in 2000-01. Developing nations play a major role in India's imports at present. Similarly, India exports more to OECD countries and developing nations. 52.7% of India's exports goes to OECD nations in 2000-01 and 26.7% to developing nations of the world.

India joining the WTO (World Trade Organisation) in 1995 as a founder member has made it obligatory to strike down all quantitative restrictions on imports and reduce import tariffs so as to open up the economy to world trade and the forces of globalisation.

The Government of India announced the new five year export-import policy covering the Tenth Five Year Plan period (2002-2007) on March 31, 2002. This policy carries a number of measures to raise India's share in global trade to 1% by 2007, up from the present 0.67%. This require increasing exports from $46 billion to over $80 billion over the Tenth Five Year Plan.

8. INDIA AND THE WORLD ECONOMY

From the Indian context, globalisation implies opening up the economy to foreign direct investment by providing facilities to foreign companies to invest in India; removing obstacles to the entry of MNCs in India; allowing Indian Companies to enter into foreign collaborations in India and encourage them to set up joint ventures abroad; carrying out massive import liberalisation programmes etc.

The economic crisis which prevailed in India during 1990-91, pushed economy into the adoption of structural adjustment programme of the IMF and World Bank. Globalisation is a part of structural adjustment programme. Since the desperate conditions prevailed in 1990 and 1991 India was pushed towards globalisation.

As the first step taken towards globalisation, Government of India opted for devaluation of rupee by 22%. Then it announced import liberalisation. India as a member of WTO has to remove the quantitative restrictions on imports and it has been totally removed by April 1, 2001. This was followed by announcement of various measures from time to time to attract foreign investors. NRIs investment restrictions were relaxed. NRI investment upto 100% of equity has been allowed in export houses, trading houses, star trading houses, hospitals, sick industries, hotels etc. 100% of foreign equity participation has been allowed for setting power plants in India.

Globalisation has led to considerable changes both positively and negatively in India. It has increased our foreign currency reserves to over $20 billion on March 10, 1995. Exporters were responding well. Liberalisation and openness have increased our self-reliance. Exports now finance over 90% of our imports, compared to 60% in later half of 1980s. International confidence in India has been restored resulting in increased foreign direct and portfolio investment.

The process of globalisation has led to an unhealthy or unequal competition between 'Giant MNCs and very small Indian enterprises. The domestic corporate sector is dominated by these MNCs. They capture the Indian Market. In the case of joint ventures, the MNCs have shown alarming speed in pushing over their Indian partners and gaining full control on the enterprise.

9. INDIA AND WTO

India has joined the WTO in 1995 as a founder member. Its impact on Indian trade can be viewed from two dimensions. First is the advantages or benefits which India can enjoy and secondly the disadvantages which India has to face.

Benefits to India

1. The GATT Secretarial has projected that there will be greater demand for clothing, agriculture, fishery products and processed food. Since India mainly exports these goods, it can expect an increase in its exports.

2. The phasing out of the Multi-Fibre Agreement by 2005 will benefit India as the exports of textiles and clothings will increase.

3. There will be improved prospects for agricultural exports as a result of likely increase in the world prices of agricultural products due to reduction in domestic subsidies and barriers to trade.

4. By strengthening the multilateral rules and disciplines, the Uruguay Round Agreement, create a more favourable environment for India in the new world economic order.

Disadvantages

WTO is now seen by many developing countries like India as a threat to their very economic existence than an opportunity.

1. There is totally ineffective implementation of many of the Agreements which are expected to benefit developing countries like India.

2. Encouraging foreign investment into a country without any control on them will result in BOP (balance of payments) crisis.

3. The extension of intellectual property rights to agriculture has serious consequences for India.

4. By April 2001, India will have to remove all quantitative restrictions and forced have most liberal import policy in the world than any western country.

5. There are very serious threats to our exports. Very soon the benefits like DEPB scheme, EPCG etc. will have to be withdrawn or modified because they are actionable under the Agreement on subsidies and countervailing measures.

6. The extent and intensity of non-tariff barriers against our exports have increased significantly.

7. It is ironical that while India is forced to reduce tariffs and face non-tariff barriers, the developed countries maintain high peak tariffs for our exportable products.

Though India is not benefiting much from WTO, it would not be a wise decision to leave WTO. Being a part of global economy, in the interest of the nation, it is better to be an active member of WTO and ensure multilateralism in trade policy. If it is not a member, it has to approach every country for concessions and it will be a very complicated affair. Developed countries attitude about non-WTO countries can not be predicted. It may affect India's exports and exchange earnings. Access may be denied for to modern technologies or delayed. Therefore, it is necessary for India to continue to be the member of WTO and insist on our legitimate rights.

SUMMARY

1. The economic planning strategy adopted by Indian economy has enabled it to achieve its targets and it is also reflected in the GDP growth rate.

2. To overcome major economic crisis in 1991, 4 important reforms are undertaken by the Indian Government. They are (i) Trade and capital flows reforms (ii) Industrial deregulation (iii) Disinvestment and public enterprise reforms and (iv) Financial sector reforms.

3. The share of NI from agriculture has gradually decreased in the last five decades. It has comedown from 59.2% in 1950-51 to 26.6% in 2000-01.

4. The share of industrial sectors to NI has increased steadily. Several industrial policy resolutions were introduced to develop industrial sector of our country. New Industrial Policy of 1991 has enabled the industrial sector to develop to a greater extent.

5. India's foreign trade has undergone several changes both in terms of composition and direction.

6. Globalisation has both positive and negative impact on Indian economy.

7. Bring a member of WTO though India has gained in certain aspects, but being a developing country it is considered as a threat to its very economic existence than an opportunity.

QUESTIONS

1. What is economic planning? How far is it helpful in achieving the objectives of development?

2. Explain the reasons for the introduction of the policy of liberalisation in Indian economy.

3. Discuss the causes for the backwardness of Indian agriculture.

4. Bring out the development of agriculture under five year plans.

5. Explain the policy of the Government in relation to industries.

6. Discuss the features of New Industrial Policy of 1991.

7. Explain the growth of industries five year plans.

8. Describe the composition and direction of India's foreign trade.

9. What measures would you suggest to increase our exports?

10. Explain the impact of globalisation on the development of Indian economy.

11. WTO a threat or an opportunity to Indian Economy. Discuss.

I. HIGHLIGHTS OF DEVELOPMENTAL ACTIVITIES OF INDIAN ECONOMY (2003-2004)

1. Economy registers record growth of 8.1 per cent during the period.
2. Strong agricultural recovery of 9.1 per cent.
3. Industry and services sectors also record higher growth.
4. Economy in resilient mode in terms of growth, inflation and BoP.
5. Continued macro-economic stability and growth momentum ensured.
6. The year saw continued relative stability of prices.
7. Inflation 4.6 per cent March end compared to 5.5 per cent average.
8. Foreign exchange reserves reach 119.3 billion dollars by May end.
9. Banks' recovery management improves considerably.
10. Combined centre and States fiscal deficit worsened to reach 10.1%.
11. Revenue deficit deteriorated more sharply than fiscal deficit.
12. Centre and several States initiate Fiscal Responsibility Acts.
13. Gross domestic savings increase to 24.2 per cent of GDP in 2002-03.
14. Gross domestic capital formation grew by 7.6 per cent in 2002-03.
15. Industrial production registers 6.9 per cent growth.
16. Mining, Electricity and Manufacturing major contributors.
17. 10th Plan poverty reduction ratio set at 5 percentage points.
18. Annual growth rate of 7-8 per cent envisaged in next five years.
19. Annual inflation rate to be contained to single digit.
20. Agricultural growth with emphasis on agro processing.
21. Expansion of industry 10 per cent annually proposed.
22. Fiscal consolidation and removal of revenue deficit get priority.
23. Private sector involvement for enhancing Investment in infrastructure.
24. Improtance to social sector in NCMP for poverty reduction.

(**Source:** Economic Survey 2003-2004.)

Planwise Growth of National Income

Trends in the growth of NI during FYPs I FYP-IX FYP (per annum)		
Plan Period	*Target Growth Rate*	*Actual Growth Rate*
I Plan	2.1%	3.6%
II Plan	4.5%	4.1%
III Plan	5.6%	2.5%
IV Plan	5.7%	3.3%
V Plan	4.4%	5.0%
VI Plan	5.2%	5.4%
VII Plan	5.0%	5.8%
VIII Plan	6.0%	6.7%
IX Plan	6.5%	5.4%

(**Source:** Government of India, Economic Survey, 2001-2002.)

First Five year plan periods are3 considered as low growth rate period. NI has not increased as per the target rate of each plan. From Sixth five year plan onwards, the increase in national income was significant. During the nineth five year plan the actual growth rate of the national income was lower than growth rate of achieved during the eighth plan. This is due to the failure of industrial sector which registered a mere 5.85% per annum increase in industrial production.

Trends in the growth of agricultural and allied sector

GDP and Agriculture growth rates (Per cent)		
Year	GDP	GDP Agriculture and Allied Sector*
1992-93	5.1	5.8
1993-94	5.9	4.1
1994-95	7.3	5.0
1995-96	7.3	-0.9
1996-97	7.8	9.6
1997-98	4.8	-2.4
1998-99	6.5	6.2
1999-00	6.1	0.3
2000-01	4.4	-0.4
2001-02	5.6	5.7
2002-03**	4.4	-3.1

*At 1993-1994 prices   **Advanced estimate

(**Source**: Central Statistical Organisation.)

Agriculture and allied sector growth is likely to register a decline of 3.1 per cent in the current year due to the severity of drought. This would adversely affect the current year's GDP growth rate. It is likely to fall to 4.4 per cent compared to 5.6 per cent in 2001-2002.

Trends in the growth of industrial production

Annual growth rate of industrial production in major sectors of industry (Based on the index of industrial production)				
Period	Mining and Quarrying	Manufacturing	Electricity	Overall
April-November				
1995-96	11.6	13.7	9.6	13.1
1996-97	-1.0	9.8	3.7	8.0
1997-98	6.1	6.9	6.4	6.8
1998-99	0.5	4.1	6.2	3.9
1999-00	0.5	6.6	8.2	6.2
2000-01	3.6	6.3	4.9	6.0
2001-02	0.7	2.6	2.5	2.5
2002-03	5.7	5.4	4.0	5.3

(**Source**: Central Statistical Organisation.)

In the year 2001-2002 India witnessed a weak industrial growth of 2.7% during 2001-02, as measured by the index of industrial production (IIP). But it has also displayed some definite signs of pick-up in the first eight months i.e., April-November of 2002. The mining and quarrying sector showed growth of 5.7% followed by 5.4% and 4.0% growth by manufacturing and electricity sector respectively during the period. Capital goods achieved a growth of 9.9% in April-November 2002.

Trends in the growth of infrastructural sector

Items	Unit	1992-98	2000-01	2002-03
Trends in the growth of infrastructural sector (in per cent)				
I Energy				
1. Coal production	Mn.Tonnes	3.6	3.5	5.1
2. Electricity generated	Bn.kwh	6.6	3.9	3.7
3. Petroleum	Mn.Tonnes	6.7%	21.8	7.3
II Steel	Mn.Tonnes	6.3	6.5	3.1
III Cement	Mn.Tonnes	9.1	-0.9	9.7
IV Transport and Communications				
1. Railway	Mn.Tonnes	5.0	3.7	6.5
2. Cargo handled at major ports	Mn.Tonnes	10.7	3.4	8.7
3. Telecommunications	'000 Nos.	27.1	27.2	17.0
4. Civil Aviation				

(**Source**: Ministry of Commerce and Industry, Railways, Shipping, Communications and Ministry of Statistics and Programme Implementation.)

Development of infrastructure is very important aspect of economic development. Because the development of other sectors depends on the development of infrastructure of a country. The New Economic Policy of Government of India has stressed the same. The quality and quantity of infrastructure services provided now-a-days shows an upward trend in this sector.

Development in an economy is not possible without human development. Realising this factor Central Government has increased its expenditure on education, health, family welfare, nutrition, sanitation, rural development, housing, social welfare etc. from Rs.9,608 crore in 1992-93 to Rs.40,370 crore in 2001-02 (RE) for 2002-03 (BE) Rs.45,642 crore have been provided. As a ratio of GDP at current market prices, the Central Government expenditure on social services increased from 1.4% in 1992-93 to 1.8% in 2001-02 (RE) and further to 1.9% in 2002-03 (BE). The ongoing economic reforms have a human face and in pursuance of the commitment towards development of human resources and enhancement of human well being, additional resources for the social services sector are being allocated by the government. In the Tenth Five Year Plan (2002-07), suitable targets for the reduction of poverty, hunger, mortality and illiteracy have also been incorporated.

Trends in Social Sectors (2002-2003)

Central Government expenditure (Plan and Non-Plan) on social sectors and rural development (Rs.Crore)

Item	1992-93 Actual	1998-99 Actual	1999-00 Actual	2000-01 Actual	2001-02 (RE)	2002-03 (BE)
1. Social Services	6397	19750	23406	26550	29267	33547
a. Education, Sports & Youth Affairs	1878	6604	7081	7696	8703	9948
b. Health and Family Welfare	1722	3993	5012	5291	5734	7038
c. Water supply, Sanitation, Housing and Urban Dev.	788	4073	4465	4932	5853	5391
d. Information & Broadcasting	371	1041	1169	1317	1331	1438
e. Welfare of SC/ST and Other Backward Classes	488	916	951	969	1133	1385
f. Labour, Employment and Labour Welfare	347	708	845	894	871	900
g. Other social services	803	2415	3883	4124	3092	2768
2. Rural Development	3211	5854	5184	4449	5729	6430
3. Basic Minimum Services (BMS)* including Slum development	—	3684	4048	321^	341	365
4. Pradhan Mantri Gramodaya Yojana (PMGY)@	—	—	—	2350^	2533	2800
Pradhan Mantri Gram Sadak Yojana (PMGSY)@	—	—	—	2500	2500	2500
5. Social Services, Rural Dev. BMS and PMGY (1+2+3+4)	9608	29288	32638	36170	40370	45642
6. Total Central Government expenditure as percentage of GDP at current market prices**	17.40	16.04	15.40	15.50	16.00	16.74
7. Social Services, Rural Dev. BMS & PMGY as a percentage of Total Expenditure**	7.8	10.5	11.0	11.1	11.1	11.1
8. Social Services, Rural Dev. BMS & PMGY as a percentage of GDP at market price$	1.4	1.7	1.7	1.7	1.8	1.9

Note: Figures for the years 1992-93, 1998-99 to 2000-01 are actuals.
* Came into operation from 1996-97.
@ Launched in 2000-01 (BE) as a new initiative for basic rural needs.
** The total Central Government Expenditure excludes the transfer of States/UTs share of small savings collections.
$ Ratios to GDP are at current market prices as released by CSO. GDP for 2002-03 is based on CSO's Advance Estimates.
^ RE figures

(**Source**: Budget documents.)

II. REVIEW OF RECENT DEVELOPMENTS IN INDIAN ECONOMY
2002-2003 AND 2003-2004

The economy appears to be in a resilient mode in terms of growth, inflation, and balance of payments, a combination that offers large scope for consolidation of the growth momentum with continued macroeconomic stability. Real Gross Domestic Product (GDP) is estimated to have grown by 8.1 per cent in 2003-04, buoyed by a strong agricultural recovery of 9.1 per cent from the drought-affected previous year. A growth rate higher than 8 per cent has been achieved in the past in only three years: 1967-68 (8.1 per cent), 1975-76 (9.0 per cent) and 1988-89 (10.5 per cent). However, the higher than expected growth in 2003-04, like in the other three years referred to above, was on the back of a year of poor growth (4.0 per cent) due to an unfavourable monsoon and fall in agricultural production. The key macro aggregates are in Table 1.1 and Figure 1.1.

Apart from agriculture, the industry and services sectors also maintained the momentum with GDP growth from these two sectors accelerating from 6.4 per cent and 7.1 per cent, respectively, in 2002-03, to 6.5 per cent and 8.4 per cent, respectively, in 2003-04 (Table 1.2). A broad-based acceleration in growth from the second to the third quarter of 2003-04 was also observed in mining and quarrying, electricity, gas and water supply, trade, hotels, transportation and communication; and financing, insurance, real estate and business services.

The quarterly GDP data released by the CSO indicate GDP growth rates at 5.7 per cent, 8.4 per cent, and 10.4 per cent respectively in the first three quarters of 2003-04. The GDP growth rate of 10.4 per cent in the 3rd quarter of 2003-04 was the highest in any quarter since at least 1997-98, when CSO started compiling quarterly estimates, and was supported by a growth of 16.9 per cent in agriculture, forestry and fishing, 6.5 per cent in industry and 9.0 per cent in the services sectors.

A benign world economic environment provided a conducive backdrop to the robust performance of the Indian economy in 2003-04. World output growth is estimated to have accelerated from 3.0 per cent in 2002 to 3.9 per cent in 2003. Strong performance by the US, China and Russia and a strong turnaround in Japan helped to brighten the world economic outlook in 2003. Volume of world trade in goods and services also grew rapidly by 4.5 per cent, compared to only 3.1 per cent in the previous year. The robust performance of India and the emerging market economies also contributed to the good performance of the world economy.

The Meteorological Department has predicted normal rainfall-100 per cent of long period average-for the current year. The pre-monsoon rainfall (March 1 to end May, 2004), which has been estimated at 25 per cent above normal, augurs well for the kharif sowing industry, which normally responds to a good agricultural year, is expected to do well along with the services sector, which has been buoyant since 2001-02. Institutional projections of GDP growth for 2004-05 vary from 5.0 to 7.4 per cent.

Table 1.2 Sectoral real growth rates in GDP (at factor cost)

Item	| Percentage change over the previous year							
	1996-1997	1997-1998	1998 1999	1999-2000	2000-2001	2001-2002 (P)	2002-2003 (Q)	2003-2004 (A)
I. Agriculture & allied	9.6	-2.4	6.2	0.3	-0.1	6.5	-5.2	9.1
II. Industry	7.1	4.3	3.7	4.8	6.5	3.4	6.4	6.5
1. Mining & Quarrying	0.5	9.8	2.8	3.3	2.4	2.2	8.8	4.0
2. Manufacturing	9.7	1.5	2.7	4.0	7.4	3.6	6.2	7.1
3. Electricity, gas & water supply	5.4	7.9	7.0	5.2	4.3	3.6	3.8	5.4
4. Construction	2.1	10.2	6.2	6.0	6.7	3.1	7.3	6.0
III. Services	7.2	9.8	8.4	10.1	5.5	6.8	7.1	8.4
5. Trade, hotels, transport & communications	7.8	7.8	7.7	8.5	6.8	8.7	7.0	10.9
6. Financial services	7.0	11.6	7.4	10.6	3.5	4.5	8.8	6.4
7. Community, social & personal services	6.3	11.7	10.4	12.2	5.2	5.6	5.8	5.9
IV. Total GDP at factor cost	7.8	4.8	6.5	6.1	4.4	5.8	4.0	8.1

A: Advance estimates; Q: Quick estimates; P: Provisional estimates

(**Source**: Central Statistical Organisation.)

The growth recovery in 2003-04 was accompanied by continued maintenance of relative stability of prices. Inflation, as measured by the wholesale price index (WPI), was 4.6 per cent at end-March 2004 over end-March 2003, and 5.5 per cent on average. The manufacturing sector was the major contributor accounting for nearly 80 per cent of the inflation. Within the manufacturing sector, the prime movers were sugar, edible oils, textiles, leather and leather products, basic metal and alloys and iron and steel.

A firming of energy and primary product prices had resulted in the inflation rate crossing 6 per cent in January 2004. However, the inflation rate softened considerably during March 2004. The high point-to-point inflation through much of 2003-04 and its sharp deceleration in March 2004 were early because of the carry over of the price increase that took place in the last quarter of 2002-03, especially in March 2003. Retail price inflation, as measured by the Consumer Price Index for Industrial Workers (CPI-IW), touched a peak of 5.1 per cent in April 2003 followed by a declining trend and reached 3.5 per cent in March 2004. CPI inflation declined further to 2.2 per cent in April 2004, compared to 5.1 per cent in April 2003, and abundant food grain stocks helped in maintaining stability in food prices.

The point-to-point inflation (WPI) was 5.5 per cent in the week ending June 5, 2004. The Reserve Bank of India (RBI), in its Annual Policy Statement for 2004-05, has placed the inflation rate, on a point to point basis, at around 5 per cent in 2004-05. After a long delay, prices of motor spirit, high speed diesel and LPG were revised upwards on June 15, 2004. The high international price of petroleum crude-for example, at around US $36 per barrel (Brent crude) on June 11, 2004-and the necessary revision of prices of LPG and kerosene as well as motor spirit and high speed diesel in line with market developments would exert upward pressure.

The weakening of the US dollar, caused mainly by widening US deficits, has affected the rupee-dollar exchange rate. The Indian rupee, which started strengthening from June 2002 onwards, had appreciated, on a monthly average basis, by 8.8 per cent against the US dollar by March 2004. On annual average basis, the rupee, after depreciating by 1.5 per cent in 2002-03, appreciated by 5.3 per cent in 2003-04 vis-a-vis the US dollar. The movements in the rupee value were smooth and orderly, avoiding undue adjustment costs. Furthermore, while the rupee appreciated against the US dollar in 2003-04, it depreciated against the currencies of major non-dollar trading partners. Given the inflation differential, the appreciation has been less pronounced in trade weighted effective terms, with the Real Effective Exchange Rate (REER) of the rupee (5-country index with base 1993-94) appreciating by around 2 per cent on an annual basis in 2003-04.

Forex reserve of our country has in recent years due to strong balance of payments (BOP) position. After a robust growth of US $21.3 billion in 2002-03, foreign exchange reserves (including gold, SDRs and Reserve position in IMF), increased by an unprecedented US $36.9 billion in 2003-04. The level of reserves crossed the US $100 billion mark on December 19, 2004 and stood at US $119.3 billion as of May 31, 2004. This accretion to reserves is attributed not only to capital inflows and current account surplus, but also to valuation gains arising from a steady appreciation of the major non-US dollar global currencies (the Euro and the Pound Sterling in particular) against the US dollar.

The focus of the monetary policy in 2003-04 was, thus, on dealing with this surge in reserves. The RBI had to moderate the impact of these inflows (Rs.124,169 crore in domestic currency terms) through open market sale of Government securities and repo operations through the Liquidity Adjustment Facility. Moreover, outward foreign investment policies were liberalized and interest spreads over LIBOR on various non-resident deposit schemes were reduced.

The current account of BOP has been in surplus since 2001-02. Fuelled by strong growth in imports, reflecting an upsurge in economic activity, the current account balance-in surplus for previous six successive quarters-turned into deficit in the first quarter of 2003-04. But the trend was quickly reversed in the subsequent months, with the current account posting a surplus of US $ 3.2 billion in the first, nine months of 2003-04. While the trade deficit increased from US $12.9 billion in the whole of 2002-03 to US $15.0 billion in April-December 2003, the deficit was neutralised by a higher surplus in the invisibles in April-December 2003. Buoyant inflows of private transfers and higher inflows from software services exports, inter alia, contributed to this buoyancy in invisibles surplus. Growth momentum of merchandise exports was also broadly sustained with exports (in US dollar value, custom basis) growing by 17.1 per cent in 2003-04 on top of a rise of 20.3 per cent in 2002-03. The growth in merchandise imports was even faster from 19.4 per cent in 2002-03 to 22.8 per cent in 2003-04.

Reserve money growth nearly doubled from 9.2 per cent in 2002-03 to 18.3 per cent in 2003-04, driven entirely by the increase in the net foreign exchange assets of the RBI. Reserve money growth in 2003-04 was the highest in recent years. Net RBI credit to the government continued to remain negative, owing to the open market sale of government securities to sterilise the foreign inflows. The declining stock of government securities held by the RBI somewhat constrained the scope of these operations. Broad money (M_3) grew by 16.4 per cent in 2003-04, higher than the targeted growth of 14.0 per cent mentioned in the annual monetary and credit policy, reflecting, primarily, the higher-than-anticipated GDP growth achieved during the year.

The money multiplier-the ratio of M_3 to reserve money-after increasing from 4.43 in 2001-02 to 4.66 in 2002-03, declined to 4.58 in 2003-04, suggesting some headroom for further expansion in M_3. The virtuous decline in income velocity of money-the ratio of gross domestic product at current market prices to the average money stock during the year-continued in 2003-04. Income velocity declined from 1.62 in 2001-02 to 1.50 in 2002-03 and further to 1.48 in 2003-04, indicating greater 'monetisation' of the Indian economy, with less of barter and more and more of M_3 being used for transactions in generating a unit of income.

Adequate liquidity in the banking system continued, and with a resurgence of growth, supported a credit pick up in 2003-04. Total bank credit (food and non-food) increased by 14.6 per cent in 2003-04 after an increase of 16.1 per cent in the previous year. Food credit, which after accelerating in 1999-2000 and 2000-01 had declined by 8.3 per cent in the 2002-03, fell by a steep 27.3 per cent in 2003-04 because of lower procurement and higher off-take of foodgrains. The flow of non-food credit, which remained subdued in the first two quarters, started picking up from the third quarter of 2003-04. Offtake of non-food credit in the last two quarters of 2003-04 amounted to Rs.1,01,407 crore, much higher than Rs.71,980 crore in the corresponding quarters of the previous year. For the year as a whole, non-food credit grew by 17.6 per cent, compared to a growth of 18.6 per cent (net of merger) in 2002-03.

The downward trend in interest rates continued in 2003-04. RBI reduced the Bank Rate from 6.25 per cent to 6.00 per cent from the close of business on April 29,2003. Also, the cash reserve ratio (CRR) was reduced by 25 basis points to 4.50 per cent in June, 2003. Lending rates have remained sticky and have not fallen by as much as the deposit rates. As a result, interest spread of commercial banks witnessed an increase in recent years. The RBI has advised scheduled commercial banks (SCBs) to announce benchmark prime lending rates based on their actual costs, and this has fortified the soft interest rate regime. A significant development in 2003-04 was the lower than budgeted market borrowings by the Central Government, which was facilitated by an improvement in the cash position. During the year 2003-04, SCBs improved their profitability on account of higher income from treasury operations and higher spread.

Equity market return was 85 per cent in 2003-04, the second highest in Asia. With good corporate earnings in 2003-04, the Sensex crossed 6,194 on January 2004, after remaining low in the first half of 2003-04. There was a revival in primary market in 2003-04 with Rs.23,271 crore raised as against Rs.4,070 crore in the previous year. The secondary market rally and primary market revival were both helped by FII inflows. Market capitalisation of listed companies rose from Rs.7.2 trillion in 2002-03 to Rs.13.8 trillion in 2003-04 (49 per cent of GDP). Spot market trading volume rose sharply, from Rs.9.3 trillion in 2002-03 to Rs.16 trillion in 2003-04.

The combined fiscal deficit of the Centre and the States, which had been decreasing in the early nineties, worsened subsequently to reach a level of 10.1 per cent in the revised estimates (RE) for 2002-03, higher than the pre-reform level of 9.4 per cent. The revenue deficit followed a more disturbing trend, deteriorating more sharply than the fiscal deficit. The combined revenue deficit as a proportion of GDP, after declining from 4.2 in 1990-91 to 3.6 per cent in 1996-97, increased to 7.0 per cent in 2001-02, to decline again to 6.7 per cent in 2002-03 (RE) and further to a budget estimate (BE) of 5.8 per cent in 2003-04. For 2003-04, the combined fiscal deficit was budgeted at Rs.2,59,265 crore, constituting 9.4 per cent of GDP. Furthermore, a declining share of capital expenditure (excluding loans) in total expenditure, from 13.5 per cent in 1990-91 to 10.3 per cent in 2001-02, suggests a worsening quality of the deficit. With sustained efforts at stepping up capital expenditure, the share subsequently improved to 11.8 per cent in 2002-03. It was budgeted to go up to 14.5 per cent in 2003-04.

Fiscal deficit of the Central Government was budgeted at 5.6 per cent of GDP (Rs.1,53,637 crore) in 2003-04, compared to Rs.1,31,306 crore amounting to 5.3 per cent of GDP in 2002-03. Revenue deficit was budgeted at 4.1 per cent of GDP as compared with 4.4 per cent of GDP in the previous year. The reduction in revenue deficit was budgeted to be achieved from higher growth in revenue receipts and lower growth in revenue expenditure. In the event, according to unaudited figures, fiscal and revenue deficits, as a proportion of GDP, are estimated to have been 4.6 per cent and 3.6 per cent in 2003-04.

The Budget for 2003-04 undertook to provide a major thrust to infrastructure, principally to roads, railways, airports, and seaports, through innovative funding mechanisms. The total cost of these projects was estimated at about Rs.60,000 crore. The scheme undertook to leverage public funds through private sector partnership through three critical components: release of public funds only when linked to specific and well-defined milestones in completion of the project, in physical terms; a sharing of the risks with the private promoters and financiers; and no open-ended Government guarantees at any stage. Implementation work on these projects has made substantial progress. NHAI has invited bids for 622 km. of highways and DPRs for 1510 km. are under preparation. The restructuring of the Mumbai and Delhi airports is under implementation. Bids have been invited for the modernisation of the Cochin port. Rail Vikas Nigam Ltd. (RVNL) is executing 61 projects.

As a ratio to total expenditure, the combined plan and non-plan expenditure of the Centre in social services (comprising education, health, family welfare, water supply, housing, social welfare, nutrition, and rural development) increased from 9.3 per cent in 1997-98 to 11.0 per cent in 2003-04.

An Interim Budget for 2004-05 seeking a vote-on-account was presented on February 3, 2004, prior to the dissolution of the Thirteenth Lok Sabha and announcement of elections. While the Budget did not contain any fresh tax proposals, revenue and fiscal deficits-as proportions of GDP-were budgeted at 2.9 per cent and 4.4 per cent for 2004-05.

Consumption, Savings and Investment

Private final consumption expenditure, at constant 1993-94 prices, increased by Rs.30,507 crore or 3.5 per cent in 2002-03 compared to an increase of Rs.47,099 crore (5.7 per cent) in 2001-02. This growth at a rate lower than that of GDP meant that private final consumption as a proportion of GDP at current market prices declined from 65.5 per cent in 2001-02 to 64.4 per cent in 2002-03. The decline in private final consumption in 2002-03 was mainly on account of lower expenditure on cereals, which declined from Rs.1,58,621 crore in 2001-02 to Rs.1,24,560 crore in drought-affected 2002-03, and reduced the share of food, beverages and tobacco in total consumption by 2.6 percentage points to 44.8 per cent. Among other major categories of consumption, share of clothing and footwear, gross rent, fuel and power, medical care and health services, transport and communication and miscellaneous goods and services increased marginally, while the share of furniture, furnishings, appliances and services, and recreation, education and cultural services remained unchanged between 2001-02 and 2002-03.

In 2002-03, gross and net domestic savings at current prices grew by 11.7 per cent and 14.2 per cent respectively.

The increase in the overall saving rate in 2002-03 was on account of a decline in the dissavings of the public sector to 1.9 per cent of GDP in 2002-03 from 2.7 per cent in the previous year. Dissavings of the public sector declined from Rs.62,704 crore in 2001-02 to Rs.45,730 crore in 2002-03.

Gross domestic capital formation (GDCF) at constant prices grew by 7.6 per cent in 2002-03. GDCF as a proportion of GDP at 1993-94 market prices was marginally higher at 25.8 per cent in 2002-03 compared with 25.1 per cent in 2001-02.

Domestic demand has been the main driver of growth in recent years (Figure 1.2). In 2002-03, among demand categories, private final consumption, by contributing 52.4 per cent of the GDP growth at current market prices, was the prime mover, followed by investment (25.6 per cent), government consumption (13.4 per cent) and external balance (2.4 per cent). The contribution of private final consumption to growth, however, was lower in 2002-03 compared to 69.6 per cent in the previous year.

The Government's current expenditure comprises consumption expenditure and current transfers. Apart from an increase in the consumption expenditure, there was also an increase in current transfers, squeezing public investment. The share of current transfers in the total expenditure of the Central Government increased from 43.0 per cent in 1990-91 to 58.0 per cent in 2002-03 and was budgeted to decline marginally to 56.7 per cent in 2003-04.

Because of the growth in consumption expenditure and transfer payments of the Central Government, the share of current expenditure in total expenditure increased from 64.3 per cent in 1990-91 to 79.2 per cent in 2002-03 (RE), and was budgeted to marginally come down to 79.0 per cent in 2003-04.

The surplus in the current account of India's BOP for three consecutive years ending in 2003-04 indicates that the rest of the world has contributed to sustaining aggregate demand. This surplus is likely to decline as investment picks up and the country transits to a sustained growth phase at a higher rate.

Production

A good monsoon helped to increase the level of foodgrains production from 174.2 million tonnes in 2002-03 to 210.8 million tonnes in 2003-04, contributed by increase in the production of both cereals and pulses. The prospects for agricultural production in 2004-05 are considered bright with a normal monsoon forecast by the Meteorological Department.

As per the index of industrial production (IIP), overall growth in the industrial sector improved from 5.7 per cent in 2002-03 to 6.9 per cent in 2003-04, supported by growth rates of 5.1 per cent in mining, 5.0 per cent in electricity and 7.2 per cent in manufacturing. As per use-based classification, industrial growth was broad-based except for consumer non-durables. Capital goods took the lead with a growth of 12.7 per cent followed by consumer durables, which recorded a growth rate of 11.6 per cent. Enhanced availability of retail loans and lower interest rates contributed to the latter's growth. Intermediate goods and basic goods also performed better in 2003-04 than in 2002-03, with growth rates of 6.2 per cent and 5.4 per cent, respectively, while the growth of consumer non-durables decelerated substantially from 12.0 per cent in 2002-03 to 5.7 per cent in 2003-04.

Both production and exports of steel continued to rise, propelled by surging demand for steel in China and a strong domestic market. In 2003-04, total finished steel production rose by 7.5 per cent, reaching 36.2 million tonnes, while exports of finished steel grew by 17.6 per cent to 5.3 million tonnes.

During 2003-04, automobile production grew by 15.1 per cent, following up on strong growth of 18.6 per cent i the previous year. Commercial vehicles grew by 35.1 per cent, while passenger cars grew by 38.3 per cent. A major development in Indian manufacturing has been the success in exports of automobile components and finished vehicles. With export of vehicles growing by 56 per cent in 2003-04, India appeared to be on its way to establishing itself as a new player in the international market for small passenger vehicles.

Six core and infrastructure industries (viz., electricity, coal, steel, cement, crude oil and petroleum products) having a total weight of 26.7 per cent in the Index of Industrial Production (IIP) registered a marginally lower average growth rate of 5.4 per cent in 2003-04 compared to 5.6 per cent in 2002-03. Among the other infrastructure sectors, new cell phone connections (with a growth of 159.2 per cent), goods traffic on railways (7.5 per cent), cargo handled at major sea ports (9.9 per cent) and air ports (5.3 per cent), and air passenger traffic at both domestic and international airports (10.3 per cent) performed well in 2003-04 due to sustained industrial growth and significant pick-up of service activities.

Major initiatives taken in 2003-04 for infrastructure development include: notification of the Electricity Act in June 2003; signing of the tripartite agreement by 28 States for one time settlement of the dues of State Electricity Boards to Central Public Sector Undertakings; launching of 50,000 MW hydro electric power initiative in May, 2003, unified access service license regime for telecommunication services; and the Bharat Jodo Project for development of 10,000 kms of roads connecting state capitals.

Many policies were announced in the Union Budget for 2003-04 to encourage industry. Major measures included: a special incentive package for textiles, garments and apparel, which have high exports and employment potential; income tax concessions to the sunrise sectors of biotechnology, pharmaceuticals and information technology; withdrawal of expenditure tax for tourism; and withdrawal of small-scale reservation from 75 items of chemicals, leather, plastics and paper products.

Employment and Poverty

It is well known that there3 was a significant decline in the poverty ratio from 36 per cent in 1993-94 to 26.1 per cent in 1999-2000. The Tenth Five Year Plan (2002-07) has set a target of reduction in poverty ratio by five percentage points by 2007 and by 15 percentage points by 2012.

Subsequently, 'thin' surveys for household consumer expenditure were conducted by the National Sample Survey Organisation (NSSO) for 2000-2001 (56th Round) and 2001-2002 (57th Round). As per the results of the 57th Round, the proportion of chronically hungry households (not getting enough to eat in any month of the year) declined to 0.5 per cent in rural areas and 0.1 per cent in urban areas. As for seasonal hunger, 16 per thousand households in rural areas and 3 per thousand households in urban areas reported getting enough food only in some months of the year.

Major initiatives taken for the social sectors during 2003-04 included: expansion of the Antyodaya Anna Yojana to cover an additional 50 lakh families; introduction of a community based Universal Health Insurance Scheme and a special pension policy called Varishtha Pension Bima Yojana; launching a National Programme for Education of Girls at Elementary Level; launching a social security scheme for the unorganised workers in January 2004 on a pilot basis in 50 districts; and initiating the setting up of All India Institute of Medical Sciences (AIIMS) like institutions in six backward states (Bihar, Chattisgarh, Madhya Pradesh, Orissa, Rajasthan and Uttaranchal).

The Economic Survey 2002-03 reported that the rate of growth of employment, on Current Daily Status (CDS) basis, declined from 2.7 per cent per annum in 1983-1994 to 1.07 per cent per annum in 1994-2000. The deceleration of the employment growth was mainly due to near stagnation of employment in agriculture, although employment growth in all the sub-sectors within services (except community, social and personal services) exceeded 5 per cent per annum.

III. RECENT POLICIES OF GOVERNMENT OF INDIA

1. THE CENTRAL GOVERNMENT BUDGET 2004-2005

The Union Budget 2004-2005 was presented on July 8, 2004 by Union Finance Minister Mr. P. Chidambaram of Congress led the United Progressive Alliance Government. The new budget presented is a well crafted budget. Finance Minister has managed to re-orient the government policies and programmes to suit the priorities outlined in the Common Minimum Programme.

The new budget lay more emphasis on the poorer sections of the society, agriculture and rural development. In the new budget there is no change in the income tax rate, instead 2 per cent education cess has been levied on all taxes-income, corporation, excise and customs duties and services. The 2 per cent cess is expected to yield about Rs.4000-5000 crore in a year. There will be no change in the rate of interest on small savings such as PPF, General Provident Fund and the Special Deposit Scheme. Senior citizens will have special bonds fetching a return of 9 per cent. There is change in the corporate tax also. The new budget has reduced the prices for some items like computers, dairy machinery and hand tools such as spades, shovels etc. Import duty on platinum is reduced while the rough coloured precious gemstones have been totally exempted. Items which will now cost more include contact lenses, vacuum flasks, scented supari, prefabricated buildings, black and white TV sets, imitation jewellery, candles and watches.

The service tax has been increased from 8 per cent to 10 per cent and the coverage expanded from the current 58 services to cover some more. To create employment opportunities a food-for-work programme will be launched in 150 most backward districts. Foreign Direct Investment limit rised in the insurance, civil aviation and telecom sectors.

Profit making PSUs will not be privatised. Other measures under consideration include exercising the call option in BALCO and some other PSUs.

In the current budget additional revenue through direct taxes in estimated to be Rs.2,000 crores this year. The plan expenditure for 2004-2005 is expected to be Rs.1,45,590 crore while non-plan expenditure would be Rs.3,22,239 crore. Revenue receipts are estimated to be Rs.3,09,332 crore and revenue expenditure Rs.3,85,493 crores, leaving a deficit of Rs.76,171 crore-equivalent to 2.5 per cent of the gross domestic product - one per cent point below the corresponding estimate of 3.5 per cent in 2003-04.

With the total expenditure expected to be Rs.4,77,829 crore, the fiscal deficit is estimated to be Rs.1,37,407 crore or 4.4 per cent of GDP.

Highlights of Union Budget 2004-2005

- Two per cent education cess imposed on income tax, corporation tax, excise duties, customs duties and service tax.

- Service tax rate hiked from eight per cent to ten per cent, tax net to include a host of services.

- Persons with taxable income of Rs.one lakh will not have to pay income tax, tax slabs and rates unchanged for others.

- No change in interest rates on small savings including PPF, GPF and special deposit scheme.

- Sectoral cap for FDI to be raised from 49 per cent to 74 per cent in tele communications; from 40 per cent to 49 per cent in civil aviation and from 26 per cent to 49 per cent in insurance.

- Investment ceiling for FIIS in debt funds to be raised from US $1 billion to US $1.75 billion.

- Equity oriented mutual funds will continue to be exempt from tax on dividends.

- Banks with strong risk management systems to be allowed greater latitude in their exposure to capital market.

- Investment commission to be established.

- 85 items to be taken out of the reserve list for small scale sector.

- Automobile industry will be entitled to 150 per cent deduction of expenditure on in-house R&D facilities.

- Request of shipping industry for the levy of tonnage tax accepted.

- New hospitals with 100 beds or more set up in rural areas to get tax benefit.

- Long-term capital gains from securities transactions to be replaced by a tax on transactions; short-term capital gains tax slashed to 10 per cent.

- Tractors, dairy machinery and hand tools such as spades to be fully exempt from excise.

- Preparation of meat, poultry and fish to attract 8 per cent excise, down from 16 per cent earlier.

- Computers to be fully exempted from excise duty; LPG gas stoves costing less than Rs.2000 and footwear upto Rs.250 to get excise relief.

- Task force to be appointed on reforms in the cooperative banking system.

- Rs.2,800 crore provided for accelerated irrigation benefit programme.

- Special economic package of Rs.3225 crore for Bihar through the Rashtriya Sam Vikas Yojana.

- North-eastern region gets Rs.650 crore from the central pool for specific projects and schemes.

- Jammu and Kashmir to get special assistance for a reasonable plan size, Baglihar project and to switch over to RBI ways and means advance.

- Additional provision of Rs.10,000 crore for programmes such as foods for work, Sarva Shiksha Abhiyan, basic health care, drinking water etc.

- Antyodaya Anna Yojana to be extended to 2 crore families.

- Pilot scheme for distributing food stamps to be introduced.

- Defence budget hiked from Rs.64,300 crore to Rs.77,000 crore.

- States share of union taxes to increase by about 30 per cent from Rs.63,758 crore to Rs.82,227 crore.

- States to pay 9 per cent interest on Government of India loans as against 10.5 per cent.

- Plan expenditure hiked to Rs.1,45,590 crore, up from Rs.1,21,507 crore in the revised estimate for 2003-04.

- Direct taxes to yield Rs.2,000 crore more, indirect tax changes to stay revenue neutral.
- Fiscal deficit pegged at 4.4 per cent, down from 4.8 per cent in 2003-04 revised estimates.
- Revenue deficit to be eliminated by 2008-09.

2. NEW FOREIGN TRADE POLICY 2004

On August 31, 2004, Kamal Nath, Union Minister from Commerce and Industry announced India's Foreign Trade Policy for the next five years. 2004-2009. It replaces the five year Export-Import Policy (2002-07), the most recent amendments to which were announced in January this year. The new policy was released with the aim of doubling India's share of global trade to 1.5 per cent in next five years. The new FTP is also designed to act as an effective instrument of economic growth by boosting employment.

Highlights of New Foreign Trade Policy

Following are the highlights or important elements of New Foreign Trade Policy 2004-09.

Highlights of Foreign Trade Policy 2004-2009

1. Strategy

(a) It is for the first time that a comprehensive Foreign Trade Policy is being notified. The Foreign Trade Policy takes an integrated view of the overall development of India's foreign trade.

(b) **The objective of the Foreign Trade Policy is two-fold:**

(i) to double India's percentage share of global merchandise trade by 2009; and

(ii) to act as an effective instrument of economic growth by giving a thrust to employment generation, especially in semi-urban and rural areas.

(c) The key strategies are.

(i) Unshackling of controls;

(ii) Creating an atmosphere of trust and transparency;

Simplifying procedures and bringing down transaction costs;

Adopting the fundamental principle that duties and levies should not be exported;

Identifying and nurturing different special focus areas to facilitate development of India as a global hub for manufacturing, trading and services.

2. Special Focus Initiatives.

(a) Sectors with significant export prospects coupled with potential for employment generation in semi-urban and rural areas have been identified as thrust sectors, and specific sectoral strategies have been prepared.

(b) Further sectoral initiatives in other sectors will be announced from time to time. For the present, Special Focus Initiatives have been prepared for Agriculture, Handicrafts, Handlooms, Gems & Jewellery and Leather & Footwear sectors.

(c) The threshold limit of designated Towns of Export Excellence is reduced from Rs.1000 crores to Rs.250 crores in these thrust sectors.

3. Package for Agriculture.

The Special Focus Initiative for Agriculture includes:

(a) A new scheme called Vishesh Krishi Upaj Yojana has been introduced to boost exports of fruits, vegetables, flowers, minor forest produce and their value added products.

(b) Duty free import of capital goods under EPCG scheme.

(c) Capital goods imported under EPCG for agriculture permitted to be installed anywhere in the Agri Export Zone.

(d) ASIDE funds to be utilized for development for Agri Export Zones also.

(e) Import of seeds, bulbs, tubers and planting material has been liberalized.

(f) Export of plant portions, derivatives and extracts has been liberalized with a view to promote export of medicinal plants and herbal products.

4. Gems & Jewellery

(a) Duty free import of consumables for metals other than gold and platinum allowed up to 2% of FOB value of exports.

(b) Duty free re-import entitlement for rejected jewellery allowed up to 2% of FOB value of exports.

(c) Duty free import of commercial samples of jewellery increased to Rs.1 lakh.

(d) Import of gold of 18 carat and above shall be allowed under the replenishment scheme.

5. Handlooms & Handicrafts

(a) Duty free import of trimmings and embellishments for Handlooms & Handicrafts sectors increased to 5% of FOB value of exports.

(b) Import of trimmings and embellishments and samples shall be exempt from CVD.

(c) Handicraft Export Promotion Council authorised to import trimmings, embellishments and samples for small manufacturers.

(d) A new Handicraft Special Economic Zone shall be established.

6. Leather & Footwear

(a) Duty free entitlements of import trimmings, embellishments and footwear components for leather industry increased to 3% of FOB value of exports.

(b) Duty free import of specified items for leather sector increased to 5% of FOB value of exports.

(c) Machinery and equipment for Effluent Treatment Plants for leather industry shall be exempt from Customs Duty.

7. Export Promotion Schemes

(a) Target Plus:

A new scheme to accelerate growth of exports called Target Plus has been introduced.

Exporters who have achieved a quantum growth in exports would be entitled to duty free credit based on incremental exports substantially higher than the general actual export target fixed. (Since the target fixed for 2004-05 is 16%, the lower limit of performance for qualifying for rewards is pegged at 20% for the current year).

Rewards will be granted based on a tiered approach. For incremental growth of over 20%, 25% and 100%, the duty free credits would be 5%, 10% and 15% of FOB value of incremental exports.

(b) Vishesh Krishi Upaj Yojana:

Another new scheme called Vishesh Krishi Upaj Yojana (Special Agricultural Produce Scheme) has been introduced to boost exports of fruits, vegetables, flowers, minor forest produce and their value added products.

Export of these products shall qualify for duty free credit entitlement equivalent to 5% of FOB value of exports.

The entitlement is freely transferable and can be used for import of a variety of inputs and goods.

(c) Served from India Scheme:

To accelerate growth in export of services so as to create a powerful and unique served from India brand instantly recognized and respected the world over, the earlier DFEC scheme for services has been revamped and re-cast into the served from India scheme.

Individual service providers who earn foreign exchange of at least Rs.5 lakhs, and other service providers who earn foreign exchange of at least Rs.10 lakhs will be eligible for a duty credit entitlement of 10% of total foreign exchange earned by them.

In the case of stand-alone restaurants, the entitlement shall be 20%, whereas in the case of hotels, it shall be 5%.

Hotels and Restaurants can use their duty credit entitlement for import of food items and alcoholic beverages.

(d) EPCG:

 (i) Additional flexibility for fulfillment of export obligation under EPCG scheme in order to reduce difficulties of exporters of goods and services.

 (ii) Technological upgradation under EPCG scheme has been facilitated and incentivised.

 (iii) Transfer of capital goods to group companies and managed hotels now permitted under EPCG.

 (iv) In case of movable capital goods in the service sector, the requirement of installation certificate from Central Excise has been done away with.

 (v) Export obligation for specified projects shall be calculated based on concessional duty permitted to them. This would improve the viability of such projects.

(e) DFRC

Import of fuel under DFRC entitlement shall be allowed to be transferred to marketing agencies authorized by the Ministry of Petroleum and Natural Gas.

(f) DEPB:

The DEPB scheme would be continued until replaced by a new scheme to be drawn up in consultation with exporters.

8. New Status Holder Categorization:

(a) A new rationalized scheme of categorization of status holders as Star Export Houses has been introduced as under,

Category Total performance over three years

One Star Export House 15 crores

Two Star Export House 100 crores

Three Star Export House 500 crores

Four Star Export House 1500 crores

Five Star Export House 5000 crores

(b) Star Export Houses shall be eligible for a number of privileges including fast-track clearance procedures, exemption from furnishing of Bank Guarantee, eligibility for consideration under Target Plus Scheme etc.

9. EOUs: (Export Oriented Units)

(a) EOUs shall be exempted from Service Tax in proportion to their exported goods and services.

(b) EOUs shall be permitted to retain 100% of export earnings in EEFC accounts.

(c) Income Tax benefits on plant and machinery shall be extended to DTA units which convert to EOUs.

(d) Import of capital goods shall be on self-certification basis for EOUs.

(e) For EOUs engaged in Textile & Garments manufacture leftover materials and fabrics upto 2% of CIF value or quantity of import shall be allowed to be disposed of on payment of duty on transaction value only.

(f) Minimum investment criteria shall not apply to Brass Hardware and Hand-made Jewellery EOUs (this facility already exists for Handicrafts, Agriculture, Floriculture, Aquaculture, Animal Husbandry, IT and Services).

10. Free Trade and Warehousing Zone

(i) A new scheme to establish Free Trade and Warehousing Zone has been introduced to create trade-related infrastructure to facilitate the import and export of goods and services with freedom to carry out trade transactions in free currency. This is aimed at making India into a global trading- hub.

(ii) FDI would be permitted up to 100% in the development and establishment of the zones and their infrastructure] facilities.

(iii) Each zone would have minimum outlay of Rs.100 crores and five lakh sq. mts. built up area.

Units in the FTWZs would qualify for all other benefits as applicable for SEZ units.

11.Import of Second hand Capital Goods

a. Import of second-hand capital goods shall be permitted without any age restrictions.

b. Minimum depreciated value for plant and machinery to be re-located into India has been reduced from Rs.50 crores to Rs.25 crores.

12. Services Export Promotion Council

An exclusive Services Export Promotion Council shall be set up in order to map opportunities for key services in key markets, and develop strategic market access programmes, including brand building, in co-ordination with sectoral players and recognized nodal bodies of the services industry.

13. Common Facilities Centre

Government shall promote the establishment of Common Facility Centres for use by home-based service providers, particularly in areas like Engineering & Architectural design, Multi-media operations, software developers etc., in State and District-level towns, to draw in a vast multitude of home-based professionals into the services export arena.

14 Procedural Simplification & Rationalisation Measures

(a) All exporters with minimum turnover of Rs.5 crores and good track record shall be exempt from furnishing Bank Guarantee in any of the schemes, so as to reduce their transactional costs.

(b) All goods and services exported, including those from DTA units, shall be exempt from Service Tax.

(c) Validity of all licences/entitlements issued under various schemes has been increased to a uniform 24 months.

(d) Number of returns and forms to be filed have been reduced. This process shall be continued in consultation with Customs & Excise.

(e) Enhanced delegation of powers to Zonal and Regional offices of DGFT for speedy and less cumbersome disposal of matters.

(f) Time bound introduction of Electronic Data Interface (EDI) for export transactions. 75% of all export transactions to be on EDI within six months.

15. Pragati Maidan

In order to showcase our industrial and trade prowess to its best advantage and leverage existing facilities, Pragati Maidan will be transformed into a world-class complex. There shall be state-of- the-art, environmentally-controlled, visitor friendly exhibition areas and marts. A huge Convention Centre to accommodate 10,000 delegates with flexible hall spaces, auditoria and meeting rooms with high-tech equipment, as well as multi-level car parking for 9,000 vehicles will be developed within the envelope of Pragati Maidan.

16. Legal Aid

Financial assistance would be provided to deserving exporters, on the recommendation of Export Promotion Councils, for meeting the costs of legal expenses connected with trade-related matters.

17. Grievance Redressal

A new mechanism for grievance redressal has been formulated and put into place by a Government Resolution to facilitate speedy redressal of grievances of trade and industry.

18. Quality Policy

(a) DGFT shall be a business-driven, transparent, corporate oriented organization.

(b) Exporters can file digitally signed applications and use Electronic Fund Transfer Mechanism for paying application fees.

(c) All DGFT offices shall be connected via a central server making application processing faster. DGFT HQ has obtained ISO 9000 certification by standardizing and automating procedures.

19. Bio Technology Parks

Biotechnology Parks to be set up which would be granted all facilities of 100% EOUs.

20. Co-acceptance/Avalisation introduced as equivalent to irrevocable letter of credit to provide wider flexibility in financial instrument for export transaction.

21. Board of Trade

The Board of Trade shall be revamped and given a clear and dynamic role. An eminent person or expert on trade policy shall be nominated as President of the Board of Trade, which shall have a Secretariat and separate Budget Head, and will be serviced by the Department of Commerce.

III. What is new in New Foreign Trade Policy of Government of India?

The new policy replaces the old Exim Policy 2002-2007. This policy comes at a time when India's Foreign Trade is growing robustly. The FTP, according to the Government is more than a change in nomenclature and has much wider connotation than the exim policy it replaces. Promising an integrated approach to trade development, the FTP hopes to double the country's percentage share of global trade within next 5 years and also generate substantial employment. For achieving these objectives, the Government will rely on some established strategies: loosen controls and create an atmosphere of trust; simplify procedure and reduce transaction costs; neutralise the incidence of levies and duties on inputs used in export products; facilitate technological and infrastructural upgradation in all the sectors of the economy. The idea is also to revitalise the Board of Trade by redefining its role.

Agriculture and services now get their due in the export promotion framework. The new initiatives announced for agriculture and other thrust areas such as handicrafts, handlooms, gem and jewellery and leather and footwear are commendable. All these sectors have proved their worth in export performance. But the promotional steps proposed are not exactly original; they involve a liberal import of capital goods and raw materials to aid export effort. The Duty Entitlement Pass-book Scheme will be persisted with until an alternative WTO compatible scheme is put in place.

The New FTP is in continuance with exim policy. Hence it does not suffer from lack of vision. However a FTP can succeed only in conjunction with other economic policies working towards similar goals. The New FTP should be supported by infrastructure development, then only foreign trade will be benefited. Moreover, with the WTO rules coming into play, fiscal and other concessions are no longer in the exclusive domain of national trade policies.

3. DISINVESTMENT POLICY OF GOVERNMENT OF INDIA

The New Industrial Policy of 1991, announced by Government of India recommended disinvestment of selected Public Sector Enterprises (PSEs) in order to provide market discipline and to improve the performance of PSEs. Accordingly government decided to disinvest PSE share in some selected units phasewise. Disinvestment (in PSEs) processes started in December 1991. Though disinvestment started in early 90s, the Department of Disinvestment was set up by BJP led United Front Government on 6th September 2001. Now the department was renamed as Ministry of Disinvestment. On 3rd September 2002, government has constituted the Cabinet Committee on Disinvestment with composition and functions.

Evolution Of Disinvestment Policy In India can be studied under two phase

I PHASE (1991-1998)

Initial Stages

The policy of the Government on disinvestment has evolved over a period and it can be briefly stated in the form of following policy statements made in the chronological order:

A. Contents of disinvestment policy in Interim Budget 1991-92

Policy : To divest up to 20% of the Government equity in selected PSEs in favour of public sector institutional investors.

Objective: To broad-base equity, improve management, enhance availability of resources for these PSEs and yield resources for the exchequer.

B. Industrial Policy Statement of 24th July, 1991

Policy: To divest part Government holdings in selected PSUs

Objective: "to provide further market discipline to the performance of public enterprises"

C. Disinvestment Policy in 1991-92 budget

Policy: To offer up to 20% of Govt. equity in selected PSUs to mutual funds and investment institutions in the public sector, as also to workers in these firms.

Objectives: "to raise resources, encourage wider public participation and promote greater accountability".

D Report of the Committee on the Disinvestment of Shares in PSEs (Rangarajan Committee): April 1993

"... emphasized the need for substantial disinvestment, and stated that while the percentage of equity to be divested should be no more than 49% for industries explicitly reserved for the public sector, it should be either 74% or 100% for others."

(E) The Common Minimum Programme of the United Front Govt.: 1996 insisted on following measures regarding disinvestment.

- To carefully examine withdrawal from non-core strategic areas
- To set up a Disinvestment Commission for advising
- To take and implement decisions to disinvest in a transparent manner
- Job security, opportunities for retraining and redeployment to be assured.

F. Disinvestment Commission Recommendations: Feb. 1997 - Oct. 1999

The disinvestment process of PSEs was carried over after the formation of Disinvestment commission. The commission recommended the following:

(i) 72 PSEs were referred to the Disinvestment Commission during 1996-99. The Disinvestment Commission gave its recommendations on 58 PSEs.

(ii) The Disinvestment Commission recommendations gave priority to strategic/trade sales, with transfer of management, instead of public offerings, as was recommended by the Rangarajan Committee in 1993 also.

The following table gives the details:

Mode of disinvestment recommended	No. of Companies
A. Involving change in own management / management	
1. Strategic sale	31
2. Trade sale	8
3. Employee buy out /strategic sale	2
B. Involving no change in ownership/ management offer of shares	5
C. No change (Disinvestment deferred)	8
D. Closure/sale of assets	4
GRADE TOTAL:	58

2.2 PHASE (1998-2003)

A. Disinvestment Policy Measures in 1998-99 budget

Policy:

- To bring down Government shareholding in the PSUs to 26% in the generality of cases, (thus facilitating ownership changes, as was recommended by the Disinvestment Commission).
- To retain majority holding in PSEs involving Strategic considerations.
- To protect the interest of workers in all cases.

B. Disinvestment Policy measures in 1999-2000 budget

Policy:

- To strengthen strategic PSUs
- To privatize non-strategic PSUs through gradual disinvestment or strategic sale
- To devise viable rehabilitation strategies for weak units

Approval of Clear Guidelines for Strategic / Non strategic Classification by the Cabinet on 16th March 1999.

Strategic & Non-strategic Classification

Cabinet classified the PSUs into strategic and non-strategic areas.

Strategic PSUS:

- Defence related
- Atomic energy related, with some exceptions
- Railway transport

Non-strategic PSUS:

- All others

Non-strategic Public Sector Undertakings

Reduction of Government stake to 26% to be worked out on a case to case basis, on the rowing considerations:

a. Whether the Industrial sector requires the presence of the public sector as a countervailing force to prevent concentration of power in private hands, and

b. Whether the Industrial sector requires a proper regulatory mechanism to protect the consumer interests before Public Sector Enterprises are privatised.

Policy: The main elements or objectives of disinvestment policy

To restructure and revive potentially viable PSUs

- To close down PSUs which cannot be revived
- To bring down Government equity in all non-strategic PSUs to 26% or lower, if necessary
- To fully protect the interest of workers
- To put in place mechanisms to raise resources from the market against the security of PSUs' assets for providing an adequate safety-net to workers and employees
- To establish a systematic policy approach to disinvestment and privatisation and to give a fresh impetus to this programme, by setting up a new Department of Disinvestment
- To emphasize increasingly on strategic sales of identified PSUs
- To use the entire receipt from disinvestment and privatisation for meeting expenditure in social sectors, restructuring of PSUs and retiring public debt

D. Disinvestment policy measures in 2001-2002 budget

Objectives

To use the proceeds from disinvestment for providing -

- Restructuring assistance to PSUs
- Safety net to workers
- Reduction of debt burden
- Additional budgetary support for the Plan, primarily in the social and infrastructure sectors (contingent upon realization of the anticipated receipt.)

E. New Disinvestment Commission

As the term of the first Disinvestment Commission expired in the year 1 999, a new Disinvestment Commission has been constituted in the month of July 2001. The Composition of the Disinvestment Commission is as under:

1. Dr. R.H. Patil   Chairman
2. Shri N.V. Iyer   Member
3. Shri T.L. Shankar   Member
4. Dr. V.V. Desai   Member
5. Prof. K.S.R. Murthy   Member
6. A. Bhattacharya   Member (Secretary) (w.e.f. April 2002)

New Terms of Reference of Commission

The terms of reference are as follows:

(i) It shall be an advisory body and its role and function would be to advise the Government on Disinvestment in those public sector units that are referred to it by the Government.

(ii) It shall also advise the Government on any other matter relating to disinvestment as may specifically be referred to it by the Government, and also carry out any such other activities relating to disinvestment as may be assigned to it by the Government.

(iii) In making its recommendations, it will also take into consideration the interest of workers, employees and other stakeholders, in the public sector unit(s).

(iv) The final decision on the recommendations of the Disinvestment Commission will vest with the Government.

- Reference of all Non-Strategic PSEs including their subsidiaries to Disinvestment Commission

- The Government has decided to refer to the Disinvestment Commission "non-strategic" Public Sector Enterprises (PSES) including their subsidiaries, excluding IOC, ONGC & GAIL. Since such PSEs would be quite large in number, the Commission would prioritise the cases and make recommendations to the Government.

- The Disinvestment Commission has, so far, given its recommendations on

1. Neyveli Lignite Corporation Ltd. (NCL),

2. Manganese Ore (India) Ltd. (MOIL),

3. Rail India Technical & Economic Services Ltd. (RITES),

4. Projects & Equipment Corporation Ltd. (PEC).

5. Central Inland Water Transport Corporation Ltd. (CIWTC)

6. Cochin Shipyard Ltd. (CSL)

7. Dredging Corporation of India Ltd. (DCI)

8. Hindustan Shipyard Ltd. (HSL)

9. IRCON International Ltd. (IRCON)

10. National Projects Construction Corporation Ltd. (NPCC)

11. Semiconductor Complex Ltd. (SCL)

12. Telecommunications Consultants India Ltd. (TCIL)

13. Cotton Corporation of India Ltd. (CCI)

14. Indian Medicines Pharmaceuticals Ltd. (IMPCL)

15. Jute Corporation of India Ltd. (JCI)

16. National Buildings Construction Corporation Ltd. (NBCC)

- Out of these cases, Government has already taken decision to disinvest 51% of shares in MOIL. Other cases are under consideration.

The disinvestment commission has recommended a new method for disinvesting government shares through "cross holding" of equity among the public sector units to ensure effective government control. This was adopted first in shipping corporation of Indian Limited. Later, the idea was further developed by commission which recommended 19 PSUs for varying degree of disinvestment.

F. Participation of PSUs in disinvestment (Present Policy)

- Cabinet decided in September,2002 that Central Public Sector Undertakings (PSUs), Central Government owned cooperative societies (where Government's ownership is 51% or more) should not be permitted to participate in the disinvestment of other PSUs as bidder. If in some specific cases any deviation from these restrictions is considered desirable in public interest, the ministry/ Department concerned may bring an appropriate proposal for consideration of the Core Group of Secretaries on Disinvestment. Recently, Cabinet decided in December, 2002 that Multi State Cooperative Societies under the Department of Fertilizers be allowed to participate in the disinvestment of fertilizer PSUS including National Fertilizers Limited (NFL).

G. Review of policy and new directions as indicated in a Suo - Moto Statement of Shri Arun Shourie, Minister of Disinvestment, Minister of Development of North Eastern Region and Minister of Commerce & Industry made in both Houses of Parliament on 9th December, 2002

- The main objective of disinvestment is to put national resources and assets to optimal use and in particular to unleash the productive potential inherent in our public sector enterprises. The policy of disinvestment specifically aims at:

- Modernization and upgradation of Public Sector Enterprises,

- Creation of new assets;

- Generating of employment; and

- Retiring of public debt.

- Government would continue to ensure that disinvestment does not result in alienation of national assets, which, through the process of disinvestment, remain where they are. It will also ensure that disinvestment does not result in private monopolies.

- In order to provide complete visibility to the Government's continued commitment of utilisation of disinvestment proceeds for social and infrastructure sectors, the Government would set up a Disinvestment Proceeds Fund. This Fund will be used for financing fresh employment opportunities and investment, and for retirement of public debt.

- For the disinvestment of natural asset companies, the Ministry of Finance and the Ministry of Disinvestment will work out guidelines.

- The Ministry of Finance will also prepare for consideration of the Cabinet Committee on

Disinvestment a paper on the feasibility and modalities of setting up an Asset Management Company to hold, manage and dispose the residual holding of the Government in the companies in which Government equity has been disinvested to a strategic partner.

Since 1991-92, the government of India could raise resources through disinvestment to the extent of Rs. 29,440 crore upto 2002-2003, which was just 37.59 percent of its target, to the extent of Rs.78,300 crores.

Critical Analysis of Disinvestment Policy of Government of India

At present the whole policy of disinvestments has undergone a sea change. In the beginning it was one of the offering a part of the equity to various private sector players both domestic and foreign. Now it is one of the outright sale of majority shares to strategic partners, with a clear commitment to ultimately off-load the rest of the shares after some time. With such a strategy, the anxiety of the present government to bridge the fiscal deficit is creating a situation of distress sale of PSEs to private hands. Therefore, it is no longer disinvestment policy, but a policy of privatisation.

The process of privatisation has become an instrument of transferring public property to private hands much to the detriment of the national interest and the industrial economy of the country in particular. And with the whole process, corruption is woven intrinsically. The very concept of privatisation of public sector units and more so the blue chip ones, in itself a bankrupt corrupt policy, perception and fraud on the people of the company.

The most strategic sectors have been engulfed under the drive for privatisation. The important among them are oil and petroleum, power, telecom, rail, road and air transport, ports and docks, airports and financial sector. This will completely cause the public sector network from the industrial map of the country. The government has declared to close down sick and loss making PSEs instead of taking efforts for their revival.

In reality the PSEs are contributing to the central exchequer in a big way on an ever increasing scale. This will totally disappear once the enterprises are sold. The cash rich profit making companies like Bharat Petroleum Corporation Ltd. (BPCL) and Hindustan Petroleum Corporation Ltd. (HPCL) and other top companies in telecommunication like VSNL etc. are under current prioritised initiative of the Government for privatisation.

Contrary to the publicity of the government the privatisation of CPSEs almost invariably involves reduction in workmen. This will add to the current unemployment problem in the country. Reduction in workforce may occur either before or after privatisation. Moreover, once these companies are privatised, the workers are forced to face humiliation and insult in the hands of the new private sector management. This may affect the employees emotionally.

To avoid all these ill effects of disinvestment policy. Government should conduct referendum to take the opinion of the people on the government policy and steps of privatisation of public sector.

Disinvestment in Public Sector Undertakings

The following table indicates the actual disinvestment from 1991-92 till date, the methodologies adopted for such disinvestment and the extent of disinvestment in different CPSUs:

Actual Disinvestment from April 1991 onwards and Methodologies Adopted

Year	No.of Companies in which equity sold	Target receipt for the year (Rs.in Crore)	Actual receipts (Rs.in Crore)	Methodology
1991-92	47 (31 in one trance and 16 in other)	2500	3038	Minority shares sold by auction method in bundles of "very good", "good", and "average" companies.
1992-93	35 (in 3 tranches)	2500	1913	Bundling of shares abandoned. Shares sold separately for each company by auction method.
1993-94	-	3500	0	Equity of 7 companies sold by open auction but proceeds received in 1994-95.
1994-95	13	4000	4843	Sale through auction method, in which NRIs and other persons legally permitted to buy, hold or sell equity, allowed to participate.
1995-96	5	7000	361	Equities of 4 companies auctioned and Government piggy backed in the IDBI fixed price offering for the fifth company.
1996-97	1	5000	380	GDR (VSNL) in international market.
1997-98	1	4800	902	GDR (MTNL) in international market.
1998-99	5	5000	5371	GDR (VSNL)/Domestic offerings with the participation of FIIs (CONCOR, GAIL). Cross purchase by 3 Oil sector companies i.e. GAIL, ONGC & Indian Oil Corporation.
1999-00#	4	10000	1860	GDR-GAIL, VSNL-domestic issue, BALCO restructuring, MFILs strategic sale and others.
2000-01	4	10000	1871	Strategic sale of BALCO, LJMC; Takeover-KRL (CRL), CPCL (MRL), BRPL.
2001-02#	9	12000	5632	Strategic sale of CMC-51%, HTL-74%, VSNL-25%, IBP-33.58%, PPL-74%, and sale by other modes: ITDC & HCI; surplus reserves: STC and MMTC.
2002-03	6	12000	3348	Strategic sale: HZL-26%, MFIL-26%, IPCL-25%, HCI, UTDC, Maruti: control premium from renunciation of rights issue, ESOP:HZL,CMC.

2003-04	9	13200	15547	Maruti-IPO(27.5%), Jessop & Co. Ltd. (Strategic sale-72%), HZL (Call Option of SP-18.92%), Public Offers-IPCL, (28.95%) CMC(26%),UBP(26%), DRDG(20%), GAIL(10%), ONGC(10%), ICI(9.2%).
Total#	48*	91500	45066	

* Total number of companies in which disinvestment has taken place so far.

Figures (inclusive of control premium, dividend/dividend tax, restructuring and transfer of surplus cash reserves prior to disinvestment etc.)

* Total number of companies in which disinvestment has taken place so far.

Figures (inclusive of amount expected to be realised, control premium, dividend/dividend tax and transfer of surplus cash reserves prior to disinvestment etc.)(Rs.31 crore taxes from BALCO).

The Government had finalised the privatisation/disinvestment of the following 12 companies through strategic sales and 18 hotels of ITDC and 3 of HCI through demerger/slump sale (till 15th July 2002):

Strategic Sale of PSEs Year 2000 Onwards

Sl.No.	Name of PSE	Date	Ratio of paid up Equity Sold %	Face value of Equity Sold (Rs.in Crore)	Realisation (Rs.Crores)
1a	Modern Food Industries Ltd. (MFIL)	Jan.2000	74	9.63	105.45
1b	MFIL-Phase-II		26	3.38	44.07
2	Lagan Jute Machinery Corporation	Jul.2000	74	0.70	2.53
3	BALCO^	Mar.2001	51	112.52	826.50
4a	CMC	Oct.2001	51	7.73	152.00
4b	CMC$		61	0.91	6.07
5	HTL	Oct.2001	74	11.10	55.00
6	VSNL^	Feb.2002	25	71.20	3689.00
7	IBP	Feb.2002	33.6	7.40	1153.68
8	PPL	Feb.2002	74	320.10	151.70
9	Jessop	Aug.2003	74	68.10	18.18
10a	HZL	Apr.2002	26	109.80	445.00
10b	HZL***	Nov.2003	18.92	79.90	323.88
10c	HZL$	Apr.2003	1.5	6.17	6.19
11	IPCL	May 2002	26	64.50	1490.84
12a	Maruti Udyog Phase-I	Mar.2002	-	-	1000.00
12b	Maruti Udyog Phase-II	Jul.2003	27.5	39.73	993.34
13	State Trading Corporation of India(STC)#	Mar.2003			40.00
14	MMTC Ltd.#	Mar.2003			60.00
15-17	HCI(3 Hotels)	2001-02 various dates	100	14.70	242.51

18-36	ITDC(19 Hotels)	2001-02 various dates	100	27.10 444.17	
37	ICI	Oct.2003	9.2	3.76	77.10
38	IPCL	Mar.2004	28.95	71.85	1202.85
39	IBP Co.Ltd.	Mar.2004	26	5.80	350.66
40	CMC Ltd.	Mar.2004	26.25	3.98	190.44
41	DCI	Mar.2004	20	5.60	221.20
42	GAIL	Mar.2004	10	84.60	1627.36
43	ONGC	Mar.2004	10	142.60	10542.40
	Total			1272.86	25462.12

^ Including dividend & Civi. Tax/withdrawal of surplus cash prior to disinvestment.

*** Realisation from call option

$ Disinvestment in favour of employees

The receipt is on account of transfer of cash reserves.

4. NEW EXIM POLICY 2002-2007

External sector is becoming increasingly important for the growth of the Indian economy. Its share (exports plus imports) accounted for 22.8 per cent of Gross Domestic Product in 2000-01 as against only 14.6 per cent in 1990-91. It is, therefore, imperative that two-digit growth rate in exports are achieved if India aspires to record a GDP growth rate of around 8 per cent per annum. An increase in exports also brings in its wake a rise in imports because the import contents of many export products are fairly high. A low tariff and free of licensing import regime which allows Indian exporters access to the global supply market is, therefore, a crucial element of the export promotion strategy.

The Exim Policy for 2002-07 is the first policy which had to be formulated keeping in view all the commitments India had made under the WTO. Last year, all quantitative restrictions on imports were removed. In the current year's budget, the Government has announced its plan to bring down tariff rates substantially over the next few years. While such integration process is expected to increase imports, the export performance in 2001-02 has been dismal. As against a growth rate of 19.6 per cent in US dollar terms in 2001-02, the rate has slumped to 0.6 per cent during April-December 2001 period. The Ministry of Commerce has recently announced a Medium Term Export Promotion Strategy which aims at raising India's share in global exports from the current level of 0.6 per cent to 1 per cent by the end of Tenth Five Year Plan (2002-07). This will involve raising exports from $44.5 billion in 2000-01 to $80 billion in 2002-07, by recording a compound annual growth rate of 11.9 per cent. The Export-Import Policy announced on 31st March 2002 by the BJP led NDA Government provides the blueprint of initiatives that the Government will take to achieve this objective.

The new policy announced by the Government includes, lifting of export restrictions, initiatives to boost agriculture, hardware and gems exports, continuation and simplification of existing duty neutralisation schemes, steps to decrease transaction cost, incentives to attract more investments in Special Economic Zones (SEZs) etc. The new policy aims at diversifying markets with new programmes for exports and also provides more benefits to industrial dusters, cottage industry and handicrafts exports and hardware sector.

Highlights of New Exim Policy 2002-2007

Following are the important features of new five year Exim Policy (2002-2007):

(i) The Current Policy retains the popular DEPB (Duty Entitlement Pass Book) scheme, because it was found to be WTO-consistent. Since the complete VAT system is still not in operation, the Scheme has to be retained. Other export promotion schemes, such as EPCG (Export Promotion Capital Goods) will also continue to operate.

(ii) Providing subsidy to reduce freight disadvantage for exports is allowed under the WTO rates. Taking advantage of this provision, the Policy extends export freight subsidy to several agricultural products including floricultural, horticultural and dairy products. Further, the Policy proposes to work out suitable transport allowance for export of the large accumulated stocks of rice and wheat, currently available with the Food Corporation of India.

(iii) Several sector specific measures for important export products have been taken. These include duty-free import of rough diamonds and reducing the value addition norms for both plain and studded jewellery.

(iv) All quantitative restrictions on agricultural product exports have been removed, except on a few items.

(v) Several support measures to promote exports from the Cottage and Handicraft sector have been introduced. An amount of Rs.Five crore has been allocated for the promotion of items falling under the Khadi and Village industries Commission. Handicraft units will be eligible for Export House status with a lower turnover of Rs.Five crore as against the normal level of Rs.15 crore.

(vi) Concept of industrial clusters for exports will be used. To begin with, Tirupur for hosiery, Panipat for blankets and Ludhiana for Woollen knit wear have been identified which will be given special privileges, like eligibility to EPCG (Export Promotion Capital Goods) scheme, market access initiative funds etc.

(vii) Special Economic zones will continue to constitute the main institutional form to promote exports. Several new fiscal concessions have been granted to SEZs in this year's policy.

(viii) For the first time in India, Overseas Banking unit will be permitted under this year's Policy to be set up in Special Economic Zones. These units will practically act as branches of foreign banks. They will be able to provide world-class financing facilities to SEZ units as well as the private sector firms which will be involved in developing infrastructure in SEZs.

(ix) To promote agro-exports, the concept of Agro-Processing Zones was introduced last year. 20 such Zones have already been set up. The Policy proposes to catalyse the development of infrastructure in these zones, flow of credit and other facilities in consultation with the respective State Government where these zones are located.

(x) The Policy has schemes to promote export of computer hardware from India. The Electronic Hardware Technology Park (EHTP) Scheme will be strengthened. Units in the EHTP will be allowed several procedural liberalisation.

(xi) With a view to diversifying India's export markets, Focus Africa has been launched in the line of Focus Latin America which is currently in operation. The first phase of the

Programme will cover seven countries with large export potential. The countries are Nigeria, South Africa, Mauritius, Kenya, Ethiopia, Tanzania and Ghana.

(xii) The Market Access Initiative was introduced in 2001. The Initiative finances activities directed to export market promotion based on country-products focus. The scheme is also being strengthened with an outlay of Rs.42 crore in 2002-03.

(xiii) The ASIDE (Assistance to States for Infrastructural Development for Exports) is being strengthened. ASIDE would provide funds to the States based on the twin criteria of gross exports and the rate of growth of exports of each state. 80 per cent of the total funds would be disbursed based on these criteria while the rest 20 per cent will be utilised by the Centre for infrastructural development. Rs.330 crore have been allocated to this scheme for 2002-03.

(xiv) Reducing the high incidence of transaction costs has been a major area of concern for the last few years. The new Exim Policy has made a concerted effort to tackle this issue.

Measures to be taken include (a) adoption of a new commodity classification for imports and exports by Central Board of Excise and Customs, DGFT and Directorate General of Commercial Intelligence. This will eliminate the possibility of disputes arising out of classification of commodities, (b) simplification of all export promotion schemes, (c) reduction of the maximum fee limit for application under various schemes, (d) licence being issued within 24 hours in all regional offices of DGFT, (e) reduction in percentage of physical examination of export cargo, (f) fixation of brand drawback rate within 15 days, (g) exporters will be allowed to negotiate export documents directly, thereby saving back charges.

(xv) Designated exporters will now allowed to retain 100 per cent of the amount in the EEFC (Export Earners' Foreign Currency) accounts. They will be also be allowed to bring back to India export proceeds within a period of 360 days, as against 180 days earlier.

CASE STUDY 1

On Competition and Diversification

Raman runs an auto spares factory at Bangalore. Seventy five per cent of the spares produced are sold in domestic market and the rest is exported to foreign countries.

Government has changed the Export-Import policy allowing foreign manufacturers to operate in the country. This policy will affect the products of Raman firm.

In this emerging scenario, what precautions the firm should take to protect their market share in domestic market vis-a-vis foreign market?

Hints

The change in Exim Policy will definitely affect the market of Raman's firm. Therefore, Raman should follow the steps.

    (i) Examine the possible magnitude of threat from foreign goods.
    (ii) Assess the possible loss of market share from the competition.
    (iii) Explore the possibility of improving export share.
    (iv) Examine the possibility of improving or diversifying the product and market.

CASE STUDY 2

Market Situation and Government Policy

A controlled economy has market clearance equations built over years. The policy makers looked at the domestic markets and found that product markets are almost perfect and that technical rate of substitution has been advantageous. The economic fundamentals were strong enough to open up the economy. There was opposition attributing to inconsistency from "outside". The debate were on the following questions:

    (i) What are macro-economic fundamentals?
    (ii) Could market equations are the same after "opening up" of the economy?
    (iii) What if the economy is closed for some more time?   *(BU, MBA)*

Solution

Open economy is one that interacts with other economies around the world.

1. Fundamentals to be examined are (i) closed economy (ii) open economy (iii) Exports (iv) Imports (v) Net exports (vi) Trade Balance (vii) Trade Deficit (viii) Balance of Payments (ix) Foreign Exchange Resources.

2. Market equations are different in open economy. In open economy, Market for Loanable Funds (MLF) and market for foreign currency exchange (MFCE) are very important. In MLF there will be an adjustment of interest rate to supply of LF (from internal savings) and the demand for loanable funds (from domestic investment and net foreign investments). MFCE real exchange rate adjusts to balance the supply of rupee (net foreign investment) and the demand for loanable funds (Net foreign exports). Net foreign export connects these two markets.

3. Economy is rise to open in the said situation. Or it can be closed for some more time.

CASE STUDY 3

Shift in Demand

The government, as a social obligation, will be releasing messages to the public that "continuing alcohol destroys families." This message can be implemented in two ways.

One action to reduce the consumption of alcohol by the people is to shift the demand curve for alcohol. This may be made by prohibition of drinking alcohol, mandatory health warnings on liquor bottles and sachets, banning liquor advertising on television. If government succeeds, these actions shift the demand curve for liquor to the left.

Alternatively, the government may raise the price of liquor by imposing more tax which raises the price of liquor. This prohibits the consumers of liquor to drink more. This will not cause shift in demand. The price moves along the same demand curve of liquor to a point with higher price and lower quantity.

1. Do you consider that change in price shifts the demand curve?
2. How the price of liquor affects the demand for illicit liquor?

Hints

1. Demand curve will not shift. Prove moves along the same demand curve as the price and quantity demanded have inverse relationship.
2. High price of liquor encourages the use of illicit liquor. Both are substitutes. Only those who care for health may reduce the consumption of liquor.

Determinants that affect quantity demanded	Change in the determinant
Price	Moves along the demand curve.
Income	Shifts the demand curve.
Price of related goods	Shifts the demand curve.
Expectations	Shifts the demand curve.
Number of consumers	Shifts the demand curve.
Tastes and preferences	Shifts the demand curve.

CASE STUDY 4

Market Equilibrium

Market equilibrium is a concept which indicates the balancing of supply and demand for a product, for a given price in a given point of time.

1. The price at which demand and supply curves cross is called EQUILIBRIUM PRICE. This is a market clearing price.
2. Quantity demanded at equilibrium price is called EQUILIBRIUM QUANTITY.

There are three situations in which equilibrium shifts.

(i) When only supply curve shifts.

(ii) When only demand curve shifts.

(iii) When both demand and supply curve shift.

Case 1 (when only supply curve shifts)

Case Incident: In mid-point of winter weather will be very cold or say biting cold. How this affects the woolen blanket and pullovers market?

Solution

Three situations can be viewed to analyse the market equilibrium.

(i) Cold weather affects the demand curve of pullovers and blankets. Demand for these products increase and buy at a given price. But supply curve remains same. Demand curve shifts to the right.

(ii) Increase in demand raises the price of the products.

(iii) Quantity sold also increases, even at higher prices.

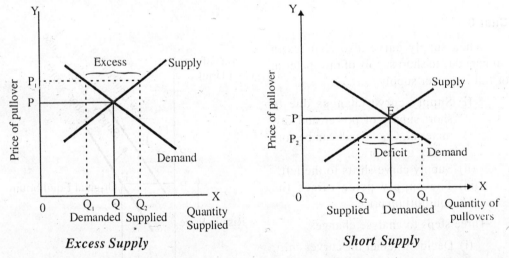

Excess Supply   *Short Supply*

Further, these two diagrams indicate that market is not in equilibrium. In the first figure, the supply exceeds demand and there is an excess supply. Therefore marketers reduce the price from P_1 to P to increase the sales to reach equilibrium.

In the second figure short supply of pullovers is shown. Because the market price (P_2) is below the equilibrium price. The quantity demand (Q_1) exceeds the quantity supplied (Q_2). Suppliers take advantage of the situation to raise price (P) to reach market equilibrium.

Therefore, in both cases, the price adjustment moves the market towards the equilibrium of demand and supply.

Case 2 (when only demand curve shifts)

Case Incident: In summer the demand for cool drinks increases. This changes the demand curve of the product. The situation prevails in the following manner.

(i) The supply curve does not change as the weather does not directly affect. The firms that sell cool drinks.

(ii) As people drink more cool drinks, demand curve moves towards right. This indicates that demand is higher at every price.

(iii) The price of cool drinks as well as quantity of consumption increase in summer.

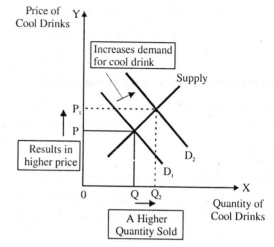

Change in Demand

Case 3

When supply curve also changes in summer due to short supply of raw material or fall in power supply.

(i) Supply curve changes due to short supply of power and raw material. Cool drink can be sold at any given price.

(ii) Supply curve shifts to the left.

(iii) The supply price raises the equilibrium price.

Three steps to analyse changes:

(i) Decide whether the curves shift.

(ii) Show the direction in which the curve moves.

(iii) Develop a diagram to show the shift in curves.

In both these cases, the equilibrium price changes. In case 2, demand curve shifts to right and results in higher price (P_1) as the supply being constant. In Case 3, supply curve shifts to left resulting in movement of price to higher level. Equilibrium point also moves from E to E_1.

Case Let 4 (Change in both supply and demand)

Case Incident: Suppose, if there is a labour problem in garment factory the supply of garments in the market may be reduced. If that occurs during any festival season, (there will be increase in demand for readymade garments) there will be simultaneous increase in demand and decrease in supply. How this affect the readymade garments market? Analyse this situation.

Solution

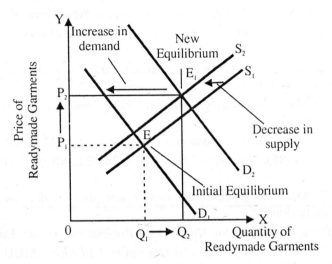

Fig. Readymade Garments

1. There will be a shift in the demand curve towards right side due to increase in demand.
2. The supply curve will be shifted backward due to shortage of supply.
3. Because of these two reasons, there will be a shift in equilibrium position and also price changes.

The diagram clearly shows that, the equilibrium price rises from P_1 to P_2 and the equilibrium quantity rises from Q_1 to Q_2. There is a shift in the equilibrium position also from E to E_1.

1. Analyse a similar situation when there is a shortfall of supply of raw materials and power during earthquake and the demand for the same product increases in the same period.

2. Will the change in supply and demand for a commodity always results in change in equilibrium and price in the market?

To conclude we can say that above caselets helps to know how to use supply and demand curves to analyse a change in equilibrium. Whenever an event shifts the supply curve, demand curve, or perhaps both curves, you can use these tools to predict how the event will alter the amount sold in equilibrium and the price at which the product is sold.

BIBLIOGRAPHY AND REFERENCES

1. Banmol,W.J. (1982), *Economic Theory and Operations Analysis*, 4th Ed., New Delhi, Prentice Hall.

2. Gupta, R.D. (1988), *Keynes Post-Keynesian Economics*. New Delhi, Kalyani Publishers.

3. Misra, S.K. and Puri, V.K. (2001), *Advanced Micro Economic Theory*, New Delhi, Himalaya Publishing House.

4. Mote,V.L., Paul,S. and Gupta,G.S. (1963), *Managerial Economics-Concepts and Cases*, New Delhi, Tata McGraw-Hill.

5. Kotler, P. (1991), *Marketing Management:Analysis, Planning and Control*, 7th Ed., New York, Prentice-Hall.

6. Gupta, G.S. (1990), *Managerial Economics*, New Delhi, Tata McGraw-Hill.

7. Habib-ur-Rahman, (1986), *Managerial Economics*, 2nd Ed., Mumbai, Himalaya Publishing House.

8. Mithani, D.M. (2003), *Managerial Economics — Theory and Applications*, 2nd Ed., Nagpur, Himalaya Publishing House.

9. Crowson, P. (1985), *Economics for Managers:A Professional Guide*, London, MacMillan.

10. Gupta, R.D., 'Rational Expectations — An Operational Illusion,' MDU Research Journal, Vol. 2, No.2, Oct.1987.

11. Jude Wanniski, (1978), 'The Way the World Works,' New York, Basic Books.

12. Kreiger, R.A. (1981), *Supply Side Economics*, Choice.

13. Gilder George, (1982), 'Wealth and Poverty', New Delhi, Kalyani Publishers.

14. Bhagawali, J.N. (1970), 'Oligopoly Theory, Entry Prevention and Growth,' Oxford Economic Papers.

15. Hall, R.L. and Hitch, C.I. (1939), 'Price Theory and Business Behaviour', Oxford Economic Papers.

16. Barback, "The Pricing of Manufactures', p. 36, Essays in Positive Economics.

17. Milton Friedman, "The Methodology of Positive Economics," Essays in Positive Economics.

18. Alchian, A. (1950), "Uncertainty, Evolution and Economic Theory", Journal of Political Economy, pp. 211-221.

19. Lekhi, R.K. and Aggarwal, S.L. (2002), *Business Economics*, New Delhi, Kalyani Publishers.

20. Edith Penrose (1952), "Biological Analogies in the Theory of the Firm", American Economic Review, pp. 804-19.

21. Machcup, F. (1946) "Marginal Analysis and Empirical Managerialist Behavioural", American Economic Review.

22. Hicks, J.R. (1939), *Value and Capital*, London, The English Language Book Society.

23. Varshney, R.L. and Maheswari, K.L. (2002), *Managerial Economics*, New Delhi, Sultan Chand and Sons.

24. Misra, S.K. and Puri (2003), *Indian Economy — Its Development Experience*, New Delhi, Himalaya Publishing House.

25. Misra, S.K. and Puri,V.K. (2002), Economics of Development and Planning (Theory and Practice), Mumbai, Himalaya Publishing House.

26. Economic Survey, *Government of India*, 2001-2002, 2002-2003.

OBJECTIVE QUESTIONS

1. Managerial Economics deals with application of:
   (a) Economic theory to business management
   (b) Economic theory to financial accounting
   (c) Economic theory to organised behaviour
   (d) Economic theory to statistics and management.

2. Business Economics is:
   (a) A science only
   (b) A science and an art
   (c) An art only
   (d) None of the above.

3. Opportunity Cost is:
   (a) Cost of alternatives sacrificed or foregone
   (b) Cost of particular decision taken
   (c) Total cost of a decision
   (d) Loss incurred/profit evaded by adopting a specific decision.

4. The nature of Managerial Economics is:
   (a) Micro
   (b) Macro
   (c) Normative and Micro
   (d) Only normative.

5. Demand Curve shows the relationship between:
   (a) Price and demand for the commodity
   (b) Price and Income of the commodity
   (c) Price, taste and preference
   (d) Both (a) & (c).

6. Extension in demand is due to:
   (a) Extension in price
   (b) Extension in supply
   (c) Fall in price of the commodity
   (d) Increase in income of the customer.

7. Demand effected by price of the related good is known as:
   (a) Price demand
   (b) Income demand
   (c) Gross demand
   (d) None of the above

8. Price elasticity of demand is equal to zero when:
   (a) When quantity demanded changes with no changes in price
   (b) When there is no change in quantity demanded inspite of price changes
   (c) When quantity demanded changes with changes in income
   (d) None of the above.

9. Labour as a factor of production is:
   (a) Active factor
   (b) Perishable factor
   (c) Both (a) and (b)
   (d) Neither (a) nor (b).

10. Function of an Entrepreneur is:
    (a) To bear risk and uncertainty
    (b) To control and manage efficiently
    (c) To increase co-ordination
    (d) All of the above.

11. Law of diminishing returns specially apply in Agriculture:
    (a) True
    (b) False
    (c) May be true
    (d) Only (a) or (b).

12. Under law of diminishing returns:
    (a) Marginal cost rises eventually
    (b) Marginal cost diminishes
    (c) Marginal cost decreases but increases later on
    (d) Average cost diminishes.

13. Differential cost is due to:
    (a) Difference in cost due to increase or decrease in cost
    (b) Increase in cost only
    (c) Decrease in cost only
    (d) Fall in production activity.

14. Semi variable cost is one which is:
    (a) Fixed cost
    (b) Variable cost
    (c) Partly fixed cost and partly variable
    (d) Direct cost.

15. Absorption costing implies:
    (a) Treatment of cost as a part of production of goods
    (b) Total cost incurred in production of goods
    (c) Average cost incurred in production of goods
    (d) Increase in total cost with changing levels of activity.

16. Which of the following is not included in managerial economics:
    (a) Elementary supply and demand
    (b) Cost of production
    (c) Profit planning and control
    (d) Factors influencing national product
    (e) Market forms.

17. Marginal cost is most closely related to:
    (a) Fixed costs
    (b) Variable costs
    (c) Total costs.

18. The objective of cash discount is:
    (a) To extend the good will of a firm
    (b) To reduce the price of product
    (c) To encourage the customers to make profit payment of the bill
    (d) To increase the number of customers.

19. The law of demand states that:
    (a) When income rises demand rises
    (b) When price rise demand fall
    (c) When price rises demand rises
    (d) When income and price rise demand rises.

20. The equilibrium of firm occurs when:
    (a) P=MC
    (b) MC=MR
    (c) P=MR
    (d) AC=MC.

21. Input-output analysis is for:
    (a) Inter industry relations
    (b) Intra industry relations
    (c) Sectoral comparison of different industry
    (d) Analysing revenue structure of the economy.

22. Price discrimination in monopoly refers:
    (a) Charging same price from different buyers
    (b) Charging different prices from different buyers for same goods
    (c) Charging different price for different products from the buyers
    (d) When demand price are similar.

23. How would you indicate relatively elastic demand by using one of the following measures:
    (a) E=Zero
    (b) E is less than 1
    (c) E is greater than 1
    (d) E=1
    (e) E=infinity

24. Prices can be increased to shift excise duty to the consumers if the product subjected to duty is:
    (a) Relatively in elastic demand
    (b) In relatively elastic supply
    (c) Of perishable nature
    (d) Widely used
    (e) A luxury item.

25. We can say with certainty that when the demand for cars increases, in the long run prices:
    (a) Will go down without the knowledge of elasticity
    (b) Will go up
    (c) Settle at the original level
    (d) Change proportionally
    (e) Cannot be predicted.

26. The optimum size of a firm:
    (a) Can exist only under monopoly
    (b) Can exist only under perfect competition
    (c) Can exist only under imperfect competition
    (d) Can exist under all types of Market structures

27. The demand for a commodity is said to be elastic if the total amount spent on the commodity is:
    (a) Less when the price is low when the price is high
    (b) The same whether the price is high or low
    (c) More when the price is low than when the price is high.

28. The basic cost accounting method in which the fixed overhead cost is added to inventory is:
    (a) Absorption or full costing
    (b) Direct costing
    (c) Job order costing
    (d) Process costing

29. Total Cost is:
    (a) The overall cost associate with a given level output
    (b) Equal to Marginal cost times the quantity of output
    (c) Determined by adding marginal cost and average cost
    (d) None of these.

30. Which of the following factors is not likely to influence your decision on whether to borrow money for investment:
    (a) Bank rate
    (b) Cost of borrowing
    (c) Profit expectation
    (d) Existing capital gearing
    (e) Dividend freeze.

31. Equi Marginal principle states:
    (a) Adjustment of cost with equal time value
    (b) Future cost and revenues are adjusted equally
    (c) Input allocated is same for last unit in all the cases
    (d) Equal sacrifice of alternative cost.

32. Macro Economics deals with:
    (a) Study of aggregates and averages concerning the entire economy
    (b) Study of aggregates of various firms
    (c) Study of specific market condition
    (d) Study of particular production process.

33. Micro Economics deals with:
    (a) Study of industry as a whole
    (b) Study of individual firms and small group of individuals
    (c) Study of full production activity
    (d) Study of entire economy.

34. Which inter disciplinary approache is not applied to managerial Economics:
    (a) Statistics and mathematics
    (b) Accounting
    (c) Operation research
    (d) Anthropology

35. Demand analysis means:
    (a) Analysis of factors affecting demand of a product
    (b) Allocation of resource according to forecasted demand
    (c) Planning and decision making
    (d) Maintaining Market share.

36. Capital Management in Business Economics implies:
    (a) Planning and Control of Profit Management
    (b) Planning and Control of Capital expenditure
    (c) Planning and Control of Cost of production
    (d) Increasing profits by proper Capital management.

37. The demand for a commodity is said to be elastic if the total amount spent on the commodity is:
    (a) Less when the price is low than when the price is high
    (b) The same whether the price is high.

38. External Economies of scale arises when:
    (a) Expansion of output of one firm improves the efficiency of others
    (b) A large firm acquires monopoly advantage
    (c) To encourage the customer to make prompt payment of bill
    (d) To increase the number of customers.

39. Which of the following assumption is not necessary for the existence of perfect competition:
    (a) Products are homogeneous
    (b) Buyers have no preference between different sellers
    (c) Each producer is aware of the profits made by the other
    (d) Buyers have knowledge of prices in every part of the market.

40. The opportunity cost of a factor of production with specific use is:
    (a) Very high
    (b) Infinite
    (c) Zero
    (d) Constant

41. How would you indicate relatively elastic demand by using one of the following measures.
    (a) E = zero
    (b) E is less than one
    (c) E is greater than one
    (d) E = 0
    (e) E = inifinity

42. Marginal cost curve cuts average cost curve:
    (a) At the left of its lowest point
    (b) At its lowest point
    (c) At the right of its lowest point.

43. Break even point is:
    (a) Where total revenue equals total cost
    (b) Where total contribution equals variable cost
    (c) Where total revenue equals fixed cost.

44. In an Oligopolistic Market there are:
    (a) A large number of sellers and few buyers
    (b) Few sellers and few buyers
    (c) Few sellers and a large number of buyers.

45. In a perfect competitive market the firm will be:
    (a) A price maker
    (b) Attempting to maximise profits
    (c) A price taker
    (d) Restricting freedom of entry into market.

46. Giffen Goods are Goods:
    (a) For which demand increases as price increases
    (b) Which have a high income elasticity of demand
    (c) Which have a low cross elasticity of demand
    (d) Which are short supply.

47. Complementary goods are those:
    (a) Which are demanded seperately
    (b) Which are demanded jointly
    (c) Which are demanded at different times
    (d) None of the above.

48. Elasticity of demand measures:
    (a) A change in amount demanded in response to given prices
    (b) Changes in amount demanded due to government policy
    (c) Only (a)
    (d) Only (b)
    (e) Change in taste and preference.

49. Rectangular Hyperbola Curve occurs when:
    (a) $E = \infty$
    (b) $E > 1$
    (c) $E < 1$
    (d) $E = 1$.

50. Demand for superior Goods increases:
    (a) With demand in Consumers income
    (b) With rise in price of goods
    (c) With decrease in price of related goods
    (d) With increase in Consumers income.

Answers

(1) a	(11) a	(21) a	(31) c	(41) c
(2) c	(12) c	(22) b	(32) a	(42) b
(3) a	(13) a	(23) c	(33) b	(43) a
(4) c	(14) c	(24) c	(34) d	(44) c
(5) a	(15) a	(25) c	(35) a	(45) c
(6) c	(16) d	(26) d	(36) b	(46) a
(7) c	(17) b	(27) c	(37) a	(47) b
(8) b	(18) d	(28) a	(38) a	(48) a
(9) c	(19) b	(29) a	(39) b	(49) b
(10) a	(20) b	(30) d	(40) c	(50) a